A·N·N·U·A·L E·D·I·T·I·O·N·S

American Foreign Policy

02/03

Eighth Edition

EDITOR

Glenn P. Hastedt

James Madison University

Glenn Hastedt received his Ph.D. from Indiana University. He is professor of political science at James Madison University, where he teaches courses on U.S. foreign policy, national security policy, and international relations. His special area of interest is on the workings of the intelligence community and the problems of strategic surprise and learning from intelligence failures. In addition to having published articles on these topics, he is the author of *American Foreign Policy: Past, Present, Future*; coauthor of *Dimensions of World Politics*; and editor and contributor to *Controlling Intelligence*. He has also published two volumes of readings, *Toward the Twenty-First Century* and *One World, Many Voices*.

McGraw-Hill/Dushkin

530 Old Whitfield Street, Guilford, Connecticut 06437

Visit us on the Internet
http://www.dushkin.com

Credits

1. **The United States and the World: Strategic Choicest**
   Unit photo—© 2002 PhotoDisc, Inc.
2. **The United States and the World: Regional and Bilateral Relations**
   Unit photo—© United Nations photo.
3. **The Domestic Side of American Foreign Policy**
   Unit photo—Courtesy of The White House.
4. **The Institutional Context of American Foreign Policy**
   Unit photo—Courtesy of K. Jewell/U.S. House of Representative.
5. **The Foreign Policy–Making Process**
   Unit photo—AP photo/Pool, David Brauchli.
6. **U.S. International Economic Strategy**
   Unit photo—© 2002 PhotoDisc, Inc.
7. **U.S. Post–Cold War Military Strategy**
   Unit photo—Courtesy of Northrop Corporation.

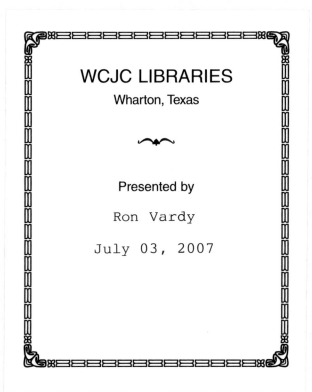

Copyright

Cataloging in Publication Data
Main entry under title: Annual Editions: American Foreign Policy 2002/2003.
1. U.S. Foreign Relations–Periodicals. I. Hastedt, Glenn P., *comp.* II. Title: American foreign policy
ISBN 0–07–250716–0   658'.05   ISSN 1075–5225

Eighth Edition

Cover image © 2002 by PhotoDisc, Inc.
Printed in the United States of America   1234567890BAHBAH5432   Printed on Recycled Paper

To the Reader

In publishing ANNUAL EDITIONS we recognize the enormous role played by the magazines, newspapers, and journals of the public press in providing current, first-rate educational information in a broad spectrum of interest areas. Many of these articles are appropriate for students, researchers, and professionals seeking accurate, current material to help bridge the gap between principles and theories and the real world. These articles, however, become more useful for study when those of lasting value are carefully collected, organized, indexed, and reproduced in a low-cost format, which provides easy and permanent access when the material is needed. That is the role played by ANNUAL EDITIONS.

This eighth volume of *Annual Editions: American Foreign Policy* presents an overview of American foreign policy. It is a foreign policy in transition, but it is a very different transition from what was taking place before September 11, 2001. Prior to the terrorist attacks on the World Trade Center and the Pentagon, the foreign policy debate centered on a selection of strategies and tactics that could guide the United States in the transition period between the end of the cold war and the emergence of a post–cold war era. It was a debate largely conducted in the language of academics and it was one that did not engage large numbers of the American public.

Today the debate over the proper course of American foreign policy is conducted in passionate tones and is seen as important by virtually all Americans. Its immediate focus is on combating and eradicating terrorism. At first glance, the urgency of this challenge may make it appear that there is little left to discuss about the future direction of American foreign policy. The reality is quite different. Only by fully understanding the strategic and tactical choices available to the United States, the perspectives of other countries, the strengths and weaknesses of our own society and institutions, and the possible shapes that the international system may take during and after the war on terrorism can U.S. foreign policy succeed. Differing views exist on all of these points.

Annual Editions: American Foreign Policy 02/03 examines the many issues and problems involved in making this transition from an ill-defined post–cold war world into a world defined by a war against global terrorism. It is divided into seven units. The first unit addresses questions of grand strategy. The second unit focuses on selected regional and bilateral relations. In the third unit, our attention shifts inward to the ways in which domestic forces affect the content of American foreign policy. The fourth unit looks at the institutions that make American foreign policy. In the fifth unit, the process by which American foreign policy is made is illustrated by accounts of recent foreign policy decisions. The sixth and seventh units provide an overview of the economic and military issues confronting the United States today. Together the readings in these seven units provide students with an up-to-date overview of key events in American foreign policy, the forces that shape it, and the policy problems on the agenda. The essays were chosen for their ability to inform students and spark debate. They are not designed to advance any particular interpretation of American foreign policy.

I would like to thank Ian Nielsen for supporting the concept of an *Annual Editions: American Foreign Policy* and for helping to oversee the process of putting this volume together. Also deserving of thanks are the many people at McGraw-Hill/Dushkin who worked to make the project a success and those faculty on the Advisory Board who provided input on the selection of articles. In the end, the success of *Annual Editions: American Foreign Policy* depends upon the views of the faculty and students who use it. I encourage you to let me know what worked and what did not so that each successive volume will be better than its predecessor. Please complete and return the postage-paid *article rating form* at the end of this book.

Glenn Hastedt

Glenn Hastedt
Editor

Contents

To the Reader   iv

Topic Guide   xi

Selected World Wide Web Sites   xiv

UNIT 1
The United States and the World: Strategic Choices

Five articles review some of the foreign policy choices the United States has today.

Unit Overview   xvi

1. **The American Way of Victory: A Twentieth-Century Trilogy,**
   James Kurth, *The National Interest,* Summer 2000
   James Kurth provides a panoramic view of the twentieth century and of the successful as well as the flawed "victory strategies" the United States and other major political powers implemented after the two **world wars.** He draws lessons about these **military and economic strategies** to evaluate United States policy following its victory in the cold war.   2

2. **War on Terrorism,** David Masci and Kenneth Jost, *CQ Researcher,*
   October 12, 2001
   The September 11, 2001, attack on the United States has created a challenge of how to define and respond to war. Evidence has pointed to **Osama bin Laden** and his **global terrorist network, Al Qaeda,** as being responsible for masterminding the attacks. Al Qaeda has been sanctioned by the Taliban, the Islamic fundamentalist rulers in Afghanistan. In response to the attack, a **"war on terrorism"** was declared, and an air and ground attack by U.S. and British forces began on Afghanistan soil.   10

3. **Different Drummers, Same Drum,** Andrew J. Bacevich, *The National Interest,* Summer 2001
   The author argues that in spite of George W. Bush's pledge to jettison the Clinton Doctrine if elected, his presidency shares Clinton's view of the proper role of the United States in world affairs. This has not happened because **Bush and Clinton share the same worldview** but because they both accept five elements that constitute today's foreign policy consensus in the United States.   18

4. **In From the Cold: A New Approach to Relations With Russia and China,** Robert S. McNamara and James G. Blight, *World Policy Journal,* Spring 2001
   The authors note that Woodrow Wilson and other American leaders failed to establish a sustainable peace after World War I. Avoiding their missteps requires that **American policymakers ensure that neither Russia nor China comes to feel as betrayed as Germany did in 1919.** Their answer is to employ a strategy of "realistic empathy."   25

5. **The Lonely Superpower,** Samuel P. Huntington, *Foreign Affairs,* March/April 1999
   Samuel Huntington argues that while the world is not unipolar, the United States is acting as if it is. In doing so, the **United States is becoming increasingly isolated** from other states, and it is taking on the characteristics of a rogue superpower.   33

The concepts in bold italics are developed in the article. For further expansion, please refer to the Topic Guide and the Index.

UNIT 2
The United States and the World: Regional and Bilateral Relations

Eight selections consider U.S. relations with Russia, Europe, Asia, and the South.

Unit Overview   38

Part A.   Russia

6. **Russian Foreign Policy: Promise or Peril?,** Paula J. Dobriansky, *The Washington Quarterly,* Winter 2000
Democracy in Russia has provided a setting for domestic political and economic factors to shape Russian foreign policy. Paula Dobriansky asserts that Russia is fundamentally disinterested in promoting international stability in the context of a U.S.–led international system. *The current U.S.–Russian agenda closely resembles that of the 1970s.*   40

7. **Against Russophobia,** Anatol Lieven, *World Policy Journal,* Winter 2000/01
Anatol Lieven decries *two traits that dominate American foreign policy toward Russia.* First, there exists a blind, dogmatic hostility toward Russia on the part of "residual foreign policy elites" that are found predominantly in the Republican Party. Second, there is a tendency to believe that the United States is not influenced by national prejudices; that it stands "taller" than other states.   45

Part B.   Europe

8. **Europe: Superstate or Superpower?,** Martin Walker, *World Policy Journal,* Winter 2000/01
Martin Walker raises the fundamental question of *how close Europe is to being a superpower* and not just a large state. The EU army might be just large enough to get into trouble but too small to get itself out of trouble. Walker observes that this situation has come about in part because the United States has pushed Europe to take more responsibility for the military burdens of the Atlantic Alliance.   51

9. **The Lesser Evil: The Best Way Out of the Balkans,** Richard K. Betts, *The National Interest,* Summer 2001
What is the future of the Balkans? Will it resemble that of Palestine, Kashmir, Tibet, South Africa, or somewhere else? Richard Betts asserts that a potential solution in the Balkans requires forging a connection between self-government and interstate stability. He presents three exit scenarios but cautions that *there is no way out of the Balkans that does not entail a high cost in either honor or effort.*   58

Part C.   Asia

10. **East Asia: Security and Complexity,** Marvin C. Ott, *Current History,* April 2001
The author argues that in the coming decade U.S. security concerns will shift away from Europe and toward Asia. *Three key flashpoints are identified*: South Korea, Taiwan, and the South China Sea. The combination of Russian decline and Japanese strategic paralysis are seen as giving China the strategic freedom to exert its influence in each of these areas.   67

11. **To Be an Enlightened Superpower,** Wu Xinbo, *The Washington Quarterly,* Summer 2001
The author, a professor in China, asserts that while the world recognizes American primacy, it also recognizes that primacy is full of contradictions. He notes that China has always been upset by the oversimplified black-and-white view the United States holds of it. Paying particular attention to Taiwan, Wu Xinbo discusses *the future of Sino-American relations and how the United States should conduct itself.*   73

The concepts in bold italics are developed in the article. For further expansion, please refer to the Topic Guide and the Index.

Part D. The South

12. **A Small Peace for the Middle East,** Arthur Hertzberg, *Foreign Affairs,* January/February 2001
The author argues that the **conflict between the Israelis and Palestinians has been made worse by the dream of a perfect peace.** Arthur Hertzberg argues that the only hope for the future lies in taking small pragmatic steps. The best way for the United States to contribute to peace is to deemphasize the conflict. **78**

13. **Bush's Global Agenda: Bad News for Africa,** Salih Booker, *Current History,* May 2001
Salih Booker argues that the promotion of peace, democracy, and development in Africa is necessary to combat the global threats that face the United States. Yet, George W. Bush's decision not to embrace multilateral collaborative solutions to problems such as the environment and population does more than push Africa off the American foreign policy agenda. It amounts to **a de facto war on Africa.** **82**

UNIT 3
The Domestic Side of American Foreign Policy

Three selections examine the domestic impact of American foreign policy.

Unit Overview **88**

14. **On American Principles,** George F. Kennan, *Foreign Affairs,* March/April 1995
George Kennan calls a principle **"a general rule of conduct"** that defines the limits within which foreign policy ought to operate. Building on a position argued by John Quincy Adams, Kennan argues that the best way for a big country such as the United States to help smaller ones is by the **power of example.** **90**

15. **The New Apathy,** James M. Lindsay, *Foreign Affairs,* September/October 2000
An **apathetic internationalism** has come to dominate the politics of American foreign policy. It encourages policymakers to neglect foreign policy, empowers those who make the most noise, and makes it harder for presidents to lead. Together these consequences prevent the United States from capitalizing on its position of power in the international system. **95**

16. **Allies in Search of a Strategy,** *The Economist,* September 22, 2001
After the September 11, 2001 tragedy in New York and Washington, D.C., **the challenge to build a coalition** was the goal of President George W. Bush. Maintaining that coalition would prove to be a difficult problem. **99**

UNIT 4
The Institutional Context of American Foreign Policy

Seven articles examine how the courts, Congress, the presidency, and bureaucracy affect U.S. foreign policy.

Unit Overview **103**

Part A. Law and the Court

17. **The Pitfalls of Universal Jurisdiction,** Henry A. Kissinger, *Foreign Affairs,* July/August 2001
One of the most controversial developments in the field of international law is the establishment of a permanent international criminal court. Of major concern to opponents is its relationship to the American legal system. Henry Kissinger warns that its creation may not produce international peace but simply **substitute the tyranny of judges for that of governments.** **105**

The concepts in bold italics are developed in the article. For further expansion, please refer to the Topic Guide and the Index.

18. **States' Rights and Foreign Policy: Some Things Should Be Left to Washington,** Brannon P. Denning and Jack H. McCall, *Foreign Affairs,* January/February 2000

In the early 1990s, **many state and local governments entered the field of foreign affairs by establishing "economic sanctions"** against countries whose human rights policies they found to be objectionable. This article asserts that states should stay out of foreign policy. In 2000, the **Supreme Court** agreed and ruled against **a Massachusetts ban on trade with Burma.** 109

Part B.   Congress

19. **The Folk Who Live on the Hill,** James Kitfield, *The National Interest,* Winter 1999/2000

James Kitfield examines **the growing split within Republican congressional ranks between aging assertive internationalists and newer international minimalists.** Nowhere is the gap greater than on the question of using military force. Kitfield discusses the **Hutchinson Doctrine,** which would place the United States behind a missile defense shield and leave peacekeeping to others. 113

20. **Farewell to the Helmsman,** Christopher Hitchens, *Foreign Policy,* September/October 2001

Written prior to Republican senator Jesse Helms's announcement that he planned to retire from the Senate, this article surveys his views on American foreign policy. **Helms is described as an isolationist-interventionist** who always placed protecting American sovereignty at the center of his foreign policy agenda. 119

Part C.   The Presidency

21. **Perils of Presidential Transition,** Glenn P. Hastedt and Anthony J. Eksterowicz, *Seton Hall Journal of Diplomacy and International Relations,* Winter/Spring 2001

Important foreign policy decisions are often made in the first months of a president's term in office. These decisions are heavily influenced by events occurring during the presidential campaign and transition period. This article examines and **compares recent two-party presidential transitions involving Carter, Reagan, and Clinton, and their resulting foreign policies.** 122

Part D.   Bureaucracy

22. **The One Percent Solution: Shirking the Cost of World Leadership,** Richard N. Gardner, *Foreign Affairs,* July/August 2000

Richard Gardner sees a dangerous game being played in Washington where **leaders are trying to craft a successful foreign policy that uses only one percent of the federal budget.** He calls for greater international affairs spending and presents a plan for doing so. 133

23. **America's Postmodern Military,** Don M. Snider, *World Policy Journal,* Spring 2000

The postmodern American military is likely to be smaller, focused on peacekeeping missions, enjoying tepid public support. It seems to be led by officers whose values may differ greatly from those of the rest of American society. Retired military officer Don Snider looks at these trends and sees a strong need for civilians to reconnect with the military. 139

The concepts in bold italics are developed in the article. For further expansion, please refer to the Topic Guide and the Index.

UNIT 5
The Foreign Policy–Making Process

Three selections review some of the elements that influence the process of American foreign policy.

Unit Overview   **145**

24. **NATO Expansion: The Anatomy of a Decision,** James M. Goldgeier, *The Washington Quarterly,* Winter 1998

Relying on interviews with major players in the Clinton administration, James Goldgeier recounts the three key phases in the decision-making process that led to support for **NATO expansion.** He finds that this decision was made because a few key people supported it and that it was taken over **widespread bureaucratic opposition.**   **147**

25. **Outmaneuvered, Outgunned, and Out of View: Test Ban Debacle,** Stephen I. Schwartz, *The Bulletin of the Atomic Scientists,* January/February 2000

Policy making occurs in **Congress** as well as in the White House. This essay examines the political maneuvering that took place in Congress leading up to the vote to reject the **Comprehensive Test Ban Treaty** in October 1999. Author Stephen Schwartz is critical of the Clinton administration's handling of the vote.   **155**

26. **A Four-Star Foreign Policy?,** Dana Priest, *Washington Post,* September 28, 2000

Using examples from Europe, Africa, and Latin America, this article highlights the **growing political influence that high-ranking military officers** who command America's regional commands have in making U.S. foreign policy. These "proconsuls" have achieved their positions of influence at the expense of the State Department and separate military services. They report directly to the president and secretary of defense.   **162**

UNIT 6
U.S. International Economic Strategy

Four selections discuss how American foreign policy choices are affected by economics and trade strategies.

Unit Overview   **169**

27. **Q: Should the United States Renew the Iran Libya Sanctions Act?,** Kenneth R. Timmerman and Archie Dunham, *Insight,* July 2–9, 2001

The authors debate whether or not U.S. **economic sanctions against Iran and Libya** should be lifted. They address such issues as whether the sanctions have worked, the degree of reform that has occurred in these societies, and the broader economic impact of the sanctions on the U.S. and global economies.   **171**

28. **The U.S. Trade Deficit: A Dangerous Obsession,** Joseph Quinlan and Marc Chandler, *Foreign Affairs,* May/June 2001

A large trade deficit has become a persistent feature of U.S. trade policy. To many it is an important indicator of the health of the U.S. economy. The authors assert that this is incorrect and that **the trade balance is no longer a valid index for measuring American global competitiveness.** The United States is better positioned than ever to compete in the global marketplace.   **175**

29. **The Death of the Washington Consensus?,** Robin Broad and John Cavanagh, *World Policy Journal,* Fall 1999

The Washington Consensus refers to the belief that creating unrestricted free markets is the key ingredient for any development strategy. The authors contend that over the past few years this strategy has lost some of its legitimacy and that an alternative development strategy has now emerged.   **180**

The concepts in bold italics are developed in the article. For further expansion, please refer to the Topic Guide and the Index.

30. **Globalization After Seattle,** Jacob Park, *The Washington Quarterly,* Spring 2000

The 1999 meeting of the World Trade Organization (WTO) in Seattle brought out a tide of protest from environmental and labor groups. Jacob Park discusses what lies ahead for the WTO. The key to the future lies in the ability of American policymakers to wield *"soft power."* **187**

UNIT 7
U.S. Post–Cold War Military Strategy

Five articles examine U.S. military planning in the context of the post–cold war era.

Unit Overview **189**

Part A. The Use of Military Power

31. **Responding to Terrorism,** David Tucker, *The Washington Quarterly,* Winter 1998

David Tucker is a staff member of the assistant secretary of defense for special operations and low-intensity conflict. He reviews and evaluates the *effectiveness of three current and six past U.S. policies designed to combat terrorism.* Tucker recommends a combination of elements from many of these strategies. **191**

32. **War on America: The New Enemy,** *The Economist,* September 15, 2001

The assault on the World Trade Center in New York and the Pentagon in Washington, D.C., on September 11, 2001, will forever change the way America looks at itself and at the world. As this special report points out, the extent of current terrorism is a form of war that the United States has never had to deal with in the past. **199**

33. **Musclebound: The Limits of U.S. Power,** Stephen M. Walt, *The Bulletin of the Atomic Scientists,* March/April 1999

The extraordinary power position of the United States does not guarantee that it can achieve its objectives. Among the reasons for this are that other states may care more about an issue than does the United States, other states fear U.S. hegemony, and the United States has pursued an overly ambitious set of goals. **203**

Part B. Arms Control

34. **Ending the Nuclear Nightmare: A Strategy for the Bush Administration,** Jim Wurst and John Burroughs, *World Policy Journal,* Spring 2001

The authors present an alternative to building a national ballistic missile defense system (BMD). It is centered on affirming and expanding the principles found in Article VI of the *Nuclear Non-Proliferation Treaty.* They argue that by eroding the nonproliferation regime, a BMD will create the very nuclear threat to U.S. national security that it is intended to protect against. **208**

35. **Mission Impossible,** Henry D. Sokolski, *The Bulletin of the Atomic Scientists,* March/April 2001

In 1993, the United States announced that it would supplement arms control with a policy of counterproliferation. This article provides an overview of 8 years of politics within the Clinton administration's national security bureaucracy over *how to define counterproliferation and implement the initiative.* In the process it became transformed from an offensive military capability into a damage-limitation one. **214**

Index **219**
Test Your Knowledge Form **222**
Article Rating Form **223**

The concepts in bold italics are developed in the article. For further expansion, please refer to the Topic Guide and the Index.

Topic Guide

This topic guide suggests how the selections in this book relate to the subjects covered in your course. You may want to use the topics listed on these pages to search the Web more easily.

On the following pages a number of Web sites have been gathered specifically for this book. They are arranged to reflect the units of this *Annual Edition.* You can link to these sites by going to the DUSHKIN ONLINE support site at *http://www.dushkin.com/online/.*

ALL THE ARTICLES THAT RELATE TO EACH TOPIC ARE LISTED BELOW THE BOLD-FACED TERM.

Afghanistan
2. War on Terrorism

Africa
13. Bush's Global Agenda: Bad News for Africa
26. A Four-Star Foreign Policy?

Al Qaeda
2. War on Terrorism

Arms control
6. Russian Foreign Policy: Promise or Peril?
25. Outmaneuvered, Outgunned, and Out of View: Test Ban Debacle
34. Ending the Nuclear Nightmare: A Strategy for the Bush Administration
35. Mission Impossible

Asia
5. The Lonely Superpower
10. East Asia: Security and Complexity
11. To Be an Enlightened Superpower
26. A Four-Star Foreign Policy?
28. The U.S. Trade Deficit: A Dangerous Obsession

Balkans
4. In From the Cold: A New Approach to Relations With Russia and China
8. Europe: Superstate or Superpower?
9. The Lesser Evil: The Best Way Out of the Balkans
17. The Pitfalls of Universal Jurisdiction
21. Perils of Presidential Transition

China
4. In From the Cold: A New Approach to Relations With Russia and China
10. East Asia: Security and Complexity
11. To Be an Enlightened Superpower
28. The U.S. Trade Deficit: A Dangerous Obsession

Congress
15. The New Apathy
19. The Folk Who Live on the Hill
20. Farewell to the Helmsman
25. Outmaneuvered, Outgunned, and Out of View: Test Ban Debacle

Counterterrorism
2. War on Terrorism
31. Responding to Terrorism
32. War on America: The New Enemy

Court system
17. The Pitfalls of Universal Jurisdiction
18. States' Rights and Foreign Policy: Some Things Should Be Left to Washington

Defense department
22. The One Percent Solution: Shirking the Cost of World Leadership
23. America's Postmodern Military
26. A Four-Star Foreign Policy?
35. Mission Impossible

Defense policy
33. Musclebound: The Limits of U.S. Power

Democracy
6. Russian Foreign Policy: Promise or Peril?

Diplomacy
22. The One Percent Solution: Shirking the Cost of World Leadership
26. A Four-Star Foreign Policy?
29. The Death of the Washington Consensus?

Domestic policy, American
15. The New Apathy
18. States' Rights and Foreign Policy: Some Things Should Be Left to Washington
23. America's Postmodern Military
30. Globalization After Seattle

Economics
1. The American Way of Victory: A Twentieth-Century Trilogy

Economic sanctions
18. States' Rights and Foreign Policy: Some Things Should Be Left to Washington
27. Q: Should the United States Renew the Iran Libya Sanctions Act?

Europe
5. The Lonely Superpower
8. Europe: Superstate or Superpower?
9. The Lesser Evil: The Best Way Out of the Balkans
24. NATO Expansion: The Anatomy of a Decision
28. The U.S. Trade Deficit: A Dangerous Obsession

Foreign aid
22. The One Percent Solution: Shirking the Cost of World Leadership
29. The Death of the Washington Consensus?

Foreign policy
3. Different Drummers, Same Drum
13. Bush's Global Agenda: Bad News for Africa
15. The New Apathy
18. States' Rights and Foreign Policy: Some Things Should Be Left to Washington
21. Perils of Presidential Transition
23. America's Postmodern Military
30. Globalization After Seattle
33. Musclebound: The Limits of U.S. Power

Fundamentalism

2. War on Terrorism

Future

1. The American Way of Victory: A Twentieth-Century Trilogy

Globalization

3. Different Drummers, Same Drum
13. Bush's Global Agenda: Bad News for Africa
30. Globalization After Seattle

Human rights

14. On American Principles
17. The Pitfalls of Universal Jurisdiction
18. States' Rights and Foreign Policy: Some Things Should Be Left to Washington

International aid

1. The American Way of Victory: A Twentieth-Century Trilogy

International coalition

16. Allies in Search of a Strategy

International economy

1. The American Way of Victory: A Twentieth-Century Trilogy

International relations

2. War on Terrorism

International trade

18. States' Rights and Foreign Policy: Some Things Should Be Left to Washington
27. Q: Should the United States Renew the Iran Libya Sanctions Act?
28. The U.S. Trade Deficit: A Dangerous Obsession
29. The Death of the Washington Consensus?
30. Globalization After Seattle

Iraq

3. Different Drummers, Same Drum

Latin America

9. The Lesser Evil: The Best Way Out of the Balkans
17. The Pitfalls of Universal Jurisdiction
28. The U.S. Trade Deficit: A Dangerous Obsession

Middle East

5. The Lonely Superpower
12. A Small Peace for the Middle East
26. A Four-Star Foreign Policy?
27. Q: Should the United States Renew the Iran Libya Sanctions Act?

Military

1. The American Way of Victory: A Twentieth-Century Trilogy

Military power

5. The Lonely Superpower
9. The Lesser Evil: The Best Way Out of the Balkans
19. The Folk Who Live on the Hill
23. America's Postmodern Military
24. NATO Expansion: The Anatomy of a Decision
33. Musclebound: The Limits of U.S. Power
35. Mission Impossible

Missile defense

19. The Folk Who Live on the Hill
25. Outmaneuvered, Outgunned, and Out of View: Test Ban Debacle
34. Ending the Nuclear Nightmare: A Strategy for the Bush Administration
35. Mission Impossible

National interest

4. In From the Cold: A New Approach to Relations With Russia and China
5. The Lonely Superpower
7. Against Russophobia
11. To Be an Enlightened Superpower
13. Bush's Global Agenda: Bad News for Africa
14. On American Principles
15. The New Apathy
17. The Pitfalls of Universal Jurisdiction

National values

4. In From the Cold: A New Approach to Relations With Russia and China
5. The Lonely Superpower
7. Against Russophobia
11. To Be an Enlightened Superpower
13. Bush's Global Agenda: Bad News for Africa
14. On American Principles
15. The New Apathy
17. The Pitfalls of Universal Jurisdiction

NATO

6. Russian Foreign Policy: Promise or Peril?
8. Europe: Superstate or Superpower?
9. The Lesser Evil: The Best Way Out of the Balkans
17. The Pitfalls of Universal Jurisdiction
24. NATO Expansion: The Anatomy of a Decision

Natural resources

27. Q: Should the United States Renew the Iran Libya Sanctions Act?

North Atlantic Treaty Organization

9. The Lesser Evil: The Best Way Out of the Balkans
17. The Pitfalls of Universal Jurisdiction
24. NATO Expansion: The Anatomy of a Decision

Nuclear weapons

6. Russian Foreign Policy: Promise or Peril?
34. Ending the Nuclear Nightmare: A Strategy for the Bush Administration

Peacekeeping

9. The Lesser Evil: The Best Way Out of the Balkans
17. The Pitfalls of Universal Jurisdiction
19. The Folk Who Live on the Hill
23. America's Postmodern Military

Policy making

23. America's Postmodern Military
24. NATO Expansion: The Anatomy of a Decision
25. Outmaneuvered, Outgunned, and Out of View: Test Ban Debacle
26. A Four-Star Foreign Policy?
35. Mission Impossible

Presidency

21. Perils of Presidential Transition
25. Outmaneuvered, Outgunned, and Out of View: Test Ban Debacle

Public opinion

15. The New Apathy

Russia

4. In From the Cold: A New Approach to Relations With Russia and China
6. Russian Foreign Policy: Promise or Peril?
7. Against Russophobia
24. NATO Expansion: The Anatomy of a Decision
35. Mission Impossible

State Department

16. Allies in Search of a Strategy
22. The One Percent Solution: Shirking the Cost of World Leadership
26. A Four-Star Foreign Policy?
29. The Death of the Washington Consensus?

Taiwan

10. East Asia: Security and Complexity
11. To Be an Enlightened Superpower

Taliban

2. War on Terrorism

Terrorism

1. The American Way of Victory: A Twentieth-Century Trilogy
2. War on Terrorism
16. Allies in Search of a Strategy
27. Q: Should the United States Renew the Iran Libya Sanctions Act?
31. Responding to Terrorism
32. War on America: The New Enemy

Terrorist attacks

2. War on Terrorism
31. Responding to Terrorism
32. War on America: The New Enemy

Terrorists

2. War on Terrorism
31. Responding to Terrorism

Trade

1. The American Way of Victory: A Twentieth-Century Trilogy
18. States' Rights and Foreign Policy: Some Things Should Be Left to Washington
29. The Death of the Washington Consensus?
30. Globalization After Seattle

United Nations

9. The Lesser Evil: The Best Way Out of the Balkans
17. The Pitfalls of Universal Jurisdiction
22. The One Percent Solution: Shirking the Cost of World Leadership

Warfare

1. The American Way of Victory: A Twentieth-Century Trilogy

War on terrorism

2. War on Terrorism
32. War on America: The New Enemy

World Wide Web Sites

The following World Wide Web sites have been carefully researched and selected to support the articles found in this reader. The easiest way to access these selected sites is to go to our DUSHKIN ONLINE support site at *http://www.dushkin.com/online/*.

AE: American Foreign Policy 02/03

The following sites were available at the time of publication. Visit our Web site—we update DUSHKIN ONLINE regularly to reflect any changes.

General Sources

The Federal Web Locator
http://www.infoctr.edu/fwl/

Use this handy site as a launching pad for the Web sites of federal U.S. agencies, departments, and organizations. It is well organized and easy to use for informational and research purposes.

Foreign Affairs
http://www.foreignaffairs.org

The *Foreign Affairs* site allows users to search the magazine's archives and provides access to the field's leading journals, documents, online resources, and so on. Links to dozens of other related Web sites are possible from here.

International Information Programs
http://usinfo.state.gov

This wide-ranging page offered by the State Department provides definitions, related documentation, and a discussion of topics of concern to students of foreign policy and foreign affairs. It addresses today's hot topics as well as ongoing issues that form the foundation of the field. Many Web links are provided.

Oneworld.net
http://www.oneworld.net/front.shtml

Information and news about issues related to human sustainable development throughout the world is available at this site by topic or by country.

U.S. International Affairs
http://www.state.gov/www/regions/internat.html

Data on U.S. foreign policy around the world are available here. Some of the areas covered are arms control, economics and trade, international organizations, environmental issues, terrorism, current treaties, and international women's issues.

UNIT 1: The United States and the World: Strategic Choices

The Bulletin of the Atomic Scientists
http://www.bullatomsci.org

This site allows you to read more about the Doomsday Clock and other issues as well as topics related to nuclear weaponry, arms control, and disarmament.

The Henry L. Stimson Center
http://www.stimson.org

The Stimson Center, a nonprofit and (self-described) nonpartisan organization, focuses on issues where policy, technology, and politics intersect. Use this site to find assessments of U.S. foreign policy in the post–cold war world and to research many other topics.

ISN International Relations and Security Network
http://www.isn.ethz.ch

Maintained by the Center for Security Studies and Conflict Research, this site is a clearinghouse for information on international relations and security policy. The many topics are listed by category (Traditional Dimensions of Security and New Dimensions of Security) and by major world regions.

UNIT 2: The United States and the World: Regional and Bilateral Relations

Center for Russian, East European, and Eurasian Studies
http://reenic.utexas.edu/reenic.html

Information ranging from women's issues to foreign relations and covering more than two dozen countries in Central/Eastern Europe and Eurasia may be found here. Also check out University of Texas/Austin's site on Broader Asia (*http://asnic.utexas.edu/asnic/index.html*) for more insight into bilateral/regional relations.

Inter-American Dialogue (IAD)
http://www.iadialog.org

This IAD Web site provides data on U.S. policy analysis, communication, and exchange in Western Hemisphere affairs. The organization has helped to shape the agenda of issues and choices in hemispheric relations.

World Wide Web Virtual Library: International Affairs Resources
http://www.etown.edu/vl/

Extensive links to learn about specific countries and regions, to research for various think tanks, and to study such vital topics as international law, development, the international economy, human rights, and peacekeeping are available here.

UNIT 3: The Domestic Side of American Foreign Policy

American Diplomacy
http://www.unc.edu/depts/diplomat/

American Diplomacy is an online journal of commentary, analysis, and research on U.S. foreign policy and its results around the world. It provides discussion and information on such topics as Life in the Foreign Service and Americanism and Strategy Security.

Carnegie Endowment for International Peace (CEIP)
http://www.ceip.org

One of the most important goals of CEIP is to stimulate discussion and learning among both experts and the public on a range of international issues. This site provides links to the magazine *Foreign Policy,* to the Moscow Center, and to descriptions of various programs.

RAND
http://www.rand.org

RAND, a nonprofit institution that works to improve public policy through research and analysis, offers links to certain topics and descriptions of RAND activities as well as major research areas (such as international relations and strategic defense policy).

www.dushkin.com/online/

UNIT 4: The Institutional Context of American Foreign Policy

Central Intelligence Agency (CIA)
http://www.cia.gov

Use this official CIA page to learn about many facets of the agency and to connect to other sites and resources.

The NATO Integrated Data Service (NIDS)
http://www.nato.int/structur/nids/nids.htm

NIDS was created to bring information on security-related matters within easy reach of the widest possible audience. Check out this Web site to review North Atlantic Treaty Organization documentation of all kinds, to read *NATO Review* magazine, and to explore key issues in the field of European security and transatlantic cooperation.

United States Department of State
http://www.state.gov/index.html

This State Department page is a must for any student of foreign affairs. Explore this site to find out what the department does, what services it provides, what it says about U.S. interests around the world, and much more.

United States Institute of Peace (USIP)
http://www.usip.org

The USIP, which was created by Congress to promote peaceful resolution of international conflicts, seeks to educate people and disseminate information on how to achieve peace.

UNIT 5: The Foreign Policy–Making Process

Belfer Center for Science and International Affairs (BCSIA)
http://ksgwww.harvard.edu/csia/

BCSIA is the hub of the John F. Kennedy School of Government's research, teaching, and training in international affairs and is related to security, environment, and technology. This site provides insight into the development of leadership in policy making.

InterAction
http://www.interaction.org

InterAction encourages grassroots action and engages government bodies and policymakers on various advocacy issues, including initiatives to expand international humanitarian relief, refugee, and development assistance programs.

National Archives and Records Administration (NARA)
http://www.nara.gov/nara/welcome.html

This official site, which oversees the management of all federal records, offers easy access to background information for students interested in the policy-making process, including a search of federal documents and speeches, and much more.

UNIT 6: U.S. International Economic Strategy

International Monetary Fund (IMF)
http://www.imf.org

This Web site is essential reading for anyone wishing to learn more about this important body's effects on foreign policy and the global economy. It provides information about the IMF, directs readers to various publications and current issues, and suggests links to other organizations.

United States Agency for International Development
http://www.info.usaid.gov

Information about broad and overlapping issues such as Democracy, Population and Health, Economic Growth, Development, and Regions and Countries is available here.

United States Trade Representative
http://www.ustr.gov

The mission of the U.S. Trade Representative is presented on this site. Background information on international trade agreements and links to other sites may be accessed.

World Bank
http://www.worldbank.org

News (including press releases, summaries of new projects, and speeches), publications, and coverage of numerous topics regarding development, countries, and regions are provided at this Web site. It also contains links to other important global financial organizations.

UNIT 7: U.S. Post–Cold War Military Strategy

Arms Control and Disarmament Agency (ACDA)
http://dosfan.lib.uic.edu/acda/

This archival ACDA page provides links to information on arms control and disarmament. Researchers can examine texts of various speeches, treaties, and historical documents. For further current information, go to the Bureau of Arms Control page at *http://www.state.gov/global/arms/bureauac.html.*

The Commission on Global Governance
http://www.cgg.ch

Access to *The Report of the Commission on Global Governance,* produced by an international group of leaders who want to find ways in which the global community can better manage its affairs, is possible on this site. It pays particular attention to reform of the United Nations.

Counterterrorism Page
http://counterterrorism.com

A summary of worldwide terrorism events, groups, and terrorism strategies and tactics, including articles from 1989 to the present of American and international origin, plus links to related Web sites and graphs are available on this Web site.

DefenseLINK
http://www.defenselink.mil/news/

Learn about the Department of Defense at this site. News, publications, and other related sites of interest are noted. BosniaLINK and GulfLINK can also be found here.

Federation of American Scientists (FAS)
http://www.fas.org

FAS, a nonprofit policy organization, maintains this site to provide coverage of such topics as Global Security, Peace and Security, and Governance in the post–cold war world.

Human Rights Web
http://www.hrweb.org

The history of the human rights movement, text on seminal figures, landmark legal and political documents, and ideas on how individuals can get involved in helping to protect human rights around the world can be found here.

We highly recommend that you review our Web site for expanded information and our other product lines. We are continually updating and adding links to our Web site in order to offer you the most usable and useful information that will support and expand the value of your Annual Editions. You can reach us at: *http://www.dushkin.com/annualeditions/.*

UNIT 1

The United States and the World: Strategic Choices

Unit Selections

1. **The American Way of Victory: A Twentieth-Century Trilogy**, James Kurth
2. **War on Terrorism**, David Masci and Kenneth Jost
3. **Different Drummers, Same Drum**, Andrew J. Bacevich
4. **In From the Cold: A New Approach to Relations With Russia and China**, Robert S. McNamara and James G. Blight
5. **The Lonely Superpower**, Samuel P. Huntington

Key Points to Consider

- Make a scorecard of the successes and failures of the Bush administration's foreign policy to date. Defend your choices and explain why these policies turned out as they did.

- Where are the major fault lines of international conflict found today? Discuss this in the light of events since the attacks of September 11, 2001, on the World Trade Center and the Pentagon.

- Has the United States become a rogue superpower? Defend your answer.

- What principles do you think should guide American foreign policy when it conducts humanitarian operations? Should we be involved in these type of efforts at all? Why or why not?

- How much does the past serve as a guide to the future in constructing foreign policy strategies?

 **Links: www.dushkin.com/online/**
These sites are annotated in the World Wide Web pages.

The Bulletin of the Atomic Scientists
http://www.bullatomsci.org
The Henry L. Stimson Center
http://www.stimson.org
ISN International Relations and Security Network
http://www.isn.ethz.ch

Choice in foreign policy is always present. The September 11, 2001, terrorist attacks on the World Trade Center and the Pentagon have not changed this reality. Debate will continue over the wisdom of specific tactics and the strategic vision underlying the war against terrorism. We should also expect debate over the shape of the future world that the United States wishes to see come into existence.

For much of the cold war, the foreign policy debate focused on tactics. A consensus had formed around the policy of containment. It was a policy that identified communism and the Soviet Union as the primary threats to American national interests and that prescribed a strategy of constant vigilance, global competition, and unparalleled military strength. But, there were still choices. Rolling back the iron curtain was a minority view during the 1950s, and cooperation with the Soviet Union was advocated by some during the immediate post–World War II period. In the late 1960s, détente emerged as a serious competitor to containment and succeeded in supplanting it for a brief period of time.

No single vision of American foreign policy emerged as dominant in the first decade of the post–cold war era. R. James Woolsey, President Clinton's first director of the Central Intelligence Agency, has suggested that rather than having to contend with a single menacing dragon, the United States now faces a jungle filled with many poisonous snakes. Instead of containing the dragon, the test for any U.S. foreign policy would be how well it handles these snakes. For neoidealists, the 1990s represented a moment to be seized. It was a time in which the strategies of conflict and confrontation of the cold war could be replaced by strategies designed to foster cooperation among states and to lift the human condition. For neoisolationists, the 1990s provided the United States with the long-awaited opportunity to walk away from the distracting and corrupting influence of international affairs and focus instead on domestic concerns and embrace traditional American values.

Thus, when it entered office, the Bush administration found itself in the position of continuing the search for a strategic framework around which to organize American foreign policy. Its early initiatives suggested it would pursue a foreign policy based on unilateralist principles and favoring disengagement from global problem-solving efforts. This was evidenced in its withdrawal from the Kyoto protocol and its stated desire to extract the United States from involvement in the Balkans, the negotiations with North Korea, and the brokering of a Middle East peace accord. Pursuit of a national ballistic missile defense system in face of global opposition further reinforced this perception.

The terrorist attacks of September 11, 2001, fundamentally altered the Bush administration's foreign policy and domestic agenda. It will now view choices and visions of the future through a different set of lenses. One danger to be avoided is to dismissing as irrelevant all foreign policy thoughts that preceded the attack. They are particularly valuable for their ability to focus our thinking on the range of alternative futures open to us and for alerting us to missteps in the conduct of American foreign policy.

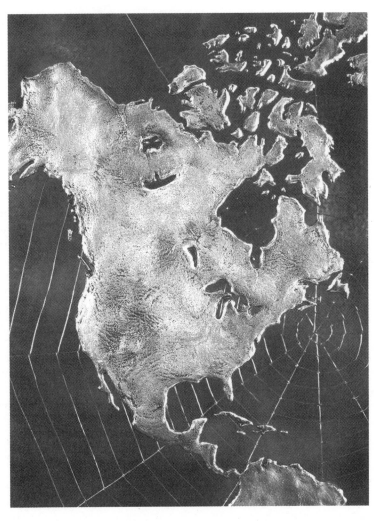

The essays in this unit introduce us to the scope of the contemporary debate over the shape of the world and the choices open to the United States. The first article, "The American Way of Victory: A Twentieth-Century Trilogy," is a panoramic view of military and economic strategies used after the two world wars. This article is followed by "War on Terrorism," by David Masci and Kenneth Jost, which brings history to the U.S. and British air and ground attacks on Afghanistan on October 7, 2001.

The next article, "Different Drummers, Same Drum," raises the question of just how different Clinton and Bush are in their thinking about foreign policy. Robert McNamara and James Blight, in "In From the Cold," call for a new strategic approach for dealing with Russia and China. In the fifth article, "The Lonely Superpower," Samuel Huntington argues that the world is not unipolar but that the United States is behaving as if it were. This is creating resentment among other states and creating a situation in which the United States has become a rogue superpower. Huntington examines the response of other states to American foreign policy and puts forward a strategy for the United States to follow.

The American Way of Victory: A Twentieth-Century Trilogy

James Kurth

THE TWENTIETH century, the first American century, was also the century of three world wars. The United States was not only victorious in the First World War, the Second World War and the Cold War, but it was more victorious than any of the other victor powers. As the pre-eminent victor power, the subsequent strategies of the United States did much to shape the three postwar worlds. They therefore also did much to prepare the ground for the second and third world wars in the sequence. Now, ten years after the American victory in that third, cold, world war, it is time to evaluate the U.S. victor strategies of the 1990s and to consider if they will make the twenty-first century a second American century, this time one of world peace and prosperity, or if they could lead, sometime in the next few decades, to a fourth world war.

The First and Second British Centuries

LIKE America at the beginning of the twenty-first century, Britain in the early nineteenth century had passed through a century of three wars that were worldwide in scope—the War of the Spanish Succession (1702–13), the Seven Years' War (1756–63) and the successive Wars of the French Revolution and Napoleonic Wars (1792–1815). Britain had been victorious in each of these wars, making the eighteenth century something of a British one. The victor strategy that Britain pursued after the Napoleonic Wars laid the foundations for what has been called "the Hundred Years Peace" (1815–1914), making the second British century as peaceful as the first one had been war-like.[1]

The central elements of the British victor strategy were four; two involved international security and two involved the international economy.[2] The security elements were established immediately after the victory over Napoleon. They were, first, a British-managed balance of power system on the European continent, and, second, British naval supremacy in the rest of the world. The eco-

nomic elements were established about a generation later. They involved, third, British industrial supremacy operating in an open international economy (Britain serving as "the workshop of the world"), and, fourth, British financial supremacy, also operating in an open international economy (the City of London serving as "the world's central bank").

By the beginning of the twentieth century, however, British naval and industrial supremacy were threatened by the spectacular growth of German military and economic power. When in August 1914 it appeared that Germany was about to destroy the Continental balance of power system with its invasion of Belgium and France, Britain went to war to stop it. The Hundred Years Peace and the second British century came to a crashing and catastrophic end with the First World War.

Victory therefore presents a profound challenge to a victor power, especially to a pre-eminent one: it must create a victor strategy to order the postwar world in a way that does not lead to a new major war. The British victor strategy after the Napoleonic Wars was successful in meeting this challenge for almost a century. But even this sophisticated strategy ultimately proved inadequate to the task of managing the problems posed by the rise of a new and very assertive power. As shall be discussed below, the American victor strategies after the First and Second World Wars were similar to the earlier British one in their efforts to combine several different dimensions of international security and economy; indeed, the American strategies relied upon some of the same elements, particularly naval, industrial and financial supremacy. They did not, however, succeed in preventing the Second World War and the Cold War. The fundamental question for our time is whether the American victor strategies after the Cold War will succeed in preventing some kind of a new world war in the next century.

As it happens, the Spring 2000 issue of *The National Interest* contained an array of articles that can help us address this question. In considering the lessons that can be drawn from the earlier American experiences of living with victory, I shall be making use of them. In particular, these lessons underline the importance of managing the rise of Chinese military and economic power and of doing so in ways similar to those that Zbigniew Brzezinski advocates in his "Living With China." They also underline the danger but potential relevance of the arguments that Robert Kagan and William Kristol advance in their essay, "The Present Danger."

Living With Victory After the First World War

IT TOOK FOUR years of war and the massive engagement of the United States before, in November 1918, the Western Allies succeeded in defeating Germany. But even in defeat, the nation whose rise to military and economic power Britain had failed to manage still retained most of its inherent strengths. The German problem, which had been at the center of international relations before the war, was redefined by the Allied victory, but it was still there, and Western victory still had to focus upon the German reality.

Germany remained the central nation on the European continent. Demographically, it had the largest and best educated population in Europe. (Russia, although it had a larger population, was convulsed by revolution and civil war.) Economically, it had the largest and most advanced industry in Europe. Strategically, it faced formidable powers to the west (France and Britain), but to the east lay only new and weak states (Poland and Czechoslovakia). In this sense, Germany's strategic position was actually better after its defeat in the First World War than it had been before the war began, when to the east it had faced Russia as a great power. It would only be a matter of time before Germany recovered its political unity, gathered up its inherent strengths, and once again converted these into military and economic power. This was the long-term reality that the victorious Allies had to consider as they composed their victor strategies.

There were four basic strategies that different allies employed at different times: territorial dismemberment, military containment, security cooperation and economic engagement. These were not new inventions; they derived from the strategies employed by victor powers after earlier wars. The first two derived from territorial annexations and frontier fortifications, strategies that the Continental powers had used against each other in the eighteenth and nineteenth centuries. The last two derived from the "concert of Europe", or balance of power system, and the open international economy that Britain had managed in the nineteenth century. But these strategies were not obsolescent conceptions; the latter three prefigured the victor strategies that the United States would employ after the Second World War and after the Cold War.

Territorial dismemberment and military containment.

One apparent solution to the German problem was territorial dismemberment. This was the strategy preferred by France. The dismemberment of a defeated enemy can sometimes be carried out by victorious powers, and the Allies did so with that other Central Power in World War I, the Austro-Hungarian monarchy. But while this division destroyed a former adversary, it unleashed a sort of international anarchy in southeastern Europe that still reverberates today. Dismemberment is also what happened to the Soviet Union after the Cold War. Here too, while this division greatly diminished a former adversary, it has unleashed internal and international anarchy in the Caucasus and Central Asia.

Whatever might be the advantages of dismemberment as a victor strategy, they were not applicable to Germany in 1919. By that time, the German nation had become a solid reality with a solid identity; it could not be permanently undone by artificial territorial divisions, unless these were enforced by military occupation (which is how the division of Germany was to be enforced after the Second World War). There are today a few international analysts who argue that the United States should encourage the territorial division of troublesome powers, particularly Russia and China. There are, however, hardly any specialists on China or even Russia who believe that a permanent division of these nations is possible.

An alternative but closely related solution to the German problem was military containment. This was the objective of the Treaty of Versailles, which set up what was known as the Versailles system to carry it out. Military containment was another victor strategy chosen by France, and in the early 1920s the French were quite active at implementing it, as in their military occupation of the Ruhr in 1923.

The Democratic administration of President Woodrow Wilson advanced a kinder, gentler version of the Versailles system in its proposals for a League of Nations and a U.S. security guarantee to France and Britain. The military containment of Germany embodied in the security guarantee would be institutionalized and legitimatized in a collective security system embodied in the League. But, of course, the Republican-controlled U.S. Senate rejected these proposals, and the United States never again considered the strategy of military containment as a solution to the German problem.

Economic engagement and security cooperation.

Instead, a few years later, the United States addressed the German problem (now accentuated by the unstable French occupation of the Ruhr) with a strategy of economic engagement. This took the form of the Dawes Plan, an ingenious project for financial recycling, in which American banks loaned capital to Germany, Germany paid war reparations to France and Britain, and France and Britain repaid war debts to the American banks. The Dawes Plan thus encouraged an open international economy among the most advanced economies, and it sought to integrate Germany into this mutually beneficial system.[3]

The Dawes Plan succeeded very well from 1924 to 1929. It formed the basis for Germany's reintegration not only into the international economic system but into the international security system as well. It encouraged France and Britain to develop a new strategy of security cooperation toward Germany. In 1925 they signed the Lucarno security treaty with Germany, and in 1926 Germany entered the League of Nations. The new American strategy of economic engagement seemed to be working far better than the earlier French strategy of military containment.

But as Charles Kindleberger famously demonstrated in his 1973 book, *The World in Depression 1929–1939*, an open international economic system requires an "economic hegemon" to keep it running, in bad times as well as good. The economic hegemon performs three essential functions: (1) providing long-term loans and investments (as in the Dawes Plan); (2) providing short-term credits and foreign exchange in times of currency crises; and (3) opening its markets to receive the exports of economies that are passing through recession. Britain had performed these functions before the First World War, and they in turn had provided the economic foundations for the Hundred Years Peace. After the war, however, Britain no longer had the economic strength to play the hegemon role, even though it still had the will. Conversely, the United States now had the economic strength but had not yet developed the will. The Dawes Plan was only one step in the right direction, and it was a step in only one dimension. Still, for a few years in the prosperous 1920s, the international economy seemed to be operating well enough without an economic hegemon.

The prosperous and open international economic system of the 1920s allowed the victor powers to engage in a strategy of security cooperation (or even appeasement, then still an innocuous term). Given the success of the strategies of economic engagement and security cooperation, the strategy of military containment appeared unnecessary or even counterproductive, and it was largely abandoned even by France. But, with the exception of the Dawes Plan, neither Britain nor the United States stepped forward to assume leadership in managing either the German problem or the international economy, in good times or bad.

With the beginning of the Great Depression (which Kindleberger ascribed to the failure of the United States to act as an economic hegemon), the prosperous and open economic system of the 1920s collapsed and was replaced with the impoverished and closed economic system of the 1930s. Whereas the prosperity system had permitted a strategy of appeasement, the poverty system required a strategy of containment. But for political reasons (polarization between the Left and the Right), France in the 1930s no longer had the political will to provide leadership for such a strategy.

Leadership in managing the German problem fell by default to Britain, which had never been a strong believer in the strategy of military containment. It chose instead a modest version of the strategy of economic engagement, at a time when the conditions of the Depression made this no longer adequate and attractive for Germany. Further, economic engagement seemed to imply a strategy of security appeasement, which was now even less appropriate for Germany. As for the United States, with the collapse of the Dawes Plan it gave up on any effort to manage the German problem at all.

Thus, by the early 1930s, none of the three victor powers from World War I—France, Britain and the United States—was pursuing a coherent and consistent strategy to preserve its victory. With the coming to power of the National Socialist regime, Germany decided to manage the German problem in its own way. The Second World War was the result.

ON THE OTHER side of the world in East Asia, the United States pursued a quite different strategy. Here it faced the rising power of Japan, which had been an ally of Britain since 1902 and which was one of the victor powers in the First World War. Japan's growing military and economic strengths and its ambitions in China presented a serious challenge to the dominant powers in East Asia in the early 1920s, the United States and Britain.

The Republican administration of President Warren G. Harding, and particularly his secretary of state, Charles Evans Hughes, took the lead in designing an innovative strategy of security cooperation to deal with Japan.[4] It convened a conference in Washington in 1921–22, out of which came the following security elements: the Washington Naval Treaty, an agreement between the United States, Britain and Japan to limit the numbers of their battleships; the Four-Power Treaty, which provided for consultations on security issues among these three powers plus France; and the Nine-Power Treaty, which provided for common principles and cooperation in regard to China. These arrangements, which were later called "the Washington system", were an elaboration of the U.S. strategy of security cooperation. However, the United States did not develop a comparable strategy of economic engagement for Japan, to serve as the basis for this security strategy. Instead, it largely relied on conventional international trade between the two nations, which seemed sufficient in the prosperous and open international economy of the 1920s. But with the beginning of the Great Depression, this international trade largely collapsed, and the collapse of the Washington system of security cooperation soon followed.

Thus by the mid-1920s, the United States had conceived of some important elements for a victor strategy. In Europe, the Dawes Plan echoed the nineteenth-century

British use of financial power in an open international economy. In East Asia, the Washington system echoed the nineteenth-century British use of naval power and balance of power management. But there was not much of a U.S. security strategy in Europe or of a U.S. economic strategy in East Asia. The U.S. victor strategies after the First World War had not added up to a grand design. They failed to prevent the Great Depression and the ensuing Second World War.

Why did the United States fail to adopt a coherent and consistent victor strategy after World War I? The traditional explanation blames American immaturity and "idealism", and the resulting "isolationism." A related explanation blames the isolationism and protectionism of the Republican Party. However, the Dawes Plan and the Washington system were quite sophisticated projects (even by British standards) that can hardly be described as isolationist—and these were projects advanced by Republican administrations.

The main reason why the United States did not have a coherent and consistent victor strategy was that its victory in 1918 was *too* complete. As a result, in the 1920s the United States faced no obvious great power adversary or "peer competitor", which could have concentrated the American mind and provided the desirable coherence and consistency. Conversely, in the 1930s the Great Depression produced a real American isolationism. It also produced real great power adversaries (Germany and Japan), but these posed quite different strategic threats in quite different regions. This too made it difficult for the United States to compose a coherent and consistent strategy.

Living With Victory After the Second World War

THE UNITED States learned profound lessons from the failure of the Versailles and Washington systems to manage the German and Japanese problems and to prevent the Second World War. As it turned out, these lessons were largely expanded versions of the lessons that the Wilson administration, the Harding administration and the American bankers had already learned from the First World War. As World War II was drawing to a close, the United States took the lead in establishing a number of international institutions that would complete the first but abortive steps taken after the previous war.

Security cooperation and economic engagement.

On the security dimension, the United Nations was to succeed and perfect the League of Nations. On the economic dimension, three organizations were to help the United States perform the role of economic hegemon, one for each of the three functions identified by Kindleberger. The task of long-term lending would be promoted by the International Bank for Reconstruction and Development (the World Bank); the task of short-term currency support would be promoted by the International Monetary Fund; and the task of opening trade would be promoted by an International Trade Organization (ITO). Together, the three organizations were known as the Bretton Woods system. As it happened, the Republican-controlled U.S. Senate rejected the ITO treaty in 1947, but a less institutionalized arrangement, the General Agreement on Tariffs and Trade, took its place. (Almost fifty years later, the World Trade Organization was established, and this at last completed the original grand design.) The overall victor strategy of the United States was one of security cooperation based upon economic engagement.

This strategy—and its elaborate United Nations and Bretton Woods system—might have been perfect for dealing with the German and Japanese problems that existed after the First World War. But the problems that now existed were altogether different. Whereas after the first war Germany was not defeated enough, after the second it was defeated too much. The victorious allies, including the United States, could easily, and almost automatically, impose the alternative and simpler victor strategy of territorial division and military occupation, and at first they did so.

Conversely, whereas after the first war Russia was in a sense doubly defeated (first by the German army and then by the chaos of the Russian Revolution and Civil War), after the second it was doubly victorious (first by defeating Germany and then by occupying or annexing—along with its soon-to-be involuntary allies, Poland and Czechoslovakia—the eastern half of it). The German problem suddenly ceased to be the central problem of international security and instead became a subordinate part of the new central problem, which was the Russian one.

The United States initially tried to apply its overall strategy of security cooperation and economic engagement to this new Russian problem. But it was crucial to this strategy that it be implemented through international institutions led by the United States, i.e., the United Nations and the Bretton Woods system. Both the strategy and its systems were incompatible with the interests of the Soviet Union, as those were defined by Stalin. Security cooperation and economic engagement required some degree of an open society and a free market, and these contradicted the closed society and command economy that characterized the Soviet Union. Instead, the worldwide reach of the American system was aborted by the Cold War and the establishment of the Soviet bloc.

The United States therefore was only able to apply its strategy and system to the Free World, especially the First World. In Europe, the United Nations was replaced by NATO, and the Bretton Woods system was reinforced by the Marshall Plan. NATO represented a sort of second coming of Wilson's abortive security guarantee to France and Britain, as was the Marshall Plan a second coming of the Dawes Plan. In East Asia, the United States concluded a series of bilateral security treaties and bilateral economic aid programs (including the Dodge Plan for Japan). The ensemble of security treaties echoed the earlier Washington system, and since it was based upon U.S. naval supremacy in the Pacific, it also echoed earlier British strategies based upon naval supremacy.

This American strategy and this system, whose prototypes had been aborted after the First World War and whose applications were confined to only half the world after the Second World War, were extraordinarily successful where they did operate. They certainly helped to solve a good part of the old German and Japanese problems. However, they could not solve the new Russian problem (some historians think that they even accentuated it). The result was the Cold War.

Military containment.

The Russian problem was addressed by a version of the alternative victor strategy, military containment—in this case, containment not of the recently defeated enemy but of the victorious ally. By 1948 there had already been the sudden reversal of the alliance between the Western Allies (Britain and the United States) and the Soviet Union against Germany into an emerging alliance between the Western Allies and Germany against the Soviet Union. The rapidity of the transformation was quite breathtaking, but it was readily accepted by the American public. (In his famous novel, *1984*, written in 1948 as this transformation was being completed, George Orwell portrayed the sudden reversal of the alliance between Oceania and Eastasia against Eurasia into an alliance between Oceania and Eurasia against Eastasia.)

When the communists came to power on the Chinese mainland in 1949, they presented a new security problem. For a brief time, the Truman administration was inclined to hope that some version of the strategy of security cooperation (perhaps based upon traditional Chinese suspicions of Russia) and economic engagement would work to solve this new Chinese problem, but this hope was aborted by Mao's alliance with Stalin in January 1950, the Chinese entry into the Korean War in November 1950, and the closed society and command economy that characterized communist China.

The prosperous and open international economic system of the 1920s had permitted a strategy of security cooperation or appeasement toward Germany and Japan. But this was because these two nations had capitalist economies and were willing to engage with a prosperous and open international economy. When the international economy ceased to be so, the basis for a strategy of security appeasement disappeared; the only effective alternative would have been a strategy of military containment.

The Soviet Union and communist China in the 1940s–50s, on the other hand, were command economies. Because of this, they were not willing to engage with an open international economy, even one that was prosper-

ous. Consequently, there was no basis for a strategy of security cooperation (or appeasement). The alternative strategy of military containment therefore became necessary. But although containment of the Soviet Union and communist China was necessary, it did present problems of its own. Military containment once led to defeat for the United States (the Vietnam War) and once led to near disaster for the world (the Cuban Missile Crisis). And military containment by itself was not sufficient to defeat the Soviet Union, to reform communist China, and to bring about a U.S. victory in the Cold War. The successful and sustained operation of the free market and open international economy in the First or Free World, in contrast with the gradual but steady exhaustion of the command and closed economic systems in the Second or Communist World, exerted a magnetic force upon the Soviet Union and China, and drove them by the 1980s, each in its own way, to reform their economies and to engage in the American-led international economic system. But of course this did not happen quickly or easily. Forty years of Cold War and military containment were the price.

Why did the United States succeed in adopting a generally coherent and consistent victor strategy after the Second World War? The main reason was that its victory was in some sense a Pyrrhic one. The German enemy was replaced almost immediately by the Russian one, and the Japanese enemy was soon replaced by the Chinese one. Even more, since both enemies were communist and initially were in alliance, they could easily be seen as one enormous enemy. This wonderfully concentrated the American mind into a generally coherent and consistent strategy in the late 1940s and 1950s.

Living With Victory After the Cold War

THE circumstances of victory and defeat after the Cold War had more in common with those pertaining after the First World War than those after the Second.

The redefined Russian problem.

Russia was more defeated after the Cold War than Germany after the First World War (but less defeated than Germany after the Second). As the Soviet Union was reinvented as Russia, it lost a quarter of its territory and half of its population. The Russian economy in the 1990s was beset both by deep depression and by high inflation, and the Russian military was beset by weakness and incompetence, with only an arsenal of nuclear weapons remaining as the legacy from the era of Soviet power. The strategic position of Russia was removed from the center to the periphery of the European continent, and it remained the central nation only in the emptiness of Central Asia. The Russian problem was redefined from being one of organized power into one of organized crime. Only in 2000—with a new president, Vladimir Putin, modest economic recovery and ambiguous military success in the Chechnya war—are there signs that Russia may have begun a revival to the degree that Germany did in the mid-1920s.

The U.S. victor strategy toward this "Weimar Russia" has been a variation of that adopted toward Weimar Germany, a new version of the strategy of security cooperation and economic engagement. Russia's generally positive role in the United Nations echoes Germany's role in the League. However, the enlargement of NATO into Eastern Europe (really a form of military containment of Russia) echoes Wilson's abortive security guarantee to Western Europe (really a form of military containment of Germany). The extensive U.S. and international economic aid to Russia echoes the Dawes Plan (although it has not been nearly as extensive and effective as the Marshall Plan). But just as the U.S. victor strategy toward Germany in the 1920s depended upon integrating that nation into an international economy that remained open and prosperous, so too does the contemporary U.S. victor strategy toward Russia. It would fail if either the international economy collapsed into one that was closed and depressed (like the 1930s), or if the Russian economy reverted into one that was closed and command (like the 1940s–70s).

The new Chinese problem.

In East Asia, the United States faces the rising power of China, a situation not unlike that it faced with Japan after the First World War. China's growing economic and military strengths, and its goals regarding Taiwan and the South China Sea, have presented a serious challenge. Indeed, the Chinese problem after the Cold War has been an even greater challenge for the United States than the Japanese problem was after the First World War (although it is not nearly as threatening as the Russian problem was after the Second).

The U.S. strategy toward China that evolved in the 1990s has in some sense been an inversion of the U.S. strategy toward Japan in the 1920s (and an expansion of the U.S. strategy toward Weimar Germany). Whereas the strategy toward Japan provided for an elaborate system of security cooperation (the Washington system) but only for relatively simple economic engagement (conventional international trade), the strategy toward China provides for an elaborate system of economic engagement ("the Washington consensus", including the admission of China into the World Trade Organization), but for relatively simple security cooperation (conventional military visits). In a more important sense, however, the U.S. strategy involves an innovative combination of economic engagement and military containment (particularly in respect to Taiwan and the South China Sea). But since China thinks of Taiwan as being properly part of China, what the United States perceives as its strategy of military containment, China perceives as a strategy of territorial dismemberment.

Probably the most difficult single challenge facing the contemporary U.S. victor strategy is how to sustain this innovative and complex combination of economic engagement and military containment in regard to China. The article by Zbigniew Brzezinski, "Living With China", is a sustained and eminently sensible analysis of this problem. In essence, he hopes that the Taiwan independence question can be dissolved into the World Trade Organization, that the tensions from military containment can themselves be contained by the rewards of economic engagement. His proposals are thus very different from those of Robert Kagan and William Kristol in "The Present Danger", who hardly consider the international economy at all. Consequently, they advocate a pure strategy of military containment toward China, including U.S. efforts to bring about a "regime change."

We have seen that the U.S. strategies toward Germany and Japan in the 1920s depended upon integrating those nations into an open and prosperous international economy, and that the U.S. contemporary strategy toward Russia depends upon the same. To an even greater extent, the U.S. strategy toward China has as its foundation the integration of that giant nation—one with more and more of a nationalist mentality—into such a global economy. If the global economy were to exclude China from its benefits, or if it were to become a closed and depressed one, the entire complex U.S. strategy toward China would collapse. The United States would be driven, at best, to the classic alternative, a simple strategy of military containment, or, at worst, as was the case in the 1930s in regard to both Germany and Japan, to no strategy at all. At that point, the proposals of Brzezinski would become obsolete, and the proposals of Kagan and Kristol could appear to be necessary. The management of the new China problem therefore depends upon the management of the new global economy, and the development of any real Sino-American security cooperation depends upon the performance of the United States as the global economic hegemon.

Challenges to the Victor

The culminating point of victory.

EVEN when a victor power conceives a victor strategy that is sound and appropriate to the military and economic realities of the time, there will be challenges that arise from how it is implemented. The first of these challenges is to determine what is, in Clausewitz's phrase, "the culminating point of victory", and to not go beyond it. Victor powers are prone to succumb to "the victory disease"; they continue to pursue the strategies that brought them victory in the utterly new and inappropriate circumstances that the victory has created. Concentration in war becomes compulsion in victory. The most famous example of the twentieth century was Hitler following his successful blitzkriegs of Poland and France with his disastrous invasion of the Soviet Union. The most familiar American example was MacArthur following his successful landing at Inchon and recovery of South Korea with his disastrous drive to the Yalu River and the Chinese border, resulting in China's entry into the war.

A contemporary American example of going beyond the culminating point of victory could be the enlargement of NATO. Although the admission of Poland, the Czech Republic and Hungary may not have passed that point, a "second round of enlargement" including the Baltic states and reaching the most sensitive borders of Russia probably would do so. This kind of victory disorder may also be developing with the U.S. promotion of human rights over national sovereignty, and especially with the use of military force for the purpose of humanitarian intervention. The 1995 U.S.-led humanitarian intervention in Bosnia was accepted by all of the other major powers. The 1999 U.S.-led humanitarian intervention in Kosovo was greatly resented, and in some measure rejected, by Russia and China. A third such intervention anytime soon, especially in a country traditionally in the sphere of influence of Russia (e.g., the Caucasus and Central Asia) or of China (e.g., the South China Sea), very likely would go beyond the culminating point of victory; it would represent a humanitarian disease.

The realistic range of opportunities.

The second challenge for the victor power is in some sense the opposite of the first. It is to determine what is the realistic range of opportunities resulting from victory. The victor power is suddenly in a position where all things seem possible, where there are too many options. It may erratically pursue this objective, then that, and then another. Versatility in war becomes diffusion, even dissipation, in victory. This is an error to which pluralist democracies, with their different interest groups, are especially prone.

It has often been argued that Britain succumbed to this victory disorder in the nineteenth century. The British continued to expand their colonial empire, one of the opportunities that came with their victory in the Napoleonic Wars, until they entered into the condition of "imperial overstretch." One result was that Britain had to undertake numerous and continuous military operations on "the turbulent frontier." Another result, more serious in its long-run consequences, was that the ample British investment capital was diffused across a wide range of colonies and foreign countries, rather than concentrated upon the development of new technologies and industries within Britain itself. Such new technologies and industries would have better suited Britain for its competition with Germany.

A contemporary American example of the error of diffusion or dissipation seems to be developing with the U.S. promotion of every aspect of the American way of life in every part of the world. The promotion of economic globalization may be inherent in the U.S. performance as economic hegemon, but it does weaken the economic conditions and social bonds of many Americans. Even more, the promotion of social and cultural globalization—of the American way of expressive individualism, popular culture and the dysfunctional family—has generated resentment and resistance in a wide arc of countries in the Middle East, South Asia and East Asia. This, it seems, is the American way of producing a turbulent frontier.

The balancing effect.

The third challenge is the most familiar and the most fundamental, although Americans are inclined to think that they are exempt from it. It is derived from the well-known balancing effect. Victory brings the pre-eminent victor power hegemony, which in turn can initiate a realignment of the lesser victor powers against it (perhaps joined by the defeated one). The balancing effect was always especially pronounced among the continental powers of Europe. However, since Britain was an offshore power with no ambitions for territorial acquisitions on the continent, its victories did not initiate this balancing process. Indeed, its role as an "offshore balancer" helped it on occasion to exercise a sort of offshore hegemony.

The United States has served as an offshore or rather overseas balancer for Europe and also for East Asia. Even more than Britain, its remote position has permitted it to exercise an overseas hegemony over the nations of Western Europe (while balancing against the Soviet Union) and over those of East Asia (while balancing against China). Indeed, the United States continues to exercise this overseas hegemony, now over all of Europe, even with the collapse of the Soviet Union and with no other power to balance at all. By historical comparison with the European past, this hegemonic security system is an extraordinary achievement on the part of the United States. Were America located on the continent where France is, or even thirty miles offshore where Britain is, it probably would not have occurred; it can exist because the United States is located an ocean away and in another hemisphere. The U.S. hegemonic security system in East Asia continues to include Japan, South Korea, the Philippines and the problematic Taiwan; it provides the basis for any strategy of military containment of China.

The overseas location of the United States thus enables it to avoid the balancing effect and instead to perform the role of security hegemon in Europe, parts of East Asia and, in more complicated conditions, parts of the Middle East (as in the Gulf War and the continuing air strikes against Iraq). Of course, the United States also acts as the security hegemon in Latin America, where there is no prospect of a balancing effect against "the colossus of the North" (a case of an opposite phenomenon, which international relations specialists call the "bandwagoning effect").

Hegemony versus hyper-victory.

The U.S. role as the security hegemon in several regions of the globe complements the U.S. role as the economic hegemon in the global economy. America's security hegemony is acceptable because of its unique overseas location and the sustained peace that it has provided. Its economic hegemony is acceptable because of the unique economic functions that it performs and the sustained prosperity that it has produced. The United States has operated the security and economic dimensions of hegemony together to consolidate and preserve its great victory after the Cold War. It does so in ways reminiscent of Britain coordinating the security and economic dimensions of its supremacy to consolidate and preserve its great victory after the Napoleonic Wars.

This splendid achievement of the United States could be undermined, however, by its own actions. The victory disorders of compulsion and dissipation could eventually overcome even the powerful U.S. advantages of overseas position and economic performance, and drive some major powers—most obviously China and Russia—into the balancing effect and even into a sort of containment policy directed at the United States. This was the prospect put forward by Samuel Huntington in his famous argument about the "clash of civilizations." Huntington was concerned that American excesses could bring about a Sino-Islamic alliance or even "the West versus the Rest." These prospects would become even more likely if the prosperous and open international economy should turn into a poor and closed one—if the "New Economy" of the 1990s, based upon the computer and the Internet, should suddenly collapse, as the "New Era" economy of the 1920s, based upon the automobile and the radio, had done.

Whatever form a balancing effect or containment coalition might take, however, at its core would be China. It would be the new Central Power on the Eurasian land mass, just as it was once the Middle Kingdom. The arrival of this coalition on the international scene would mean that the U.S. victory after the first cold war would have been followed by a second cold war (or worse), and this in turn would mean another war on a global scale. This alone makes living with China the single most important challenge facing a United States that is still living with victory, and which is still expecting to do so for decades to come.

Notes

1. Karl Polanyi, *The Great Transformation: The Political and Economic Origins of Our Time* (Boston: Beacon Press, 1957), chapter 1.
2. Realist theories of international relations focus on international security; liberal theories focus on the international economy. In practice, however, successful strategies have combined both, e.g., the British strategy of the nineteenth century and the American strategy during the Cold War. At its best, the Anglo-American tradition in international relations has been *both* realist and liberal. See my "Inside the Cave: The Banality of I.R. Studies", *The National Interest* (Fall 1998).
3. P.M.H. Bell, *The Origins of the Second World War in Europe*, second edition (New York: Longman, 1997), chapter 3.
4. Akira Iriye, *The Origins of the Second World War in Asia and the Pacific* (New York: Longman, 1987), chapter 1.

James Kurth is Claude Smith Professor of Political Science at Swarthmore College.

War on Terrorism

BY DAVID MASCI AND KENNETH JOST

THE ISSUES

The images of Sept. 11 will be seared into the nation's collective consciousness for generations to come. Two hijacked airplanes, one after the other, smashing into the World Trade Center's twin towers in the heart of New York City's financial district; the two 110-story skyscrapers erupting in flames and then collapsing into a vast cloud of billowing smoke and debris. And in Arlington, Va., an entire section of the massive Pentagon crushed and in flames after being hit by a third plane.*

As the magnitude of the terrorist attacks became clear, Americans reacted with shock and grief. By evening, those emotions had been forged into a sense of national unity, as well as intense anger at the perpetrators of the most devastating terrorist episode in U.S. history. Indeed, the death toll exceeds 5,500 and the economic losses could top $100 billion.

On the night of the attacks, President Bush pledged in brief televised remarks that the government would find the perpetrators, as the first step in a wider "war on terrorism." Although Bush mentioned no suspects, investigators said that the attacks likely were the handiwork of Saudi exile Osama bin Laden and his global terrorist network, Al Qaeda ("the base"). (*See "Bin Laden's War on America"*). The Islamic fundamentalist rulers of Afghanistan, the Taliban, who are protecting bin Laden, also quickly drew U.S. attention.[1]

On Sunday, Oct. 7, Bush launched the war he had been promising. At about noon Eastern Time, the White House announced that the United States and Great Britain had attacked military targets in Afghanistan using land- and sea-based planes and missiles, as well as special ground forces.

"These carefully targeted actions are designed to disrupt the use of Afghanistan as a terrorist base of operations and to attack the military capability of the Taliban regime," Bush said in a televised statement from the White House, about a halfhour after the strikes began. The United States had warned the Taliban, he said, to surrender bin Laden, stop supporting terrorism and release foreign aid workers they were holding. "None of these demands were met," Bush said. "And now, the Taliban will pay a price."

The United States has been the occasional target of terrorists, both at home and overseas, for years.[2] But before Sept. 11, the country largely ignored the issue. Suddenly, fighting terrorism—defined in federal law as premeditated, politically motivated violence typically perpetrated against civilians—had become the nation's top priority.

In the weeks following the terrorist attacks, the United States said it had solidified a case against bin Laden, Al Qaeda and, by association, their Taliban supporters. The U.S. military positioned dozens of ships, hundreds of planes and thousands of troops around Afghanistan with the intention of capturing or killing bin Laden, destroying Al Qaeda's infrastructure and weakening or overthrowing the Taliban. In addition, the U.S. assembled a coalition of European allies—led by British Prime Minister Tony Blair—and moderate Islamic states to support American efforts.

Some analysts argue that the United States cannot just target bin Laden, Al Qaeda and other terrorist groups but also must take military action against those states—like Afghanistan, Iraq and Syria—that support terrorists. The governments of such nations must be overthrown, they say, because they provide the financial and logistical assistance needed to mount complex terrorist operations.

"Without state support, these groups couldn't do the things we saw on Sept. 11," says Jack Spencer, a defense policy analyst at the Heritage Foundation, a conservative think tank. "If we don't deal with state sponsors of terrorism, we're not going to win this fight."

But other experts say that overthrowing governments will cause untold suffering for civilians and disrupt those countries for years to

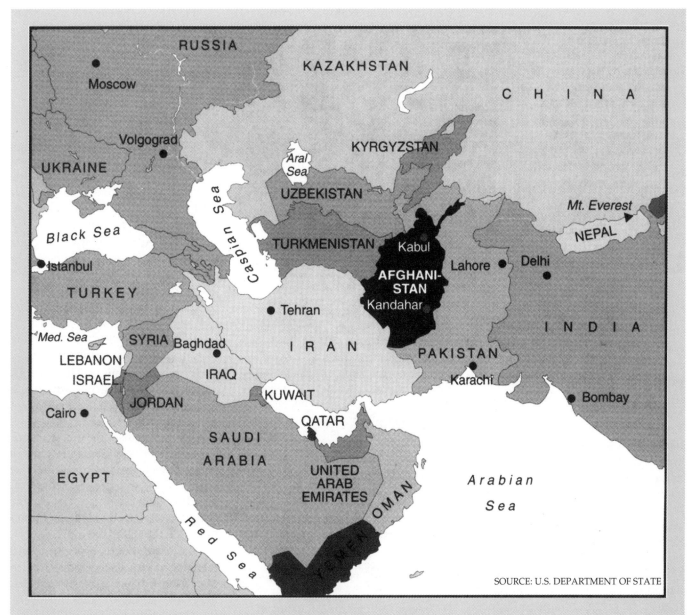

The Middle East's Ring of Terror

The Afghanistan-based Al Qaeda network is the prime suspect in the Sept. 11 attacks on the United States. Founded in 1987 by Osama bin Laden and Egyptian militants, it bombed the U.S. embassies in Kenya and Tanzania in 1998 and the USS *Cole* in 2000 and maintains cells in some 60 countries. Several other terrorist organizations operate in and around the Middle east, many with ties to Al Qaeda, and threaten American and Western interests.

come. In addition, they say, action by the United States will probably lead to more terrorism against America and her allies. "We're going to end up creating more terrorists because so many people will be outraged by this and want to do something about it," says Dan Smith, chief of research at the Center for Defense Information, a think tank.

Within the United States, the administration launched what Bush and Attorney General John Ashcroft called the most massive law enforcement investigation in U.S. history. In his televised Sept. 11 address, Bush said he had "directed the full resources of our intelligence and law enforcement communities to find those responsible and to bring them to justice."

Over the course of the next three weeks, the government identified the 19 hijackers—all men in their 20s and 30s with Middle Eastern names. They had commandeered four flights, steering three to their targets but failing with a fourth; terrorists, passengers and crews all perished. Investigators fanned out across the country. By early October, more than

600 people had been questioned—several were charged with immigration violations but none were linked directly to the terrorist attacks. In Britain, however, the government arrested an Algerian pilot who they said gave flying instructions to four of the hijackers.

The administration also asked Congress to pass a broad anti-terrorism bill that would ease prosecutions, lengthen sentences, expand electronic surveillance and simplify deportation of immigrants. "Our laws fail to make defeating terrorism a national priority," Ashcroft told the House Judiciary Committee on Sept. 24.

Civil liberties advocates sharply criticized some of the proposals, as did some terrorism experts. "The terrorist will have at least a small victory if we change any of our principles just because they've frightened us," says Neal Pollard, founding director of the Terrorism Research Center. Still, Congress seemed likely to pass a bill later this month embodying most of what the administration requested.

Bush also has moved to strengthen domestic defenses against terrorism, beefing up security at airports and along the borders. In addition, he announced the creation of an Office of Homeland Security to coordinate and direct anti-terrorism efforts at home. The president tapped Republican Pennsylvania Gov. Tom Ridge to the Cabinet-level job.

While terrorism experts widely support the new office, they caution that Ridge will have little long-term impact unless he has some institutional authority over the 40-plus agencies, from the FBI to the Federal Emergency Management Agency (FEMA), that deal with terrorism. Some analysts, like James Lindsay, a senior fellow at the Brookings Institution, argue that the new office needs power over relevant agency budgets. "Without some sort of lever like that, they're simply not going to listen to him," he says.

Others, like former Sen. Gary Hart, D-Colo., who co-chaired the

Commission on National Security in the 21st Century, go further, saying the office should be a new department, with a huge budget and staff.

Major Terrorist Groups

Abu Nidal—Based in Iraq and Lebanon, Abu Nidal, also known as Fatah and Black September, has carried out attacks in 20 countries, including the murders of 11 Israeli athletes at the 1972 Olympic games in Munich and a 1986 Pan Am hijacking in Pakistan that left 22 people dead.

Al-Jihad—Egyptian group works closely with Al Qaeda to replace the Egyptian government with an Islamic state; assassinated Egyptian President Sadat in 1981.

Hamas—Operating in Israel and the Occupied Territories, it has staged many suicide bombings against Israeli targets and seeks to replace Israel with an Islamic Palestinian nation.

Hezbollah—Also known as Islamic Jihad, the radical Shiite Party of God is based in southern Lebanon and allied with Iran. It is suspected in hundreds of attacks against Israel as well as the 1983 bombing of the U.S. Embassy and Marine barracks in Beirut, killing 241 people.

Popular Front for the Liberation of Palestine General Command—Headquartered in Syria, with bases in Lebanon, the PFLP-GC conducts raids against Israel and opposes Yasser Arafat's PLO.

SOURCE: U.S. DEPARTMENT OF STATE

But some analysts say that another big bureaucracy is not the answer. Instead, they say, Ridge should be charged with setting the direction and goals of anti-terrorism efforts at home and coordinating agencies' efforts to meet those goals. In addition, they say, Ridge will have enough power so long as terrorism is a national priority.

"He'll have the ear and support of the president to back him up," says Rep. Ike Skelton, D-Mo., ranking Democrat on the House Armed Services Committee. "How much more power does he need?"

Despite the intense focus on terrorism, both at home and overseas, administration officials—including Ashcroft—and others have warned that new terrorist attacks against the United States are likely in the near future. "We all know it's going to happen again," Skelton says.

In particular, terrorism experts worry about chemical, biological or even nuclear attacks.[3] "If we don't get on this now, the likelihood of attack using weapons of mass destruction will grow," Spencer says. "I wouldn't be shocked if something like this happened tomorrow."

But others dismiss such concerns. "When an enemy strikes, there is a tendency to ascribe to that enemy capabilities that they don't possess," says Amy Smithson, a senior associate at the Henry L. Stimson Center, a national security think tank. "These kinds of attacks require an infrastructure and scientific knowledge that groups like Al Qaeda just don't possess."

As government officials and terrorism experts grapple with the prospect of future attacks, here are some of the questions they are asking:

Should the U.S. topple foreign governments that harbor or support terrorists?

On the evening of Sept. 11, with the fires still burning in New York and Washington, President Bush threw down the gauntlet: "We will make no distinction between the terrorists who committed these acts and those who harbor them," he told the nation and the world.

The president's remarks, backed by statements from top national security aides, were intended to put Afghanistan and other states sus-

Bin Laden's War on America

Americans view him as a murderous religious fanatic, the presumed mastermind of the Sept. 11 attacks on the World Trade Center and Pentagon and other terrorist incidents over the past decade.

Within the Muslim world, however, Osama bin Laden is a hero in some quarters: a man of courage and piety willing to fight outside infidels in the name of their true faith.

The exiled Saudi multimillionaire "articulates the frustrations of people in the Middle East who resent being left behind while the West takes over the world," says David Little, a professor of religion and international affairs at Harvard University. "Their frustration is disorganized and beyond people's control. Bin Laden provides a point of reference and shows that something can be done."

"Bin Laden does not have religious training or recognition within the theological community of any country," explains Suzanne Maloney, a specialist on Persian Gulf politics at the Brookings Institution. Instead, his appeal stems from his proven sincerity, she explains. "He has battle credentials and has been willing to suffer" for his obsession with defending the Muslim world from alleged domination by the United States.

Bin Laden was born in Riyadh, Saudi Arabia, probably in 1957, one of 52 or 53 children of the 10 wives of a prominent construction magnate originally from Yemen.[1] When his father died in the late 1960s, bin Laden may have inherited as much as $300 million—though some authorities estimate the inheritance at much less.

As a teenager living in Beirut, Lebanon, in the early 1970s, he made his mark as a carouser and womanizer. He later studied civil engineering and business administration at King Abdul Aziz University in Jeddah, Saudi Arabia, where he was drawn to radical Islam.

Enraged by the Soviet invasion of predominantly Muslim Afghanistan in 1979, bin Laden began organizing the Afghan resistance alongside U.S.-backed guerrillas, known as *mujaheddin*. Dazzling locals with his wealth, he brought in 9,000 Arab fighters, sent in supplies, helped build arms facilities and recruited Sunni Muslims. The legend of his bravery soon spread, along with reports that he had proposed the Reagan administration's eventual policy of arming the *mujaheddin* with Stinger missiles.

While in Afghanistan, bin Laden came under the influence of the Egyptian Islamic Jihad, the militant group responsible for the assassination of President Anwar el-Sadat in 1981. Working with the Egyptians, in 1987 he founded Al Qaeda—Arabic for "the base"—to serve as the organizational base for a global Islamic crusade.

After the Russian retreat from Afghanistan in 1989, bin Laden ended up back in Saudi Arabia, distributing videotapes extolling his military exploits. In a few years, his likeness had become common in shops and on T-shirts all over the Muslim world.

The Persian Gulf War of 1990–91 sharpened bin Laden's focus on the United States. He deeply resented the Saudi government's willingness to host U.S. troops in the campaign to remove Iraqi forces occupying Kuwait. He

viewed his country's cooperation with the United States as an affront to its guardianship of the holy cities of Mecca and Medina.

After the Saudi government expelled bin Laden for anti-government views in 1991, he fled to Sudan, where he ran global businesses in banking, construction and agriculture while allegedly siphoning off funds from Muslim charities. In 1994 he was stripped of his Saudi citizenship for smuggling weapons and spreading terrorist propaganda.

Soon his network was linked—though not conclusively—to co-conspirators responsible for attacks on U.S. soldiers in Somalia, plans to assassinate the pope and President Bill Clinton and bomb U.S. passenger jetliners, the 1993 bombing of New York's World Trade Center and the 1995 bombing of the Khobar Towers, a U.S. military barracks in Saudi Arabia.[2] When U.S. pressure forced him out of Sudan, he moved to Afghanistan again, which was in the midst of a civil war.

In 1996, bin Laden issued his first major *fatwa*—an Islamic religious ruling typically issued by trained or senior clerks—declaring a holy war on "Americans occupying the land of the two holy places." Two years later, he broadened the threat to target not just soldiers but all Americans.

In 1998, he told ABC-TV reporter John Miller that his campaign of violence would "inevitably move... to American soil."[3] He also publicly cultivated suicide terrorists, telling followers in a video last summer, "You should love the other world, and you should not be afraid to die."[4]

(continued on next page)

pected of supporting terrorism on notice that the United States would consider them legitimate military targets.

"We've essentially been at war with states that support terrorism and didn't know it until now," says the Heritage Foundation's Spencer. "President Bush is finally articulating this new reality."

Spencer argues that nations like Iraq, Syria and Iran have used terror-

ist groups as proxies to make war against the United states. "We have to understand that these states see themselves in a war with us," he says.

Supporters of targeting states in the war against terrorism also say that a strategy that only focuses on groups and individuals is doomed to fail because terrorists depend upon government support. "These groups could never pull off these sophisti-

cated operations if there was no place where they could support their network," Spencer says.

"The fact is, we often think of terrorists as sleeping in caves, like bin Laden in Afghanistan," said Richard Perle, a former assistant secretary of Defense in the Reagan administration. "Terrorists go to office blocks, where they have modern communications technology, where they have the ability to move money around

Al Qaeda serves indirectly as the instrument of bin Laden's war on America.[5] Rather than carrying out attacks itself, bin Laden's group provides financial and other assistance that allows smaller independent organizations to operate.

"Al Qaeda is a Ford Foundation for terrorist groups," says Stephen P. Cohen, a South Asia expert at the Brookings Institution. "They take money that they've raised—from Muslim charitable contributions and other sources—and direct it to specific groups for specific missions."

The organization also provides other terrorist groups with military and other training from bases in Afghanistan. "They train people in camps in Afghanistan and then often send them to serve with the Taliban," Cohen says.

Groups supported by Al Qaeda operate in more than 60 countries, including the United States, Canada and Western Europe.[6] While some are thought to be based in Egypt, Algeria and Saudi Arabia, members include citizens of most Middle Eastern countries as well as militants from Muslim populations in the Philippines and Indonesia, the world's most populous Muslim nation.

Al Qaeda and similar groups represent a change in the nature of terrorism over the last few decades—away from direct state sponsorship and toward non-state terrorism. "If you consider what we were worried about even 15 years ago—Libya, Syria—that's just not the same kind of factor anymore," said Paul R. Pillar, national intelligence officer for the Near East and South Asia

for the Central Intelligence Agency (CIA).[7] Today, instead of carrying out the acts of terror themselves, certain states now assist groups like Al Qaeda.

The United States has had bin Laden in its sights since the mid-1990s, but so far to no avail. Sudan made a back-channel offer to arrest bin Laden in 1996 and turn him over to Saudi Arabia. The Saudis declined, and the Clinton administration concluded it had no basis to indict bin Laden in this country.[8]

President Clinton personally authorized a cruise missile attack on suspected training camps in Afghanistan in August 1998 in response to the U.S. embassy bombings earlier in the month. Bin Laden himself was the intended target, but—contrary to the pre-attack intelligence—he had left the site hours earlier. A year later, the CIA trained Pakistani intelligence agents to capture bin Laden, but the plan was abandoned after the Pakistani government fell in a coup Oct. 12, 1999, and the new leader—Gen. Pervez Musharraf—refused to continue the operation.[9]

Within the United States, the government's focus on bin Laden—President Bush declared that he is wanted "dead or alive"—provides a recognizable symbol of the war on terrorism. For bin Laden, the failure of the U.S. initiatives so far only furthers his hopes of reducing the United States from a great power to a humbled, chaotic land.

"We anticipate a black future for America," he told ABC in 1998. "Instead of remaining United States, it shall end up separated states and shall

have to carry the bodies of its sons back to America."

—*Charles S. Clark*

Notes

1. For background, see David E. Kaplan and Kevin Whitelaw, "The CEO of Terror, Inc.," *U.S. News & World Report*, Oct. 1, 2001, pp. 18–22; Rob Nordland and Jeffrey Bartholet, "The Mesmerizer," *Newsweek*, Sept. 24, 2001, pp. 44–45; Yossef Bodansky, *Bin Laden: The Man Who Declared War on America* (1999); Simon Reeve, *The New Jackals: Ramzi Yousef, Osama bin Laden and the Future of Terrorism* (1999).
2. See U.S. Dept. of State, "Patterns of Global Terrorism 2000," 2001 ("Al Qaeda" entry in Appendix B) (www.state.gov).
3. Quoted in Michael Dobbs, "Inside the Mind of Osama bin Laden," *The Washington Post*, Sept. 20, 2001, p. A1.
4. Michael Powell, "Bin Laden Recruits With Graphic Video," *The Washington Post*, Sept. 27, 2001, p. A19.
5. For background, see Michael Dobbs, "A Few Loyal Men Direct Bin Laden's Sprawling Network," *The Washington Post*, Sept. 27, 2001, p. A1; Karen De Young and Michael Dobbs, "Bin Laden: Architect of New Global Terrorism: *The Washington Post*, Sept. 16, 2001, p. A8.
6. See Bob Woodward and Walter Pincus, "Investigators Identify 4 to 5 Groups Linked to Bin Laden Operating in U.S.," *The Washington Post*, Sept. 23, 2001, p. A1.
7. Quoted in De Young and Dobbs, *op. cit.*
8. Barton Gellman, "Sudan's Offer to Arrest Militant Fell Through After Saudis Said No," *The Washington Post*, Oct. 3, 2001, p. A1.
9. Bob Woodward and Thomas E. Ricks, "U.S. Was Foiled Multiple Times in Efforts to Capture Bin Laden or Have Him Killed," *The Washington Post*, Oct. 3, 2001, p. A1.
10. Quoted in De Young and Dobbs, *op. cit.*

the world, to obtain false documents, the technology of explosives, and the like."

Ultimately, says Dan Goure, a senior fellow at the Lexington Institute, a conservative think tank in Arlington, Va., states that succor terrorists must be overthrown. "To just go after terrorist groups without dealing with the countries that help them is like fighting fleas on a dog one at a time," he says. "You spray the whole dog."

But opponents say that toppling another government would almost

certainly inflame tensions throughout the Middle East and create even more terrorism in the long run. "Opposition to the U.S. in the region grows out of a perception that we misuse our power," says the Center for Defense Information's Smith, referring to American military action in the Persian Gulf fighting a decade ago.[4] Large-scale military actions will only contribute to "the sense of powerlessness that already exists among individuals and even countries" and breed more terrorism, he adds.

Moreover, critics say, massive U.S. military action could destabilize or even topple key U.S. allies in the region like Pakistan, Saudi Arabia or even Egypt, making it harder for America to dismantle terrorist groups in the future. "These states all have large numbers of Islamic fundamentalists who could, in a worst-case scenario, even topple one of these moderate regimes," says Ivan Eland, director of defense policy studies at the CATO Institute, a libertarian think tank. "At the very least, it would mean that we would lose some of our allies in the region as they pulled away [from the U.S.] to avoid upsetting their own internal opposition. So we might find ourselves trying to operate in, say, Afghanistan without having Pakistan to support us, which would make doing that impossible."

In short, Eland says, invading another country is exactly what the terrorists want. "Doing something like that is playing into bin Laden's hands because it will lead to instability and strengthen the hand of the extremists."

"This could get completely out of hand," agrees Anthony Cordesman, a senior analyst at the Center for Strategic and International Studies (CSIS). "You could find yourself at war with the entire Arab world if you're not careful."

Finally, opponents say, U.S. military action, even if successful, usually doesn't solve the problem in the long term. "When the U.S. has toppled governments in the past, they have usually ended up wreaking much more havoc than existed before," says Martha Honey, director of peace and security at the Institute for Policy Studies, a liberal think tank.

Cordesman agrees. "This is a trip that is infinitely easier to start than it is to finish," he says, adding that countries like Afghanistan or Iraq could be broken up into a number of pieces if their regimes are cavalierly overturned.

But supporters of military action argue that creating greater instability or more potential terrorists would be a worthwhile tradeoff if the states that sponsor terrorism were replaced with friendlier regimes.

"If you replace the states that do support terrorism with those that don't, you deny terrorists the kind of support that allows them to mount big operations against us," Goure says. "So even if you have more terrorists, if they can't do anything against us, that's much better."

Will tougher wiretapping and immigration laws help fight terrorism without unduly infringing on civil liberties?

Two days after the Sept. 11 attacks, the Senate approved with little debate a bill significantly expanding the government's power to track suspects' communications on the Internet. The measure—still pending in Congress—was rushed through in the evening hours of Sept. 13 despite questions from Democratic senators about making electronic surveillance easier not only in terrorism cases but also in criminal investigations generally.

When Ashcroft came to Capitol Hill two weeks later with an omnibus anti-terrorism bill, however, skeptics were more insistent. Republican and Democratic lawmakers combined to slow the bill—and eventually force substantial compromises—by complaining that some of the provisions would curtail individual liberties while doing little to prevent future attacks.[5]

The administration's partial retreat followed a buzz saw of criticism from civil liberties organizations on the right and the left. "The civil liberties that we value so much as a society are at stake," said Rachel King, legislative counsel at the American Civil Liberties Union (ACLU). Charles Peña, a defense policy analyst at the Cato Institute, voiced similar caution: "We need to be very careful about rushing to give up some of our liberties in exchange for security," he said.

The Justice Department bill covered a range of topics—including a broader definition of terrorism crimes, maximum life sentences and no time limits for prosecutions. The major controversies, however, centered on provisions to make it easier for the government to engage in electronic surveillance and detain aliens.

Ashcroft told lawmakers the provisions were necessary to deal with the "clear and present danger" of

terrorism. "We need to unleash every possible tool against terrorism, and we need to do that promptly," he warned the House Judiciary Committee on Sept. 24.

The immigration provisions called for allowing the attorney general to order the indefinite detention of any non-citizen if he had "reason to believe" the person "may commit, further or facilitate" terrorist acts. The bill also permitted deporting any alien who gave "material support" to a terrorist organization. "The ability of alien terrorists to move freely across our borders and operate within the United States is critical to their capacity to inflict damage on our citizens and facilities," Ashcroft said.

Immigrants'-rights advocates sharply criticized the proposed detention power. The bill "would basically allow unilateral detention of anyone on the attorney general's say-so," said David Cole, a Georgetown University law professor who has represented Palestinians in a number of deportation cases. Cole also criticized the "material support" provision, which he described as "guilt by association."

Some conservatives were also critical. "I am against permanent detention without cause," said Todd Gaziano, director of legal studies at the Heritage Foundation.

Some terrorism experts also said the immigration provisions went too far. "There are things that America stands for: land of the free, home of the brave, the melting pot," Pollard of the Terrorism Research Center said. "That's one of the things that has resulted in such strong international support."

The electronic-surveillance section of the administration bill was both broader and more complex. It included provisions for so-called "roving" wiretaps—court orders to wiretap any phone that a suspect might use rather than requiring separate permission for each. Another provision called for allowing the government to obtain a warrant or court order for nationwide electronic surveillance rather than having to obtain authorization in individual judicial districts. And the Justice Department asked for the power to subpoena Internet service providers for the names and e-mail addresses of people in communication with a terrorism suspect.

Ashcroft said that the provisions would help law enforcement powers adapt to new technologies and tactics. "Terrorists are trained to change cell phones frequently, to route e-mail through different Internet computers in order to defeat surveillance," he testified. "We are not asking the law to expand, just to grow as technology grows."

Civil liberties groups said the provisions would reduce judicial protections against privacy-invading surveillance. Nationwide surveillance orders would amount to "a blank check," King said. The Center for Democracy and Technology noted that the government could get a subpoena for Internet contacts with less evidence than would be needed for a search warrant. "The idea that you can go from service provider to service provider without a judge ever actually asking what leads you to believe there's criminal conduct, we said that was too much," said Deputy Director James Dempsey.[6]

The administration appeared to have been surprised by the strength of civil liberties sentiment both from lawmakers and outside groups. In a late-night session on Oct. 1, House Judiciary Committee negotiators reached bipartisan agreement on a bill that modified some of the most controversial provisions in the administration's proposal. In one major change, the new bill would allow detention of immigrants for seven days (not indefinitely) if the attorney general had "reasonable grounds" (rather than "reason to believe") for suspecting terrorist activity.

The House bill, however, retained most of the administration's original package, however, leaving civil lib-

erties groups still discontented. "The compromise bill would have a long-term negative impact on basic freedom in America that cannot be justified," said Laura Murphy, head of the ACLU's Washington office.

For its part, the administration said it was encouraged by the bipartisan support for stronger counter-terrorism laws, but voiced concern about a "sunset" provision calling for the new provisions to expire at the end of 2003 without congressional reauthorization.

Will the new Office of Homeland Security have the authority it needs to protect the country from terrorists?

On Sept. 20, before a joint session of Congress, President Bush set out the government's strategy for combating terrorism. One of the cornerstones of that plan, the president said, was a new office to direct U.S. counterterrorism efforts.[7]

"Today, dozens of federal departments and agencies, as well as state and local governments, have responsibilities affecting homeland security," Bush said. "These efforts must be coordinated at the highest levels. So tonight I announce the creation of a Cabinet-level position reporting directly to me."

In the week following the speech, the administration fleshed out its plan for the office, likening it to the National Security Council, with relevant department and agency heads—such as the secretaries of Defense and Treasury and the attorney general—working with the new coordinating body.

To underscore the importance of the office, Bush selected the experienced and popular Ridge, a close friend who will certainly have the president's ear. Still, Ridge, who resigned as governor and was sworn in on Oct. 8, faces a daunting task. More than 40 agencies within 20 departments—from the FBI to the Small Business Administration—have some hand in protecting the

country from terrorist attack or mitigating any damage done.

Moreover, many analysts say, the fact that Ridge is simply a "counter-terrorism czar," someone like the current drug czar who coordinates government agencies in a particular effort, makes it likely that he will play only a small role in shaping policy. These pessimists argue that, at the very least, Ridge needs some authority over the budgets of relevant agencies, which would give him the leverage to influence their policies.

"Unless you give this new office budgetary authority, Ridge will be little more than a cheerleader from the sidelines, because these agency heads and others won't listen to him," says Brookings' Lindsay. "At a place like the Department of Defense, where assistant secretaries can't even get the services to listen to them, do you think this guy from the outside will have even a chance if he doesn't have some control over their money?" he adds.

The most efficient way to bring Ridge into the process, Lindsay says, would be to let him examine agency budgets when they reach the Office of Management and Budget. "The OMB already plays a key role in making all agency budgets, so why not let Ridge help them then."

But some, including Lindsay, argue that budgetary authority alone will probably not be enough to make Ridge effective. According to Cordesman of CSIS, the governor will need specific delineated powers to help departments make major policy decisions. "If Ridge doesn't have the authority to shape programs over the whole structure of federal agencies, then he might as well resign right now," he says.

Some say that the office will not acquire the policy power it needs unless it becomes a full-blown agency. "If you want to get a job done, there's no substitute for having an agency with a budget," said Sen. Joseph I. Lieberman, D-Conn., chairman of the Senate Governmental Affairs Committee.[8]

Indeed, a commission report issued in January by Hart and former Sen. Warren Rudman, R-N.H., recommended the creation of a new federal department to deal with homeland security issues. The commission proposed folding the Coast Guard, Border Patrol, FEMA and Customs Service into the new agency.[9]

"I think anyone who understands how the national government works sees the difference between a czar who seeks to create task forces and working groups among disparate agencies, and the head of an agency who has accountability, statutory responsibility, budget authority and is directly accountable to the president and the people of the United States," Hart said on Fox Television's "Hardball with Chris Matthews" on Sept. 26. "And I think that agency approach which we strongly believe in is the way the president will find he has to go. I simply hope it happens before the next attack occurs."

But those who oppose creating a powerful new entity contend that the focus should be on working better with existing agencies, not trying to create a new one. "This isn't brain surgery," says Missouri Rep. Skelton. "There are so many agencies involved in [combating terrorism] that the right hand doesn't know what the left is doing. We need someone to tie all of these agencies together and direct them."

According to Skelton and others, generating yet another bureaucracy within the federal government is unnecessary and could be counterproductive. "We have trouble enough with bureaucracies that don't talk to each other," says Stephen P. Cohen, a senior fellow at the Brookings Institution. "We don't need to create another bureaucracy—some supra-

interior minister—we need someone who could facilitate coordination."

Pollard of the Terrorism Research Center agrees, adding that a new department would just generate unnecessary interagency rivalries. "It should not be a full department, because if it's a new agency, then it will just compete with other agencies that already exist."

Opponents also say that it is unnecessary to give the office authority over other agencies' budgets. Indeed, they warn, conferring budgetary authority could very well hurt other agencies that have many missions—like the Coast Guard—by forcing them to neglect their other duties in order to combat terrorism. "You cannot allow this to cause an agency to change its main mission," Skelton says. "The threat of terrorism is a very real threat, but it's one that has to be handled and coordinated separately."

Moreover, Pollard says, terrorism czar with the president's ear can have tremendous influence over future spending on terrorism. "I'll tell you already who has budgetary authority—the president," he says. "If [Ridge] makes an analysis, sets a strategy and then says, this is the strategy and this is how all the resources of the federal government should be orchestrated, then he can take his case to the president and I can guarantee to you that the president [can] make those budgetary changes."

And, opponents say, given the magnitude of the Sept. 11 attacks, Ridge will have tremendous political heft. "In the short run, he has all the authority he could ever have," says Sen. Judd Gregg, R-N.H. "The president is standing right beside him, and whatever he wants right now, he's

going to get out of the administration."[10]

Notes

1. For background, see David Masci, "Islamic Fundamentalism," *The CQ Researcher*, March 24, 2000, pp. 241–264, and Ahmed Rashid, *Taliban: Militant Islam, Oil and Fundamentalism in Central Asia* (2000).
2. For background, see Mary H. Cooper, "Combating Terrorism," *The CQ Researcher*, July 21, 1995, pp. 633–656.
3. For background, see Mary H. Cooper, "Missile Defense," *The CQ Researcher*, Sept. 8, 2000, pp. 689–712, and Mary H. Cooper, "Chemical and Biological Weapons," *The CQ Researcher*, Jan. 31, 1997, pp. 73–96.
4. For background, see David Masci, "Middle East Conflict," *The CQ Researcher*, April 6, 2001, pp. 273–296, and Patrick G. Marshall, "Calculating the Costs of the Gulf War," *The CQ Researcher*, March 15, 1991, pp. 145–168.
5. For coverage, see Adriel Bettelheim and Elizabeth A. Palmer, "Balancing Liberty and Security," *CQ Weekly*, Sept. 22, 2001, pp. 2210–2214; Elizabeth A. Palmer, "Committees Taking a Critical Look at Ashcroft's Request for Broad New Powers," *CQ Weekly*, Sept. 29, 2001, pp. 2263–2265.
6. Quoted in Alison Mitchel and Todd S. Purdum, "Ashcroft Seeking Broad Powers, Says Congress Must Act Quickly," *The New York Times*, Oct. 1, 2001, p. A1.
7. For background, see Kenneth Jost, "Bush Presidency," *The CQ Researcher*, Feb. 2, 2001, pp. 65–88.
8. Quoted in Karen Tumulty, "Looking Out for Next Time," *Time*, Oct. 1, 2001.
9. U.S. Commission on National Security/21st Century, "Roadmap for National Security, Feb. 1, 2001.
10. Quoted in Chuck McCutcheon, "Defining Homeland Security," *CQ Weekly*, Sept. 29, 2001, pp. 2252–2254.

* [A fourth hijacked plane, possibly heading for the White House or Capitol, crashed in western Pennsylvania after passengers overpowered the hijackers.]

Different Drummers, Same Drum

Andrew J. Bacevich

WHEN, on February 16, George W. Bush ordered U.S. combat aircraft to attack targets in Iraq, White House staffers let it be known that the new President was putting Baghdad on notice. In Washington, the "adults" had once again grasped the reins of power. The bombing of a handful of Iraqi air defense facilities was indeed an important signal, but not because it marked any notable departure from past practice. On the contrary, taken in conjunction with other early indicators, the incident suggests that when it comes to foreign policy, the new Bush administration will hew more closely to precedents established during the Clinton era than either its supporters had hoped or its detractors are likely to acknowledge. The emerging story is one of continuity, not change. Understanding why is crucial to comprehending the essential nature of American foreign policy after the Cold War.

Throughout eight years during which Democrats controlled the White House, few things raised greater ire among Republicans than the fecklessness with which Bill Clinton employed U.S. military power. Attracting particular ridicule was Clinton's penchant for pinprick air attacks portrayed as demonstrations of toughness and resolve. The effort to contain Saddam Hussein displayed this tactic at its worst. As a symbol of allied vigilance, American (and British) pilots flying nearly daily combat patrols over the so-called no-fly zone have launched dozens of attacks against Iraqi military installations, in effect waging an open-ended war of attrition. Saddam's response has been to mount ever bolder acts of defiance. Determined to sustain the fiction that Saddam remains securely in his "box", but unwilling to risk a showdown, Bill Clinton relied on faux air power to camouflage the deteriorating situation in the Gulf. The impact on Saddam and his regime was demonstrably nil.

During the run-up to the 2000 election, Bush and his surrogates let it be known that, if elected, they would jettison this amateurish Clinton doctrine. When it came to using force, George W. Bush would exhibit the prudence and sound judgment that had characterized his father's administration. By implication, a second Bush presidency would revive some variant of the Powell Doctrine, using military power only when vital U.S. interests are at stake, and then doing so overwhelmingly and decisively. Bush's appointment of Colin Powell, the doctrine's namesake, as secretary of state seemingly affirmed this intention. When it came to Saddam, the Bush team promised to have done with the temporizing and vacillation. Two words sufficed to define the essence of a more assertive policy toward Iraq: "regime change."

But the adults have now had their chance, and the results show a remarkable resemblance to the lamentable practices of the Clinton era. In explaining his decision to bomb Iraq, President Bush took pains to emphasize that doing so had long since become simply "routine." Indeed, the media discovered that the February 16 bombing was by no means the "first" of Bush's presidency, that on several other occasions after January 20, U.S. warplanes had hit targets inside Iraq. Insisting that endless American air patrols form "part of a strategy", President Bush vowed that "we will continue to enforce the no-fly zone." Reporters present for these remarks politely refrained from pressing Bush to explain exactly what that strategy might be.

But within weeks the answer to that question became clear. During the course of Secretary Powell's first trip to the Persian Gulf in February, tough talk about removing Saddam from power was notable by its absence. Instead, Powell touted the administration's plans for "retooling" the sanctions regime established during the first Bush presidency and continued by Bill Clinton. Although Saddam over the past decade has evinced extraordinary skill in evading that regime, Secretary Powell promised that a new set of unspecified "smart sanctions" would deny Baghdad access to arms and militarily relevant technology, keeping Saddam from causing further mischief while easing the hardships of the long-suffering Iraqi people. Yet stripped of the flourishes intended to convey a sense of novelty, the smart sanctions policy amounts to little more than a promise to try harder.

Thus is the Bush team, in the apt judgment of a March 4 *Washington Post* editorial, well "on its way to adopting the same Iraq policy pursued in recent years by the Clinton administration—a policy President Bush and his top aides repeatedly and vociferously condemned." Why the apparent flip-flop?

SEVERAL plausible explanations exist. The first and most obvious is the different perspective that results from assuming the mantle of power. Advocacy when free of responsibility is one thing; action when one will be held to account for the consequences is, to put it mildly, something else. Employed as a basis for actual decisions, campaign rhetoric is as likely to produce disaster as sound policy. John F. Kennedy ran for the presidency vowing to get tough on Castro, a stance that landed him in the Bay of Pigs. Skeptics warn that attempting to overthrow Saddam Hussein could well produce a comparable debacle—a Bay of Goats. That George W. Bush, wary of such a prospect, might discover hitherto overlooked virtues in the Iraq policy of his predecessor is eminently understandable.

A realistic appraisal of the facts on the ground provides a second possible explanation for Bush's about-face on Iraq. Although viewed in Washington as an event of cosmic importance, the inauguration of a new president left those facts unchanged, chief among them the strength of the security apparatus sustaining Saddam's grip on power; the haplessness of the Iraqi opposition; the limited appetite of the American people for another large-scale Persian Gulf war; and the cost-benefit calculus persuading other nations that the time has come to cut a deal with Saddam. Just as candidate Clinton, after berating the elder Bush for coddling the "butchers of Beijing", discovered once in office the merits of "engaging" China, so too the younger Bush, who denounced Clinton for being soft on Saddam, is finding practical alternatives to containing Iraq to be few and risky.

But there is a third explanation, one that looks beyond the particular problems posed by Iraq. To an extent that neither partisan supporters nor members of the chattering classes are willing to concede, Bush and his chief advisers conceive of America's proper role in a post-Cold War world in terms nearly identical to those used by Clinton and his advisers. They assume the same intimate connection between U.S. foreign policy and America's domestic well-being; they embrace the same myths about the past; they voice similar expectations for the future, ascribing the shape of that future to the same set of factors. To a remarkable extent, they agree on the basic aims that should inform U.S. policy and the principles that should guide its conduct. Even when it comes to overlooking or ignoring inconvenient facts, Bush and Clinton share the same blind spots.

Thus, it is not really surprising that when setting its foreign policy azimuth the Bush administration spent its first weeks tacking away from the positions taken during the campaign, back toward the course previously charted by the Clinton administration. This was true not simply with regard to Iraq but on a number of other issues. Would a Bush administration act promptly to return U.S. forces to their true vocation as warfighters and leave peacekeeping to others, as Condoleezza Rice, Bush's national security adviser, had hinted during the campaign? Not really: President Bush announced that he had no immediate plan to withdraw U.S. troops from the Balkans and assured NATO that any changes would occur only after thoroughgoing allied consultation—a signal for nervous Europeans to rest easy. Would the new administration reverse the Clinton policy of showering North Korea with blandishments whenever Pyongyang hints darkly about acquiring nuclear weapons? Not according to Secretary Powell, who announced in early March that the new team would "pick up where President Clinton and his administration left off."[1] Would Bush act quickly to fix the gaping problems with military readiness that had excited Republicans during the campaign? No again: for now, the final defense budget submitted by President Clinton will serve quite nicely, thank you. Is Colombia another Democratic quagmire in the making, with Clinton's $1.3 billion program of military aid the first step toward plunging the United States into an intractable civil war? Perhaps, but the Bush administration is not going to take the rap for "losing" Colombia or for neglecting the war on drugs. The commitment stays. And then there is China. Republicans had mocked Clinton for categorizing China as a "strategic partner." Candidate Bush had classified the regime as a "strategic competitor." When the "spy plane" incident in April offered Bush an opportunity to show just what that formulation means, his administration demonstrated a Clintonesque penchant for conciliation.

Put another way, Bush and Clinton each fit comfortably within the foreign policy consensus that prevails today in all quarters to the Left of the tattered remnant of hard-core isolationists and to the Right of those few beleaguered radicals still pining for the glory days of the 1960s—that is to say, across the entire spectrum of opinion deemed respectable. That consensus defines the parameters within which the policy debate occurs and provides the language that shapes foreign policy discourse. It establishes priorities and defines options. It focuses, disciplines and excludes. As such, it transcends partisan affiliation and subsumes labels such as liberal and conservative. It renders moot old distinctions between realists and idealists, nationalists and internationalists. To be sure, not every adherent to that consensus agrees on every detail; but on those things that matter most, agreement is well nigh unanimous.

THIS CONSENSUS constitutes the substructure of present-day U.S. foreign policy, superseding an earlier consensus that prevailed from the mid-1940s through the 1980s (although for a time fractured by the Vietnam War). Yet the new consensus has not so much displaced the old as renewed and expanded it. So pervasive as to be all but taken for granted, so authoritative as to be virtually immune to challenge, the renewal of this consensus forms the true centerpiece of the foreign policy legacy left by Bill Clinton. It promises to be the most durable element of that legacy as well.

The consensus consists of five distinctive elements. Each figured prominently in the policies of the Clinton era. Each has now been embraced by the Bush camp.

First, *America as historical vanguard.* According to this notion, history has a discernible direction and destination. Uniquely among all the nations of the world, the United States comprehends and manifests history's purpose. That purpose is freedom, achieved through the spread of democratic capitalism, and embodied in the American Way of Life. As that way of life mutates so too does the meaning of freedom.

The conviction that America is, in Melville's phrase, "the Israel of our time", possesses a distinguished pedigree, but it is one to which the end of the Cold War, victory in the Persian Gulf War, and the prosperity of the 1990s imparted fresh life. During the Clinton era, that conviction gave rise to all manner of gaudy claims about America's indispensability and its providentially endowed mission. Clinton believed that, as the nation that defines what he called "the right side of history", the United States possesses an inescapable mandate to enlighten those who have thus far failed to decipher history's meaning. Thus, as president, Clinton publicly reproached the Chinese government for languishing on "the wrong side of history." On the eve of this 1998 trip to the People's Republic, he explained his personal obligation to the Chinese "to create for them a new and different historical reality." Revising China's view of the past, Clinton said, would enable the government in Beijing to "feel more confident in doing what I believe is the morally right thing to do."

Setting himself up as a source of instruction on the finer points of morality exemplifies the sort of effrontery that triggered paroxysms of disbelief among Clinton's many critics. But the conviction that the United States has indeed solved the riddle of history finds equal favor at the highest levels of the Bush administration. Speaking at the Reagan Library on November 19, 1999, then-Governor Bush was explicit on this point: "We firmly believe that our nation is on the right side of history." For Republicans, too, the point is not merely to claim an honorific; with it comes responsibilities. Condoleezza Rice wonders "if we are going to accept responsibility for being on the right side of history" and expresses concern about the willingness of Americans to step up to the task. Should they fail to do so, should they squander the opportunity to seal the triumph of democratic capitalism, she warns that future generations will be asking "why we were on the right side of history, and did not take care of this."[2]

Colin Powell entertains a similarly expansive conception of America's purpose. During his tenure as chairman of the Joint Chiefs of Staff, General Powell acquired a well-earned reputation as cautious and circumspect. Upon his appointment to be secretary of state, he shed his soldierly inhibitions to reveal his Wilsonian inner self. In his confirmation hearing testimony before the Senate Foreign Relations Committee, for example, Powell waxed eloquent: "There is no country on earth that is not touched by America, for we have become the motive force for freedom and democracy in the world." As such, he said,

> We are attached by a thousand cords to the world at large, to its teeming cities, to its remotest regions, to its oldest civilizations, to its newest cries for freedom. This means that we have an interest in every place on this Earth, that we need to lead, to guide, to help in every country that has a desire to be free, open, and prosperous.

What might leading, guiding and helping entail? When it comes to China, Powell endorses a tutelary approach not unlike that pursued by Clinton. The key, he explained to the committee, lies in "exposing them to the powerful forces of a free enterprise system in democracy, so they can see that this is the proper direction in which to move."

SECOND, *the promise of openness and integration.* Previous U.S. efforts to lead, guide and help others toward the right side of history have achieved mixed results. Americans take pride in their contribution to democratizing Germany and Japan after World War II. Yet earnest and determined efforts during the decades before the war to teach Latin Americans to elect good men yielded resentment and reaction. A Herculean attempt after the war to graft liberal institutions onto South Vietnam failed spectacularly. Efforts closer to home in a much earlier time to lead, guide and help Native Americans produced a disaster of such magnitude that Americans are able to assimilate the outcome only by practicing a form of cognitive dissonance, acknowledging the facts as incontrovertible and then shrugging them off as irrelevant. Given this spotty record, heeding present-day American calls to hop aboard the express train of history might strike some as an iffy proposition. Not so, according to members of the policy elite: climbing aboard has never been easier, nor has the prospective journey been more exhilarating. Thanks for that goes to that signal phenomenon of the post-Cold War era: globalization.

Combined with its fraternal twin the information revolution, globalization is accelerating the inexorable process of international integration. In so doing, it enhances the appeal of America's message, investing it with an allure that is well nigh irresistible. As President Clinton never tired of declaiming, globalization sweeps aside barriers impeding the movement of goods, capital, ideas and culture. It creates boundless new opportunities for the creation of wealth. But globalization also does much more: it imprints onto its beneficiaries the expectations and sensibilities of the nation acting as the project's chief sponsor, namely, the United States. A world opened up by the forces of globalization will not only be more affluent; it will also be freer, as Americans define freedom. It will be more democratic, as we understand democracy. It will be more peaceful, as we ourselves are a peaceful people.

Clinton and his advisers frequently voiced these expectations; Bush and his advisers concur. Thus in December 2000, upon being introduced as the next secretary of state, Powell, with nary an acknowledging footnote, appropriated the clichés that Clinton himself had never tired of reiterating. According to Powell, the "information and technology revolutions… are reshaping the world as we know it, destroying political boundaries and all kinds of other boundaries as we are able to move information and capital data around the world at the speed of light." Removing boundaries fosters free trade, to which Bush, like his father before him and like Clinton, evinces a cult-like devotion. Like them, Bush also attributes to openness benefits that extend beyond mere commercial opportunity. "Free trade brings greater political and personal freedom", he told the Congress in February. Or, as he stated it more grandly in the November Reagan Library speech, his own approach to foreign policy derives from a "vision in which people and capital and information can move freely, creating bonds of progress, ties of culture and momentum toward democracy."

But the creation of an open world is not just about creating ties of culture. Globalization is not social work. The pursuit of openness is first of all about Americans doing well; that an open world might also enable them to do good qualifies at best as incidental. As Raymond Aron observed over a quarter century ago, "A world without frontiers is a situation in which the strongest capitalism prevails."[3] An open global order in which American enterprise enjoys free rein and in which American values and tastes enjoy pride of place is a world in which the United States remains pre-eminent. Clinton and his advisers knew this. So do their successors.

THIRD, *the duality of openness.* As senior members of the Clinton administration acknowledged, openness is a two-edged sword. The prospect of a world remade in America's image does not strike all with equanimity. Although post-ideological Washington cannot conceive of the future harboring any significant secret or surprise—have not all of the big questions been settled once and for all?— elsewhere History remains hotly contested.

So, even in the absence of any viable alternative to democratic capitalism or of any remotely comparable great power, America's enthusiastic promotion of openness incites resistance. Based on the record of the Clinton era, opponents fall into one of three distinct categories. In the first are those, such as adherents of radical Islam, who advance an altogether different view of history's purpose and their own distinctive claims to truth. Speaking on behalf of such groups, critics—some honest, some dishonest—assert that the values that America exports have less to do with authentic freedom than with a popular culture that they view as vulgar and meretricious, where not simply debased and dehumanizing. They are determined to prevent that culture from inundating their own.

The second category of opposition to openness includes those who reject universalism of any stripe and cling ferociously to their own particularistic vision. The perverse attempt by Kosovar guerrillas to carve out a Greater Albania offers only the most recent illustration of this phenomenon. Since the end of the Cold War there have been countless others: bloody purges fueled by tribal hatred in Africa, violent separatist movements across Asia, and, most vividly, the intractable conflict between Israelis and Palestinians, who, we are told, have no choice but to live together but who regularly choose to do otherwise. Not for these groups the tolerant pluralism and easygoing multiculturalism that is the ultimate promise of an open world. They will not condone any blurring of the distinctions between "us" and "them." They persist in believing that identity is indelible, sacred and worth fighting for.

The final category of opposition includes various parties intent simply on grabbing their share of the loot. Although Americans take it as a given that the United States should benefit disproportionately from the spoils that globalization throws up in such profusion, to others the logic of this arrangement is not self-evident. Some opponents in this category are merely aggravating—like the industrious Asian entrepreneurs who pirate the latest CDs, videos and software and thereby siphon off profits rightfully belonging to Hollywood or Silicon Valley. Others—like the narcotraffickers of Latin America—pose a far more insidious threat.

The various elements forming this opposition differ in their capacity to act. They also differ in the means that they employ. But all are alike in rejecting the norms that the United States insists are necessary for globalization to work.[4]

Openness greatly complicates the task of suppressing these adversaries. Removing barriers to commercial activity likewise removes barriers that once protected everyday life within the borders of the United States. Openness exacerbates existing vulnerabilities and creates new ones. It facilitates the theft of technology, the transport of contraband, and the acquisition of weapons. It eases intelligence collection and infiltration. Thus, thanks to openness, and despite the absence of any single power capable of directly challenging the United States, Americans today ostensibly find themselves less secure than during the bad old days of the Cold War. At least one would think so as evidenced by the senior officials who issue stern warnings about fanatics releasing anthrax in downtown Washington or paint lurid scenarios in which hackers acting on a whim disable the nation's financial networks.

This depiction of the United States as besieged by "new threats" is very much the handiwork of the Clinton years. Yet the idea is one that the Bush administration has adopted without reservation. On the campaign trail in September, Bush depicted the twenty-first century as "an era of car bombers and plutonium merchants and cyber terrorists and drug cartels and unbalanced dictators." Once in office, the new President affirmed that the dangers facing the United States in this new era "are more widespread and less certain." Cribbing a term invented by the Clinton administration, Bush has cited the great danger posed by "rogue nations" intent on acquiring weapons of mass destruction, the "rogue" label obviating any need actually to evaluate the capabilities of nations such as North Korea that fall into this category. When it comes to terror, Bush likewise endorses his predecessor's view, ignoring (as did Clinton) data indicating that the incidence of international terrorism is actually on the wane. For Bush, as for Clinton, the utopia implicit in the vision of a globalized world will, it appears, be a precarious one.

FOURTH, *the necessity of military supremacy.* Even as openness exposes the United States to what Bush has called "all the unconventional and invisible threats of new technologies and old hatreds", it remains an abiding imperative. Once having decided that the protective barriers must go, there can be no retreat. To do so would be to jeopardize domestic prosperity, unsustainable absent ever expanding access to global markets. Furthermore, the most effective way to defend the open order (and to promote economic growth) is to continuously expand its perimeter.

Policing the perimeter and pushing it outward requires power, above all coercive power. As a result, the passing of the Cold War has accelerated the transformation of the U.S. military from an institution charged with providing for the common defense into an instrument of power projection and political influence. Begun haphazardly in 1898 when American soldiers set sail to liberate Cuba, that transformation reached a culminating point of sorts in the 1990s when the Pentagon promulgated its "strategy of engagement", formally charging U.S. forces with responsibility for "shaping" the international environment.

Formalized during the Clinton years, the notion of using the military to sustain the momentum toward openness and integration under the aegis of the United States is by no means the exclusive property of liberal Democrats. It commands bipartisan support. Consider the post-Cold War U.S. military presence and activities in Europe. A half century after World War II, with Europe prosperous, democratic, stable and easily able to defend itself, leaders of both parties take it for granted that the United States should maintain in perpetuity a European garrison

of 100,000 soldiers. Similarly, leaders of both parties agree on the wisdom of expanding the "Europe" that the United States is committed to defend. A decade ago, the elder Bush first proposed the program of NATO enlargement. Clinton converted that idea into reality. But Clinton went even further: he also enlarged NATO's charter, exploiting the opportunities presented in Bosnia and Kosovo to convert a defensive alliance into a vehicle for policing Europe's periphery. The younger Bush—who supported the war for Kosovo—shows little sign of undoing the work that Clinton began.

This reorientation of purpose—not simply in Europe, but in Asia, the Persian Gulf, the Western Hemisphere and even, to a lesser extent, in Africa—has profound implications. In contrast to the soldier's traditional stance—awaiting the summons—engagement requires an activist posture. In contrast to the soldier's traditional expectations—responding to the occasional war or emergency—engagement entails continuous exertion. Thus engagement implies a continuing need for a large, highly capable and highly professional, even praetorian, military establishment, charged with shouldering a wider array of responsibilities.

On this score, too, the elite consensus is firm. Indeed, to judge by the most recent national elections, the proposition that the United States must remain militarily supreme attracts something close to universal assent. In mainstream American politics, there is nothing even remotely resembling an anti-military party. Nor does either national party contain an antimilitary wing or faction. Indeed, in all of American public life there is hardly a single prominent figure who finds fault with the notion of the United States remaining the world's sole military superpower until the end of time.

If disagreement exists, it concerns not the ends of strategy but the means to achieve those ends. Critics have charged Clinton with having left the U.S. military in a parlous state. Stripped of its partisan underpinnings, that charge is difficult to sustain. By any conceivable measure, the United States ended the Clinton era as it began it—as easily the strongest military power on the planet while far and away outspending allies and adversaries alike in its determination to maintain that status.

Yet critics can quite justifiably fault Clinton's stewardship on another score: Throughout his two terms in office, efforts to transform the way that the American military thinks, organizes and operates have lagged well behind the actually ongoing transformation of what U.S. strategy calls upon the military to do. A combination of factors—lackluster civilian leadership, obstructionism on the part of hidebound senior officers, and the military's distracting involvement in the culture wars—has impeded efforts to restructure the services for their expanded role. In short, although Clinton succeeded in broadening the purposes that U.S. military power would serve, his efforts to adapt the armed services to those new purposes foundered.

The Bush administration has forcefully declared its intention to close this gap, if necessary bludgeoning the services into discarding the Cold War era structure to which they have clung. But in vowing to create, in Deputy Secretary of Defense Paul Wolfowitz's words, "a future force that is at once more agile, more lethal and more rapidly deployable", the Bush national security team is reciting the very same litany of qualities that the Clinton administration had long since identified as essential for effective global interventionism. In other words, although on defense matters notable differences do exist between Bush and his predecessor, it is easy to make more of these differences than they deserve.

Ballistic missile defense—the signature initiative of the Bush-Cheney-Rumsfeld Pentagon—offers a case in point. The new administration's commitment to missile defense does not signify an abandonment of Clinton's paradigm regarding the proper role of American forces; if anything, it affirms that paradigm. The true purpose of missile defense after all is not to permit the United States to withdraw behind the ramparts of Fortress America. It is not a step toward isolationism. Rather, ballistic missile defense will facilitate the more effective application of U.S. military power abroad. By insulating the homeland from reprisal—albeit in a limited way—missile defense will underwrite the capacity and willingness of the United States to "shape" the environment elsewhere. As Lawrence F. Kaplan, writing in *The New Republic,* has correctly discerned, "Missile defense isn't really meant to protect America. It's a tool for global dominance."[5] Credit the Bush administration with having a better appreciation of what military tools dominance requires. But do not credit it with changing the larger purpose to which the tools will be put.

FIFTH, *the imperative of American "leadership."* The final element of the consensus to which leaders of the Clinton administration and of both Bush administrations have subscribed stipulates that there exists no alternative to global U.S. leadership. To be sure, during his first year in office, Clinton dallied briefly with "assertive multilateralism." But any fanciful notions that Washington would routinely work with or through the United Nations did not survive the debacle of Mogadishu in October 1993. Subsequent to that chastening experience, the Clinton administration acted unilaterally or at the head of a coalition, working in concert with international organizations only as it saw fit. In speech after speech and in crisis after crisis, members of Clinton's team and the President himself made it clear that the United States would defer to no one.

What the Clinton administration never could bring itself to acknowledge is that leadership is really a code word, one whose use honors the cherished tradition according to which the United States is not and cannot be an empire. Leadership has become a euphemism for hegemony.

In the public statements of senior officials, the word "hegemon" figures only by way of identifying threats that the United States must anticipate and deflect. For example, Condoleezza Rice has stated that the paramount aim of U.S. foreign policy should be to "make certain that the international system remains stable and secure... so that no hegemon can rise to threaten stability."[6] But what is the exercise of U.S. power to maintain global stability and security if not itself hegemony? There is today no region of strategic significance in which the United States is not pre-eminent. Thanks to NATO, the United States remains the leading power in Europe. With its permanent commitment of 100,000 troops in the Pacific, it is the leading power in East Asia. With its various bases and garrisons established subsequent to the Persian Gulf War, it is the guarantor of order and stability in that region as well. And that does not even count America's sway over the Western Hemisphere.

Back in the days when President Bush's father was in the White House, the Pentagon prepared a document suggesting (in so many words) that something approximating global hegemony offered a useful principle around which to organize U.S. strategy after the Cold War. The document leaked, the *New York Times* professed great shock, and Democrats pilloried its chief author, then Undersecretary of Defense Paul Wolfowitz. Eight years later Wolfowitz is back in the Pentagon as deputy secretary of defense, and there is no evidence that he has modified his views. What has changed is the climate of informed opinion. Were Wolfowitz today to publish a new draft of the strategy he devised in 1992, it would produce nary a ripple. As a result of the Clinton era, hegemony—although few dare to call it by its rightful name—has gone mainstream.

The Theater of Continuity

IN THE aftermath of the Cold War, public discourse about U.S. foreign policy retains a strong element of theater. Especially when it comes to political campaigns, the parts are prescribed, the players know their roles, and everyone sticks to the script, sustaining the fiction that in the forthcoming balloting the differences separating the candidates are large and the stakes profound. Thus in the fall of 2000, during the second of the three debates between Bush and Gore, the moderator charged the two presidential candidates with identifying the "guiding principles" of U.S. foreign policy. Governor Bush, coached to play the role of hardheaded realist, explained that, "The first question is what's in the best interests of the United States." The vice president—ostentatiously donning the mantle of progressivism—demurred: "I see it as a question of values."

Thus do candidates pretend to differ. After the fact, partisans in both camps pretend that those differences actually matter. Journalists chime in with commentary pretending to spin out the weighty implications. In fact, comparing the actual views of Bush and Gore, or more generally comparing the views of Democratic foreign policy experts with those of their Republican counterparts, is akin to comparing the primetime programming of competing television networks.[7] Some differences exist—after all, people actually make a living contrasting the finer points of sitcoms—but enumerating those differences does not go very far toward identifying the true nature of the enterprise known as commercial television. Similarly, some people actually make a living parsing the differences between where Democrats and Republicans stand on foreign policy. But doing so does not get you very far toward understanding the essential nature of U.S. foreign policy after the Cold War.

In the period following World War II, the pivotal year for U.S. foreign policy was not 1947, the year of "Mr. X", the Truman Doctrine and the Marshall Plan. Nor was it 1950, the year of NSC-68 and the Korean intervention. Rather, the defining moment occurred in 1953. In January of that year, Republicans, after a long and frustrating absence from power, reclaimed the White House. For years, they had been charging that on the paramount issue of the day—responding to the threat of communism—the Truman administration had been pusillanimous and inept. During the presidential campaign, Dwight D. Eisenhower had hinted at a new approach: his administration would seek ways to "roll back" communism. Privately, Eisenhower favored lowering the U.S. profile abroad, even toying with the idea of phasing American troops out of Europe. Once in office, he did neither more nor less. Instead, Eisenhower embraced the logic of the strategy that his predecessor had devised: containment. In doing so, Eisenhower paid his predecessor a very large if backhanded compliment. More important, he invested U.S. policy with a continuity that it would retain—with the exception of a brief period following the Vietnam War—until the end of the Cold War.

In a similar sense, 2001 may well prove to be the pivotal year in fixing the azimuth of U.S. policy in the emerging global era. Historians may well look back on the transfer of power from Clinton to Bush as the moment in which conservative Republicans, after a long and frustrating absence from power, after years of complaining about pusillanimity and ineptness, affirmed the course set by liberal Democrats—and in doing so made manifest the new consensus underlying U.S. strategy.

When President-elect Bush introduced Colin Powell as his nominee to be secretary of state, the retired four-star general let it be know[n] that "the world marches to new drummers, drummers of democracy and the free enterprise system." In Washington a new set of drummers may have picked up the sticks, but, to a far greater extent than they are willing to acknowledge, the rhythms that they are tapping out do not differ appreciably from those favored by their predecessors.

Notes

1. The White House subsequently seemed to distance itself from Powell's position. But any differences in the Bush take on North Korea are ones of tone rather than substance. "All that has happened", one observer noted, "is that the public enthusiasm of President Clinton—which masked the private skepticism of everyone else—is gone, replaced by the public skepticism of President Bush." Anne Applebaum, "Ping Pyongyang", Slate, March 30, 2001.
2. Rice, "American Foreign Policy in the 21st Century", Speech at Los Angeles World Affairs Council, January 15, 1999.
3. Aron, The Imperial Republic: The United States and the World, 1945–1973 (Englewood Cliffs, NJ: Prentice Hall, 1974), p. 176.
4. Some might see Europe as possessing the potential to oppose the United States. In terms of aggregate wealth and population, it does. In its resentment of perceived American highhandedness and arrogance—expressed most vigorously by France—it would seem to possess a motive of sorts. But Europe lacks political will. It talks, but actions seldom match words. The proposed European defense identity is a case in point. Who among the Europeans is willing to pay for it?
5. Cover text, New Republic, March 12, 2001.
6. Interview by Haim Zaltzman with Rice, "The Future of Foreign Policy", Hoover Digest (Fall 1999), www-hoover.stanford.edu/publications/digest/994/rice.html
7. Once the campaign ends, so does the posturing. Once safely elected, but even before his inauguration, Bush declared that, "American values always are at the center of our foreign policy."

Andrew J. Bacevich teaches at Boston University and is currently writing a book about U.S. foreign policy since the end of the Cold War.

REFLECTIONS

In from the Cold: A New Approach to Relations with Russia and China

Robert S. McNamara and James G. Blight

The ghost of Woodrow Wilson, whose presidency encompassed the whole of the First World War and its immediate aftermath, has haunted world leaders from his day to ours. The message of Wilson's ghost is this: beware of the blindness and folly that led Europe's leaders into the First World War, a disaster theretofore without compare in world history; and beware of the temptation to believe that sustainable peace will be maintained simply by plotting to achieve an alleged "balance of power," without a strong international organization to enforce it. That message has gone unheeded. Not only did the twentieth century become the bloodiest century by far in all of human history, but we enter the twenty-first century with conflicts breaking out around the globe—so far, largely within states—and with the capacity utterly to destroy ourselves in a nuclear holocaust.

As the twenty-first century begins, Wilson's ghost may continue to haunt us if we do not now begin to ask ourselves how a great power conflict might begin and what must be done to prevent it. Understanding Wilson's vision, however, can help us immeasurably in finally laying to rest Wilson's ghost. Woodrow Wilson and the other Allied leaders failed after the First World War to establish a sustainable peace with their defeated adversary, Germany. Almost alone among his contemporaries, Wilson understood the problem: if Germany was not, in the phrase of our own day, brought "in from the cold," if the Germans were instead to be humiliated, to feel betrayed, and to become ever more paranoid as they looked out on the world then, said Wilson, "I do not hesitate to say that the war we have just been through, though it was shot through with terror of every kind, is not to be compared with the war we would have to face next time."[1] Tragically, this is exactly what happened. The Allies' treatment of Germany after the First World War is a parable of how not to prevent great power conflict, the lessons of which apply to a principal task of

the United States and the West in the twenty-first century: bringing Russia and China in from the cold.

Here, in roughest outline, is how the seeds were planted that grew into the Second World War. On November 9, 1918, Kaiser Wilhelm II abdicated his throne as German emperor in the wake of a popular uprising. There followed a meeting in a railway car in the forest of Compiègne, in France, where a representative of the new German government signed an armistice by the terms of which Germany agreed to lay down its arms. The German government, in signing the armistice, had put its faith in Woodrow Wilson's "Fourteen Points" which, according to Wilson, "would lead to a peace without victors," chiefly by means of a nonpunitive peace treaty, which would leave Germany with the capacity to rebuild itself into a democratic republic, and via the establishment of the League of Nations, which would enforce the European peace thereafter. However, to the representatives of France, Britain, and Italy—the three major allies of the United States—the Treaty of Versailles could have but one purpose: to punish Germany by extracting as much of its wealth and territory as possible, thereby leaving it too weak and destitute to threaten its neighbors thereafter.

As the Yale historian Donald Kagan has written, the treaty "was neither conciliatory enough to remove the desire for change, even at the cost of war, nor harsh enough to make another war impossible."[2] In humiliating Germany, in pressing for every conceivable momentary advantage from her, and in giving rise to her feelings of betrayal and the need for vengeance, the Allies at Versailles helped sow the seeds of their own devastation at Germany's hands in the Second World War.

If the lessons of this Wilsonian parable are not heeded, a Third World War could result sometime in the twenty-first century. Such an event may seem highly improbable at the moment and may remain so for some time. But we nevertheless discern an eerie resonance between Germany's feelings of betrayal in 1919 with those of Russia and China following the Cold War. Even more troubling, we also see similarities between the victors' enthusiasm for humiliating Germany in 1919 and the lack of empathy so far shown in the West—particularly by the United States—for the situation of the major communist "losers" in the half-century-long Cold War. For these reasons, we believe, a great power conflict between Russia or China (or both) and the United States is not impossible and, in fact, the risk of such a conflict may rise over time, unless we act to lower that risk. In 1919, as the combatants in the First World War sat down to negotiate in Paris, the risk of another great power conflict was also low. By 1933, with the ascension of the Nazis to power, it may have been too late to prevent it. This, therefore, should be our objective: to prevent the twenty-first century from ever arriving at its own figurative "1933."

Before the astounding events of 1989, for example, little serious thought was given in the West, and particularly in the United States, to the reconciliation or integration of Russia and China into an international system of shared values, beliefs, and institutions. The communist "bloc" was the enemy, and it had its own system—its own mutual security and economic organizations. A principal purpose of such organizations, on both sides, was to prevent anything resembling integration between the two systems. Reconciliation on terms acceptable to both blocs was generally seen as an impossible pipe dream and suggestions to the contrary were customarily regarded on both sides as seditious, as caving in to the enemy. The emphasis was on intra-bloc solidarity, not inter-bloc integration.

The Cold War's principal surprise is that it never erupted into a full-blown military conflict between two or more of the great powers on either side. The Soviet Union collapsed, and communist ideology was globally and irreversibly discredited (although communist parties retained power in a few countries, including China). All this happened without Western military conquest and occupation, without any kind of official "surrender." That all this happened peacefully was both a shock and a blessing.

Yet this supreme blessing of the Cold War—its relative "coldness," including its peaceful conclusion—is, in a sense, the post-Cold War era's curse, because it mimics, in an eerie way, the conclusion and aftermath of the First World War. Just as the other Great Power signatories of the Treaty of Versailles ensured that Germany entered the 1920s humiliated, destabilized, bankrupt, and bitter, Russia and China after the Cold War seem in many respects to feel alienated—politically, economically, militarily, socially, and psychologically—from the global community established by the other great powers. Russia and China, in their individual ways, still feel very much "out in the cold," just as Germany did 80 years before.

It is useful to keep in mind why the end of the previous great power conflict, the Second World War, does not, in most respects, offer useful lessons for those seeking guidance on how to achieve integration and reconciliation for Russia and China in the twenty-first century. The difference is obvious but critically important: the unconditional surrender, and subsequent extended occupation, of Germany and Japan made it possible for the United States and the West to force quick integration and eventual reconciliation with their former enemies. No such possibility exists with regard to Russia's and China's entrance into the mainstream of the twenty-first century.

In the absence of military occupation of Russia and China, and the consequent impossibility of their enforced tutelage in Western-style civil society, and political and economic affairs, by what indirect means might the United States and the West bring these powers in from the cold? How might this be accomplished, moreover, before Russia's and China's alienation from, and suspicion of, the United States and the West provoke a crisis, possibly leading to a military confrontation? If we cannot forcibly remold Russia and China according to Western political values, how can we reach them, make contact with them, develop a dialogue of mutual exploration, by the conclusion of which their integration and reconciliation might be achieved?

Realistic Empathy

Our answer is to deploy "realistic empathy," a process that, we believe, must lie at the heart of any successful strategy of bringing Russia and China in from the cold. With occupation not a realistic (or desirable) option, a policy based on empathy is an idea whose time has come. Think of it this way: a policy whose objective is not to preach but to listen; to learn something of the history and culture of Russia and China, rather than to proclaim the virtues of our history and systems; to treat them, in effect, as our equals, as peoples and cultures who seek peace and tranquility but also dignity and respect.

Empathy has nothing to do with sympathy, with which it is often confused. Ralph K. White, a former U.S. Information Agency official, later a political scientist and psychologist at George Washington University, was for a generation the foremost advocate of realistic empathy in foreign affairs, and he made exactly the distinction that must be made between empathy and sympathy. According to White: "Empathy is the great corrective for all forms of war-promoting misperception. It means simply understanding the thoughts and feelings of others. It is distinguished from sympathy, which is defined as feeling with others—as being in agreement with them. Empathy with opponents is therefore psychologically possible even when a conflict is so intense that sympathy is out of the question. We are nor talking about warmth or approval, and certainly not about agreeing with, or siding with, but only about realistic understanding.[3]

The great philosopher of empathy, Sir Isaiah Berlin, wrote that in addition to knowing the mind of an adversary, empathy requires one to grasp "the particular vision of the universe which lies at the heart of [an adversary's] thought." This capacity, he said, permits one "to some degree re-enact the states of mind of men" who are fundamentally at odds with oneself.[4] This is what we call the "deployment" of empathy, the "occupation" of a mindset whose assumptions are fundamentally alien from one's own. The journalist and scholar Michael Ignarieff has written that to act uninformed by empathy, to refuse to occupy as fully as possible the mindset of an actual or potential adversary, is to submit to what he calls "autism," the behavior of those who are "so locked into their own myths… that they can't listen, can't hear, can't learn from anybody outside themselves." In these instances, "What is denied is the possibility of empathy: that human understanding is capable of penetrating the bell jars of separate identities."[5]

The United States is at present the world's only superpower and is commonly regarded by friends and foes alike as arrogant and lacking in objectivity toward itself. Thus, it is possible that a principal benefit to Americans of the deployment of a strategy of realistic empathy would be an unprecedented "honest look at oneself." Should this occur, it could easily have a stunning effect upon the Russians and the Chinese. When empathy is embraced it is possible to construct a peaceful solution even when all the momentum of history, politics, and military alerting schedules seem to be forcing the parties involved toward calamitous hostilities.

Anticipating Inadvertent Conflict

This is our second imperative for preventing great power conflict: anticipate that any military confrontation between the United States and either Russia or China may occur inadvertently. Inadvertent conflict is not "accidental" conflict. Rather, it is conflict that occurs due to the unintended consequences of actions taken by many actors, over an extended period, at the outset of which none of the actors will have anticipated a crisis leading to heightened risk of war between two or more of them.

It is becoming increasingly apparent that the gravest dangers to great power security, and to the peace of the world, derive not from threats uttered or implied at the moment, but from inadvertence—from the unintended consequences of hugely complicated interactions of policies, pronouncements, and actions taken over time by a multilateral cast of players. In fact, often some of the most important actions leading to conflict are taken years, decades, or centuries before the shooting begins. History—incommensurable interpretations of the "same" history—must also be taken into account as a potentially

explosive factor in a process leading to increased risk of conflict.

It is a perversely fascinating fact of life as we enter the twenty-first century that, while our capacity to destroy our fellow human beings is in effect infinite, and the globalization and interconnection of the world is now almost beyond comprehension—in spite of these developments, concepts of national security and foreign policy still rely almost exclusively on assumptions of direct threat, counterthreat, and the like. To an extent, new ideas appeared in the late 1950s, as U.S. specialists began to study the implications of endeavoring to "defend" the country in a situation where there could be no meaningful defense against Soviet ballistic missiles tipped with nuclear warheads. In this singularly uncomfortable fact lay the origins of the so-called theory of nuclear deterrence, according to which each side in the Cold War sought to convince its adversary that an attack by the opponent very probably would result in unacceptable damage inflicted in a retaliatory strike.

The bottom line from these developments was even less comforting to Americans than the knowledge that the Russians (after 1949) and the Chinese (after 1964) had nuclear weapons. It was this: that in order to avoid nuclear destruction, one must rely on the sanity and discretion of the enemy not to launch a devastating first strike against the United States. The Russians and Chinese, in other words, had to become our collaborators, and we had to become theirs, in pursuit of our mutual survival. We had to trust each other—no easy task for either side then or now.

Straining the Imagination

In the twenty-first century, the most destructive type of conflict would involve two or more great powers, armed with nuclear weapons, who find their interests so irreconcilable, their situation so perverse and nonnegotiable, that the least bad option at some critical moment seems to be to go to war with one another. It strains the imagination of many at the moment to articulate plausible scenarios by which the United States might become involved in a war with potential enemies that are, or likely will be, great military powers during the course of the twenty-first century. The leading candidates—virtually the only plausible candidates at present—are Russia and China, America's former Cold War rivals. Yet Russia is in terrible straits economically, psychologically, and militarily, whereas China remains militarily inferior to the United States at every level and also faces deep uncertainty about the future of its social, political, and economic systems. Each may be said to be, relative to the position of the United States and the West, deeply inferior, hardly in a position to risk war with the United States.

But what is not adequately appreciated, especially in the United States, is the potential significance of the reaction in Russia and China to what both perceive as post-Cold War U.S. unilateralism. The key elements of their common reaction are: first, that due to the way the Cold War ended, the United States has become triumphalist and increasingly arrogant in the prosecution of its foreign policy, especially toward Russia and China, the "losers" in the Cold War struggle; and second, that this U.S. arrogance is not only irritating, it is also dangerous because it threatens a number of interests Russia and China consider vital. U.S. arrogance, in their view, is displayed most ominously in its betrayal of both Russia and China on pivotal and contentious issues, betrayals that demonstrate a U.S. disregard for its international commitments. To Russian and Chinese eyes, America appears to believe that as the world's only remaining superpower, it need not adhere to accepted norms of international behavior among great powers.

Many contentious issues divide the United States and the West from Russia and China. Both oppose the building of a U.S. national missile defense: Russia, because it will violate the terms of the 1972 Anti-Ballistic Missile Treaty between the United States and the Soviet Union; China because Beijing believes it will compromise China's relatively small nuclear deterrent force. Russia resents U.S. and Western accusations of human rights abuses in the ongoing war in Chechnya, which Russia regards as a purely internal matter. China takes the same dim view of Western criticism of its governance of Tibet. Beijing also objects strenuously to the 1996 renewal of the U.S.-Japan Security Alliance, believing that it represents an attempt to encircle and contain China.

In 1997, Prime Minister Li Peng stated emphatically to Robert McNamara during a visit to his country that, whereas initially the treaty might have been directed against the Soviet Union, with the end of the Cold War it could have no purpose other than to contain and, ultimately, threaten China. He supported his argument by emphasizing that in contrast to Germany, Japan had never admitted or accepted responsibility for its role in the Second World War. To this day, the majority of Japanese citizens are ignorant of the degree to which their country's actions contributed to the initiation of the war in the Pacific.

The lists of Russian and Chinese grievances are long and their resentment is, in some cases, strong—leaving open the question of whether it is justified. Our purpose here is not to try to "resolve" all these issues, but rather to penetrate as deeply as we can in a brief space into the Russian and Chinese mindsets that harbor this substantial resentment toward the United States. We are convinced that the resentment is real and growing. It is in many ways remarkable that in the space of a single decade since the conclusion of the Cold War, U.S. relations with Russia and China have plummeted from an initial heady optimism to their present testy, occasionally very tense state. It would be an exaggeration to say that we are in the midst of a new Cold War with either country. But we believe that Russian president

Boris Yeltsin did not exaggerate when he warned in December 1994 of an imminent descent into a "cold peace," caused, he said, by attempts of the United States and the West to "bury democracy in Russia."[6] As we see it, the cold peace predicted by Yeltsin in late 1994 has now arrived.

We will focus briefly on two issues: the reaction of Russia to the U.S. decision to enlarge the North Atlantic Treaty Organization (NATO); and the reaction of China to what it perceives as a shift in U.S. policy toward Taiwan, from the "one China" policy inaugurated by the Nixon administration, to one favoring independence for the island.

To reiterate: We do not necessarily agree with these Russian and Chinese assessments. In fact, we do not believe that their accuracy—as to whether they represent a true understanding of U.S. motives—should be the principal issue, either for scholars of foreign policy or U.S. and Western foreign policymakers themselves. Far more important, in our view, is this: we believe Russia and China see the United States and, to a lesser extent, the other Western powers, as pushing them into a corner over these issues, raising the risk not only of regional confrontations but also of a military clash that would not be in the interest of any of the countries involved. Such a clash would almost certainly be a disaster for all sides. This is why we emphasize the primacy of comprehending the Russian and Chinese views, rather than arguing with or lecturing Russia and China. An ounce of empathy and anticipation of inadvertent paths to conflict will be worth a pound of disputation, and a ton of traditional "deterrence."

The "Betrayal" of Russia

According to former deputy secretary of state Strobe Talbott, the Clinton administration's coordinator of Russia policy, the post-Cold War preservation and expansion of NATO was required to provide "the means of deterring or, if necessary, defeating threats to our common security," and to provide "newly liberated and democratic states… [with] the security that the Alliance affords."[7]

The Russian view is totally different. Russia sees NATO expansion as part of an American post-Cold War doctrine of neo-containment, whose purpose is the encirclement and neutralization of Russia in its traditional European sphere of influence. Any Russian diplomat can recite the litany of ostensible U.S. betrayals leading up to NATO expansion. In 1989–90, for example, the Soviet government believed that the United States had pledged never to expand NATO eastward, if Moscow would agree to the unification of Germany.

The former director of Russia's Institute of the USA and Canada, Sergey Rogov, has written of NATO's decision to expand: "It is very difficult to not interpret this step as an expression of deep Western skepticism about future developments in Russia and as a kind of delayed containment, containment in a different form."[8] Many Americans share Rogov's assessment. During the 1998 congressional debate over NATO expansion, Senator Dale Bumpers of Arkansas, typically a supporter of the Clinton administration's foreign policy initiatives, made a speech criticizing expansion. "The Russians would have to be incredibly naive beyond all imagination," he asserted, "not to believe that... NATO enlargement is designed to hem Russia in."[9]

The next critical act of betrayal began in May 1997, with the signing in Paris of the "Founding Act" of cooperation between Russia and the West, in which Russia sought to obtain a written commitment that the United States and NATO would limit the expansion of its military capabilities even as its membership grew; disavow any intention to use force against any state except in self-defense or unless authorized by the U.N. Security Council; and grant Russia a role in NATO's political decision making. Russia achieved the first two objectives but failed in the third.[10]

The result, in the Russian view, was another betrayal in March 1999, when NATO began its bombing campaign against the Serb government in Belgrade, in an effort to force the Serbs to stop their ethnic cleansing of Albanians in Kosovo. In the West, the intervention was portrayed as an attempt to avert a humanitarian disaster caused by the racist and fascist policies of Serb leader Slobodan Milosevic. To the Russians, however, the NATO intervention was, first, an outrage, in part because it was directed against their fellow Slavs, the Serbs, but more important, because it flagrantly violated the Founding Act's commitment that both NATO and Russia would refrain "from the threat or use of force against each other as well as against any other state, its sovereignty, territorial integrity or political independence in any manner inconsistent with the United Nations Charter."[11]

But Kosovo, for the Russians, was also more than a little frightening. They watched helplessly, as NATO conducted a high-tech air war against the Serbs, seemingly invulnerable to any sort of defense the Serbs, using their antiquated Russian equipment, could muster. One principal implication of NATO's success was drawn by Russian defense minister Igor Sergeev, following Russian maneuvers in June 1999, which simulated a NATO attack on Russia in the Kaliningrad Oblast region, using only conventional forces. "Russia was able to defend itself," he said of the training maneuvers, "only by using nuclear weapons."[12] This led Russian president Vladimir Putin to endorse in 2000 what he calls Russia's "new concept of security," renouncing its stated policy of "no-first-use" of nuclear weapons and relying increasingly on early use of such weapons if Russia should be attacked, presumably by NATO forces.[13] More recently, Putin authorized a 15-year plan to modernize Russian conventional forces, while reducing the strategic nuclear arsenal to approximately 1,500 warheads.[14] The Harvard Russia

specialist Celeste Wallander draws the bottom line. "For Russia," she says, "the lesson of Kosovo is that power matters," including both nuclear power and conventional military power.[15]

Sergey Rogov said recently that this perceived history of betrayal has led the Russian foreign policy establishment to begin to contemplate, for the first time since the end of the Cold War, "a new geopolitical split of the world... between the West on one side and Russia, China and India on the other"—a new Cold War.[16]

Jack F. Matlock, Jr., former American ambassador to the Soviet Union, recently wrote that many U.S. difficulties with Russia derive from American historical blindness, our inability to understand and appreciate the significance of the fact that "the Cold War we won was against the Soviet Union, not Russia."[17] For just this reason, the historian and diplomat George Kennan has called NATO expansion "the most fateful error of American policy in the entire post-Cold War era."[18] What particularly worries Kennan, and worries us, is the emphasis placed by the United States on NATO, on the military dimension of its relations with its European allies and with Russia. Treating Russia more or less as it treated the Soviet Union—by giving the Russians the impression that they are being encircled and "contained" once again by the military might of a technologically superior West, Kennan says, "can only have suicidal significance."[19]

The "Betrayal" of China

Ever since the 1972 opening to China by the Nixon administration, the formal U.S. position on Taiwan has been one of "strategic ambiguity." According to this policy, the United States recognizes "one China" whose capital is in Beijing, a China to which Taiwan belongs. At the same time, the United States provides military hardware and political backing for the (now) democratically elected and (at times) independence-minded government in Taipei, in an effort to deter Beijing from attempting to conquer the island by force. Washington has hoped thereby to delay indefinitely a final resolution of its contradictory policy, which it regards as reflecting the reality of Taiwan—this disputed remnant of the still incompletely resolved Chinese civil war between Mao Zedong's Communists and Chiang Kai-shek's Nationalists, a war that began before the Second World War.

Yet in Beijing, the feeling of U.S. betrayal on the central issue of Taiwan is powerful and growing. It derives from the U.S. failure (at least in China's eyes) to adhere to the "one China" policy it agreed to in 1972. Indeed, Beijing believes that the United States, through its arms sales and military advice to Taiwan, has sought instead to make the island an impregnable fortress and in this way to force Beijing into accepting an eventual "two-China" reality.

As further proof of the validity of this view of U.S. motives, Chinese officials cite the continued U.S. military presence in East Asia. Especially worrisome to the Chinese was the reaffirmation of the U.S.-Japan Security Alliance in 1996, which the Chinese regard as directed principally against themselves, and especially at their efforts at reunification with Taiwan. In this way, Beijing's feeling of U.S. betrayal on the Taiwan question has fueled broader suspicions that the United States has "hegemonic" objectives in East Asia. While the situation is intermittently tense, the governments in Taipei, Beijing, and Washington have, at least so far, backed off at key moments.

Many believe, however, that the day of reckoning over Taiwan is coming. Increasingly, the Beijing government threatens to intervene militarily if the Taipei government and its more than 20 million constituents choose independence. Once every four years, during Taiwan's presidential elections, some political candidates court voters with pledges to move toward the full independence that Beijing says it will never permit. The United States is, as always, caught in the middle. It seeks better relations with an increasingly prosperous and powerful China, but it is also committed to protecting Taiwan militarily, should Beijing try to conquer it by force. One analyst has maintained that "the question of Taiwan's affiliation" is "the single most serious jurisdictional issue to survive the Cold War."[20] It is a very dangerous situation.

In recent years, the perpetually smoldering danger has twice exploded into crises. Beijing believes that the U.S. betrayal began in earnest in 1995 when, under pressure from Congress, the Clinton administration authorized the visit of Taiwan's president Lee Teng-hui to the United States, ostensibly on an "unofficial" visit to attend a class reunion at Cornell University. But Lee had just previously raised the ante in the war of words between Taipei and Beijing by seeming to Beijing to have openly advocated separatism, and by initiating a campaign to get Taiwan readmitted to the United Nations, where it had been replaced by Beijing in 1971. In retaliation, the Chinese government flexed its muscles in the lead-up to Taiwan's March 1996 election by firing three intermediate-range M-11 missiles at what they called "target zones" in the Taiwan Strait. The United States responded by deploying two aircraft carrier battle groups nearby and by warning Beijing not to deepen the crisis.

In a recent memoir, former U.S. secretary of defense William Perry has written that "in retrospect it seems clear that Chinese government officials had misunderstood the seriousness with which the United States viewed unprovoked military actions against Taiwan. The CBG [carrier battle group] deployment straightened out that misunderstanding."[21] In fact, however, the Chinese by no means regarded their actions as unprovoked. They viewed them as required by the shrillness and boldness of the pre-election rhetoric of several presidential candidates in Taiwan urging a declaration of full independence

from Beijing. Predictably, the Chinese then regarded deployment of a U.S. carrier battle group as a provocation. Prime Minister Li Peng responded by reminding the Americans that "with a concentrated fire of guided missiles and artillery, the People's Liberation Army can bury an intruder in a sea of fire."[22] The confrontation ended in a standoff. The United States had signaled its willingness to use force to protect Taiwan from a forcible takeover. China had indicated that any move toward Taiwanese independence would be regarded in Beijing as an act of war by both Taiwan and the United States.

The Beijing government's view of the Taiwan problem mirrors Russia's perception of NATO expansion. Beijing believes that U.S. policy since 1995 represents a betrayal—a unilateral reversal of U.S. pledges and written commitments over nearly three decades. It believes it has a strong case. Here is a relevant passage from the "Shanghai Communiqué" of February 27, 1972, that concluded the epochal visit of President Nixon to China and established the ground rules for U.S.-China relations ever since: "The U.S. acknowledges that all Chinese on either side of the Taiwan Strait maintain there is but one China and that Taiwan is part of China. The U.S. Government does not challenge that position. It reaffirms its interest in a peaceful settlement of the Taiwan question by the Chinese themselves. With this prospect in mind, it affirms the ultimate objective of the withdrawal of all U.S. forces and military institutions from Taiwan."

The meaning seemed transparently clear to the Chinese: politically, the United States had committed itself, during the so-called transitional era leading to reunification, to a steady withdrawal of its presence. Beijing believed it would be followed quickly by Beijing's recovery of its sovereignty over Taiwan. This was reinforced in two subsequent documents: the Joint Communiqué on the Establishment of Diplomatic Relations Between China and the United States of 1979, and the Joint Communique of August 1982 concerning U.S. arms sales to Taiwan. In all these agreements, the United States agreed that "there is but one China and Taiwan is part of China." The identical phrase appears in all three documents. These are the agreements that Beijing felt were being violated by U.S. support of separatist sentiments voiced by Taiwanese leaders in March 1996 and March 2000.

Yet the U.S. commitment to Beijing in these three communiqués is contradicted by the language of the Taiwan Relations Act of 1979, which governs the U.S. relationship with the Taiwanese government itself. According to this act of Congress: "It is the policy of the United States… to consider any effort to determine the future of Taiwan by other than peaceful means, including boycotts or embargoes, a threat to the peace and security of the Western Pacific area and of grave concern to the United States [and]… to maintain the capacity of the United States to resist any resort to force or other forms of coercion that would jeopardize the security, or the social and economic system, of the people on Taiwan." In other words, Taiwan believes that the United States has made a commitment to Taiwan that, in the event of hostilities between Taiwan and China, the United States is legally bound to enter the conflict on the side of Taiwan. Taiwan looks upon this as an iron-clad security commitment, of the sort that characterized the security relationship among the NATO countries during the Cold War, in the event of an attack on any of them by Soviet forces.

What is the solution to this downward spiral of relations that is driven by the Taiwan issue? What should be done about what seems to be a "crisis in slow motion," with a steadily increasing risk of a conflict involving the United States and China?[23] The late Michel Oksenberg of Stanford University, a leading American specialist on China, believed that above all else, Americans must begin to show more "empathy and understanding… in thinking about the problems the leaders of China confront."[24] In particular, he points our, we must try to understand their sense of betrayal, and how it feeds suspicions going back to the nineteenth century, when China, which had long seen itself as the "Middle Kingdom," the center of civilization, entered the modern world only to be occupied, humiliated, and exploited.

In addition, there seems to be considerable concern within the post-Cold War leadership in Beijing regarding the firmness of their grip on power and the possibility that China might follow in the path of the Soviet Union, breaking up into pieces, no one of which approaches the power and influence of the former union.[25] This is a potentially deadly combination: the aspiration to recover the past glory and position of China, coexisting with the fear that even its current position could be undermined by U.S. and Japanese "encirclement." Taiwan symbolizes everything the Chinese leadership seeks (reunification and recovery of at least its past geographical borders) and fears (the loss of Taiwan, loss of face and prestige, and loss of the credibility even of its claim to regional hegemony, let alone great power status). Whether or not one agrees with the policies of the communist government in Beijing, empathy for the pressure its leaders feel seems to us a bare minimum for lowering the odds of conflict over Taiwan. At a minimum, the United States should urge Taiwan to avoid actions that appear to be contradictory to a one-China policy.

The ambiguous status quo may not be completely satisfying to either side, but it is surely better than a war—which is likely if Taiwan proceeds down the road to independence and/or Beijing continues periodically to threaten the island militarily. The former U.S. assistant secretary of defense Joseph S. Nye, Jr. (currently the dean of the Harvard's Kennedy School of Government), has proposed a useful formula: Beijing should pledge not to use force against Taiwan, which, in turn, should pledge not to declare independence.[26] While this is not an ultimate solution, it would buy much precious time that is needed to arrive at one.

Finally, we believe the United States should strive to play the role of mediator in pursuit of such an ultimate solution. In the past, Beijing has rejected U.S. mediation because it has claimed, not without reason, that the United States is far from neutral in the dispute. Yet we believe it is well worth exploring with both Beijing and Taiwan whether U.S. mediation might be useful if the first interim objective were an agreement along the lines suggested by Nye.[27]

The Difficulty Before Us

We should have no illusions about the difficulty before us. Just how difficult is illustrated in the following story of the evolution of one individual's thinking. At a 1991 meeting called by the Carnegie Corporation of New York to discuss post-Cold War security needs, a participant suggested to the assembled group a program somewhat similar to the one we propose here. The chair of the meeting, Senator Sam Nunn of Georgia, stifled any further proposals along these lines by replying: "Well, you have human nature and all of history going against you there. What have you got going for you?"[28] That was in 1991. In the summer of 1999, Senator Nunn (since retired from elective office) again chaired a meeting of specialists in international security, this time under the auspices of the Aspen Strategy Group. On this occasion, having witnessed the devolution of the 1990s into escalating tension between Russia and China, on the one hand, and the United States and the West on the other, he said simply, "We must reverse the course of history."[29]

Notes

1. Quoted in Frank Ninkovich, *The Wilsonian Century: U.S. Foreign Policy since 1900* (Chicago: University of Chicago Press, 1999), p. 75.

2. Donald Kagan, *On the Origins of War and the Preservation of Peace* (New York: Doubleday, 1995), p. 297.

3. Ralph K. White, *Fearful Warriors: A Psychological Profile of U.S.-Soviet Relations* (New York: Free Press, 1984), p. 160.

4. Quoted in Michael Ignatieff, "The Ends of Empathy," *New Republic*, April 29, 1991, pp. 33–34. See also Berlin's classic essay on the significance of empathy, "Herder and the Enlightenment," in *The Proper Study of Mankind: An Anthology of Essays by Isaiah Berlin*, ed. Henry Hardy and Roger Hausheer (New York: Farrar, Straus and Giroux, 1998), pp. 359–435, esp. 389–405.

5. Michael Ignatieff, *The Warrior's Honor: Ethnic War and the Modern Conscience* (New York: Metropolitan Books, 1997), p. 60.

6. Boris N. Yeltsin, statement of December 5, 1994, in Budapest, at a meeting of the Conference on Security and Cooperation in Europe (csce[&stop])—now the Organization of Security and Cooperation in Europe (osce[&stop]). Quoted in William G. Hyland, *Clinton's World: Remaking American Foreign Policy* (Westport, Conn.: Praeger, 1999), p. 99.

7. Strobe Talbott, "The Crooked Timber: A Carpenter's Perspective," speech given at All Soul's College, Oxford University, January 21, 2000, p. 9 (manuscript available from the author).

8. Sergey Rogov, "The Challenge of Russia's Foreign Policy," in *U.S.-Russia Relations*, ed. Michael Mandelbaum (Washington, D.C.: Aspen Institute, 1999), p. 14.

9. Quoted in Hyland, *Clinton's World*, p. 104.

10. Celleste Wallander, "Russian Foreign Policy in the Wake of the Kosovo Crisis," in Mandelbaum, ed., *U.S.-Russia Relations*, p. 6.

11. Ibid. p.7.

12. Igor Sergeev, in *Krasnaya Zvezda*, July 10, 1999, trans. Svetlana Savranskaya.

13. Quoted in William Pfaff, "Nothing Very Romantic about Putin's Nationalism," *International Herald Tribune*, February 28, 2000.

14. Daniel Williams, "Russia to Rebuild Conventional Forces," *International Herald Tribune*, August 14, 2000.

15. Wallander, "Russian Foreign Policy in the Wake of the Kosovo Crisis," p. 7.

16. Rogov, "Challenges to Russia's Foreign Policy," p. 16.

17. Jack F. Matlock, Jr., "Russia and the CIS," in *Preparing America's Foreign Policy for the 21st Century*, ed. David L. Boren and Edward J. Perkins (Norman: University of Oklahoma Press, 1999), p. 26.

18. Quoted in James M. Goldgeier, "The U.S. Decision to Enlarge NATO: How, When, Why, and What Next?" *Brookings Review*, vol. 17 (summer 1998), p. 18.

19. George F. Kennan, *At Century's Ending* (New York: Norton, 1996), p. 330.

20. John D. Steinbruner, *Principles of Global Security* (Washington, D.C.: Brookings, 2000), p. 214.

21. Ashton B. Carter and William J. Perry, *Preventive Defense: A New Security Strategy for America* (Washington, D.C.: Brookings, 1999), p. 99.

22. Quoted in Richard Bernstein and Ross H. Munro, *The Coming Conflict with China* (New York: Vintage, 1998), p. 154.

23. On "crises in slow motion," see Robert H. McNamara, James G. Blight, and Robert K. Brigham, *Argument Without End: In Search of Answers to the Vietnam Tragedy* (New York: PublicAffairs, 1999), pp. 396–97.

24. Michel Oksenberg, "The American View of China," in Boren and Perkins, eds., *Preparing America's Foreign Policy for the 21st Century*, p. 64.

25. According to Thérèse Delpech of the Centre d'Etudes et Recherches Internationales, at the Fondation Narionale des Sciences Politiques in Paris, this was the conclusion of French leaders, following 17 hours of intense discussion with Chinese president Jiang Zemin during a state visit to Paris in the fall of 1999. See Joseph Fitchett, "Europe Fears Fallout from Taiwan Tensions," *International Herald Tribune*, March 17, 2000.

26. Joseph S. Nye, Jr., "Clear Up the Dangerous Ambiguity about Taiwan," *International Herald Tribune*, March 12, 1998. See also Robert A. Pastor, "The Paradox of the Double Triangle" *World Policy Journal*, vol. 17 (spring 2000), pp. 19–30.

27. We are grateful to China specialist Harry Harding, dean of the Elliott School of International Affairs, George Washington University, for suggesting this possibility.

28. Quoted in Steinbruner, *Principles of Global Security*, p. 2.

29. Ibid.

Excerpted from the forthcoming book, *Wilson's Ghost: Reducing the Risk of Conflict, Killing and Catastrophe in the 21st Century*. Copyright © 2001 by Robert S. McNamara and James G. Blight. To be published in June by PublicAffairs, a member of the Perseus Books Group. All rights reserved.

Robert S. McNamara was secretary of defense to Presidents Kennedy and Johnson. James G. Blight is professor of international relations at the Watson Institute for International Studies at Brown University.

The Lonely Superpower

Samuel P. Huntington

THE NEW DIMENSION OF POWER

DURING THE past decade global politics has changed fundamentally in two ways. First, it has been substantially reconfigured along cultural and civilizational lines, as I have highlighted in the pages of this journal and documented at length in *The Clash of Civilizations and the Remaking of World Order*. Second, as argued in that book, global politics is also always about power and the struggle for power, and today international relations is changing along that crucial dimension. The global structure of power in the Cold War was basically bipolar; the emerging structure is very different.

There is now only one superpower. But that does not mean that the world is *unipolar*. A unipolar system would have one superpower, no significant major powers, and many minor powers. As a result, the superpower could effectively resolve important international issues alone, and no combination of other states would have the power to prevent it from doing so. For several centuries the classical world under Rome, and at times East Asia under China, approximated this model. A *bipolar* system like the Cold War has two superpowers, and the relations between them are central to international politics. Each superpower dominates a coalition of allied states and competes with the other superpower for influence among nonaligned countries. A *multipolar* system has several major powers of comparable strength that cooperate and compete with each other in shifting patterns. A coalition of major states

is necessary to resolve important international issues. European politics approximated this model for several centuries.

Contemporary international politics does not fit any of these three models. It is instead a strange hybrid, a *uni-multipolar* system with one superpower and several major powers. The settlement of key international issues requires action by the single superpower but always with some combination of other major states; the single superpower can, however, veto action on key issues by combinations of other states. The United States, of course, is the sole state with preeminence in every domain of power—economic, military, diplomatic, ideological, technological, and cultural—with the reach and capabilities to promote its interests in virtually every part of the world. At a second level are major regional powers that are preeminent in areas of the world without being able to extend their interests and capabilities as globally as the United States. They include the German-French condominium in Europe, Russia in Eurasia, China and potentially Japan in East Asia, India in South Asia, Iran in Southwest Asia, Brazil in Latin America, and South Africa and Nigeria in Africa. At a third level are secondary regional powers whose interests often conflict with the more powerful regional states. These include Britain in relation to the German-French combination, Ukraine in relation to Russia, Japan in relation to China, South Korea in relation to Japan, Pakistan in relation to India, Saudi Arabia in relation to Iran, and Argentina in relation to Brazil.

The superpower or hegemon in a unipolar system, lacking any major powers challenging it, is normally able to maintain its dominance over minor states for a long time until it is weakened by internal decay or by forces from outside the system, both of which happened to fifth-century Rome and nineteenth-century China. In a multipolar system, each state might prefer a unipolar system with itself as the single dominant power but the other major states will act to prevent that from happening, as was often the case in European politics. In the Cold War, each superpower quite explicitly preferred a unipolar system under its hegemony. However, the dynamics of the competition and their early awareness that an effort to create a unipolar system by armed force would be disastrous for both enabled bipolarity to endure for four decades until one state no longer could sustain the rivalry.

In each of these systems, the most powerful actors had an interest in maintaining the system. In a uni-multipolar system, this is less true. The United States would clearly prefer a unipolar system in which it would be the hegemon and often acts as if such a system existed. The major powers, on the other hand, would prefer a multipolar system in which they could pursue their interests, unilaterally and collectively, without being subject to constraints, coercion, and pressure by the stronger superpower. They feel threatened by what they see as the American pursuit of global hegemony. American officials feel frustrated by their failure to achieve that hegemony. None of the principal power-wielders in world affairs is happy with the status quo.

The superpower's efforts to create a unipolar system stimulate greater effort by the major powers to move toward a multipolar one. Virtually all major regional powers are increasingly asserting themselves to promote their own distinct interests, which often conflict with those of the United States. Global politics has thus moved from the bipolar system of the Cold War through a unipolar moment—highlighted by the Gulf War—and is now passing through one or two uni-multipolar decades before it enters a truly multipolar 21st century. The United States, as Zbigniew Brzezinski has said, will be the first, last, and only global superpower.

NOT SO BENIGN

AMERICAN OFFICIALS quite naturally tend to act as if the world were unipolar. They boast of American power and American virtue, hailing the United States as a benevolent hegemon. They lecture other countries on the universal validity of American principles, practices, and institutions. At the 1997 G-7 summit in Denver, President Clinton boasted about the success of the American economy as a model for others. Secretary of State Madeleine K. Albright has called the United States "the indispensable nation" and said that "we stand tall and hence see further than other nations." This statement is true in the narrow sense that the United States is an indispensable participant in any effort to tackle major global problems. It is false in also implying that other nations are dispensable—the United States needs the cooperation of some major countries in handling any issue—and that American indispensability is the source of wisdom.

Addressing the problem of foreign perceptions of American "hegemonism," Deputy Secretary of State Strobe Talbott set forth this rationale: "In a fashion and to an extent that is unique in the history of Great Powers, the United States defines its strength—indeed, its very greatness—not in terms of its ability to achieve or maintain dominance over others, but in terms of its ability to work *with* others in the interests of the international community as a whole.... American foreign policy is consciously intended to advance *universal* values [his italics]." The most concise statement of the "benign hegemon" syndrome was made by Deputy Secretary of the Treasury Lawrence H. Summers when he called the United States the "first non-imperialist superpower"—a claim that

manages in three words to exalt American uniqueness, American virtue, and American power.

American foreign policy is in considerable measure driven by such beliefs. In the past few years the United States has, among other things, attempted or been perceived as attempting more or less unilaterally to do the following: pressure other countries to adopt American values and practices regarding human rights and democracy; prevent other countries from acquiring military capabilities that could counter American conventional superiority; enforce American law extraterritorially in other societies; grade countries according to their adherence to American standards on human rights, drugs, terrorism, nuclear proliferation, missile proliferation, and now religious freedom; apply sanctions against countries that do not meet American standards on these issues; promote American corporate interests under the slogans of free trade and open markets; shape World Bank and International Monetary Fund policies to serve those same corporate interests; intervene in local conflicts in which it has relatively little direct interest; bludgeon other countries to adopt economic policies and social policies that will benefit American economic interests; promote American arms sales abroad while attempting to prevent comparable sales by other countries; force out one U.N. secretary-general and dictate the appointment of his successor; expand NATO initially to include Poland, Hungary; and the Czech Republic and no one else; undertake military action against Iraq and later maintain harsh economic sanctions against the regime; and categorize certain countries as "rogue states," excluding them from global institutions because they refuse to kowtow to American wishes.

In the unipolar moment at the end of the Cold War and the collapse of the Soviet Union, the United States was often able to impose its will on other countries. That moment has passed. The two principal tools of coercion that the United States now attempts to use are economic sanctions and military intervention. Sanctions work, however, only when other countries also support them, and that is decreasingly the case. Hence, the United States either applies them unilaterally to the detriment of its economic interests and its relations with its allies, or it does not enforce them, in which case they become symbols of American weakness.

At relatively low cost the United States can launch bombing or cruise missile at-

tacks against its enemies. By themselves, however, such actions achieve little. More serious military interventions have to meet three conditions: They have to be legitimated through some international organization, such as the United Nations where they are subject to Russian, Chinese, or French veto; they also require the participation of allied forces, which may or may not be forthcoming; and they have to involve no American casualties and virtually no "collateral" casualties. Even if the United States meets all three conditions, it risks stirring up not only criticism at home but widespread political and popular backlash abroad.

American officials seem peculiarly blind to the fact that often the more the United States attacks a foreign leader, the more his popularity soars among his countrymen who applaud him for standing tall against the greatest power on earth. The demonizing of leaders has so far failed to shorten their tenure in power, from Fidel Castro (who has survived eight American presidents) to Slobodan Milošević and Saddam Hussein. Indeed, the best way for a dictator of a small country to prolong his tenure in power may be to provoke the United States into denouncing him as the leader of a "rogue regime" and a threat to global peace.

Neither the Clinton administration nor Congress nor the public is willing to pay the costs and accept the risks of unilateral global leadership. Some advocates of American leadership argue for increasing defense expenditures by 50 percent, but that is a nonstarter. The American public clearly sees no need to expend effort and resources to achieve American hegemony. In one 1997 poll, only 13 percent said they preferred a preeminent role for the United States in world affairs, while 74 percent said they wanted the United States to share power with other countries.

Other polls have produced similar results. Public disinterest in international affairs is pervasive, abetted by the drastically shrinking media coverage of foreign events. Majorities of 55 to 66 percent of the public say that what happens in western Europe, Asia, Mexico, and Canada has little or no impact on their lives. However much foreign policy elites may ignore or deplore it, the United States lacks the domestic political base to create a unipolar world. American leaders repeatedly make threats, promise action, and fail to deliver. The result is a foreign policy of "rhetoric and retreat" and a growing reputation as a "hollow hegemon."

THE ROGUE SUPERPOWER

IN ACTING as if this were a unipolar world, the United States is also becoming increasingly alone in the world. American leaders constantly claim to be speaking on behalf of "the international community." But whom do they have in mind? China? Russia? India? Pakistan? Iran? The Arab world? The Association of Southeast Asian Nations? Africa? Latin America? France? Do any of these countries or regions see the United States as the spokesman for a community of which they are a part? The community for which the United States speaks includes, at best, its Anglo-Saxon cousins (Britain, Canada, Australia, New Zealand) on most issues, Germany and some smaller European democracies on many issues, Israel on some Middle Eastern questions, and Japan on the implementation of U.N. resolutions. These are important states, but they fall far short of being the global international community.

In the eyes of many countries America is the rogue superpower.

On issue after issue, the United States has found itself increasingly alone, with one or a few partners, opposing most of the rest of the world's states and peoples. These issues include U.N. dues; sanctions against Cuba, Iran, Iraq, and Libya; the land mines treaty; global warming; an international war crimes tribunal; the Middle East; the use of force against Iraq and Yugoslavia; and the targeting of 35 countries with new economic sanctions between 1993 and 1996. On these and other issues, much of the international community is on one side and the United States is on the other. The circle of governments who see their interests coinciding with American interests is shrinking. This is manifest, among other ways, in the central lineup among the permanent members of the U.N. Security Council. During the first decades of the Cold War, it was 4:1—the United States, the United Kingdom, France, and China against the Soviet Union. After Mao's communist government took China's seat, the lineup became 3:1:1, with China in a shifting middle position. Now it is 2:1:2, with the United States and the United Kingdom opposing China and Russia, and France in the middle spot.

While the United States regularly denounces various countries as "rogue states," in the eyes of many countries it is becoming the rogue superpower. One of Japan's most distinguished diplomats, Ambassador Hisashi Owada, has argued that after World War II, the United States pursued a policy of "unilateral globalism," providing public goods in the form of security, opposition to communism, an open global economy, aid for economic development, and stronger international institutions. Now it is pursuing a policy of "global unilateralism," promoting its own particular interests with little reference to those of others. The United States is unlikely to become an isolationist country, withdrawing from the world. But it could become an isolated country, out of step with much of the world.

If a unipolar world were unavoidable, many countries might prefer the United States as the hegemon. But this is mostly because it is distant from them and hence unlikely to attempt to acquire any of their territory. American power is also valued by the secondary regional states as a constraint on the dominance of other major regional states. Benign hegemony, however, is in the eye of the hegemon. "One reads about the world's desire for American leadership only in the United States," one British diplomat observed. "Everywhere else one reads about American arrogance and unilateralism."

Political and intellectual leaders in most countries strongly resist the prospect of a unipolar world and favor the emergence of true multipolarity. At a 1997 Harvard conference, scholars reported that the elites of countries comprising at least two-thirds of the world's people—Chinese, Russians, Indians, Arabs, Muslims, and Africans—see the United States as the single greatest external threat to their societies. They do not regard America as a military threat but as a menace to their integrity, autonomy, prosperity, and freedom of action. They view the United States as intrusive, interventionist, exploitative, unilateralist, hegemonic, hypocritical, and applying double standards, engaging in what they label "financial imperialism" and "intellectual colonialism," with a foreign policy driven overwhelmingly by domestic politics. For Indian elites, an Indian scholar reported, "the United States represents the major diplomatic and political threat. On virtually every issue of concern to India, the United States has 'veto' or mobilizational power, whether it is on nuclear, technological, economic, environmental, or political

matters. That is, the United States can deny India its objectives and can rally others to join it in punishing India." Its sins are "power, hubris, and greed." From the Russian perspective, a Moscow participant said, the United States pursues a policy of "coercive cooperation." All Russians oppose "a world based on a dominant U.S. leadership which would border on hegemony." In similar terms, the Beijing participant said Chinese leaders believe that the principal threats to peace, stability, and China are "hegemonism and power politics," meaning U.S. policies, which they say are designed to undermine and create disunity in the socialist states and developing countries. Arab elites see the United States as an evil force in world affairs, while the Japanese public rated in 1997 the United States as a threat to Japan second only to North Korea.

Such reactions are to be expected. American leaders believe that the world's business is their business. Other countries believe that what happens in their part of the world is their business, not America's, and quite explicitly respond. As Nelson Mandela said, his country rejects another state's having "the arrogance to tell us where we should go or which countries should be our friends.... We cannot accept that a state assumes the role of the world's policeman." In a bipolar world, many countries welcomed the United States as their protector against the other superpower. In a uni-multipolar world, in contrast, the world's only superpower is automatically a threat to other major powers. One by one, the major regional powers are making it clear that they do not want the United States messing around in regions where their interests are predominant. Iran, for instance, strongly opposes the U.S. military presence in the Persian Gulf. The current bad relations between the United States and Iran are the product of the Iranian revolution. If, however, the Shah or his son now ruled Iran, those relations would probably be deteriorating because Iran would see the American presence in the Gulf as a threat to its own hegemony there.

FLEXIBLE RESPONSES

COUNTRIES RESPOND in various ways to American superpowerdom. At a relatively low level are widespread feelings of fear, resentment, and envy. These ensure that when at some point the United States suffers a humiliating rebuff from a Saddam or a Milošević, many countries think, "They finally got what they had coming to them!" At a somewhat higher level, resentment may turn into dissent, with other countries, including allies, refusing to cooperate with the United States on the Persian Gulf, Cuba, Libya, Iran, extraterritoriality, nuclear proliferation, human rights, trade policies, and other issues. In a few cases, dissent has turned into outright opposition as countries attempt to defeat U.S. policy. The highest level of response would be the formation of an antihegemonic coalition involving several major powers. Such a grouping is impossible in a unipolar world because the other states are too weak to mount it. It appears in a multipolar world only when one state begins to become strong and troublesome enough to provoke it. It would, however, appear to be a natural phenomenon in a uni-multipolar world. Throughout history, major powers have tended to balance against the attempted domination by the strongest among them.

Some antihegemonic cooperation has occurred. Relations among non-Western societies are in general improving. Gatherings occur from which the United States is conspicuously absent, ranging from the Moscow meeting of the leaders of Germany, France, and Russia (which also excluded America's closest ally, Britain) to the bilateral meetings of China and Russia and of China and India. There have been recent rapprochements between Iran and Saudi Arabia and Iran and Iraq. The highly successful meeting of the Organization of the Islamic Conference hosted by Iran coincided with the disastrous Qatar meeting on Middle Eastern economic development sponsored by the United States. Russian Prime Minister Yevgeni Primakov has promoted Russia, China, and India as a "strategic triangle" to counterbalance the United States, and the "Primakov doctrine" reportedly enjoys substantial support across the entire Russian political spectrum.

Undoubtedly the single most important move toward an antihegemonic coalition, however, antedates the end of the Cold War: the formation of the European Union and the creation of a common European currency. As French Foreign Minister Hubert Védrine has said, Europe must come together on its own and create a counterweight to stop the United States from dominating a multipolar world. Clearly the euro could pose an important challenge to the hegemony of the dollar in global finance.

Despite all these antihegemonic rumblings, however, a more broad-based, active, and formal anti-American coalition has yet to emerge. Several possible explanations come to mind.

First, it may be too soon. Over time the response to American hegemony may escalate from resentment and dissent to opposition and collective counteraction. The American hegemonic threat is less immediate and more diffuse than the prospect of imminent military conquest posed by European hegemons in the past. Hence, other powers can be more relaxed about forming a coalition to counter American dominance.

Second, while countries may resent U.S. power and wealth, they also want to benefit from them. The United States rewards countries that follow its leadership with access to the American market, foreign aid, military assistance, exemption from sanctions, silence about deviations from U.S. norms (as with Saudi human rights abuses and Israeli nuclear weapons), support for membership in international organizations, and bribes and White House visits for political leaders. Each major regional power also has an interest in securing U.S. support in conflicts with other regional powers. Given the benefits that the United States can distribute, the sensible course for other countries may well be, in international-relations lingo, not to "balance" against the United States but to "bandwagon" with it. Over time, however, as U.S. power declines, the benefits to be gained by cooperating with the United States will also decline, as will the costs of opposing it. Hence, this factor reinforces the possibility that an antihegemonic coalition could emerge in the future.

Third, the international-relations theory that predicts balancing under the current circumstances is a theory developed in the context of the European Westphalian system established in 1648. All the countries in that system shared a common European culture that distinguished them sharply from the Ottoman Turks and other peoples. They also took the nation-state as the basic unit in international relations and accepted the legal and theoretical equality of states despite their obvious differences in size, wealth, and power. Cultural commonality and legal equality thus facilitated the operation of a balance-of-power system to counter the emergence of a single hegemon, and even then it often operated quite imperfectly.

Global politics is now multicivilizational. France, Russia, and China may well have common interests in challenging U.S. hegemony, but their very different cultures are likely to make it difficult for them to organize an effective coalition. In addition, the idea of the sovereign legal equality of nation-states has not played a significant role in relations among non-Western societies, which see hierarchy rather than equality as the natural relation among peoples. The central questions in a relationship are: who is number one? who is number two? At least one factor that led to the breakup of the Sino-Soviet alliance at the end of the 1950s was Mao Zedong's unwillingness to play second fiddle to Stalin's successors in the Kremlin. Similarly, an obstacle to an anti-U.S. coalition between China and Russia now is Russian reluctance to be the junior partner of a much more populous and economically dynamic China. Cultural differences, jealousies, and rivalries may thwart the major powers from coalescing against the superpower.

Fourth, the principal source of contention between the superpower and the major regional powers is the former's intervention to limit, counter, or shape the actions of the latter. For the secondary regional powers, on the other hand, superpower intervention is a resource that they potentially can mobilize against their region's major power. The superpower and the secondary regional powers will thus often, although not always, share converging interests against major regional powers, and secondary regional powers will have little incentive to join in a coalition against the superpower.

THE LONELY SHERIFF

THE INTERPLAY of power and culture will decisively mold patterns of alliance and antagonism among states in the coming years. In terms of culture, cooperation is more likely between countries with cultural commonalties; antagonism is more likely between countries with widely different cultures. In terms of power, the United States and the secondary regional powers have common interests in limiting the dominance of the major states in their regions. Thus the United States has warned China by strengthening its military alliance with Japan and supporting the modest extension of Japanese military capabilities. The U.S. special relationship with Britain provides leverage against the emerging power of a united Europe. America is working to develop close relations with Ukraine to counter any expansion of Russian power. With the emergence of Brazil as the dominant state in Latin America,

U.S. relations with Argentina have greatly improved and the United States has designated Argentina a non-NATO military ally. The United States cooperates closely with Saudi Arabia to counter Iran's power in the Gulf and, less successfully, has worked with Pakistan to balance India in South Asia. In all these cases, cooperation serves mutual interests in containing the influence of the major regional power.

Most of the world does not want America to be its policeman.

This interplay of power and culture suggests that the United States is likely to have difficult relations with the major regional powers, though less so with the European Union and Brazil than with the others. On the other hand, the United States should have reasonably cooperative relations with all the secondary regional powers, but have closer relations with the secondary regional powers that have similar cultures (Britain, Argentina, and possibly Ukraine) than those that have different cultures (Japan, South Korea, Saudi Arabia, Pakistan). Finally, relations between major and secondary regional powers of the same civilization (the EU and Britain, Russia and Ukraine, Brazil and Argentina, Iran and Saudi Arabia) should be less antagonistic than those between countries of different civilizations (China and Japan; Japan and Korea; India and Pakistan; Israel and the Arab states).

What are the implications of a uni-multipolar world for American policy?

First, it would behoove Americans to stop acting and talking as if this were a unipolar world. It is not. To deal with any major global issue, the United States needs the cooperation of at least some major powers. Unilateral sanctions and interventions are recipes for foreign policy disasters. Second, American leaders should abandon the benign hegemon illusion that a natural congruity exists between their interests and values and those of the rest of the world. It does not. At times, American actions may promote public goods and serve more widely accepted ends. But often they will not, in part because of the unique moralistic component in American

policy but also simply because America is the only superpower, and hence its interests necessarily differ from those of other countries. This makes America unique but not benign in the eyes of those countries.

Third, while the United States cannot create a unipolar world, it is in U.S. interests to take advantage of its position as the only superpower in the existing international order and to use its resources to elicit cooperation from other countries to deal with global issues in ways that satisfy American interests. This would essentially involve the Bismarckian strategy recommended by Josef Joffe, but it would also require Bismarckian talents to carry out, and, in any event, cannot be maintained indefinitely.

Fourth, the interaction of power and culture has special relevance for European-American relations. The dynamics of power encourage rivalry; cultural commonalities facilitate cooperation. The achievement of almost any major American goal depends on the triumph of the latter over the former. The relation with Europe is central to the success of American foreign policy and given the pro- and anti-American outlooks of Britain and France, respectively, America's relations with Germany are central to its relations with Europe. Healthy cooperation with Europe is the prime antidote for the loneliness of American superpowerdom.

Richard N. Haass has argued that the United States should act as a global sheriff, rounding up "posses" of other states to handle major international issues as they arise. Haass handled Persian Gulf matters at the White House in the Bush administration, and this proposal reflects the experience and success of that administration in putting together a heterogeneous global posse to force Saddam out of Kuwait. But that was then, in the unipolar moment. What happened then contrasts dramatically with the Iraqi crisis in the winter of 1998, when France, Russia, and China opposed the use of force and America assembled an Anglo-Saxon posse, not a global one. In December 1998 support for U.S. and British air strikes against Saddam was also limited and criticism widespread. Most strikingly, no Arab government, including Kuwait, endorsed the action. Saudi Arabia refused to allow the United States to use its fighter planes based there. Efforts at rallying future posses are far more likely to resemble what happened in 1998 than what happened in 1990–91. Most of the

world, as Mandela said, does not want the United States to be its policeman.

As a multipolar system emerges, the appropriate replacement for a global sheriff is community policing, with the major regional powers assuming primary responsibility for order in their own regions. Haass criticizes this suggestion on the grounds that the other states in a region, which I have called the secondary regional powers, will object to being policed by the leading regional powers. As I have indicated, their interests often do conflict. But the same tension is likely to hold in the relationship between the United States and major regional powers. There is no reason why Americans should take responsibility for maintaining order if it can be done locally. While geography does not coincide exactly with culture, there is considerable overlap between regions and civilizations. For the reasons I set forth in my book, the core state of a civilization can better maintain order among the members of its extended family than can someone outside the family. There are also signs in some regions such as Africa, Southeast Asia, and perhaps even the Balkans that countries are beginning to develop collective means to maintain security. American intervention could then be restricted to those situations of potential violence, such as the Middle East and South Asia, involving major states of different civilizations.

In the multipolar world of the 21st century, the major powers will inevitably compete, clash, and coalesce with each other in various permutations and combinations. Such a world, however, will lack the tension and conflict between the superpower and the major regional powers that are the defining characteristic of a uni-multipolar world. For that reason, the United States could find life as a major power in a multipolar world less demanding, less contentious, and more rewarding than it was as the world's only superpower.

SAMUEL P. HUNTINGTON is the Albert J. Weatherhead III University Professor at Harvard University, where he is also Director of the John M. Olin Institute for Strategic Studies and Chairman of the Harvard Academy for International and Area Studies.

Reprinted by permission of *Foreign Affairs*, March/April 1999, pp. 35–49. © 1999 by the Council on Foreign Relations, Inc.

UNIT 2

The United States and the World: Regional and Bilateral Relations

Unit Selections

6. **Russian Foreign Policy: Promise or Peril?** Paula J. Dobriansky
7. **Against Russophobia**, Anatol Lieven
8. **Europe: Superstate or Superpower?** Martin Walker
9. **The Lesser Evil: The Best Way Out of the Balkans**, Richard K. Betts
10. **East Asia: Security and Complexity**, Marvin C. Ott
11. **To Be an Enlightened Superpower**, Wu Xinbo
12. **A Small Peace for the Middle East**, Arthur Hertzberg
13. **Bush's Global Agenda: Bad News for Africa**, Salih Booker

Key Points to Consider

- Construct a list of the top five regional or bilateral problems facing the United States. Justify your selections. How does this list compare to one that you might have composed 5 or 10 years ago?

- What is the most underappreciated regional or bilateral foreign policy problem facing the United States? How should the United States go about addressing it?

- What should the United States expect from Russia? Should Russia be seen as a new friend or is it still a foe?

- Construct an exit policy from the Balkan conflict that protects American national interests.

- What do you see as the emerging power structure in Asia? Is this good or bad for the United States?

- How important is Africa to U.S. foreign policy? What is the greatest challenge facing the United States there?

- If you were secretary of state, how would you try to bring about peace in the Middle East between Israel and the Palestinians?

 **Links: www.dushkin.com/online/**
These sites are annotated in the World Wide Web pages.

Center for Russian, East European, and Eurasian Studies
http://reenic.utexas.edu/reenic.html

Inter-American Dialogue (IAD)
http://www.iadialog.org

World Wide Web Virtual Library: International Affairs Resources
http://www.etown.edu/vl/

Possession of a clear strategic vision of world politics is only one requirement for a successful foreign policy. Another is the ability to translate that vision into coherent bilateral and regional foreign policies. What looks clear-cut and simple from the perspective of grand strategy, however, begins to take on various shades of gray as policymakers grapple with the domestic and international realities of formulating specific foreign policy.

This will be particularly true in seeking to organize and maintain a global coalition of states for a war against terrorism. The United States is the world's only superpower but that does not translate into total power. It needs the cooperation of others in such a war and this cooperation will often come at a price. That price may be as simple as increased access to U.S. officials or it may carry very real military and economic price tags. It may take the form of demands for American acquiescence to the foreign or domestic policies of others.

Success will also demand that the Bush administration and its allies in the war against terrorism trust one another. In its rush to fulfill campaign promises, the first months of the Bush administration's dealings with other states produced a series of negative responses that pointed to an absence of trust. At issue were both the content of these decisions and the manner in which they were arrived at. Consultation with allies was frequently absent and the Bush administration often found itself on the defensive in meetings with other states as they pressed the administration to modify its position on such policies as withdrawal from the Kyoto protocol, building a national ballistic missile defense system, removing U.S. forces from Bosnia, and stopping talks with North Korea.

No single formula exists to guide the Bush administration in constructing a successful foreign policy for dealing with other states and organizations. Still, it is possible to identify three questions that should be asked in formulating a foreign policy. First, what are the primary problems that the United States needs to be aware of in constructing its foreign policy toward a given country or region? Second, what does the United States want from this relationship? That is, what priorities should guide the formulation of that policy? Third, what type of "architecture" should be set up to deal with these problems and realize these goals? Should the United States act unilaterally, with selected allies, or by joining a regional organization?

Each succeeding question is more difficult to answer. Problems are easily cataloged. The challenge is to distinguish between real and imagined ones. Prioritizing goals is more difficult because it forces us to examine critically what we want to achieve with our foreign policy and what price we are willing to pay. Constructing an architecture is even more difficult because of the range of choices available and the inherent uncertainty that the chosen plan will work.

The readings in this section direct our attention to some of the most pressing bilateral and regional problem areas in American foreign policy today. Which of these is most important to the American national interest is a hotly debated topic.

The first two readings in this unit examine U.S. relations with Russia. Paula Dobriansky in "Russian Foreign Policy: Promise or Peril?" argues that Russia is fundamentally not interested in promoting international stability in a world dominated by the United States. In "Against Russophobia," Anatol Lieven argues that the United States needs to drop its sense of moral superiority in dealing with Russia and liberate itself from cold war stereotypes about Russia. The next set of readings examine U.S. relations with Europe. "Europe: Superpower or Superstate?" by Martin Walker raises the question of what type of Europe the United States will soon have to deal with. He is concerned that Europe will become militarily powerful enough to get itself into trouble but too small to get out of trouble. Richard Betts, in "The Lesser Evil," looks at possible exit strategies from the Balkans and discusses the more general problem of when the United States should intervene in such conflicts.

The next section examines U.S. foreign policy toward Asia. In "East Asia: Security and Complexity," Marvin Ott presents a survey of the geopolitics of the region. He focuses on China and the proper U.S. role in East Asia. "To Be an Enlightened Superpower" is written by a Chinese academic and presents a Chinese view of U.S. foreign policy. He calls for a greater realism on the part of the United States and recommends changes in policy.

The final two readings examine the complex issues of dealing with the South. In the first essay, "A Small Peace for the Middle East," Arthur Hertzberg argues that one of the key roadblocks to peace in that region has been the dream of a perfect peace, and he presents an alternative agenda. Salih Booker, in "Bush's Global Agenda: Bad News for Africa," argues that Bush's unwillingness to give a high priority to issues such as AIDS and global warming does more than marginalize Africa on the foreign policy agenda; it amounts to a declaration of war against Africa.

Russian Foreign Policy: Promise or Peril?

Paula J. Dobriansky

Conventional wisdom is that the Kosovo conflict has damaged U.S.-Russian relations, with the only salient question being to what extent. At first blush, this claim appears to be well grounded. During the conflict, Russian commentators of all political stripes vented emotional, anti-U.S. rhetoric, displaying humiliation and anger and making claims that all of Russia's oft-expressed concerns about North Atlantic Treaty Organization (NATO) enlargement and the alliance's post-Cold War "offensive" orientation were coming true. Another common lamentation was that Kosovo was but a harbinger of things to come, with the United States striving, under the guise of protecting human rights, to impose its will on any recalcitrant country. Russian military publications also drew an alarming set of conclusions, noting that NATO's ability to defeat Serb air defenses with seeming impunity evidenced the growing margin of U.S. military superiority and reinforced similar beliefs extrapolated from the Persian Gulf War.

Meanwhile, polls taken during the conflict showed that Russian public opinion turned sharply against the United States. Going beyond rhetoric, Russia temporarily suspended its relations with NATO. All of these facts cannot be dismissed lightly. A careful examination of the evolution of U.S.-Russian relations demonstrates that a long-term negative trend has been underway for years and that the Kosovo conflict, far from being its sole or even major cause, has merely helped to highlight much more fundamental, long-term problems. Additionally, in the foreseeable future, any sustained improvement in U.S.-Russian relations, or even in the overall tenor of Moscow's relations with the West, is unlikely.

The Evolving Context for Russian Foreign Policy

The question of what factors shaped Soviet and now shape Russian foreign policy has provoked countless debates. Most scholars agree that, during the Soviet period, foreign policy was driven by Communist ideology, which helped both to define the Soviet *raison d'état* and provided an all-encompassing analyt-

ical framework for discerning international trends, identifying problems, and devising solutions. Thus, contrary to the Western sovietologists' endless preoccupation with tracking the rise and fall of the Politburo's various "hawks and doves," personalities did not seem to matter much in Soviet foreign policy. Likewise, with a few exceptions, Moscow's international endeavors were largely immune from domestic opinion.

By contrast, Russia's developing democracy has provided a context for domestic conditions to influence Russian foreign policy. Indeed, more than any other traditional international-related factor, it is the dismal failure of Russia's economic[1] and political reforms, as perceived by the Russian people, that has been responsible for the palpable worsening of U.S.-Russian relations. Had the Russian economy shown a decent performance, U.S.-Russian relations, while probably not as euphoric as in the early post-Communist years, would have remained quite amicable.

An economically successful Russia would have had to focus on international economic and institutional issues.[2] In the foreign policy realm, it would have been mostly interested in the near abroad and Europe. Contentious matters, such as relationships with rogue states, the Middle East peace process, or the Balkan crisis, while not necessarily drawing identical responses from Moscow and Washington, probably would have been minor irritants.

However, given Moscow's virtual economic and political collapse, foreign policy-related disputes have come to be viewed quite differently. Russia's economic demise has bred feelings of resentment and suspicion that the United States has deliberately undermined the Russian economy. Meanwhile, contrary to oft-expressed opinions, Russia's dire need for Western economic aid, while perhaps serving as a temporary constraint on Moscow's international behavior, in the long run is certain to exert a negative influence on U.S.-Russian relations. Overall, Russia's economic and political crises have been important factors pushing Moscow's entire foreign policy agenda toward a much more anti-Western course. Hence, the best way to predict the possible evolution of Russian foreign policy is to examine Moscow's evolving economic and political trends and the range of possible future outcomes.

Among the negative trends, one can discern a near-total loss of legitimacy by all governmental institutions and widespread apathy, as well as anger and disenchantment with Western "democratic" approaches to politics and economic reforms capped by the August 1998 meltdown of the Russian economy. Despite many dire predictions, the good news is that the Russian political system has demonstrated considerable democratic resilience. Since the August 1991 collapse of the Soviet Union, there have been dozens of local, regional, and national elections. Except for Boris Yeltsin's victory in 1996, these elections have produced mixed results, in which Yeltsin and his allies have fared rather poorly. Yet, while corruption, electoral and campaign irregularities, and media-related shenanigans are widespread, with the exception of the October 1993 confrontation between Yeltsin and the Duma, no major political player has tried to resort to extraconstitutional means. More important, Russians appear to have developed a real taste for the most basic rudiment of democracy: free, albeit by no means fair, elections. Moreover, decades of communist rule, punctuated by periods of terrorism and repression, seem to have left most Russians with little appetite for bloodletting. Unfortunately, they also have equally little appetite for sacrifice or heroism.

Russians appear to have developed a taste for the most basic rudiments of democracy.

Another relevant feature of the Russian political landscape is the apparent vulnerability of the Russian executive branch, coupled with the Duma's unwillingness to pass any serious legislation. While the reshuffling of Yeltsin's prime ministers has reached a farcical level, Russian governmental and institutional weaknesses have been a longstanding problem. A related but distinct problem is the dearth of capable leaders at the national level and the absence of democratic mechanisms by which competent local and regional politicians can move up to the national scene.

Meanwhile, overall institutional arrangements for dealing with foreign policy are flawed. In the past, the Communist Party was the key player, with the military, the KGB, Foreign Ministry, and industrial managers serving as pivotal interests groups that advanced their respective agendas through their own channels, as well as through alliances and coalitions with various prominent party patrons. Here again, the current situation is much more confusing and uncertain. The Communist Party is no longer in power and no single institution has been able to assume a leading foreign-policy role. The military, the Federal Security Service, and the Foreign Ministry have different foreign-policy agendas and some opportunities to influence them. The same is true of the media, the old-fashioned industrial man-

agers, and the new, post-Communist oligarchs. The problem is one of policy coordination and development. On paper, given the strong "executive" nature of the Russian government, it is the president, the prime minister, and the foreign minister who should be able to carry out a thoughtful, well-coordinated foreign policy. While this had happened at least during some portions of Yevgeny Primakov's tenures as foreign minister and prime minister, the current Russian government has made this more of the exception than the rule. One recent example is the widely divergent Russian statements about the dispatch of their troops into Kosovo that emanated from various ministries in Moscow.

Other important factors influencing Russian foreign policy are the opinions of the elite, a small segment of whom are preoccupied with international politics, and the vast majority of Russians who do not appear to have a strong interest in the world. Of all foreign policy-related issues, developments in the near abroad and the treatment of Russian minorities command the most attention. Yet, even with regard to these matters, perhaps due to the generally restrained nature of the policies for dealing with Russian minorities adopted by key newly independent states (NIS) governments, as well as the rather lukewarm nature of Russian nationalism, most Russians are strongly opposed to any military intervention outside of Russia. Meanwhile, memories of the first Chechen war appear to have dampened the Russian public's enthusiasm for putting down rebellions even on the territory of the Russian Federation. The current upsurge in public support for Prime Minister Vladimir Putin's second invasion of Chechnya is attributable to the understandable outrage over the wave of terrorist bombings in Moscow—ascribed to the alleged Chechen perpetrators.

While foreign policy-related concerns are limited to a fairly small segment of the Russian elite, these individuals appear to exhibit a growing sense of anti-Western and anti-U.S. sentiments. Even a casual perusal of the Russian media illustrates a profoundly disturbing phenomenon: Russian commentators, both pro-Communist and pro-government, are hostile to U.S. goals and policies. They routinely grouse about the unipolar nature of the existing international system, cite the evils of U.S. hegemonism, and muse about the need to create offsetting power centers, such as an anti-U.S. alliance comprised of such powers as Russia, France, Germany, and China.

Most Russians seem to equate reform and democracy with failure and misery.

While the most commonly discussed issue in Western debates over "who lost Russia"—whether the West was stingy or, conversely, too generous with economic aid—Russian commentators usually focus on U.S. support of President Yeltsin and other corrupt Russian politicians. A somewhat broader criticism is that Washington chose to support a small number of "pro-U.S." Russian politicians instead of Russian democratic institutions and processes. Given the ample evidence of Russian corruption and the virtual collapse of Russia's governing institutions, this criticism is not entirely unfair.

The view that the biggest mistakes committed by the Clinton administration in its dealings with Russia were political rather than economic in nature is now embraced by some U.S. commentators. Dimitri Simes, in an excellent article entitled "Russia's Crisis, America's Complicity," observed that the Clinton administration "endorsed Yeltsin's unconstitutional dissolution of the Congress of People's Deputies in 1993, his shelling of the Russian White House (where the parliament was located), and his virtual imposition of a new constitution granting the Russian President almost dictatorial powers." Simes argued that "the administration clearly gave priority to its notion of economic reform over democracy, and to Yeltsin's personal fortunes over respect for Russia's constitution—and over the obvious U.S. interest in the establishment of political checks and balances that would discourage a future Russian autocracy from returning to an aggressive foreign policy."[3]

It is indeed the case that the United States has failed to do everything in its power to combat corruption and cronyism in Russia. One of the best analyses of this problem has been authored by Fritz W. Ermarth, a former senior Central Intelligence Agency (CIA) official. He details a range of bureaucratic, political, and policy reasons responsible for "overlooking the darker side of Russian realities with respect to the Yeltsin regime, the reform team… the real nature of privatization, the fiscal and financial environment, and flaws in elections."[4] By now, with all of the revelations about Russian money-laundering, the claim that Washington has failed to do enough to stem corruption in Russia appears to be widely accepted. Yet, although it is not clear that even the most rigorous anticorruption U.S. strategy would have made a significant difference in Russia's economic fortunes, this approach would have at least made it difficult for anybody in Moscow to blame the United States for aiding and abetting Russian corruption.

Those analysts who have been arguing that no combination of Western aid and enlightened policies would have been sufficient to overcome Moscow's post-Communist economic and political ills may be right. What is far more unfortunate, though, is that Western policies and rhetoric have caused large segments of Russian society to blame the West for supporting the worst tendencies in Russia's post-Communist development, with a sizeable minority thinking that the United States was deliberately trying to destroy Russia.

Now, many Russians no longer subscribe to the view that it is Communism and its legacy that are to be blamed for Moscow's current standing. Unfortunately, most Russians seem to equate reform and democracy with failure and misery. Instead of attributing their current plight to specific mistakes made by their political leaders, they are trying it to overall attempts at democratic and market reforms. The loss of anti-Communist zeal and the concomitant abandonment of pro-democratic euphoria is not a phenomenon unique to Russia; it is common to most post-Communist countries.

What is remarkable, however, is the speed and scope of this transformation.

The World as Seen from Moscow

Despite the dizzying succession of Russian governments, engineered by an increasingly erratic Yeltsin, Moscow's global outlook has remained essentially unchanged since the mid-1990s. In the early post-Gorbachev period, Russian foreign policy was largely driven by then-Foreign Minister Andrei Kozyrev. When looking back nostalgically at his tenure, Western observers usually focus on Kozyrev's avowed interest in a strategic partnership with the West. However, even more importantly, Kozyrev appears to have accepted several key foreign-policy-related conceptual premises, championed by a number of Western scholars in the post-Cold War days, such as the desirability of bolstering multilateral institutions and the espousal of universal human values as distinct from narrow national goals.

These views came to be strongly criticized as naïve even while Kozyrev was still in office and they were decisively abandoned once Primakov became foreign minister in January 1996. The notion of universal human values was discarded in exchange for the promotion of Russia's national interest. Moscow's new world view came very close to resembling a rather crude and mechanistic "balance of power" concept. Alleged U.S. hegemony, combined with Russia's perilous domestic state, became Moscow's major international problem for the twenty-first century. Meanwhile, the overall tenor of Russian strategic assessments has become nothing less than dire. According to Alexei Arbatov, a well-known Russian analyst and an influential Duma member, "Besides domestic instability and decline, Russia feels vulnerable in the south, threatened in the west, potentially endangered in the east, and progressively inferior at the global strategic level. The West is domestically robust, invulnerable, and superior vis-à-vis Russia."

The foreign policy agenda resembles the U.S.-Soviet diplomatic minuet of the 1970s and 1980s.

Meanwhile, Russian analysts have been arguing that U.S. international dominance was neither benign nor likely to endure.[5] Russia's preferred solution to U.S. hegemony has been the promotion of multipolarity—the building of a grand coalition of several regional powers to confront and reduce U.S. international preponderance. In Primakov's vision, the imperative of offsetting U.S. hegemony was so paramount that such countries as Russia, France, China, and even India which otherwise share divergent regional interests, might become members of a common anti-U.S. front.

Another point, which Russian spokesmen tirelessly emphasize these days, is the need to resolve all international problems diplomatically rather than through the use of force. It is easy to dismiss such musings as hypocritical. After all, what is the point of negotiating with the likes of Saddam Hussein or Slobodan Milosevic when they have broken almost every international commitment they have made and subscribe to goals and aspirations fundamentally incompatible with core Western objectives of respect for human rights and regional stability? Yet, Moscow's policy prescriptions for dealing with rogue states becomes much easier to understand once one grasps that Russia is fundamentally disinterested in the promotion of international stability in the context of a U.S.-led global system. In fact, the more friction and instability, up to a certain point, plague the international system, the better it is for Moscow. In a perverse way, post-Communist Russia appears to have embraced essentially the same zero-sum, anti-U.S. approach to international relations as its Soviet predecessors.

However, there is no nostalgia for Moscow's superpower past. Something more than realism is involved here. The fact that analysts are content with calling Russia a major power, emphasizing the need to advance its economic interests and stressing its preeminent role only in the near abroad, suggests that Moscow is not interested in completely overturning the established international order.

Key Russian Foreign Policy Issues

The U.S.-Russian foreign policy agenda resembles the U.S.-Soviet diplomatic minuet of the 1970s and 1980s. It is dominated by arms-control issues with a few regional conflicts thrown into the mix. Not surprisingly, Russia's current political and economic environment and its outlook on international relations do not provide much hope for either good U.S.-Russian relations or the harmonization of U.S. and Russian approaches to various regional and global problems. This is not to say that no progress can be made on select bilateral and global issues.

As far as arms control is concerned, the prospects of any immediate breakthroughs on either offensive nuclear forces or strategic defenses remain rather dim. There are, however, important long-term differences in these two areas. While the Duma has not moved since 1993 to ratify the START II Treaty, this inaction is primarily attributable to the fundamental disharmony between the Duma and the Kremlin. In essence, Yeltsin rules through administrative dictat, both drawing upon and even exceeding the ample constitutional powers of the presidency. While the Duma has been unable to block some of his initiatives, Yeltsin has been similarly unsuccessful in securing the legislature's approval for his proposed legislation.

Assuming that a more competent government emerges in a post-Yeltsin Russia, it would be entirely plausible both to get START II ratified and negotiate START III. The START III-envisioned reductions to the 2,500 nuclear warheads are entirely consistent with Moscow's economic and strategic imperatives. The Russian military budget in 1998 was around four

billion dollars and falling. In fact, without any arms control regime in place, Moscow would find it difficult to support and maintain a force of even 1,500 long-range nuclear weapons by the early twenty-first century. While Russia's glaring conventional military weaknesses have prompted it to articulate a doctrinal posture that is heavily nuclear in emphasis and embrace a launch-on-warning policy, there are good reasons to believe that Moscow is primarily interested in fine-tuning its declaratory strategy so as to squeeze as much of an extended deterrent as possible from its rather meager force posture. Stated differently, Moscow is not serious about retaining a credible nuclear-war-fighting capability. Hence, there is no reason to believe that it would not find cuts even lower than those envisioned by START III strategically palatable.

The situation with strategic defenses is much more complicated. The official Russian attitude toward ballistic missile defense deployment has been one of unrelenting hostility. Russian officials have extolled the virtues of the 1972 Anti-Ballistic Missile Treaty and have insisted that Washington's real purpose in reopening ballistic missile defense-related issues is nothing short of negating the only area in which Russia can still lay a legitimate claim to being a great power, the possession of sizeable nuclear forces. With Russia's foreign policy mindset and its evident inability to deploy in the foreseeable future anything resembling capable conventional forces, Moscow's unwillingness to give up its nuclear crutch is not particularly surprising.

Yet, Moscow's post-Soviet views on ballistic missile defense have been far more complex than has been commonly acknowledged. For example, until Clinton's inauguration in January 1993, U.S. and Russian negotiators made a number of important breakthroughs in the bilateral defense and space talks. These discussions were discontinued by the U.S., not the Russian, side. From time to time in the last several years, senior Russian officials and scholars have provided, in private settings, tantalizing hints to U.S. interlocutors that Moscow might be willing to deploy some strategic defenses, provided that certain important conditions (the United States bears most of the costs for new defense deployments; the overall offense/ defense ratios are such that Russia will still retain a robust assured-destruction capability against the United States) were met. However, current political and economic conditions in Moscow make it extremely unlikely that any major arms control-related breakthroughs would occur in the near future.

As far as Russia's policy toward rogue states and regional conflicts are concerned, these are likely to remain ad hoc in nature, long on anti-U.S. rhetoric while short on action. It is probably inevitable that even a pro-U.S. Russian government would be unable for years to come to ensure its country's full compliance with international economic sanctions. To do so, the Russian government would be able to control the bureaucracy and the private sector through the rule of law.

What About the Future?

The evolution of Russian foreign policy is likely to be largely driven by Russia's economic development. Changes will occur in the next year with the December Duma elections, the presidential elections slated for next summer, and Yeltsin's increasingly precarious health. Unfortunately, the current circumstances do not appear to augur well for the victory of a capable Russian leader who would be able to carry out major political and economic reforms. Russian political parties are underdeveloped, state institutions lack legitimacy, and politics in general is discredited to an unimaginable point. Political parties associated with the government have been particularly stigmatized by Yeltsin's economic record. General Lebed, one of Russia's most charismatic politicians, has no real political organization. To be sure, the recent alliance between Primakov and Moscow's popular mayor, Yuri Luzhkov, has the potential of creating a very strong political block. It is not clear, though, how these two ambitious politicians would cooperate in the presidential elections when both of them want the same job. While the Communist Party remains the best organized political force, its leader Gennadiy Zhuganov and his colleagues are probably among the least impressive Russian politicians.

Even though anti-Americanism is certain to be in evidence during the elections, enough Russian politicians have embraced it, making it almost irrelevant as a political force. In any case, the real reason that Russian liberals are not likely to do well in the near future is the dismal failure of the economic reforms, for which they are—fairly or unfairly—being blamed.

Assuming that an able leader replaces Yeltsin next year and advances a modicum of political and economic progress, opportunities would be created for a gradual improvement in Russian foreign policy. To be sure, the most likely evolution would be, to borrow Leon Aron's analogy, toward a Gaullist foreign policy, cooperative on most issues, contentious on some, whose bark is much worse than its bite, rather than toward a U.S.-Russian strategic partnership. Alternatively, if no economic and political improvements materialize, Russian foreign policy would remain essentially the same. The only wild card in this equation is the possibility of further fragmentation of the Russian Federation—an option that, given the conflict in Dagestan and renewed fighting in Chechnya, is quite feasible. Since Moscow in the past was able to buy the loyalties of various local elite with generous economic handouts, Russia's future economic performance is also a key variable. If Russia were to fragment further, all bets about its foreign policy would be off.

Notes

1. It should be noted that some keen observers of Russian affairs dispute the argument that Russia's current economic situation is disastrous. For example, Leon Aron points out that, objectively speaking, most Russian economic indicators today—such as average salary, availability of foodstuffs and basic consumer products, car and computer ownership—are better than in the waning days of Soviet rule. See "Is Russia Really 'Lost'?" *Weekly Standard*, October 4, 1999. The problem with this argument is that it ignores the rising expectations and public passions, unleashed by Russian democratic reforms. Indeed, throughout history, revolutions and other upheavals occurred precisely at times when political and economic conditions, while improving, could not keep pace with rising expectations.

2. This is not to say that Henry Kissinger was wrong when he observed that "in Russia, democratization and a restrained foreign policy may not necessarily go hand in hand." Henry Kissinger, *Diplomacy* (New York: Simon & Schuster, 1994), p. 817, quoted in Dimitri K. Simes, *After the Collapse: Russia Seeks Its Place as a Great Power* (New York: Simon & Schuster, 1999), p. 228. Observers such as Dimitri Simes take this argument one step further and opine that it is precisely the "underdevelopment of democracy in Russia [that] has in fact helped the Clinton Administration... win Russian acquiescence in U.S. foreign policy actions." While this claim has some merit, it ignores the broader implications of possible Russian economic prosperity—a more politically accountable government in Moscow may well be more nationalistic, but a more prosperous Russian citizenry is likely to be much less interested in foreign policy adventures of all stripes.

3. Dimitri K. Simes, "Russia's Crisis, America's Complicity," *National Interest* (Winter 1998/99): 12.

4. Fritz W. Ermarth, "Seeing Russia Plain," *National Interest* (Spring 1999): 13.

5. One oft-repeated Russian observation is that the United States is making the same mistake as was made by the Soviet Union in the bygone days, equating a few favorable and temporary international developments with a long-term shift in the international correlation of forces.

Paula Dobriansky is the vice president and Washington director of the Council on Foreign Relations, and the Council's first George F. Kennan Senior Fellow for Russian and Eurasian Studies. She served as director of European and Soviet affairs at the National Security Council in the Reagan administration.

From *The Washington Quarterly*, Winter 2000, pp. 135–144. © 2000 by the Center for Strategic and International Studies. Reprinted by permission.

Against Russophobia

Anatol Lieven

Ever since the Cold War ended, Western officials and commentators have been telling the Russians how they need to grow out of their Cold War attitudes toward the West and Western institutions, and learn to see things in a "modern" and "normal" way. And there is a good deal of truth in this. At the same time, it would have been good if we had subjected our own inherited attitudes toward Russia to a more rigorous scrutiny. For like any other inherited hatred, blind, dogmatic hostility toward Russia leads to bad policies, bad journalism, and the corruption of honest debate—and there is all too much of this hatred in Western portrayals of and comments on Russia.

From this point of view, an analysis of Russophobia has implications that go far beyond Russia. Much of the U.S. foreign policy debate, especially on the Republican side, is structured around the belief that American policy should be rooted in a robust defense of national interest—and this is probably also the belief of most ordinary Americans. However, this straightforward view coexists with another, equally widespread, view that dominates the media. It is, in Secretary of State Madeleine Albright's words, that "the United States stands taller than other nations, and therefore sees further." The unspoken assumption here is that America is not only wise but also objective, at least in its perceptions: that U.S. policy is influenced by values, but never by national prejudices. The assumption behind much American (and Western) reporting of foreign conflicts is that the writer is morally engaged but ethnically uncommitted and able to turn a benign, all-seeing eye from above on the squabbles of humanity.

It is impossible to exaggerate how irritating this attitude is elsewhere in the world, or how misleading and dangerous it is for Western audiences who believe it. Not only does it contribute to mistaken policies, but it renders both policymakers and ordinary citizens incapable of understanding the opposition of other nations to those policies. Concerning the Middle East, it seems likely that most Americans genuinely believe that the United States is a neutral and objective broker in relations between Israelis and Palestinians—which can only appear to an Arab as an almost fantastically bad joke. This belief makes it much more difficult for Americans to comprehend the reasons for Palestinian and Arab fury at

both the United States and Israel. It encourages a Western interpretation of this anger as the manipulation of sheep-like masses by elites. At worst, it can encourage a kind of racism, in which certain nations are classed as irrationally, irredeemably savage and wicked.

Concerning Russia, the main thrust of the official Western rhetoric with respect to the enlargement of NATO, and Russia's response, has been that the alliance is no longer a Cold War organization or a threat to Russia, that NATO enlargement has nothing to do with Russia, that Russia should welcome enlargement, and that Russian opposition is not merely groundless but foolish and irrational. It is of course true that Russian fears of NATO expansion have been exaggerated, and some of the rhetoric has been wild. Still, given the attitudes toward Russia reflected in much of the Western media (especially among the many supporters of NATO enlargement), a Russian would have to be a moron or a traitor to approve the expansion of NATO without demanding guarantees of Russian interests and security.[1]

This is not to deny that there has been a great deal to condemn in many aspects of Russian behavior over the past decade, the war in Chechnya being the most ghastly example. But justifiable Western criticism has all too often been marred by attacks that have been hysterical and one-sided, and it has taken too little account of the genuine problems and threats with which Russians have had to struggle. This has been especially true of comment on the latest Chechen war, which began in the summer of 1999.

Outworn Stereotypes

Western Russophobia has various roots. One shoot is the continuing influence of what the political scientist Michael Mandelbaum has called "residual elites": groups and individuals who rose to prominence during the Cold War and have lacked the flexibility to adapt to a new reality. To these can be added others who have sought to carve out careers by advocating the expansion of U.S. influence into the lands of the former Soviet Union, in direct competition with Russia. Then there are various ethnic lobbies, whose members hate and distrust Russia for historical reasons and whose sole remaining raison d'être is to urge an anti-Russian geopolitical agenda.

Finally, there are those individuals who need a great enemy, whether from some collective interest or out of personal psychological need.

Much of the intellectual basis for, and even the specific phraseology of, Russophobia was put forward in Britain in the nineteenth century, growing out of its rivalry with the Russian Empire.[2] Given Britain's own record of imperial aggression and suppression of national revolt (in Ireland, let alone in India or Africa), the argument from the British side was a notable example of the kettle calling the pot black. Many contemporary Russophobe references to Russian expansionism are almost word-for-word repetitions of nineteenth-century British propaganda [3] (though many pre-1917 Russians were almost as bad, weeping copious crocodile tears over Britain's defeat of the Boers shortly before Russia itself crushed Polish aspirations for the fourth time in a hundred years).

When it comes to Western images of other nations and races, there has been an effort in recent decades to move from hostile nineteenth-century stereotypes, especially when linked to "essentialist" historical and even quasi-racist stereotypes about the allegedly unchanging nature and irredeemable wickedness of certain peoples (though it seems that this enlightened attitude does not apply to widespread American attitudes toward Arabs).

If outworn stereotypes persist in the case of Russia, it is not only because of Cold War hostility toward the Soviet Union (identified crudely and unthinkingly with "Russia," although this was a gross oversimplification). It is also the legacy of Soviet and Russian studies within Western academe. Its practitioners were often deeply ideological (whether to the right or left) and closely linked to Western policy debates and to the Western intelligence and diplomatic communities. On the right, there was a tendency, exemplified by the Harvard historian Richard Pipes, to see Soviet communism as a uniquely Russian product, produced and prefigured by a millennium of Russian history. In a 1996 article, Professor Pipes wrote of an apparently fixed and unchanging "Russian political culture" leading both to the adoption of the Leninist form of Marxism in 1917 and to the problems of Russian democracy in 1996—as if this culture had not changed in the past 80 years, and as if the vote of ordinary Russians for the Communists in 1996 was motivated by the same passions that possessed Lenin's Red Guards.[4] Even after the Soviet collapse, this tendency has persisted, and developments in post-Soviet Russia are seen as a seamless continuation of specifically Soviet and tsarist patterns—patterns which, it goes without saying, are also specifically and uniquely wicked.[5]

To be sure, many of the crimes of communism in Russia and in the Soviet bloc *were* uniquely wicked. But the behavior of the tsarist empire and the dissolution of its Soviet version in the 1990s can only be validly judged in the context of European and North American imperialism, decolonization, and neo-colonialism. Pre-1917 imperial Russia's expansionism was contemporaneous with that of Spain, France, Holland, Belgium, Britain, and the United States. As far as the Soviet Union's disintegration is concerned, Russophobes cannot have it both ways. If the Soviet Union was to a considerable extent a Russian empire, then the legitimate context for the study of its disintegration is the retreat of other empires and their attempts to create post- or neo-colonial systems. In this context—particularly bearing in mind France's retreat from its Asian and African empire—the notion that the Soviet/Russian decolonization process has been uniquely savage becomes absurd. Such comparisons are essential in attempting to determine what has been specifically Soviet, or specifically Russian, about this process, and what reflects wider historical realities.

A Historicist Approach

These comparisons are rarely made. References to allegedly unique and unchanging historical patterns in Russian behavior are an ongoing trope of much of Western journalistic and academic comment. Take for example a recent statement by Henry Kissinger: "For four centuries, imperialism has been Russia's basic foreign policy as it has expanded from the region around Moscow to the shores of the Pacific, the gates of the Middle East and the center of Europe, relentlessly subjugating weaker neighbors and seeking to overawe those not under its direct control."[6] This not only implies that expansionism was uniquely Russian but that it represents an unchangeable pattern. Yet for virtually this entire period, the same remark could have been made about the British, the French, or (within North and Central America at least) the United States. It is also extremely odd that in 1989–93, "Russia" conducted what was probably the greatest, and most bloodless imperial retreats in history and that this has simply vanished from Kissinger's account. At worst, such attitudes can approach a kind of racism, as in the conservative political commentator George Will's statement that "expansionism is in the Russians' DNA."[7]

Another example of such thinking is former national security adviser Zbigniew Brzezinski's statement that "[the Russians] have denied many, many times now that they have committed atrocities [in Chechnya].... In 1941, they killed 15,000 Polish prisoners, officers in Katyn, and they denied that for 50 years."[8] In his account, "the Russians" as a collectivity are fully responsible for the crimes committed by the Soviet Union under the Communist dictatorship of Joseph Stalin—an ethnic Georgian who at the time of the massacre at Katyn was also responsible for murdering or imprisoning millions of ethnic Russians who were accused of hostility toward communism or toward Stalin himself. This Stalinist past is then made part of a seamless continuity of "Russian" behavior, running unchanged through the years since Stalin's death. The condemnation of Stalinism by Nikita Khrushchev, the reforms of Mikhail Gorbachev, the peaceful Soviet withdrawal from Poland, the Russian recognition of the independence of the other Soviet republics—all this is ignored.

As Brzezinski's statement illustrates, this essentialist attitude toward Russia has played a major part in the reporting of and commentary on, the latest Chechen war. Take, for example, a recent editorial in the *Los Angeles Times*: "Russians also fight brutally because that is part of the Russian military ethos, a tradition of total war fought with every means and without moral restraints."[9] Unlike, of course, the exquisite care for civilian lives displayed by the French and American air forces during the wars in Indo-China, Korea, and Algeria, the strict adherence to legality in the treatment of prisoners, and so on. The editorial read as if the wars against guerrillas and partisans involving Western powers had been wiped from the record. (What was most depressing was that it followed two articles on Russian and Chechen atrocities by Maura Reynolds and Robyn Dixon in the same newspaper that were the very models of careful, objective—and utterly harrowing—reportage).[10]

This historicist approach toward Russia also reflects the decline of history as an area of study, an ignorance of history on the part of international relations scholars, and the unwillingness of too many historians themselves to step beyond their own narrow fields. The attitudes it reveals also spring from a widespread feeling that Russophobia is somehow legitimized by the past Western struggle against Communist totalitarianism, a struggle I strongly supported. This is deeply mistaken. With communism dead as a world ideology, dealing with Russia—or China for that matter—has become the much more familiar, historically commonplace question of dealing with nations and states, which we on occasion may have to oppose and condemn, but whose behavior is governed by the same interests and patterns that historically have influenced the behavior of our own countries. In fact, both the policy and the statements of Russian generals with respect to Chechnya not only recall those of French generals during the Algerian War of Independence (1954–62), but of Turkish generals during the recent war against the Kurdish PKK: the ruthless prosecution of the war (including in the Turkish case major attacks on PKK bases in Iraq); a refusal to negotiate with the enemy; no role whatsoever for international organizations. None of this is, or ever was, praiseworthy, but "communism" plays no role in it.

I might add that many old hard-line Cold Warriors-turned-Russophobes like Brzezinski and Kissinger have in any case rendered their pretensions to anticommunist morality dubious by the warmth with which they embrace the Chinese state, as well as their wooing of hard-line ex-Communist dictators in Central Asia and elsewhere.[11]

Architectures of Hatred

Russophobia today is therefore rooted not in ideological differences but in national hatred of a kind that is sadly too common. In these architectures of hatred, selected or invented historical "facts" about the "enemy" nation, its culture, and its racial nature are taken out of context and slotted into prearranged intellectual structures to arraign the unchanging wickedness of the other side. Meanwhile, any counterarguments, or memories of the crimes of one's own are suppressed. This is no more legitimate when directed by Russophobes against Russia than when it is directed by Serb, Greek, or Armenian chauvinists against Turkey, Arabs against Jews, or Jews against Arabs.

The most worrying aspect of Western Russophobia is that it demonstrates the capacity of too many Western journalists and intellectuals to betray their own professed standards and behave like Victorian jingoists or Balkan nationalists when their own national loyalties and hatreds are involved. And these tendencies in turn serve wider needs. Overall, we are living in an exceptionally benign period in human history so far as our own interests are concerned. Yet one cannot live in Washington without becoming aware of the desperate need of certain members of Western elites for new enemies, or resuscitated old ones. This is certainly not the wish of most Americans—nor of any other Westerners—and it is dangerous. For of one thing we can be sure: a country that is seen to need enemies will sooner or later find them everywhere.

As an antidote, Western journalists and commentators writing on the Chechen wars might read Alistair Horne's *A Savage War of Peace* (about the French war in Algeria), Max Hastings's *Korean War* (especially the passages dealing with the capture of Seoul in 1950 and the U.S. air campaign), any serious book on the U.S. war in Vietnam or French policies in Africa, or more general works like V. G. Kiernan's *Colonial Empires and Armies*. With regard to Russian crimes in Chechnya, they could also read some of the remarks on the inherent cruelty of urban warfare by Western officers in journals like the *Marine Corps Gazette* and *Parameters*. Neither Horne nor Hastings (both patriotic conservatives) were "soft on communism"; nor are most military writers "soft on Russia." They are true professionals with a commitment to present the facts, however uncomfortable—and they have the moral courage to do so. Concerning the pre-1917 Russian Empire in the context of European imperial expansion in general, I could also recommend (by way of a family advertisement and to reveal my own intellectual influences) my brother Dominic Lieven's recent book, *Empire: The Russian Empire and Its Rivals*.[12]

A familiar counterargument to this approach is that Western colonial and neocolonial crimes are long past, and that we have atoned for them. To this there are a number of responses, the first of which is that some allowance has to be made for the fact that Russia only emerged from Communist isolation about ten years ago, whereas at the time of their crimes the Western colonial powers were democracies and longstanding members of the "free world." And while some have excused the crimes of other former communist states on the nature of the system they have abjured, such leniency has not been shown toward Russia.

Then there is geography. Western powers escaped involvement in ex-colonial conflicts by putting the sea between themselves and their former colonies. Britain, for examples, was not directly affected by wars in any former colonies except Ireland, because they occurred at a distance. Russia thought it was making a similar break when it withdrew from Chechnya in 1996—but in its case of course there was no ocean in between. If France had had a land border with Algeria, the war there might well have gone on far longer than it did.

I believe that the Russian invasion of Chechnya in October 1999 was a terrible mistake, and that the government in Moscow ought to have done everything in its power to find other ways of dealing with the Chechen threat. At the same time, any honest account must recognize that forces based in Chechnya had carried out attacks on Russia that would have provoked most other states in the world—including the United States—to respond forcefully. How would France have reacted if the French withdrawal from Algeria had been immediately followed by Algerian raids into France?[13]

And then there is the question of the brutal way in which the Russians conducted the war, especially the destruction of Grozny. Since the early 1970s, it has been difficult to say whether the Western conduct of antipartisan wars or urban operations has improved because, as a result of Vietnam, Americans have taken enormous care to avoid involvement in such wars—and once again, geography has given the United States that option. But when American soldiers became involved in a lethal urban fight in Mogadishu in 1994, the indiscriminate way in which retaliatory firepower was used meant that Somali casualties (the great majority of them civilian) outnumbered U.S. casualties by between twenty-five and fifty to one.[14] In other words, to some extent the degree of carnage in Chechnya reflects not inherent and historical Russian brutality, but the nature of urban warfare.

That the Russians have been extremely brutal in Chechnya is beyond question—but explanations for this should be sought less in Russian history than in the common roots that produced U.S. atrocities in Vietnam— a demoralized army under attack from hidden enemies operating from within the civilian population. I have no doubt that even in Chechnya, Western troops would have behaved much better than the Russians. But then again, the West's soldiers come from proud, well-paid services, and are honored and supported by their societies. If American, French, or British troops had undergone the treatment by their own state that Russian soldiers suffered in the 1990s (notably the catastrophic decline in spending on the armed forces, and especially on military pay), and were then thrown into a bloody partisan war, one would not like to answer for their behavior.

Moreover, especially with regard to the French and their sphere of influence in Africa, it is not true that Western crimes are necessarily long in the past. If one examines French "sphere-of-influence" policies toward Rwanda before and during the 1994 genocide (as analyzed by Gerard Prunier, Philip Gourevitch, and others), one finds a record uglier than anything Russia has done since 1991 beyond its own borders. Why should Russians listen to French lectures? In France, leading figures deeply implicated in the Algerian debacle—like former president François Mitterrand—continued to play leading roles until their deaths. In both Algeria and Vietnam (and in British campaigns such as that against the Mau Mau), the punishments meted out to Western officers accused of atrocities were either derisory or nonexistent. Is this of no relevance to present demands that Russia punish its soldiers for atrocities in Chechnya?

To draw these parallels in no way justifies Russian crimes in Chechnya or elsewhere—and I firmly believe that the Russian state should try to punish some of the officers directly responsible for crimes in Chechnya— both as a matter of justice and morality, and as a means of reimposing order on what too often resembles an armed rabble more than a modern organized force. I also believe, however, that Western pressure for this would be better phrased in the terms used by President Clinton during a visit to Turkey. When he criticized the Turkish government and military for their policies toward the Kurds, he made it clear that he was doing so not from a position of moral superiority but as the representative of a country which itself had been guilty of racism and ethnic suppression.

This I believe is a more honorable and effective way of making the point. In contrast, I would condemn the statements of certain German and Belgian politicians who oppose Turkish membership in the European Union— not for economic reasons or because of particular actions by contemporary Turkish governments, but because of supposedly innate, unchanging Turkish national features such as adherence to a negatively stereotyped Islam.

Rejecting Bigotry

Rejecting this sort of bigotry with regard to Russia, and insisting on proper balance and use of evidence, is what has led me to the extremely unwelcome position of appearing to defend some aspects of Russian policy in the Caucasus—not because I wish to defend Russian crimes (which have been legion) but because I cannot accept that Russia should be judged by utterly different standards than those applied to other countries.

The crimes of a General Massu against Algerian civilians in the 1950s do not justify the crimes of a General Kvashnin in Chechnya, any more than the crimes of a General Kitchener against South Africans during the Boer War justified those of Massu. Nor do French sphere-of-influence policies in Africa in themselves justify similar Russian policies in its "Near Abroad." In fact, if the French (for example) who harangue Russia on its sins would make some reference to their country's own past crimes, it would actually make their arguments stronger. Then, one could have a rational argument with a Russian about historical, ethnic, political, and geographical similarities *and* differences between, say, Algeria and Chechnya, and about what are Russian crimes, what is truly in Russia's interest, and how Russia should reasonably be expected to handle Chechnya.

Such a comparative approach would eliminate the essentialist, or chauvinist/historicist/racist element in critiques of Russia. It would allow an analysis based on common moral standards and, equally important, common standards of evidence and logic in the reporting and analysis of Chechnya and other issues involving Russia. This, in turn, would permit a policy toward Russia based on reason and Western interest, not on bigotry, hysteria, and nationalist lobbies.

An example of how blind hostility toward Russia—and the absence of any comparison to other postcolonial situations—can warp Western reporting may be seen in the following passage from the *Economist* of last September: "Russia may be using still dodgier tactics elsewhere. Uzbekistan, an autocratically run and independent-minded country in Central Asia, is facing a mysterious Islamic insurgency. Its president, Islam Karimov, said crossly this week that Russia was exaggerating the threat, and was trying to intimidate his country into accepting Russian bases."[15] As Sen. Daniel Patrick Moynihan once said, "Everyone is entitled to his own opinion, but not his own facts." I do not know of a single shred of evidence or the testimony of a single reputable expert to support this insinuation, which is in any case counterintuitive, given the Islamic Movement of Uzbekistan's links to Russia's most bitter enemies. It is a passage reminiscent of the baroque Russian conspiracy theories suggesting, among other things, that the CIA is actually behind the terrorist Osama bin Laden.[16]

Instead, we would do better to listen to Owen Harries, editor of the *National Interest*, a conservative who was a tough anticommunist and is certainly no Russophile:

> During the Cold War, a struggle against what was truly an evil empire, there was some justification in maintaining that similar behavior by Washington and Moscow should be judged differently, because the intrinsic moral character of the two actors was so different. But that was due less to the unique virtues of the United States

than to the special vileness of the Soviet Union, and even then applying double standards was a tricky business, easily abused. In the more mundane world of today there is no justification for applying one standard to the rest of the world and another to America. Not only does insistence on double standards seem hypocritical to others, thereby diminishing American credibility and prestige, but even more seriously, it makes it impossible to think sensibly and coherently about international affairs. And that is a fatal drawback for an indispensable nation.[17]

Hatred of Soviet communism helped take me to Afghanistan in 1988 as a journalist covering the war from the side of the anti-Soviet resistance, and then to the Baltic States and the Caucasus in 1990. In the 1970s and 1980s, I was prepared to justify nasty Western crimes as a regrettable part of the struggle against communism. But I never pretended these crimes did not occur, or that the reasons for them did not include a good measure of crude traditional national power politics.

The Cold War was a profoundly necessary struggle, but it was also one in which Western morality suffered and Western soldiers on occasion behaved badly. Westerners greeted their qualified but peaceful victory with overwhelming joy and relief. Ten years after the end of the Cold War, it is time to liberate ourselves from Cold War attitudes and to remember that whether as journalists or academics, our first duty is not to spread propaganda but to hold to the highest professional standards.

Notes

1. See, for example, the attitudes toward Russia reflected in Ariel Cohen, Thomas Moore, John Hillen, John Sweeney, James Phillips, and James Przystup, "Making the World Safe for America," in *Issues '96: The Candidate's Briefing Book* (Washington, D.C., Heritage Foundation).

2. The classic study of this tradition remains John Howard Gleason, *The Genesis of Russophobia in Great Britain: A Study of the Interaction of Policy and Opinion* (Cambridge: Harvard University Press, 1950).

3. A favorite example of mine—and one beloved of anti-Russian geopoliticians then and now—is Captain Fred Burnaby, a British Guards officer who traveled extensively in the Ottoman Empire and Central Asia, and wrote some brilliantly vivid accounts of his experiences with a strongly anti-Russian cast. Burnaby was later killed fighting with a British expedition to the Sudan. What was he doing there, one may ask? Well, he was trying to introduce Christian civilization to the Sudanese with the help of the Maxim gun and the Martini-Henry rifle. This of course bore no relationship whatsoever in his own mind to Russia's introduction of Christian civilization in Central Asia with the help of slightly different brands of armaments. See his *A Ride to Khiva*, first published London 1877 (republished, London: Century Hutchinson, 1983).

4. Richard Pipes, "Russia's Past, Russia's Future," *Commentary*, June 1996. See also his "A Nation with One Foot Stuck in the Past," *Sunday* (London) *Times*, October 20, 1996. For a similar historicist view, see Mark Galeotti, *The Age of Anxiety: Security and Politics in Soviet and Post-Soviet Russia* (New York: Longman, 1995), esp. pp. 3–24.

5. For a milder version of such thinking, see Laurent Murawiec, "Putin's Precursors," *The National Interest*, no. 60 (summer 2000), in which the Putin regime is slotted into a desperately simplistic theory of a division between "Westernizers" and "Slavophiles" that allegedly runs continuously from the eighteenth century through the era of the Soviet Union to the present.

6. Henry Kissinger, "Mission to Moscow: Clinton Must Lay the Groundwork for a New Relationship with Russia," *Washington Post*, May 15, 2000.

7. George Will, "Eastward-Ho—And Soon," *Washington Post*, June 13, 1996.

8. Interview with Gene Randall on CNN, February 26, 2000.

9. "The World Must Not Look Away," editorial, *Los Angeles Times*, September 19, 2000.

10. Maura Reynolds, "War Has No Rules for Russian Forces Fighting in Chechnya," and Robyn Dixon, "Chechnya's Grimmest Industry," *Los Angeles Times*, September 17 and 18, 2000, respectively.

11. For the contrast between Brzezinski's approach to human rights abuses in Russia and in China, or in the states of Central Asia he wishes to turn into anti-Russian allies, see, for example, his testimony to the Senate Finance Committee's hearing on Trade Relations with China, July 9, 1998, or his interview in *Cyber-Caravan: News and Analysis from Central Asia and the Caucasus*, vol. 1, no. 2, February 18, 1998.

12. Dominic Lieven, *Empire: The Russian Empire and Its Rivals* (London: Macmillan, 2000).

13. See my essay, "Nightmare in the Caucasus," *Washington Quarterly* vol. 23 (winter 2000).

14. See Mark Bowden, *Black Hawk Down: A Story of Modern War* (New York: Atlantic Monthly Press, 1999).

15. "Russia and Its Neighbours: Frost and Friction," *Economist*, September 30, 2000.

16. See, for example, Konstantin Truyevtsev, "Ben Laden v Kontekste Chechni," *Nezavisimaya Gazeta*, November 30, 1999.

17. Owen Harries, "America Should Practice the Foreign Policy It Preaches," *International Herald Tribune*, August 24, 1999.

Anatol Lieven is a senior associate at the Carnegie Endowment for International Peace in Washington, D.C. He reported on the Chechen war of 1994–96 for The Times (*London*). *His most recent book,* Chechnya: Tombstone of Russian Power, *was published in paperback in 1999 by Yale University Press.*

From *World Policy Journal*, Winter 2000/01, Vol. XVII, No. 4, pp. 25-31. © 2000/01 by World Policy Institute at New School University. Reprinted by permission of Anatol Lieven.

Europe: Superstate or Superpower?

Martin Walker

Tony Blair, the most enthusiastically European of British prime ministers since the Conservative premier Edward Heath who took Britain into the European Economic Community almost 30 years ago, has devised the new vogue phrase that captures Europe's somewhat ambivalent ambition. Speaking to the Warsaw Stock Exchange in October, a venue which itself illuminates the transformations that old continent has undergone since the end of the Cold War, Blair said that he saw Europe as "a superpower, not a superstate." The phrase has since been widely echoed across Europe, notably by the former Italian premier Romano Prodi, who currently presides over the European Commission in Brussels, the institution that sees itself as the custodian of the European project.[1]

The European Union (EU), in terms of the combined wealth of its constituent member states, has been an economic superpower for decades. Its current total population of 376 million slightly out-produces the 275 million Americans in total GDP. But it has long chosen to be a military pygmy and a political dwarf, content to leave its security to NATO and American leadership. That curious combination of wealth without power is now being reconsidered, and a European superpower is beginning to take uneasy and so far ungainly shape.

The process is sporadic, and far from guaranteed of success. But its implications are compelling for Europeans, for the current lone superpower of the United States, and for Europe's neighbors in Russia, the Middle East, and North Africa. In the course of the twentieth century, the world gained two new great powers and lost several more. The former nation-state powers of Europe declined with defeat and the shedding of their colonial empires. The old power of Russia assumed monstrous shape under Soviet rule and has sunk into what will be a long, if temporary, eclipse. Japan could not long sustain its great-power status and now emulates what Europe used to be, a lopsided (and currently stumbling) economic giant with atrophied limbs where its military prowess and strategic pretensions once flourished. The two new regional powers of China and India are already forces to be reckoned with in the global equation.

But the prospect of a European superpower is fundamentally and qualitatively different. Europe's combination of wealth and high technology, and its prominent role in global trade and finance, puts it at least potentially into the category now occupied by the United States alone. Once the current crop of applicants for membership (13 states are now seeking entry) join the EU, a process that should be close to completion within 20 years, its population will swell to over 520 million, almost twice that of the United States today.[2]

The traditional qualifications for sovereignty have been a single political will, combined with a double monopoly over arms and money. The first asserts the sole right to violence to keep order at home and wage war abroad; the second asserts the sole right to mint coin, regulate the currency, and levy taxes. The EU, despite its constitutionally curious shape as a strong confederacy (or weak federation) of nation-states, is now close to meeting all of these classic definitions. There is a series of founding treaties, to which national legislative bodies are subject, and a supranational court to whose judgments national courts must conform. It is developing a single political will in the form of a Common Foreign and Security Policy (CFSP), with an official, the high representative—Javier Solana now holds the position—appointed by the EU's council of the heads of government of the 15 member states (the Council), to devise and run it. It is developing its own, so far modest, military force. It has a single currency, run by an independent European Central Bank, which includes 11 of the members, and a common Economic and Monetary Policy, which includes all of them. It so far has only modest powers to tax, through a levy on the common sales tax imposed by each of the member states, but is actively seeking to increase them. It is becoming a single judicial space, and all of its citizens have the right to live and work anywhere within its borders, with all enjoying free movement of goods and capital.

The words "developing" and "becoming" should be stressed. This is ambition and momentum combining into a process, rather than accomplished fact. And this process is very far from having the full-hearted support of the citizens of the member states or their national governments, hence Tony Blair's interesting conception of Europe as a superpower rather than a superstate. The fig leaf of national sovereignty will remain for a long time, however impressive the growth of the physical entity behind it.

The ambition was clearly defined in the Maastricht Treaty, as agreed by the Council in December 1991 and ratified in 1992. It addressed the core issues of sovereignty, by asserting a common citizenship and enshrining Economic and Monetary Union (EMU) and the Common Foreign and Security Policy as strategic objectives. EMU was given force with the launch of the single currency, the euro, in January 1999, and CFSP finally graduated from concept to institution at the end of the same year.

The crucial decision was made at the EU summit in Helsinki in December 1999: "For the Union to have an autonomous capacity to take decisions, and where NATO as a whole is not engaged, to launch and then conduct EU-led military operations in response to international crises." The formal text of the summit conclusions went on to emphasize that "NATO remains the foundation of the collective defense of its members and will continue to have an important role in crisis management…. Further steps will be taken to ensure full mutual consultation, cooperation and transparency between the United States and NATO."[3]

The European Force

By the year 2003, the 15 nations of the European Union are pledged to deploy a multinational force of at least 60,000 troops, organized into 15 brigades of infantry, armor and artillery, and combat engineers. Designated as an army corps, it will be provided with appropriate command, control, and intelligence capabilities, along with logistical and combat support. It may be backed up by 15 warships and some 500 military aircraft, organized into 15 squadrons. The member states have agreed to purchase over 200 large Airbus jet aircraft, configured as military transports, and to provide the staffing and logistics capable of maintaining such an expeditionary force for at least 12 months. To achieve that goal, at least three times the number of troops—and probably as many as 200,000—will have to be routinely assigned to EU force duties, whether training for missions, on standby for deployment, or preparing to replace other units.[4]

Along with this main-force concept, various kinds of smaller rapid-reaction units are being discussed. Lightly armed logistics teams to assist in natural disasters, heavily armed smaller units to evacuate EU citizens from danger spots, and battalion-size (up to 1,000 troops able to deploy in 2–5 days) and brigade-size (up to 4,000 troops able to deploy in 5–15 days) forces are the priorities. It is worth noting that even the maximum force envisaged would not have been able to sustain the 1999 air campaign against Serbia. It would, in theory, be able to carry out the peacekeeping mission in Kosovo, so long as the environment was not hostile; if it were to become

so, the EU force would have no heavy reserves on hand either to support its peacekeepers or to extricate, them.

Assembling the basic force should not be difficult. The EU nations among them have 2 million troops under arms, about one-third more than the United States, although the U.S. defense budget, at $280 billion, is almost twice as large as Europe's combined defense budgets of $148 billion. The EU's total air forces are slightly larger than the U.S. Air Force, although its combined naval force is significantly smaller. But the British and French armies are highly respected and have long experience of carrying out missions far from home. Last November, the British sent 25,000 troops, over 100 warplanes, and 30 Royal Navy ships to Oman to conduct Operation Safe Sword, a large training exercise that could have been mounted so far from home by no other power except the United States.

The German army, although still designed for a grinding homeland defense against a Red Army tank assault, retains some of its traditional prowess as it moves toward a predominantly professional force. The Swedes and Finns mount formidable and well-equipped citizens' armies. Two of the EU nations, Britain and France, are nuclear powers, with ballistic-missile submarines. Britain deploys three aircraft carriers, France has two, and Spain and Italy have one each. Even combined, these seven EU carrier units would have difficulty holding their own against a single U.S. Navy carrier task force. And as demonstrated by the 1999 bombing campaign against Serbia, in which over 80 percent of the munitions were delivered by U.S. warplanes, the Europeans are a technological generation behind their American allies. But the EU's combined nuclear weapons, aircraft carriers, and generally high-tech infrastructure make it the only serious putative challenger for U.S. military dominance for the foreseeable future?[5]

A Distinctly Modest Army

Challenging the United States is not the EU's strategic goal, and few if any EU members would want to be part of any arrangement that furthered such an ambition. It is a distinctly modest army the EU is preparing to deploy, aimed more at the modest tasks of aid, rescue, and peacekeeping than at the sharp end of peace enforcement. Since the EU is already the world's leading donor of humanitarian funds, such a force could play a distinctive and useful role in responding to natural disasters and not-too-threatening emergencies. Here, however, Americans will recall the unhappy involvement in Somalia that began as a humanitarian mission. The EU force might well be big enough to get itself into trouble but too small to get itself out.

There are three more potential difficulties with the prospective EU force. First, since it so far lacks the logistical and military assets to undertake anything other than token missions, the United States (and other NATO members like Turkey, Canada, and Norway that are not in the EU) will retain a practical veto over "autonomous" EU operations for some years to come. Even if the EU powers were to agree to increase their defense budgets, of which there is so far little sign, EU operations will depend on borrowed NATO assets—from AWACS planes to communications systems. Since NATO makes all decisions by consensus, this will require broad strategic approval of EU missions by all NATO members. William Cohen, the outgoing U.S. defense secretary, has sensibly proposed establishing a common NATO-EU planning staff. The EU response awaits the outcome of its internal consultation process and discussions between Javier Solana and the new EU Political-Military Committee on the details of the EU staff structure. (It has been announced that a German, Gen. Rainer Schuwirth, will command the force; a Briton, Gen. Graham Messervy-Whiting is to be deputy commander.)[6]

The second difficulty is that the EU proposes to tackle missions that are serious enough to induce all EU members to agree to a military deployment but not serious enough to involve the United States. But here it is not easy to concoct credible scenarios. Consider the arc of potential crisis that stretches from Murmansk in northern Russia, through the Baltic states, Ukraine, the Balkans, the Caucasus, the Middle East, and North Africa. Anything involving Russia, Israel, or oil supplies in the Persian Gulf or the Caspian region would automatically trigger U.S. interest. The United States and NATO are also now militarily committed in the Balkans. This leaves little scope for a solo EU operation in Europe's immediate neighborhood. Africa may therefore become the prime—although doubtless controversial—focus of EU interest.

However, operations like the Sierra Leone peace-keeping mission have so far been handled by the United Nations. In its Helsinki policy statement, the EU "recognize[d] the primary responsibility of the United Nations Security Council for the maintenance of international peace and security." So the third problematic issue will involve mandates. During the recent Kosovo crisis, a majority of EU member states felt the political and legal need for a formal U.N. mandate in order to participate in military operations. But this raises another question: if there is a U.N. mandate in a particular circumstance, why an EU—rather than a U.N.—peacekeeping force? However, when there is no U.N. mandate, it is not clear that the EU will be able to agree to mount a mission.[7]

Weighing together the lack of obvious scenarios for its use and the problems of mandates, the EU force starts to look like a political concept in search of a military rationale, possibly leading to that traditionally troublesome entity, an army in search of a mission. How did this state of affairs come about? It was the direct consequence of three separate decisions in London, Paris, and Washington, and each decision signaled the end of a long-held strategic principle.

London Beginnings

The idea for a European force began in Britain in the course of 1998, as a means for the new government of Tony Blair to demonstrate its strongly pro-European credentials despite its refusal to join Europe's single currency. The project emerged from a paper written by Roger Cooper, a fast-rising civil servant in the Foreign Office, who suggested that Britain's impressive military capabilities were an underused asset available to the British government in its European diplomacy. Cooper argued that Britain's traditional reluctance to embrace any European military formation that might challenge or weaken the NATO alliance and its commitment to the United States had become outdated with the end of the Cold War. With careful drafting, a European Security and Defense Identity (ESDI) could be concocted that would reinforce, rather than weaken, NATO. It could, for example, be presented as a way to meet longstanding U.S. complaints that the European allies were not adequately sharing the burden of the joint defense. The financial strength and existing military resources of the 15 EU nations could be far more effectively deployed.

Cooper's argument gathered weight as the Kosovo crisis developed. The British chiefs of staff warned the prime minister in October 1998, as NATO first threatened an air offensive against Serbia, that the EU air forces alone would be unable to prevail; any credible threat of a bombing campaign would depend on the United States. Knowing this, U.S. envoy Richard Holbrooke was dominating the diplomacy of the Kosovo crisis. His brusqueness left the Europeans in general, and the British in particular, feeling aggrieved and marginalized. An element of pique may therefore have contributed to Blair's decision. But fundamentally, his decision to commit Britain to an EU force was based on the view that this could serve British interests in Brussels without damaging them in Washington.[8]

The French Weigh In

The second decision was made in Paris, where the traditional Gaullist suspicion of NATO and the U.S. strategic leadership it entailed has slowly and fitfully given way to a more nuanced approach. France in 1995 sought to reenter the NATO military command structure, which it had left in 1966 when President Charles de Gaulle expelled NATO headquarters from French soil. That reentry into NATO failed when Washington refused to pay the French price of appointing a French commander for NATO forces in the Mediterranean. But despite the visceral Gaullist reflexes at the Quai d'Orsay, the French foreign ministry, the French military was already far advanced in a reintegration into NATO by stealth. French officers serve at the British (and thus NATO) air defense headquarters, and it has been reported (although not officially confirmed) that the British and French ballistic nuclear submarines coordinate their patrol schedules.[9]

But reentering NATO was not the prime French concern. In Paris, other motives came into play. First was the acceptance that German reunification made it very difficult for France to continue playing its traditional leading role in Europe. The price President Francois Mitterrand exacted from Chancellor Helmut Kohl (who was eager to pay it) was that France would approve unification so long as the dominant deutschmark disappeared into a single European currency. France's traditional fears of Germany would be eased if Germany were locked into European institutions, and a European defense structure fit the bill. Second, the Gaullist tradition has never quite died in Paris. Thus the appeal of an EU force that could carve out a space for an autonomous European strategy, independent of the dominant American ally.

Over 35 years have passed since de Gaulle declared: "Europe requires a common defense system for which France has the responsibility of determining the guidelines and designating the leader." There was, however, a clear, if distant, echo of de Gaulle's words in the speech delivered last year by President Jacques Chirac to the European Parliament: "The European Union cannot fully exist until it possesses autonomous capacity for action in the field of defense." The echoes reverberated the more loudly in the speeches of Foreign Minister Hubert Vedrine on the need for Europe to balance the American "hyperpower." In September 1997, Vedrine told an assembly of French diplomats: "There is only one great power nowadays, the United States, but unless it is counterbalanced, that power brings with it the risks of monopoly domination." The EU, he said, "must gradually affirm itself as a center of power."[10]

The complex French motives in agreeing, at the summit in St. Malo in December 1998, to the British proposal for a European force, can thus be portrayed as the policy equivalent of the official French government poster used in the campaign for a "Yes" vote in the (narrowly won) 1992 referendum on the Maastricht Treaty. The poster depicted the globe being squashed by a caricature American in a cowboy hat, and the caption read: *"Faire l'Europe, c'est faire le poids"* (Building Europe gives us weight).

It must be emphasized that the motives behind the British and French decisions are so divergent that they may prove to be incompatible. For France, the decision to embrace the British plan was a means to give Europe the eventual option of strategic independence from the United States. The British, on the other hand, see their plan as a way to strengthen NATO, through the Europeans assuming more of the common security burden hitherto shouldered by the United Stares. For the Blair government, it was a neat device to have its European cake while continuing to eat it at the transatlantic table. In November, Blair announced a breathtakingly large commitment of British resources to the EU: 12,500 troops, 72 aircraft, and 18 warships—or, a quarter of the British

army and air force, and half of the Royal Navy. This move was seen in Britain as an attempt to preempt French ambitions to dominate the new force.[11]

Washington Reacts

The third crucial decision was made in Washington. Since 1956, when the United States had objected to the Franco-British attack on the Suez Canal and engineered runs on the pound and the franc to frustrate it, Washington has opposed European attempts to take independent strategic decisions. Up to 1993, it had opposed the emergence of any separate European security identity that might become a threat to the primacy of NATO. While the Maastricht Treaty was being negotiated in 1991, the Bush administration issued what became known as the Bartholomew Memorandum, after the undersecretary of state who drafted this firm warning that the U.S. commitment to the Atlantic Alliance could be at risk if the plans for the Common Foreign and Security Policy went so far as to duplicate or threaten to replace NATO.[12] The Clinton administration proved to be far more relaxed about CFSP, accepting that so long as NATO remained the linchpin of transatlantic security, a European security system could play a useful role.

A number of factors went into this decision. First was President Clinton's conviction that the end of the Cold War had transformed the security environment in which NATO had its being. NATO, he informed me during an interview in the White House in May 1997, "is in transition from a defensive military alliance against the Soviet Union into a transatlantic security system which can include Russia."[13] Second, the difficulty in winning congressional approval for the U.S. military interventions in the Balkans gave new force to the longstanding demands for more burden sharing by the Europeans themselves. Third, the enlargement of NATO was seen as going hand-in-hand with the enlargement of the EU into Central and Eastern Europe, spreading stability and prosperity in their wake. The adherence of countries like Poland, and eventually the Baltic states, who preferred the U.S.-backed security of NATO membership over the vaguer and untried aspirations of a purely European security system, was seen as adding weight to Atlanticist voices in Europe. They would, it was thought, overwhelm, if not silence, the neo-Gaullist ones.

These considerations all merged into a far stronger current, which had been a cardinal principle of U.S. grand strategy since the late 1940s: that European integration was good for Europe, good for global stability, and therefore good for the United States.

President Clinton's deputy secretary of state, Strobe Talbott, asserted this principle anew in 1997:

When our Administration says we support European integration, we mean both deepening and broadening; we mean both the consolidation of international institutions and the expansion, or enlargement, of those institutions. That means we encourage our friends in Europe to embrace the broadest, most expansive, most outward-looking, most inclusive possible version of integration.... We have done so for reasons of our own self-interest. A politically united Europe will be a stronger partner to advance common goals. An economically united Europe creates a much more attractive environment for American investment.... But I will be quite frank: We have an ulterior motive as well. We hope that the enlargement of NATO, of which we are a member, will contribute to the conditions for the enlargement of the EU, of which we are not a member, but in which we have such a profound—I'd even say vital—interest.... From our vantage point, NATO enlargement and EU expansion are separate but parallel processes in support of the same overall cause, which is a broader, deeper transatlantic community.[14]

This has become such an article of faith for American policymakers that its premises are now seldom questioned.

The pursuit of vital American interests meant exerting influence on the EU to grow in ways the United States found congenial. The Clinton administration persistently urged the speedy inclusion of the East and Central European states, and also pressed the far more controversial cause of Turkey. This advocacy went considerably beyond routine diplomatic pressure. During the 1998 EU summit in Cardiff, Wales, President Clinton startled some European leaders with his unprecedented intervention into their affairs. He telephoned the Greek premier, Costas Simitis, to urge him to soften his opposition to EU attempts to release some $350 million in promised compensation for tariff losses from a customs agreement with Turkey.

Earlier, acknowledging that on EU membership "the U.S. doesn't have a vote but it certainly has interests," Strobe Talbott, in May 1997, had issued a firm warning: "There are those who resist vehemently the idea that any nations to the east of what might called 'traditional Europe' can ever truly be part of a larger, 21st-century Europe. We believe that view is quite wrong—and potentially quite dangerous."[15] President Clinton also pressed Turkey's claims repeatedly in meetings with EU leaders, and in particular with Germany's new Social Democrat chancellor Gerhard Schroeder after Helmut Kohl's electoral defeat in 1998. Along with the Clinton administration's efforts to mediate the problem of Cyprus, this has been the most assiduous use of American leverage upon the European allies on behalf of another country. The only parallels are the Kennedy administration's support of British attempts to join the European

Economic Community in the early 1960s and the Bush administration's pressure on Britain and France to accept German unification in 1990.[16]

This pressure worked, to the degree that the EU Council formally accepted Turkey as a candidate member state, to be included on exactly the same terms as Poland or Hungary, at the Helsinki Summit in December 1999. Perhaps emboldened by this success, President Clinton seized upon the occasion of being awarded the Charlemagne Prize (for services to European integration) in Aachen, Germany, in June 2000, to chart an even grander course for Europe's future. The first U.S. president to receive the prestigious prize, he startled his audience, which included Chancellor Schroeder, Czech president Vaclav Havel, and the king of Spain, by calling on the EU and NATO to bring Russia and Ukraine into their ranks. Clinton sketched out a vision of a Greater Europe. The Europe he had in mind would be bigger still than the one currently envisioned; in addition to the 13 new member states, this Europe would include the former constituent states of Yugoslavia and stretch eastward into the vast steppes of Russia.

"The first piece of unfinished business is to make Southeast Europe fully, finally and forever apart of the rest of Europe," the president said, stressing that "Turkey must also be included." Then he turned to "a Russia that should be, indeed must be, fully part of Europe. That means no doors can be sealed shut to Russia—not NATO's, not the EU's." All this, he went on, was such a grand and important challenge that the United States and the EU must work together to achieve it. "The steps necessary to bring Southeast Europe and Russia into the embrace of European unity illustrate the continued importance of the transatlantic alliance to both Europe and America."[17]

What Is New

Americans have yet seriously to ponder the implications of this speech, and of the Greater Europe—with a geographic reach that includes the Baltic, the Black Sea, Central Asia, and the Middle East—that it summons into being. The European allies have always been fortunate in that there are no areas where their vital interests might clash with those of the United States. Indeed, their association and alliance was based on the common vital interest in ensuring that continental Europe did not fall under Soviet sway. However, the formal acceptance of Turkey as a candidate for EU membership brings within sight the day when Iraq, Iran, and Syria will be immediate neighbors of the EU. The oil wealth of the Persian Gulf, and of the Caspian basin, will then be in the EU's backyard, and the Middle East in general will become an immediate and close EU concern. This is new.

While their participation in the Gulf War showed that Britain and France viewed the security of Gulf oil as a vital national interest, this was not sufficient to trigger the participation of some other EU members. Europeans and Americans have traditionally not seen eye to eye on their Middle East and Persian Gulf policies. In 1973, during the Yom Kippur War, the Europeans—even Britain—refused landing rights to U.S. aircraft taking vital supplies to Israel, which had its back to the wall. (Only Britain offered landing rights to U.S. bombers staging their strike on Libya in 1985.) Differences with all the Europeans except Britain over sanctions against Iraq, and with the entire EU over sanctions against Iran, point to the possible conflicts of interest that could challenge the Atlantic Alliance when Greater Europe takes shape. The traditional closeness between Turkey and the United States may keep such differences under control, but it appears that Washington's concept of Greater Europe may not have been thought through.

Russia's inclusion may have even more serious consequences. Russian membership would make the EU a neighbor of China. Russian membership in NATO, with its crucial Article 5 provision for mutual defense against aggression, would mean a commitment to help defend Russia's Siberian frontiers against Chinese or other threats.

While NATO, trade and investment links, cultural values, and sheer habit, should keep this Greater Europe anchored to the United States, its strategic concerns now threaten to drive it to the east and south, into intimate and neighborly relations with Russia, the Middle East, the Persian Gulf, and Central Asia. These are regions where the United States is accustomed to primacy, rather than the equal partnership that a Greater Europe is likely to demand.

Like it or not, and thanks in no small degree to consistent American policy, future administrations are going to have to come to terms with the EU as a Eurasian power, with its own interests to assert. The irony is that the United States has brought this new and potentially delicate strategic situation upon itself. Washington is deliberately steering the Europeans into commitments and neighborhoods that the United States has been at pains to keep to itself. Irony piles upon irony. Europe's new military capability, feeble as it is, follows directly from American demands that Europe shoulder more of the military burden and responsibilities of the Atlantic Alliance. Europe is being molded by Washington into a new shape, pushed into a role and directed into new terrain that Americans may someday come to regret.

Serious Risks

Some thoughtful U.S. officials have considered these problems and concluded that a Greater Europe will serve American interests. "For decades," Ron Asmus, the deputy assistant secretary for European affairs, noted in Stockholm last November, "The United States has concentrated on the task of what we can do for Europe, in essence to 'fix' Europe through, for example, the Marshall Plan, deterring Soviet power through NATO, and

supporting European integration. Today, we don't really see ourselves as being in Europe to 'fix' Europe. The United States sees itself as being in Europe as part of a partnership and the question is, What can we do with Europe?… Though the United States is the sole remaining superpower in the world, we don't want, to go it alone." [18]

Others see the new Greater Europe sharing America's core interests to the degree that the Atlantic Alliance in future could become an even deeper partnership, extending its security umbrella to new regions and defining new common enemies. Zbigniew Bzrezinski, President Jimmy Carter's national security adviser, has suggested that Israel might be the next candidate for EU membership. [19]

As Robert Hunter, former U.S. ambassador to NATO, notes, "The NATO allies also have the task of deciding whether to act beyond the confines of Europe, potentially in North Africa, the Transcaucasus and Central Asia, and the Middle East and the Persian Gulf." Hunter points out that NATO already has an involvement, if not yet a responsibility, in Central Asia, where all the former Soviet states except Tajikistan are members of the Partnership for Peace: "Turning to the Middle East, allied debate is no longer theoretical nor certain to remain limited to discretionary action not covered by the founding treaty. The NATO provisions for collective defense apply to armed attacks on any ally from whatever quarter, and that includes attacks with weapons of mass destruction (nuclear, biological, chemical)." [20]

But speeches and articles by the most thoughtful of those in the U.S. policy loop are not quite the same thing as a vigorous public debate. Congress, let alone the American people, has yet to consider whether the United States should continue to further a Greater Europe that could challenge U.S. primacy and will certainly want a greater say in policymaking in more and more parts of the world.

Nor have Europe's citizens considered these matters, perhaps because the prolonged process of EU enlargement has pushed such concerns into the remote future, perhaps because such prospects resemble that vague and empty diplomatic rhetoric that inspired former secretary of state James Baker to evoke in 1990 a new Northern Hemisphere security partnership "from Vancouver to Vladivostock."

But like the Greater European superpower itself, such conceptions are already taking shape in the thoughts and speeches and decisions of policymakers. *Grosseuropa* may not work; if it does, two serious risks will emerge.

The strategic interests of the American and Greater Europe superpowers may diverge in the new regions of Eurasia into which the EU is being pressed to extend its influence. This would strain and could damage the Atlantic Alliance, and might come to be seen as the Gaullist revenge.

Or the United States and the EU may manage to exert their joint dominance in harmony, irritating those other powers, whether India or China or some future Islamic grouping, where the phrase "Vancouver to Vladivostock" sounds ominously like a white folks' club. This might come to be seen as Jörg Haider's revenge.

In either event, even if Britain manages to straddle the gap between its European and its Atlantic vocations, Tony Blair is likely to be remembered for reasons far more consequential than his ingenious distinction between the EU as superpower and superstate.

Notes

1. See *The Times* (London), October 7 and 18, 2000.
2. Eurostat, 1999 (www.eurostat.int.eu)
3. EU Council, *Presidency Conclusions*, Helsinki, December 1999.
4. A pledging conference of EU defense ministers in Brussels on November 19, 2000, oversubscribed these goals, offering 110,000 troops, 400 warplanes, and over 100 ships.
5. *The Military Balance, 1999* (London: International Institute of Strategic Studies, 1999).
6. William S. Cohen, address to the NATO Defense Ministers' Meeting, Birmingham, England, October 10, 2000.
7. I have discussed these matters at greater length in *NATO and Europe in the 21st Century*, (Washington, D.C.: Woodrow Wilson International Center for Scholars, 2000), pp. 17–22.
8. I am indebted to my colleague at the Woodrow Wilson International Center for Scholars, Sir Michael Quinlan, formerly permanent undersecretary of Britain's Ministry of Defense, for his insights into this matter.
9. See Robert Tiersky, *The Mitterrand Legacy and the Future of French National Security Policy*, McNair Paper 43, (Washington, D.C.: National Defense University, 1995). chap. 4.
10. Cited in Walker, *NATO and Europe in the 21st Century*. See also Martin Walker, "What Europeans Think of America," World Policy Journal, vol. 17 (summer 2000).
11. See "Blair's Security Risk," *Daily Telegraph* (London), November 18, 2000.
12. Robert L. Hutchings, *American Diplomacy and the End of the Cold War: An Insider's Account of U.S. Policy in Europe, 1982–1992* (Washington, D.C.: Woodrow Wilson Center Press, 1997), p. 277.
13. Interview with the author, May 1997.
14. Strobe Talbott, "The US-EU and Our Common Challenges," address before Bridging the Atlantic Conference, Washington, D.C., May 6, 1997.
15. Ibid.
16. Martin Walker, "The Turkish Miracle," *Wilson Quarterly*, vol. 24 (autumn 2000).
17. William Jefferson Clinton, *Papers of the Presidency*, address on receiving the Charlemagne Prize, Aachen, Germany, June 2, 2000.
18. Ronald Asmus, address to Baltic Sea Conference, Stockholm, November 4, 1999.
19. Zbigniew Bzrezinski, "Living with a New Europe," *The National Interest*, no. 60 (summer 2000), p. 27.
20. Ronald Hunter, "Maximizing *NATO*," *Foreign Affairs*, vol. 78 (May-June 1999).

Martin Walker, former U.S. bureau chief and European editor of The Guardian (*London*), *is a public policy fellow at the Woodrow Wilson International Center for Scholars in Washington, D.C.*

From *World Policy Journal*, Winter 2000/01, Vol. XVII, No. 4, pp. 7-16. © 2000/01 by World Policy Institute at New School University. Reprinted by permission of Martin Walker.

The Lesser Evil

The Best Way Out of the Balkans

Richard K. Betts

PEACE IN Bosnia and Kosovo, such as it is, has rested these past several years on an uneasy conspiracy to prop up, but never openly discuss, a set of irreconcilable contradictions. Inhabitants and intervenors have conspired to live with political practices that contradict constitutional principles, and to prolong foreign occupation while genuflecting to the aims of democracy and self-determination. The American foreign policy elite on both sides of the political spectrum has been complicit. Clintonites promoted the conspiracy in order to do something like the right thing without overstepping the seeming bounds of domestic support. The new Bush team disapproves of entanglement in peacekeeping, but it wants to maintain American primacy on the world stage—a contradiction of its own that blocks a graceful exit. And now, Albanian guerrillas subverting southern Serbia and northern Macedonia, and Croat rioters in Bosnia, are disturbing the calm that had preserved inertial peacekeeping as the path of least resistance.

In 1995 President Clinton justified sending American troops to Bosnia with the assurance that they would be out within a year. He mistook an exit date for an exit strategy. As a result, for six years in Bosnia and two years in Kosovo, the United States has continued to collaborate with other occupying powers without an exit strategy, far beyond the passing of the exit date. Unlike the occupations of Germany and Japan after 1945, NATO and the UN have settled into operations in the Balkans that are best understood as institutionalized temporizing. There have been noteworthy efforts at economic reconstruction, but attempts at political reconstruction have been limited and confused.

In fact, the confused political status of these areas has been a vital necessity. It lets occupiers and inhabitants pursue separate agendas. The Western presence has been sustainable because it rests on unresolved contradictions between the *de jure* and *de facto* settlements of the two wars: Bosnia is in principle a single state but in practice a partitioned one, while Kosovo in principle remains a province of Yugoslavia but in practice is not. These contradictions allow the inhabitants of Bosnia and Kosovo to avoid organizing their societies in the ways that the occupiers want, while allowing the occupiers to pretend that they are supervising a transition to the type of social organization of which the West approves.

Resolving these contradictions has proved too daunting, so temporizing is the result. Rather than face an unpalatable choice between the much stronger efforts that cultivating political stability would require and a withdrawal that might reignite war, the United States, NATO and the UN drifted toward open-ended occupation. This has been the path of least resistance, however, only because the costs have been modest—little treasure and no blood. Without U.S. casualties, and with surpluses suppressing urges to wield sharp budgetary pencils, the American public has no reason yet to rue the occupations. The odds that these fortuitous, permissive conditions will continue indefinitely are low.

Around Kosovo, Albanian action to support their kin in Serbia and Macedonia has already undermined postwar stability. In Bosnia, Croats have already challenged the status quo. Economic decline could easily produce greater popular unrest and protests against the outside powers, thus catapulting the region back onto the front pages of American newspapers and highlighting the risk of further trouble. It would raise the dormant question of whether Americans wish to run that risk.

Despite such dangers, some believe that there is no need to rush to a resolution and that, indeed, getting out would be a bad thing. In this view, it is good that unchallenged global dominance enables the United States to contemplate an indefinite mission. Now, in the absence of any serious opposition, is the time to use American power to shape world order. Why not start in the Balkans?

During the Cold War, the United States was often accused of neo-imperialism. At the time, this was a bad rap. U.S. interventions often found the client's tail wagging the patron's dog, as Washington became mired in support of problematic Third World governments, while not having any direct or real governing authority over them. Today, however, we are engaged in *real* neo-imperialism, although a quite peculiar multilateral and humanitarian form of it. Under the aegis of international organizations, the United States is collaborating with other governments in the direct control of Bosnia and Kosovo, a return of the Western powers to the tutelary administration of backward nations—rather like a League of Nations mandate. There is certainly no economic benefit to the imperial metropoles. Rather, the Western presence represents a new *mission civilisatrice* for a new imperium. In effect, beneficent recolonization is the regional security strategy that the "international community" offers up at the turn of the twenty-first century. But is this a solution that we should embrace, or a wrong turn from which we should escape?

For its part, and despite rhetorical backing and filling, the Clinton administration embraced the idea. Indeed, it was the implicit rationale for maintaining American primacy that animated the belief shared by Holbrooke, Berger and Albright in the United States as "the indispensable nation." The new Bush administration rejects the enthusiasm for intervention in principle, yet it endorses the importance of American primacy just as forcefully as its predecessor. This makes it awkward to shed current responsibilities. (And although intervention in Bosnia was a Clinton project, the U.S. commitment to protect Kosovo goes back to the administration of Bush the Elder.) Beneficent recolonization can serve primacy if the United States and its rich allies are willing to invest heavily and sacrifice significantly to make it work; otherwise, half-hearted recolonization exposes a hollowness at the core of primacy. The dirty little secret of American foreign policy is that exercising primacy is popular across the domestic political spectrum, but only as long as it is cheap. When national assertion—whether for altruistic or narcissistic purposes—hits a costly snag, people notice that it is not all that much fun, and begin to see more merit in less meddling.

To get out of the Balkans, the United States should aim at achieving six main objectives:

Establish self-government to end the occupation. The United States should not be an imperial power and should not accept an indefinite responsibility to administer foreign countries.

Stabilize external security and peace for local states. The prime motive to intervene in the Balkans was to end the violence there. Withdrawal that allowed war to erupt again would therefore represent failure.

Minimize damage to relations with other great powers. The main reasons for intervention were humanitarian, but good deeds should not incur significant costs in those aspects of international politics that count most.

Withdraw U.S. forces. Aside from the moral interest in ending occupation, we have a material interest in reducing the strains on U.S. military forces—particularly on the personnel rotation system and training in the army—that are imposed by prolonged peacekeeping expeditions.

Honor moral obligations. As long as the cost is low, at least, there is no reason not to keep faith with those for whom we intervened.

Honor legal obligations. Other considerations being equal, it is in the interest of the United States to observe the terms of international agreements that it has signed if it wishes such agreements to be useful instruments in the future. But other considerations in the Balkans are not equal. To realist critics, "legalism and moralism" are often lumped together as impediments to the wise pursuit of material interests. In Kosovo, however, legal obligations to Belgrade conflict starkly with moral obligations to the Albanian population. This is a vexation for realists, a dilemma for idealists.

Some would add preservation of NATO's "credibility" and America's "leadership" to this list of objectives. Indeed, some cite these as the most important ones. Mortgaging the mission to these buzzwords, however, is to put the cart before the horse. It reflects a penchant for self-entrapment that is not unique to involvement in the Balkans, but is a problem of U.S. foreign policy in general. We should, by now, recognize that credibility is not served by re-inforcing failure. Just because the costs were measured on an entirely different scale does not mean that Vietnam's lessons on this score are irrelevant. Credibility should serve the pursuit of substantive objectives, but it should not dictate what those objectives are. Leadership means convincing others to want what we want, not changing what we want in order to keep followers faithful. If we could succeed in meeting the six objectives listed above, leadership would be evident and credibility would follow.

The problems with this list of objectives, however, are, first, that each one is hard to achieve in itself, and, second, that it is impossible to achieve some of them without undercutting others. One or more of them will have to be sacrificed. How, then, to proceed?

Sovereignty and Stability

THE HINGE of a potential solution in the Balkans is forging a connection between sovereign self-government and interstate stability (meshing the first, second and fourth of the objectives listed above). Establishment of self-government has already occurred to a degree, but it is a sharply limited kind reminiscent of colonies in the more enlightened of the old European empires. Self-government in Bosnia and Kosovo so far remains subject to the higher authority of the occupying forces. NATO officials skew elections, disqualify candidates, close down radio and television stations, and so on. The benefit in this is that it prevents self-government from re-energizing local conflict; the cost is that it defers resolution of the essential issue. *Genuine* self-government requires decolonization —termination of the controlling role of the occupying powers.

Self-government and stability are at odds because it was conflict over the conditions of self-government—the lack of congruence between cultural and political communities—that caused the explosions in the first place. The essential issues are the number, form and boundaries of independent governments—that is, which units constitute the "selves" of self-government—when sovereignty ceases to be limited by occupation. Would the solution be autonomy for ethnically defined territorial areas within a Bosnia and a Yugoslavia that are organized as loose confederations (the current situation in Bosnia, the official aim of the outside powers for Kosovo)? Or self-government for a genuinely unified Bosnia and a Yugoslavia that includes the province of Kosovo, both as multi-ethnic states? Or self-government of smaller, ethnically defined states in formal partitions of the larger units that are currently the juridically legitimate ones?

At present, peace in both Bosnia and Kosovo depends on a blatant contradiction between principle and practice. As long as outside powers continue to run the region, these contradictions can be finessed and may even be useful. If full self-government is ever to develop, however, they have to be resolved. In Bosnia it will be hard to honor legal obligations while meeting the other criteria for success, unless the Dayton agreement is revised. In Kosovo it will be impossible to honor legal obligations to Belgrade without betraying the Albanian population for whom the war was allegedly fought in the first place.

Bosnia remains at peace only because the unified political structure established by the Dayton Accord does not function. Officially the single state is composed of two "entities"—the Muslim-Croat Federation and the Republika Srpska—but each has veto rights over actions of the central government. (There are actually three entities, as the Federation has broken down into Croat and Muslim areas that cooperate only minimally, with the Croat side increasingly asserting its separateness.) What is the real function of the unified state, if any, when the fundamental divisions behind the war remain in place during the peace? As Ivo Daalder observes, "By incorporating rather than resolving the fundamental disagreement among the parties about Bosnia's future, Dayton assured that its implementation would become little more than the continuation of conflict by other means."[1] What makes this situation preferable to formal partition, other than a belief that a hypocritical liberal fiction is better than a legitimized reactionary reality?

Kosovo remains at peace because its internationally recognized status as a component of the Yugoslav state— the price of getting Belgrade to end the 1999 war—is a fiction. The crucial concession that Belgrade got was the elimination of the Rambouillet ultimatum's provision for eventual disposition of sovereignty over Kosovo according to the will of the province's people—a prescription for eventual independence. Annex II of Security Council Resolution 1244, adopted June 10, 1999, affirms the aim of "substantial self-government for Kosovo", but recognizes "the principles of sovereignty and territorial integrity of the Federal Republic of Yugoslavia" and stipulates "the demilitarization of UCK."[2] This is an inherent contradiction even greater than that in the Dayton Accord. Only in a wishful scenario of assured self-restraint by Belgrade could Kosovo's juridical status as part of Yugoslavia be made real without betraying the Albanians of Kosovo. Only with a potent army of its own would Kosovo have any reason for confidence that its autonomy would be safe.

Now, in contrast to the scheme embodied in the Rambouillet ultimatum, occupying powers cannot grant Kosovo independence without violating the terms of the agreement that ended the 1999 war. Nor can NATO violate that provision of the agreement without expelling the UN from jurisdiction, since the Security Council has a central legal role in the occupation. And, as Barry Posen has explained, unless Russia and China agree otherwise, the Security Council cannot relinquish responsibility: "Paragraph 19 of the Security Council resolution of June 10, 1999, declares that 'the international civil and security presences are established for an initial period of 12 months, to continue thereafter until the Security Council decides otherwise.' Thus, if either the Chinese or Russians choose not to decide otherwise, insofar as both have veto power, Security Council control over Kosovo will last forever."[3]

The overlapping UN and NATO roles in the Balkans reflect the complex novelty of multilateral humanitarian intervention. Two observers argue that "Trusteeship is a new weapon in the armoury of international intervention, and Bosnia is its first arena."[4] This is only partially correct. After all, one of the original institutions of the United Nations was its Trusteeship Council, toothless for most of its existence, and inactive since 1994, just as the point was reached when such an organ might be useful. Moreover, Bosnia is not trusteeship's "first arena" even in the post-Cold War era; that distinction belongs to the United Nations Transitional Administration for Cambodia (UNTAC) in the early 1990s. In Cambodia, the UN did manage to facilitate a truce among three sets of contenders, preside over a temporary receivership of the country, and organize elections and a new political start. The terms of the UN-supervised settlement, however, were imperfectly honored during the UNTAC mission and crumbled rapidly after its termination. Worse, Cambodia did not make the transition to peaceful democratic competition envisioned by the UNTAC plan. Rather, the victory of the strongest of the three main political groups over the others carried the day. Cambodia is not a disastrous precedent for the Balkans, but it is not a good one either.

Models to Emulate—or Avoid

IF TRUSTEESHIP is not a trustworthy solution for problems such as those of the Balkans, what are the remaining options?

Optimism is a bad bet, but not a ridiculous one. Over the past dozen years some bitter, epochal conflicts turned in far more positive directions than most experts would have predicted: the end of the Cold War, the peaceful democratization of South Africa, the ebbing of civil wars in Central America. But where do we look for a basis on which to predict how sectarian and ethnic conflict in the Balkans will be settled? Liberal optimists tend to rely on logic: domestic peace and international aid, both secured by peacekeeping missions, should foster civil cooperation and tolerance because they make better sense than destructive parochialism. Conservative pessimists tend to look more for precedents. What similar cases have yielded the desired result?

If the aim is to make viable multinational states out of riven polities in the region, few encouraging examples spring to mind. Switzerland and the United States may be cited as models, but their achievements are surely too distant in time and circumstances to be convincing analogues. Neither has suffered a war among its constituent groups that still lives in personal memories. Satisfactory political integration in the American South took more than a hundred years after the Civil War, and social integration remains elusive to this day. The settlement in Zimbabwe has crumbled as the Mugabe government expropriates land from white farmers. South Africa so far offers the best example of hope, but even if reconciliation there proves durable, it is arguably less similar to the Balkans than the many examples of failure.

Those who would bank on joining contending ethnic groups into functioning polities bear the burden of providing relevant examples of successful integration. Other ethnically divided states and regions of the twentieth century generally give rise to skepticism about secular integration after bitter civil wars. This is especially true if the states emerging from the resolution are to be democratic and genuinely self-governing. A multisectarian Lebanon is stable now compared to its previous decades of civil strife, but that is largely because Syria keeps the country under its thumb—just as NATO does in the Balkans. Yugoslavia before the 1990s was united and stable in no small part because it was not democratic, and because secular communism suppressed regional particularisms.

Some relevant lessons might be sought among cases of wars ended by partition along ethnic lines, for example, in Palestine, Kashmir and Cyprus. The mention of these unhappy, controversial and unsettled places would undoubtedly prompt many to reject formal partition as a model for Bosnia or Yugoslavia and Kosovo. A closer look, however, leads to a more equivocal conclusion.

The partition of Palestine in 1947 was immediately revised by the 1948 war. It was altered again by the Six-Day War, the Camp David accords, and the Oslo Agreement—and it still remains in question. Does this suggest that Bosnia would do better to avoid partition and insist on an integrated multinational state? Could anything have been much worse than the past half century of tension and periodic war in the Middle East? Well, yes. An internationally enforced creation of an integrated Arab-Jewish state in the 1940s (no harder to imagine at the time than the integration of Serbs and Albanians in Kosovo today) probably would not have been less violent or more viable than what developed.

Kashmir, too, has remained a dangerous cauldron of conflict. In this case either a more careful plan for the partition of India in 1947 that allocated the area to Pakistan (on grounds of ethnic affiliation), or a more decisive war that left it fully within India (as Israel's gains in the 1948 war overcame the nonviable non-contiguity of the partition plan's territorial divisions in Palestine), might have yielded more stability. An independent Kashmir or an accepted division of the area between India and Pakistan are additional hypothetical alternatives, though not real ones. The analogous choices in Kosovo would be union with Albania, reincorporation into Yugoslavia, or independence. (The first or third of these could include partition of Kosovo itself, with a slice in the north going back to Serbian Yugoslavia.) There is no good analogy in Bosnia, since the Muslims—who have no supporting external state comparable to Croatia or Serbia—create an unbalanced tripolar situation more complicated than Kashmir or Kosovo.

If one takes the UN role in Cyprus seriously, that case presents the model of indefinite peacekeeping; UN forces have been in the country for nearly forty years. During that time the mission has been eased by its irrelevance to the main security issues on Cyprus—it has not had the powerful controlling role of the West in the Balkans, and did not stop either the Greek coup on the island or the Turkish invasion of 1974. More relevant is the unilateral Turkish partition imposed in 1974. Unacceptable as that partition may be on legal grounds (it remains unrecognized by virtually the entire world outside Turkey), it has ensured peace on the island for more than a quarter century. If justice is to take precedence over peace, what is the solution for Cyprus—to return to the unitary state that preceded the Greek coup? If so, what mechanism would protect the Turkish minority more satisfactorily than has Ankara's intervention? If peace is to take precedence over justice, there is a strong case for international recognition of the partition and the legitimacy of the Turkish Republic of Northern Cyprus. If justice and peace are to rank equally, a solution is nowhere in sight—after nearly four decades of impotent UN presence.

PERHAPS the best illustration by analogy of choices for Kosovo comes from the untidy periphery of contemporary China. Is Kosovo's future best exemplified by Tibet, Hong Kong or Taiwan? Since 1950 Tibet has suffered the fate which NATO was concerned to save Kosovo from when it went to war in 1999. Hong Kong represents the hope of the temporizers in the Balkans—in that case an escape from the choice between betraying the Kosovar Albanians and violating the agreement that ended the war with Belgrade; in the Hong Kong case the promise of indefinite actual autonomy under nominal Chinese sovereignty. Taiwan represents *de facto* autonomy without *de jure* independence; but autonomy guarded by force rather than, as in Hong Kong, by Beijing's sufferance. The analogy would be a Kosovo recognized internationally as a province of Yugoslavia, but armed and able to prevent Belgrade from imposing its writ. Unlike Taiwan, however, Kosovo lacks the geographic conditions (a hundred miles of water) to make self-defense without foreign forces feasible.

With the choice cast in these terms, most outsiders would be drawn to the Hong Kong model. But would Belgrade remain as restrained as Beijing has with respect to Hong Kong? Hong Kong's special status is of great economic importance to China while Kosovo has no such importance for Serbia. Further, China has incentives for good behavior as long as it seeks a peaceful re-incorporation of Taiwan. Could we count on Serbia to abstain from encroachment unless the West extends a security guarantee to Kosovo—in effect negating Yugoslav sovereignty?

Legal issues aside, is formal partition the lesser evil? Clearly, the history of partitions in the twentieth century is mostly a sorry one.[5] Several wars followed the 1947 partitions in Palestine and on the Indian subcontinent, Northern Ireland remains violently unsettled eighty years after its separation, and so forth. The relevant question, however, is the counterfactual: Would history in these sorry cases have been better or worse if the states had not been partitioned? The argument for partition is not that it is good or desirable. It is that it may be less horrendous than keeping the warring communities in the same state, or that it is preferable to the indefinite foreign occupation of an artificial and uneasy confederation.[6]

U.S. National Security

MORAL INTERESTS were the prime reason for NATO and UN intervention in the Balkans—the humanitarian imperative to suppress atrocities (although why this imperative should be irresistible in Europe, but not in Rwanda, Sudan or other places plagued by even worse atrocities, has never been made clear). Some observers believed that intervention in the Balkans was warranted as well by material interests, traditional security concerns about the international balance of power and the need to keep local chaos from expanding into conflict among major states. This argument, however, has it backwards. Intervention worsened conflict among great powers instead of dampening it. It would be nice if moral and material interests re-inforced each other, but in reality they have been in tension. Moral interests have prevailed in NATO capitals mainly because material interests have not been seriously threatened.

If the objective had been to prevent escalation of the local conflict to confrontation with a major adversary, there was never reason to assume that Western intervention would accomplish this, or would do so more effectively than diplomatic collusion to insulate the conflict by foreswearing intervention by *any* of the great powers. It is disingenuous to argue that intervention by the West need not aggravate already disagreeable strategic relations between NATO and Russia.

Luckily, worsened relations with Russia are not a crucial problem in today's world, and some may consider them a price worth paying for the moral benefit of keeping the locals from butchering each other. Russia is weak and has few plausible options for responding to its alienation in a way that can threaten NATO. The West does not have to worry about maintaining a balance of power, reassuring Russia about its security, or pandering to Moscow's wounded *amour propre*. In short, NATO may take advantage of its hegemonic position and leave the Russians to lump it if they don't like it. Indeed, as it was, Moscow had no choice but to accept the Dayton Accord and participate in both occupation missions. Although the Kosovo war infuriated the Russians, there was little they could do about it.

It is useful to recall, however, that the Russian *coup de main* in seizing the Pristina airport at the end of the war, and the short-circuiting by the British of General Clark's plan to have NATO forces challenge them, raised the specter of potential unintended military confrontation. Beyond that, the most important question is whether NATO should count on indefinite Russian weakness, or attempt to stabilize relations on a more equitable and cooperative basis before an aggrieved and resurgent Russia regains options of its own.

The Kosovo war brought a large and unanticipated cost to America's relations with another potential great power adversary: China. The accidental bombing of the Chinese embassy (which the Chinese will never accept as accidental) had a gratuitously damaging impact not only on diplomatic relations, but on Chinese public opinion. Moreover, the entire rationale for Western intervention in Kosovo represents a threat in principle to Chinese sovereignty. The rationale could just as easily be applied to justify humanitarian intervention on behalf of the ethnically oppressed populations of Tibet and Xinjiang, or Taiwan's claim to autonomy (in the same way as it impugns Russia's sovereign right to pacify Chechnya).

The burden on Sino-American relations notwithstanding, the American public has supported U.S. operations in the Balkans so far because the costs have been low. But they would also have supported them if the apparent benefits were high—especially in shoring up genuine security interests—even if it had been a more costly enterprise. As John Mueller has argued in these pages, the notion that voters will not tolerate any venture that brings Americans home in body bags is a myth.[7] What voters reject are military operations that appear inconclusive, unsuccessful and bloody, for purposes of dubious importance. Thus, if the perceived benefits of policing the Balkans are low, but the costs rise abruptly, public tolerance will wane. Throwaway rhetoric notwithstanding, no administration has seriously tried to convince the public that humanitarian intervention—if it happens to get messy—is an interest that is truly important to Americans. Leaving support for intervention hostage to endless good luck on the cost side of the equation is therefore a fragile basis for long-term involvement. That is why we need to think seriously about finding a way out.

Ways Out

RECOGNIZING a reality that admits of no good strategy, two analysts of the situation are reduced to recommending that we avoid the question: "Kosovo may now have shattered the exit strategy concept…. Not only is it impossible to say when NATO troops will leave Kosovo, it is also impossible to specify under what circumstances they will do so…. One cannot say; it would be unwise at this point even to try."[8] Such a plaintive note is a sign of false maturity. We *do* have to try, unless we want to occupy the region for decades.

There is no way out of the Balkans for the United States that does not entail high cost in either effort or honor. There is no evidence of support for a much stronger effort, so the price will probably have to be paid in honor. In that light, there are three general options: worst, bad and not quite so bad.

Inertia: open-ended occupation. This has seemed the path of least resistance, but it puts us at the mercy of events. It is foolish to assume that either the locals or American voters will want us in place forever, or that the costs on the ground will remain low. The Albanian insurgencies in southern Serbia and northern Macedonia suggest the dangers that can arise to complicate the peace that peacekeeping affords.

If there is a rationale for this option other than mindless inertia, it is a long-term tutelage designed to transform the local societies and allow eventual disengagement and durable peace. If a long period of neo-imperial tutelage has high odds of civilizing the lo-

cals and making the next generation willing practitioners of secular liberalism, it might be worthwhile to gamble on it, to view institutionalized temporizing as gradual behavior modification. To give such a gamble a chance, however, suggests a bigger effort rather than a dwindling one: a much more muscular tutelage, forcing the locals to be free as we forced the Germans and the Japanese after 1945. That means forcing them to be free on our terms of liberal, secular, democracy; cracking the heads of the few but crucial nationalist fanatics in all areas; intervening inventively in civics education; imposing the equivalent of denazification ruthlessly on all the local communities, rather than leaving them to shelter indicted war criminals; decisively crushing subversive activism by the Albanians for whom NATO fought in 1999; and changing the political culture to root protections for minorities in custom rather than foreign fiat.

This would be a tall order even under better circumstances. Contrary to the implicit logic of enthusiasts for limited intervention, there is no evidence that a liberal, tolerant, de-ethnicized political order is the natural default option once a peaceful truce is attained, no evidence that it is what societies will necessarily fall into if given the chance by temporary international policing and reconstruction. This conclusion does not rely on the common exaggeration of the historic depth of animosity among ethnic groups in the Balkans; indeed, the assumption that intense centuries-old group hatreds there are irrepressible is in some respects a myth.[9] For whatever tragic reasons of criminal manipulation or fear, however, members of these groups have killed each other in large enough numbers in recent times to prevent easy re-establishment of civic trust. To create secular liberalism in the Balkans amounts to remaking the societies—nation-building and state-building—the ambitious, hubris-laden mission that Vietnam made anathema to the American military.

While doing this is not impossible, even long and strenuous effort cannot guarantee success. Unlike the case in the Balkans, neither Germany nor Japan—the two success stories usually evoked in this context—was an ethnically divided society. Nor does duration of occupation correspond to the durability of reform. A dozen years of Reconstruction in the American South did not consolidate emancipation or prevent the replacement of slavery by virtual serfdom. Nearly twenty years of American occupation in the interwar period left Haiti neither more just nor more durably stable than it had been at the outset—and rather the same may be said for more recent efforts in that country.

More to the point, there is no reason to believe that the responsible powers will permit the more ambitious form and degree of nation-building. Will the UN, with Russia and China involved, work effectively to impose the Western vision of democratic liberalism in the Balkans, or allow NATO to do it while it watches? Will American or European governments really make an all-out effort even if the Security Council sanctions it? No. The force of inertia is toward the thinning out of occupation efforts, not their intensification. Even before the surge of violence around Kosovo's borders, the path of least resistance seemed to be a permanent presence only because it was an attenuating one. Given the long odds, it makes no sense to stay indefinitely, leaving policy and forces exposed to whatever surprises political developments may throw up—even as the occupation becomes progressively less capable of shaping such developments.

Formal partition. Partition is the fallback position if the odds against creating integrated liberal societies within currently segregated ones are too low—and if we will not make the strenuous effort required to raise those odds. Phony multinational states are not harmless. They fool few and make no one happy but the lawyers, diplomats or foreign moralists who prefer a shameless fiction to an imperfect reality. Partition would make *de jure* political lines congruent with *de facto* social lines; political separation would reduce exaggerated expectations of day-to-day cooperation among the communities whose antagonism was the source of the wars of the 1990s.

Partition, however, is still a bad option.[10] To make states both ethnically homogeneous and territorially defensible (that is, geographically coherent rather than a checkerboard collection of noncontiguous or strategically vulnerable swatches of land) would require revised borders and forced population transfers. This would contravene international law and Western moral sensibilities to a degree that makes it a fanciful option. The kind of partition that might be salable diplomatically for Bosnia would likely be one etched along current lines. This would make for an awkwardly shaped Muslim Bosniac state lacking access to the sea and difficult to defend. It would require a Western military guarantee to that state, regardless of whether the Croat sections and the Republika Srpska joined Croatia and Serbia.

In one sense, partition of Kosovo would be easier, if only because ethnic cleansing was more extensive there. The 1999 war and its aftermath concentrated the province's majority and minority in relatively distinct zones, and more or less exchanged ethnic cleansing of Albanians by Serbs for the reverse. A partition deal would carve off a northern slice for Serbia and give independence to the remaining Albanian bulk of Kosovo. This would have to be engineered, however, in the context of an imbalance of power between independent Kosovo and Serbian Yugoslavia. It would also require the violation of the Western peace agreement with Belgrade and face the prospect that the Albanian Kosovars—who have already been mounting attacks into Serbia and Macedonia—would refuse to concede any territory. With both sides having good reason to fear revanchism by the other, anything but a craven retreat would require NATO to provide security guarantees of some sort to both sides—something much easier to do in theory than in practice.

Finally, partition of Bosnia and Kosovo would further undermine the shaky foundation of Macedonian statehood, and could energize a crack-up there as nasty as what happened elsewhere in Yugoslavia in the 1990s. The rationale for propping up that multinational amalgam would be hard to sustain after giving up on the other two.

Hand over to the European Union. This—a modified bugout—is also a bad solution, only less bad than the others. It would involve a plan for American withdrawal over the course of, say, six months, and a declaration that policing the periphery of Europe is a perfect mission for a European Union currently groping toward an independent "defense identity." This would be a rather shameful escape for the United States, which led the charge to the Dayton agreement and the Rambouillet ultimatum. In material terms, however, there is no reason that a Europe whose unity is worth anything, and whose collective resources exceed those of the United States, could not be expected to handle a neighborhood problem without us, just as we intervene in our neighborhood (Central America and the Caribbean) without them. Nonetheless, there are two problems with this option.

The first is that our European allies would scream bloody murder, and might well refuse to take the baton, instead evacuating when we do. This would leave the hope that the locals would see the wisdom of keeping the current peace, and forgo new attempts to rectify old grievances by force. If optimists who prefer continued occupation are right to believe that it has been justified by progress toward stability, then there should be some chance of this. The plan for U.S. withdrawal over six months could include an accelerated schedule for doing whatever remains to be done in political transition. If, after all this time in Bosnia, we do not know what still needs to be done, we have no business being there. If we do know, the answer is just to *do* it. In Kosovo, if the European members of NATO refuse to continue the occupation on their own, the UN would have the ball in its court and could try multilateral trusteeship again. In any case, the U.S. withdrawal should include an offer of assistance in resettling Serbs who fear what Kosovo's Albanians will do to them without NATO protection.

Despite these possibilities of peace, the withdrawal leaves the distinct likelihood that the locals will go at it again. That would make the NATO efforts of the past six years—including the only war NATO ever fought—appear to have been a waste.

Should our European allies not be even more inclined to avoid such a waste? If proximity does not make their interest in pacifying the edge of Europe greater than ours, this will simply reflect the weakness of current commitments and the danger that, by standing pat with a minimal effort and no exit strategy, we will eventually be embroiled in a disaster as bad as what might follow withdrawal now. If the Europeans refuse to take the handoff, U.S. withdrawal would need to arm and supply the weaker of the local states to give them a chance of surviving.

Time to Stop Digging

"Balkan War Looms", say the headlines, as they have done intermittently for a century and a quarter. Nothing in this area is ever entirely new: just the manner in which it is done.

And it isn't simply the local contenders who exhibit the same old instincts. The Western powers (the Great Powers, as they would once have been called) are behaving in similar fashion as well—with one big difference: they are not, for once, fighting each other by proxy. Instead, they are bewildered, timid, reluctant, and have a terrible conviction that whatever they do will turn out to be wrong. In that, at least, they seem likely to be proved correct....

Everyone knows that Kosovo is a mess that is going to get worse, and no one really wants to be there when it does. We should think of the conflict between the Republic of Macedonia and the Albanian extremists as the War of Clinton's Succession: as much a part of his approach to things as the pardons that he gave to sundry crooks and sleazeballs.

All the moral bombast that surrounded the idea of trying to settle a complicated, ugly little ethnic conflict by bombing Serbia from 15,000 ft. has fallen away now. We're left with the consequences. And we don't like them.

—John Simpson, World Affairs Editor of the BBC, *Sunday Telegraph*, March 18, 2001

The second problem is that the Bush administration is, to say the least, skittish about encouraging European military activism outside the NATO framework, and about reducing American leadership of the alliance. Too bad. We cannot have it both ways. On this the Europeans are right: If we want to run the show, we have to shoulder the burden. Bush and his foreign policy team have to face the choice in Europe between fortifying American primacy or moving toward a balance of power strategy. If they want the former, they should move toward more decisive intervention in the Balkans—the muscular nation-building version of recolonization—rather than backing away from the area altogether.

THE BALKANS are just one reminder of the uncertain function of U.S. primacy. There is only one global superpower, involved strategically everywhere in the world, but the variety of its involvements tends to limit the effort it can make in any one. The United States is one of a coalition of great powers in each region of importance outside North America. The post-Cold War world is thus unipolar globally, but multipolar regionally.[11] Or as Shin'ichi Ogawa has said, since the end of the Cold War the international economy has been globalized but security has been regionalized. Clintonites lurched prematurely toward the mirage of political globalization, conflating American leadership with multilateralism, committing the United States to humanitarian activism ambitious in aims but limited in action. Half-measures leave us bogged down in the Balkans. The Bush team risks promoting hollow primacy: a hefty affirmation of America as number one, ever ready to do deserts but not mountains—in a world where conflicts occur far more often in the latter.

Unless the projection of moral force is backed by material force that is decisive rather than hesitant, intervention risks ineffectiveness and embarrassment. The Clinton administration never fully faced this problem, and it certainly did not solve it. By the same token, American primacy is hard either to keep or to justify unless it is exercised when challenges to American preferences arise. Some on the Bush team have been reluctant to accept this. Even for those willing to intervene forcefully, however, the puzzle in the post-Cold War world has been how to decide the standard for selection. There are more disastrous political disorders around the world than can be dealt with decisively. The Clintonite answer to this was that just because we cannot do everything does not mean that we should do nothing. But then how to choose? If Bosnia, why not Burundi—or any number of other divided societies on the brink of violence?

A weak answer, but probably the only politically sustainable one, is that we should intervene where probable benefits exceed probable costs by a hefty margin. Estimating those probabilities in advance, of course, is hard. Keeping the costs low in turn, may often require compromising moral principles and privileging peace over justice in the hierarchy of objectives. For example, interventions that separate antagonistic communities and allow them independence may face fewer obstacles to success than ones that try to impose Western standards of civic decency and re-integration of communities that have recently soaked each other in blood.

To reject humanitarian intervention altogether, even under this cautious standard, is unnecessarily callous. To demand more is to raise the question of how to marshal the international will and resources to make frequent and decisive intervention feasible—rather than guarantee spotty, limited and ineffective interventions that may harm all they touch. Those focused on material interests must deal with the former point, and those focused on moral interests must deal with the latter. Neither material nor moral interests alone can make a foreign policy that works, and that is truly American.

Notes

1. Ivo H. Daalder, *Getting to Dayton* (Washington, DC: Brookings Institution Press, 2000), p. 180.
2. UCK is the Albanian acronym for the Kosovo Liberation Army.
3. Posen, "The War for Kosovo: Serbia's Political-Military Strategy", *International Security* (Spring 2000), p. 79.
4. Gerald Knaus and Marcus Cox, "Whither Bosnia?", *NATO Review* (Winter 2000-2001), p. 11.
5. See Radha Kumar, "The Troubled History of Partition", *Foreign Affairs* (January/February 1997).
6. See Chaim Kaufmann, "Possible and Impossible Solutions to Ethnic Civil Wars", *International Security* (Spring 1996); and Kaufmann, "When All Else Fails: Ethnic Population Transfers and Partitions in the Twentieth Century", *International Security* (Fall 1998).
7. Mueller, "The Common Sense", *The National Interest* (Spring 1997).
8. Ivo H. Daalder and Michael E. O'Hanlon, *Winning Ugly: NATO's War to Save Kosovo* (Washington, DC: Brookings Institution Press, 2000), p. 216.
9. John Mueller, "The Banality of Ethnic War", *International Security* (Summer 2000).
10. See Richard Holbrooke, *To End a War* (New York: Modern Library, 1999), p. 365.
11. See my "Wealth, Power, and Instability", *International Security* (Winter 1993/94), p. 41.

Richard K. Betts is director of the Institute of War and Peace Studies at Columbia University. Another version of this article will appear in a volume edited by Stephen Blank and published by the U.S. Army War College.

East Asia: Security and Complexity

"In Southeast Asia, the United States and China are natural geopolitical rivals. For United States security planners based in Honolulu and Washington, this creates a remarkably challenging environment. The stakes are high, the uncertainties and ambiguities are everywhere, and the pace of change is rapid and accelerating."

MARVIN C. OTT

The next decade will in all likelihood see the locus of United States security strategy and concerns shift toward Asia. The nearly half century of cold-war preoccupation with the Soviet Union and the fate of Europe is over. Russia has entered a prolonged period of attempting to build a viable nation on the wreckage of a collapsed Soviet Empire. The struggle for Europe has been won and the continent's energies are focused on building the institutions of a united Europe. The Middle East will continue to be a security concern because of oil, the Arab-Israeli conflict, and the ambitions of regional despots and terrorists. Latin America and particularly Africa will remain marginal players in the global geopolitical drama.

> *Clearly, volatility and the potential for explosive change on a vast scale must be added to the list of reasons why Asia matters.*

Asia, however, is another story. Important parts of the region, notably Japan, South Korea, and to some degree China and the nations of Southeast Asia, have mastered the core technological and institutional competencies of the West. No great multilateral corporations are indigenous to the Middle East, but there is a long list in Japan alone. The region has an inherent weight that also comes from sheer scale. The world's most populous country, China, is East Asian. More important, for the last three decades the world's highest rates of economic growth have been recorded in Asia. For tens of millions of Asians,

living standards have quadrupled in a generation. Never before in human history have so many lives been transformed in so short a time. Japan has long been the world's second-largest economy—40 percent larger than Germany's. Today South Korea's GDP is one and a half times that of Italy's, and Singapore's GDP per capita exceeds Great Britain's.

Yet this picture of economic success was severely shaken by the financial crisis that rolled across much of Asia in 1997–1998. The most severe consequences were felt in Indonesia, the fourth most populous country in the world; there the crisis broke the back of the long-entrenched Suharto regime and has unleashed political forces that threaten to dismember this huge archipelago nation. Clearly, volatility and the potential for explosive change on a vast scale must be added to the list of reasons why Asia matters.

History also underlines the strategic importance of Asia. The United States has fought three major wars in the region since 1941. Southeast Asia, in particular, was an important arena in the cold war. From the early 1950s through the 1970s, every country in this region was the focus of a serious effort by communist groups to overthrow the existing government; in Vietnam, Cambodia, and Laos, communist regimes did seize power. China was an adversary of United States forces directly in Korea and indirectly in Indochina. As a consequence of this history, the United States has established and maintained a farflung military presence in Asia headquartered in Hawaii but forward deployed from Japan's Hokkaido island to Australia and from Guam to Diego Garcia. The mission includes the protection of the world's busiest commercial sea-lanes, which run from the Indian Ocean through the Straits of Malacca and northward to Japan.

CHINA STANDS UP

The recent emergence of China as a regional great power and aspiring superpower has been the central development in the East Asian security picture. After the humiliation of Western colonial administration and Japanese military occupation, China has sought to reassert its historical prominence. Mao Zedong's first words on leading his victorious armies into Beijing were: "China has stood up." Nevertheless, for most of the following four decades China was preoccupied with domestic difficulties and disasters (largely self-inflicted) and economic development. But with the consolidation of the economic reforms of paramount leader Deng Xiaoping in the late 1980s, China launched an unmistakable effort to increase its power. Chinese GDP growth for the last decade has averaged over 10 percent annually While other major nations were reducing their military budgets in the post–cold war environment, China was rapidly increasing its own. Today Chinese military expenditures place it among the top five countries worldwide (and maybe as high as second when China's very low personnel costs are taken into account). The effect has been to alter the regional security calculus much as the rise of Prussia and imperial Japan did so in an earlier period.

> *As China becomes less communist it is probably becoming more dangerous.*

The centrality of China is revealed in three of the region's most dangerous potential flashpoints: South Korea, Taiwan, and the South China Sea. Each of these concerns is increasingly dynamic. In the case of Korea, the most recent developments have been dramatically positive, with North Korea suddenly opening up to hold high-level substantive contacts with South Korea and the United States. But hope that the exceedingly dangerous standoff on the peninsula can be resolved must be tempered by the fact that thus far no change has occurred in the actual disposition of the massive military forces confronting each other across the demilitarized zone separating North from South Korea. Nor have any concrete steps been taken to freeze North Korea's ballistic missile program.

In the case of Taiwan, no comparable easing of tension has occurred. The root of the problem lies in the climactic events of 1949–1950, when the communist armies under Mao completed their conquest of China and the defeated forces of the Republic of China under Chiang Kai-shek retreated to Taiwan and a last stand. The final battle never came, largely because North Korean armies attacked the south in an attempt to forcibly unite the Korean peninsula under communist rule. The Truman administration saw the threats to South Korea and Taiwan as part of a coordinated communist offensive and responded by throwing United States ground and air units into the defense of the South Korean regime and moving the Seventh Fleet into the Taiwan Straits. For more than half a century since, Taiwan has remained beyond Beijing's reach because of United States security support.

For most of this period tensions have been contained by Beijing's avowed willingness to take a long view of the dispute and an American affirmation beginning with the visits of national security adviser Henry Kissinger and President Richard Nixon in the early 1970s that there was only one China, which included Taiwan. The timetable and modalities of Taiwan's reintegration into the "mainland" remained in dispute but there was tacit agreement that a final resolution might be decades away. In the meantime the United States asserted a limited right to provide Taiwan with the means to defend itself.

This relatively relaxed situation has given way to growing tension because of four factors. The first is Chinese nationalism. As communism has disappeared from the map of Europe and Russia, its salience and appeal within China have faded. Ironically, as China becomes less communist it is probably becoming more dangerous—at least regarding Taiwan. A regime in Beijing that justified its rule ideologically did not need to recapture Taiwan in the short term, but a regime that relies on appeals to national pride and aspirations to legitimate its authority is under much greater pressure to recover the national patrimony. Mao once even suggested that Taiwan might go its own way, and Deng Xiaoping talked about a 50-year timetable to recover the island. But China's current president, Jiang Zemin, is pressing hard for "reunification" in the near future.

A second factor concerns developments on Taiwan itself. Politically Taiwan has undergone a dramatic transition from a tough authoritarian regime in the 1950s through the 1970s to a multiparty democracy with a popularly elected president. The election of President Chen Shui-bian in March 2000 marked the transfer of power from the long-governing Kuomintang to the opposition. This momentous change highlighted a demographic transition as aged "mainlanders" who came to Taiwan with Chiang Kai-shek have given way to a Taiwan-born generation. The net effect is pregnant with implications for China. The new Taiwan electorate and leadership regard Taiwan as their homeland and are instinctively skeptical, if not hostile, toward the "one-China" formula. For Beijing this can only suggest that time is not on its side. China could afford to be relatively relaxed about Taiwan as long as it was convinced that growing communication and economic interaction with Taiwan would inexorably draw the island toward China. Instead, time and the status quo have become the enemy.

A third factor—the changing climate in United States–China relations—has also given Beijing a new sense of urgency. From the Nixon opening to China until the end of the cold war, Beijing and Washington developed a close strategic partnership aimed at the Soviet Union. With this overriding common interest, China was unlikely to provoke a dispute with the United States over Taiwan. But 1989 saw both the end of the cold war and the Tiananmen tragedy. In an instant Sino-American relations turned sour—and have remained so. In this new adverse climate Chinese suspicions concerning United States intentions toward Taiwan grew. They were seemingly validated when the first Bush administration decided to sell F-16s to Taiwan in clear violation of an earlier understanding between Beijing and

Washington. In 1996, in a blatant attempt to intimidate the Taiwan electorate, China fired a number of ballistic missiles over the northern tip of the island to impact a short distance offshore. The United States reacted by deploying two aircraft carriers near Taiwan. That response seemed to surprise Beijing and probably convinced the Chinese leadership that the United States would, in fact, defend Taiwan if the island were attacked. Put another way, a successful Chinese attack on Taiwan would have to defeat or outmaneuver an expected American military response. In this context, China's recent acquisition of Russian destroyers equipped with missile systems specifically designed to attack United States carriers has generated considerable attention—as have growing Chinese missile deployments opposite Taiwan.

The South China Sea—the fourth factor—is, from all evidence, a matter of less urgency and priority for Beijing. Nevertheless, the issues are substantial. Malaysia, the Philippines, Brunei, and Vietnam all have claims to various coral reefs and islets that make up the Spratly Islands group in the South China Sea. China, however, claims the entire sea and all its outcroppings as sovereign Chinese territory. The world's busiest commercial sea-lanes transit the South China Sea, and major maritime countries, including the United States, have always regarded these lanes as international waters. This position clashes directly with China's assertion of territorial waters.

In support of its position, China has fought two naval engagements with Vietnam (in 1974 and 1988) and has built structures on Mischief Reef claimed by the Philippines. A series of confrontations between Chinese "fishing boats" and Philippine naval craft produced a round of unproductive negotiations between Manila and Beijing. Meanwhile other claimants, notably Malaysia, have been energetically establishing a physical presence on various other outcroppings. A few years ago it was generally believed that the seabed under the South China Sea contained large oil deposits. Limited exploration has so far failed to validate that expectation. If a major oil find were to occur, the Spratlys dispute can be expected to heat up rapidly.

REDRAWING THE GEOPOLITICAL MAP

The foregoing must be understood in the context of a remarkably dynamic Asian geopolitical environment. Crudely put, the balance of power in Asia is being transformed with the growth of Chinese power both absolutely and relative to other national actors—notably Japan and Russia.

The deterioration in Russia's power and prestige since the heyday of the Soviet Union is evident. By every measure except the size and lethality of its strategic (nuclear) rocket forces, Russia is much diminished. As late as the mid-1980s the Soviet Pacific Fleet was a major strategic factor in East Asia, including maintaining a substantial physical presence at Cam Ranh Bay in Vietnam. Vietnam and Cambodia were Soviet client states, and Tokyo's perception of the security threats facing Japan began and ended with Moscow. But today Russia figures into the region's strategic equation mainly in speculation about whether

Moscow can maintain effective control over its vast and ever-more thinly populated Far Eastern provinces. One key exception to this generalization is Russian weapons sales. These transfers have clearly augmented China's modern military capabilities, although the degree and significance of that improvement remains a matter of intense debate among specialists. But beyond its role as a military supplier to Beijing, Moscow has essentially dropped off the strategic map of East Asia.

Japan presents a more puzzling and uncertain picture. Japan has long boasted an economy second only to the United States in size and technological sophistication. The phrase "economic superpower" was coined about 20 years ago specifically to characterize Japan. At the height of the Japanese economic boom of the late 1980s, Japan was painted as an ominous predatory threat to the global economy and the Western world. Then Japan's "bubble economy" burst in 1990. The Japanese economy, burdened by bad commercial debt and huge government deficits, has not grown since. Nevertheless, living standards remain high and the electorate's relative passivity has left the political system in the hands of an entrenched group of conservative politicians deeply averse to any far-reaching reforms.

In terms of security policy, Japan is again largely frozen in place. Fifty-six years after its World War II surrender, Tokyo remains committed to a constitutional restriction that prevents its military from employing force for any purpose other than the actual defense of the home islands. This posture has been sustainable because of the protection afforded by the American alliance and by a general assessment that the security environment in Northeast Asia over the last decade, while certainly not benign, has not been immediately threatening. That assumption has been seriously challenged by two developments.

The first and most obvious was evidence of new North Korean strategic nuclear and missile capabilities. In the mid-1990s the determination by the International Atomic Energy Agency and United States intelligence that Pyongyang was producing fissile material usable in nuclear weapons produced a tense contest of wills on the Korean peninsula. Ultimately a deal first brokered in June 1994 by former President Jimmy Carter in conversations with North Korea's "Great Leader" Kim Il Sung eased the crisis. Despite this apparent breakthrough, Japanese opinion generally remained ill-disposed toward North Korea due in part to Pyongyang's refusal to account for Japanese citizens believed to have been kidnapped during the 1960s and taken to North Korea for use as language instructors for foreign agents. Then, in August 1998, North Korea launched a ballistic missile over Japan to the shock of Japanese authorities and the public alike.

More important in strategic terms has been the evident rise in China's military power coupled with an almost belligerent posture toward Japan, including demands for repeated apologies for Japan's World War II occupation of China. The growth of Chinese power presents a geopolitical situation without precedent in Japanese experience, at least since the height of the Ming Dynasty in the fifteenth century. Increased Chinese pressure on Taiwan has produced growing uneasiness in defense and security circles in Japan. Taiwan was under Japanese rule from 1895 until the end of World War II. But Japan's interest in Taiwan is not simply historic and nostalgic. If Taiwan were to come under Beijing's control, the regional security environment would be greatly altered to Japan's detriment.

The expected response of a nation with Japan's inherent capabilities would be twofold. First, it would improve the nation's defense capabilities with substantially greater military expenditures. Second, it would seek allies willing and able to act as a counterweight to growing Chinese power. The first option is foreclosed by Japanese constitutional limitations buttressed by domestic political opinion (and a static economy). Japan's wartime legacy likewise forecloses any defense collaboration with the only two possible candidates in the region—South Korea and Taiwan.

Japan does have a third option—to try to win China's goodwill largely through economic measures designed to foster China's modernization and its evolution as an increasingly "satisfied" power. In a sense Japan has been doing this since the 1970s by providing substantial economic assistance and investment to China while striving to avoid offending China's diplomatic and political sensibilities. A final option—to accommodate growing Chinese geopolitical ambition (including subordination to China's strategic interests) is from all evidence unacceptable to the Japanese leadership or populace.

Japan thus has one remaining strategic choice: strengthen its defense ties with the United States. A review of the United States–Japan Guidelines for Defense Cooperation in 1996–1997 was designed to make Japan a more effective security partner of the United States. Despite this effort at clarification, if the United States were to become involved in a serious conflict and needed Japan's military assistance, neither Washington nor Tokyo knows for sure how far Japan would go.[1] The tough decisions have been avoided simply because they are so tough. In short, Japan remains a potential great power that is unable to act like one despite an increasingly problematic regional security environment.

CHINA LOOKS SOUTH

Russia's decline and Japan's strategic paralysis have removed the two overriding threats that have preoccupied China historically. China now has the strategic freedom and the emerging capability to pursue its natural inclination to assert influence and interests to the south. Aside from Taiwan, Southeast Asia will feel the greatest impact from China's emergence.

From China's perspective, Southeast Asia is attractive, vulnerable, and nearby. Southern China abuts Southeast Asia along the northern borders of Burma (Myanmar), Laos, and Vietnam. Many Chinese phrases characterize the *nanyang* (South Seas) as golden lands of opportunity. For three decades Southeast Asia has been a region of rapidly growing wealth, much of it generated and owned by large Chinese-emigrant populations in major urban centers. As was noted, the world's busiest sealanes traverse the region, and even after the wholesale despoilation of tropical forests and other natural endowments, the physical resources of Southeast Asia remain impressive. With

the exception of Indonesia, individual states that comprise the political map of Southeast Asia are only a fraction the size of China.

Historically, China's presence and influence in Southeast Asia have waxed and waned for more than two millennia. During China's long imperial epoch, strong dynasties asserted a kind of cultural-political suzerainty through the "tribute system." Southeast Asian monarchs, chieftains, and sultans gave symbolic deference to the Celestial Throne as the apogee of human civilization. But as a general rule China did not attempt to exert actual physical control on the ground. The principal exception was in northern Vietnam, which was long treated by China as a province of the Middle Kingdom. After a struggle waged episodically for 1,000 years, the Vietnamese finally wrested political independence from China in A.D. 939.

With the 1949 communist revolution in China, an unsettling new era dawned. Initially, the People's Republic embraced Moscow's grand design of providing support for communist insurrections in the third world. China gave political, moral, and sometimes material backing to communist guerrillas and urban revolutionaries seeking to topple noncommunist regimes throughout Southeast Asia.

From the vantage point of Southeast Asia, the early cold-war period was one of regional conflict and pervasive security threats emanating from international communism in various guises. By the late 1980s and early 1990s, this picture had changed dramatically. With the Vietnamese military withdrawal from Cambodia in 1989, the region's last significant military conflict came to an end (Vietnam had invaded the country in 1978 ostensibly to end the Khmer Rouge's bloody revolution). For the first time the Southeast Asian countries did not face any major security threats from within or outside the region. With relatively marginal exceptions, governments were secure, societies stable, the status quo accepted, economies were growing, and external powers posed no immediate danger. To an exceptional degree, the Southeast Asian states had developed regional institutions and patterns of interaction that gave the region increasing coherence as a single political, economic, and even security entity. The centerpiece of that achievement was the establishment of the Association of Southeast Asian Nations (ASEAN) in 1967. Meanwhile, China was preoccupied with the task of consolidating the far-reaching domestic reforms initiated by Deng Xiaoping. By any historical measure, this was an extraordinary moment, with peace, prosperity, and security ascendant.

The fragility of that moment was quickly demonstrated when the financial crisis that began in Thailand in late summer 1997 swept across the region. The crisis and its aftermath have been deeply unsettling and have revealed that the extraordinary economic growth of the last three decades—a phenomenon characterized by the World Bank as the "Asian Miracle"—was not as solid as nearly everyone believed. The image of a stable and productive modernizing region gave way to a quite different picture of ineffective regulatory institutions, illusory bank balance sheets, wildly irrational investments, excessive corruption, and conspicuous consumption. As the value of the bath, rupiah, and ringgit collapsed, Southeast Asians were reminded that not just living standards, but social order, political stability, and even national security rested ultimately on economic performance.

The political dangers embedded in economic failure were graphically revealed in Indonesia. For 32 years the New Order regime of President Suharto had been a fixture of the Southeast Asian scene. Indonesia had been politically stable (if not static), economically successful, and socially quiescent. But under the impact of the financial crisis, the framework of Suharto's New Order regime cracked, triggering mass political demonstrations, widespread street violence, and the downfall of Suharto himself. In the nearly three years since, Indonesia has grappled with a transition from autocracy to electoral democracy accompanied by lethal ethnoreligious conflict and increasingly violent separatist movements—all exacerbated by severe administrative ineptitude and corruption. Paradoxically, the economy is showing signs of recovery, with certain sectors, notably small business, performing surprisingly well. Still, by mid-2001 it could no longer be assumed that Indonesia would even remain a single sovereign entity.[2] At best, the largest and most important country in Southeast Asia faces the prospect of years of putting the pieces back together and learning how to govern itself democratically.

Indonesia has long been the cornerstone of ASEAN. Not surprisingly, the spectacular decline in Indonesia's fortunes coincided with a deterioration in ASEAN's standing. The association proved unable to deal effectively with the financial crisis, and its ill-timed decision to expand its membership to 10 countries, first made in 1997, had the effect of undercutting the cohesion and like-mindedness that had been the organization's core strength. The admission of Burma and Cambodia, in particular, brought two nations with poor human rights records inside ASEAN. The result has been tension within the organization and with both the United States and Europe, which have been highly critical of developments within Burma in particular.

In geopolitical terms the potential beneficiary of Southeast Asia's difficulty is China. China is simply too large and too near not to be a major factor in the Southeast Asian equation—and not to be viewed with some trepidation. China's postwar support for communist revolutionary movements in the region marked the reappearance of Chinese power in Southeast Asia after it had disappeared during the nearly three centuries of European colonial dominance of Southeast Asia. This, coupled with the presence of economically influential Chinese populations in nearly every Southeast Asian city, has bred distrust. Beijing's claim to the entire South China Sea (and its refusal to disavow the use of force to back up that claim) has caused alarm in a number of quarters. Growing Chinese influence in Burma and Cambodia has been a further source of concern. Finally, the growth of China's economy in recent years has been welcomed by some (mostly ethnic Chinese) Southeast Asian businesspeople as a major new investment opportunity, while being feared by others because of the potent competition from ultra-low-wage Chinese industries.

In security terms, the emergence of China as a powerful "colossus of the north" has obvious implications. For the Southeast Asian countries the optimal circumstances with regard to China

existed in the 1980s and early 1990s. Its economy was expanding but China remained, overall, poor, relatively weak, and preoccupied with a daunting array of domestic problems. A stronger, more confident, more outward-looking China can be expected to do what all major powers have done—assert its interests with growing effect in adjacent regions.

Whether China becomes a "threat" to Southeast Asia depends not only on capabilities but also intentions. The public posture of the ASEAN governments on this score has been to repeatedly express confidence that China's intentions are benign. The basic argument is that China does not have a history of imperial expansion and that it stands to gain economically from a stable, peaceful Southeast Asia. As more than one Southeast Asian official has put it, "We can all get rich together." The ASEAN governments have supported this proposition with what might be termed a "Gulliver" strategy of lashing China to Southeast Asia with myriad ties of mutual interest. These include investments, trade, cultural exchanges, arms purchases, visits by senior leaders and officials, and a far-ranging discourse with China on economic and security issues in a variety of regional forums. The expectation is that an increasingly prosperous China will see its interests and future tied to an economically successful and peaceful Southeast Asia. China, in short, will complete its transformation from revolutionary firebrand to guardian of the status quo.

Any strategy cannot simply assume favorable outcomes, however. The most important task for strategists and policymakers is to plan against the failure of optimistic assumptions. Southeast Asian governments have tried to do this by strengthening their national military and economic capabilities (building national "resilience" in the parlance of the region), and by maintaining a cooperative relationship with the United States military presence in the region.

WHAT ROLE FOR AMERICA?

At the most basic level, United States objectives in East Asia have remained consistent over the last five decades: prevent the emergence of a regional hegemony; keep open the sea and air routes that transit the area; maintain commercial access to the economies of the region and the peace and stability that commerce requires; and preserve and strengthen security ties with allies and friends in the region.

Any discussion of the American security role in East Asia must begin with the security treaty between Japan and the United States signed in September 1951. Since the end of World War II, the United States and Japan have forged a unique alliance. Under its terms Japan has assumed responsibility for the conventional defense of Japan itself but has forsworn the development of nuclear weapons, a strategic offensive capability, or any military role in the security and stability of East Asia more broadly. For the United States the alliance has long been the cornerstone of American security strategy for East Asia. Japan allows the United States to maintain a force of approximately 40,000 military personnel in Japan, including nearly 20,000 marines on Okinawa. An aircraft carrier battle group is "homeported" in Yokosuka (with an amphibious-ready group in Sasebo) while the air force supports nearly 14,000 personnel at several airfields in the home islands and Okinawa.

Despite the importance both countries attach to the alliance, its operational role (and future) is replete with uncertainties. The marine presence on Okinawa has come under increasing and understandable pressure from the local populace that finds such a large foreign military deployment in such a small place burdensome. Despite various agreements between American and Japanese officials dealing with the issue, the medium-term future of the marine presence is far from certain.

In operational terms the alliance would be tested in the event of a military conflict involving United States forces in the defense of South Korea. Despite the best efforts of defense officials in Washington and Tokyo, it remains unclear exactly what role, if any, Japanese forces would assume in support of their United States allies. The same is true to an even greater extent regarding a Taiwan contingency. This is strategic ambiguity of a very high order. Potential steps toward the eventual unification of the Korean peninsula raise another set of uncertainties. Would United States forces remain in Korea if tensions ease to the point that unification becomes a realistic possibility? North Korean leader Kim Jong Il has told his South Korean counterpart that a continuation of the United States military presence would be acceptable. China, however, may have a different view.

Taiwan occupies a uniquely ambiguous position in United States security strategy. The United States has no formal obligation or commitment to defend Taiwan. However, the 1979 Taiwan Relations Act, passed by Congress and signed by President Carter, contains the following language: "It is the policy of the United States… to consider any effort to determine the future of Taiwan by other than peaceful means… a threat to the peace and security of the Western Pacific area and of grave concern to the United States;… to provide Taiwan with arms of a defensive character; and… to maintain the capacity of the United States to resist any resort to force or other forms of coercion that would jeopardize the security, or the social or economic system, of the people on Taiwan."

Whether the United States would actively assist in the defense of Taiwan if the island were attacked remains uncertain. The sensitivity of the issue makes it difficult for the Defense Department to do the comprehensive, detailed operational planning that such a large commitment of forces would require.

In 1991 the Philippines refused to renew the leases under which United States forces were based in that country. Conse-quently the United States lost its two principal bases in Southeast Asia—at Clark Field and Subic Bay. This has greatly complicated the task of maintaining forward deployments by United States forces. The vacuum was filled in part by a series of access agreements that provided for port visits, including refitting and supply in most Southeast Asian countries as well as joint exercises and other forms of contact with local militaries. In a recent development Singapore has constructed a pier specifically to accommodate United States aircraft carriers.

In Northeast Asia the United States is generally credited with providing a vital element of security and stability in a region where historical animosities run deep. With regard to Taiwan and Southeast Asia, the United States role as a security guarantor has taken on a different character. In effect, the United States armed forces stand as an obstacle to Chinese strategic ambitions in the region—including the South China Sea. Put another way, in Southeast Asia, the United States and China are natural geopolitical rivals.

For United States security planners based in Honolulu and Washington, this creates a remarkably challenging environment. The stakes are high, the uncertainties and ambiguities are everywhere, and the pace of change is rapid and accelerating. The one constant since World War II has been a United States military presence serving as a kind of offshore gendarme insuring against the outbreak of serious international conflict or the assertion of hegemonic ambition. Whether the United States can continue to play such a demanding role effectively into the future remains to be seen.

Notes

1. The prevailing interpretation of the Japanese constitution precludes "collective self-defense." This creates a major question whether Japanese forces could act in concert with United States forces in a combat situation.

2. One former province of Indonesia, East Timor, is in the process of achieving independence with UN assistance. Because it was not part of the original Dutch East Indies, East Timor's secession may not establish a useful precedent for Indonesia's other discontented regions.

MARVIN C. OTT *is a professor of national security policy at the National War College in Washington, D.C. The views expressed are the author's.*

To Be an Enlightened Superpower

Wu Xinbo

The twentieth century passed with a vivid U.S. finger-print on almost every aspect of human life. As we move into the twenty-first century, the magic of globalization and the information age has rendered U.S. influence omnipresent on the earth. The United States' primary role in world affairs is understood, but for many observers, it is full of contradictions. The United States pledges to stand for human rights and democracy, but this promise is coupled with a certain degree of hypocrisy. The United States claims to promote peace and stability but often intrudes into the internal affairs of others by abusing its supreme military power or waving the stick of sanctions. The United States cherishes a high degree of self-pride but often neglects to show respect to, and consideration for, the national feelings of others. Washington tends to seek absolute security for itself but is inclined to dismiss the legitimate security concerns of other countries.

Without the United States the world might be less stable and prosperous; but Washington certainly can do better in promoting peace, harmony, and prosperity in the world. Hypothetically, how can the United States act as an enlightened superpower? In particular, from a Chinese perspective, what are the ideal policies the United States should undertake in dealing with China and the Asia–Pacific region? To explore what an ideal U.S. policy should look like, the baseline must necessarily be current U.S. policy.

Neither Rosy nor Grimy Glasses

An ideal U.S. policy toward China should be based on a correct perception of China. The United States should develop a full appreciation of three issues before a sound China policy can be developed: how to understand progress and problems in a fast-changing China, how to treat a rising China with respect, and how to define the nature of Sino–U.S. relations.

The Chinese have always been upset by an oversimplified U.S. view of China. From 1979 to the spring of 1989, the United States had viewed China through rose-colored glasses. In that light, China was a country embracing economic reform, political liberalization, and a diversified social life. After the Tiananmen Square conflict, the United States swung to the other extreme, looking at China through a grimy lens and seeing a country that violates human rights, restricts religious freedom, pollutes the environment, and bullies Taiwan.

Washington is inclined to dismiss the legitimate security concerns of other countries.

In fact, understanding China has never been that simple. China has made huge progress over the past two decades toward turning itself into a modern country. At the same time, it has been carrying too much historical baggage and now faces many new challenges. China is not as good as U.S. observers used to believe in the 1980s, but it is not as bad as they assume in the post-Tiananmen period.

In the real world, the Americans, affected by their cultural background, may never be able to overcome a black-and-white approach to understanding China. In an ideal world, policymakers in Washington would take a more balanced view of China's achievements and problems and be reasonably patient when expecting more fundamental and positive changes in this country. Moreover, U.S. policy would be geared to facilitate China's progress, not to hamper it. For example, on the issue of human rights, the United States should welcome China's progress, while acknowledging the complexity of this issue and help China develop its social, economic, and political conditions to improve human rights even further. U.S. human rights policy should not be focused on sponsoring anti-China bills at the annual Geneva conference of the United Nations Human Rights Commission and on supporting a handful of political dissidents.

A second problem is the U.S. attitude toward a rising China. In the 1980s, the U.S. political elite stated that a strong China would help promote regional stability and serve U.S. interests. At the time, they perceived that a more powerful China would contribute to U.S. efforts to contain the Soviet Union. With the end of the Cold War, U.S. policymakers no longer publicly claimed that they would like to see the emergence of a strong China. Instead, many U.S. strategists expressed concern, either publicly or privately, over the "China threat." Absent a strategic necessity to play the China card against a more threatening power, some U.S. policymakers worry that a stronger China would undermine the paramount U.S. position in East Asia and pose a challenge to U.S. interests in the region. In the real world, such a selfish and parochial view does have its currency; in an ideal world, however, the U.S. political elite would put China's rise in a broad perspective. First and foremost, they would come to realize that a stronger China will benefit the Chinese people. Having suffered from poverty and weakness in their modern history, the Chinese are eager to make their country wealthy and strong, and there is nothing wrong with their genuine wishes to reach this goal.

Moreover, a strong China would promote regional stability. The past has shown that, when China was poor and weak, a power vacuum emerged in the East Asia region. Chaos and turmoil prevailed in the midst of various powers' efforts to build their spheres of influence. Contrary to the concern of those who perceive a "China threat," a strong China is unlikely to be detrimental to regional stability. As Ambassador Chas W. Freeman convincingly argued, "China is not Germany, Japan, the USSR, or even the United States. China does not seek lebensraum; is not pursuing its manifest destiny; does not want to incorporate additional non-Han peoples into its territory; has no ideology to export; and is certainly not a colonizer and does not station any troops overseas."[1]

> **A**n ideal U.S. policy should encourage Japan to remain a civilian and pacifist country.

Most importantly, the reemergence of China as a major power coincides with China's integration into the world community, which means that, as China accumulates greater material strength, it is also learning to become a responsible power. The past two decades have shown that China has become more responsive to, and cooperative with, international society. Based on this understanding, first, the United States should view the rise of China as an inevitable trend, welcome it, and interpret it as a great opportunity for peace and prosperity. Second, it should facilitate rather than obstruct China's growth into a world power and be sympathetic to China's pursuit of its legitimate national interests. Third, the United States should, through its own conduct, provide China with a model of behavior as a responsible power in the international community.

The third issue is the U.S. understanding of its relations with China. Two assumptions tend to complicate Sino–U.S. ties: that China and the United States have no common values and therefore cannot develop intimate relations; and that U.S. relations with China should be second to U.S. relations with historical allies in the region, such as Japan, South Korea, and Australia. The first assumption is flawed because, in fact, common interests do exist between these two countries. Although differing in ideology and political system, China and the United States have a wide range of common interests at the global, regional, and bilateral levels. History demonstrates that ideology has not impeded Sino–U.S. cooperation on many important issues that serve mutual interests. In international relations, what matters is not a country's ideology and political system, but its external behavior.

The second assumption is fallacious because it overlooks the fact that China is geopolitically more influential than any of the three U.S. allies in the region: Japan, the Republic of Korea, or Australia. For peace and stability in Northeast Asia, Southeast Asia, South Asia, or Central Asia, Beijing can play a more important role than Tokyo, Seoul, or Canberra. As China's economic boom grows, so will its weight in regional economic affairs, as demonstrated by its performance in the Asian financial crisis in 1997–1998. By refraining from devaluing its currency in the midst of the crisis, China helped prevent the already deteriorating regional economies from worsening.

In an ideal world, both the liberal and conservative wings of the U.S. political elite would judge the China–U.S. relationship on its own merits, not by political or security ideology. Washington would not predetermine China as either a "strategic partner" or "strategic competitor" but would define it through comprehensive interaction with Beijing. Although it would be prepared to handle ups and downs in bilateral relations, the United States would seek a better future for one of the most important relationships in the world. Finally, the U.S. political elite in the ideal world would prioritize statesmanship over domestic political disputes in relations with China, thus ameliorating the environment in which to develop Sino–U.S. ties.

The Taiwan Question

Questions surrounding two crucial policy issues—Taiwan and Asia–Pacific regional security—will determine the future of Sino–U.S. ties.[2] The Taiwan question is the crux of U.S.–China security problems. It is probably the only issue that may ignite a major military conflict between China and the United States and completely destroy bilateral ties.

In general, the Chinese hold three assumptions about U.S. policy toward Taiwan. Strategically, China believes the United States still views Taiwan as part of its "sphere of influence" in the western Pacific, a quasi-ally in the region. Politically, China believes the United States favors Taiwan's independence. Although the United States does not want to fight for Taiwan's independence, it prefers the maintenance of the status quo, namely, the de facto independence of Taiwan. Militarily, China believes the United States will continue to provide Taiwan with assistance, including the transfer of advanced arms and military technology, intelligence, and training. Should China resort to the use of force to integrate Taiwan, the United States would certainly intervene. Those assumptions, true or not, reflect the mainstream Chinese interpretation of U.S.–Taiwan policy.

Ideally, the United States would think differently about the Taiwan headache and view the problem basically as a matter of nation-building for China, not as a U.S. issue in either a geopolitical or ideological sense. The United States would also understand that, in the long run, for Taiwan to gain security, international space, and greater economic opportunities, it must accept some association with the mainland while preserving its utmost political autonomy. If Taiwan seeks formal independence, Beijing will almost certainly resort to the use of force. If those events come to pass, even if China is not able to take over Taiwan, it certainly is able to throw the island into chaos.

Chinese have always been upset by an oversimplified U.S. view of China.

Should the United States intervene at that point, it will have to make an extremely difficult decision about what price it is willing to pay to maintain, at a minimum, the present situation on Taiwan. U.S. military involvement, which would create even more trouble in the Taiwan Strait, will not end the problem. Compared with such a horrible scenario, peaceful reunification is in the best interests of Beijing, Taipei, and Washington.

Most importantly, U.S. policymakers would realize that, as long as the current U.S. Taiwan policy continues, Washington can never place its relations with a rising power on a solid basis. Beijing will remain suspicious of, and concerned about, the U.S. security presence in East Asia. The U.S. leadership would also not be able to expect Beijing's endorsement on strategic initiatives in regional and global affairs. Should the Taiwan issue be resolved peacefully, however, China will become a status quo power in the political–security sense; Sino–U.S. relations will be far more stable, healthy, and constructive; and China–U.S. cooperation will stand as a strong force for regional security and prosperity.

Based on this wisdom, an ideal U.S. Taiwan policy would adopt a refreshing new outlook. First, Washington would reorient its goal on the Taiwan issue from a "peaceful solution" to "peaceful reunification," because

"peaceful solution" implies two possibilities: Taiwan's peaceful independence or peaceful reunification with China. By unequivocally pledging to support China's peaceful reunification with Taiwan, the United States would dismiss the ambiguity in, and Chinese suspicion of, its Taiwan policy. Only by so doing can there be a peaceful solution for the disputes across the Taiwan Strait. Second, Washington would encourage Taipei to negotiate a reasonable arrangement for reunification with Beijing. Washington can act as an honest broker by presenting useful and creative ideas about reconciliation across the Taiwan Strait, or it can exert pressure from behind the scenes on both sides when dilemmas stall the negotiations. If Taipei tries to push the envelope and provoke China, the United States would ideally stop it.

On the issue of arms sales to Taiwan, in an ideal world, the United States would adopt a more sensible and responsible approach. Washington would ardently honor its commitment to China in the 1982 Communiqué not to carry out a long-term policy of arms sales to Taiwan and gradually to reduce its arms sales to Taiwan, leading, over a period of time, to a final resolution.[3] Also, Washington would make its arms sale policy compatible with the ultimate goal of Taiwan's peaceful reunification with China.

Regional Issues

On the issue of regional security, several questions will test U.S. policymakers: how to restructure the U.S. military presence in the western Pacific in a changing security context; how to manage its security alliances in a new geopolitical setting; how to encourage Japan to play a larger role in regional security without upsetting existing balances; and, finally, how to deal with the issue of theater missile defense (TMD) in East Asia.

In an ideal world, the United States would no longer view its military presence in the western Pacific as a means of bolstering its strategic interests in the region. With the ongoing reconciliation and inevitable reunification of the Korean Peninsula and the resumption of a normal regional security role for Japan, the United States would understand that a large-scale, permanent military presence would not be politically sustainable either domestically or internationally. Ideally, as the international environment changes, Washington will try to find new ways to preserve its influence. For instance, a base-access arrangement in the region for U.S. forces would be more feasible politically and less expensive financially than maintaining a permanent presence in East Asia. The revolution in military affairs and the improvement of rapid-reaction capability will negate the need for the United States to keep a large armed force on foreign soil. Most importantly, Washington policymakers would understand that, in a time of growing economic interdependence and deepening regional integration, it is more relevant for the United States to lead by shaping the rules of the game and building a security community than to seek influence by showing off its military muscle.

Building security communities also affects the role of U.S. security alliances in the region. Washington's redefinition of its security alliance with Japan and others has clearly alarmed and alienated states such as China that have become very suspicious of U.S. strategic intentions. As countries feel threatened, they naturally respond by aligning with each other. The Chinese–Russian partnership, although still far from being an alliance, has become more substantive over the past several years in response to perceived aggressiveness by the United States in Asia and Europe. As a result, at a time when members in the Asia–Pacific region are supposed to build a community that promotes the security of all the regional members, U.S. reliance on alliances is deepening regional divisions.

What matters is not a country's ideology and political system, but its external behavior.

In an ideal world, the United States would seek to promote common security (security for all), not unilateral security or collective security (security for some countries at the expense of others). In this context, Washington will play down the importance of security alliances. For existing alliances, the United States would stress their political rather than their military function and would seek closer diplomatic consultation and coordination among allies in dealing with regional issues, abstaining from rattling the alliance saber against a third party. Most importantly, policymakers in Washington would realize that a sound trilateral relationship among China, Japan, and the United States is crucial to peace and stability in the Asia–Pacific region. Therefore, instead of uniting with Japan against China, Washington would spare no efforts to promote constructive interactions among the three parties.

The notion of a "pluralistic security community" would ideally prevail in U.S. security ideology. Like an Asia–Pacific economic community that benefits all economies in the region, a security community would advance equal security for all regional members. As Admiral Dennis Blair argues, "[S]ecurity communities are the right way ahead for the Asia–Pacific region." According to him, the goal is to build upon the current set of principally bilateral security relationships in the Asia–Pacific region to form a web of partnerships leading to mature security communities.[4] In this context, "pluralistic" means that the community is not based on a single pillar, but on several variables such as the consensus of major powers, the role of security alliances, regional or subregional mechanisms, and so forth. Differences in ideology and political systems should not obstruct cooperation on security is-

sues. The United States would still play a significant role—not as a hegemonist, but as a key player.

In both the real and ideal worlds, Japan inevitably features prominently in U.S. policy configurations. The redefinition of the U.S.–Japan alliance, coupled with the rise of conservative political influence and nationalism in Japan as well as the perceived shift in Japan's security environment, has been driving Japan to become a traditional political–military power. An ideal U.S. policy toward Japan, however, would encourage Japan to remain a civilian and pacifist country. Realizing that Japan will and should become a normal state, the United States would advise Japan to be serious and responsible in dealing with its World War II legacy and to be sensitive to its Asian neighbors' concerns about Japan's future behavior. Although expecting Japan to play a larger and more active role in regional affairs, Washington would avoid pushing Japan to assume a high profile on security issues and to expand its already impressive military capability. With regard to the revision of Japan's Peace Constitution—particularly Article IX—Washington would urge Tokyo to take into account the possible negative impact of such an action on regional stability as well as Japan's future. The U.S. administration would advise Japan's political elite to be cautious and responsible in dealing with one of the most important political legacies of modern Japan.

U.S. reliance on alliances is deepening regional divisions.

In an ideal world, Washington would not be addicted to the idea of deploying TMD in East Asia because it would understand the high risk of altering the existing strategic stability in the region and inviting an arms race. Even though security challenges to U.S. interests in the region will still exist, as a responsible power, the United States would be inclined to respond to such challenges mainly through nonmilitary means. For instance, Washington would seek to improve political relations with regional members, encourage economic cooperation and regional integration, develop a security community, and promote arms control measures. U.S. policymakers would firmly believe that U.S. security interests and regional stability were best preserved through arms reduction, not arms buildup.

Beyond Hegemony

Economic factors have become the most powerful engine for China–U.S. relations. The development of economic ties, however, has been invariably constrained by the conservative attitude of the United States on technology transfers and the politicization of economic issues. In both bilateral and multilateral settings, Washington has been pushing the agenda for trade and investment liberalization while neglecting the call from developing economies for bolder technology transfer on the part of developed countries. In particular, the United States maintains a discriminatory technology transfer policy toward China on the pretext of national security. The U.S. debate over whether to give China permanent normal trade relations and to facilitate its World Trade Organization membership was an example of efforts to politicize economic relations.

In a best-case scenario, however, the United States would consider the advanced science and technology it has developed as a public good it can provide to all countries. While benefiting from such technology, those countries would work cooperatively and wholeheartedly to build world peace in return. In other words, advanced science and technology would no longer be a monopoly of the developed countries, but a means to promote peace, harmony, and prosperity on earth. Moreover, economic relations would not be affected by political considerations.

The twentieth century has often been characterized as the "American Century." In the twenty-first century, like it or not, the United States will continue to play a leading role in the world. The question for the United States and others is not whether it should play a role in world affairs, but how it should play this role. In reality, Washington may never see the world from this perspective, but the United States certainly will want to be a benign superpower, as some Americans often claim. To achieve that goal, Washington should not be content with the way it has been doing business. It should keep learning about the perspective of others, thus serving the interests of the United States and the rest of the world as well.

Notes

3. Chas W. Freeman Jr., "An Interest-Based China Policy" in Hans Binnendijk and Ronald N. Montaperto, eds., *Strategic Trends in China* (Washington, D.C.: National Defense University Press, 1998), 123–124.
4. Wu Xinbo, "U.S. Security Policy in Asia: Implications for China–U.S. Relations" *Contemporary Southeast Asia* 22 (December 2000): 3.
5. "United States–China Joint Communiqué on United States Arms Sales to Taiwan" in Harry Harding, *A Fragile Relationship: The United States and China Since 1972* (Washington, D.C.: The Brookings Institution), 383–385.
6. Dennis C. Blair and John T. Hanley Jr., "From Wheels to Webs: Reconstructing Asia–Pacific Security Arrangements," *Washington Quarterly* 24, no. 1 (Winter 2001).

Wu Xinbo is a professor at the Center for American Studies at Fudan University in China.

From *The Washington Quarterly*, Summer 2001, Vol. 24, No. 3, pp. 63-71. © 2001 by MIT Press Journals, Cambridge, MA 02142-1407, for the Center for Strategic and International Studies. Reprinted by permission.

A Small Peace
for the Middle East

Arthur Hertzberg

THE CLASH OF ABSOLUTES

THE DREAM of perfect peace is also the enemy of peace. The world can no longer avoid the somber insight of Isaiah Berlin, who wrote that any ideal taken to its very end brings not redemption, but pain and horror. Great conflicts, as Berlin realized, are insoluble because they involve absolutist principles and uncompromising visions. In wars of religion, no peace can be made between true faith and idolatry. In wars of ideology, no true revolutionary can compromise with false visions. And so wars continue, endlessly and insolubly. The only way to stop them is to abandon ideals—whatever they may be—and to make, in the here and now, pragmatic arrangements that stop the killing.

Unlike the Jews, the Palestinians have no messianic vision—they simply want to be left alone.

This precept holds for the conflict between the Israelis and the Palestinians, which has been made worse, unutterably worse, by such a dream of perfect peace. In this case, the dream took the form of one of the most glorious and creative movements of the last century: modern Zionism. A hundred years ago, some of the most vital elements in the Jewish community all over the world attempted to join the modern world by rejecting the passivity of their ancient messianic religion. They embraced modern nationalism with great enthusiasm and entered the lists of modern politics in order to establish a "normal" nation in the ancient homeland of the Jews, a goal that would free their people from confined existence in ghettos. The Zionists thought that Jews would achieve a kind of redemption by ceasing to be different from and persecuted by the nations of the world. Somehow, they thought, the inevitable discomforts and conflicts with the Arabs would be resolved. The Jews would find peace and acceptance in the land where their ancestors had once fashioned their religion and culture. But it was not to be.

Instead, from its very beginning to this very day, Zionism has confronted a century of war.

The Palestinians have no corresponding messianic vision, no contemporary secular dream of a resurgent Islamic society. They simply want to be left alone in the land they believe was taken from them in wars of conquest. The results of these conquests can never be accepted by the Palestinians. Neither the Christian crusaders nine centuries ago nor the Jews in this century ever acquired title to the land. No international decision made at Versailles or by the United Nations can change the minds of those who belong, religiously, culturally, and historically, to the world on which Islam set its fundamental stamp. Palestine is irrevocably a part of the realm of the believers, especially since Jerusalem is the home of the third holiest shrine in Islam: the mountain from which the Prophet Muhammad ascended to heaven.

The claim of the Jews on the land of Palestine is more complex but equally non-negotiable. The religious believe that God once promised the land to the children of Abraham. The nationalists believe that the Jewish people will be endangered unless their base is re-established in their ancient homeland. Thus neither group can ever grant the ultimate Palestinian demand that the Jews cease their aggression and go elsewhere. Modern Zionism began with the vision of a "normalized" Jewish people, a nation among nations that would be part of the world as of right. The most important Jewish demand is therefore that at the end of the peace process, the Arabs agree that the Jews' existence in the region is permanent and can never again be questioned. Without such a pledge, the vision of the Zionist enterprise—that modern Israel be established as a legitimate member of the family of nations—will remain unrealized.

RETURN AND REVENGE

FOR YEARS, Yasir Arafat, chairman of the Palestinian Authority, has spoken the language of peace and compromise in his declarations in Western languages, while saying in Arabic that Jerusalem is totally inalienable and that not one acre of Palestine rightfully belongs to the Jews. Jewish hard-liners have seized on these statements to prove that Arafat does not want peace and never intended to negotiate an end to the conflict. Jewish moderates have countered that these statements in Arabic are merely intended to temporarily satisfy Arafat's own constituency and that despite them, he is negotiating peace in good faith.

Both assessments of Arafat's policies are wrong, but not for the reasons that are sometimes given: namely, that he is either a man of peace who cannot deliver it, or an unregenerate man of war who occasionally hides behind the rhetoric of peace. In fact, Arafat wants neither peace nor war, nor even a permanent peace process. All that he, or any successor, can deliver are de facto arrangements that tamp down the conflict but leave the ultimate ideological issues unsolved. This is because no Palestinian political leader can possibly declare that the Jews have a right to settle permanently in Palestine as its newest conquerors. This would fly in the face of the Koran and the various forms of Arab nationalism that are its heirs. Such thinking should not be hard to comprehend. Indeed, after the Roman conquest of Judea and the destruction of the Second Temple in the year 70, rabbinic law refused to acknowledge the Romans' legal title to the land. The land of the Jews remained in the hands of the Jews, at least theoretically, and the Romans and all others who came after them had no claim to sovereignty. Why should Islam and its successors be any less tough-minded about their own claims?

The vehemence of the Palestinian position has never really been faced by the Israelis and their supporters throughout the world. Zionists, both in Israel and abroad, are essentially Westerners who believe that problems have rational solutions and that age-old religious or nationalist quarrels can ultimately be solved by compromise. To think otherwise is to take a tragic view of politics. But the whole point of the Zionist enterprise is to end the tragedy of Jewish existence as a persecuted minority in the Diaspora, and to win acceptance for the Jews.

The Zionists want to remake the Jewish people as a "normal" entity. Israel has recognized that this change is not happening quickly. But until recently, Israel firmly believed that the day would come when a global settlement of the conflict would be negotiated. Although Arab refugees from Palestine have not found new homes in the Arab countries to which they fled, Israelis believed that some resettlement and much compensation would resolve the question. In August 2000, at Camp David, Prime Minister Ehud Barak was bold enough to try to lead Israel into a settlement in which he gave away much of the Old City of Jerusalem itself to Palestinian control. Barak could not believe that the Palestinians would reject what was clearly the most generous settlement that any Israeli prime minister could ever offer them.

Had the Palestinians accepted the deal, their agreement would have allowed Barak to vanquish his domestic enemies by waving before them an unimaginable victory: an Israel finally at home in the Arab world. But it did not happen. Would it have happened if Israel had better treated the Arab populations in its pre-1967 borders? No, for Arafat could not deliver permanent peace to the four million refugees outside Israel's borders. These refugees have sustained themselves during a half-century

of misery on the dream of return and revenge. This dream Arafat dared not take away from them. Thus, the most that Israel was able to offer the Palestinians was not enough to make permanent peace.

The result of this failure within Israel and the Jewish world was simple and dramatic. It seemed to confirm the view of hard-liners within the Jewish community who have long said that peace is not possible, and that the only response to Arab riots and guerrilla warfare is to intensify the military struggle. Meanwhile, the moderates, the "peace party" among the Jews, were plunged into deep trouble. They always believed that a generous offer from the Israeli side would bring permanent peace. But Barak's offer did not. Now some of the members of the peace camp profess bitter disappointment in their Arab comrades. Others, however, still believe that mutual acceptance is possible. They must believe it—for the very essence of the Zionist dream is crumbling before them.

Israel now faces many of the same difficulties as did the Diaspora for many centuries. The Zionist state will have to live with uncertainty, insecurity, and the remaking of its safety year by year, perhaps even day by day. Of course, such instability is not Israel's lot alone. Many other states and nations live in lasting discomfort and even danger. The difference is that Zionism did not ask those who took up its cause to live with uncertainty. It promised them just the opposite. Thus the chaos today seems to give the lie to the pledge made by the Balfour Declaration in November 1917, when the Jews were told that they could look forward to the happiness and stability of a national home of their own.

MUDDLING THROUGH

Is THERE ANY HOPE for the future? Yes, but only if all sides abandon messianic dreams and remember Isaiah Berlin's message that we cannot resolve great ideological problems. We can only make pragmatic arrangements that bring some calm to the world.

What would be the outlines of such a pragmatic arrangement in the Middle East? At the very core of the lasting quarrel between Israel and the Palestinians—and the Arab world as a whole—is the question of what is to be done for the Palestinian refugees. Indeed, the central goal of Israeli diplomacy since 1948 has been to find a way to convince the Arabs to take the refugees off Israeli hands. The time is overdue for all parties concerned—Israelis, Arabs, and the powers of the world, led by the United States—to stop talking about grand solutions. It would be more than enough, now, to simply make life better for some of the Palestinians who have lived in camps for half a century. An international effort should be made to offer them technical education in such popular fields as electronics, where the skills learned are immediately useable all over the world. Such education should be given on the broadest basis to young people in the refugee camps, especially in the West Bank and Gaza. It would offer hope to people who have long sat, trapped in anger.

Such an educational program would be seen by some as an attempt to weaken Palestinian nationalism, by offering young people the promise of careers outside the camps. But it will give younger Palestinians, and their families, a realistic choice between throwing rocks or shooting at Israeli patrols, and training for a productive life. Those who accept such training may insist that they will never forget the homes that their grandparents once occupied in Jaffa, even if their careers take them to Silicon Valley. The opportunity should still be offered to them, without demanding as a precondition the end of their attachment to their nationalist dream.

On the extremely difficult question of Jerusalem, a very simple suggestion is that nothing be done. The arrangement that Defense Minister Moshe Dayan worked out after the Six-Day War in 1967 for the care and management of that most sacred and most fought-over place—the Temple Mount, which the Muslims call Haram al-Sharif—has held up. Why should the dreamers of the dream of ultimate peace now want to change it? The very worst way to solve the problem would be an international commission of the major religions of the world, or a U.N. body. Both such formulas would produce conflict, because all sides involved would have their own agendas. If there must be some international oversight, let the least partisan and self-interested groups be the referees between Israelis and Palestinians. It would be much better, however, for Jews and Arabs to keep muddling along on their own.

The current arrangement for Jerusalem has worked better than any of the alternatives proposed.

Barak's proposal, that control of much of the Old City be given to the Palestinians in return for their agreement to final peace, was greeted with disdain on both sides. The Arab world found the offer to be too little. Arabs regard the whole of al-Quds, the holy city at the center of Jerusalem, to be non-negotiable. On the other side, Jews, from the right to very nearly the extreme left, made it clear that they would reject any proposal that surrendered the Old City to Arab rule. Both sides prefer war to even the most generous proposal for peace that might be advanced by the other. Would it be horrible, then, if Jews and Arabs simply agreed to live with the current arrangement in Jerusalem, which, although unsatisfactory, they have tolerated since 1967, rather than attempt to move toward a glorious new future, when such movement will clearly bring untrammeled war?

Let everyone—Jews, Arabs, and international leaders—face reality: the 1967 arrangement, for Arabs to administer the shrines on the Temple Mount and for Jews to exercise police power in Jerusalem as a whole, has worked far better than any of the alternatives that keep being proposed. Think of how many people will remain alive if the sensible choice is made to continue with the inglorious muddle that now exists.

The other major problem in peacemaking is what to do with the Jewish settlements on the West Bank, in the territory that Israel conquered from Jordan in the Six-Day War. It is tempting to say that here, too, the combatants should desist from making

any changes and somehow muddle through. But such a suggestion will not work. Whenever the Israeli hard-liners are given the slightest leeway, they establish new settlements, sometimes in the guise of beefing up older communities, sometimes for some other reason, such as contributing to Israel's security by protecting lines of communication. Among the Palestinians, the anger at the loss of more and more of the West Bank into the hands of Israeli settlers, and the loss of more and more water into the swimming pools and gardens of beautiful model suburbs, has passed the explosion point. Making a pragmatic peace now between the two sides will require an agreement that this creeping annexation must end. Otherwise, the riots and guerilla warfare will continue. Such an arrangement need not foreshadow the dismantling of all Jewish settlements. But it must end the argument that Israel's security requires more and more strongholds on the West Bank.

No one except Jewish nationalist ideologues really believes that the whole West Bank venture is about Israel's security. Likud Prime Minister Menachem Begin made it very clear in 1977, when he first came to power, that the purpose of putting Jews on the West Bank was not to make Israel more defensible. Begin said, without hesitation, that he had been elected prime minister of Israel in order to carry out an ideological policy: that the land of Israel, from the Mediterranean Sea to the Jordan River, was inalienably Jewish. He would defend that policy even if the actions it required sometimes seemed to compromise Israel's security. Even Israel's general staff recognized that although maintaining some strong points on the hills would be useful to Israel's defense, the military effort needed to protect a large number of settlers on the West Bank would be greater than would be their contribution to Israel's safety.

On this issue, the time has come for Israel to make a clear-cut and pragmatic choice in its own interest. Although the upcoming election may further limit Israel's flexibility, it must abandon the idea that a settlement or two in the Gaza Strip, in the very midst of hundreds of thousands of angry Palestinians, is a boon for its security. Israel must make a distinction between settlements on the outskirts of Jerusalem and other Israeli population centers, and those isolated settlements that were scattered about in order to divide up the land of the West Bank and prevent the formation of a cohesive Palestinian territory. Such a decision may not inspire Arabs to see the dawn of peace, but it will give them less Israeli traffic on their roads to shoot at. Fewer Palestinians and Israelis will die.

ON THEIR OWN

THE SUGGESTIONS made above may seem strange, because they will not require major American diplomacy to effect or American money to fund. Superior education for Palestinian refugees will certainly cost some millions of dollars, but this is not beyond the resources of foundations interested in the Middle East, or of European governments eager to show what they can achieve on their own. Meanwhile, packing up some of the most provocative of the settlements will cost Israel less money than it has spent to maintain them. Even if Israel decides to pay to return the settlers to homes inside the country and to compensate them for their losses, these sums will not add up to billions. And the payoff will be high: a radical and welcome change in the nature of this deep-seated conflict. Israelis and Palestinians will be forced to work things out on their own, unable to nurture the hope of a grandiose peace requiring such deep concessions on either side that only the Americans have the resources to pay for it.

Perhaps the best way that the United States can contribute to peace between Jews and Arabs is to de-emphasize the conflict. At the very least, Washington should dispel the impression that it will offer grand prizes for those who help realize its vision of a fundamental peace settlement, announced with drama and fanfare on the lawn of the White House. The way to make peace is for Israeli settlements and Arab villages to work out between them, on their dusty streets, an end to the shooting.

The more grandiose a solution to the conflict, the more likely that it will require massive U.S. involvement, with Americans monitoring the arrangements and safeguarding the newly defined borders. The great virtue of the more modest deals proposed here is that they will not require large third-party involvement. If peace is ever to come to this region, Israelis and Palestinians must decide to relieve themselves of the burdens they have borne, with great discomfort, for quite a while. Temporary arrangements and compromises may seem to chart a long and plodding road toward peace. But they are likely to achieve their goal faster than the interminable peace process followed thus far, during which young diplomats have grown old and gray.

De-emphasizing the grandiose expectations of the American leadership has become even more plausible in these days of uncertainty that have succeeded the U.S. presidential election. Neither party now has a decisive mandate in the White House or Congress. The United States is in no position to define a bold plan or to insist that the protagonists in the Middle East conflict follow an American lead. The stars have conspired to produce an occasion for caution, both in the region and on the international scene. We should therefore move forward in pragmatic steps. The power for miraculous solutions is not in our hands.

ARTHUR HERTZBERg is Bronfman Visiting Professor of the Humanities at New York University and the author of many books, including *The Zionist Idea*. He is currently working on a memoir to be published in 2002.

Bush's Global Agenda: Bad News for Africa

"Today's 'global' issues, from HIV/AIDS to global warming, and from trade policies to the failure of international peacekeeping, have their most immediate and devastating consequences in Africa.... These vital challenges must be addressed in Africa, in solidarity with Africans, if they are not to overwhelm the world."

SALIH BOOKER

The greatest international challenge facing the United States in the twenty-first century is to devise a strategy to overcome the world's structural inequities that perpetuate extreme poverty. In a world where race, place, class, and gender are the major determinants of people's access to the full spectrum of human rights needed to escape poverty, Africa should be at the top of the United States foreign policy agenda. In a way—albeit the wrong way—it already is.

To find the substance of United States foreign policy toward the nations and peoples of Africa, however, one must know where to look. During the tenure of the previous administration it was necessary to see beyond the travel itineraries of cabinet secretaries and President Bill Clinton himself to the parsimonious management of the budget and the rising death toll from conflicts and AIDS in Africa to discern the yawning gap between rhetoric in Washington and reality in Africa. With the new administration it will be necessary to look past the conventional categories of what it will call Africa policy—conflict resolution, political reform, and economic and commercial relations—to the broader use of United States power in determining matters of global governance. Today's "global" issues, from HIV/AIDS to global warming, and from trade policies to the failure of international peacekeeping, have their most immediate and devastating consequences in Africa. And it is equally true that these vital challenges must be addressed in Africa, in solidarity with Africans, if they are not to overwhelm the world.

Africa policy is thus no longer to be found at the margins of United States global politics but in the mainstream. At present, however, this is bad news for Africa.

When the snow caps of Mt. Kilimanjaro melt in a decade or two, the damage done by the real Africa policies of the world's sole superpower at the dawn of this new century will be manifest. The floods that have devastated Mozambique and many other southern African countries in the past two years are but omens of that future. Like the AIDS pandemic that is wreaking havoc on African societies and economies, global warming is also taking its toll primarily among poor countries in the South, mainly in Africa. These consequences are not merely the result of "natural" disasters compounded by neglect on the part of the richest country on earth. Rather they are the strange fruit of what amounts to years of aggressive and irresponsible United States behavior.

THE NATIONAL INTEREST

During the electoral campaign, George W. Bush and his advisers repeatedly stressed that Africa did not "fit into the national strategic interests" of America. During the televised presidential debates he said Africa was not a priority, and that he would not intervene to prevent or stop genocide in Africa should such a threat—as occurred in Rwanda in 1994—develop. Since he took office, a few officials, Secretary of State Colin Powell most notable among them, have tried to amend this statement with reassurances that African concerns, such as AIDS, will be taken seriously by this administration.

Other Bush supporters have noted, correctly, that although the Clinton administration gave much attention to Africa, it was slow to deliver in practical terms. They hold out hope that Bush will promise less and deliver more. Thus far the new administration has only promised

WHO ARE THESE PEOPLE?

Looking at the lineup of policymakers now responsible for global affairs and Africa policies, it would be unrealistic to expect much progress in United States policy toward Africa were it not for the rise in public activism on African and Africa-related issues such as AIDs and foreign debt.

The president himself has little foreign policy experience and, as with domestic policy, is likely to follow the lead of his vice president. Vice President Dick Cheney's perspective on Africa is illustrated by his support for keeping Nelson Mandela in prison and his opposition to sanctions against apartheid South Africa while he was a member of Congress. More recently, as CEO of Halliburton, the world's largest oil services company, he was complicit in lining the pockets of the dictatorship of the late General Sani Abacha in Nigeria. National Security Adviser Condoleezza Rice was, until this year, a director of Chevron, another oil company that buttressed military rule in Nigeria and even hired the regime's soldiers for crowd-control work—work that including firing on unarmed protesters at the sites of its operations in Nigeria. (A Chevron oil tanker even bears her name.) With Bush himself coming from the oil industry, oil is likely to top the list of United States interests in Africa as defined by the Bush "oiligarchy."

Neither Rice nor Secretary of State Colin Powell, both African Americans, has demonstrated a particular interest in or special knowledge of Africa. Moreover, both Powell and Rice are loyal Republicans with a shared orientation toward international affairs that derives from a narrow militaristic understanding of security. They are also unilateralists at a time when the need in Africa is for multilateral support for peace and security.

The person chosen to become the top Africa policymaker at the State Department, Walter Kansteiner III, comes out of the right-wing Institute on Religion and Democracy in Washington, where he criticized mainline Christian denominations for supporting democratic change in apartheid South Africa. A commodity trader and adviser on privatization in Africa, Kansteiner also served in the White House under Bush's father. Like Cheney, he opposed sanctions against apartheid South Africa years after they were in place and as late as 1990 considered the prodemocracy movement in South Africa, led by Nelson Mandela's African National Congress, to be unrepresentative of most South Africans. With analytical skills like those, he appears singularly unqualified for the job except that he fits the profile of many new Bush staff: conservative ideologues who served Bush's father. *S. B.*

a substantive Africa policy without revealing much in the way of details and taking no early positive actions.

A fundamental problem is that the team of President George Bush and Vice President Dick Cheney will, like all its predecessors, shape United States foreign policy based on its own version of the national interest. At times the administration will slant it to concentrate on strategic or security interests. At other moments economic interests will get top billing. And on some occasions political interests, even values, will be put forward as the core of the national interest. But all these interpretations will share the limitations that stem from who participates in crafting these subjective definitions of the national interest, and who is excluded. With a cabinet composed of so many people recycled from his father's administration and the cold-war era preceding it (when rank racism more visibly defined the American approach to African affairs), it is understandable that some observers have the impression that Africa will now be off the agenda.

But Africa is not "off" the Bush administration agenda. It is worse than that. The net effect of the administration's broader policies already amount to a de facto war on Africa.

Consider President Bush's decision in March not to seek reductions in carbon dioxide emissions—as he had

explicitly promised he would during the electoral campaign. Media commentators quickly noted how the move would arouse criticism from domestic and European environmentalists and doom hopes of completing negotiations on the Kyoto Protocol, the as-yet-unratified treaty that would require signatory states to cut their greenhouse gas emissions—including carbon dioxide—below 1990 levels by the year 2012. Such gases are believed by most scientists to be responsible for the increased warming of the earth's atmosphere during the last century.

But few recalled the recent warning from Klaus Toepfer, executive director of the UN Environment Program, that Africa would suffer the most from the effects of global warming: "Africa's share of the global population is 14 percent but it is responsible for only 3.2 percent of global CO_2 emissions. Africans face the most direct consequences with regard to extreme weather conditions, with regard to drought and storms." Developed countries, principally the United States, produce the vast majority of the greenhouse gas emissions.

In February, just weeks before Bush's policy reversal, glaciologist Lonnie Thompson of Ohio State University released a study predicting that the glacier ice atop Mt. Kilimanjaro would disappear entirely between 2010 and

2020. And massive floods in Mozambique for the second consecutive year demonstrated the region's vulnerability to extreme weather, which global warming may exacerbate. A January report by the Intergovernmental Panel on Climate Change laid out a long list of predicted damage for Africa, ranging from water shortages and declines in food production to expanded ranges for malaria and other vector-borne diseases. The decision on CO_2 emissions makes the United States a rogue state in global environmental terms as far as Africans are concerned.

WAR ON REPRODUCTIVE HEALTH

George W. Bush's first full working day as president of the United States was also the twenty-eighth anniversary of *Roe v. Wade,* the Supreme Court decision that first established a women's constitutional right to abortion. On that day his first exercise of authority was to impose the contentious abortion politics of one narrow domestic constituency on millions of people in the poor countries of the world. By reinstating the "global gag rule"—slashing funding for family-planning services overseas—Bush did not really intend to reduce the number of abortions; rather his true purpose was to advance the ideological agenda of the antichoice religious fundamentalists who are among his strongest supporters.

Although AIDS is a global threat that knows no borders and does not discriminate by race, at present it is mainly killing black people. And that is the cruel truth about why the world has failed to respond with dispatch.

The rule was first imposed by President Ronald Reagan in 1984 during a population conference in Mexico City, sustained by Bush's father, President George H. W. Bush, but reversed by Clinton in 1993. The measure (also known as the Mexico City Policy) denies federal funding to international organizations that provide public health and family-planning services if they also provide reproductive health education and abortion services through their own funds.

As a result of Bush's action, organizations delivering important health-care assistance in Africa will lose funding. Projects providing contraceptives will be cut, which will contribute to a greater demand for abortions. More unsafe abortions will occur, as happened during the last period this policy was enforced. And with the decrease in the full range of family-planning services, there will be an increase in the incidence of HIV/AIDS infections on a continent that is already experiencing unprecedented suffering and social destruction because of the AIDS pandemic.

Congresswoman Nita Lowey D-NY said the president was "declaring war on the reproductive health of the world's poorest women." When members of Congress from both parties moved to stop Bush's move, the White House announced that it would reissue the order through an executive memorandum, which is not subject to congressional review. The unseemly rush to reimpose the gag rule offers evidence of just how antagonistic the Bush administration is to the interests of poor people, especially black people. It is clear that the president was emboldened to take this decision in part because those who will become its casualties are poor people of color in Africa and Asia. This was a small price to pay for rewarding a favored band of fundamentalists for their loyalty and silence during the campaign.

THE BLACK PLAGUE

The gag rule suggests even deadlier future policies against what may become the defining human struggle of the new century, the fight for Africans' right to health, indeed to life. While many global issues are important in United States relations with Africa, no issue is of greater immediate importance than HIV/AIDS. Addressing the AIDS pandemic is not just a question of what to do, but of whether members of the international community—especially the United States—are committed to do all that is necessary to defeat it in Africa.

During the past two decades 17 million people have died in Africa due to AIDS-related illnesses. Africans infected with HIV had been deemed as "untreatable" because of the artificially high prices of the anti-AIDS medications that became available five years ago. Now, responding to sharply falling AIDS drug prices brought on by competition from developing-country producers of generic versions; by African government moves to ignore patent rights to save lives; and by militant activism in the West—home to the world's largest and richest drug companies—public policymakers the world over are under pressure to produce a plan to stop the AIDS pandemic.

The World AIDS Conference in Durban, South Africa in July 2000 and the African Development Forum in Addis Ababa, Ethiopia in December increased public attention about the pandemic last year, both globally and within Africa. News reports stressed not only the overwhelmingly disproportionate effect of AIDS on Africa, but also the failure of the international community to respond with more than token action. Drug companies were targeted by activists and exposed by the media for blocking efforts to provide affordable treatment drugs to combat the effects of AIDS. The "Statement of Concern on Women and HIV/AIDS" issued at the conference drew particular attention to the significance of gender inequalities in the spread of the disease and to the fact that women and girls are placed at greatest risk of contracting it because of these disparities. But whether there is real progress during the year will depend on:

- the extent to which other African countries emulate Senegal and Uganda in putting into effect comprehensive AIDS prevention programs that combine access to condoms, sex education, treatment of opportunistic infections, safe injections, counseling, testing, and efforts to prevent mother-to-child transmission of HIV with highly visible political leadership and partnerships with civil society;

- whether wealthy countries and multilateral agencies even approach the $3 billion a year estimated to be needed for HIV prevention and the $4.5 billion a year for treatment (current funding levels are probably less than 10 percent of this for prevention, and almost none for treatment); and

- whether drug companies and the international community can be pressured to respond to the demand to reduce the prices of AIDS medicines to a level commensurate with their production costs.

AIDS is the black plague. Its epicenter is Africa; the region with the next-highest infection rate is the Caribbean. In the United States, HIV/AIDS infection rates are increasing mainly among young men and women of color. Although AIDS is a global threat that knows no borders and does not discriminate by race, at present it is mainly killing black people. And that is the cruel truth about why the world has failed to respond with dispatch.

This global crisis poses the question of how much inequality the United States is prepared to accept in the world and the obvious corollary: do Americans believe that Africa is part of their common humanity? But to see how much inequality the United States government is prepared to accept globally, one only has to look at how much inequality it accepts at home.

The glacial pace of the international response to AIDS has exposed an entrenched racial double standard. As Dr. Peter Piot of the UN AIDS program remarked just before the Durban World AIDS conference, "If this would have happened… with white people, the reaction would have been different."

The AIDS crisis in Africa is a stark reminder of the racial double standard that has marginalized African lives for the past 500 years. This double standard divides the world between rich and poor, white and black. The past five centuries have brought not only progress, but also considerable suffering—and Africa has suffered disproportionately, and still does. The consequences of slavery, colonialism, and imperialism have kept Africa underdeveloped and poor, although African leaders are certainly not blameless. Now AIDS threatens Africa's very survival.

TREATING THE CRISIS

The Bush administration has entered office at a moment of truth in the global struggle against HIV/AIDS. For Africa, the question of how the poor can get cheaper, safer, and effective medicines is vital. What steps can the United States take?

The Clinton administration's proposal in August 2000 to lend Africa $1 billion annually at commercial rates for the purchase of antiretroviral drugs was a cruel hoax and a vivid example of government-subsidized corporate greed. The plan sought to protect American pharmaceutical companies that were threatened by African rights under the World Trade Organization's rules to pursue parallel imports and compulsory licensing of anti-AIDS drugs. But the plan showed that the United States government was prepared to push Africa further into debt to prevent Africans from purchasing cheaper drugs from Brazil or India or from licensing local firms to produce generic versions at home. Some of the World Bank's anti-AIDS programs are largely financed along similar lines, causing some countries, such as Malawi, to reject them as worse than unsustainable. As Peter Walshe of the University of Notre Dame wrote in the February 2001 issue of *Common Sense,* "One is hard pressed to imagine a more cynical example of usury—the sin of lending surplus funds to take advantage of another's disadvantage."

The initial steps of the Bush White House have been no better. Within days of issuing the gag rule, the president expanded his assault on global public health by initiating a review of a May 2000 Clinton executive order mandating that the United States not challenge African countries seeking to exercise their rights to obtain cheaper versions of essential medications still under United States patent (Clinton issued the order to support Al Gore's presidential bid after anti-AIDS activists targeted Gore's early campaign rallies). Following a storm of protest, the White House announced that it would not reverse the executive order at this time.

One way in which elected officials can begin to address the pandemic is to dedicate a modest 5 percent of the budget surplus—approximately $9.5 billion in 2001—to a global health emergency fund. This would still fall short of what is needed, but it would be a leap above the paltry $325 million the United States is providing for AIDS efforts worldwide. Such funding will be necessary to help finance the acquisition of AIDS medications, either through bulk-purchasing mechanisms used for international vaccine programs, or through regional and national mechanisms. In any case purchases should be from the safest and cheapest source available regardless of patents (which would require a major policy shift by Washington). Such a policy will ensure that prices continue to fall to levels realistically accessible to African countries.

LIFE AFTER DEBT

The other key elements of an appropriate United States policy response to Africa would include the cancellation of African countries' bilateral debts to the United States and a leadership role in pressing for the outright cancellation of Africa's debts to the other creditors, especially the international financial institutions and European governments. The average African government spends more annually to finance its foreign debts than on national health care, and many spend more on debt servicing than on health and education combined. Zambia spends 40 percent of its total revenue on debt payments, while Cameroon, Guinea, Senegal, and Malawi all spend between 25 and 35 percent of theirs in the same manner.

These are mostly illegitimate foreign debts, contracted during the cold war by unrepresentative governments from Western creditors that sought to buy geopolitical loyalties, not to finance development in countries previously set back by Western colonialism. They beg the question: Who owes whom?

Early gains in health care in the 1960s have been all but negated by the free-market reforms imposed by international creditors beginning in the 1980s. The "one-size-fits-all" structural adjustment policies that African countries were forced to implement generally included currency devaluations, reductions in government spending (slashing public investments in health and education), privatization of many government services, and a focus on export-oriented agricultural development undermining food self-sufficiency. The AIDS pandemic now finds African states unable to cope.

At the end of 2000, the debt burden remained a pervasive obstacle to Africa's capacity to deal with other issues, despite additional relief won from creditors. The $34-billion package announced under the Heavily Indebted Poor Countries HIPC initiative included $25 billion for 18 African countries, almost half the outstanding debt owed by those countries. HIPC is the predominant international approach to debt relief and poses as a scheme to reduce the debt of world's most impoverished countries to "sustainable" levels by offering deep cuts in their total debt stock (including that held by the international financial institutions, governments, and private creditors) and pegging future payments to projected export earnings. The program is conditioned, however, on the lengthy implementation of economic austerity measures. In reality, HIPC seeks to protect creditors by using formulas designed to extract the maximum possible in debt payments from the world's poorest economies, and by continuing to use debt as leverage to prescribe economic policies for African countries.

Overall, the creditors' announcements of progress have satisfied neither debtor countries nor activists engaged on the issue, because their programs do not provide sustainable solutions. In fact, HIPC should be pronounced dead.

A continentwide meeting of debt-cancellation activists in Dakar, Senegal in December called not only for cancellation of illegitimate debts but also for reparations from rich countries for damage to Africa. Worldwide the demand is rising for a new mechanism to deal with the debt. In September UN Secretary General Kofi Annan called for the immediate suspension of all debt payments by HIPC countries and others that should be added to the list, and for an independent body—not controlled by creditor countries—to consider new ways to address the debt. Substantial debt cancellation would not only free up resources for public investments in health infrastructure and education, but would liberate African countries from the imperial economic dictates of the international financial institutions, which currently undermine democratic development. It would also restore commercial creditworthiness to countries still requiring a mix of grant and loan financing for long-term development efforts. The cancellation of German debts after World War II, or those of Poland toward the end of the cold war, are examples of previous Western willingness to provide a new lease on economic life to select deeply indebted states.

DANGEROUS LIAISONS

While most African countries are not at war, the effects of those that are embroiled in conflict touch the entire continent. Fragile cease-fires punctuated by episodes of violence, rather than open war, prevail in earlier conflict zones in West Africa (for example, Sierra Leone and the Casamance region of Senegal). A peace treaty between Ethiopia and Eritrea to end the 1998 border dispute that had escalated into a massive war claiming tens of thousands of lives was finally signed at the end of 2000, and deployment of UN observers began. The largest interlinked set of unresolved conflicts in Africa today include Angola in west central Africa; the Democratic Republic of Congo in the heart of the continent; Burundi and Rwanda in the Great lakes region (tying in not only to eastern Congo but also to Uganda and to Sudan); and the perennial war in Sudan itself.

If Secretary of State Powell is serious about contributing to peace in Africa, as he has suggested in appearances before Congress and elsewhere, then Washington must first pay its membership fees to the United Nations, including back dues for peacekeeping. Beyond paying its arrears, the administration will also need to give new and substantial financial, diplomatic, and security support to African and UN peacemaking efforts endorsed by the Organization of African Unity and legitimate subregional organizations. There should also be immediate restrictions on arms transfers to African countries, and greater public scrutiny of all American military training and education activities in Africa and for Africans in the United States. The Bush administration's intention to continue the Clinton policy of training and equipping select African forces as a way to avoid greater responsibility-sharing for international peace efforts in Africa risks turning an unaccountable and unreformed Nigerian military into Africa's Gurkhas. And the administration's evident interest in Sudan could actually jeopardize a democratic solution to the conflict if military measures are mistakenly given more weight than diplomacy and economic pressures, especially against foreign oil companies now financing Khartoum's war.

THE AFRICAN CENTURY

Despite the severe challenges Africa faces—or perhaps because of them and their centrality to global progress—there is no reason to despair of the continent's prospects for transformation in the twenty-first century. For American and international engagement with Africa to have the most positive impact, however, much greater leadership is required from African countries themselves. A number of developments suggest such leadership is forthcoming. The heads of state of three of Africa's subregional superpowers—Nigeria, South Africa, and Algeria—have been drafting what they call Africa's Millennium Plan, an effort to promote a continentwide consensus on development and security priorities and on mechanisms for financing Africa's economic growth while solving its debt crisis. The plan is likely to emphasize strengthening subregional institutions (in which they constitute dominant influential powers). Another initiative, sponsored by Libya's Muammar Qaddafi, proposes the establishment of a continental United States of Africa with mechanisms for cooperation similar to institutions of the European Union.

These and other efforts reveal just how acutely aware African leaders are of the weak positions they will continue to occupy on the global stage absent a greater collective voice. In addition, African civil society actors—from human rights organizations to African entrepreneurs—are tackling immediate problems such as AIDS education, constitutional reform, poverty eradication, and conflict resolution. Nearly every African conflict has a peace plan and process crafted by Africans themselves, but which lack adequate international support.

The promotion of peace, democracy, and development in Africa is necessary and vital to combat the global threats that will challenge the United States in the century ahead. The attainment of these goals is desirable on their own merits because of the economic and social benefits the United States will realize through savings from reduced expenditures on emergency relief activities, through the development of regional institutions able to cooperate more productively with the United States on various international issues, and through the expanding markets and investment opportunities that will help the United States sustain its economy while supporting African economic growth as well. Withdrawal, or neglect, would aid the establishment of a global apartheid that creates economic, social, and security disparities throughout the world and within countries along the color line—and that would put American democracy itself at risk.

SALIH BOOKER *is the executive director of Africa Action in Washington. He was previously senior fellow and director of the Africa studies program at the Council on Foreign Relations.*

Reprinted with permission from *Current History* magazine, May 2001, pp. 195-200. © 2001 by Current History, Inc.

UNIT 3

The Domestic Side of American Foreign Policy

Unit Selections

14. **On American Principles**, George F. Kennan
15. **The New Apathy**, James M. Lindsay
16. **Allies in Search of a Strategy**, The Economist

Key Points to Consider

- Should policymakers listen to the U.S. public in making foreign policy decisions? Defend your answer.

- What types of issues are the American public most informed about?

- Construct a public opinion poll to measure the relative support for internationalism and isolationism among students. What do you expect to find? Were your expectations correct?

- In what ways is U.S. foreign policy true to traditional American values?

- What is the most effective way for Americans to express their views to policymakers on foreign policy?

- What role should patriotism play in international humanitarian efforts? Is patriotism incompatible with Wilsonianism?

 **Links: www.dushkin.com/online/**
These sites are annotated in the World Wide Web pages.

American Diplomacy
http://www.unc.edu/depts/diplomat/
Carnegie Endowment for International Peace (CEIP)
http://www.ceip.org
RAND
http://www.rand.org

Conventional political wisdom holds that foreign policy and domestic policy are two very different policy arenas. Not only are the origins and gravity of the problems different, but the political rules for seeking solutions are dissimilar. Where partisan politics, lobbying, and the weight of public opinion are held to play legitimate roles in the formulation of health, education, or welfare policy, they are seen as corrupting influences in the making of foreign policy. An effective foreign policy demands a quiescent public, one that gives knowledgeable professionals the needed leeway to bring their expertise to bear on the problem. It demands a Congress that unites behind presidential foreign policy doctrines rather than one that investigates failures or pursues its own agenda. In brief, if American foreign policy is to succeed, politics must stop "at the water's edge."

This conventional wisdom has never been shared by all who write on American foreign policy. Two very different groups of scholars have dissented from this inclination to neglect the importance of domestic influences on American foreign policy. One group holds that the essence of democracy lies in the ability of the public to hold policymakers accountable for their decisions, and therefore that elections, interest group lobbying, and other forms of political expression are just as central to the study of foreign policy as they are to the study of domestic policy. A second group of scholars sees domestic forces as important because they feel that the fundamental nature of a society determines a country's foreign policy. These scholars direct their attention to studying the influence of such forces as capitalism, American national style, and the structure of elite values.

The influence of domestic politics was highly visible in the first 6 months of the Bush administration, which was accused of seeking to attract Hispanic voters by ending the Navy's bombing on the Puerto Rican island of Vieques and of promoting a plan to grant amnesty to illegal Mexicans in the United States. Pressure from the trucking industry led Congress to reject an administration proposal that would have allowed Mexican trucks into the United States as called for in the NAFTA treaty. Demonstrators took to the streets in Washington and Ottawa to protest globalization and the policies of the IMF and World Bank. And

pressure from U.S. industry contributed to Bush's decision to withdraw from the Kyoto protocol.

The terrorist attacks of September 11, 2001, altered the domestic politics of American foreign policy at least for the short run. Unity replaced division in the aftermath of the attacks as the public rallied behind President Bush. However, we can expect that controversial foreign policy issues unrelated to the war effort will continue to surface. A major challenge facing Bush will be to extend this sense of wartime unity and support for his leadership to these other foreign and domestic policy problems. It is a task that his father was unable to accomplish.

The readings in this section provide us with an overview of the ways in which U.S. domestic politics and foreign policy interact.

The first reading in this unit focus on the enduring influence that American values have on U.S. foreign policy. In "On American Principles," George Kennan, one of the leading architects of containment, asserts that the best way for the United States to help small states is to lead by the power of example. James Lindsay in "The New Apathy," examines the contemporary state of American public opinion on foreign policy matters. He characterizes it as apathetic internationalism and discusses its consequences for how American foreign policy is made. The final reading, "Allies in Search of a Strategy," explores the toughest challenge faced by President Bush in the aftermath of the terror attacks—maintaining the international coalition.

On American Principles

George F. Kennan

THE HISTORICAL EXPERIENCE

AT A LARGE dinner given in New York in recognition of his ninetieth birthday, the author of these lines ventured to say that what our country needed at this point was not primarily policies, "much less a single policy." What we needed, he argued, were principles—sound principles—" principles that accorded with the nature, the needs, the interests, and the limitations of our country." This rather cryptic statement could surely benefit from a few words of elucidation.

The place that principle has taken in the conduct of American foreign policy in past years and decades can perhaps best be explained by a single example from American history. In the aftermath of the Napoleonic wars, and particularly in the period beginning about 1815–25, there set in a weakening of the ties that had previously held the Spanish empire together, and demands were raised by certain of the American colonies for complete independence. Pressure was brought on Washington to take the lead not only in recognizing their independence at an early stage, but also in giving them political and presumably military aid in their efforts to consolidate their independence in the face of whatever resistance might be put up by the Spanish government.

These questions presented themselves with particular intensity when James Monroe was president (1817–25). At that time the office of secretary of state was occupied by John Quincy Adams. In view of his exceptional qualities and experience, and the high respect with which he was held in Washington and throughout the country, much of the burden of designing the U.S. response to those pressures rested on him.

Adams realized that the U.S. historical experience left no choice but to welcome and give moral support to these South American peoples in their struggle for the recognition and consolidation of their independence. But he had little confidence in the ability of the new revolutionary leaders to shape these communities at any early date into mature, orderly, and firmly established states. For this reason, he was determined that America not be drawn too deeply into their armed conflicts with Spain, domestic political squabbles, or sometimes complicated

relationships with their neighbors. Adams took his position, incidentally, not just with regard to the emerging South American countries, but also in relation to similar conflicts in Europe, particularly the efforts of Greek patriots to break away from the Turkish empire and establish an independent state.

These attitudes on Adams' part did not fail to meet with opposition in portions of the American political establishment. Some people, including the influential speaker of the House, Henry Clay, remembering America's own recent struggle for independence, felt strongly that the United States should take an active part in the similar struggles of other peoples. This, of course, was directly opposed to Adams' views. For this reason, Adams felt the need to take the problem to a wider audience and enlist public support for his views. In 1823, when he was invited by a committee of citizens to deliver a Fourth of July address in the nation's capital, he promptly agreed. The address was delivered in the premises of the House of Representatives, although not before a formal session of that body. The talk was presented as a personal statement, not an official one; and Adams took care to see that the text was printed and made widely available to the public.

A considerable part of the address was devoted to the questions I have just mentioned. On this subject Adams had some firm views. America, he said, had always extended to these new candidates for statehood "the hand of honest friendship, of equal freedom, and of generous reciprocity." It had spoken to them in "the language of equal liberty, of equal justice, and of equal rights." It had respected their independence. It had abstained from interference with their undertakings even when these were being conducted "for principles to which she [America] clings, as to the last vital drop that visits the heart." Why? Because, he explained, "America goes not abroad in search of monsters to destroy. She is the well-wisher to the freedom and independence of all. She is the champion and vindicator only of her own. She will recommend the general cause by the countenance of her voice, and the benignant sympathy of her example. She well knows that by once enlisting under other banners than her own, were they even the banners of foreign independence, she would involve herself beyond the power of extrication, in all the wars of interest and intrigue, of individual avarice, envy, and ambition, which assumed the colors and usurped the standards of freedom.... She might become the dictatress of the world. She would be no longer the ruler of her own spirit."

A government cannot play fast and loose with the interests of its people.

The relevance of this statement to many current problems—in such places as Iraq, Lebanon, Somalia, Bosnia, Rwanda, and even Haiti—is obvious. But that is not the reason why attention is being drawn to the statement at this point. What Adams was doing in those passages of his address was enunciating a principle of American foreign policy: namely, that, while it was "the well-wisher to the freedom and independence of all," America was also "the champion and vindicator only of her own." Those words seem to provide as clear an example as any of what the term "principle" might mean in relation to the diplomacy of this country or any other.

THE IDEAL VS. REALITY

HOW, THEN, using Adams' statement as a model, would the term "principle" be defined? One might say that a principle is a general rule of conduct of its relations with other countries. There are several aspects of the term, one or two of them touched on in this definition, others not, that require elucidation.

A principle was just defined as a general rule of conduct. That means that whoever adopts a principle does not specify any particular situation, problem, or bilateral relationship to which this rule should apply. It is designed to cover the entirety of possible or presumptive situations. It merely defines certain limits, positive and negative, within which policy, when those situations present themselves, ought to operate.

A principle, then, is a rule of conduct. But it is not an absolute one. The possibility is not precluded that situations might arise—unforeseeable situations, in particular—to which the adopted principle might not seem applicable or to the meeting of which the resources of the government in question were clearly inadequate. In such cases, exceptions might have to be made. This is not, after all, a perfect world. People make mistakes in judgment. And there is always the unforeseeable and unexpected.

But as new situations and challenges present themselves, and as government is confronted with the necessity of devising actions or policies with which to meet them, established principle is something that should have the first and the most authoritative claim on the attention and respect of the policymaker. Barring special circumstances, principle should be automatically applied, and whoever proposes to set it aside or violate it should explain why such violation seems unavoidable.

Second, a principle is, by definition, self-engendered. It is not something that requires, or would even admit of, any sort of communication, negotiation, or formal agreement with another government. In the case of the individual person (because individuals have principles, just as governments do), the principles that guide his life are a matter of conscience and self-respect. They flow from the individual's view of himself; the nature of his inner commitments, and his concept of the way he ought to behave if he is to be at peace with himself.

Now, the principles of a government are not entirely the same as those of an individual. The individual, in choosing his principles, engages only himself. He is at liberty to sacrifice his own practical interests in the service of some higher and more unselfish ideal. But this sort of sacrifice is one that a responsible government, and a democratic government in particular, is unable to take upon itself. It is an agent, not a principal. It is only a representative of others.

When a government speaks, it speaks not only for itself but for the people of the country. It cannot play fast and loose with their interests. Yet a country, too, can have a predominant collective sense of itself—what sort of a country it conceives itself or would like itself to be—and what sort of behavior would fit that concept. The place where this self-image finds its most natural reflection is in the principles that a country chooses to adopt and, to the extent possible, to follow. Principle represents, in other words, the ideal, if not always, alas, the reality, of the rules and restraints a country adopts. Once established, those rules and restraints require no explanation or defense to others. They are one's own business.

A drawing that appeared in *The New Yorker* magazine many years ago showed a cringing subordinate standing before the desk of an irate officer, presumably a colonel, who was banging the desk with his fist and saying: "There is no reason, damn it; it's just our policy."

Well, as a statement about policy, this was ridiculous. But had the colonel been referring to a principle instead of a policy, the statement might not have been so out of place. It would not be unusual, for example, for someone in authority in Washington today to say to the representative of a foreign government, when the situation warranted it, "I am sorry, but for us, this is a matter of principle, and I am afraid we will have to go on from there."

Let me also point out that principles can have negative as well as positive aspects. There can be certain things that a country can make it a matter of principle not to do. In many instances these negative aspects of principle may be more important than the positive ones. The positive ones normally suggest or involve action; actions have a way of carrying over almost imperceptibly from the realm of principle into that of policy, where they develop a momentum of their own in which the original considerations of principle either are forgotten or are compelled to yield to what appear to be necessities of the moment. In other words, it is sometimes clearer and simpler to define on principle the kinds of things a country will not go in for—the things that would fit with neither its standards nor its pretensions—than it is to define ways in which it will act positively, whatever the circumstances. The basic function of principles is, after all, to establish the parameters within which the policies of a country may be normally conducted. This is essentially a negative, rather than a positive, determination.

Another quality of a principle that deserves notice is that it is not, and cannot be, the product of the normal workings of the political process in any democratic country. It could not be decided by a plebiscite or even by legislative action. You would never get agreement on it if it came under that sort of debate, and whatever results might be achieved would deprive the concept of the degree of flexibility it requires to serve its purpose.

A principle is something that can only be declared, and then only by a political leader. It represents, of necessity, his own view of what sort of a country his is, and how it should conduct itself in the international arena. But the principle finds its reality, if it finds it at all, in the degree of acceptance, tacit or otherwise, that its proclamation ultimately receives from the remainder of the political establishment and from the populace at large. If that acceptance and support are not forthcoming in sufficient degree, a principle ceases to have reality. The statesman who proclaims it, therefore, has to be reasonably confident that, in putting it forward, he is interpreting, appealing to, and expressing the sentiment of a large proportion of the people for whom he speaks. This task of defining a principle must be seen as not just a privilege, but also a duty of political leadership.

Adams' statement certainly had this quality. The concept was indeed his own. But his formulation of it met wide and enthusiastic support among the people of his time, as he probably thought it would. The same could be said of similar declarations of principle from a number of other American statesmen, then and later. One has only to think, for example, of George Washington's statements in his farewell address, Thomas Jefferson's language in the Declaration of Independence, or Abraham Lincoln's in his Gettysburg speech. In each of those instances, the leaders, in putting forward their idea of principle, were speaking from their own estimate—a well-informed estimate—of what would find a sufficient response on the part of a large body, and not just a partisan body, of American opinion.

In no way other than by advocacy or proclamation from high office could such professions of principle be usefully formulated and brought forward. The rest of us may have our thoughts from time to time about the principles America ought to follow in its relations with the world, but none of us could state these principles in a manner that would give them significance for the behavior of the country at large.

THE POWER OF EXAMPLE

SO MUCH, then, for the essential characteristics of a principle and the manner in which it can be established. But there are those who will not be content with this abstract description of what a principle is, and who will want an example of what a principle valid for adoption by the United States of our day might look like.

The principle cited from Secretary Adams' Fourth of July speech was one that was applicable, in his view, to the situation then. The world now is, of course, different from his in many respects. There are those who will hold the gloomy view that such is the variety of our population and such are the differences among its various components, racial, social, and political, that it is idle to suppose that there could be any consensus among them on matters of principle. They have too little in common. There is much to be said for that view. This writer has at times been inclined to it himself. But further reflection suggests that there are certain feelings that we Americans or the great majority of us share, living as we do under the same political system and enjoying the same national consciousness, even though we are not always aware of having them. One may further suspect that if the translation of these feelings into principles of American behavior on the world scene were to be put forward from the highest governmental levels and adequately explained to the people at large, it might evoke a surprisingly strong response.

The best way for a larger country to help smaller ones is by the power of example.

But this understanding and support cannot be expected to come spontaneously from below. It will not be likely to emerge from a public media dominated by advertisers and the entertainment industry. It will not be likely to emerge from legislative bodies extensively beholden to special interests, precisely because what would be at stake here would be the feelings and interests of the nation as a whole and not those of any particular and limited bodies of the citizenry. An adequate consensus on principles, in other words, could come from below only by way of response to suggestions from above, brought forward by a leadership that would take responsibility for educating and forming popular opinion, rather than merely trying to assess its existing moods and prejudices and play up to them.

Now, coming back to the model of Adams' Fourth of July speech, the problems now facing this country show a strong resemblance to ones Adams had in mind when he gave that address in 1823. At that time the dissolution of the great empires was only just beginning, and few—at the most half a dozen—of the newly emerging states were looking to us for assistance. In the period between Adams' time and our own, and particularly in the wake of the Second World War, the process of decolonization has preceded at a dizzying pace, casting onto the surface of international life dozens of new states, many of them poorly prepared, as were those of Adams' time, for the responsibilities of independent statehood. This has led to many situations of instability, including civil wars and armed conflicts with neighbors, and there have been, accordingly, a great many appeals to us for political, economic, or military support.

To what extent, then, could Adams' principle of nonintervention, as set forth in 1823, be relevant to our situation today?

One cannot ignore the many respects in which our present situation differs from that which Adams was obliged to face. This writer is well aware of the increasingly global nature of our problems and the myriad involvements connecting our people and government with foreign countries. I do not mean to suggest a great reduction in those minor involvements. But what is at stake here are major political-military interventions by our government in the affairs of smaller countries. These are very different things.

First of all, we do not approach these questions with entirely free hands. We have conducted a number of such interventions in recent years, and at least three of these—Korea, Iraq, and Haiti—have led to new commitments that are still weighty and active.

There are several things to note about these interventions and commitments. First, while some may well have helped preserve peace or promote stability in local military relationships, this has not always been their stated purpose; in a number of instances, in particular, where we have portrayed them as efforts to promote democracy or human rights, they seem to have had little enduring success.

Second, lest there be any misunderstanding about this, the interventions in which we are now engaged or committed represent serious responsibilities. Any abrupt withdrawal from them would be a violation of these responsibilities; and there is no intention here to recommend anything of that sort. On the contrary, it should be a matter of principle for this government to meet to the best of its ability any responsibilities it has already incurred. Only when we have succeeded in extracting ourselves from the existing ones with dignity and honor will the question of further interventions present itself to us in the way that it did to Mr. Adams.

Third, instances where we have undertaken or committed ourselves to intervene represent only a small proportion of the demands and expectations that have come to rest on us. This is a great and confused world, and there are many other peoples and countries clamoring for our assistance. Yet it is clear that even these involvements stretch to the limit our economic and military resources, not to mention the goodwill of our people. And even if this were not a compelling limitation, there would still be the question of consistency. Are there any considerations being presented as justifications for our present involvement that would not, if consistently applied, be found to be relevant to many other situations as well? And if not, the question arises: If we cannot meet all the demands of this sort coming to rest upon us, should we attempt to meet any at all? The answer many would give to this question would be: yes, but only when our vital national interests are clearly threatened.

And last, beyond all these considerations, we have the general proposition that clearly underlay John Quincy Adams' response to similar problems so many years ago—his recognition that it is very difficult for one country to help another by intervening directly in its domestic affairs or in its conflicts with its neighbors. It is particularly difficult to do this without creating new and unwelcome embarrassments and burdens for the country endeavoring to help. The best way for a larger country to help smaller ones is surely by the power of example. Adams made this clear in the address cited above. One will recall his urging that the best response we could give to those appealing to us for support would be to give them what he called "the benign sympathy of our example." To go further, he warned, and try to give direct assistance would be to involve ourselves beyond the power of extrication "in all the wars of interest and intrigue, of individual avarice, envy, and ambition, which assumed the colors and usurped the standards of freedom." Who, today, looking at our involvements of recent years, could maintain that the fears these words expressed were any less applicable in our time than in his?

These, then, are some of the considerations bearing on the relevance of Adams' principle to the present problems of our country. This writer, for one, finds Adams' principle, albeit with certain adjustments to meet our present circumstances and commitments, entirely suitable and indeed greatly needed as a guide for American policy in the coming period. This examination of what Adams said, and its relevance to the problems of our own age, will in any case have served to illustrate what the word "principle" meant in his time and what it could, in this case or others, mean in our own.

One last word: the example offered above of what a principle might be revolved primarily around our relations with smaller countries that felt, or professed to feel, the need for our help in furthering their places in the modern world. These demands have indeed taken a leading place in our diplomacy of this post-Cold War era. But one should not be left with the impression that these relationships were all that counted in our present problems with diplomacy. Also at stake are our relations with the other great powers, and these place even more important demands on our attention, policies, and resources.

The present moment is marked, most happily, by the fact that there are no great conflicts among the great powers. This situation is without precedent in recent countries, and it is essential that it be cherished, nurtured, and preserved. Such is the destructive potential of advanced modern weapons that another great conflict between any of the leading powers could well do irreparable damage to the entire structure of modern civilization.

Intimately connected with those problems, of course, is the necessity of restraining, and eventually halting, the proliferation of weapons of mass destruction and of achieving their eventual total removal from national arsenals. And finally, also connected with these problems but going beyond them in many respects, there is the great environmental crisis our world is entering. To this crisis, too, adequate answers must be found if modern civilization is to have a future.

All of these challenges stand before us. Until they are met, even the many smaller and weaker countries can have no happy future. Our priorities must be shaped accordingly. Only when these wider problems have found their answers will any efforts we make to solve the problems of humane and civil government in the rest of the world have hopes of success.

George F. Kennan is Professor Emeritus in the School of Historical Studies at the Institute for Advanced Study in Princeton, N.J. This is his nineteenth article for Foreign Affairs. His first, "The Sources of Soviet Conduct," appeared in July 1947 under the pseudonym X.

From *Foreign Affairs*, March/April 1995, pp. 116–126. © 1995 by George F. Kennan. Reprinted by permission.

The New Apathy

How an Uninterested Public Is Reshaping Foreign Policy

James M. Lindsay

Americans and their leaders disagree on foreign policy. Polls show that 80 percent of Americans support the Comprehensive Test Ban Treaty (CTBT), but the Senate overwhelmingly rejected it. Two-thirds of Americans want to pay their country's back dues to the United Nations, but Congress took three years to appropriate the money and then demanded that the U.N. write off more than $400 million in bad debt. Nearly half of all Americans supported using ground troops in Kosovo, but the Clinton administration resisted admitting that it was even considering the option.

What explains this gap between what Americans want and what Washington does? The common answer—that politicians are misreading the public—is as mistaken as it is popular. It rests on the flawed premise that in politics, majority preferences trump all. But politicians worry less about what the public thinks about an issue than about how intensely it cares. And therein lies the great irony of the post-Cold War era: at the very moment that the United States has more influence than ever on international affairs, Americans have lost much of their interest in the world around them.

This apathetic internationalism is reshaping the politics of American foreign policy—encouraging the neglect of foreign affairs, distorting policy choices to favor the noisy few over the quiet many, and making it harder for presidents to lead. Left unchecked, these impulses will prevent the United States from capitalizing on its great power. So the most important foreign policy challenge facing the next president is not encouraging democracy in Russia, coping with a rising China, or advancing a liberal economic order. Instead, it is persuading the American people to pay more than lip service to their internationalist beliefs.

THE INTERNATIONALIST HABIT

Despite fears that Americans would turn inward when the Cold War ended, they still consistently support an internationalist foreign policy. Since 1947, the Gallup polling organization has periodically asked, "Do you think it will be best for the future of this country if we take an active part in world affairs or if we stay out of world affairs?" In 1999, 61 percent of those surveyed responded that active American involvement in the world was criti-cal—roughly in the middle of the range of responses recorded over the past 50 years.

The public's internationalist inclinations hold up when one moves from the abstract to the specific. During the Kosovo war, Gallup found that public support for "U.S. participation in NATO air strikes in Yugoslavia" reached as high as 61 percent, and the war always had more supporters than foes, despite widespread criticism of the Clinton administration's strategy. The Pew Research Center found in February that 64 percent of Americans think free trade is good for the country; 62 percent say the same about U.S. membership in the World Trade Organization. These numbers are virtually identical to those in polls taken before the failed WTO meeting in Seattle last year.

Unlike many on Capitol Hill, Americans have not embraced unilateralism. A 1998 poll by the Chicago Council on Foreign Relations found that 72 percent of Americans say that the United States should not act in international crises without its allies' support. This multilateralist preference also carries over to support for international organizations, which most Americans, as polls consistently show, want to strengthen, not weaken.

Moreover, the American public's internationalist attitudes span all parts of the country and key demographic groups. Despite fears that "Generation X" would turn its back on the world because it came of age after the Cold War, polls show it to be as internationalist, if not more so, than the World War II generation. And nothing in the polls suggests that isolationism or unilateralism has much appeal.

ELIANATION

Why, then, has the public's embrace of internationalism not translated into greater political support in Washington for American engagement abroad? The answer lies in a basic rule of politics: What really counts is not how many people line up on each side of an issue but how intensely each side holds its opinions. Politicians know that opposing impassioned voters may mean looking for a new job, so silent majorities get ignored. In politics, as in the rest of life, squeaky wheels get the grease.

Consider the saga of Elián González. Roughly two out of three Americans favored sending the six-year-old back to Cuba to live with his father. But while many politicians raced to the cameras to demand that Elián be allowed to stay in the United States, few argued publicly for returning him to Cuba—because the minority of Americans who backed Elián's Miami relatives cared passionately enough about the issue to reward their friends and punish their enemies. By contrast, the majority that favored returning Elián to Cuba was unlikely to remember the boy in six months, let alone use the voting booth to punish politicians who favored letting him stay.

Intensity is crucial to the politics of foreign policy today because the public's commitment to internationalism has ebbed over the past decade. During the Cold War, foreign affairs almost always topped the country's political agenda. Gallup regularly found that 10 to 20 percent—and sometimes even more—of those polled named a foreign policy issue as the most important problem facing the United States. But today most Americans dismiss foreign policy as relatively unimportant. Only two to three percent name foreign policy concerns as the most important problem facing the country, and Americans have trouble identifying foreign issues that concern them. When the Chicago Council on Foreign Relations asked people in 1998 to name the "two or three biggest foreign-policy problems facing the United States today," the most common response by far, at 21 percent, was "don't know."

The "don't know"s predominate because fewer Americans follow foreign affairs. In February 1999, as the Rambouillet summit convened, Pew found that only one in nine Americans said they followed news about Kosovo "very closely." By comparison, one in six said they closely followed the news of Joe DiMaggio's death. Or take the Senate's rejection of the CTBT, which *The New York Times* likened to the Senate's 1920 defeat of the Versailles Treaty: immediately after the CTBT vote, Pew found that half of those surveyed admitted they had heard nothing about it.

Americans ignore much of what happens overseas because they see little at stake. In September 1997, Pew asked 2,000 Americans how much impact other parts of the world had on the United States. Solid majorities answered "very little," even when asked about America's allies. (About 60 percent said that western Europe had little or no impact on their lives.)

These poll numbers all jibe with what people at both ends of Pennsylvania Avenue know firsthand: Americans endorse internationalism in theory but seldom do anything about it in practice. Americans may have wanted to pay their U.N. debt, but few wrote to Congress demanding action. Similarly, most Americans supported the CTBT, but they did not descend on Washington in busloads to save it. Americans approach foreign policy the way they approach physical fitness—they understand the benefits of being in good shape, but they still avoid exercise.

THE WASTELAND

Apathetic internationalism is reshaping American foreign policy in three ways. First, it encourages politicians, who naturally gravitate toward issues that matter to the public, to neglect foreign policy. Of course, foreign affairs still matter after the Cold War, but the political credit that once came with handling them has faded. President Bush discovered this when he was attacked in 1992 for being too interested in foreign affairs and defeated by a candidate who argued that the country should focus on domestic policy. Over his two terms, Bill Clinton largely delivered what he promised, and to judge by the polls, he did not suffer for it. Foreign policy remains a low priority in the 2000 campaign.

The neglect of foreign policy is, if anything, even worse on Capitol Hill. Both the Senate Foreign Relations Committee and the House International Relations Committee have trouble recruiting members. "Foreign Relations has been kind of a wasteland," admits Senator Chuck Hagel (R-Neb.), a staunch internationalist. "It is not a particularly strong committee to fundraise from." The House Republicans' famous "Contract with America" ignored foreign policy (save for a plug for national missile defense and a broadside against U.N. peacekeeping), and congressional Democrats have virtually purged foreign policy from their vocabulary.

Second, apathetic internationalism empowers squeaky wheels. This happens partly because politicians who abandon foreign policy for greener political pastures cede power to colleagues whose interest in foreign policy arises from personal passion. As former Representative David Skaggs (D-Colo.) noted about life on Capitol Hill, "When there are a few people who will die for the issue, and nobody else gets anywhere close to that, they can have their way."

"Skaggs' Law" clearly operated during the debates over U.N. dues and the CTBT. Once the U.N. bill passed the Senate, Representative Christopher Smith (R-N.J.) linked it to aid for international family-planning programs and for two years resisted intense pressure to back down. In the CTBT case, Senator Jon Kyl (R-Ariz.) and a few colleagues lobbied fellow Republicans and pressed Majority Leader Trent Lott (R-Miss.) to hold a vote. Their zeal—and the prospect that they would make Lott's life miserable if he postponed the vote—more than outweighed the fact that 24 Republican senators had publicly asked that the treaty be withdrawn.

Apathetic internationalism also favors the noisy few because it encourages politicians to cater to groups with narrow but intense preferences. That, after all, is where the political credit lies when the broader public is looking elsewhere. Indian-Americans have used their growing political clout (membership in the Congressional Indian Caucus is nearly double that of the Congressional Study Group on Germany) to block efforts to cut aid to India and persuade Congress to condemn Pakistani "aggression" in Kashmir. Human rights activists, labor unions, and environmentalists kept Clinton from winning "fast-track" negotiating authority in trade. The extreme right has turned U.S. participation in U.N. peacekeeping missions into political poison. Of course, narrow interests have always been part of American foreign policy. But without a countervailing push from the political center, they are fast becoming its defining feature.

Third, apathetic internationalism makes it harder for presidents to lead. During the early Cold War, both political savvy and policy arguments encouraged Congress to rally around the president; public rebuffs could embolden Moscow and bring punishment at the polls. Vietnam destroyed this knee-jerk support for the president, but congressional deference survived (albeit tattered) well into the 1980s. Ronald Reagan's great ally in fights over arms control, contra aid, and other issues was moderate Democrats' reluctance to defeat his policies outright. That caution partly stemmed from policy considerations—a major public defeat would weaken the president's standing abroad—but also reflected Democrats' fear that Reagan would blame them for playing politics with national security.

But in the 1990s, with no major threat to U.S. security on the horizon and with public interest waning, the costs of challenging the president plummeted. In April 1999, during the Kosovo war, the House refused to vote to support the bombing. Not to be outdone, the Senate voted down the CTBT in October even though President Clinton and 62 senators had asked that it be withdrawn. These episodes were major departures from past practice. When Congress sought to wrest control of foreign policy from the president on issues such as Vietnam, the MX missile, and contra aid, it had vocal public support. On Kosovo and the CTBT, Congress challenged Clinton even though most Americans backed his positions.

The decline in congressional deference has accompanied a growing politicization of foreign policy, for the same basic reason. When the public is engaged, foreign policy is a risky way to score political points; demonizing opponents and exaggerating policy differences energizes core supporters but alienates less fervent voters. But when the public is disengaged, foreign policy becomes—to paraphrase Clausewitz—the continuation of domestic politics by other means. The temptation to use foreign policy for partisan gain is hardly restricted to members of Congress or Republicans; witness Clinton's insistence, against all available evidence, that the CTBT had fallen victim to "the new isolationists in the Republican Party." And Senator Joseph Biden (D-Del.) was simply being more honest than most when he pointed out an upside to a vote against the CTBT by William Roth, a Republican senator up for reelection. "Bingo!" Biden said. "That's $200,000 worth of ads."

Without denying the enmity that many congressional Republicans reserve for Clinton, Congress is not likely to start deferring again to the White House when he leaves it. Strikingly, 45 percent of current senators and 61 percent of current representatives first took office after 1992. They have known only fractious relations with the commander in chief. Resurrecting the old norms that members should defer to presidents and leave politics at the water's edge will hardly be automatic, and members are certainly under no pressure from the public to behave. In 1998, the Chicago Council on Foreign Relations found that 43 percent of Americans thought that Congress' role in foreign policy was about right—the highest number recorded since the Council's quadrennial surveys began in 1974.

MALIGN NEGLECT

The consequences of apathetic internationalism—however much they please isolationists, pandering politicians, and ethnic groups relishing their newfound clout—should trouble anyone who believes that the United States must be engaged in world affairs. They are eroding America's capacity to lead and encouraging what Treasury Secretary Lawrence Summers has called the "malign neglect" of U.S. global standing.

International affairs spending provides a clear case in point. Just as everyone wants to go to heaven but no one wants to die, politicians routinely deride the idea that global leadership can be had on the cheap but do little to adequately fund American diplomacy. The fiscal year 2000 budget allotted only $22.3 billion to international affairs—a 40 percent drop in real spending from the peak of the mid-1980s even though the overall federal budget is running a surplus for the first time in decades. The resulting tin-cup diplomacy is penny-wise and pound-foolish. The few tens of millions the United States will save by lowering its U.N. dues, for instance, hardly make up for the damage done to the U.N. as an instrument for U.S. foreign policy.

This myopia about what the United States needs to accomplish its goals abroad goes beyond international affairs spending. Human rights, labor, and environmental groups blocked fast-track and cost the United States the opportunity to push ahead with the trade liberalization that most Americans believe will enhance their prosperity. Narrow-minded laws like the Helms-Burton sanctions, which punish other countries for trading with Cuba, needlessly squander allied goodwill while offering almost no prospect of success. How can any country sustain its foreign policy if it continually gives short shrift to its national interests?

Malign neglect also erodes the belief that the country as a whole benefits from giving the president a degree of deference in foreign affairs. Although presidents possess no monopoly on foreign policy virtue, history has shown that Congress simply cannot run foreign affairs. To be sure, Congress serves the public interest when it scrubs presidential initiatives and advances alternatives of its own. But one can have too much congressional assertiveness as well as too little. The more Congress reverses the president—especially when it does so gratuitously, as in the CTBT case—the more timid the White House will be. Moreover, presidential defeats diminish other countries' confidence in America's resolve and in the White House's ability to deliver.

Finally, malign neglect makes it easier to forget that foreign policy should be as much about shaping the world to America's liking as it is about meeting threats from abroad. America is prosperous and secure today because

Cold War internationalists, with broad public support, had a vision of the world they wanted to create. Anyone searching Washington today for a similar vision will come away disappointed. Politicians focused on domestic affairs do not see the outside world as a source of opportunity; narrow interests are not looking to transform the world. Historians will look back on the first decade of the post-Cold War era as a squandered opportunity.

KEEPING THE FAITH

The key to fighting apathetic internationalism is persuading the public to act on its internationalist preferences. If politicians believe they will be rewarded for defending broad interests and penalized for tending to narrow ones, they will pay more heed to foreign policy, and squeaky wheels will lose out to a not-so-silent majority.

But how to raise the political stakes in foreign policy? A renewed threat to American security would clearly do the trick. So might a recession. Just as people appreciate the wonders of indoor plumbing only when it breaks down, tough economic times will drive home to many Americans just how much their prosperity depends on an internationalist foreign policy. When the Asian economic crisis suddenly deprived Midwestern farmers of some of their biggest markets, they and their representatives became ardent supporters of the International Monetary Fund and new markets abroad.

It would be better and less painful, of course, to raise the political stakes on foreign policy through persuasion. But who could play this role? Certainly not the public itself, and probably not Congress. Despite congressional moderates' laudable efforts to rejuvenate the political center after the CTBT fiasco, Congress' internal divisions render it incapable of articulating a clear foreign policy message.

Business, however, could do much better. It has both the resources and the incentives to mount a campaign for internationalism. Exports account for more than ten percent of the U.S. economy, and American businesses large and small sell their products abroad. Meanwhile, the malign neglect of America's global standing is undermining the international infrastructure that promotes U.S. business expansion abroad.

But if business is going to raise the political stakes on foreign policy, it must take its case to the country. The traditional corporate strategy of focusing on trade and working the corridors of power in Washington when a major vote approached made sense when an internationalist consensus dominated Capitol Hill. It does not work when the political case for engagement is weak and its opponents vocal. Indeed, antitrade groups redefined the terms of the debate at Seattle—and put the future of freer trade at risk—not because they had the better arguments but because they were the only ones on the playing field.

Business appears to have learned from Seattle. In the battle for permanent normal trading relations for China, for example, groups such as the Business Roundtable, the Chamber of Commerce, and the American Farm Bureau mobilized executives, workers, and farmers around the country to lobby members of Congress. This grassroots approach could be broadened into a sustained campaign to remind Americans what they have at stake overseas. One initiative worth emulating and expanding is USA*Engage, a broad-based coalition of nearly 700 business and agricultural groups that opposes the proliferation of unilateral U.S. economic sanctions.

Private foundations could also pitch in by going beyond scholarly research, however important, to underwrite outreach programs to educate Americans about the importance of U.S. engagement. These efforts should be linked to similar efforts by nongovernmental organizations such as the United Nations Association and local councils on foreign relations. These education campaigns will not magically transform Americans into ardent internationalists, but they could help.

Even under the best of circumstances, however, civil society can do only so much. The ultimate responsibility for convincing the public to act on its internationalist beliefs lies with the White House. In a 500-channel world, no one can dominate the political agenda and mobilize support the way the president can. Apathetic internationalism makes it harder for presidents to lead, but it does not make it impossible. After all, Clinton scored some important foreign policy victories: enlarging NATO, ending the war in Bosnia, and securing approval for the North American Free Trade Agreement, the General Agreement on Tariffs and Trade, and the Chemical Weapons Convention, to name only the most well known. He won because, unlike in his other forays into foreign policy, he committed the full powers of his office to winning, built bipartisan coalitions in Congress, and made the case to the American public. That mix of vision and dedication—simple to sketch but difficult to do—is the recipe for future presidential leadership in foreign policy.

With Clinton's term all but over, the responsibility for persuading Americans to abandon their apathetic internationalism will lie with the next president. Both Al Gore and George W. Bush are internationalists by inclination, but their predilections are beside the point; Clinton's leanings were internationalist as well. Rather, the issue is whether the next president will devote time and political capital to persuade Congress and the public of engagement's importance. Even then, there will be no quick fix. Absent a clear and present danger, the temptation to dismiss foreign policy as a trifle will remain powerful. But the malign neglect of America's world standing will worsen badly if the next president turns out to be an apathetic internationalist.

JAMES M. LINDSAY is Senior Fellow at the Brookings Institution.

Reprinted by permission of *Foreign Affairs*, September/October 2000, Vol. 79, No. 5, pp. 2-8. © 2000 by the Council on Foreign Relations, Inc.

Allies in search of a strategy

First, build the coalition. Then, think what to do

LONDON AND WASHINGTON, DC

TWO days after the destruction of the World Trade Centre in New York and the simultaneous assault on America's military nerve centre, the Pentagon, President George Bush declared the United States to be "at war" with international terrorism. He enjoined America's soldiers, and with them the American people, to "get ready" for military conflict and for further sacrifice. At the memorial service in Washington's National Cathedral for the close to 6,000 victims of the bloodiest terrorist assault in history, the leader of the world's most powerful country declared that this conflict, "begun on the timing and terms of others… will end in a way, and at an hour, of our choosing."

Mr Bush picked his words to send a message of resolve not just to America but to the world. But what does it mean to be at war with terrorism? Who are the enemy? What are the right tools, and what is the best strategy, to fight them with? If this is indeed to be the first war of the 21st century, is victory possible against an enemy that demands neither territory nor any other recognisable war booty, and seeks only the maximum possible destruction with no calculation of restraint? And what might such a victory look like?

Mr Bush's immediate target is clear. This week he called on the Taliban, the rulers of Afghanistan, to hand over Osama bin Laden, the fugitive terrorist leader they have long sheltered—or else. He wanted Mr bin Laden, he said, "dead or alive". Other western intelligence agencies concur with the initial judgment of America's: that all the evidence gathered so far points to Mr bin Laden as the prime suspect.

But even getting at him, let alone the loosely-knit and widely-dispersed terrorist network over which he presides, will not be easy. Earlier this week, a high-level Pakistani delegation, given special United Nations dispensation to break the international embargo and travel to Afghanistan to try to talk the Taliban into handing him over, left Kabul empty-handed. Amid calls for Afghanistan to renew its *jihad* ("struggle" or "holy war") against America, the country's highest-ranking Islamic clerics, summoned by their leader, Mullah Muhammad Omar,to respond to the mounting pressure from the outside world, said that Mr bin Laden should leave voluntarily. Mr Bush is unlikely to wait long before striking back at the man and the organisation he suspects of causing the greatest number of casualties on American territory in a single day since the civil war, and at the country that harbours him. On September 20th, 100 extra American war planes were moved to the Gulf in preparation for action.

In that strict sense, America is not only sounding, but acting, as if it is going to war. Reserves are being called up. Congress has passed a resolution giving the president power to "use all necessary and appropriate force" against any individual, organisation or country that played any role in last week's attacks, and allowing for pre-emptive strikes to prevent any more. It has already appropriated $20 billion for that purpose, on top of the $20 billion assigned for rescue and clean-up operations at home. Public opinion is overwhelmingly in favour of military action against terrorists, though more nervous of using force against states that sponsor them.

International opinion is a little more varied. Even those countries that back America to the hilt are calling for coolness and deliberation before military action is taken. Others, such as Russia and China, want nothing to be done without the approval of the UN Security Council.

But NATO responded last week by invoking, for the first time in its 52-year history, Article 5 of its founding treaty, which declares the attack on America to be an attack on the alliance as a whole, and enables America to call on its allies for military support. And few would argue that America does not have the legal right, under Article 51 of the UN charter, to strike back at its tormentors. The United States is naturally reserving the right to take unilateral action; but talks are under way with many countries, from America's close allies in Europe to Islamic Pakistan and some of the countries of Central Asia and even fartherflung Australia, to gather the military support, access to bases and overflight rights that America may need.

Retaliation may indeed be justified and necessary—if only to persuade the world, and especially other would-be terrorist groups, of the strength of America's determination to fight back after such devastating attacks on its territory, its values and its institutions. But the struggle America is preparing to wage will be long, complex and dangerous. President Bush has made it clear that this is not just a war against the terrorists responsible for last week's atrocities, but against terrorism itself.

Needed: allies inside Islam

That is why this will be unlike any other war America has fought. Mr Bush has called it a "crusade", a word with just the bruising overtones that some Islamic extremists have used in the past to justify their murderous assault on America and all it represents.Yet the president has no intention of declaring war on the Islamic world. On the contrary, he is now hoping for direct help from a number of its governments, from the Middle East to Asia, in isolating and eventually eliminating groups, such as Mr bin Laden's, that use Islam as a cover for their crimes. However, both he and his senior officials have given warning that America will go after not only terrorist groups but also the governments that sponsor or support them.

Apart from Afghanistan itself, America's list of "the usual suspects" in the terrorism business has long included Iran, Iraq, Libya, Syria, North Korea, Sudan and Cuba. Since last week's attacks, the deputy secretary of defence, Paul Wolfowitz, has talked of "ending" states which sponsor terrorism. If it refused to hand over Mr bin Laden and his associates, Afghanistan's regime would be one obvious target.

Might Iraq be another? In the past there have been reported links between Iraq and Mr bin Laden. So far, there is no clear evidence of Iraqi involvement in last week's carnage. If more were to emerge, America would have little compunction about attacking a regime that is thought to be rebuilding its illegal chemical, biological and possibly nuclear weapons.

Yet most of the states on America's list—Iraq stands out as the exception—have condemned last week's attacks. For the first time in more than 20 years, worshippers in Iran failed to chant "Death to America!" at the start of their Friday prayers. Words of condolence come naturally in the aftermath of ferocious acts of terrorism. Yet this could be a chance for America to find common ground with old foes such as Iran to end some of their official and unofficial support for groups with terrorist connections—a first victory, perhaps, for America's will to prosecute this new war.

Will Mr Bush's chosen tools be diplomacy or force? He will need both. Military pressure—and possible military strikes—on Afghanistan would not just assuage Americans' demands for retaliation, but might help to deter some governments from further aid to Mr bin Laden's group or others bent on terrorism. Yet his senior aides admit that military strikes—even a whole series of them—cannot win a war with an aim as all-embracing as this one. Indeed, unless America is prepared to alienate wide swathes of the moderate Muslim world, by launching military attacks against any country suspected of having terrorists somewhere on its territory, the direct military options available to America may soon come to seem rather limited.

Pinprick missile attacks against terrorist training camps in Afghanistan and a suspected chemical-weapons plant in Sudan, launched by President Bill Clinton in 1998 after attacks on the American embassies in Kenya and Tanzania, did nothing to deter Mr bin Laden and his followers. Neither have Russia's scorched-earth tactics against rebels (Russia calls them terrorists) in Chechnya, which have reduced that country to rubble. And would the targets be the 1,000 or so operatives thought to be in Mr bin Laden's al-Qaeda network worldwide, or the wider universe of terror organisations, including Islamic Jihad and Hamas in Palestine? If simply killing terrorists were enough, Israel would by now be the safest country on earth.

Amid all the talk of war, it has been left to Cohn Powell, the secretary of state, to spell out the beginnings of a broader strategy. He has called for "a campaign that goes after not just retaliatory satisfaction, but goes after eliminating this threat by ripping it up, by going after its finances, by going after its infrastructure, by making sure we're applying all the intelligence assets we can to finding what they are up to." And the measure of its success? "No more attacks like this against the United States and our interests around the world."

In this campaign, as in the narrower military one that is about to be unleashed, America will need allies. But to qualify as a friend of America's, revulsion and words of moral support will not be enough. Mr Powell has talked of a "new benchmark": how governments now respond to America's requests for help in the war against terrorism "will be a means by which we measure our relationship with them in the future."

Cold war parallels

In many ways, the nearest parallel to America's new thinking is the determination to contain communism that marked the cold war. This was an equally all-embracing struggle that had military, diplomatic, economic and ideological elements. Of course, the cold war was also a classic military stand-off which ended when the Soviet block finally threw off communism. Islam, by contrast, is here to stay, and many of its adherents are as shocked as the rest of the world at the barbarity of the crimes just committed in its name. Still, as a way of viewing the outside world, the fight against terrorism may now come to represent for America what the cold war

did for much of the second half of the 20th century: a means of ordering defence priorities and national budgets at home; a way of organising military, political and diplomatic power abroad; a new focus for old institutions and an organising concept for new ones. Above all, a way of telling friend from foe.

Some have understood this more clearly than others. America has been particularly pleased with the support it has received from Pakistan. That country's leader, General Pervez Musharraf, was quick to offer America assistance, both in pressing the Taliban to give up Mr bin Laden and in offering America use of its air space and other support. Pakistan,through its links with Afghanistan, will have a major role if military efforts are made to dislodge the Taliban from power.

By helping America, Pakistan is taking a risk. Its own Islamic militants have close connections to Afghanistan's mullahs, and American military action could cause a backlash inside Pakistan. But Mr Musharraf understood that this was the moment he had to choose sides, and has made sterling efforts to induce his people to accept that.

If Pakistan is ever to get out from under its mountain of debt and achieve a degree of political stability, it needs the economic support of the West. Japan has already suggested it may resume some of the aid to Pakistan that was cut off after the Indian and Pakistani nuclear tests in 1998. America may do the same. And at a time when Pakistan's great rival, India, has been seeking a new connection with America, Mr Musharraf has a much-needed opportunity to strengthen his own American links. Help with the war against terrorism could earn Pakistan some American sympathy in its argument with India over Kashmir. At the least, Pakistan's response to the events of the past week may have corrected what Pakistan saw as a dangerous western tilt towards India. But Pakistan, like other countries, can expect to come under pressure to clamp down on its own extremists.

Other countries will face hard decisions, too. Israel and the Palestinians have been pressed to accept a ceasefire and open talks that could dampen down their months of fighting; America wants nothing to get in the way of its efforts to rally Arab support to the anti-terrorist cause. Saudi Arabia has long supported America's presence in the Gulf, while trying to protect its own regime by funnelling money to fundamentalist groups, including some in Pakistan. This has indirectly helped to finance outfits like Mr bin Laden's. Pressure to end

The military options
Take your pick

A tough set of choices

WASHINGTON, DC

WHAT are the ways of fighting such a war? Michael O'Hanlon of the Brookings Institution offers four:

1. Kosovo-style air strikes against Afghanistan. This could be done by aircraft carriers in the Gulf (to where many extra combat aircraft have been sent) and/or stealth bombers flying from America. The combination of precision and heavyweight bombs could almost certainly destroy Mr bin Laden's camps and the Taliban's handful of military bases. But Mr bin Laden himself might well escape, along with much of his terrorism-planning staff. So might much of the Taliban's armoury—small arms, rocket-propelled grenades, 2,000-5,000 mortars and Stinger missiles that are deadly against helicopters.

2. Bombing other countries that help or shelter terrorists, not just Afghanistan. But the wider the attacks, the louder the protests in the Muslim world and elsewhere. The possible exception is Iraq. If Saddam Hussein were found to have been involved in last week's terrorism, attacks on his palaces and his Republican Guard might improve the chances of overthrowing him.

3. Invading Afghanistan. This would be the surest way of destroying the terrorists—if it worked. But it would require bases in either Pakistan or Iran, and preferably the help of their soldiers. Mr bin Laden might slip away. And, as both Britain and Russia can record, Afghanistan is no pushover. "Lice, dirt, blood," is one Russian general's memory.

4. Commando raids plus support for the Afghan resistance. America has 5,000 Green Berets, 2,000 Rangers, 2,200 navy Seals and hundreds of men in the crack Delta Force. Britain has its own efficient special forces. Other countries might help. This is the likeliest way of killing or capturing Mr bin Laden. The anti-terrorism allies could also arm and train the anti-Taliban Northern Alliance, even though its leader, Ahmad Masoud, has just been killed. But Mr O'Hanlon reckons all this could take a long time, and cost hundreds of allied lives.

---

this practice could put Saudi Arabia's stability at risk. But difficult calculations will have to be made by many governments—including America's.

Puzzlingly, for an administration that came to office vowing to nurture old friendships and alliances, Mr Bush's team had seemed to spend its first months doing the opposite. Its decision to abandon the Kyoto protocol on global warming irritated many of its friends. So did its readiness to set aside the Anti-Ballistic Missile (ABM) treaty, and its reluctance to accept the constraints of multilateral arms-control agreements. America, it seemed, was prepared to operate on its own: happy if others wanted to tag along, unconcerned if they did not. Will this now change?

Holding onto friends

The Bush administration is already making better use of the international tools that are available. Although America will not submit its military plans to the UN Security Council for approval, it has moved quickly to speed payment of its longstanding financial arrears to the organisation, giving its new ambassador, John Negroponte, a cleaner diplomatic slate for gathering sup-

port in the fight against terrorism. The strong condemnation of the terrorist attacks by both the Security Council and the General Assembly has been appreciated. Among the UN conventions already on the books or under debate are a number designed specifically to combat terrorism. These include one, adopted in 1999, to help end the financing of terrorist organisations. America is likely to press more countries to put their names to this.

If nothing else, the assaults on the World Trade Centre and the Pentagon have demonstrated to Americans that they cannot simply look to their own defences and forget the world outside. An international terrorist onslaught needs an international response. Can America pull together such a coalition, and sustain it? Over the next few weeks there will be more at stake than Afghanistan and Mr bin Laden.

Right now, America seems to have more staunch friends and sympathisers than Mr Bush knows what to do with. France's president, Jacques Chirac, and Britain's prime minister, Tony Blair, were both in Washington to confer with Mr Bush this week. These are allies who not only possess the most deployable military forces in Europe, should America need them, but also have influence in parts of

the world, from Europe to the Middle East and Asia, that will be equally useful if America's diplomats are to turn the coalition of sympathisers into something more useful and enduring.

Yet there is still worry about the possibility of America going it alone. Despite the strong political and emotional support provided by the allies over the past week, a number of European politicians have said that this does not amount to a "blank cheque" for anything America may now wish to do. Both Mr Chirac and Mr Blair will have wanted to impress on Mr Bush this week the need for a measured and proportionate response, and for a readiness to listen to the concerns of allies. The wider and less discriminating America's military attacks are, should they come, the harder it will be to keep some of America's European allies on board. Yet, if cracks were to appear in the support for America from its NATO allies, the effects could be disastrous—for both. The worry in Europe is that this danger may be less obvious to the administration in Washington than it is to onlookers in London, Paris or Berlin.

Assuming that these dangers can be avoided, how might the change in America's thinking affect the balance of its relations with the other two big powers, Russia and China? Both have long shared America's concern with the fundamentalist threat emanating from Afghanistan, and have condemned last week's attacks. Yet both have their differences with America. Will this be taken as a time to narrow these, or exploit them?

Russia's reaction has been ambivalent. Its defence minister, Sergei Ivanov, was quick to refuse America access to military bases in Central Asia on the borders with Afghanistan—too quick, given that these bases are in supposedly sovereign countries. Uzbekistan has since sounded more ready to accommodate any American requests for help; Tajikistan, more closely under Russia's thumb, has said little.

Yet Russia's diplomats can also see some opportunities for their country in co-operating with America. Russia has long bristled at western criticism of its brutal war in Chechnya, and is clearly hoping that this will now subside if it makes common diplomatic cause with America against Islamic terrorism. It remains to be seen whether Russia will also now temper its support in the Security Council for lifting sanctions on Iraq.

Vladimir Putin, Russia's president, had already agreed to talk to America about new understandings that might amend the ABM treaty and allow America room to explore anti-missile defences. Although such defences could not have stopped the recent terrorist attacks, America is unlikely to abandon its quest for them. Indeed, its concern about future threats from unpredictably violent countries and people who are attempting to acquire long-range missiles is naturally going to intensify. So too will pressure on Russia to tighten the loopholes in its export controls that have repeatedly allowed missile and related technologies to slip through the net.

So far, Russia has been part of the problem. Can it now become part of the solution? Mr Putin may yet be hoping that, in return for Russia's co-operation in the war against terrorism and a readiness to strike a new strategic bargain over nuclear weapons and missile defences, America will heed Russian concerns by delaying or abandoning any plans to bring the Baltic states into an enlarged NATO.

The Chinese reaction has been even more ambivalent. As expected, China has called formally for America to act only with the approval of the UN Security Council (where China, like Russia, has a veto). Yet it is unlikely to press the matter. It has a keen interest in ending Afghanistan's role as a haven for Islamic terrorists, not least because it sees that as the source of much instability around the region, including in its own Xinjiang province. And it has an interest in improving ties with America after the collision in April between a Chinese fighter and an American surveillance plane off the Chinese coast.

China, too, has its own agenda. This week it pointedly called for America to help in its fight against "separatism"—a dig at continued American support for Taiwan. Despite official promises to the contrary, Chinese firms are as active as ever in supplying illicit technology to dodgy customers who may one day add to the threat the world now faces. America would like more co-operation from China in the fight against terrorism. But few people doubt that, in the longer run, America and China will remain rivals in Asia.

Outward, look

America has been redefined by disaster three times in the past 75 years. The first was in 1929, when the Wall Street crash began a decade of depression at home and isolationism abroad. That was halted by the second disaster: the Japanese attack on Pearl Harbour. Eventually, once war ended, the country saw 50 years of unparalleled domestic wealth and international engagement. This could be the third shock. There is clearly a risk that America could turn inward, driven by emotional horror at the evil the outside world can do. Yet, to judge by the first rallying of both government and people, almost the reverse is happening. America is seeing this tragedy as a reason to provide renewed leadership, to become engaged abroad, and to look resolutely outward for friends.

UNIT 4
The Institutional Context of American Foreign Policy

Unit Selections

17. **The Pitfalls of Universal Jurisdiction**, Henry A. Kissinger
18. **States' Rights and Foreign Policy: Some Things Should Be Left to Washington**, Brannon P. Denning and Jack H. McCall
19. **The Folk Who Live on the Hill**, James Kitfield
20. **Farewell to the Helmsman**, Christopher Hitchens
21. **Perils of Presidential Transition**, Glenn P. Hastedt and Anthony J. Eksterowicz
22. **The One Percent Solution: Shirking the Cost of World Leadership**, Richard N. Gardner
23. **America's Postmodern Military**, Don M. Snider

Key Points to Consider

- How relevant is the Constitution to the conduct of American foreign policy? Do courts have a legitimate role to play in determining the content of U.S. foreign policy? What role should international law play in making policy?

- If you were a Supreme Court justice, how would you rule on a case involving a state's right to conduct its own foreign policy? Explain your position.

- Is Congress best seen as an obstacle course that presidents must navigate successfully in making foreign policy? What is the proper role of Congress in making foreign policy? Is it the same for military and economic policy?

- Which of the foreign affairs bureaucracies discussed in this unit is most important? Which is the most in need of reform? Which is most incapable of being reformed?

- Prioritize which parts of the U.S. government are most in need of reform in terms of making foreign policy. In your view, are the institutions that make American foreign policy capable of being reformed? Are institutional reforms really necessary for the content of American foreign policy to change?

- Are we spending too much on foreign and defense policy? Where should we spend more? Where should we cut our spending?

- How deeply involved in the political process should the military become? What types of values should we expect professional officers to hold?

 **Links: www.dushkin.com/online/**
These sites are annotated in the World Wide Web pages.

Central Intelligence Agency (CIA)
http://www.cia.gov

The NATO Integrated Data Service (NIDS)
http://www.nato.int/structur/nids/nids.htm

United States Department of State
http://www.state.gov/index.html

United States Institute of Peace (USIP)
http://www.usip.org

Central to any study of American foreign policy are the institutions responsible for its content and conduct. The relationship between these institutions often is filled with conflict, competition, and controversy. The reasons for this are fundamental. Edwin Corwin put it best: The Constitution is an "invitation to the president and Congress to struggle over the privilege of directing U.S. foreign policy." Today, this struggle is not limited to these two institutions. At the national level the courts have emerged as a potentially important force in the making of American foreign policy. State and local governments have also become highly visible actors in world politics.

The power relationships that exist between the institutions that make American foreign policy are important for at least two reasons. First, different institutions represent different constituencies and thus advance different sets of values regarding the proper direction of American foreign policy. Second, decision makers in these institutions have different time frames when making judgments about what to do. The correct policy on peacekeeping in Kosovo or conducting a war against terrorism looks different to someone coming up for election in a year or two than it does to a professional diplomat.

Institutions and policy are so tightly intertwined that it often becomes impossible to talk about one without the other. Vietnam quickly brings to mind images of the "imperial presidency," Pearl Harbor is associated forever with the need for more coordination among the national security bureaucracies, and references to the Central Intelligence Agency (CIA) abound in any study of U.S. foreign policy toward Cuba, Angola, Chile, Iran, and Guatemala.

This close linkage between institutions and policies suggests that if American foreign policy is to conduct a war successfully against terrorism, American policy-making institutions must also change their ways. Many commentators were not confident of the ability of these institutions to respond to the apparently more benign and enemy-free character of the post–cold war period that preceded the terrorist attacks of September 11, 2001. They saw budgetary power bases and political predispositions that were rooted in the cold war as unlikely to provide a hospitable environment for policies designed to further human rights, engage in multilateral peacemaking operations, protect the environment, or open markets to American products. The same concerns exist about the ability of American institutions to conduct a war against terrorism. This war, some note, will be less like the Persian Gulf War or World War II than it will be like the war against drugs. Bipartisanship and unity will be far more difficult to maintain should that be the case, and the need for innovative change (as opposed to a return to old practices and habits) in American foreign policy institutions will be great.

The courts are the first group of institutions that we need to examine. Henry Kissinger, a former secretary of state and national security advisor, argues against the creation of an international criminal court in "The Pitfalls of Universal Jurisdiction." He, himself, has been targeted by some groups as someone who should be tried by this body. The second article examines the issues raised by an important recent Supreme Court decision that ruled against a Massachusetts law banning trade with Burma because of its human rights record. "States' Rights and Foreign Policy: Some Things Should Be Left to Washington" was written prior to the Court's reaching this decision and reaches the same conclusion.

In prioritizing institutions for change, Congress and the presidency are important as the leading protagonists in the struggle to control the content and conduct of American foreign policy. The relationship between them has varied over time with such phrases as the "imperial presidency," "bipartisanship," and "divided government" being used to describe it.

In his essay "The Folk Who Live on the Hill," James Kitfield looks at the growing split within congressional Republican ranks between the aging assertive internationalists and the newer breed of international minimalists. Christopher Hitchens, in "Farewell to the Helmsman," examines the foreign policy philosophy of Jesse Helms, one of the major foreign policy voices in Congress over the past decade. Helms, who is not seeking re-election, is described as an isolationist-internationalist. In the essay, "Perils of Presidential Transition," the authors look at how the transition process influences early foreign policy decisions in new administrations. Examples are drawn from the Carter, Reagan, and Clinton administrations.

Another set of institutions thought to be in need of change are the bureaucracies that play influential roles in making foreign policy by supplying policymakers with information, defining problems, and implementing the selected policies. The end of the cold war presents these bureaucracies with a special challenge. Old threats and enemies have declined in importance or disappeared entirely. To remain effective players in post–cold war foreign policy making, these institutions must adjust their organizational structures and ways of thinking or risk being seen by policymakers as irrelevant anachronisms. The three leading foreign policy bureaucracies of the cold war are the State Department, the Defense Department, and the Central Intelligence Agency (CIA).

What the future holds for each of these institutions is the subject of two articles in this section. Richard Gardner is critical of the amount of money spent on foreign affairs. In "The One Percent Solution: Shirking the Cost of World Leadership," he asserts that solving global problems requires leadership and that leadership costs money. The final essay in this section, "America's Postmodern Military" by Don Snider, looks at the changing role of the American military and the growing divide between the outlooks of civilian policymakers and professional officers. This changing nature of civil-military relations is one of the most talked about trends of the post–cold war era.

The Pitfalls of Universal Jurisdiction

by Henry A. Kissinger

RISKING JUDICIAL TYRANNY

IN LESS THAN a decade, an unprecedented movement has emerged to submit international politics to judicial procedures. It has spread with extraordinary speed and has not been subjected to systematic debate, partly because of the intimidating passion of its advocates. To be sure, human rights violations, war crimes, genocide, and torture have so disgraced the modern age and in such a variety of places that the effort to interpose legal norms to prevent or punish such outrages does credit to its advocates. The danger lies in pushing the effort to extremes that risk substituting the tyranny of judges for that of governments; historically, the dictatorship of the virtuous has often led to inquisitions and even witch-hunts.

The doctrine of universal jurisdiction asserts that some crimes are so heinous that their perpetrators should not escape justice by invoking doctrines of sovereign immunity or the sacrosanct nature of national frontiers. Two specific approaches to achieve this goal have emerged recently. The first seeks to apply the procedures of domestic criminal justice to violations of universal standards, some of which are embodied in United Nations conventions, by authorizing national prosecutors to bring offenders into their jurisdictions through extradition from third countries. The second approach is the International Criminal Court (ICC), the founding treaty for which was created by a conference in Rome in July 1998 and signed by 95 states, including most European countries. It has already been ratified by 30 nations and will go into effect when the total reaches 60. On December 31, 2000, President Bill Clinton signed the ICC treaty with only hours to spare before the cutoff date. But he indicated that he would neither submit it for Senate approval nor recommend that his successor do so while the treaty remains in its present form.

The very concept of universal jurisdiction is of recent vintage. The sixth edition of *Black's Law Dictionary*, published in 1990, does not contain even an entry for the term. The closest analogous concept listed is *hostes humani generis* ("enemies of the human race"). Until recently, the latter term has been applied to pirates, hijackers, and similar outlaws whose crimes were typically committed outside the territory of any state. The notion that heads of state and senior public officials should have the same standing as outlaws before the bar of justice is quite new.

In the aftermath of the Holocaust and the many atrocities committed since, major efforts have been made to find a judicial standard to deal with such catastrophes: the Nuremberg trials of 1945–46, the Universal Declaration of Human Rights of 1948, the genocide convention of 1948, and the anti-torture convention of 1988. The Final Act of the Conference on Security and Cooperation in Europe, signed in Helsinki in 1975 by President Gerald Ford on behalf of the United States, obligated the 35 signatory nations to observe certain stated human rights, subjecting violators to the pressures by which foreign policy commitments are generally sustained. In the hands of courageous groups in Eastern Europe, the Final Act became one of several weapons by which communist rule was delegitimized and eventually undermined. In the 1990s, international tribunals to punish crimes committed in the former Yugoslavia and Rwanda, established ad hoc by the U.N. Security Council, have sought to provide a system of accountability for specific regions ravaged by arbitrary violence.

But none of these steps was conceived at the time as instituting a "universal jurisdiction." It is unlikely that any of the signatories of either the U.N. conventions or the Helsinki Final Act thought it possible that national judges would use them as a basis for extradition requests regarding alleged crimes committed outside their jurisdictions. The drafters almost certainly believed that they were stating general principles, not laws that would be enforced by national courts. For example, Eleanor Roosevelt, one of the drafters of the Universal Declaration of Human Rights, referred to it as a "common standard." As one of the negotiators of the Final Act of the Helsinki conference, I can affirm that the administration I represented considered it primarily a diplomatic weapon to use to thwart the communists' attempts to pressure the Soviet and captive peoples. Even with respect to binding undertakings such as the genocide convention, it was never thought that they would subject past and future leaders of one nation to prosecution by the national magistrates of another state where the violations had not occurred. Nor, until recently, was it argued that the various U.N. declarations subjected past and future leaders to the possibility of prosecution by national magistrates of third countries without either due process safeguards or institutional restraints.

Yet this is in essence the precedent that was set by the 1998 British detention of former Chilean President Augusto Pinochet as the result of an extradition request by a Spanish judge seeking to try Pinochet for crimes committed against Spaniards on Chilean soil. For advocates of universal jurisdiction, that detention—lasting more than 16 months—was a landmark establishing a just principle. But any universal system should contain procedures not only to punish the wicked but also to constrain the righteous. It must not allow legal principles to be used as weapons to settle political scores. Questions such as these must therefore be answered: What legal norms are being applied? What are the rules of evidence? What safeguards exist for the defendant? And how will prosecutions affect other fundamental foreign policy objectives and interests?

A DANGEROUS PRECEDENT

IT IS decidedly unfashionable to express any degree of skepticism about the way the Pinochet case was handled. For almost all the parties of the European left, Augusto Pinochet is the incarnation of a right-wing assault on democracy because he led a coup d'état against an elected leader. At the time, others, including the leaders of Chile's democratic parties, viewed Salvador Allende as a radical Marxist ideologue bent on imposing a Castro-style dictatorship with the aid of Cuban-trained militias and Cuban weapons. This was why the leaders of Chile's democratic parties publicly welcomed—yes, welcomed—Allende's overthrow. (They changed their attitude only after the junta brutally maintained its autocratic rule far longer than was warranted by the invocation of an emergency.)

The world must respect Chile's own attempt to come to terms with its brutal past.

Disapproval of the Allende regime does not exonerate those who perpetrated systematic human rights abuses after it was overthrown. But neither should the applicability of universal jurisdiction as a policy be determined by one's view of the political history of Chile. The appropriate solution was arrived at in August 2000 when the Chilean Supreme Court withdrew Pinochet's senatorial immunity, making it possible to deal with the charges against him in the courts of the country most competent to judge this history and to relate its decisions to the stability and vitality of its democratic institutions.

On November 25, 1998, the judiciary committee of the British House of Lords (the United Kingdom's supreme court) concluded that "international law has made it plain that certain types of conduct... are not acceptable conduct on the part of anyone." But that principle did not oblige the lords to endow a Spanish magistrate—and presumably other magistrates elsewhere in the world—with the authority to enforce it in a country where the accused had committed no crime, and then to cause the restraint of the accused for 16 months in yet another country in which he was equally a stranger. It could have held that Chile, or an international tribunal specifically established for crimes committed in Chile on the model of the courts set up for heinous crimes in the former Yugoslavia and Rwanda, was the appropriate forum.

The unprecedented and sweeping interpretation of international law in *Exparte Pinochet* would arm any magistrate anywhere in the world with the power to demand extradition, substituting the magistrate's own judgment for the reconciliation procedures of even incontestably democratic societies where alleged violations of human rights may have occurred. It would also subject the accused to the criminal procedures of the magistrate's country, with a legal system that may be unfamiliar to the defendant and that would force the defendant to bring evidence and witnesses from long distances. Such a system goes far beyond the explicit and limited mandates established by the U.N. Security Council for the tribunals covering war crimes in the former Yugoslavia and Rwanda as well as the one being negotiated for Cambodia.

Perhaps the most important issue is the relationship of universal jurisdiction to national reconciliation procedures set up by new democratic governments to deal with their countries' questionable pasts. One would have thought that a Spanish magistrate would have been sensitive to the incongruity of a request by Spain, itself haunted by transgressions committed during the Spanish Civil War and the regime of General Francisco Franco, to try in Spanish courts alleged crimes against humanity committed elsewhere.

The decision of post-Franco Spain to avoid wholesale criminal trials for the human rights violations of the recent past was designed explicitly to foster a process of national reconciliation that undoubtedly contributed much to the present vigor of Spanish democracy. Why should Chile's attempt at national reconciliation not have been given the same opportunity? Should any outside group dissatisfied with the reconciliation procedures of, say, South Africa be free to challenge them in their own national courts or those of third countries?

It is an important principle that those who commit war crimes or systematically violate human rights should be held accountable. But the consolidation of law, domestic peace, and representative government in a nation struggling to come to terms with a brutal past has a claim as well. The instinct to punish must be related, as in every constitutional democratic political structure, to a system of checks and balances that includes other elements critical to the survival and expansion of democracy.

Another grave issue is the use in such cases of extradition procedures designed for ordinary criminals. If the Pinochet case becomes a precedent, magistrates anywhere will be in a position to put forward an extradition request without warning to the accused and regardless of the policies the accused's country might already have in place for dealing with the charges. The country from which extradition is requested then faces a seemingly technical legal decision that, in fact, amounts to the exercise of political discretion—whether to entertain the claim or not.

Once extradition procedures are in train, they develop a momentum of their own. The accused is not allowed to challenge the substantive merit of the case and instead is confined to procedural issues: that there was, say, some technical flaw in the extradition request, that the judicial system of the requesting country is incapable of providing a fair hearing, or that the crime for which the extradition is sought is not treated as a crime in the country from which extradition has been requested—thereby conceding much of the merit of the charge. Meanwhile, while these claims are being considered by the judicial system of the country from which extradition is sought, the accused remains in some form of detention, possibly for years. Such procedures provide an opportunity for political harassment long before the accused is in a position to present any defense. It would be ironic if a doctrine designed to transcend the political process turns into a means to pursue political enemies rather than universal justice.

The Pinochet precedent, if literally applied, would permit the two sides in the Arab-Israeli conflict, or those in any other passionate international controversy, to project their battles into the various national courts by pursuing adversaries with extradition requests. When discretion on what crimes are subject to universal jurisdiction and whom to prosecute is left to national prosecutors, the scope for arbitrariness is wide indeed. So far, universal jurisdiction has involved the prosecution of one fashionably reviled man of the right while scores of East European communist leaders—not to speak of Caribbean, Middle Eastern, or African leaders who inflicted their own full measures of torture and suffering—have not had to face similar prosecutions.

Some will argue that a double standard does not excuse violations of international law and that it is better to bring one malefactor to justice than to grant immunity to all. This is not an argument permitted in the domestic jurisdictions of many democracies—in Canada, for example, a charge can be thrown out of court merely by showing that a prosecution has been selective enough to amount to an abuse of process. In any case, a universal standard of justice should not be based on the proposition that a just end warrants unjust means, or that political fashion trumps fair judicial procedures.

AN INDISCRIMINATE COURT

THE IDEOLOGICAL supporters of universal jurisdiction also provide much of the intellectual compass for the emerging In-

ternational Criminal Court. Their goal is to criminalize certain types of military and political actions and thereby bring about a more humane conduct of international relations. To the extent that the ICC replaces the claim of national judges to universal jurisdiction, it greatly improves the state of international law. And, in time, it may be possible to negotiate modifications of the present statute to make the ICC more compatible with U.S. constitutional practice. But in its present form of assigning the ultimate dilemmas of international politics to unelected jurists—and to an international judiciary at that—it represents such a fundamental change in U.S. constitutional practice that a full national debate and the full participation of Congress are imperative. Such a momentous revolution should not come about by tacit acquiescence in the decision of the House of Lords or by dealing with the ICC issue through a strategy of improving specific clauses rather than as a fundamental issue of principle.

At any future time, U.S. officials involved in the NATO air campaign in Kosovo could face international prosecution.

The doctrine of universal jurisdiction is based on the proposition that the individuals or cases subject to it have been clearly identified. In some instances, especially those based on Nuremberg precedents, the definition of who can be prosecuted in an international court and in what circumstances is self-evident. But many issues are much more vague and depend on an understanding of the historical and political context. It is this fuzziness that risks arbitrariness on the part of prosecutors and judges years after the event and that became apparent with respect to existing tribunals.

For example, can any leader of the United States or of another country be hauled before international tribunals established for other purposes? This is precisely what Amnesty International implied when, in the summer of 1999, it supported a "complaint" by a group of European and Canadian law professors to Louise Arbour, then the prosecutor of the International Criminal Tribunal for the Former Yugoslavia (ICTY). The complaint alleged that crimes against humanity had been committed during the NATO air campaign in Kosovo. Arbour ordered an internal staff review, thereby implying that she did have jurisdiction if such violations could, in fact, be demonstrated. Her successor, Carla Del Ponte, in the end declined to indict any NATO official because of a general inability "to pinpoint individual responsibilities," thereby implying anew that the court had jurisdiction over NATO and American leaders in the Balkans and would have issued an indictment had it been able to identify the particular leaders allegedly involved.

Most Americans would be amazed to learn that the ICTY, created at U.S. behest in 1993 to deal with Balkan war criminals, had asserted a right to investigate U.S. political and military leaders for allegedly criminal conduct—and for the indefinite future, since no statute of limitations applies. Though the ICTY prosecutor chose not to pursue the charge—on the ambiguous ground of an inability to collect evidence—some national prosecutor may wish later to take up the matter as a valid subject for universal jurisdiction.

The pressures to achieve the widest scope for the doctrine of universal jurisdiction were demonstrated as well by a suit before the European Court of Human Rights in June 2000 by families of Argentine sailors who died in the sinking of the Argentine cruiser *General Belgano* during the Falklands War. The concept of universal jurisdiction has moved from judging alleged political crimes against humanity to second-guessing, 18 years after the event, military operations in which neither civilians nor civilian targets were involved.

Distrusting national governments, many of the advocates of universal jurisdiction seek to place politicians under the supervision of magistrates and the judicial system. But prosecutorial discretion without accountability is precisely one of the flaws of the International Criminal Court. Definitions of the relevant crimes are vague and highly susceptible to politicized application. Defendants will not enjoy due process as understood in the United States. Any signatory state has the right to trigger an investigation. As the U.S. experience with the special prosecutors investigating the executive branch shows, such a procedure is likely to develop its own momentum without time limits and can turn into an instrument of political warfare. And the extraordinary attempt of the ICC to assert jurisdiction over Americans even in the absence of U.S. accession to the treaty has already triggered legislation in Congress to resist it.

The independent prosecutor of the ICC has the power to issue indictments, subject to review only by a panel of three judges. According to the Rome statute, the Security Council has the right to quash any indictment. But since revoking an indictment is subject to the veto of any permanent Security Council member, and since the prosecutor is unlikely to issue an indictment without the backing of at least one permanent member of the Security Council, he or she has virtually unlimited discretion in practice. Another provision permits the country whose citizen is accused to take over the investigation and trial. But the ICC retains the ultimate authority on whether that function has been adequately exercised and, if it finds it has not, the ICC can reassert jurisdiction. While these procedures are taking place, which may take years, the accused will be under some restraint and certainly under grave public shadow.

The advocates of universal jurisdiction argue that the state is the basic cause of war and cannot be trusted to deliver justice.

If law replaced politics, peace and justice would prevail. But even a cursory examination of history shows that there is no evidence to support such a theory. The role of the statesman is to choose the best option when seeking to advance peace and justice, realizing that there is frequently a tension between the two and that any reconciliation is likely to be partial. The choice, however, is not simply between universal and national jurisdictions.

MODEST PROPOSALS

THE PRECEDENT SET by international tribunals established to deal with situations where the enormity of the crime is evident and the local judicial system is clearly incapable of administering justice, as in the former Yugoslavia and Rwanda, have shown that it is possible to punish without removing from the process all political judgment and experience. In time, it may be possible to renegotiate the ICC statute to avoid its shortcomings and dangers. Until then, the United States should go no further toward a more formal system than one containing the following three provisions. First, the U.N. Security Council would create a Human Rights Commission or a special subcommittee to report whenever systematic human rights violations seem to warrant judicial action. Second, when the government under which the alleged crime occurred is not authentically representative, or where the domestic judicial system is incapable of sitting in judgment on the crime, the Security Council would set up an ad hoc international tribunal on the model of those of the former Yugoslavia or Rwanda. And third, the procedures for these international tribunals as well as the scope of the prosecution should be precisely defined by the Security Council, and the accused should be entitled to the due process safeguards accorded in common jurisdictions.

In this manner, internationally agreed procedures to deal with war crimes, genocide, or other crimes against humanity could become institutionalized. Furthermore, the one-sidedness of the current pursuit of universal jurisdiction would be avoided. This pursuit could threaten the very purpose for which the concept has been developed. In the end, an excessive reliance on universal jurisdiction may undermine the political will to sustain the humane norms of international behavior so necessary to temper the violent times in which we live.

HENRY A. KISSINGER, Chairman of Kissinger Associates, Inc., is a former Secretary of State and National Security Adviser. This essay is adapted from his latest book, *Does America Need a Foreign Policy? Toward a Diplomacy for the 21st Century.*

Reprinted by permission of *Foreign Affairs*, July/August 2001, Vol. 80, No. 4, pp. 86-96. © 2001 by the Council on Foreign Relations, Inc.

States' Rights and Foreign Policy

Some Things Should Be Left to Washington

Brannon P. Denning and Jack H. McCall

In the waning days of apartheid, South Africa found itself the subject of sanctions imposed not only by Congress but by a number of U.S. states and municipalities as well. These measures ranged from requirements that the state or city in question rid itself of holdings in South Africa or in companies doing business there to requirements that corporations bidding for government contracts likewise divest. Although the apartheid regime sought to challenge some of these laws, little litigation resulted, in part because few lawyers wished to associate themselves with such a loathsome government.

Local sanctions were not unprecedented. Decades earlier, in the 1960s, U.S. states had occasionally forbidden government purchases from communist countries or required that most state materials be bought domestically. In the 1980s, at the same time as the apartheid battle, some cities declared themselves "nuclear-free zones" and sought to keep nuclear waste or atomic weapons outside city limits. Again, although the constitutionality of such ordinances was questioned, few court challenges were brought. As with the anti-apartheid sanctions, no case made it to the Supreme Court.

In the early 1990s, as first the Cold War and then apartheid ended, so did state and local forays into foreign policy. But today this subfederal assertiveness is back with a vengeance. China, Burma (Myanmar), Nigeria, North Korea, Cuba, and Switzerland have found themselves targeted by state and local sanctions adopted in the face of strong State Department criticism. This time, however, the actual subjects of the sanctions—mainly American companies faced with the Hobson's choice of abandoning overseas markets or losing lucrative government contracts—are challenging the statutes in court. And they are winning. One such case is about to be heard by the Supreme Court, and the outcome there

should be similar. Local sanctions are being struck down, as well they should. Despite their laudable motives, such laws are not only bad policy—they are unconstitutional.

LETTER OF THE LAW

In *National Foreign Trade Council* v. *Natsios*, decided in June 1999, the U.S. Court of Appeals for the First Circuit struck down a Massachusetts statute that banned companies with direct or indirect business interests in Burma from competing for state contracts. The statute's terms were so broad that if a company owned a subsidiary in Burma, the parent company would be deemed to be "doing business with Burma" and be prohibited from bidding on contracts to supply goods to Massachusetts—even if the subsidiary was in a completely different line of business.

A federal district court had first struck down the statute in November 1998, ruling it an impermissible encroachment on the federal prerogative to conduct foreign affairs. The decision reminded states that federalism is a two-way street: just as the states have spheres in which the federal government may not intrude, Washington is supreme in the areas assigned to it by the Constitution. "State interests," the district judge wrote, "no matter how noble, do not trump the federal government's exclusive foreign affairs power."

When its turn came, the court of appeals went even further. It found that in addition to transgressing the Constitution's structural boundaries, the statute discriminated against foreign commerce, which states are forbidden to do. The Constitution grants Congress the power to regulate foreign trade; courts have long inferred from that grant limitations on a state's power to discriminate in this area. (The very purpose for giving this power to Washington had been to end the conflicting state commercial policies that plagued the country under the Articles of Confederation.) The appeals court rejected Massachusetts' argument that it had a right not to support, directly or indirectly, regimes whose human rights records it found objectionable. Laudable humanitarian aims, the court held, did not license states to violate the Constitution.

Finally, the court found Massachusetts' approach contrary to the sanctions that Congress itself had adopted. According to the Constitution, federal laws are supreme; state laws expressly or implicitly in conflict with those of Congress must give way. Sometimes Congress explicitly declares an intent to preempt similar state laws. More frequently, Congress remains silent, and courts must determine whether there is any room for the states to supplement congressional action or whether such supplements would conflict with the intended congressional scheme. In *Natsios*, the court concluded that although the goals of the federal and state legislation regarding Burma were similar, the state sanctions conflicted with those of Congress and could not stand.

The appeals court offered Massachusetts the following consolation: "The passage of the Massachusetts Burma Law has resulted in significant attention being brought to the Burmese government's human rights record. Indeed, it may be that the Massachusetts law was a catalyst for federal action." The court also noted the role that Massachusetts' congressional representatives played in crafting a federal response. "Nonetheless," it concluded, "the conduct of this nation's foreign affairs cannot be effectively managed on behalf of all of the nation's citizens if each of the many state and local governments pursues its own foreign policy."

The First Circuit's decision is binding precedent only in Maine, Massachusetts, New Hampshire, Rhode Island, and Puerto Rico, and Massachusetts has appealed it to the U.S. Supreme Court, which has yet to hear the case. Meanwhile, 29 other state and local governments outside the First Circuit have passed or proposed 42 similar sanctions. Passage of 15 other such laws was attempted but has failed in 13 states or municipalities so far. Although no new statutes or ordinances have been passed since the *Natsios* decision—even in the wake of recent crises in East Timor and Pakistan, which might otherwise have provoked them—proponents of local sanctions beyond the jurisdiction of the First Circuit, vowing to fight for the right to dictate foreign policy, have refused to repeal existing laws or suspend their operation.

DELUSIONS OF GRANDEUR

What has so emboldened cities and states? Two factors stand out: the increased role for the states brought on by globalization, and the rise of nongovernmental organizations (NGOs), particularly those promoting human rights worldwide. The latter have succeeded in replacing the classical view of international relations and international law as high-level affairs conducted among elite policymakers with one in which grassroots organizations now reach millions worldwide through the Internet and the fax machine. An American-led NGO was largely responsible for the drafting and adoption of the recent treaty banning land mines, despite the opposition of the U.S. government—a result unthinkable 25 or 30 years ago. Policy entrepreneurship among NGOs out to abolish the death penalty has driven recent challenges to death sentences imposed on non-U.S. citizens, on grounds that they were arrested and held in violation of the Vienna Convention on Consular Relations (which guarantees detainees in foreign countries the right to contact their consulates). Similarly, NGOs have furnished much of the impetus for the state and local sanctions.

Meanwhile, state policymakers have been emboldened to play a more active role in foreign affairs, once thought to be the exclusive province of the federal government. And why not? After all, states compete for foreign business, many states with large urban centers host foreign consulates, and some contain large numbers of resident aliens or recent immigrants who retain close ties to their homelands. Given the new realities of international relations, defenders of the sanctions claim, state and local governments should take the lead in combating international human rights abuses. Their taxpayers, they add, should not be asked to support repressive regimes or the companies that do business with them.

Little direction in the devolution debate has come from the federal executive branch, and state and local governments have interpreted this silence as tacit approval. Apparent state disregard for the Vienna consular convention was motivated not so much by indifference to international agreements as by ignorance; the State Department, until recently, made little effort to educate state and local law enforcement agencies about their responsibilities under the convention. Likewise, although the State Department made its opposition to some local sanctions known, the Clinton administration did not file a brief in *Natsios*, apparently fearful of offending human rights activists and sanctions' congressional supporters.

TALKING 'BOUT THE CONSTITUTION

Subfederal sanctions have a visceral appeal, particularly given the horrible human rights records of targets such as Burma. Sanctions have even captured the hearts and minds of those holding wildly divergent political views: anticommunist conservatives cherish them as tools to use against nations like Cuba and China, while liberals and human rights activists invoke them to bash regimes like Indonesia's. Yet despite their peculiar transideological charm, local sanctions represent an attempt by states to co-opt the power to set foreign policy—a power that the

Constitution, as the courts have long recognized, quite clearly allocates to Washington.

Articles I and II of the Constitution place primacy for the conduct of foreign and military affairs squarely with Congress and the president. The regulation and taxation of foreign commerce, immigration, declarations of war, the appointment and reception of ambassadors, the definition and punishment of offenses against international law, the command of U.S. military forces, the negotiation and approval of treaties—all are left to the federal government. The federal, not the state, judiciary hears cases involving ambassadors, consuls, public ministers, and controversies involving states and foreign countries, citizens, or subjects. Moreover, states are expressly forbidden by Article I, Section 10, of the Constitution from entering into treaties, alliances, agreements, or compacts with foreign powers; from making war; and from laying certain taxes on foreign commerce without congressional consent.

It is hardly credible to look at the Constitution's assignment of power and its proscriptions on state involvement in foreign affairs and to argue that, absent an express ban, states are free to impose sanctions on foreign countries. Such an argument epitomizes interpretative literalism at its most wooden and ignores the historical context in which constitutional powers were assigned. For all that the original supporters and opponents of constitutional ratification disagreed, both sides would have accepted the absolute necessity for uniformity in the conduct of foreign relations. Few dissented from James Madison's statement in the Federalist no. 42 that the powers to conduct foreign affairs constitute "an obvious and essential branch of the federal administration." "If we are to be one nation in any respect," Madison wrote, "it clearly ought to be in respect to other nations." Alexander Hamilton noted elsewhere that since the actions of the individual states in the foreign policy arena would be charged against the United States as a whole, the power to set policy must reside at the federal level. In the Supreme Court's contemporary phraseology, the United States must speak "with one voice" on such matters.

Proponents of state and local sanctions today dismiss Hamilton's concerns, arguing that international actors are now much more sophisticated. Yet when Japan and the European Union protested Massachusetts' Burma law before the World Trade Organization (WTO), the action was brought against the United States, since Massachusetts, as a subnational government, has no WTO standing. Similarly, when Switzerland was hit with local sanctions in 1998 for not releasing the bank accounts of Holocaust victims, a major Swiss retailer responded by boycotting American products from states that had neither imposed nor intended to impose sanctions.

There are other, more esoteric, constitutional objections to laws like Massachusetts'. Sanctions burden foreign commerce. As discussed in the *Natsios* decision,

the Supreme Court has sharply limited states' powers to regulate interstate and foreign trade. State regulation touching foreign commerce has historically been more tightly circumscribed than that affecting commerce between states. After all, a babble of state regulations would drown out the "one voice" of the federal government.

Even where regulations are allowed, states must not *discriminate* against trading partners from other states or countries. Yet the current subfederal sanctions do just that. To argue that the restrictions apply to interstate and foreign companies alike (i.e., to anyone who trades with Burma) is to miss the point. The relevant discrimination, which Supreme Court case law prohibits, is between companies (foreign or domestic) engaged in foreign commerce and those that are not, or at least not with the pariah regimes targeted by the statute.

Nor, as *Natsios* recognized, does the narrow "market-participant" doctrine apply here to excuse the discrimination. (This doctrine allows states some leeway to interfere with commerce when they themselves are directly involved in the transaction.) The Supreme Court has refused to apply the exception to foreign commerce; moreover, sanctions, like taxes, constitute a "primeval governmental activity" of the sort unavailable to ordinary commercial actors and are thus beyond the scope of the exception.

INTERDICTING IMBECILITY

The First Circuit's decision in *Natsios* should remind states that just as there are constitutionally mandated realms into which the federal government cannot intrude, the federal government also has its own exclusive provinces. Furthermore, policing the demarcation between federal and subfederal governments, as the First Circuit has done, is the appropriate province of the judiciary. Although Congress has the unquestioned power to halt all sanctions initiatives if it wishes, doing so would divert legislative resources from other national concerns or force Congress to react long after damage has been done to the nation's foreign policy. In this case, moreover, the executive branch proved an unreliable guardian of its prerogatives: the Clinton administration, wary of unfavorable publicity, declined to get involved.

Of course, to invalidate sanctions like Massachusetts' Burma law does not leave state and local governments without reasonable alternatives. Subnational governments can, of course, craft nonbinding resolutions to condemn repressive foreign regimes. More effectively, their officials can lobby congressional representatives—who would ignore such requests at their peril, come election time—to act. These options are not foreclosed by the First Circuit's decision. If state and local governments wish to exercise their constitutional rights in calling for a cohesive foreign policy against oppressive governments, they can use means other than sanctions. Private citizens and NGOs, too, can organize boycotts to pressure businesses to quit countries with poor human rights records. Such measures can have a powerful effect, as apartheid-era activism demonstrated.

Supreme Court Justice Joseph Story, in his influential 1833 treatise on the Constitution, wrote that "notwithstanding our boasts of freedom and independence," Americans were victims "of our own imbecility" in relations with other countries under the Articles of Confederation, because states insisted on conducting foreign policy themselves. Despite the otherwise welcome invigoration of federalism in the legislative and judicial branches of government, Washington still must be given pride of place in the conduct of foreign affairs and the regulation of foreign commerce. Without the central government's lead, the United States risks returning to the Balkanization of its national interests that necessitated the Constitution in the first place.

BRANNON P. DENNING *is Assistant Professor at Southern Illinois University School of Law.* JACK H. MCCALL *is an Associate at Hunton & Williams in Knoxville, Tennessee.*

Reprinted by permission of *Foreign Affairs*, January/February 2000, pp. 9–14. © 2000 by the Council on Foreign Relations, Inc.

The Folk Who Live on the Hill

James Kitfield

WHEN Theodore Roosevelt ushered in the American Century as the nation's youngest president in 1901, he promptly rallied the Republican Party behind his unique brand of foreign affairs activism. In short order, the former Rough Rider and hero of the Spanish-American War put down insurrection in the Philippines, abetted a revolution in Panama that led to U.S. acquisition of the Panama Canal, and won the Nobel Peace Price for mediating the quarrel between Russia and Japan. In 1907 he dispatched the Great White Fleet on a cruise around the world. An America in the "prime of our lusty youth," Roosevelt proclaimed, would "speak softly and carry a big stick" in world affairs.

At the end of the twentieth century, with American power and influence ascendant to a degree unimaginable in Teddy Roosevelt's time, emissaries from a far different Republican Party called a Capitol Hill press conference to allege presidential malfeasance. This time it was not campaign finance irregularities, personal indiscretions or technology transfers that were denounced by Senators Jeff Sessions (R-Ala.), Craig Thomas (R-Wyo.) and Larry E. Craig (R-Idaho). What irked the three Republicans was, rather, the discovery that the President of the United States had been spending too much money on trips to faraway places like China, Africa and Chile.

When queried about their own official travels, Thomas and Craig exhibited a disdain for the world beyond America's borders that is increasingly echoed in Republican ranks. Both boasted through staff that they had ventured out of the country only twice in the previous two years. This despite the fact that Thomas is chairman of the Senate Foreign Relations Subcommittee on East Asian and Pacific Affairs, and Craig is a member of the Senate Appropriations Committee with jurisdiction over foreign operations, foreign aid and defense.

The press conference was revealing, too, as political theater. That three Republican senators thought there were political points to be scored by criticizing the travel budget of the leader of the sole remaining superpower says much about the mood of the Republican Party today.

Indeed, theirs was but the latest shrug in a string of gestures of indifference made by Republicans, who seem rapidly to be tiring of the burdens that attend America's status as lone superpower. After refusing to support U.S. involvement in the Kosovo conflict, which a number of prominent Republicans dubbed "Mr. Clinton's war", many in the GOP began espousing an anti-interventionist doctrine that would preclude U.S. military action save when a narrowly defined set of vital interests is threatened.

Proposed Republican cuts in next year's foreign affairs budget would abdicate U.S. commitments to the Middle East peace process, slash funding for the National Endowment for Democracy, and abandon a program to dismantle Russian nuclear weapons. Republican leaders have refused to pay back dues to the United Nations for so long that the United States is in danger of losing its vote in the General Assembly, where Republicans had left U.S. interests unrepresented for a year by holding up the nomination of UN Ambassador Richard Holbrooke.

Despite the fact that a Republican serves as secretary of defense, congressional indifference to national security matters extends to the Pentagon as well. Uniformed leaders who once counted congressional Republicans as their most reliable boosters were shaken by recent Republican-led efforts to kill the air force's next generation F-22 fighter plane; to pass a tax cut that would have reduced military spending by nearly $600 billion over the next decade; to shutter the army's School of the Americas; and to slash funding for the production of a theater-based missile defense system. Republican leaders have also continually blocked efforts by the Pentagon in recent years to close obsolete military bases and production lines in order to save desperately needed funds. And in a move that echoed one of the most infamous roll calls in history—the 1941 vote in which a majority of congressional Republicans refused to support military conscription—the Republican-led House recently voted 232 to 187 to stop requiring young Americans to register for the draft.

What accounts for this transformation of a party that not so long ago promoted itself as a champion of muscular internationalism? Explanations include the retirement of an aging cadre of internationalists within the party; the ascendance of a generation of Republican lawmakers with minimal interest in foreign and defense matters and an instinctive aversion to big government; an American public largely indifferent to the world around it; and, finally, a deeply held animus toward Bill Clinton. Sen. John McCain (R-Ariz.), a candidate for the Republican presidential nomination and long-time Senate Armed Services Committee member, discerns an ominous current in Republican thinking. As McCain noted,

> Partly out of dislike and distrust of President Clinton, and an understandable feeling that his foreign policy has been conducted on an *ad hoc* basis, I am concerned by what I see as a growing isolationism in the Republican Party.... Fewer and fewer members of Congress today have any real interest in national security issues, and they don't appreciate that we live in a less dangerous but far less predictable world.

A Historical Pendulum

CONFRONTATIONS between the legislative and executive branches over the extent of America's international entanglements are of course as old as the Republic itself. When Congress threatened to withhold funding for the proposed around-the-world tour by U.S. naval forces in the early 1900s, for instance, Teddy Roosevelt reportedly promised to pay for half the trip out of executive funds, daring Congress not to appropriate monies to bring the fleet home. More recently, in the 1970s Congress withdrew the funding necessary to back U.S. military commitments to South Vietnam as U.S. forces exited the region.

Such partisan showdowns have on occasion reshaped the essential world-view of the political parties. When, for example, Senate Republican Henry Cabot Lodge took the lead in rejecting the League of Nations after World War I, as Professor Donald Kagan has observed, it was less because he was a committed isolationist than because "he was just so damn angry at Woodrow Wilson that he wanted to deny Wilson a victory. But that helped drive the Republican Party into a flight from American responsibilities around the world." The analogy is apt. Indeed, a year after Lodge's defeat of the League of Nations, Republican presidential candidate Warren G. Harding won the White House running on a rallying cry of "a return to normalcy."

By the 1930s "normalcy" for the Republican Party had evolved into a strident isolationism that culminated in GOP sponsorship of the Neutrality Acts of 1935. The creed's chief exponent was Senator Robert Taft (R-Ohio), son of Republican President William Howard Taft. Known as "Mr. Republican", Taft was himself a three-time candidate for the Republican presidential nomination, and his isolationism persisted well into the Cold War. But the 1952 election of war hero Dwight Eisenhower set the Republican Party back on the path of American leadership. Having organized the forces of NATO as its Supreme Allied Commander, Eisenhower ended the Korean War, adopted the Truman administration's policy of containment, committed the United States to an active role in the Middle East, and authorized numerous covert interventions.

After the trauma of Vietnam it was the Democrats' turn to flirt with isolationism, a phase neatly exemplified by presidential candidate George McGovern's 1972 summons to "Come Home America" (penned by current National Security Adviser Samuel Berger), and President Jimmy Carter's defense cutbacks and threats to pull U.S. troops out of South Korea. The modern zenith of Republican internationalism, meanwhile, came with President Reagan's massive defense build-up and aggressively anti-communist policies in the 1980s. Apart from strengthening U.S. forces in Europe and the Far East, deploying medium-range nuclear missiles to Europe, and nearly accomplishing the aim of a six hundred-ship navy; Reagan deployed peacekeepers to the Middle East, bombed Libya, supported anti-communist insurgencies in Central America and Afghanistan, and invaded Grenada.

The New Minimalists

THE RECENT furor surrounding Pat Buchanan's latest book, *A Republic, Not An Empire: Reclaiming America's Destiny*, is but one symptom of a new tug of war within the GOP. Arguing that the United States need not have been drawn into World War II, Buchanan was swiftly denounced by the major Republican presidential candidates. Buchanan's primary contention, however, is that "arrogant" elites have committed America to going to war in regions where the nation has no vital interests, while tying its fortunes to agencies of "an embryonic new world government."

Rep. Herbert H. Bateman (R-VA.), chairman of the House Armed Services Subcommittee on Military Readiness, has heard much the same argument from his colleagues in Congress:

> I'm very much aware of a body of opinion within the Republican Party which holds that America is trying to be the world's policeman, and too often we do undertake missions that are not really vital to U.S. national security.... At the same time, I've certainly never been an isolationist or 'Fortress America' type, and it's a major embar-

rassment that a meaningful number of Republicans can be identified as the 'Get out of the United Nations crowd.' It embarrasses me that those people even exist in the Republican Party.

But they do. Republicans were set philosophically adrift with the demise of the Soviet threat. The defeat just three years later of Republican standard-bearer George Bush by Democrat Bill Clinton, whose campaign mantra was "It's the economy, stupid," taught Republicans an important lesson: foreign policy activism no longer has a political constituency. That the GOP had taken this lesson to heart became evident with the Republican takeover of Congress in 1994. The "Contract with America"—Newt Gingrich's poll-tested battle plan for electoral success— barely mentions foreign policy or national security apart from a cursory plug for the national missile defense system popularized by Reagan. Even more important, the Republican revolution of 1994 signaled a generational transition within the Republican Party, shifting power from an aging cadre of cold warriors to a younger generation, which proved more committed than its predecessors to reducing the size and scope of the federal government. And these reformers soon discovered that no government agencies were larger and more costly than those that maintain America's superpower status.

Douglas Bandow, a senior fellow at the libertarian Cato Institute, believes that the Republican Class of '94 sympathizes with Cato's limited view of America's role in the world and its calls for reduced military expenditures:

> Because they didn't spend their political careers at a time when the Cold War was the reigning paradigm, and are willing to see that period as an anomaly in our history, a lot of the younger Republicans elected in 1994 are more skeptical of these massive government institutions and interventionist policies that went along with the Cold War…. A lot of older Republicans, however, still can't imagine a world where the United States is not totally predominant. They have a very hard time giving up that notion. I think those two groups represent a real cleavage in the Republican Party today.

Though an internationalist himself, then-House Speaker Gingrich may have furthered that divide by concentrating so much power in his own office, bypassing the committee seniority system, and elevating trusted allies to the chairmanships of key committees such as Appropriations, Commerce and the Judiciary. Gingrich further undermined the committee structure by limiting the terms of chairmen and affording the new class of Republican revolutionaries greater leeway to challenge their committee chairs on legislation. When Gingrich retired, this power promptly reverted to House leaders with a decidedly less internationalist bent, such as Majority Whip Tom DeLay (R-TX.) and Majority Leader Richard Armey (R-TX.). After being queried last year about his opposition to additional funding for the International Monetary Fund, Armey responded with the increasingly familiar Republican refrain: he had not traveled outside the United States since 1986, his freshman year in the House. "I've been to Europe once, I don't need to go again," Armey claimed, adding a similar comment about Asia. Soon after, it was revealed that a sizeable number of House Republicans had never held a passport.

Significantly, in the early days of the Republican revolution the seniority system was left intact in the House International Affairs and Armed Services Committees. In fact, the average age of the chairmen of the four primary committees with jurisdiction at that time over foreign affairs and national security was eighty. As opposed to years past when the heads of these committees were revered as lions within the party, the new chairmen—Sen. Jesse Helms (R-NC.), Sen. Strom Thurmond (R-SC.), Rep. Floyd Spence (R-SC.) and Rep. Benjamin Gilman (R-NY.)—seemed neither predisposed nor sufficiently powerful to protect their committees from the efforts of the younger Republican revolutionaries.

As a former majority staffer on the House Armed Services Committee under Chairman Spence for much of the 1990s, Thomas Donnelly experienced that marginalization first-hand:

> When Newt Gingrich came in and pushed aside guys who were in line for seniority on various committees, he didn't bother with the foreign affairs or defense committees. Great American that Mr. Spence is, he worked tirelessly to try and increase defense spending and stop the decline of our military forces. But he was unable to carry the day. It just wasn't a high priority for the Republican leadership in Congress.

This divide between an aging cadre of internationalists and a younger generation of Republican lawmakers with little interest in foreign or defense affairs, but a natural skepticism toward big government, will surely become more pronounced as the former group recedes from the stage. Noted retirements from the internationalist wing of the party in recent years include Senators Mark Hatfield (R-OR.), Nancy Kassebaum (R-KA.), William Cohen (R-ME), Alan Simpson (R-WY.) and Robert Dole (R-KA.). "I don't think there's any doubt that there's a serious identity crisis in the Republican Party right now, and it's probably been worsened by the departure of committed internationalist leaders like Bob Dole and Newt Gingrich," says Norman Ornstein, a senior fellow at the American Enterprise Institute. The Cold War generation, he notes, "is being replaced by a new generation of political leaders that is just not deeply involved in foreign policy issues. They don't see American leadership in the world as particularly important."

Atlas Shrugs

BOTH THE SENATE and House voted this summer to cut the administration's budget for international affairs by nearly 14 percent, or more than $2 billion. These cuts come despite the fact that the United States devotes less than one-tenth as much of its GDP to foreign aid today than it did a generation ago, putting it last among industrialized nations in this category. Fundamental disagreements about the level of foreign affairs funding have been sharpest on the subject of paying arrears to the United Nations, to which the United States owes approximately $1.7 billion in back dues. Republicans in general, and Senate Foreign Relations Chairman Jesse Helms in particular, have traditionally cast a skeptical if not jaundiced eye toward the UN. But Helms and ranking committee Democrat Sen. Joseph Biden (Del.) fashioned a compromise bill two years ago that combined payment of U.S. funds with demands for stringent UN reform. And for two years running, the bill has been held up by anti-abortion language attached at the behest of Rep. Christopher H. Smith (R-NJ.). This is the kind of freelancing that would have been rapidly quashed in the days of Arthur Vandenburg. As it was, the stalemate lasted for most of Clinton's second term, before a tentative agreement was reached in November 1999.

Chairman Helms has also deftly used his power to block administration nominations, thwart arms control agreements, and reorganize the State Department. Yet, the Senate Foreign Relations Committee has not reported out a foreign aid authorization bill in nearly fifteen years. Former Chairman Richard Lugar (R-Ind.) notes that the committee today is a faint echo of its activist predecessors. As Lugar says,

> In fairness Chairman Helms hasn't been feeling well, but the truth is the committee hardly meets anymore.... Back in those days I would travel around the world as chairman at the President's request, helping take care of crises in the Philippines or Guatemala, or being on hand for the transition to democracy in Latin America or South Africa. That just doesn't happen anymore.

Then, too, there is the waning Republican attachment to matters of national defense. Republican lawmakers become irate when their *bona fides* as champions of a strong military are called into question. To be sure, Republicans have twisted the administration's arm on behalf of a national missile defense system. But the ongoing efforts of budget hawks such as Chairman of the

House Budget Committee John Kasich (R-OH)—who in 1995 joined with eighty like-minded Republicans in an attempt to kill the B-2 bomber program—beg the question nonetheless. Republican budget cutters have been aided in their efforts to slash military spending by the Defense Working Group, a group of libertarian-minded Republicans who advocate lasting reductions in Pentagon expenditures.

That Republicans would attempt to kill the F-22 aircraft and enact a major tax cut, especially at a time when the armed forces are desperately short of funds and the nation is running a budget surplus, struck many observers as an indication that Republican budget hawks have already triumphed in the struggle for the party's soul. Defense proponents were particularly alarmed by an analysis of the proposed Republican tax cut by the Center for Strategic and Budgetary Assessments, an independent policy research group in Washington, which suggested that not only would the Republican tax plan allocate $174 billion less for defense over the next decade than the administration's proposal, but unless highly unlikely cuts in domestic programs were secured, another $595 billion in defense cuts might be required:

In the words of Rep. Bateman,

> Because I think it was larger than it needed to be, I voted for the tax cut with a great deal of reluctance, and some degree of certainty that it was not the tax cut that would be ultimately approved.... If you look closely at the Republican conference, you'll also find Republicans from the Midwest who vote for every amendment to reduce the size of the defense budget, because they don't see a threat to justify it.... As for defense hawks—if that term even applies anymore—it is demonstrably the case that we are not as dominant or effective today as we were in the 1970s and 1980s.

The Hutchison Doctrine

DISAGREEMENTS among Republicans are nowhere more pronounced than over the question of when to use military force. These tensions boiled over recently in a bizarre showdown during the war in Kosovo, when the House voted to require congressional approval for the use of ground troops; deadlocked on a vote authorizing U.S. involvement in the air war despite the fact that it was already under way; and yet doubled the emergency funds that the Clinton administration had requested to conduct that war. "Give peace a chance"—in this instance the words of Senate Majority Leader Trent Lott (R-MS), not of some fringe pacifist group—became the Republican war cry.

Clearly exasperated by what they complain is a promiscuous use of military force by the Clinton administration, a number of Republican leaders have articulated an anti-interventionist policy that would preclude military entanglements in all cases except where vital U.S. interests are directly at stake. In their view, only a dramatic reduction of military deployments can avert a looming crisis in military preparedness.

Certainly there is ample evidence to suggest that America's military is nearing a critical phase as it enters the twenty-first century. In recent years the armed services have suffered chronic shortfalls in the areas of recruiting, military readiness, and equipment modernization and acquisition. At the same time, the rate of overseas deployments has increased more than 300 percent over the Cold War average. Lately, for example, the U.S. military has been entangled in stressful and draining conflicts in, among other places, Yugoslavia, Bosnia, Iraq, Haiti and Somalia. Despite this expanding catalogue of missions, the armed forces still have as their primary responsibility deterring, and if necessary fighting and winning, two major theater wars, a task that requires the maintenance of forward-deployed, combat-ready forces in Asia and the Middle East.

Sen. Kay Bailey Hutchison (R-TX.), a member of the Armed Forces Committee, says,

> We are stretching our forces so thin today that we have a crisis in military readiness, retention and recruitment.... We've so dissipated our resources and energies by getting involved in regional conflicts and misguided peacekeeping operations that our allies and others could do as well as the United States, that we've threatened our core capability to accomplish those missions that only a superpower can do.

Hutchison has in fact been among the most vocal of the Republican proponents of a minimalist foreign policy. In some ways her efforts hearken back to a doctrine promulgated by Reagan-era Defense Secretary Caspar Weinberger, who detailed six "tests" that should be passed before the United States placed its forces in harm's way. The county's vital interests must be imperiled, and the United States must be willing to commit sufficient forces to triumph quickly. Both the political and military objectives of the mission should be clearly defined and the military forces structured to achieve them. There must also be a reasonable likelihood that the American public will support an intervention, and, finally, U.S. forces will be committed to action only as a last resort.

The strategy advanced by Hutchison goes even further. Under her proposal, the United States would redefine its strategic role by providing itself and its allies protection under a missile defense umbrella, while maintaining air superiority and strategic lift capabilities. But the United States would leave the burden of pacifying regional conflicts and the vast majority of peacekeeping operations to its allies. Hence, in the Fiscal Year 2000

Defense Authorization, Hutchison inserted a provision calling on the administration to examine where the United States might reduce its global commitments and withdraw its forces from missions whose time has passed, including those in South Korea and Saudi Arabia.

Given the obvious strains on the military resulting from a frenetic pace of deployments and operations, such a hard-headed and realistic approach to military intervention is certainly defensible. It is nonetheless difficult to fathom exactly how America is to retain its superpower status if it eschews all regional crises and insists that its allies shoulder the risks on the ground. For nearly three years, the Clinton administration adopted such an arms-length policy while Bosnia burned, European allies vacillated, and the Balkans imploded. The calamitous results of this indifference are by now well known.

MANY Republican internationalists claim that if one of their own were to win the White House in 2000, the non-interventionist wing of the party would be vanquished, *à la* Taft and the Old Guard. In this view, the Republicans would benefit from the unifying influence of a commander in chief in the White House, much as the election of Bill. Clinton masked fissures between globalists and protectionists in the Democratic Party.

And, indeed, the leading Republican presidential candidates have all proclaimed fealty to a robust brand of internationalism. In officially announcing his candidacy in September, Sen. McCain devoted much of his speech to the importance of American leadership. If elected, McCain has promised to spend more on defense, military training and missile defense:

> I believe that President Clinton has failed his first responsibility to the nation by weakening our defenses, but he's not the only one to blame. Both parties in Congress have wasted scarce defense dollars on unneeded weapons systems and other pork projects while 12,000 enlisted personnel, proud young men and women, subsist on food stamps. That's a disgrace.

As for George W. Bush, despite his disdainful references to peacekeeping and nation-building operations, and his apparently tenuous grasp of world affairs, the Texas governor has assembled a brain trust that reads like a "Who's Who" of assertive internationalists. The team includes former Defense Secretary Richard Cheney, former Secretary of State George Schultz, former National Security Council analyst Condoleezza Rice, former Undersecretary of Defense Paul Wolfowitz and former Assistant Secretary of Defense Richard Perle. On issues ranging from relations with China and Russia to confronting rogue states, they depict a Bush foreign policy as one that will be more muscular and assertive than the Clinton-Gore approach in its promotion of American interests. As Rice was at pains to assure:

> I think Governor Bush is one of those people who believe that America pursues its national interests best by involvement in the international system, rather than letting that system buffet us around because we withdrew from it and left a huge, global vacuum. At the same time, I think he'll work very hard to establish a more coherent foreign policy driven by some central priorities, because despite our unmatched historical power, there's a sense of drift in American foreign policy right now.

Of course, two other possibilities exist. One is that, even if a Republican president were to be elected in 2000, he would soon find his foreign policy aims being undermined by an obstructionist Republican Congress. Representative Joe Scarborough (R-FL.), who has lately been directing the crusade to close down the army's School of the Americas, explained: "Any Republican president who expects the House members and probably the newer members of the Senate to merrily go along and rubber-stamp" his national security policies "will be very disappointed." The second possibility is that a Democrat will win the presidency, in which case, after four more years of partisan positioning on foreign policy issues, the Republican Party may find itself drifting into unsettling but all too familiar waters. Just as Henry Cabot Lodge's fierce opposition to Woodrow Wilson begat Warren Harding's "return to normalcy", and opposition to Franklin Roosevelt yielded Robert Taft's anti-interventionism, so might strident Republican opposition to Bill Clinton's successor herald a new era of isolation. The party has been down that road before, with nearly disastrous results for the nation.

James Kitfield is national security correspondent for *National Journal*, and two-time recipient of the Gerald R. Ford Award for Distinguished Reporting on National Defense.

Farewell to the Helmsman

During his 22 years on the Senate Foreign Relations Committee, Sen. Jesse Helms has had a fairly simple political philosophy: the only sovereignty that matters is America's own. Now Helms is no longer chairman and may soon be out of a job. But he leaves behind a storied legacy as latter-day America's quintessential isolationist-interventionist.

By Christopher Hitchens

In relinquishing his Republican allegiance last May, Sen. James Jeffords of Vermont did not refer explicitly to the senior senator from North Carolina. But it is hard to imagine that he did not have Jesse Helms somewhere in mind when he spoke of his former party's conservative extremism, and the end of Helms's six-year reign over the Foreign Relations Committee is one of the most salient results of the post-Jeffords alignment.

It is slightly too easy to say that Helms, who may not seek re-election next year, is a man one will miss. True, he enjoyed giving the impression of the three Cs—courteous, colorful, yet curmudgeonly—as if playing a Dixie boss in some remake of *Advise and Consent*. (A one-time smoker himself, he would never forget to say " 'Preciate it" when anyone lit up a fine tobacco product in his presence.) However, the other big C, the Confederacy, not cancer, somewhat qualified this effect. It was Helms who ran, with the help of political consultant Dick Morris, the notorious "white hands" TV spot in the election of 1990, showing two gnarled Caucasian mitts crumpling a rejection letter from an employer who had perforce selected "a minority" hire. Nor was the dignity of the deliberative body much enhanced when Helms began yodeling about the land of cotton in a Senate elevator in 1993, in order, as he put it, to make Carol Moseley-Braun, the Senate's first female African-American member, cry.

Apart from his lifelong Senate role as chief whip of the Old Right (he began political life as a local radio broadcaster inveighing against the Red-inspired civil rights movement and didn't hire a black staffer until well into the 1980s), Helms's two most conspicuous interests were the preservation of America's splendid isolationism and the blocking of nomina-

tions. Who can forget his long attack on the Kissinger Commission on Central America for its role in spreading socialism throughout the isthmus? Or his dogged campaigns against the United Nations, the Kyoto Protocol, the Comprehensive Test Ban Treaty, the treaty to ban land mines, and the International Criminal Court? Then there was his adamant opposition to the ambassadorship of the liberal Republican William Weld and, somewhat earlier, his deep and dark suspicion of the nomination of Richard Burt to be an assistant secretary at the State Department. I actually attended the hearing in 1982 when Helms made an issue of Burt's supposed relationship with a female writer for the *New York Times*. "It ain't over," he growled, "until the fat lady sings."

In a typically unctuous article for the *Times* last April ("Why the World Is Better for Jesse Helms"), Council on Foreign Relations Senior Fellow Walter Russell Mead made two mistakes. Posing as an anti-elitist, he said that "hating Jesse Helms remains a parlor sport in Georgetown, Cambridge and Manhattan." Leaving aside the way in which former Secretary of State Madeleine Albright and her spokesperson Jamie Rubin—popular in all three locations—had fawned on Helms during the second Clinton administration, Mead might have cared to collect opinions among, say, black voters in the Raleigh-Durham area. His second mistake was to say that the Senate needs to reflect the anti-internationalist temper of a large segment of American opinion.

That is not a mistake in itself, of course. But did such a worldview have to be expressed in a parochial, chauvinist, and philistine manner? On the Senate floor in 1995, Helms introduced Pakistan's then Prime Minister Benazir Bhutto as "the

Prime Minister of India" and five minutes later said he had had "a delightful hour-and-a-half" conversation talking about India. In March 1995, reading a prepared statement on North Korea, he had some harsh words for a man named "Kim Jong Two." Embarrassed staffers spun this as a pun on the monarchical succession from Kim Il Sung but took care to annotate Helms's next script with the phonetic spelling "Kim Jong ILL." Like a champ, the old warhorse got to this passage and declared: "We are entitled to know the nature of President Clinton's commitment to North Korean dictator Kim Jong the Third."

Two years previously, he became pugnacious during the confirmation hearings of Pamela Harriman to be ambassador to France. Ever suspicious of supranational authority, he opened one line of questioning like this:

Helms: "I know that you are involved in the Monnet Society. Monnet, of course, was one of the spiritual founders of the European Community?"

Harriman: "Senator, I do not think I am involved in the Monnet Society. I have never heard of it, frankly."

Helms: "I believe the information submitted says that. Is that not correct?"

Harriman: "Oh, it is Claude Monet, Senator. It is the painter—the artist. His home is in France. It is called Giverny, where he lived and painted. And I have given a contribution to help restore his home."

Perhaps there were a few refined titters in Georgetown that evening. And what about when, in November of the same year, Helms wanted to know why Washington had recognized the "murderer" Jean-Bertrand Aristide as president of Haiti:

Warren Christopher: "Our support for him is based on the fact that he won a democratic election… "

Helms: "So did Hitler."

Christopher: "… with about 70 percent of the vote—"

Helms: "So did Hitler."

Of course, as Christopher might have pointed out, the Nazi party never won an electoral majority (though, even without this legitimizing formality, it did enjoy considerable "understanding" among American isolationists).

The fundamental mistake made by Mead was to view Helms as a kind of reincarnation of Sen. Arthur Vandenberg, the Republican majority leader who made himself so indispensable to the promulgation of the Truman Doctrine and who is remembered for one of those untrue truisms that pepper the conversation of the supposedly wised-up. (The same Washington hand who will inform you, as if for the first time, that "all politics is local" is liable to instruct you that "politics stops at the water's edge.") Of course, politics ever since at least the War of 1812 has begun with "water's edge" questions: witness other pseudo concepts such as "the Vietnam syndrome." And the celebrated distinction between interventionist and isolationist turns out upon examination to be a distinction about whether or not to intervene in *Europe*, or in wars being fought by others. The old "isolationists" were all for an American empire in the Philippines; Pat Buchanan may have thought the Second World War a snare and a delusion for the United States, but he was 100 percent for intervention in Nicaragua. Senator Helms's own

Weltanschauung, to employ a word that he would avoid, has always been of this sort. There is even an act that bears his name, enjoining European and other nations from doing business with, or in, Cuba. Not much hydrophobia there; the water's edge is no deterrent either to extreme partisanship or extreme meddling in the affairs of other states.

In a January 2001 address to the American Enterprise Institute, Helms made this notion explicit by praising President George W. Bush's "faith-based" domestic policy and saying that "this 'compassionate conservative' vision must not stop at the water's edge." He went on to laud the export, via aid programs in the Third World, of American-style Christian fundamentalism. Thus the work of Billy Graham's son Franklin, in defending Christians in the Sudan, gets much praise while the work of the Graham missions to North Korea does not. (Senator Helms has not, in the era of Kim Dae Jung's "sunshine policy," relaxed his dire views of the wisdom of negotiating with Kim Jong Il.) On Cuba, the senator took credit for the existence of the new administration, saying that thanks to Bush's support of the embargo, "Cuban-Americans recognized the real thing when they saw it, and they turned out in record numbers to support him in Florida—giving Mr. Bush the margin that secured Florida's 25 electoral votes *and the White House*." The italics, as well as the highly inventive concept, are in the original.

And naturally, Helms is a devoted supporter of national missile defense (NMD). He publicly told Clinton last year that he would be wasting his time in renegotiating the ABM treaty. He is unimpressed by Russian apprehensions but considers the United States to be more immediately threatened by countries with missiles yet unbuilt. In a way, the mentality of the NMD partisans is a perfect fusion of isolationist and interventionist psyches: We can build a shield over "our" country while reserving the right to intervene at will around the globe. In this way, the parochial and the imperial instincts are jointly served. Helms makes the perfect representative for this unashamed policy of having it both ways.

The same mentality is on show when it comes to human rights questions. Iraqi leader Saddam Hussein must be overthrown, to be sure. But the United States must exempt itself from the Rome Treaty on war crimes and refuse any definition of universal jurisdiction. Helms is never more eloquent and angry than when raising, for conservative audiences, the illusory threat of American soldiers being led off in chains by pesky bleeding-heart international lawyers. The fact is that the comparison of Helms with Senator Vandenberg is wrong (even if that senator does have an NMD proving-ground base in California named after him). The political antecedents of Jesse Helms are, aside from Jefferson Davis, to be found in an unholy synthesis of William Jennings Bryan and Charles Lindbergh. I say "unholy" perhaps unfairly: Helms continues to lard his speeches with references to Armageddon and with flattering references to the television-evangelical faction. It is undoubtedly this element of missionary zeal—including the opportunity to do overseas what is impossible in the United States and forbid funding for family planning and abortion by fiat—that

Want to Know More?

A good introduction to the life and times of Jesse Helms can be found in Ernest Ferguson's *Hard Right: The Rise of Jesse Helms* (New York: W.W. Norton, 1986) and Seth Effron's, ed., *One-Hundred-One Proof Pure Old Jess: Jesse Helms Quoted* (Raleigh: *The News & Observer*, 1994). Walter Russell Mead's article "Why the World Is Better for Jesse Helms," which appeared in the April 22, 2001, edition of the *New York Times*, is available on the Web site of the Council on Foreign Relations.

Jesse Helms sets out his views on foreign policy in his newly published book, *Empire for Liberty: A Sovereign America and Her Moral Mission* (Washington: Regnery, 2001). His speech to the American Enterprise Institute, "Towards a Compassionate Conservative Foreign Policy," is available at the Senate Committee on Foreign Relations minority Web site. In "Saving the U.N." (Foreign Affairs, September/October 1996), Senator Helms argues the United Nations threatens American interests and does not deserve U.S. support. Readers should also consult "When Worlds Collide" (FOREIGN POLICY, March/April 2001), a debate on sovereignty and multilateral institutions between Marc A. Thiessen, Helms's former staff member and spokesperson, and Mark Leonard, director of Great Britain's Foreign Policy Centre, a think tank launched by British Prime Minister Tony Blair and former Foreign Minister Robin Cook.

An excellent, highly readable overview of the history of U.S. foreign policy can be found in the four-volume *Cambridge History of American Foreign Relations* (Cambridge: Cambridge University Press, 1993). Two more recent, if very different, manifestos can be found in Patrick Buchanan's *A Republic, Not an Empire* (Washington: Regnery, 1999) and Henry Kissinger's most recent work, *Does America Need a Foreign Policy? Toward a Diplomacy for the 21st Century* (New York: Simon & Schuster, 2001).

Christopher Hitchens's recent writings on U.S. and world affairs include *The Trial of Henry Kissinger* (New York: Verso Press, 2001), *No One Left to Lie To: The Values of the Worst Family* (New York: Verso Press, 2000), *The Missionary Position: Mother Teresa in Theory and Practice* (New York: Verso Press, 1997), and *Hostage to History: Cyprus from the Ottomans to Kissinger* (New York: Verso Press, 1997).

• For links to relevant Web sites, as well as a comprehensive index of related Foreign Policy articles, access www.foreign policy.com.

has energized his interest in international charity. Here again, the provincial ambitions can be dovetailed, however crudely, with the interventionist and activist ones.

This unsubtle "America First" duality helps explain what is sometimes misunderstood as a mellowing on the senator's part. Let us agree that, in the late autumn of his career, he did show some symptoms of, well, softening. Helms consented to a compromise on back dues owed by the United States (and shortly thereafter enjoyed the unprecedented opportunity to take the podium at the United Nations). He affected elaborate gallantries with Albright. He sponsored a cordial joint meeting with the Mexican Senate's equivalent committee, perhaps relieved by the reflection that there is no "water's edge" between the United States and Mexico. And he became positively moist about debt relief for poor nations, succumbing to the appeal of Bono and his band U2 by agreeing to attend his first and only rock concert. (Pointless to speculate whether he thought Bono to be a member of a well-known Republican House dynasty and the band a spy plane devoted to aerial reconnaissance of our unsleeping foes.) It would therefore only be generous to concede that little became his tenure as chairman like the leaving of it. But also, it is only fair to observe that his newfound political standing, in the eyes of some, has resulted from his, at any rate partially, ceasing to be himself.

Christopher Hitchens is a columnist for Vanity Fair *and* The Nation. *His most recent book is* The Trial of Henry Kissinger *(New York: Verso Press, 2001).*

Perils of Presidential Transition

by Glenn P. Hastedt and Anthony J. Eksterowicz

The first months of a new presidency are a unique time in American politics. It is a period of great presidential activism, with appointments and policy initiatives announced on almost a daily basis. It is a "honeymoon" period, when the president's relationships with Congress and the media are at least cordial if not deferential. It is a period when campaign promises come due and domestic politics are on everyone's mind. It can also be a period of great frustration as newly elected presidents struggle with recalcitrant staffs and large, unfamiliar bureaucracies.

It is also a period in which foreign policy challenges and opportunities may arise that demand a presidential response. The extent to which a successful response is crafted heavily depends upon the planning and learning that takes place in advance, during the transition from one administration to another. This period, from the first Tuesday in November until January 20, lasts precisely eleven weeks.

Transition efforts in modern presidential campaigns begin well before Election Day.

The 2000 presidential election represents a unique challenge for transition efforts. Due to the uncertainty of the electoral vote, open transition efforts were highly criticized. For example, George W. Bush sought to create an image of leadership by openly discussing his possible Cabinet choices in the days immediately following the undecided election—discussions criticized by the media as premature.[1] What such criticism did not recognize, however, is that transition efforts in modern presidential campaigns begin well before Election Day.

The concern over presidential transitions is relatively new, and their consequences for the conduct of American foreign policy have gone largely unexamined. Far more attention is given to the impact of presidential personality, bureaucratic politics, and small-group decision-making procedures. To address this void in the literature, we examine the problems and pitfalls associated with modern presidential transitions as they specifically apply to the making of foreign policy. We argue that a three-part transition syndrome exists in the area of foreign policy that has serious consequences for the conduct of American diplomacy. We conclude by presenting lessons aimed at alleviating the problems encountered by modern presidential administrations in transition.

DIAGNOSING THE SYNDROME

Since 1935, when the Twentieth Amendment shortened the presidential transition period from sixteen to eleven weeks, there have been just six interparty transitions: the Eisenhower, Kennedy, Nixon, Carter, Reagan, and Clinton presidencies. If we concentrate upon modern administrations, that is, those that have approached this process in a systematic fashion, the number is reduced to four: Carter, Reagan, Bush, and Clinton. Of these, only three represent transitions from one party to another: Carter, Reagan, and Clinton.

What can we expect from a new president as he begins to construct a foreign policy? Richard Neustadt is one of the few scholars who has written on the perils facing incoming presidential administrations in their transition phase. He argues that regardless of their background, most first-term presidents and all interparty presidential successors will be new to the policy process at the presidential level. Thus, the presidents-elect are prone to be caught by surprise by events in the domestic or foreign policy realm. Secondly, presidents may face pressures to act in haste: a new president will be eager to show his capacity to act "presidential." Thirdly, most presidents will face the problem of hubris, or the feeling that they or their administration know best how to organize and respond to policy problems.[2]

These qualities of hubris, haste, and naïveté tend to produce a three-part transition syndrome in the area of foreign policy. First, key policy positions are adopted during the transition period on the basis of broad strategic principles or campaign themes before the realities of governing have a chance to replace the euphoria of victory. Secondly, desiring to separate itself from its predecessor, the incoming administration commits itself to deal with policies before it has established procedures for policy guidance, coordination, or implementation. Thirdly, the tendency to pursue foreign policy options with little regard for how the solution will be viewed in other countries is accentuated because the administration has yet to establish personal or bureaucratic relations with other states.

To see how this syndrome manifests itself in reality, we will examine how Presidents Carter, Reagan, and Clinton set foreign policy priorities and acted on them in the early days of their administrations.

THE CARTER ADMINISTRATION

The Mandate. Jimmy Carter did not have a strong claim to a presidential mandate. He received approximately 50 percent of the vote to Gerald Ford's 48 percent, and 297 electoral votes to Ford's 241. But he did have a Democratic majority in both houses of Congress. In addition, he had an 80 percent public approval rating at the time of his inauguration.[3] Carter campaigned as a Washington outsider pledging to clean up the mess in the nation's capital. Yet, to be effective in terms of policy, he had to work within the confines of Washington's political culture.

Hubris, haste, and naïveté tend to produce a three-part transition syndrome in the area of foreign policy.

The Transition. Carter was the first modern president to think systematically about his transition. As early as the summer of 1976, he diverted financial resources from his campaign to a transition effort under the direction of Jack Watson, who then assembled a staff of approximately fifty people. One of Watson's responsibilities was to compile inventories on personnel, known as the Talent Inventory Program.[4] There was a downside to this early action, however: it created tension between the transition organization and the campaign organization under the direction of Hamilton Jordan. As the power struggle ensued, Jordan began to win and the effort that Watson oversaw, namely, the systematic search for personnel, suffered. In the end, Carter appointed campaign people to White House positions. The recognition of the importance of advanced planning came into conflict with the need to win a presidential campaign.[5]

The relationship between the incoming and outgoing presidents was, at the outset, quite cold. When the Ford staff attempted to give their counterparts advice and information, it fell on deaf ears.[6] The hubris that Neustadt identifies was probably at work here. There was also the problem of naïveté in the Carter administration. This Georgian who had campaigned as an outsider had no prior understanding of the inner workings of Congress, and his staff had problems dealing with the modern reform-minded Congress in particular. Executive/legislature relationships were strained, and as a result, there was a considerable learning curve.[7] This was attributable in part to the new

president's propensity to appoint young and inexperienced Georgian outsiders and campaign workers to White House staff positions.

Policy Priority: The Panama Canal Treaty. Carter's first foreign policy initiative, and the subject of his National Security Council's initial Presidential Review Memorandum,[8] was the decision to conclude a Panama Canal Treaty. Just days after the inauguration, on January 27, 1977, the Policy Review Committee met and recommended that a new treaty be negotiated "in good faith and rapidly."[9] In the campaign, the status of the Panama Canal had not been a major point in Carter's foreign policy critiques of the Nixon/Ford administrations. Instead, Carter had sounded a bipartisan theme, indicating that did not foresee relinquishing practical control of the Panama Canal Zone while at the same time endorsing the 1974 Kissinger framework for the future of the canal.

What changed Carter's position by the time he became president-elect? Zbiegniew Brzezsinski, his national security advisor, notes that during the transition, Carter decided that negotiating a new treaty would be an early priority of his new administration. The primary conceptual force behind this turnabout was the Commission on U.S.-Latin American Relations, which called for a new U.S. foreign policy toward the region that recognized Latin American states as active and independent participants in an interdependent world.[10] The commission was quite persuasive: Robert Pastor notes that twenty-seven of its twenty-eight recommendations became administration policy.[11]

The speed with which an agreement was reached created a serious problem for the Carter administration.

In January, the report's chief architect, Sol Linowitz, was designated as Carter's special representative to the treaty negotiations, joining Ellsworth Bunker, who had been given this assignment in 1973. Linowitz was designated as a temporary ambassador with an appointment not to exceed six months. As such, his appointment was not put before the Senate for confirmation. This action, while legal and fitting given the speed with which the Carter administration wished to proceed, was politically naïve and created problems for the administration with the Senate. Some members objected to Linowitz's appointment because of his close ties with the Marine Midland bank. Senator Jesse Helms (R-NC), for example, argued that a major purpose of a new Panama Canal Treaty was to bail out American banks, which were concerned about Panama's willingness to repay loans.[12] Others were concerned that the six-month limit on Linowitz's tenure placed unwarranted pressure on American negotiators to conclude a treaty and would result in the United States' paying too high a price for a new agreement.[13]

Also contributing to Carter's sudden embrace of a new Panama Canal treaty were personality factors and the worldviews of key appointees. Pastor, who served in the Carter administration as director of Latin American and Caribbean Affairs on the National Security Council (NSC), notes that Carter was "a man who delighted in trying to accomplish more than anyone thought possible."[14] With respect to the Panama Canal treaties, Robert Strong adds that Carter was fully aware of the unpopularity of the initiative and that it was fully in keeping with his character to "take on the Panama treaties early in his administration, even though conventional wisdom in Washington had it that Panama was a second-term issue."[15] Still other scholars, such as Richard Melanson, note that Carter deliberately took on hard issues and that for him, the Panama Canal treaties "symbolized not retreat or surrender but the generosity of a strong, confident nation."[16]

Negotiations with Panama stretched through the winter, spring, and summer of 1977. According to participants, Carter did not involve himself heavily in the negotiations. Bunker and Linowitz were given the authority to use their own judgment in resolving U.S.-Panamanian differences so long as the final treaty was "generous, fair, and appropriate."[17] On August 9, one day before his appointment expired, Linowitz announced that an agreement had been reached on two new treaties.

One might expect that Linowitz's limited tenure would have prepared the Carter administration for a speedy resolution of the negotiations. It did not. In fact, the speed with which an agreement was reached created a serious problem for the Carter administration, as a disjuncture arose between process and product. Simply put, the administration was not prepared to engage Congress in a treaty ratification battle. Strong notes that once presented with the agreements, the administration's first move was to lobby for time. The prospect of defeat was very real, and senators were asked not to commit themselves until the administration had a chance to lay out all of the facts.[18]

The Carter administration's lobbying effort was described as badly handled. Meetings with legislators and staffers were described as "one-way communications" with no effort to solicit advice on how to handle specific treaty issues. Rumors of deal making and vote buying were rampant, and in the end, one of the most powerful arguments put forward to support the treaty was the need to protect the president from an embarrassing defeat.

Panamanian politics also complicated the ratification process. The proposed new treaties met with opposition in Panama, where a national referendum on their acceptance was held. In an effort to garner additional support and minimize some of the unpalatable compromises that negotiators made, government officials publicly put forward interpretations of controversial treaty provisions that were at odds with those given by Bunker and Linowitz. Matters degenerated to the point that a meeting between Carter and Panama's military leader, General Omar Torrijos, was hastily arranged so that a common interpretation could be announced.

In its handling of the Panama Canal treaties, one can see the mutually reinforcing influence of haste, hubris, and naïveté. Carter moved with such speed that his administration was unprepared politically to put the treaty before Congress. Full of self-confidence and a sense of purpose after his electoral victory, he elevated to highest priority an issue that had received little press during the campaign, and in the process raised suspicions both in Washington and throughout the Americas over his intentions.

THE REAGAN ADMINISTRATION

The Mandate. Ronald Reagan won a three-way presidential race in 1980 with 51 percent of the popular vote and an impressive 489 electoral votes. The 97th Congress was split, however, with Democrats controlling the House 243 to 192 and Republicans controlling the Senate 53 to 47. President Reagan quickly claimed a mandate for governmental reform. Like his predecessor, he campaigned as a Washington outsider attacking "big government" entrenched in the nation's capital.

The Transition. The Reagan transition effort was distinguished by its willingness to learn from the Carter team's mistakes. Reagan's pretransition planning occurred earlier than Carter's and was systematically organized. In April 1980, candidate Reagan initiated an ambitious set of task forces to advise him on budget and foreign policies. What began as an operation of seventy quickly grew to 132. Think tanks like The Heritage Foundation also contributed to policy recommendations. To finance such a grand effort, Reagan campaign associates gathered contributions to a "Presidential Transition Trust." This trust raised $1 million in addition to the monies obtained under the Presidential Transition Act, which specifically provides for presidential transition funding. All told, it was the most aggressive, early, and expensive transition effort, aimed at allowing the new president to hit the ground running. In the end, approximately 1,500 people were involved in the Reagan transition,[19] including pre- and postelection efforts.

During the transition, the relationship between Reagan and Carter was strained. When the two met after the election, Carter is said to have thought Reagan to be detached and uninterested in the issues that were discussed.[20] However, the relationship between Reagan's transition team and the Carter administration was generally positive. Advice was given, some of which was even taken. However, the Reagan team was, as a whole, more experienced in federal government than the Carter people had been.

Though its rhetoric was heated, the Reagan administration adopted a less activist foreign policy stance in its first months in office than had the Carter administration. Still, the influence of the transition was evident in its handling of two major inherited issues: the sale of the Airborne Warning and Control System (AWACS) to Saudi Arabia and U.S. policy toward El Salvador.

Policy Priority 1: AWACS. The first major foreign policy crisis for the new Reagan administration was a self-inflicted blow that had its roots in the transition process. At issue was an $8.5 million arms sale to Saudi Arabia that involved tanker planes, fuel tanks, and sophisticated air-to-air missiles for 60 F-15 fighters, whose transfer Congress had already approved, and AWACS reconnaissance aircraft.

The basis for the arms deal had been laid in the last half of the Carter administration. In 1978, to overcome congressional opposition to the sale, the Carter administration agreed to place operational restrictions on the aircraft. Secretary of Defense Harold Brown told Congress in May 1978 that "Saudi Arabia has not requested nor do we intend to sell any other systems that would increase the range or enhance the ground attack capability of the F-15s."[21]

The fall of the shah of Iran and the Soviet invasion of Afghanistan changed the strategic picture in the Middle East and led to a new round of negotiations over arms sales between the Carter administration and Saudi Arabia. Saudi Arabia now requested that the F-15s be upgraded, and the Carter administration indicated that it was sympathetic to the plan.[22] Locked in a tight reelection campaign and with sixty-eight senators urging him to reject the proposed arms sales, Carter got Saudi officials to withdraw their request until after the election.

One of Reagan's complaints about Carter's foreign policy had been its moralizing quality. That administration's arms sales policy very much fit this profile. By presidential directive, arms sales were not to be a normal part of American foreign policy, and dollar limits were set.[23] During the campaign, Reagan had opposed placing constraints on arms sales, and once elected, he directed the State Department to come up with a different policy. He placed Under Secretary of State James Buckley in charge of this task. Buckley presented the outlines in a May 1981 speech, and it became official policy in July, when the Reagan administration rescinded Carter's Presidential Directive 13 and put its own guidelines in place.[24]

Reagan's was the most aggressive, early, and expensive transition effort, aimed at allowing the new president to hit the ground running.

In its haste to act, and perhaps overconfident of the merits of its proposed change in policy, the Reagan administration did not wait for Buckley's review to be completed or for its findings to be approved before making decisions on specific arms sales. It approved several sales that the Carter administration had not acted upon, among them the proposed Saudi arms sale. During the transition, incoming secretary of state Alexander Haig met with Carter administration officials to talk about the Saudi sale. Press reports indicate that the latter offered to put the sale before a postelection lame duck session of Congress in order to save the new Reagan administration from having to deal with what was known to be an unpopular proposal.[25]

Nothing came of the Carter administration's offer, and on February 25, 1981, Reagan announced that he had approved the sale of additional weapons systems and refinements to Saudi Arabia. Michael Klare states that Reagan was surprised by the opposition with which his announcement was met.[26] Under pressure from lobbyists who argued that the proposed arms sale would provide Saudi Arabia with an offensive capability that threatened Israeli security, Reagan first scaled back the package and then announced on March 2 that he would put it on hold while his advisors took a closer look at the proposed sale.

In April, with Buckley's review still incomplete, the Reagan administration announced that it would supply Saudi Arabia not only with the requested upgrades but also with five AWACS, seven tankers, and twenty-two ground radar stations. Once again, Klare states, Reagan was caught off guard by the opposition to his proposal.[27] This view was echoed by many in the Senate, including supporters of the sale, who acknowledged that "the administration failed from the outset to recognize its repercussions."[28] So intense was the opposition that Reagan did not formally notify Congress of the arms sale until October.

Visible here are two hallmarks that we have identified of a foreign policy in transition: the new administration's haste to put its own stamp on policy and its unfamiliarity with the legislative environment. These factors exacted a toll on the administration's lobbying effort. Senator John Glenn, who voted against the arms sale, characterized the effort by remarking, "I know of no one on either side who does not think this has been grossly mishandled."[29] Ultimately, Congress approved the sale by a vote of 52 to 48. The argument was similar to that during the Panama Canal Treaty debate: to defeat Reagan on his first major foreign policy initiative could cripple U.S. foreign policy for the remainder of his term.

Reagan's embrace of the Saudi arms sale appears largely to have been based on two factors consistent with the transition syndrome. First, as mentioned above, was the new administration's desire to separate itself from the previous administration by quick action. Secondly, the Reagan administration's strategic outlook gave primacy to the need to bolster key U.S. allies and reestablish American leadership. Trying to explain the Reagan administration's position, Henry Kissinger argued that for it to reject the AWACS sale "would have involved unacceptable costs in the relationship to Saudi Arabia." Larry Speaks, Reagan's press spokesman, sated that Reagan felt the sale was crucial given the "serious deterioration over the last year or so of security conditions in the Middle East and Persian Gulf region and the growing threats to our friends from the Soviets and other pressures."[30]

The emphasis on strategic principles as a guide to action came at the expense of attention to the political realities of the proposed arms sale. J. Brian Atwood, who lobbied Congress on behalf of the State Department during the Carter administration, observed that Reagan might not have realized the political costs of letting the opposition become so organized. Moreover, he observed, "a lot of those senators who reversed themselves under great pressure [to support the sale] have been embarrassed by this whole thing and they're going to suffer the political consequences of it."[31] He predicted that in the future, they would be less willing to take risks for Reagan.[32] At least as far as Middle East arms sales were concerned, Atwood's prediction was more accurate than those that saw the foundation for a new foreign policy consensus: between 1983 and 1985, three arms sales packages to Lebanon had to be withdrawn due to congressional opposition, and a 1985 arms sale to Saudi Arabia was voted down in the House.

Lastly, it can be noted that the strategic arguments put forward in support of the arms sales failed to materialize in large part because the administration did not consider how the policy would be received abroad. U.S.-Israeli relations became strained. Prime Minister Menachem Begin told the State Department that the arms sale was a "serious threat" to his country's security. Israel's June 1981 raid on an Iraqi nuclear reactor and July 1981 raid on PLO headquarters in Beirut were described as undertaken in part to demonstrate Israel's frustration with the Reagan administration's efforts to attract the support of Arab states.[33] The arms sale did not have the intended effect of increasing U.S. influence with Saudi Arabia. In 1982, the Saudis rejected Secretary of Defense Casper Weinberger's proposal that Saudi Arabia actively join in support of Reagan's Middle East policy of promoting regional consensus opposed to the expansion of Soviet influence in the area. Moreover, Saudi leaders refused to enter into discussions on placing limits on how the AWACS might be used.[34]

Policy Priority 2: El Salvador. Central American had gradually worked its way up the Carter administration's foreign policy agenda. The NSC met five times between September 1978 and July 1979 to deal with the growing influence of the Sandinistas in Nicaragua. Relations between the new Sandinista government and the Carter administration had soured to the point that in his final days in office, Carter suspended the final installment of a $75 million aid package and authorized a secret intelligence finding that permitted the CIA to support anti-Sandinista forces within Nicaragua.

Melanson observes that "presidential candidate Ronald Reagan may have lacked foreign policy experience but he surely did not lack opinions about America's role in the world."[35] And one area where Reagan had definite opinions was Latin America. As Pastor notes, "to Reagan, the Monroe Doctrine was a living guide of almost spiritual importance."[36] One of the most important aspects of the transition syndrome is that it allows such opinions to become the basis of policy without subjecting them to the usual give-and-take of the policymaking process.

Reagan's personal views were reinforced by a report issued by the Committee of Santa Fe in July 1980.[37] Formed to correct what it saw as the leftist bias of the Commission on U.S.-Latin American Relations, the group warned that the Caribbean was becoming a "Marxist-Leninist lake" and that developments throughout the region constituted a threat to U.S. security interests. The 1980 Republican platform endorsed the committee's analysis, using similar language to criticize Carter's Latin American policies. All five of its leading authors would join the new administration.

According to Rowland Evans and Robert Novak, Reagan "wanted an immediate plan on the disastrous unraveling of central authority in Central America."[38] El Salvador became the first test case for reversing the course of American foreign policy in the region. In February 1981, the State Department issued a White Paper based on documents that it considered authoritative, which indicated that in late 1980 the Soviet Union and Cuba had agreed to deliver tons of weapons to the Marxist-led guerrillas in El Salvador.

Spearheading the administration's new approach to Latin America was Secretary of State Haig, who saw the "morning of administrations" as the best time to send foreign policy signals, particularly to the Soviet Union.[39] Haig remarked on the risk taken by the Soviet Union in support of the revolutionaries. Describing the problem as one of "externally-managed and orchestrated interventionism," he promised to "deal with it at its source."[40]

The White Paper sparked much controversy. On March 6, 1981, *New York Times* columnist Flora Lewis reported on the existence of a twenty-nine-page dissent paper drawn up in November 1980 by the NSC, State Department, Defense Department, and CIA personnel. In June, *The Washington Post* and *The Wall Street Journal* published articles criticizing the White Paper for questionable translations and misidentifying authorship on various articles. Most serious were questions about the Soviet Union's true role in supporting the guerrillas. Eventually, U.S. officials acknowledged that the administration had "overreacted" to the evidence in blaming the Soviet Union, but they defended the correctness of the White Paper's central conclusion: Cuba and Nicaragua did give aid to El Salvadoran guerrillas in November and December 1980.[41]

Congress also reacted with skepticism to the Reagan administration's attempt to redirect American foreign policy in Central America. The House Appropriations Subcommittee on Foreign Operations, Export Financing and Related Programs approved Reagan's request to shift additional military funding to El Salvador by a vote of eight to seven. The vote was a harbinger of the strained relationship that would settle in between the Reagan White House and Congress over Nicaragua. As Bruce Jentleson notes, the "virtual war between the branches" on Nicaragua was not typical of congressional-executive interactions during the Reagan administration, nor was it inevitable.[42] It was the product of "highly counterproductive strategies both sides opted for."

Lastly, this attempt to reverse American foreign policy did not reflect the full reality of what was transpiring in El Salvador. The problem was not simply that of a government challenged by left-wing guerrillas, but of an authoritarian government under siege from both the Left and the Right.

From a military point of view, the greater threat came from the Right, with the leftist guerrillas' having been defeated in a January 1981 offensive. Rightist forces interpreted the singular focus on the leftist challenge as a statement of support for their position. Roberto D'Aubuisson, a right-wing leader, told the press that based on his conversations with Reagan administration officials, the United States "would not be bothered by a takeover." The State Department quickly moved to counter this interpretation of U.S. foreign policy but the White House was less firm, stating, "We don't have a view on that."[43]

One can see all the aspects of the foreign policy transition syndrome at work here. Spurred by Haig's conviction that time was of the essence, the newly formed Reagan administration moved so quickly on El Salvador that it disregarded facts and confidently expected that its word would carry the day. When this did not happen, the administration found itself locked in the first phase of a long-running battle with Congress over control of U.S. policy toward Latin America.

THE CLINTON ADMINISTRATION

The Mandate. President Clinton received 43.3 percent of the popular vote to George Bush's 37.7 percent and Ross Perot's 19 percent. The electoral victory was larger, with Clinton's receiving 370 electoral votes to Bush's 168. This was an election with a disillusioned electorate, and while Clinton claimed a mandate for change, the numbers belied much of that claim, as did his relatively low personal popularity ratings for a new president. The Clinton congressional coattails were nonexistent. Ten House seats were lost in the 1992 election, leaving the new president with 258 Democrats in the House and 57 in the Senate, the lowest margin of congressional Democratic support since 1966.

The Transition. The Clinton-Gore Pre-Transition Planning Foundation took action during the fall campaign to assess Carter's mistakes and Reagan's successes.[44] Even earlier, during the summer of 1992, Democrats with experience in previous White Houses organized to help Clinton with his potential transition to the presidency. James Pfiffner notes that the Clinton campaign was not actively involved in these efforts but did establish a low-level effort of its own.[45] Overall, however, very little work was accomplished on crucial personnel issues during the pre-election period.

Even after the Clinton victory, a transition team was slow in forming. The effort was composed of three levels or branches. The *policy* branch consisted of four "cluster" coordinators for economic, domestic, health, and national security policy.[46] An *operations* branch was composed of ten cluster coordinators overseeing work on such areas as economics and international trade, science and space, justice and civil rights, etc.[47] Third was a *personnel* group under the direction of Richard Riley. These cluster teams were slow to organize. For example, with only thirty-two work-ing days left in the transition, most of the ten operations clusters had not yet initiated their status reviews of government agencies and departments.[48]

The appointment process was also slow, due, in large part, to Clinton's insistence on being directly involved in the appointments and his agonizingly slow and methodical deliberations over his own candidates.[49] Further complicating the transition process was the decision to conduct it from Little Rock, Arkansas, a move that some in the administration retrospectively regretted.[50]

There was an effort by members the Clinton transition team to meet with their departing counterparts shortly after the election while President-Elect Clinton met with President Bush. The Bush people presented a brief primer on personnel issues. One of the Bush participants noted that the Clinton people asked little and made no demands.[51]

Policy Priority 1: Gays in the Military. While conventionally treated as a domestic policy issue, the question of gays in the military was also very much a foreign policy problem. It cut to the heart of questions about military effectiveness and spilled over into a broader debate over Clinton's capability to serve as commander-in-chief.

At a 1991 campaign stop at Harvard University's John F. Kennedy School of Government, presidential candidate Bill Clinton indicated that if elected, he would lift the ban on homosexuals in the military. Clinton's statement was made in response to a student's question and, according to Clinton, was offered without prior consultation with campaign aides or consideration of the broader issues involved. Nevertheless, that promise soon became a staple on the campaign trail. In responding to a January 1992 questionnaire, the candidate indicated his intention to sign an executive order lifting the ban and his belief that "patriotic Americans should have the right to serve the country as a member of the armed forces, without regard to sexual or affectional orientation."[52] His first formal written statement on the subject came in February 1992, when he wrote, "People should be free to pursue their personal lives without government interference."[53] A campaign position paper called for "an immediate repeal of the ban on gays and lesbians serving in the United States Armed Forces.[54]

Instead of circumventing the opposition, the Clinton administration's efforts to act quickly only served to reinforce congressional fear.

Clinton's potentially explosive campaign promise generated remarkably little negative publicity during the post-convention phase of the campaign. All of that changed shortly after the election. Members of the Joint Chiefs of Staff (JCS) voiced their dissent through retired Admiral William J. Crowe, who publicly supported Clinton during the campaign but opposed lifting the ban, and Rep. Dave Mc-

Curdy (D-OK). Reportedly, they urged Clinton to appoint a presidential commission to examine the issue over a one- or two-year period.[55]

The tone of these discussions was not conducive to compromise. Clinton's transition team placed John Holum, a Washington lawyer, in charge of preparing a plan for lifting the ban. He met with General Colin Powell, the JCS, and other military leaders; Chairman of the Senate Armed Services Committee Sam Nunn (D-GA); and gay rights groups. Holum's position was that he "wasn't there to ask whether it should be done... [but] how it could be done to minimize the impact on combat effectiveness."[56] Such a stance highlights the new administration's hubris and inflexibility. Holum's report was finished in early January and sent to Little Rock for Clinton to read. It contained warnings of the danger ahead by two of Secretary of Defense Les Aspin's advisors. They urged the new administration to develop a strategy for heading off the impending conflict with the Congress.

> Early legislative action on this issue will be detrimental... to the president's long-term relations with Congress, his relationship with the military as commander-in-chief and may hinder the intended policy of change.[57]

The incoming administration's early efforts to lift the ban on gays in the military were also hampered by its naïveté about the nature of governing. Concerned primarily with keeping its campaign promise, the Clinton administration felt compelled to move quickly out of a fear that conservative Republicans and Democrats in Congress would write the existing administrative ban on gays into law by attaching it as an amendment to an early piece of legislation. Instead of circumventing the opposition, the Clinton administration's efforts to act quickly only served to reinforce congressional fear about the consequences of this move. The new administration's reassurances to gay rights groups of Clinton's continued support further reduced the room for compromise with Congress.

Aspin's aides recommended a meeting among President Clinton, Senator Nunn, Senate Majority Leader George Mitchell, and Senator Ted Kennedy to plot out a strategy. No such meeting took place. In fact, Clinton did not meet face-to-face with the JCS on this issue until January 18, a delay that angered the chiefs and their supporters in Congress, who felt that they should have been consulted from the outset about a major change in military policy. Aspin himself urged Clinton to approach this meeting not as a negotiation but "as the first step in the consultation that you have promised."[58]

Senator Nunn, without whose support the administration had no chance of succeeding, was reportedly angered by Clinton's failure to consult Congress; and Senator Dan Coats (R-IN), who led the Republican opposition to lifting the ban on gays in the military, complained about the new administration's "in-your-face" approach:

> During Aspin's confirmation they said they would consult and hold hearing... it was really a surprise when the president simply announced he was going to do it immediately.[59]

The need for compromise was not lost on all members of the new administration. The voice of Secretary Aspin, a veteran of Capitol Hill, is conspicuous. He noted on January 18 that

> the votes in Congress, if it comes to it, are overwhelmingly against it.... The point you've got to understand is that as a practical matter we are not going to be able to force this down the throat of the Congress.... If Congress does not like it, it isn't going to happen.[60]

In the end, Clinton compromised and set July 15 as the date for a formal executive order lifting the ban on gays in the military. His action allowed Majority Leader Mitchell to postpone any votes on the subject with the argument that the administration's position was not yet in place. The six-month breather also allowed for congressional hearings and for continued negotiations between Aspin and the JCS. These tense meetings produced the "don't ask, don't tell" policy, an agreement under which soldiers are not asked about their sexual orientation but would be dismissed for homosexual conduct.

The foreign policy issue that offered the most openings to criticize the Bush record was Bosnia.

Clinton's naïveté about the process of governing and building a consensus in Washington and his highly developed sense of confidence in his own political abilities were very much in evidence in the handling of this issue. Clinton proceeded initially as if campaign promises would automatically and painlessly translate into policy by virtue of his electoral victory.

Policy Priority 2. Bosnia. Vacillation is a common critique of the Clinton administration's foreign policy, and its policy toward Bosnia was no exception. However, Clinton's early Bosnia policy shows the influence of electoral politics and the transition. In fact, the Clinton transition can be read as a missed opportunity to control and channel the influence of Clinton's personality on foreign policy.

Sandy Berger, candidate Clinton's advisor on national security affairs, correctly predicted that President Bush would try to portray Clinton as inexperienced and unqualified to deal with foreign policy problems. To counteract this argument, Clinton brought together a small group to work on national security issues. Its core consisted of Berger, Anthony Lake, and Richard Holbrooke. They agreed that Clinton should follow a two-pronged strategy: criticize the Bush record where it was weak and adopt a more forward-look-ing position on some foreign policy issues than did Bush.[61] Holbrooke notes that in the summer of 1992, the issue that offered the most openings on both counts was Bosnia.[62]

Clinton proceeded to attack the Bush administration on Bosnia for "turning its back on violations of basic human rights" and "being slow on the uptake," and he promised to "make the United States the catalyst for a collective stand against aggression."[63] Fearing that the actions of a Clinton presidency might not match its campaign rhetoric, in Au-gust 1992 Holbrooke wrote a memo to Clinton urging him to adopt a more vigorous policy against Serb aggression and counselling him that the choice was not between "Vietnam and doing nothing."[64]

Holbrooke notes that after the election he had little contact with his campaign colleagues, who were now deep in the transition process. Returning from a December trip to Sarajevo and Zagreb, Holbrooke wrote another memo, this time to the soon-to-be National Security Advi-sor Lake and Secretary to State Warren Christopher, one week before inauguration. He was told by associates that the Clinton team was deeply immersed in its own discus-sions over Bosnia and did not want to hear anyone else's views.[65] As predicted, no one responded. Weeks into the new administration, Holbrooke contacted Lake to find out if the memo had been received. He was told that it was "useful" but that some of his recommendations "undercut us at the U.N."[66]

On Bosnia, the subject that preoccupied the president-elect's foreign policy team was whether or not to support the Vance-Owen peace plan. Bush had supported the plan, and in an interview on January 13, 1993, Clinton indicated that he did as well.[67] Lake also voiced support for the plan just prior to his taking office.[68] Yet, beneath these public pronouncements of support, disunity existed.

Internal conflict over what to do about Bosnia came from three sources. The first can be found in the outlooks of the key members of Clinton's foreign policy team. Secretary As-pin wanted to do as little as possible on Bosnia; Lake favored strong action; and Christopher "was on different sides at dif-ferent times."[69] Secondly, there was a desire on the part of many people surrounding Clinton to distance the new ad-ministration as far as possible from the Carter administra-tion, of which Cyrus Vance was a part. Elizabeth Drew notes that "generally speaking, people who served in the Carter administration were not held in high regard" when it came to filling cabinet posts.[70] David Owen writes that Vance was seen as an "old-style Democrat," something the "new-style Clinton Democrats" wanted to put behind them:

Clinton, himself, and the people in the White House closest to him, unlike Christopher, Tony Lake, and Les Aspin, barely knew Cy Vance. They were from the South and West, were not influenced by the East Coast foreign affairs establishment and were determined not to be la-belled a Carter Mark II administration.[71]

The third source of internal discord on Bosnia was the general sense of hubris that is so common following vic-tory. A senior White House official noted:

There was a legend developing from the fact that we won… and it carried over into the administration. It sug-gested that we were more masters of our own fate than reality allows…. We weren't ready—emotionally, intel-lectually, organizationally, or substantively.[72]

That the emerging Bosnia policy would be driven by general strategic principles and personal beliefs with little attention paid to the ongoing diplomatic initiatives surfaced in a February 1, 1993, meeting between Owen and Chris-topher in New York—a meeting that Owen describes as "disillusioning." He comments that as the discussion pro-gressed it became "painfully apparent" that in spite of the administration's criticisms of the Vance-Owen peace plan, Christopher knew "very little about the details."[73] Owen at-tributes part of Christopher's ignorance to the time de-mands of running the transition operation in Little Rock following the election.[74]

The Clinton administration's first major decision on Bosnia was made on February 5, 1993, and was arrived at in a rather casual fashion.[75] Policymaking on Bosnia was the province of the Principals Committee, whose core members were Lake, Aspin, Christopher, Powell, CIA Di-rector James Woolsey, and UN ambassador Madeline Al-bright. On that day, at the conclusion of the third principals meeting on Bosnia, Clinton joined the discus-sion and indicated that the United States must take the lead in the humanitarian effort. He then made a number of de-cisions, including becoming directly involved in humani-tarian action; asking the UN to authorize a no-fly zone, and trying to get economic sanctions tightened.[76]

The impact of decisions did not match the rhetoric surrounding them.

The impact of these decisions did not match the rhetoric surrounding them, and so a series of meetings were held through April in which more options were formulated. Clinton, however, kept postponing a decision. At the same time, the president's public pronouncements about the moral need for strong action were creating pressures to act.

The two primary options to emerge were 1) a combina-tion of lifting the embargo and launching bombing strikes against the Serbs and 2) a ceasefire and protection of the Muslim enclaves. A five-hour May 1 meeting at which Clin-ton had committed himself to making a decision led to the selection of the "lift and strike" option. The decision appar-ently was made with little regard for the difficulty of selling this policy to U.S. allies. Christopher was immediately dis-patched to Europe to try to do so. He had been warned by British and French leaders not to arrive with a fait accompli, especially if it was the lift-and-strike option, and his mission met with little success. The newly minted U.S. policy already was unraveling in the White House itself, as Clinton began having second thoughts.[77] With little support for lift-and-stroke at home or abroad, after his return from Europe Christopher "moved methodically to shut down the Bosnia policy."[78]

LESSONS

Transition. All three transitions under scrutiny here are of the interparty type and are similar in many respects. All three presidents were outsiders campaigning against the Washington establishment and claiming a mandate for change. All three presidents had trouble, to varying degrees, assimilating to the Washington political culture and in particular dealing with an aggressive Congress. All three were unfamiliar with the process of forming policy on a national scale. All suffered setbacks and mistakes in foreign policy during their first year. While the causes of these mistakes can be found in many quarters, for each of these administrations, the manner in which the transition was handled proved to be an important contributing factor.

Foreign Policy Similarities. The cases examined here represent a cross section of the foreign policy issues facing recent presidents. They include relations with Third World states (Panama, Saudi Arabia, and El Salvador), a foreign policy problem laden with domestic overtones (gays in the military), and a post–cold war dilemma over intervention (Bosnia). In spite of the considerable variation that can be found in the details of each case, similarities emerge.

As suggested at the outset, interparty transitions are at particular risk for the foreign policy transition syndrome. Key decisions are made during the campaign and transition period. Personality plays a role here, but it is also clear that the transition is a time when nongovernmental organizations can be particularly influential. The Commission on U.S.-Latin American Relations influenced Carter's Panama Canal decision; during Reagan's transition, the Committee of Santa Fe played a similar role. Clinton's decision to reform the policy on gays in the military was made with little forethought during the campaign, and his Bosnia policy was formed largely with an eye toward distancing himself from the Bush and Carter administrations.

Time and again, new presidents have sought delays in order to allow process to catch up with policy.

Secondly, key decisions were made before the foreign policy team and decisionmaking process were in place. Reagan, for example, made key decisions on arms sales before the Buckley review was completed. Clinton acted on gays in the military without consulting leading military officers who opposed the move, and his transition team in Washington

had soured on the Vance-Owen peace plan even as top appointees continued to voice their support for it.

New administrations, perhaps heady with victory, are often surprised by the opposition their initiatives encounter in Congress. Neither Reagan nor Clinton appeared prepared for the hostile response with which their policy initiatives were met. Carter appeared to realize that a new Panama Canal treaty would be unpopular, but he was no more prepared than other presidents to deal with Congress. Time and again, new presidents have sought delays in order to allow process to catch up with policy.

Lastly, when crucial decisions were being made, scant attention was paid to how the new policy would be received in the affected state or whether the policy made sense in terms of the realities of the situation. Power and size did not make a difference here. The views of the Soviet Union and major European allies were no more considered than were those of Panama, and the realities of politics in El Salvador were ignored just as easily as those in the Middle East.

RECOMMENDATIONS

Future presidents-elect, including the one preparing to take office as this issue goes to press, must acknowledge that the transition period is becoming more important. It should no longer be taken for granted as a honeymoon; it must be managed well. The United States is the sole remaining superpower, and other countries look to it for leadership on many matters, whether the government is in a transition period or not.

It is clear from this review that there exists a clear dichotomy between policy and process. As such, any efforts to avoid the perils associated with early foreign policy initiatives must address both sides of the problem. Even prior to the election, the candidates should devote time to learning the foreign policy process. Those persons who have been involved in transitions or who have written about them suggest that candidates' advisers and staff members are much more willing to discuss process rather than policy at this early stage.[79] These efforts must be bipartisan in nature and include experts and current representatives from the Congress. They should be available to both presidential candidates and to their transition teams (if in place) and campaign staffs.

It is only after the election that the focus should shift to specific foreign policy problems and detailed programs. Transition teams should be formalized early and begin work on appointments quickly. During this time, a foreign policy summit should be held on the model of Clinton's economic summit, which explored various options for the president's economic agenda. The intent would be to garner knowledge for policy options that would later be submitted for legislative action. During the post-election transition phase, the number of participants must be enlarged to include members of interest groups, experts, and the people writ large. These meetings would provide an important pregoverning forum for reviewing and critiquing the policies advocated by the various foreign policy advisory groups that inevitably emerge during the campaign.

Presidential transitions are very fragile periods. The time frame of eleven weeks is simply inadequate for extensive planning in the policy or process areas. Presidential candidates need to do all they can to ensure an orderly, organized, and politically profitable transition. They should strive to begin the process early and focus on issues of political process. The emphasis in this early phase should be upon learning the Washington policy process. If presidential candidates are successful, then their presidencies can begin on a confident note. If they are unsuccessful, foreign policy issues may overwhelm them and their presidencies.

Notes

1. For example, William Schneider on CNN's *Inside Politics*, November 8, 2000; and Brian McGrory, "Both Rivals Failing Test," *The Boston Globe,* November 14, 2000.
2. Richard E. Neustadt, "Presidential Transitions: Are the Risks Rising?" *Miller Center Journal,* 1994, p. 4.
3. Larry Berman, *The New American Presidency* (Boston, Mass.: Addison-Wesley, 1987), p. 312.
4. James P. Pfiffner, "Taking Over the Government: Key Tools for a New Administration," in *Some Views From the Campus,* vol. IV of *Papers on Presidential Transitions in Foreign Policy* (Lanham, Md: University of American Press, 1987), p. 63.
5. Carl M. Brauer, *Presidential Transitions: Eisenhower Through Reagan* (New York: Oxford University Press, 1986), pp. 180–183.
6. Ibid.
7. William F. Mullen, "Perceptions of Carter's Legislative Success and Failures: Views from the Hill and the Liaison Staff," *Presidential Studies Quarterly,* 1982, pp. 522–533.
8. Robert A. Pastor, *Whirlpool: U.S. Foreign Policy Toward Latin America and the Caribbean* (Princeton, N.J.: Princeton University Press, 1992), p. 45.
9. Ibid., p. 46.
10. Commission on U.S.-Latin American Relations, *The Americas in a Changing World* (New York: Center for Inter-American Relations, 1974).
11. Pastor, *Whirlpool,* p. 45.
12. William L. Furlong, "Negotiations and Ratifications of the Panama Canal Treaties," in *Congress, the Presidency, and American Foreign Policy,* John Spanier and Joseph Nogee, Eds. (New York: Pergamon, 1981), p. 81.
13. Ibid.
14. Ibid.
15. Robert A. Strong, *Decisions and Dilemmas: Case Studies in Presidential Foreign Policy Making* (Englewood Cliffs, N.J.: Prentice-Hall, 192, p. 158).
16. Richard A. Melanson, *Reconstructing Consensus: American Foreign Policy Since Vietnam* (New York: St. Martin's Press, 1991), p. 102.
17. Strong, *Decisions and Dilemmas,* p. 146.
18. Ibid.
19. Frederick C, Mosher *et al., Presidential Transitions and Foreign Affairs* (Baton Rouge: Louisiana State University Press, 1997), pp. 58–59.
20. Lou Cannon, *President Reagan: The Role of a Lifetime* (New York: Simon and Schuster, 1991), pp. 105–106.
21. Michael Klare, *American Arms Supermarket* (Austin: University of Texas Press, 1984), p. 149.
22. Ibid., p. 150.
23. Ibid., pp. 3, 42.
24. Ibid., p. 97.
25. Ibid., 150.
26. Ibid., p. 151.
27. Ibid., p. 152.
28. *Reagan's First Year* (Washington, D.C.: Congressional Quarterly Press, 1982), p. 20.
29. Ibid.
30. Klare, *American Arms Supermarket,* p. 151, 153.
31. Ibid., pp. 153–154.
32. *Reagan's First Year,* p. 20.
33. Ibid., 45.
34. Klare, *American Arms Supermarket,* p. 154.
35. Melanson, *Reconstructing Consensus,* p. 138.
36. Pastor, *Whirlpool,* p. 66.
37. The Committee of Santa Fe, *A New Inter-American Policy for the Eighties* (Washington, D.C.: Council for Inter-American Security, 1980).
38. Roland Evans and Robert Novak, *The Reagan Revolution* (New York: E. P. Dutton, 1981), p. 165.
39. Alexander Haig, *Caveat* (New York: Macmillan, 1984), p. 96.
40. Pastor, *Whirlpool,* p. 68.
41. Glenn P. Hastedt, *American Foreign Policy: Past, Present, Future,* 4th ed. (Upper Saddle River, N.J.: Prentice-Hall, 2000), pp. 154–155.
42. Bruce Jentleson, "American Diplomacy: Around the World and Along Pennsylvania Avenue," *A Question of Balance: The President, the Congress, and Foreign Policy,* Thomas Mann, Ed. (Washington, D.C.: The Brookings Institution, 1990).
43. Pastor, *Whirlpool,* p. 69.
44. Al Kamen, "Some Expert Advice for Clinton: Get it Right Before Jan. 20," *The Washington Post,* November 5, 1992, p. A21.
45. James P. Pfiffner, *The Strategic Presidency: Hitting the Ground Running,* 2nd ed. (Lawrenceville: University of Kansas Press, 1996), pp. 164–165.
46. Who's Who in President-Elect Clinton's Transition Team," *The Washington Post,* November 13, 1992, p. A25.
47. "Clinton's Cluster Coordinators," *The Washington Post,* November 26, 1992, p. A27.
48. "Talking to Those Who Have Been There," *The Washington Post,* December 17, 1992.
49. Ibid.
50. Ibid.
51. Ann Devroy, "Bush, Clinton Confer on the Transition of Power," *The Washington Post,* November 19, 1992, p. A1.
52. Ann Devroy, "President Opens Military to Gays," *The Washington Post,* July 20, 1993, p. A11.
53. Ibid.
54. Ibid.
55. Barton Gellman, "Clinton Says He'll Consult on Military Gay Policy," *The Washington Post,* November 13, 1992, p. A1.
56. Dan Balz, "A Promise That Held Inevitable Collision," *The Washington Post,* January 28, 1993, p. A6.
57. Ibid.
58. Stephen Barr, "Hill Backs Gay Ban, Aspin Says," *The Washington Post,* January 25, 1993, p. A1.
59. Ann Devroy, "Joint Chiefs Voice Concern to Clinton on Lifting Gay Ban," *The Washington Post,* January 23, 1993, p. A1.
60. Barr, "Hill Backs Gay Ban, Aspin Says."

61. Richard Holbrooke, *To End a War* (New York: Random House, 1998), pp. 40–41.
62. Ibid., p. 41.
63. Ibid., pp. 41–42.
64. Ibid., p. 41.
65. Ibid., p. 50.
66. Ibid., p. 53.
67. David Owen, *Balkan Odyssey* (New York: Harcourt, Brace & Company, 1995), p. 96.
68. Ibid., p. 98.
69. Elizabeth Drew, *On the Edge: The Clinton Presidency* (New York: Simon and Schuster, 1994), p. 142.
70. Ibid., pp. 28–29.
71. Ibid., p. 108.
72. Ibid., p. 37.
73. Owen, *Balkan Odyssey*, p. 106.
74. Ibid., pp. 106–107.
75. Drew, *On the Edge*, p. 146.
76. Ibid., p. 186.
77. Ibid., pp. 197–198.
78. Ibid., p. 160.
79. Victor Kirk, "After the Victory," *The National Journal*, November 28, 1988, pp. 2390–2391.

Glenn P. Hastedt and **Anthony J. Eksterowicz** are professors of political science at James Madison University, Harrisonburg, VA.

From *Seton Hall Journal of Diplomacy and International Relations*, Winter/Spring 2001, Vol. II, No. 1, pp. 67-85. © 2001 by Seton Hall University. Reprinted by permission.

The One Percent Solution

SHIRKING THE COST OF WORLD LEADERSHIP

Richard N. Gardner

A dangerous game is being played in Washington with America's national security. Call it the "one percent solution"—the fallacy that a successful U.S. foreign policy can be carried out with barely one percent of the federal budget. Unless the next president moves urgently to end this charade, he will find himself in a financial straitjacket that frustrates his ability to promote American interests and values in an increasingly uncertain world.

Ultimately, the only way to end the dangerous one percent solution game is to develop a new national consensus that sees the international affairs budget as part of the national security budget—because the failure to build solid international partnerships to treat the causes of conflict today will mean costly military responses tomorrow. Those who play the one percent solution game do not understand a post–Cold War world in which a host of international problems now affects Americans' domestic welfare, from financial crises and the closing of markets to global warming, AIDS, terrorism, drug trafficking, and the spread of weapons of mass destruction. Solving these problems will require leadership, and that will cost.

MONEY CHANGES EVERYTHING

If this all sounds exaggerated, consider the way the one percent solution game is being played this year, when America has a GDP of nearly $10 trillion and a federal budget of over $1.8 trillion. Secretary of State Madeleine Albright asked the Office of Management and Budget (OMB) for $25 billion in the budget for fiscal year (FY) 2001, which begins October 1, for the so-called 150 Account, which covers the nonmilitary costs of protecting U.S. national security. OMB cut that figure to $22.8 billion to fit President Clinton's commitment to continued fiscal

responsibility and limited budgetary growth. The congressional budget committees cut it further to $20 billion, or $2.3 billion less than the $22.3 billion approved for FY 2000. At the same time, the budget committees raised defense spending authority for FY 2001 to $310.8 billion—$4.5 billion more than the administration requested.

Clinton and Albright strongly protested the congressional cuts. They will undoubtedly protest even more when the appropriations committees of the Senate and the House divide up the meager 150 Account pie into inadequate slices for essential foreign affairs functions. At the end of this congressional session, $1 billion or so of the foreign affairs cuts may be restored if Clinton threatens to veto the appropriation bills—not easy to do in an election year. Of course, the next president could make another familiar move in the one percent solution game—ask for a small supplemental appropriation to restore the previous cuts. But if the past is any guide, Congress will do its best to force the next administration to accommodate most of its supplemental spending within the existing budget. (This year, for instance, Congress resisted additional spending to pay for the U.S. share of multilateral projects such as more U.N. peacekeeping and debt reduction for the poorest countries.)

Even more discouraging for the next president are the projections for the 150 Account that the Clinton administration and the budget committees have presented as spending guidelines until 2005. The president's projected foreign affairs spending request of $24.5 billion for 2005 hardly keeps up with inflation, and the budget committees' target of $20 billion means a decrease of nearly 20 percent from FY 2000, adjusted for inflation. By contrast, the administration's projected defense spending authority goes up to $331 billion in FY

2005; the budget committees' defense projection is comparable. Thus the ratio of military spending to foreign affairs spending would continue to increase in the next few years, rising to more than 16 to 1.

The percentage of the U.S. budget devoted to international affairs has been declining for four decades. In the 1960s, the 150 Account made up 4 percent of the federal budget; in the 1970s, it averaged about 2 percent; during the first half of the 1990s, it went down to 1 percent, with only a slight recovery in FYs 1999 and 2000. The international affairs budget is now about 20 percent less in today's dollars than it was on average during the late 1970s and the 1980s.

A nation's budget, like that of a corporation or an individual, reflects its priorities. Both main political parties share a broad consensus that assuring U.S. national security in the post–Cold War era requires a strong military and the willingness to use it to defend important U.S. interests and values. The Clinton administration and Congress have therefore supported recent increases in the defense budget to pay for more generous salaries and a better quality of life in order to attract and retain quality personnel; fund necessary research, training, and weapons maintenance; and procure new and improved weapons systems. Politicians and military experts may differ on the utility and cost-effectiveness of particular weapons, but after the catch-up defense increases of the last several years, Washington appears to be on an agreed course to keep the defense budget growing modestly to keep up with the rate of inflation.

Why then, at a time of unprecedented prosperity and budget surpluses, can Washington not generate a similar consensus on the need to adequately fund the nonmilitary component of national security? Apparently spending on foreign affairs is not regarded as spending for national security. Compounding the problem is Washington's commendable new commitment to fiscal responsibility after years of huge budget deficits—a commitment reflected in the tight cap that Congress placed on discretionary spending in 1997. Even though that cap is already being violated and will undoubtedly be revised upward this year, the new bipartisan agreement to lock up the Social Security surplus to meet the retirement costs of the baby boomers will continue to make for difficult budget choices and leave limited room for increased spending elsewhere, foreign affairs included.

The non-Social Security surplus—estimated at something more than $700 billion during the decade 2000–2010—will barely cover some modest tax cuts while keeping Medicare solvent and paying for some new spending on health care and education. Fortunately, higher-than-expected GDP growth may add $20–30 billion per year to the non-Social Security surplus, affording some additional budgetary wiggle room. Even so, that windfall could be entirely eaten up by larger tax cuts, more domestic spending, or unanticipated defense budget increases—unless foreign affairs spending becomes a higher priority now.

More money is not a substitute for an effective foreign policy, but an effective foreign policy will simply be impossible without more money. Foreign policy experts therefore disdain "boring budget arithmetic" at their peril.

The State Department recently set forth seven fundamental national interests in its foreign affairs strategic plan: national security; economic prosperity and freer trade; protection of U.S. citizens abroad and safeguarding of U.S. borders; the fight against international terrorism, crime, and drug trafficking; the establishment and consolidation of democracies and the upholding of human rights; the provision of humanitarian assistance to victims of crisis and disaster; and finally, the improvement of the global environment, stabilization of world population growth, and protection of human health. This is a sensible list, but in the political climate of today's Washington, few in the executive branch or Congress dare ask how much money will really be required to support it. Rather, the question usually asked is how much the political traffic will bear.

Going on this way will force unacceptable foreign policy choices—either adequate funding for secure embassies and modern communications systems for diplomats or adequate funding for U.N. peacekeeping in Kosovo, East Timor, and Africa; either adequate funding for the Middle East peace process or adequate funding to safeguard nuclear weapons and materials in Russia; either adequate funding for family planning to control world population growth or adequate funding to save refugees and displaced persons. The world's greatest power need not and should not accept a situation in which it has to make these kinds of choices.

THE STATE OF STATE

Ideally, a bipartisan, expert study would tell us what a properly funded foreign affairs budget would look like. In the absence of such a study, consider the following a rough estimate of the increases now required in the two main parts of the 150 Account. The first part is the State Department budget, which includes not only the cost of U.S. diplomacy but also U.S. assessed contributions to international organizations and peacekeeping. The second part is the foreign operations budget, which includes bilateral development aid, the bilateral economic support fund for special foreign policy priorities, bilateral military aid, and contributions to voluntary U.N. programs and multilateral development banks.

Take State's budget first. The United States maintains 250 embassies and other posts in 160 countries. Far from being rendered less important by the end of the Cold War or today's instant communications, these diplomatic posts and the State Department that directs them are more essential than ever in promoting the seven fundamental U.S. foreign policy interests identified above.

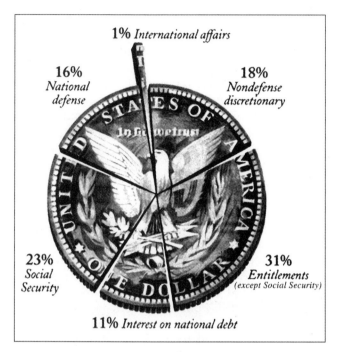

1% International affairs

16% National defense

18% Nondefense discretionary

23% Social Security

31% Entitlements (except Social Security)

11% Interest on national debt

Note: Figures are estimates for FY 2001.

Ambassadors and their staffs have to play multiple roles today—as the "eyes and ears" of the president and secretary of state, advocates for U.S. policies in the upper reaches of the host government, resourceful negotiators, and intellectual, educational, and cultural emissaries in public diplomacy with key interest groups, opinion leaders, and the public at large. As Albright put it in recent congressional testimony, the Foreign Service, the Civil Service, and the foreign nationals serving in U.S. overseas posts contribute daily to the welfare of the American people "through the dangers they help contain; the crimes they help prevent; the deals they help close; the rights they help protect; and the travelers they just plain help."

Following the tragic August 1998 bombings of American embassies in Nairobi and Dar es Salaam, the secretary of state, with the support of the president and Congress, established the Overseas Presence Advisory Panel (OPAP), composed of current and former diplomats and private-sector representatives, to recommend improvements in America's overseas diplomatic establishment. "The United States overseas presence, which has provided the essential underpinnings of U.S. foreign policy for many decades, is near a state of crisis," the panel warned. "Insecure and often decrepit facilities, obsolete information technology, outmoded administrative and human resources practices, poor allocation of resources, and competition from the private sector for

talented staff threaten to cripple America's overseas capability, with far-reaching consequences for national security and prosperity."

The OPAP report focused more on reforms than on money, but many of its recommendations have price tags. The report called for $1.3 billion per year for embassy construction and security upgrades—probably $100 million too little, since an earlier and more authoritative study by the Accountability Review Boards under former Joint Chiefs of Staff Chair William Crowe proposed $1.4 billion annually for that purpose. OPAP also called for another $330 million over several years to provide unclassified and secure Internet and e-mail information networks linking all U.S. agencies and overseas posts.

Moreover, OPAP proposed establishing an interagency panel chaired by the secretary of state to evaluate the size, location, and composition of America's overseas presence. Visitors who see many people in U.S. embassies often do not realize that the State Department accounts for only 42 percent of America's total overseas personnel; the Defense Department accounts for 37 percent, and more than two dozen other agencies such as the Agency for International Development and the departments of Commerce, Treasury, and Justice make up the rest. If one includes the foreign nationals hired as support staff, State Department personnel in some large U.S. embassies are less than 15 percent of the employees, and many of them are administrators.

The State Department's FY 2001 budget of $6.8 billion provides $3.2 billion for administering foreign affairs. Of that, even after the East Africa bombings, only $1.1 billion will go toward embassy construction and security upgrades, even though $1.4 billion is needed. Moreover, only $17 million is provided for new communications infrastructure, although $330 million is needed. Almost nothing is included to fill a 700-position shortfall of qualified personnel. The State Department therefore requires another $500 million just to meet its minimal needs.

The FY 2001 State Department budget contains a small but inadequate increase—from $204 million in FY 2000 to $225 million—for the educational and cultural exchanges formerly administered by the U.S. Information Agency. Most of this money will go to the Fulbright academic program and the International Visitors Program, which brings future foreign leaders in politics, the media, trade unions, and other nongovernmental organizations (NGOs) to meet with their American counterparts. These valuable and cost-effective exchanges have been slashed from their 1960s and 1970s heights. A near-doubling of these programs' size—with disproportionate increases for exchanges with especially important countries such as Russia and China—would clearly serve U.S. national security interests. A sensible annual budget increase for educational and cultural exchanges would be $200 million.

The budget includes $946 million for assessed contributions to international organizations, of which $300 million is for the U.N. itself and $380 million more is for U.N.-affiliated agencies such as the International Labor Organization, the World Health Organization, the International Atomic Energy Agency, and the war crimes tribunals for Rwanda and the Balkans. Other bodies such as NATO, the Organization for Economic Cooperation and Development (OECD), and the World Trade Organization (WTO) account for the rest.

Richard Holbrooke, the able American ambassador to the U.N., is currently deep in difficult negotiations to reduce the assessed U.S. share of the regular U.N. budget and the budgets of major specialized U.N. agencies from 25 percent to 22 percent—a precondition required by the Helms-Biden legislation for paying America's U.N. arrears. If Holbrooke succeeds, U.S. contributions to international organizations will drop slightly.

But this reduction will be more than offset by the need to pay for modest U.N. budget increases. The zero nominal growth requirement that Congress slapped on U.N. budgets is now becoming counterproductive. To take just one example, the U.N. Department of Peacekeeping Operations is now short at least 100 staffers, which leaves it ill-prepared to handle the increased number and scale of peacekeeping operations. If Washington could agree to let U.N. budgets rise by inflation plus a percent or two in the years ahead and to channel the increase to programs of particular U.S. interest, America would have more influence and the U.N. would be more effective. Some non-U.N. organizations, such as NATO, the OECD, and the WTO, also require budget increases beyond the rate of inflation to do their jobs properly. Moreover, America should rejoin the U.N. Educational, Scientific, and Cultural Organization (UNESCO), given the growing foreign policy importance of its concerns and the role that new communications technology can play in helping developing countries. The increased annual cost of UNESCO membership ($70 million) and of permitting small annual increases in the U.N.'s and other international organizations' budgets ($30 million) comes to another $100 million.

Selling this will take leadership. In particular, a showdown is brewing with Congress over the costs of U.N. peacekeeping. After reaching a high of 80,000 in 1993 and then dropping to 13,000 in 1998, the number of U.N. peacekeepers is rising again to 30,000 or more as a result of new missions in Kosovo, East Timor, Sierra Leone, and the proposed mission in the Democratic Republic of the Congo (DRC). So the State Department had to ask Congress for $739 million for U.N. peacekeeping in the FY 2001 budget, compared to the $500 million it received in FY 2000. (The White House also requested a FY 2000 budget supplement of $143 million, which has not yet been approved.) But even these sums fall well short of what Washington will have to pay for peacekeeping this year and next. In Kosovo, the mission is seriously underfunded; the U.N. peacekeeping force in southern Lebanon will have to be beefed up after an Israeli

withdrawal; and new or expanded missions could be required for conflicts in Sierra Leone, Ethiopia-Eritrea, and the DRC. So total U.N. peacekeeping costs could rise to $3.5–4 billion per year. With the United States paying for 25 percent of peacekeeping (although it is still assessed at the rate of 31 percent, which is unduly high), these new challenges could cost taxpayers at least $200 million per year more than the amount currently budgeted. Washington should, of course, watch the number, cost, and effectiveness of U.N. peacekeeping operations, but the existing and proposed operations serve U.S. interests and must be adequately funded.

Add up all these sums and one finds that the State Department budget needs an increase of $1 billion, for a total of $7.8 billion per year.

A DECENT RESPECT

The Clinton administration has asked for $15.1 billion for the foreign operations budget for FY 2001—the second part of the 150 Account. Excluding $3.7 billion for military aid and $1 billion for the Export-Import Bank, that leaves about $10.4 billion in international development and humanitarian assistance. This includes various categories of bilateral aid: $2.1 billion for sustainable development; $658 million for migration and refugee assistance; $830 million to promote free-market democracies and secure nuclear materials in the countries of the former Soviet Union; and $610 million of support for eastern Europe and the Balkans. It also covers about $1.4 billion for multilateral development banks, including $800 million for the International Development Association, the World Bank affiliate for lending to the poorest countries. Another $350 million goes to international organizations and programs such as the U.N. Development Program ($90 million), the U.N. Children's Fund ($110 million), the U.N. Population Fund ($25 million), and the U.N. Environment Program ($10 million).

The $10.4 billion for development and humanitarian aid is just 0.11 percent of U.S. GDP and 0.60 percent of federal budget outlays. This figure is now near record lows. In 1962, foreign aid amounted to $18.5 billion in current dollars, or 0.58 percent of GDP and 3.06 percent of federal spending. In the 1980s, it averaged just over $13 billion a year in current dollars, or 0.20 percent of GDP and 0.92 percent of federal spending. Washington's current 0.11 percent aid-to-GDP share compares unflatteringly with the average of 0.30 percent in the other OECD donor countries. On a per capita basis, each American contributes about $29 per year to development and humanitarian aid, compared to a median of $70 in the other OECD countries. According to the Clinton administration's own budget forecasts, the FY 2001 aid figure of $10.4 billion will drop even further in FY 2005, to $9.7 billion. Congress' low target for total international spending that year will almost certainly cut the FY 2005 aid figure even more.

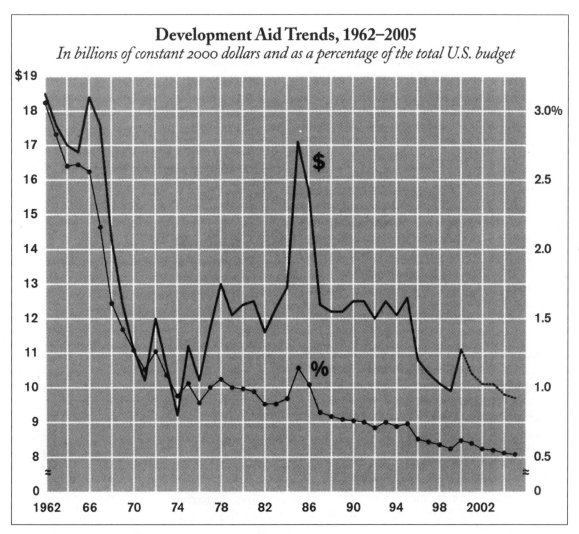

Development Aid Trends, 1962–2005
In billions of constant 2000 dollars and as a percentage of the total U.S. budget

Note: Broken lines indicate estimated figures.

Source: Center on Budget and Policy Priorities analysis of Office of Management and Budget data.

Considering current economic and social trends in the world's poor countries, these low and declining aid levels are unjustifiable. World Bank President James Wolfensohn is right: the global struggle to reduce poverty and save the environment is being lost. Although hundreds of millions of people in the developing world escaped from poverty in recent years, half of the six billion people on Earth still live on less than $2 a day. Two billion are not connected to any energy system. One and a half billion lack clean water. More than a billion lack basic education, health care, or modern birth control methods.

The world's population, which grows by about 75 million a year, will probably reach about 9 billion by 2050; most will live in the world's poorest countries. If present trends continue, we can expect more abject poverty, environmental damage, epidemics, political instability, drug trafficking, ethnic violence, religious fundamentalism, and terrorism. This is not the kind of world Americans want their children to inherit. The Declaration of Independence speaks of "a decent respect for the

opinion of mankind." Today's political leaders need a decent respect for future generations.

To be sure, the principal responsibility for progress in the developing countries rests with those countries themselves. But their commitments to pursue sound economic policies and humane social policies will fall short without more and better-designed development aid—as well as more generous trade concessions—from the United States and its wealthy partners. At the main industrialized nations' summit last year in Birmingham, U.K., the G-8 (the G-7 group of highly industrialized countries plus Russia) endorsed such U.N.-backed goals as halving the number of people suffering from illiteracy, malnutrition, and extreme poverty by 2015.

Beyond these broad goals, America's next president should earmark proposed increases in U.S. development aid for specific programs that promote fundamental American interests and values and that powerful domestic constituencies could be mobilized to support. These would include programs that promote clean energy technologies to help fight global warming; combat the spread of diseases such as AIDS, which is ravaging Africa; assure primary education for all children, without the present widespread discrimination against girls; bridge the "digital divide" and stimulate development by bringing information technology and the Internet to schools, libraries, and hospitals; provide universal maternal and child care, as well as family planning for all those who wish to use it, thus reducing unwanted pregnancies and unsafe abortions; support democracy and the rule of law; establish better corporate governance, banking regulations, and accounting standards; and protect basic worker rights.

What would the G-8 and U.N. targets and these specific programs mean for the U.S. foreign operations budget? Answering this question is much harder than estimating an adequate State Department budget. Doing so requires more information on total requirements, appropriate burden-sharing between developed and developing countries, the share that can be assumed by business and NGOs, the absorptive capacity of countries, and aid agencies' ability to handle more assistance effectively.

Still, there are fairly reliable estimates of total aid needs in many areas. For example, the 1994 Cairo Conference on Population and Development endorsed an expert estimate that $17 billion per year is now required to provide universal access to voluntary family planning in the developing world, with $5.7 billion of it to be supplied by developed countries. Were the United States to contribute based on its share of donor-country GDP, U.S. aid in this sector would rise to about $1.9 billion annually. By contrast, U.S. foreign family-planning funding in FY 2000 was only $372 million; the Clinton administration has requested $541 million for FY 2001.

We already know enough about aid requirements in other sectors to suggest that doing Washington's fair share in sustainable-development programs would require about $10 billion more per year by FY 2005, which would bring its total aid spending up to some $20 billion annually. This would raise U.S. aid levels from their present 0.11 percent of GDP to about 0.20 percent, the level of U.S. aid 20 years ago. That total could be reached by annual increases of $2 billion per year, starting with a $1.6 billion foreign-aid supplement for FY 2001 and conditioning each annual increase on appropriate management reforms and appropriate increases in aid from other donors.

An FY 2005 target of $20 billion for development and humanitarian aid would mean a foreign operations budget that year of about $25 billion; total foreign affairs spending that year would be about $33 billion. This sounds like a lot of money, but it would be less than the United States spent on foreign affairs in real terms in 1985. As a percentage of the FY 2005 federal budget, it would still be less than average annual U.S. foreign affairs spending in the late 1970s and 1980s.

STICKER SHOCK

For a newly elected George W. Bush or Al Gore, asking for $2.6 billion in additional supplemental funds for FY 2001 on top of reversing this year's budget cuts—thus adding $1 billion for the State Department and $1.6 billion more for foreign operations—would produce serious "sticker shock" in the congressional budget and appropriations committees. So would seeking $27 billion for the 150 Account for FY 2002 and additional annual increases of $2 billion per year in order to reach a total of $33 billion in FY 2005. How could Congress be persuaded?

The new president—Democrat or Republican—would have to pave the way in meetings with congressional leaders between election day and his inauguration, justifying the additional expenditures in national security terms. He would need to make the case with opinion leaders and the public, explaining in a series of speeches and press conferences that America is entering not just a new century but also a new era of global interaction. He would need to energize the business community, unions, and the religious and civic groups who are the main constituencies for a more adequate foreign affairs budget. Last but not least, he would need to emphasize reforms in the State Department, in foreign-aid programs, and in international agencies to provide confidence that the additional money would be spent wisely.

Starting off a presidency this way would be a gamble, of course. But most presidents get the benefit of the doubt immediately after their first election. Anyway, without this kind of risk-taking, the new commander in chief would be condemning his administration to playing the old one percent solution game, almost certainly crippling U.S. foreign policy for the remainder of his term. The one percent solution is no solution at all.

RICHARD N. GARDNER, Of Counsel to Morgan, Lewis, and Bockius and Professor of Law and International Organization at Columbia University, has been U.S. Ambassador to Italy and Spain and Deputy Assistant Secretary of State for International Organization Affairs. Last year, he served on the Secretary of State's Overseas Presence Advisory Panel, which made recommendations on the reform and funding of U.S. diplomacy.

America's Postmodern Military

Don M. Snider

The first decade of the new millennium promises to be a turbulent period for U.S. military institutions and for the militaries of the Western democracies generally. During recent months there have been many startling reports:

•Several researchers, seeking reasons for the continuing shortage of volunteer recruits for the U.S. armed forces, have found that while Americans still have great respect for their military institutions, they are increasingly unwilling to support them personally. A few even predict the imminent demise of the all-volunteer force, which has been in place since 1973.[1]

•Academics studying the civil-military "gap" report that the American officer corps is abandoning its traditional political neutrality, and that its members are increasingly identifying themselves as Republicans, a shift very much at odds with the civilian elites in America, a majority of whom still identify themselves as independents or as Democrats.[2]

•On the campaign trail, Al Gore and Bill Bradley, engaged in a public contest for the gay vote, have both promised to bring U.S. military leaders to heel on the issue of gays serving openly in the military. By implication, the candidates are questioning the obedience of the military, or, at the very least, suggesting that the military has been permitted too much autonomy under the Clinton administration.

•"Gap researchers" also report that a resounding 75–80 percent of officers strongly oppose gays serving openly in the American military, and over a quarter say they will resign if gays are allowed to do so, thereby disrupting the cohesion they believe to be critical to the success of the military's mission.

•A recent empirical study, *American Military Culture in the 21st Century*, documents the low morale, and the chasms of mistrust between the bottom and the top, of the U.S. military services.[3] It presents a picture of a "stressed and over-committed" institution suffering from declining professionalism.

•Contrary to history and tradition, the British government, bowing to the rulings of the European Court of Justice, announced in early January that gays would no longer be banned from serving in the British armed forces. In a similar manner and for similar reasons, the German government recently announced that females will now be permitted to serve in the Bundeswehr.

What is happening, and why is there such significant change and adaptation now? What factors are influencing military institutions and their organizational structures, and how are they doing so? How is the interested American, accustomed for decades to hearing about the military primarily, if not solely, in terms of budget battles between the Pentagon and Capitol Hill, to understand the welter of information coming from Washington and other capitals about changing military institutions?

Competing Imperatives

It has long been accepted that military institutions under democratic regimes are shaped by two competing imperatives, one from the society they serve and the other growing out of the socially useful function—protecting the nation-state and defending its people and their interests—they perform.[4]

Military institutions reflect—as they must—the societies from which they are drawn and are sworn to serve and protect. Given that armies are primarily human institutions, the existence of this social imperative should not be surprising. The method used to provide soldiers—conscription, voluntary service, or some combination of the two—does over time influence the degree to which a military is representative of the society it serves. "They" are "we," or at least a part of us. In America, the ideal and tradition of the citizen-soldier remains strong in our affections, though much less so within the military today than in the past.

Democratic societies do not want, nor are they comfortable with, "their" militaries being too different or too separate from them. The "supremacy of civilian values" has long been bedrock to the Western, and American, approach to civil-military relations.[5] The citizenry is sovereign, thus its values and way of life are what the military is defending. But soldiers will not be inclined to defend those values, particularly at the risk of death, unless they hold them dear, as being worthy of their individual and corporate self-sacrifice.

At the same time, militaries—responding to the functional imperative—are influenced and shaped by the demands of winning wars, a societal endeavor so illogical and irrational as to have its own "grammar," if not its own logic. Thus, military culture, and its central ethic, focuses on what is required to accomplish its mission. As Gen. Douglas MacArthur once said in an address to the cadets at West Point: "Yours is the profession of arms, the will to win, the sure knowledge that in war there is no substitute for victory, that if you lose the nation will be destroyed, that the very obsession of your public service must be Duty, Honor, and Country."[6] Self-abnegation and self-sacrifice are inherent in the soldier's concept of duty. The moral obligation exists not only to do one's duty when called upon by society, but also to be prepared at all times to be so called.

The study of the military art and of history has for decades convinced military professionals of the necessity of well-trained and disciplined soldiers organized into the cohesive and responsive units, the well-integrated teams and weapons crews with which wars are now fought and won. Thus, the needs of the mission and the unit are always more important than those of the individual. The military ethic is cooperative and cohesive in spirit, meritocratic, and fundamentally anti-individualist and anti-careerist. It holds dear the concept of devotion to duty, the ideals of honor, integrity, trustworthiness, and allegiance to country.

There is a stark, but potentially healthy, tension between the two imperatives and the character and ethos of their respective cultures, civilian and military. This is the tension between the freedoms and individualism so esteemed in America, whereby individual citizens can flourish, and the corporate nature of the military that demands sacrifice, that the individual soldier abnegate self to the higher good of his mission.

The "Postmodern Military"

While always reflecting this inherent tension, military institutions within democratic states also evolve and change over time in identifiable, if often unpredictable, ways.[7] A typology comparing the American military of the Second World War era to that of the late Cold War era reveals several important differences between the two.[8] The earlier type of military focused on threats of attack upon or invasion of America's homeland; it was a mass, conscripted force; it had a supportive public; and officers saw themselves as combat leaders. There were few civilians within military institutions; women were segregated or excluded; and families were not a part of the military, except for those of officers, which were considered integral to military society.

In contrast, at the height of the Cold War in the late 1980s, the military was focused on the prevention of nuclear war and a conventional invasion of Europe. The forces were all-volunteer; their mission was to contain communism "well forward" along the "Iron Curtain";

officers viewed themselves as managers of violence; and, given the nuclear dimension, public support for the military had become increasingly ambivalent. There were a significant number of civilians within military organizations, even overseas; women were partially integrated into the services; and families of all ranks were becoming integral to military society.

More to the point, the question now is what will the American armed forces look like at the end of this decade, when the current evolution toward a "postmodern military" will have been completed. Observers of the military, particularly sociologists, now believe that the historic tension between the social and functional imperatives will be resolved in quite different ways than before. This is primarily because the threat has changed so remarkably since the end of the Cold War. Even though the American military has not often changed rapidly, when it has done so, the catalyst for significant institutional adaptation and evolution has always been just such a stark change in the security environment.

Simply stated, there is now a consensus that no direct threat exists to the security of the United States, nor to its interests abroad.[9] If judged in terms of how the military has been used since the end of the Gulf War, the new "threat" is not a direct one but one of conflict and instability in regions of interest to the United States. Thus, the military's new task, the one catalyzing current change, is to be able to act, in concert with allies, within a context of increased subnational conflict and violence, often to enable transitions to liberal democratic regimes and economic orders. Such constabulary missions, using very limited military force for very limited political objectives—and most often with inconclusive results—are a major change from the warfighting focus of American armed forces for the past six decades. Thus, the nature of the military imperative has changed markedly.

At the same time, the military recognizes the possibility of renewed great-power conflict at some point in the future, for an engagement potentially fought with high-technology weapons in vastly extended battle spaces. But there is, as yet, little or no political consensus as to the likelihood or timing of such a conflict, or even as to the potential opponents. Given these two very different missions, and in the absence of well-established civilian priorities, it is no surprise that the military is not adapting effectively for either one.[10]

A Shifting Balance

Further, since Americans feel no lack of security, well-organized minorities have been demanding changes to make the military "less different and separate"—a request now more tolerated by the larger public than in the past. The balance between the social imperative and the military imperative has shifted in favor of the former. Not surprisingly, with the Cold War successfully concluded, and with no neutral middle in the political spectrum where the military might be treated as more than "pork,"[11] the military has again become a battlefield upon which the nation's cultural wars are being fought.

The postmodern military is likely to focus primarily on peacekeeping and humanitarian missions; to be a smaller, all-volunteer force of professionals, with officers who see themselves as soldier-statesmen rather than as combat leaders or managers of violence; and to enjoy only tepid public support (or worse, outright indifference— witness recent recruiting failures). Civilians will be well integrated into military organizations, female soldiers will be fully integrated into the services, and gays will be able to serve openly under the same standards of conduct as heterosexual soldiers.

Those who study the military expect the social imperative to continue to exert the stronger influence during the next decade, at least until the nation's security situation comes into greater focus and the functional imperative can be more clearly defined—at which time, the question will be: are American forces to be mid-tech constables policing U.S. interests globally or high-tech warriors facing a certain adversary?

The Civil-Military Gap

Many gaps in values and perspectives exist between those in the military and the members of the larger society. As noted earlier, many of these gaps are well known and expected because of the unique nature of the military's function. Thus, not all observed gaps are dangerous; at the same time, not all convergences between the two cultures are functional and thus desirable.

But since the end of the Cold War, the tensions between civilian and military leaders (particularly during the first Clinton administration), and between American society and its military subsociety have increased. At the leadership level, the tensions have been most clearly seen in the president's inability to change the military's policy banning openly gay behavior and in the reluctance of the military in 1992 to send U.S. forces into Bosnia.[12] At the societal level, the tensions were most obvious as progressive advocates pushed aspects of the "not too different or too separate" social imperative in an effort to change military institutions and their unique cultures, and as the military expressed its occasionally disdainful views toward the society it was defending.

With private foundation support, a group of scholars under the auspices of the Triangle Institute of Security Studies (TISS) in Chapel Hill, North Carolina, have recently completed a massive research project into the values, attitudes, and opinions of American society and its military subsociety.[13] The project, in which researchers questioned military leaders, civilian leaders, and members of the public, was designed to determine if there were growing gaps between the two societies that were contributing to these observed tensions. The results are instructive as to the likely character of the emerging postmodern military.

The first finding, which was somewhat surprising given the observed civilian-military tensions, was that a broad consensus exists between the two sets of leaders on a wide range of foreign policy and defense issues. Many of these issues—such as preventing nuclear proliferation, strengthening the United Nations, and the importance of cohesion, discipline and tradition to the effectiveness of military institutions—were quite contentious ones during the Cold War.

Similarly, the two leadership groups agree on the relative efficacy of military and nonmilitary tools in addressing current threats to our national security, and on the success of military institutions in adapting to changes in American society in the last half-century. For instance, they agree that using the military for "social engineering"—redressing historical discrimination—is not now a very important goal: very few civilian (7 percent) and military leaders (1 percent) see it as "very important," although somewhat greater percentages of both groups (civilian, 23 percent; military 14 percent) believe it to be "important." Further, while military leaders are considerably more conservative than civilian leaders, their conservatism compares well with that of the public; in fact, on some civil rights issues officers are more liberal than the general public.

Thus, the researchers believe it unlikely that there will be future conflict between the two societies over basic civic values or foreign and defense policies, and that the military continues to adapt well to the broad changes in America's security environment.

The second finding was that there is the potential for civil-military estrangement in the near future. The researchers found that beneath the surface expressions of mutual confidence and respect, military and civilian leaders view each other's culture negatively and hold strong negative stereotypes of the other. Military officers believe American society has broken down, that the military could help restore it by "leading by example," and that "civilian society would be better off" by adopting "more of the military's customs and values." Civilian leaders share the concern over a moral decline, but they do not see military institutions as having a role in cultural reformation. Officers are more likely to believe that military leaders, rather than civilian political leaders, share the values of the American people.

Because attitude and value gaps are widest between active-duty military leaders and civilian nonveteran leaders (a group increasing in size as fewer and fewer Americans serve in the military), estrangement will grow unless efforts are taken to keep the two leadership elites connected. (Since 1995, and for the first time in the twentieth century, the makeup of Congress underrepresents the percentage of veterans in the general population. Thus, the historic "veteran's bonus" has disappeared.)

The researchers believe that such estrangement is likely to lead to continued recruiting problems for the military; a decline in public confidence in military institutions whose leaders hold occasionally condescending attitudes about American society; a continued decline in public interest in and understanding of military affairs and issues; and difficulty in attracting and retaining the best of American youth to the officer corps. There is also the potential for new policies that could disrupt the armed forces. For example, on the issue of gays serving openly in the military, 75 percent of military leaders are opposed to changing the current policy, but 57 percent of the public and 54 percent of civilian leaders are in favor of doing so.

The third finding revealed that the two sets of leaders are in conflict over issues involving the use of military force. Contrary to the traditions of the American civil-military relationship (wherein the responsibility of uniformed officers was only to advise civilian decision-makers through official, nonpublic channels before executing an approved policy), a majority of the senior officers polled now believe it proper to engage in a public discussion of military policy, either to explain or defend government policy or to advocate policies they think best for the country. As for the use of force, a majority of officers also think it proper to go beyond giving advice and to insist on a role for the military in setting rules of engagement, developing exit strategies, establishing clear military goals, and selecting the type of forces to be used in any given situation.

The public is even more permissive of uniformed participation in public advocacy and of turning over considerations of the application of force to the military. At the same time, a majority believe the military will try to avoid carrying out orders it dislikes. Forty-six percent of the public does not believe "that civilian control of the military is absolutely safe and secure in the United States."

Less Neutral Officers

In the past quarter-century, officers have grown less neutral and more partisan in their political identification and are now more apt to identify (64 percent) with a political party than either civilian leaders or the mass public. Thus, on such issues as the use of force for humanitarian intervention, over which the two major U.S. political parties are often sharply divided, the professional military is increasingly perceived as unable to remain a neutral advisor.

Unfortunately, the implications of the third finding are for weakened civilian control of the military; continued friction in senior-level decisionmaking; and a possible decline in support for military institutions if the

military is perceived as just another interest group pursuing narrowly defined institutional interests.

The fourth finding is more complex than the first three, and was drawn from the data on casualty aversion. The study confirmed what academics have known for some time but have been unable to convince either the military or civilian leaders of—that the American public is *not* casualty-averse. Further, the data confirmed that for such nonwarfighting missions as peacekeeping and humanitarian intervention, *military leaders* are much more casualty-averse than civilian leaders or the public. Why this is so is not clear, but it is possible that it is because military leaders equate casualties with failure or because they believe that such nontraditional missions as they are increasingly being asked to undertake are not strongly in the nation's interest and are therefore not worth the loss of soldiers' lives.

The studies also parsed another issue from the data: from 1816 to the present, the differences in opinion between veterans and nonveterans within the nation's political leadership have strongly influenced both the nation's propensity to use force and how that force has been applied, either massively or with restraint. The fewer the number of veterans, the more likely it was that force would be used, but that it would be used with restraint. This fact, combined with the differences already noted with respect to casualty aversion, means there is likely to be continued civil-military friction over the decision to intervene abroad—which poses potential difficulties for alliance relationships and global leadership. Moreover, so long as the myth that the public is casualty-averse prevails, this can only encourage potential future U.S. adversaries.

So how is the emerging postmodern military to be understood and engaged by those interested in it, and in the nation's future security? I think there are three conclusions that can be drawn from what we see today, including from the research discussed above about the current gaps between the military and society at large.

Alienation and Its Effects

First, it is clear that during the past decade the social, rather than the functional, imperative has become more influential in the thinking of policymakers with respect to military institutions. We cannot know whether this is due to the particular fiscal, social, and intervention policies pursued by the Clinton administration, to the inexplicable reluctance of military leaders to represent effectively the needs of the functional imperative, or to such factors as the absence of a publicly perceived threat. But, irrespective of cause, this fact would be considered a negative if war loomed. Currently, however, it can be considered a positive in that it is forcing the military to address human resource issues it has treated cavalierly in the past. The services can no longer take recruiting for granted, nor can they afford to put other than the best leaders into unit command, the very place that the competition between the social and functional imperatives must be resolved every day.

Further, the services appear to be learning to take very seriously the quality of the workplace within which soldiers serve, regardless of their race, gender, or sexual orientation. Only when all of the services establish and maintain standards of performance and conduct in which all soldiers are seen to be treated meritocratically—males the same as females, heterosexuals the same as homosexuals, and latinos and blacks the same as whites—will the social imperative be met. And, not incidentally, these standards, fairly enforced, will at the same time be most conducive to meeting the needs of the functional imperative. Unfortunately, this fact is not yet recognized within all of our military institutions.

The second conclusion is that the professionalism of the military has declined since the end of the Gulf War, and markedly so. Whether measured by military-technical (warfighting), ethical, or sociopolitical standards of professionalism, this decline can be readily seen. And while to a degree this is to be expected in a transitional, peacetime period, one only has to understand America's role in the world today and then recall the horrors of our military unpreparedness during the early days of the Korean War to be very concerned about this decline.

Here the "gap literature" reveals two problems—one of attitude and one of understanding—about which we ought to be concerned. First, there appears to exist within the officer corps the belief that because the services have dealt effectively with many of the ills still too prevalent in American society—drug abuse, gang culture, racial discord, sexual harassment, poor schools—their military subsociety is now somehow "better" than the American society it serves. Obviously, this is a pernicious attitude, undermining the very basis of the military ethic, which is characterized by self-abnegating service to the nation-state.

Second, both military cadets and senior officers appear to hold an incorrect understanding of the acceptable role of military officers engaged in the decisionmaking process with civilian leaders. This is no longer an issue just for senior officers, given the number of captains and majors in decentralized advisory roles in constabulary missions (in Bosnia and Kosovo, for example). The data make clear that officers today believe it appropriate to do more than just advise civilian leaders; indeed, that they should publicly advocate a preferred policy. But they cannot do so, if history is any guide, without further politicizing the military, which will only make it more difficult to address the decline in professionalism.

Thus, restoring professionalism in all three of its components emerges as the single most urgently needed response from the officer corps in charge of our armed forces. But, as noted earlier, in this era of "divided government," in which the absence of a politically neutral middle supportive of a reprofessionalized military is only too apparent, this will indeed be a daunting task for military leaders.

A Wasted Decade

The "gap literature" shows quite clearly the likelihood of continued and even increased alienation between civilian and military leaders. Increasingly uninformed about, and out of contact with, the military profession, civilian leaders may become so "willfully ignorant" that they fail to understand the need for limited autonomy for the military so that professionalism can be restored.[14] And restored it must be if the services are to do a better job of adapting themselves to fight future wars than they did over the past decade. As one astute observer of our military institutions said of that period: "The result has been a wasted decade—not wasted as the 1930s were, for no challenger looms who has exploited this time wisely, but time frittered away nonetheless. That, and a slow seeping away of effectiveness and confidence among the armed forces in its uniformed and civilian leadership, a slackening of morale and warrior spirit, a dulling of the intellectual, as well as the practical edge of the sword."[15]

Thus, it is imperative for civilians—intellectual, business, media, and political leaders—to reconnect with our military institutions and their leaders, to understand what they need and why, and to provide determined political leadership so as to arrive—despite the military's own reluctance—at a new balance between the social and functional imperatives. Only then will we be assured of having a military equal to the challenges of the twenty-first century.

Notes

The views expressed in this article are the author's own and do not reflect the views of the Department of the Army or the Department of Defense.

1. M. Thomas Davis, "Operation Dire Straits," *Washington Post*, January 16, 2000.
2. Peter D. Feaver and Richard H. Kohn, "Project on the Gap between the Military and Civilian Society: Digest of Findings and Studies" (Chapel Hill, N.C.: Triangle Institute of Security Studies, October 1999), at http://www.poli.duke.edu/civmil.
3. *American Military Culture in the 21st Century* (Washington, D.C.: Center for Strategic and International Studies, January 2000).
4. Samuel P. Huntington, *The Soldier and The State: The Theory and Politics of Civil-Military Relations* (Cambridge: Harvard University Press, 1957), chap. 1.
5. Allan R. Millett, "The American Political System and Civilian Control of the Military: A Historical Perspective," A Mershon Center Position Paper in the Policy Sciences, no. 4 (Columbus: Ohio State University, April 1997), pp. 1–4.

6. Gen. Douglas MacArthur, "Address to the Corps of Cadets, West Point, N.Y., May 12, 1962," in *Lend Me Your Ears: Great Speeches in History*, ed. William Safire (New York: Norton, 1962), pp. 74–78.

7. Steven P. Rosen, *Winning the Next War: Innovation and the Modern Military* (Ithaca: Cornell University Press, 1991); Williamson Murray and Allan R. Millett, eds., *Military Innovation in the Interwar Period*, (London: Cambridge University Press, 1996).

8. Charles Moskos, John Allen Williams, David R. Segal, eds., *The Postmodern Military* (Oxford: Oxford University Press, 2000), chaps. 1–2.

9. James Chace, "The Age of Anxiety," *World Policy Journal*, vol. 16 (spring 1999), pp. 107–108.

10. Don M. Snider, John A. Nagl, and Tony Pfaff, *Army Professionalism, The Military Ethic and Officership in the 21st Century* (Carlisle, Penn.: Army War College, Strategic Studies Institute, December 1999).

11. Peter Connolly, "Clinton and the Two Nations," *Dissent*, vol. 46 (winter 1999), pp. 8–13.

12. Richard H. Kohn, "Out of Control," *National Interest*, vol. 35 (spring 1994), pp. 3–17.

13. See note 2.

14. Judith Hicks Stiehm, "The Civilian Mind," *It's Our Military Too! Women and the U.S. Military*, ed. Judith Hicks Stiehm (Philadelphia: Temple University Press, 1996).

15. Elliott A. Cohen, "Prepared for the Last (Cold) War," *Wall Street Journal*, November 12, 1999.

Don M. Snider, a retired officer, is professor of political science at the United States Military Academy at West Point.

From *World Policy Journal*, Spring 2000, pp. 47–53. © 2000 by the World Policy Institute. Reprinted by permission.

UNIT 5

The Foreign Policy–Making Process

Unit Selections

24. **NATO Expansion: The Anatomy of a Decision**, James M. Goldgeier
25. **Outmaneuvered, Outgunned, and Out of View: Test Ban Debacle**, Stephen I. Schwartz
26. **A Four-Star Foreign Policy?** Dana Priest

Key Points to Consider

- Construct an ideal foreign policy–making process. How close does the United States come to this ideal? Is it possible for the United States to act in the ideal manner? If not, is the failing due to individuals who make foreign policy or to the institutions in which they work? Explain.

- What is the single largest failing of the foreign policy–making process? How can it be corrected? What is the single largest strength of the foreign policy–making process?

- Does the foreign policy–making process operate the same way in all policy areas (human rights, foreign aid, military intervention, etc)? Should it? Explain.

- What changes, if any, are necessary in the U.S. foreign policy–making process if the United States is to act effectively with other countries in multilateral efforts?

- Should the United States try to be more like other countries in how it makes foreign policy decisions? If so, what countries should serve as a model?

- What advice would you give to the president before submitting a treaty for ratification?

 **Links: www.dushkin.com/online/**
These sites are annotated in the World Wide Web pages.

Belfer Center for Science and International Affairs (BCSIA)
http://ksgwww.harvard.edu/csia/
InterAction
http://www.interaction.org
National Archives and Records Administration (NARA)
http://www.nara.gov/nara/welcome.html

We easily slip into the habit of assuming that an underlying rationality is at work in the conduct of foreign policy. A situation is identified as unacceptable or needing change. Goals are established, policy options are listed, the implications of competing courses of action are assessed, a conscious choice is made as to which policy to adopt, and then the policy is implemented correctly. This assumption is comforting because it implies that policymakers are in control of events and that solutions do exist. Moreover, it allows us to assign responsibility for policy decisions and hold policymakers accountable for the success or failure of their actions.

Comforting as this assumption is, it is also false. Driven by domestic, international, and institutional forces, as well as by chance and accident, perfect rationality is an elusive quality. Often policymakers will knowingly be forced to settle for a satisfactory or sufficient solution to a problem rather than the optimum one. At other times, the most pressing task may not be that of solving the problem but of getting all of the involved parties to agree on a course of action—any course of action.

Even when decisions are made out of the public spotlight, rationality can be difficult to achieve. This is true regardless of whether the decision is made in a small group setting or by large bureaucracies. Small groups are created when the scope of the foreign policy problem appears to lie beyond the expertise of any single individual. This is frequently the case in crisis situations. The essence of the decision-making problem here lies in the overriding desire of group members to get along. Determined to be a productive member of the team and not to rock the boat, individual group members suppress personal doubts about the wisdom of what is being considered and become less critical of the information before them than they would be if they alone were responsible for the decision. They may stereotype the enemy, assume that the policy cannot fail, or believe that all members of the group are in agreement on what must be done.

The absence of rationality in decision making by large bureaucracies stems from their dual nature. On the one hand, bureaucracies are politically neutral institutions that exist to serve the president and other senior officials by providing them with information and implementing their policies. On the other hand, they have goals and interests of their own that may not only conflict with the positions taken by other bureaucracies but may be inconsistent with the official position taken by policymakers. Because not every bureaucracy sees a foreign policy problem in the same way, policies must be negotiated into existence, and implementation becomes anything but automatic. While essential for building a foreign policy consensus, this exercise in bureaucratic politics robs the policy process of much of the rationality that we look for in government decision making.

Not only is the difficulty of structuring the foreign policy decision-making process to produce high-quality decisions an ongoing one, it is one that exists irrespective of the type of foreign policy problem. It is as much a problem for dealing with immigration questions, as it is for stopping human rights violations, improving trade relations, or defeating terrorism.

In some respects, the problem of trying to organize the policy process to conduct a war against terrorism is an especially daunting task. In part this is because the enormity of the terrorist

attack on September 11, 2001, and the language of war embraced by the Bush administration leads to expectations of an equally stunning countermove. Rationality is also strained by the offsetting pressures for secrecy and the need for a speedy response on the one hand and the need to harmonize large numbers of competing interests on the other. Finally, no matter how many resources are directed at the war against terrorism, there will continue to be the need to balance resources and goals. Priorities will need to be established and trade-offs accepted. There is no neutral equation or formula by which this can be accomplished. It will be made through a political process of bargaining and consensus building in which political rationality rather than any type of substantive rationality will triumph.

The readings in this unit provide insight into the process by which foreign policy decisions are made by highlighting the activity that went into several recent important foreign policy decisions. As such, they provide us with a point of reference for thinking about decision making in the war against terrorism and other undertakings by the Bush administration. James Goldgeier, in "NATO Expansion: The Anatomy of a Decision" traces the manner in which the government responded to President Clinton's decision to seek NATO enlargement. He gives special attention to the role that the bureaucracy and presidential advisers played in this decision. Stephen Schwartz in "Outmaneuvered, Outgunned, and Out of View: Test Ban Debacle," recounts the political activity that went on in Congress leading up to the defeat of the Comprehensive Test Ban Treaty. His essay is an important reminder that policy making is not something that only takes place in the White House. The final reading, "A Four-Star Foreign Policy," is the first of a series of articles that appeared in the *Washington Post* examining the growing influence of high-ranking military officers on U.S. foreign policy. They are likened to the Roman Empire's proconsuls, who operated as semiautonomous power centers.

NATO Expansion:
The Anatomy of a Decision

James M. Goldgeier

In deciding to enlarge the North Atlantic Treaty Organization (NATO) Bill Clinton's administration followed through on one of its most significant foreign policy initiatives and the most important political-military decision for the United States since the collapse of the Soviet Union. The policy has involved a difficult tradeoff for the administration between wanting to ensure that political and economic reform succeeds in Central and Eastern Europe and not wanting to antagonize Russia, which has received billions of dollars to assist its transition to a democratic, market-oriented Western partner. Skeptics of the NATO expansion policy within the government also worried about its costs, its effect on the cohesiveness of the Atlantic Alliance, and the wisdom of extending security guarantees to new countries. How did President Clinton, often criticized for a lack of attention to foreign policy and for vacillation on important issues, come to make a decision with far-reaching consequences for all of Europe at a time when NATO faced no military threat and in the context of diminishing resources for foreign policy?

This article analyzes the process the U.S. government followed that led to this major foreign policy initiative. I have based my findings largely on interviews I conducted in 1997 with several dozen current and former U.S. government officials, from desk officers deep inside the State

and Defense Departments all the way up to President Clinton's top foreign policy advisers.[1] The interviews reveal that the administration decided to expand NATO despite widespread bureaucratic opposition, because a few key people wanted it to happen, the most important being the president and his national security adviser, Anthony Lake. Other senior officials—particularly those in the State Department—became important supporters and implementers of NATO expansion, but Lake's intervention proved critical early in the process. Keenly interested in pushing NATO's expansion as part of the administration's strategy of enlarging the community of democracies, Lake encouraged the president to make statements supporting expansion and then used those statements to direct the National Security Council (NSC) staff to develop a plan and a timetable for putting these ideas into action. The president, once convinced that this policy was the right thing to do, led the alliance on this mission into the territory of the former Warsaw Pact and sought to make NATO's traditional adversary part of the process through his personal relationship with Russian president Boris Yeltsin.

Rather than being a story of a single decision, this policy initiative came about through a series of decisions and presidential statements made during three key phases of the process in 1993 and 1994. During the summer and fall of 1993, the

need to prepare for Clinton's January 1994 summit meetings in Brussels pushed the bureaucracy into action. The product of this bureaucratic activity was the October 1993 proposal to develop the Partnership for Peace (PFP), which would increase military ties between NATO and its former adversaries. In the second phase, which culminated in his January 1994 trip to Europe, Clinton first signaled U.S. seriousness about NATO expansion by saying the question was no longer "whether" but "when."

The final phase discussed here encompasses the period from April to October 1994, when key supporters of NATO expansion attempted to turn this presidential rhetoric into reality. At the end of this period, the newly installed assistant secretary of state for European affairs, Richard Holbrooke, bludgeoned the bureaucracy into understanding that expansion was presidential policy, and an idea that had been bandied about for a year and a half finally started to become reality.

Phase One:
Bureaucratic Debate and
Endorsement of the PFP

In the first few months of his administration, President Clinton had not given much thought to the issue of NATO's future.

Then, in late April 1993, at the opening of the Holocaust Museum in Washington, he met one-on-one with a series of Central and Eastern European leaders, including the highly regarded leaders of Poland and the Czech Republic, Lech Walesa and Vaclav Havel. These two, having struggled so long to throw off the Soviet yoke, carried a moral authority matched by few others around the world. Each leader delivered the same message to Clinton: Their top priority was NATO membership. After the meetings, Clinton told Lake how impressed he had been with the vehemence with which these leaders spoke, and Lake says Clinton was inclined to think positively toward expansion from that moment.

At the June 1993 meeting of the North Atlantic Council (NAC) foreign ministers in Athens, Greece, U.S. secretary of state Warren Christopher said enlarging NATO's membership was "not now on the agenda." But Christopher understood that NATO needed to assess its future, and with White House endorsement, he pushed his fellow foreign ministers to announce that their heads of state would meet six months later, in January 1994.[2] This announcement set in motion a process back in Washington to discuss the contentious issue of expansion. At the White House, Lake wrote in the margins of Christopher's statement, "Why not now?," and his senior director for European affairs, Jenonne Walker, convened an interagency working group (IWG) to prepare for the January 1994 meeting in Brussels and to recommend what the president should do there. The working group involved representatives from the NSC staff, the State Department, and the Pentagon. According to several participants, Walker informed the group at the start that both the president and Lake were interested in pursuing expansion.

On September 21, 1993, nine months into the Clinton administration, Lake gave his first major foreign policy speech, in which he developed ideas on promoting democracy and market economies that Clinton had enunciated during his campaign. Clinton had stressed the theme that democracies do not go to war with one another and thus that U.S. foreign policy strategy should focus on promoting democracy. Lake had helped to develop this approach, which leading campaign officials saw as a foreign policy initiative behind which different wings of the Democratic party could rally. In the 1993 speech, Lake argued that "the successor to a doctrine of containment must be a strategy of enlargement—enlargement of the world's free community of market democracies." And he added, "At the NATO summit that the president has called for this January, we will seek to update NATO, so that there continues behind the enlargement of market democracies an essential collective security."[3]

Although Lake tried rhetorically to push the process along, the bureaucracy greatly resisted expanding the alliance. Officials at the Pentagon unanimously favored the Partnership for Peace proposal developing largely through the efforts of Gen. John Shalikashvili and his staff, first from Shalikashvili's perch as Supreme Allied Commander in Europe and then as chairman of the Joint Chiefs of Staff. PFP proponents sought to foster increased ties to all the former Warsaw Pact states as well as to the traditional European neutrals, and to ensure that NATO did not have to differentiate among its former adversaries or "draw new lines" in Europe. Every state that accepted its general principles could join the PFP, and the countries themselves could decide their level of participation. Many officials viewed the partnership as a means of strengthening and making operational the North Atlantic Cooperation Council (NACC), which had been NATO's fist formal outreach effort to the East, undertaken in 1991. From the Pentagon's standpoint, it did not make sense to talk about expansion until after NATO had established the type of military-to-military relationships that would enable new countries to integrate effectively into the alliance. Several participants in the IWG say that Pentagon representatives made clear that both Secretary of Defense Les Aspin and General Shalikashvili opposed expansion and, in particular, feared diluting the effectiveness of NATO.[4] As NSC staffer and PFP supporter Charles Kupchan would write after leaving the government, "The partnership was deliberately designed to enable member states to put off questions of formal enlargement and of NATO's ultimate disposition in post-Cold War Europe."[5]

In addition to concern about NATO's future military effectiveness, the bureaucracy also feared that expansion would antagonize Russia and bolster nationalists and Communists there. Many State Department debates at this time focused on this fear, and views on expansion there were more divided than those in the Pentagon. In September, Yeltsin had written a letter to Clinton and other NATO heads of state backtracking on positive remarks he had made in Warsaw on Polish membership in NATO and suggesting that if NATO expanded, Russia should be on the same fast track as the Central Europeans. Then, in early October, Yeltsin's troops fired on his opposition in Parliament, and it appeared to many that the political situation in Russia was deteriorating.

During this period, a small group at the State Department—including Lynn Davis, the under secretary for arms control and international security affairs, Thomas Donilon, the chief of staff, and Stephen Flanagan, a member of the Policy Planning Staff—advocated a fast-track approach to expansion. This group argued that in January 1994, NATO should lay out criteria, put forward a clear timetable, and perhaps even offer "associate membership" to a first set of countries. At a series of lunches with Secretary Christopher, organized to present him with the pros and cons of expansion, these individuals pressed him to move the process forward as quickly as possible, saying, as one participant recalls, that NATO should "strike while the iron is hot."

Flanagan had served on the Policy Planning Staff in the previous administration and had first publicly floated ideas about expansion in an article in *The Washington Quarterly* in spring 1992, arguing that NATO would have to address the membership issue "at some point." "No one is under any illusion," he wrote, "that the membership issue will go away as long as NATO is perceived by Eastern states as the bedrock institution of European security."[6] He laid out the basis for what would become a key element of the NATO expansion strategy: putting the onus for not drawing closer to the West on those countries themselves. As Flanagan wrote, "Any European states outside the Alliance would not be excluded by a geostrategic gambit; rather states would exclude themselves from the new collective security pact by their failure to realize or uphold the expanded Alliance principles."[7]

Flanagan, Donilon, and Davis worried that without the prospect of membership in a key Western institution, Central and Eastern Europe would lose the momentum for reform. NATO and the European Union (EU) were the premier institutions in Europe, and the EU, absorbed in the internal problems associated with the Maastricht Treaty, would clearly postpone its own expansion. These officials wanted to encourage states such as Poland and Hungary to continue on the path of reform—to adopt civilian control of the military, to build a free polity and economy, and to settle border disputes—by providing the carrot of NATO membership if they succeeded.

This pro-expansion group also drew on compelling arguments from two other government officials. Charles Gati, a specialist on Eastern Europe serving on the Policy Planning Staff, had written a memo in September 1993 arguing that the new democracies were fragile, that the ex-Communists were likely to gain power in Poland, and that if NATO helped Poland succeed in carrying out reforms, it would have a huge impact on the rest of the region. Donilon took this memo straight to Christopher, who found the reasoning impressive. When the ex-Communists did win parliamentary elections in Poland weeks later, Gati's words carried even greater weight.

The other argument came from Dennis Ross, the special Middle East coordinator for the Clinton administration, who had been director of policy planning under Secretary of State James A. Baker III. Given his involvement in the German unification process and the development of the NACC, Ross attended two of the Christopher lunches on NATO. During one, he reminded the group that critics had believed that NATO could not successfully bring in a united Germany in 1990, but it did, and without damaging U.S.-Soviet relations. He suggested that NATO involve Russia in the expansion process rather than confront its former enemy. Ross argued that the previous administration's experience with German unification offered good reason to believe that the current administration could overcome problems with Russia.

Inside the State Department's regional bureaus dealing with Europe and with the New Independent States (NIS), however, bureaucrats expressed tremendous opposition to a fast-track approach and in a number of cases to any idea of expansion. Many who worked on NATO issues feared problems of managing the alliance if Clinton pushed ahead with this contentious issue. Those who worked on Russia issues thought expansion would undermine reform efforts there.

In these State Department debates, the most important proponent of a much more cautious and gradualist approach to expansion was Strobe Talbott, then ambassador-at-large for the NIS. Talbott proved important for two reasons: As a longtime friend, he had direct access to Clinton, and as a former journalist, he could write quickly, clearly, and persuasively. Christopher

asked Talbott and Nicholas Burns—the senior director for Russian, Ukrainian, and Eurasian Affairs at the NSC—to comment on the fast-track approach. He and Burns argued to both Christopher and Lake that Russia would not understand a quick expansion, which would impair the U.S.-Russia relationship and, given the domestic turmoil in Russia in late September and early October, might push Russia over the edge.

One Saturday in mid-October, when Talbott was out of town, Lynn Davis forcefully argued to Christopher at a NATO discussion lunch that NACC and the PFP were simply not enough. When Talbott returned that afternoon and learned about the thrust of the meeting, he quickly wrote a paper reiterating the importance of a gradual approach to expansion. The next day, he delivered a memo to Christopher, stating, "Laying down criteria could be quite provocative, and badly timed with what is going on in Russia." Instead, he suggested, "Take the one new idea that seems to be universally accepted, PFP, and make that the centerpiece of our NATO position." Talbott argued that the administration should not put forward any criteria on NATO membership that would automatically exclude Russia and Ukraine, and that the administration could never manage the relationship if it did not offer Russia the prospect of joining the alliance at a future date. He firmly believed that Clinton should mention neither dates nor names in Brussels.[8]

Lake wrote in the margins of Christopher's statement, Why not now?

By Monday morning, October 18, Christopher had decided to support the gradual rather than fast-track approach, which meant that any agreement among leading officials would place the policy emphasis on the PFP. Among Clinton's top foreign-policy advisers, Lake sought to push ahead with expansion, Aspin and Shalikashvili sought to delay consideration of expansion and instead supported the PFP, and Christopher fell somewhere in between, open to gradual expansion but concerned about Russia's reaction. At the White House later that day, Clinton endorsed the consensus of his principal foreign policy advisers that, at the January summit, the alliance should formally present the PFP, and he should announce

NATO's intention eventually to expand. This decision reflected the consensus that had emerged from the bargaining within agencies and in the IWG, which had easily agreed on the PFP, but which could not agree on issues such as criteria, a timetable, or "associate membership" status. In the end, the IWG agreed on what its principals in turn could accept: to put forward the PFP and to say something general about NATO's eventual expansion.

The bureaucracy resisted expanding the alliance.

The consensus emerged because, as with many decisions, opponents and proponents of expansion had different interpretations of what they had decided, and this ambiguity created support for the decision throughout the bureaucracy. Vociferous opponents of NATO expansion believed the administration's principals had decided to promote the PFP while postponing a decision on enlargement. Those in the middle, who could live with expansion but did not want to do anything concrete in 1994, also saw the October decision as consistent with their preferences. Finally, the decision that Clinton should comment on expansion pleased proponents of near-term enlargement, as they believed such a statement would help to move the process along on a faster track.

The October 18 meeting would be the last of its kind on NATO expansion for another year. Given the meeting's ambiguous outcome—the foreign policy principals had not given the president a timetable to endorse—confusion reigned concerning the policy's direction. For the moment, the decision to develop the PFP was the Clinton administration's NATO outreach policy.

Yet from the moment the participants went their separate ways observers could tell they interpreted the decision differently. Secretary of State Christopher's entourage, on its way to Budapest to brief the Central Europeans (and then on to Moscow to explain the policy to Yeltsin), said the January summit would send the signal that NATO's door would open at some future date (and apparently even State Department officials on Christopher's plane disagreed about how to present the decision). The senior official conducting the airborne press briefing stated, "We believe that the summit should formally open the door to NATO expansion as an evolutionary process."[9] Meanwhile, Secretary of Defense Aspin and his advisers, attending the NATO defense ministers' meeting in Travamünde, Germany, to gain alliance endorsement of the PFP, emphasized that NATO would not enlarge soon. According to one report, Lake called Aspin in a pique saying the secretary of defense had veered from the script.[10]

Phase Two:
The President Speaks

After mid-October, administration officials knew the president would say something about NATO enlargement on his trip to Europe in January. But no one was sure how much he would say and how specific he would be. After all, the bureaucratic wrangling had produced a decision that the president should emphasize the PFP while delivering a vague statement that NATO could eventually take in new members.

Advocates worried that Central and Eastern Europe would lose the momentum for reform.

The first official statement prior to the summit came from Secretary Christopher at the plenary session of the Conference on Security and Cooperation in Europe (CSCE) in Rome on November 30. Noting that the United States was proposing a Partnership for Peace, he also stated, "At the same time, we propose to open the door to an evolutionary expansion of NATO's membership."[11] Two days later, at the NAC ministerial in Brussels, he said, "The Partnership is an important step in its own right. But it can also be a key step toward NATO membership."[12]

Meanwhile, prominent figures from previous administrations pressured Clinton to be more forthcoming on expansion at the summit. Former secretary of state Henry Kissinger complained in an op-ed piece that the PFP "would dilute what is left of the Atlantic Alliance into a vague multilateralism," and he called for movement to bring Poland, Hungary, and the Czech Republic into some form of "qualified membership." Former national security adviser Zbigniew Brzezinski urged NATO members to sign a formal treaty of alliance with Russia and to lay out a more explicit path to full NATO membership for

the leading Central European candidates. Former secretary of state James Baker also made the case for a "clear road map" with "clear benchmarks" for the prospective members.[13]

During this time, Brzezinski had been meeting with Lake to share ideas about his two-track approach to expansion, and he also invited Lake to his home to meet a number of Central and Eastern European leaders. Since the debate at the White House focused more on "whether" than concretely "how," these meetings with Brzezinski helped Lake to clarify his own thinking and emphasized to him the importance of keeping the process moving forward. Significantly, Brzezinski argued that Russia would be more likely to develop as a stable, democratic presence in Europe if the West removed all temptations to reassert imperial control and precluded Russia's ability to intimidate its former satellites.

In late December, Lake's staff members, who were in general opposed to moving expansion onto the near-term agenda, presented him with the draft briefing memoranda for the different stops on the president's upcoming trip to Europe. Several of his staffers say he threw a fit on seeing the initial work, because the memos emphasized the Partnership for Peace. According to Nicholas Burns, Lake wanted a presidential statement in January that would leave no doubt about the policy's direction.

But high-level opposition to any push toward expansion continued to color the agenda. The Pentagon appeared unanimously to share the view that the policy should be sequential; countries would participate in the PFP for a number of years and then the alliance might start addressing the issue of expansion. General Shalikashvili, at a White House press briefing on January 4, emphasized the value of the Partnership for Peace as a way of ensuring that the alliance create no new divisions in Europe, and he suggested postponing discussions of membership to a future date:

I think it is important that everyone understand—and I hope that our newfound friends in the East will understand that the reason that partnership is defined as it is, is to avoid at all costs the establishment of a new line, a new division that in turn, then, would create new tensions and fuel new conflicts.

But, he added, in words that Clinton would make much more significant a week later, "It is useful to remember that we are

talking so much less today about whether extension of the alliance [should take place], but so much more about how and when." Pentagon officials, however, had a much different view of what "when" meant than did proponents of expansion at the NSC and State, believing the PFP should operate for several years before the alliance began thinking about expansion.

Prior to the summit, even Clinton still seemed unsure of how far he wanted to go. The strong showing of nationalists and Communists in the December 1993 Russian parliamentary elections had sent shockwaves through the administration. On January 4, Clinton said in an exchange with reporters at the White House,

I'm not against expanding NATO. I just think that if you look at the consensus of the NATO members at this time, there's not a consensus to expand NATO at this time and we don't want to give the impression that we're creating another dividing line in Europe after we've worked for decades to get rid of the one that existed before.[14]

This was hardly the signal the Central Europeans had hoped to receive.

Just prior to his trip, Clinton sent Polish-born General Shalikashvili, Czech-born U.S. ambassador to the UN Madeleine Albright, and Hungarian-born State Department adviser Charles Gati to Central Europe to explain the administration's policy and to quell criticisms stemming from this region prior to the summit. Albright argued forcefully to the Central European leaders that the Partnership for Peace would provide the best vehicle for these countries to gain future NATO membership, and she reiterated that it was not a question of whether, but when.

In Brussels, Clinton said that the PFP "sets in motion a process that leads to the enlargement of NATO." According to Donilon, Lake wanted the president to make a more forceful statement in Prague to give a clear impetus to expansion. Sitting around a table in Prague prior to Clinton's remarks, Lake, Donilon, and presidential speechwriter Robert Boorstin wrote the statement that Clinton agreed to deliver. Echoing what Albright had told the Central Europeans, the president said, "While the Partnership is not NATO membership, neither is it a permanent holding room. It changes the entire NATO dialogue so that now the question is no longer whether NATO will take on new members but when and how."[15]

To proponents such as Lake, this statement was a clear victory, and it laid the basis for moving the process along. He wanted the alliance to address the "when" as soon as possible. For expansion skeptics, to whom "when" meant after the PFP had created a new military environment in Europe, the president's words meant nothing specific and reflected, they believed, the outcome of the October 18 decision; they concluded that although the president had stated that expansion was theoretically possible, the administration would not undertake any actual effort to expand the alliance anytime soon. Their failure to recognize the importance of the president's remarks—at least as Lake and other expansion proponents interpreted them—would lead to their surprise later in the year that the process had been moving forward.

Administration critics would later suggest that Clinton supported expansion purely for political purposes, to woo voters of Polish, Czech, and Hungarian descent. Numerous foreign policy officials in the administration, who deny that domestic political considerations came up in their meetings on expansion, hotly disputed this claim. Lake says that although everyone knew the political context of the NATO enlargement debate, he never had "an explicit discussion" with the president about the domestic political implications of expansion.

The key proponent of a cautious approach was Strobe Talbott.

Domestic politics probably played a more complicated role in this policy decision than a simple attempt to court ethnic votes in key midwestern and northeastern states. First, for several political reasons, Clinton needed to demonstrate U.S. leadership. His administration's policy in Bosnia was failing miserably, and this failure overshadowed every other foreign policy issue at the time. Second, even if ethnic pressures did not drive the decision, Clinton would have alienated these vocal and powerful domestic constituencies had he decided against expanding NATO; Republicans thus would have gained another issue to use in congressional elections later that year. If domestic politics did not drive the decision, they gave it more resonance for the White House, and both parties certainly used the policy for political pur-

poses; Clinton's speeches in places like Cleveland and Detroit in 1995–96 provide clear evidence of the perceived value of NATO expansion to those communities, and the Republicans included NATO expansion as a plank in their Contract with America during the 1994 congressional campaign.

The bureaucratic decision-making process had not advanced much between October 1993 and the president's trip to Europe in January 1994. But regardless of where the bureaucratic consensus remained, Clinton had opened the door for expansion with his forceful remarks in Brussels and Prague. This in turn gave Lake the impetus he needed, and because of his proximity and access to the president, for the moment he could move the process along without having to gain the backing of the rest of the bureaucracy.

Phase Three: From Rhetoric to Reality

For several months after Clinton's pronouncements in January, neither his advisers nor the bureaucracy paid much attention to NATO expansion, largely because of the crises in Bosnia that winter and because of the attention they paid to getting the PFP up and running. In early spring, the NATO expansion process began moving forward again, at Lake's instigation. In April, Lake held a meeting with his deputy, Samuel R. "Sandy" Berger, and one of his staffers, Daniel Fried, a specialist on Central and Eastern Europe, to discuss how to follow up on the president's January remarks and to prepare for the president's trip to Warsaw that July. Lake asked for an action plan on enlargement, and when Fried reminded him of the bureaucracy's continued strong opposition, Lake replied that the president wanted to move forward and Lake therefore needed an action plan to make it happen.

To write the policy paper, Fried brought in two old colleagues: Burns at NSC and Alexander Vershbow, then in the European bureau of the State Department but soon to become the NSC's senior director for European affairs. Fried had known Vershbow since they were both graduate students together at Columbia University and valued his expertise on NATO. Fried had known Burns since the two worked on Central European issues at the State Department during the tumultuous events of 1989. Despite his NSC portfolio on Russian affairs, Burns was not opposed to

NATO expansion, which pleased Fried; Burns in turn appreciated that Fried accepted a gradual approach and understood that the strategy had to include a place for Russia. Unlike the authors of many policy papers that need approval, or clearance, from key actors at each of the relevant agencies, this troika worked alone, thus sidestepping the need for bureaucratic bargaining. Before the president's Warsaw trip, Lake invited Talbott and State Department Policy Planning director James Steinberg to the White House to discuss the draft paper with Fried and Burns. Talbott sought assurances that the proposed process would be gradual, consistent with the policy he had pushed the previous October.

Many people believe Talbott opposed enlargement during this time, especially because most of the Russia specialists outside government vehemently opposed expanding NATO. Talbott clearly opposed making any immediate moves and emphasized that the process must be gradual and include rather than isolate Russia. But many of Talbott's colleagues say that once he became deputy secretary of state in February 1994 and more regularly considered the broader European landscape and the needs of the Central and Eastern Europeans, he warmed to expansion. (Several of Talbott's colleagues argue that he opposed expansion, lost, and then sought to ensure that both the expansion track and the NATO-Russia track would proceed in tandem.) Talbott encouraged Christopher to bring Richard Holbrooke back from his post as ambassador to Germany to be assistant secretary of state for European affairs in summer 1994, both to fix the Bosnia policy and to work on NATO expansion. By the following year, Talbott had become one of the most articulate Clinton administration spokespersons in favor of the NATO expansion policy.

By summer, the NSC and State Department positions had converged. Thinking in more gradual terms than Lake had been pushing earlier in the year, the troika's views now coincided with the consensus that had developed in the State Department. The efforts to begin figuring out a way to develop a timetable for both the expansion track and the NATO-Russia track led to a major push in summer and fall 1994 to get an expansion policy on firmer footing.

In Warsaw in July, Clinton spoke more forcefully on the issue than many in the bureaucracy would have preferred, just as he had done in Brussels and Prague earlier in the year. In an exchange with reporters after his meeting with Lech Walesa, he said, "I have always stated my support for the idea that NATO will expand.... And now what we have to do is to get the NATO partners together and to discuss what the next steps should be."[16] By emphasizing the need to meet with U.S. allies, the president gave a green light to those who wanted a concrete plan.

Two months later, addressing a conference in Berlin, Vice President Al Gore proved even more outspoken, saying,

Everyone realizes that a military alliance, when faced with a fundamental change in the threat for which it was founded, either must define a convincing new rationale or become decrepit. Everyone knows that economic and political organizations tailored for a divided continent must now adapt to new circumstances—including acceptance of new members—or be exposed as mere bastions of privilege.[17]

Holbrooke apparently had major input on this speech, and one staffer for the Joint Chiefs says the vice president's remarks gave the military its first inkling that the administration's NATO policy had changed since January. Senior military representatives objected to the draft text of Gore's remarks, but to no avail.

Despite his inclination toward expanding the alliance, Clinton understood concerns about Russia's reaction. After all, Clinton's foreign policy had centered in part on U.S. assistance for the Yeltsin government's reform program, and he did not want to undercut Yeltsin before the 1996 Russian presidential election. In late September, Yeltsin came to Washington, and Clinton had a chance to tell him face to face that NATO was potentially open to all of Europe's new democracies, including Russia, and that it would not expand in a way that threatened Russia's interests. At a White House luncheon, Clinton told Yeltsin that he had discussed NATO expansion with key allied leaders, and he made sure Yeltsin understood that NATO would not announce the new members until after the Russian and U.S. 1996 presidential elections. At the same time, Clinton wanted to ensure that any advances in the process that might take place in the meantime—during the NATO ministerials—would not surprise the Russian president.

With Holbrooke coming back to the State Department and with Vershbow and Fried both now special assistants to the president at the NSC, expansion proponents had gained

more power within the bureaucracy than they had during the previous autumn. Lake successfully circumvented bureaucratic opposition to get Clinton to make forceful statements that expansion would occur. His troika had continued to update its action plan throughout the summer and fall, and by October 1994 its strategy paper proposed the timeline that the alliance eventually followed: a series of studies and consultations designed to lead to a membership invitation to the first group and a NATO-Russia accord in 1997. But concerns about the military dimension of expansion still existed in the Pentagon, without whose efforts to address the nuts and bolts of expanding the military alliance the decision could not have moved from theory to practice.

For their next task, proponents had to convince skeptics within the administration that the president was serious. A year earlier, one State Department official had said of the Clinton foreign policy team, "They make decisions and then they have absolutely no idea of how to get the bureaucracy to implement those decisions.... There is no enforcer."[18] For NATO expansion, the enforcer would be Holbrooke, the newly installed assistant secretary of state, whom Christopher had brought back to the department at the urging of Talbott, Donilon, and Under Secretary for Political Affairs Peter Tarnoff.

Holbrooke held his first interagency meeting on NATO expansion at the State Department in late September, almost immediately after taking office. He wanted to make clear that he would set up and run the mechanism to expand NATO, because the president wanted it to happen. Holbrooke knew that most Pentagon officials preferred concentrating on making the PFP work rather than moving ahead with expansion, and he wanted to make sure everyone understood that he was taking charge. His opportunity came at this meeting when the senior representative from the Joint Chiefs of Staff (JCS), three-star Gen. Wesley Clark, questioned Holbrooke's plans to move forward on the "when" and "how" questions of expansion. To the Pentagon's way of thinking, no one had yet made a decision that would warrant this action. Holbrooke shocked those in attendance by declaring, "That sounds like insubordination to me. Either you are on the president's program or you are not."[19]

According to participants, Deputy Assistant Secretary of Defense Joseph Kruzel, one of the key figures in developing the PFP program, argued that the issue had been debated in October 1993 and the de-

cision at that time, the last formal meeting on the subject at the highest levels, was *not* to enlarge. Other Pentagon officials in attendance argued that only the "principals" could make this decision, and thus another meeting needed to be held at the highest level. Holbrooke responded that those taking this view had not been listening to what the president had been saying. The skeptics simply could not believe that Holbrooke was resting his whole case on remarks Clinton had made in Brussels, Prague, and Warsaw. Former defense secretary William Perry still refers to Holbrooke as having "presumed" at that point that the administration had decided to enlarge NATO, whereas Clinton had made no formal decision to that effect.

After this dramatic outburst, Holbrooke asked Clark to set up a meeting to brief this interagency group on what they would need to do to implement the policy. Through this request, Holbrooke enabled the Joint Chiefs of Staff to voice their concerns but also forced them to begin acting on the issue. At the Pentagon two weeks later, a team with representatives from both the Office of the Secretary of Defense (OSD) and the JCS presented to the interagency group the full range of military requirements each country would need to meet to join NATO. The JCS briefer pointed, for example, to the 1,200 Atlantic Alliance standardization agreements the former Warsaw Pact armed forces would have to address to become compatible with NATO. Holbrooke, now playing "good cop," responded by saying that this briefing was exactly what the group needed, and he invited them to work with him to make the process a smooth one. This briefing would, in fact, serve as the basis both for the briefing to the NAC later in the fall and for the NATO study conducted the following year.

Because Pentagon officials did not believe the administration had ever made a formal decision, Perry recalls that he called Clinton and asked for a meeting of the foreign policy team to clarify the president's intentions. At the meeting, Perry presented his arguments for holding back and giving the PFP another year before deciding on enlargement. He wanted time to move forward on the NATO-Russia track and to convince Moscow that NATO did not threaten Russia's interests, before the alliance moved ahead on the expansion track. Instead, the president endorsed the two-track plan that Lake and his staff, as well as the State Department, now pushed—the plan that ultimately led to the May 1997 signing of the NATO-Russia Founding Act and the July 1997 NATO summit in Madrid inviting Poland, Hungary, and the Czech Republic to begin talks on accession to full NATO membership.

The Ambiguity of the Decision

Like so many decision-making processes, the NATO expansion process was not at all clearcut. The best evidence of its ambiguities comes from asking participants a simple question: "When did you believe that the decision to expand NATO had been made?" Their answers demonstrate that what you see depends on where you stand; attitudes toward the decision affected individuals' views of what was happening. Most supporters, including Lake, cite the period between the October 1993 meeting of the principals and Clinton's trip to Europe in January 1994. The answers of opponents, on the other hand, generally range over the second half of 1994, depending on when they finally realized the president was serious. One State Department official who opposed expansion said that when he objected to language circulating in an interagency memo on the issue in August 1994, a colleague told him it was the same language the president had used in Warsaw the previous month. At that point, he says, he understood that the policy had moved from theory to reality. Others, such as Perry, did not start to believe that expansion was on the table until after the Holbrooke interagency meeting in September 1994. In support of this last interpretation, Brzezinski pointed out at the time that until Clinton *answered* the questions "when" and "how," rather than simply *asking* them, the United States had no decisive plan for Europe.[20]

These interpretations vary so widely because the president and his top advisers did not make a formal decision about a timetable or process for expansion until long after Clinton had started saying NATO would enlarge. The when, who, how, and even why came only over time and not always through a formal decision-making process. In January 1994, when the president first said that he expected the alliance to take in new members, no consensus existed among his top advisers on the difficult questions of "when" and "how." Clinton's advisers could as reasonably believe that his remarks amounted to no more than a vague statement that NATO might someday expand as they could believe that the president wanted to begin moving forward *now*.

Whereas proponents of expansion took his statements as a signal to begin planning how to put theory into practice, the president did not make an explicit decision in the presence of his top foreign policy advisers until nearly a year later, and some opponents therefore choose to believe that the course was not set until that meeting.

Readers may find it unsatisfying that I have not uncovered either *the* moment of decision or the president's ulterior motive. Truthfully, however, most policies—even those as significant as this one—develop in a more ambiguous fashion. This process was hardly unique to the Clinton administration. White House meetings often result in participants, as well as those they inform, having conflicting understandings of what the administration has decided. Policy entrepreneurs use presidential statements to push forward an issue that remains highly contentious in the bureaucracy. Each step alone seem trivial. But cumulatively, they can result in momentous policies.

As for motive, Walesa and Havel may well have made a huge impression on a president open to emotional appeals. Still, given that Clinton cared so much about the fate of Russian reform, Walesa's appeal to bring Poland and other Central European nations into the West could hardly have been sufficient. Rather, Clinton's motive was probably more complex, and he probably had only a vague idea of when he himself made the formal commitment to expand NATO. For Clinton, the appeal by the Central Europeans to erase the line drawn for them in 1945, the need to demonstrate U.S. leadership at a time when others questioned that leadership, the domestic political consequences of the choice, and his own Wilsonian orientation toward spreading liberalism combined by the second half of 1994—if not earlier—to produce a presidential preference favoring expansion.

Much more work remained to be done, including working with allies, developing the NATO-Russia track, and eventually seeking Senate ratification. Without the 1995 Dayton Accords that ended the fighting in Bosnia, NATO may not have sustained the process underway in 1994. But once Clinton spoke out in favor of NATO expansion in January 1994, expansion supporters within the administration had what they needed to begin to turn rhetoric into reality.

Notes

1. Many of the individuals I interviewed spoke on condition of anonymity.

2. For information on Secretary Christopher's intervention at the June 1993 NAC meeting, see *U.S. Department of State Dispatch* 4, no. 25, p. 3.

3. Anthony Lake, "From Containment to Enlargement," *Vital Speeches of the Day 60* (October 15, 1993), pp. 13–19.

4. Author interviews with IWG participants William Perry, Ashton Carter, Graham Allison, and other U.S. government officials.

5. Charles A. Kupchan, "Strategic Visions," *World Policy Journal* 11 (Fall 1994), p. 113.

6. Stephen J. Flanagan, "NATO and Central and Eastern Europe: From Liaison to Security Partnership," *Washington Quarterly* (Spring 1992), p. 142.

7. Ibid, p. 149.

8. For quotations from the Talbott memo, see Michael Dobbs, "Wider Alliance Would Increase U.S. Commitments," *Washington Post*, July 5, 1995. pp. A1, 16; Michael R. Gordon, "U.S. Opposes Move to Rapidly Expand NATO Membership," *New York Times*, January 2, 1994, pp. A1, 7.

9. The official is quoted in Elaine Sciolino, "U.S. to Offer Plan on a Role in NATO for Ex-Soviet Bloc," *New York Times*, October 21, 1993, pp. A1, 9.

10. Elaine Sciolino, "3 Players Seek a Director for Foreign Policy Story," *New York Times*, November 8, 1993, pp. A1, 12; Stephen Kinzer, "NATO Favors U.S. Plan for Ties with the East, but Timing is Vague," *New York Times*, October 22, 1993, pp. A1, 8.

11. *U.S. Department of State Dispatch*, December 13, 1993.

12. Ibid.

13. See Henry Kissinger, "Not This Partnership," *Washington Post*, November 24, 1993, p. A17; Zbigniew Brzezinski, "A Bigger—and Safer—Europe," *New York Times*, December 1, 1993, p. A23; and James A. Baker III, "Expanding to the East: A New NATO," *Los Angeles Times*, December 5, 1993, p. M2.

14. Remarks by the president in a photo op with Netherlands prime minister Ruud Lubbers, January 4, 1994, *Public Papers* (1994), pp. 5–6.

15. On the Brussels statement of January 10, 1994, see U.S. Department of State Dispatch Supplement, January 1994, pp. 3–4; for the Prague remarks, see Clinton, *Public Papers* Book I (1994), p. 40.

16. For his exchange with reporters in Warsaw after meeting with Walesa on

July 6, 1994, see Clinton, *Public Papers* (1994), p. 1206.

17. *U.S. Department of State Dispatch*, September 12, 1994, pp. 597–598.

18. See Mary Curtius, "Mass. Man is Clinton's Invisible Adviser," *Boston Globe*, September 18, 1993, p. 4.

19. Quoted in Dobbs, "Wider Alliance." Confirmed by author interviews with numerous officials who attended the meeting.

20. Zbigniew Brzezinski, "A Plan for Europe," *Foreign Affairs* 74 (January/February 1995), pp. 27–28.

James M. Goldgeier is an assistant professor of political science at The George Washington University. He is currently writing a book about U.S. foreign policy decision-making.

The author would like to thank Michael Struett for his research assistance; and both the Institute for European, Russian, and Eurasian Studies and GW's Columbian School of Arts and Sciences for funding.

From the *Washington Quarterly*, Winter 1998, pp. 86–102, ©1998 by the Center for Strategic and International Studies (CSIS) and teh Massachusetts Institute of Technology.

Outmaneuvered, Outgunned, and Out of View

Test ban debacle

By Stephen I. Schwartz

WHEN PRESIDENT CLINTON became the first world leader to sign the Comprehensive Test Ban Treaty (CTBT) on September 24, 1996, he hailed the agreement as the "longest sought, hardest fought prize in arms control history." Ironically, having achieved half a victory, Clinton essentially abandoned the fight, allowing a host of personal and political issues to vie for his attention until it was too late to save the treaty. On October 13, the Senate rejected it, 51 to 48, with one member—Democrat Robert C. Byrd of West Virginia—voting "present." The treaty needed a two-thirds vote of the Senate for ratification.

Although the president and Senate Democrats blame the defeat on an ideologically driven near-party line vote, the blame runs deeper and wider. For starters, the president and his national security team said repeatedly (including in two State of the Union addresses) that the treaty was their number one foreign policy priority. But the administration barely lifted a finger to secure its ratification. Vice President Al Gore's

proclamation in his first campaign commercial (hurriedly taped in the aftermath of the vote), that "there is no more important challenge than stopping the spread of nuclear weapons," rings hollow.

Why didn't the president, the vice president, and his entire national security team back up their rhetoric with action? Why did the administration fail to anticipate that a Republican-controlled Senate that was showing greater and greater antipathy toward the president would mount an effort to defeat the treaty? The administration certainly had experience winning over skeptical senators, gained during the successful ratification of the Chemical Weapons Convention and the effort to expand NATO. In the latter instance, for example, the administration crafted a coordinated, long-term strategy (it laid the groundwork for the NATO vote a year in advance), skillfully deployed cabinet officials to lobby swing votes, and expended the necessary political capital to achieve victory.

By contrast, only in the week or so before the CTBT vote did Secretary of State Madeleine Albright and Defense Secretary William Cohen visit Capitol Hill to push for ratification. On the day of the vote itself, both were at an event at the University of Maine. By then, the outcome was a foregone conclusion. Even so, it speaks volumes about the administration's priorities.

Setting the stage

When the president submitted the CTBT for ratification in September 1997, North Carolina's Jesse Helms, the chairman of the Senate Foreign Relations Committee, made it clear that he had no intention of bringing the treaty before his committee until two other agreements—one negotiated with Russia in 1996 that would allow the deployment of limited missile defenses under the Antiballistic Missile (ABM) Treaty and the other, negotiated in 1997, concerning global climate change—were first submitted for ratification. Knowing Helms's antipathy toward both treaties, the Clinton administration responded by refusing to submit the agreements. The CTBT thus became a political hostage. By using his considerable power to block consideration, Helms tied the treaty's fate more to politics than security. The administration, by refusing to handle the treaties on his terms and by failing to mount an aggressive public campaign for ratification of the CTBT, played into his hands.

The Democrats thought that if they could just get it to a vote on the Senate floor, the test ban treaty was a shoo-in. They were wrong.

By the spring and summer of 1999, Senate Democrats were growing increasingly frustrated with Helms's tactics. Non-governmental organizations in the United States and elsewhere that had worked hard to help create the treaty were also concerned about its global prospects if the United States did not ratify soon. Beginning in June and continuing into early September, Democrat Byron Dorgan of North Dakota made at least six speeches on the floor of the Senate extolling the virtues of the treaty, castigating Republicans for refusing to schedule hearings and a debate, and urging his colleagues to help schedule a vote within the next several months.

On June 28, Dorgan and four other senators—Republicans James Jeffords of Vermont and Arlen Specter of Pennsylvania, and Democrats Edward M. Kennedy of Massachusetts and Patty Murray of Washington—wrote to Helms urging him "to hold hearings on the Comprehensive Nuclear Test Ban Treaty (CTBT) and to report it to the Senate for debate… with sufficient time to allow the United States to actively participate in the Treaty's inaugural conference of Ratifying States, which may be held as early as this September, should the Senate ratify the Treaty."

During a July 20 appearance in the Rose Garden, President Clinton stood with nine senators (seven Democrats and two Republicans) and called on the Senate to take action. Clinton argued, somewhat disingenuously, that Helms's tactic of holding the treaty "hostage to two matters that are literally not ripe for presentation to the Senate yet would be a grave error."

On the same day, at a news conference on Capitol Hill, Joseph Biden of Delaware, the senior Democrat on the Foreign Relations Committee, took a harsher line, saying that the Senate's delay was "counterintuitive; it is irresponsible and it is stupid." Added Dorgan, "There is nothing on the Senate agenda—nothing, in my opinion, that is more important than this."

Also that day, all 45 Senate Democrats sent a letter to Helms asking him to "hold hearings" on the treaty and "report it to the full Senate for debate." Helms's linguistically exotic reply six days later left little doubt that he was enjoying his role as spoiler: "I note your distress at my floccinaucinihilipilification of the CTBT," he wrote. "I do not share your enthusiasm for this treaty for a variety of reasons."

The contempt factor

In any other year, or with any other president, the impasse might have been resolved more swiftly and amicably. But since the day he took office—indeed, since the 1992 presidential campaign—Bill Clinton has been subject to unusually partisan and unusually personal attacks, as have his policies. Clinton's ability to "spin" events to his advantage, his remarkable ability to connect—or appear to connect—with the concerns of individual voters, and his ability to outmaneuver Republicans in the political arena have all infuriated the increasingly conservative Republican members of Congress, some of whom no longer hide their contempt for the president.

The Republicans have expended considerable effort to expose what they perceive to be serious transgressions by the president and his wife, his aides, and his cabinet officers. Numerous investigations have had the dual effect of energizing the Republican party, particularly its right-wing members, and sapping the strength of the administration. And after the Senate's refusal in early 1999 to convict and remove the president over lying about his relationship with Monica Lewinsky, a White House intern, relations between Democrats and Republicans grew so strained that normal bipartisan communication about routine business essentially evaporated.

In the frigid political climate that pervaded the Senate in 1999, a strategy designed to hound and embarrass Republicans into releasing the CTBT—which was already facing an uphill battle to ratification—was not an astute approach.

Nevertheless, the Democrats kept at it. On August 30, the *New York Times* published a front page article headlined, "Democrats Ready for Fight to Save Test Ban Treaty." "Armed with public opinion polls and the support of many scientists, military commanders, and arms control groups, Democrats are threatening to bring the Senate to a standstill when Congress returns next month from summer recess unless Republicans agree to hold hearings this year on the Comprehensive Test Ban Treaty, which 152 nations have signed," reported the *Times*. The article laid out the three possible avenues the Democrats could use. First, they might "generate public pressure by painting Republicans as reckless" to force Senate Majority Leader Trent Lott to overrule Helms and release the treaty for debate. Second, they might "tie the Senate floor in knots until Lott relents," a tactic that "Democrats have used successfully in the past." (Dorgan and Minority Leader Thomas Daschle were reported to be "willing to wage that kind of guerrilla warfare if needed.") Finally, the administration could negotiate changes to the ABM Treaty with Russia to allow for a limited national missile defense system, at the same time pursuing even deeper reductions in deployed nuclear weapons with a START III agreement to gain Russian acceptance of limited defensive measures. Such agreements could, in theory, reverse Republican resistance and free the CTBT. But as Biden warned in the article, "The President has to play a major role. He could affect this more than he has."

The Republicans weren't getting mad; they were getting even.

The campaign began in earnest on September 8, when Dorgan delivered a speech castigating Lott for a failure of leadership and calling once again for swift consideration and approval of the treaty before the Senate adjourned for the year. Otherwise, he warned, he would plant himself "on the floor like a potted plant" and prevent the transaction of any other Senate business.

What Dorgan—and the rest of the Democrats, the administration, and the non-governmental organizations working so diligently to generate public support for ratification—did not know was that the Senate Republicans had been working for at least four months to solidify enough opposition to the treaty to deny the Democrats the 67 votes required for ratification. The Republicans weren't getting mad; they were getting even.

Setting the trap

According to reports in the *New York Times*, the *Weekly Standard*, and the *National Review*, Republican Jon Kyl of Arizona began the effort to counter just the sort of campaign envisioned by the Democrats that had worked so well in the past on budget matters and the Chemical Weapons Convention. Working in secret, Kyl

and Paul Coverdell of Georgia met with other Republican colleagues to sound out opinions about the treaty. Sometimes they brought with them former government officials who opposed the treaty, particularly James Schlesinger, whose portfolio included heading the departments of Defense and Energy, chairing the Atomic Energy Commission, and serving as director of Central Intelligence. By May, Kyl and Coverdell reported to Lott and Helms that they had 30 definite "no" votes. According to the *Weekly Standard*, Lott "indicated for the first time that he might be willing to bring the treaty up for a vote later in the year." Helms, according to the *Times*, told them to "get me more."

During the August recess, Kyl and Coverdell recruited fellow Republicans Tim Hutchinson of Arkansas and Jeff Sessions of Alabama to their cause. They also compiled briefing books for their colleagues "containing countless articles and memos making the case against the treaty," according to the *Weekly Standard*. Much of what was in those briefing books was no doubt supplied or recommended by the Center for Security Policy, a right-wing organization headed by Frank Gaffney, a former Reagan administration official who resigned from the Defense Department in late 1987 to protest the signing of the Intermediate-range Nuclear Forces Treaty and other actions he deemed objectionable. Gaffney, who is well connected with conservative Republicans, has proven skillful over the years—especially since the Republicans took control of Congress in the 1994 elections—in promoting the "re-nuclearization" of the U.S. military, the evisceration of the ABM and START agreements, and the torpedoing of presidential nominees who in any way or at any time have appeared to question or undermine U.S. military power generally and nuclear deterrence in particular.

Following the recess, Kyl and Coverdell informed Lott and Helms that there were 34 "no" votes,

enough to deny ratification. But Lott and Helms pressed for an additional six negative votes before agreeing to the Democrats' demands. Nevertheless, the Republicans "could barely contain their glee," wrote Matthew Rees in the *Weekly Standard*, as they watched Dorgan, Biden, and Daschle press for a vote. The Democrats were unaware of the solidity of the opposition.

Meanwhile, CTBT proponents were busy encouraging newspapers to run editorials about the treaty stalemate (more than 100 were published, fewer than 10 of which opposed the treaty) and releasing polls that consistently showed 80 percent or greater public support for the treaty. (Ironically, these editorials and polling data helped spur the anti-treaty effort by convincing the Republicans, wrongly as it turned out, that the administration planned to make the CTBT a major issue.) But in Washington, the Republicans were closing ranks and focusing on the only thing that really mattered: the minds and votes of their colleagues.

Kyl and Coverdell brought two former senior officials from Lawrence Livermore National Laboratory to speak to senators and answer their questions about the treaty. On September 21, James Schlesinger gave a persuasive presentation about his concerns. According to the *Weekly Standard*, this event "was the turning point in bringing wavering Republicans round to opposing the treaty." Lott himself later remarked, "James Schlesinger was the one that had the greatest impact on me."

By late September, 44 Republicans were firmly against the treaty, although the Democrats didn't know it. On September 22, Daschle, Biden, and other treaty supporters met with Sandy Berger, Clinton's national security adviser, to plan their next steps. Biden argued for pressing forward with Dorgan's threat to bring the Senate to a standstill. "At the time, we felt we needed to bring this to a head, any way we could," he told the *Times* after the vote. Berger asked what would happen if the Republicans "call for an up or down vote" on the treaty. Biden replied, "It's not the best way, but it's better than nothing."

Showdown

One week later, Lott told Biden he would allow the treaty to come up for a vote if the Democrats abandoned their threats to obstruct Senate business. The Democrats accepted. On September 30, Lott offered a unanimous consent request (a procedural motion usually reserved for uncontroversial matters, requiring the approval of all 100 senators) for 10 hours of general debate to begin October 6, followed by an immediate vote.

Caught unprepared, the Democrats objected, which put them in the politically awkward position of appearing to be against the very thing they had been asking for—something Lott and other Republicans would repeatedly chide them about during the debate.

But what the Democrats were opposing and would continue to object to throughout the debate was the process. Normally, the Foreign Relations Committee would have held several days of hearings over a period of several weeks or months. The committee would then have voted on whether to recommend ratification to the full Senate. The Senate then would have scheduled many hours of debate, including debate over possible amendments. Under the expedited procedure Lott had crafted, the only thing guaranteed was the vote.

Still, on October 1 the Democrats accepted Lott's unanimous consent offer, though they persuaded him to increase the time for the debate to 14 hours and push the starting date back to October 8. Biden and Daschle were not comfortable with this outcome, but neither they nor their colleagues believed they had much choice. As Biden said at a press conference that day, "Our choice is to either let it die by attrition and [have]

no one be held accountable, or take a shot at it and have the president and all of us make the strongest case we can between now and the time of the vote."

Completely ignored by the Democrats in this hasty decision-making process were the non-governmental organizations that had labored, in some cases for years, to achieve the CTBT and who were, at that moment, rounding up prominent treaty supporters and preparing to launch multiple campaigns to mobilize public support for ratification.

An unnamed administration official would later tell the *Times* that "the White House didn't see this coming." That suggests two major failings of the administration's approach to ratification: not designating a single official to coordinate the effort, as was done, for example, with NATO expansion; and a lack of communication between the White House and Senate Democrats. Another failing, of course, was the lack of sustained involvement by the president.

Two of his Republican colleagues told Biden he should let the treaty "die gracefully."

For all the charges from President Clinton and Senate Democrats that partisan politics derailed the CTBT, the Democrats were not above politics themselves. Senator Biden's comments in this regard are telling. At the October 1 press conference, Biden told reporters that by agreeing to the debate, "Essentially we've accomplished one of our purposes; you're writing about this." He added, "If this gets voted down... is it reasonable that we're going to get to the point where we change people's minds within the next year, or try to bring it up next year? And my answer is, it's amazing what public opinion will do to people."

Biden also said he had been approached by two Republicans who asked him not to press for action on the treaty, telling him he should let it "die gracefully." When they told him they were going to vote no and that, with the outcome a foregone conclusion, there was no point in a vote, Biden told them, "I got it. You want us to help you kill the treaty so you're not responsible. Wonderful."

Relating this to reporters, Biden concluded, "The question is, are you going to die—do you want to die with no one knowing who shot you, or do you want to die at least with the world knowing who killed you?"

Back-tracking

The White House and the Democrats tried to muster more support for the treaty but it was soon obvious that defeat was certain if the vote were held. On October 11, Clinton sent a letter to the Senate urging a postponement:

"I believe that proceeding to a vote under these circumstances would severely harm the national security of the United States, damage our relationship with our allies, and undermine our historic leadership over 40 years, through administrations Republican and Democratic, in reducing the nuclear threat. Accordingly, I request that you postpone consideration of the Comprehensive Test Ban Treaty on the Senate floor."

On October 12, with the debate nearing its conclusion, New York Democrat Daniel Patrick Moynihan and Virginia Republican John Warner circulated a letter to their colleagues urging a similar course of action. "We support putting off final consideration [of the treaty] until the next Congress," said the letter, signed by 62 senators and submitted to Lott and Daschle.

Knowing that Lott and other Republicans were concerned about the president and the Democrats attempting to use the treaty politically in the 2000 elections, Daschle wrote to Lott on October 12. "Like the President, supporters of the CTBT have reluctantly concluded that the Senate will fail to ratify the CTBT at this time and that a vote in light of this reality risks grave damage to our national security interests. Therefore, I support the President's request to postpone the vote. Absent unforeseen changes in the international situation, I will not seek to reschedule this vote."

When Lott objected to the phrase "unforeseen changes in the international situation," Daschle changed it to "extraordinary circumstances," and explicitly said it was designed to cover a resumption of nuclear testing by India or Pakistan.

But Lott and his colleagues were not satisfied. Lott demanded an agreement with no loopholes to allow the president or the Democrats to bring up the treaty in the midst of an election year. Not surprisingly, the administration found that demand an unacceptable encroachment on the president's constitutional powers.

The most likely "unforeseen changes" or "extraordinary circumstances" would be the potential unraveling of the Nuclear Non-Proliferation Treaty (NPT) at its next review conference in May 2000. If the president felt that resubmitting the treaty could forestall a weakening of the NPT regime, he certainly did not want to do anything to make such a move impossible.

Lott was also under extreme pressure from his Republican colleagues Kyl, Coverdell, and Helms, as well as Robert Smith of New Hampshire and James Inhofe of Oklahoma, not to postpone the vote. These senators were convinced that the treaty was "fatally flawed" and that postponement was merely delaying the inevitable. Kyl also argued that as long as the treaty was pending before the Senate, the United States was bound by its terms. Only a rejection would allow the eventual resumption of underground nuclear testing. They further warned Lott of personal political repercussions should he agree to delay the vote.

Lott, who during the ratification process for the Chemical Weapons Convention had acceded to the president's request to withdraw the treaty and subsequently voted for it, much to the chagrin of his more conservative colleagues, apparently got the message and, according to *Newsweek*'s analysis, reneged on a handshake deal with Daschle to postpone the vote. A telephone call from the president two hours before the vote—the first time Clinton had spoken to Lott about the treaty since submitting it for ratification two years earlier—did nothing to change his mind.

The debate

The debate, such as it was, was anticlimactic. Senators stuck mostly to prepared texts, reading their remarks to a largely empty Senate chamber. Nevertheless, it had several striking elements.

The two main arguments against the treaty—that it was unverifiable and that it would undermine the reliability of U.S. nuclear weapons and hence deterrence—have been around since the first test ban discussions in the mid-1950s. Opponents brought little new to the debate aside from the argument that a test ban would force the United States to live with "unsafe" weapons. Proponents did little to rebut decades-old concerns that were no longer relevant or were shown long ago to be overblown if not outright wrong.

"The CTBT is just the warm-up exercise for the Anti-Ballistic Missile Treaty."

When the Republicans focused on verification or the need to retain unquestioned nuclear superiority, the Democrats generally countered with why the treaty was an important international agreement and how every president since Eisenhower had

fought for it. (This was not exactly true: Reagan supported a test ban as a long-term goal but did nothing about it while in office. Bush scaled back the testing program in 1992, but only in an unsuccessful effort to head off a pre-election vote on a testing moratorium in the Senate.)

Perhaps the most telling part of the debate was what was not said. Opponents spoke frequently about needing to ensure that U.S. nuclear weapons were as safe as possible. Safety and reliability were often lumped together, though they are very different things. Near the beginning of the debate, Kyl argued that "few people know that many of our current weapons do not contain all the safety features that already have been invented by our national laboratories. Only one of the nine [types of] weapons in the current stockpile incorporates all six available safety features.... The bottom line is that a ban on nuclear testing prevents us from making our weapons as safe as we know how to make them and creates a disincentive to making such safety improvements."

To non-experts (which must include nearly every senator), this sounds like a genuine concern. Who could not favor having the safest possible nuclear weapons?

The navy and the air force, for starters. When the weapons mentioned by Kyl were under development, officials with these services weighed increased safety with decreased operational effectiveness and chose effectiveness over safety most of the time. The navy, for example, considered using insensitive high explosives (IHEs) in the W88 warhead but ultimately opted for more volatile conventional high explosives because IHEs, which are not as energetic pound-for-pound, increased the weight and volume of each warhead, which in turn decreased the number of warheads that could be packed atop each Trident II/D-5 missile as well as the missile's range. Even after these facts were made public in 1991, when questions were first raised about the safety of a number of warheads in the arsenal, the navy decided to reduce the risk of an accidental explosion by modifying how warheads were loaded onto missiles, not by employing IHEs.

Proponents also left unchallenged claims about the efficacy of nuclear deterrence. For example, Senator Lott was one of many who asserted that "the U.S. nuclear deterrent was essential in persuading Saddam Hussein not to use chemical or biological weapons during the 1991 Gulf War, undoubtedly saving thousands of lives." Kyl quoted the former head of Iraqi military intelligence who reportedly said, "Some of the Scud missiles were loaded with chemical warheads, but they were not used. We didn't use them because the other side had a deterrent force."

This often-cited example sounds compelling, but as William Arkin has written in these pages and elsewhere, it's not true.

President Bush did threaten Iraq—in a letter to Saddam Hussein written on January 5, 1991—with the "strongest possible response" (generally considered a nuclear threat) if it used nuclear, chemical, or biological weapons, or if it should destroy the Kuwaiti oil fields. Yet just days before the start of the air campaign on January 17, 1991 (Baghdad time), Iraqi forces moved 157 bombs filled with botulinum, anthrax, and aflatoxin to airfields in western Iraq. Twenty-five warheads for A1 Hussein missiles filled with the same materials were made ready for use at additional sites. As Arkin has written, the weather at the start of the war was not conducive to using these weapons (winds would have blown the agents back on Iraqi forces that were poorly equipped with defensive measures). The speed of the air war and the allies' success in destroying much of Iraq's equipment and command-and-control network were the more likely reasons why Iraq failed to use its biological weapons. Since Iraq had deployed some biological weapons and set fire to the oil fields, it seems unlikely that the

nuclear threat made by the president weighed heavily on Saddam Hussein. (In any event, Bush had—before the start of the war—privately ruled out using nuclear weapons against Iraq.)

In a similar vein, Senator Lott argued that it was nuclear deterrence that guaranteed the security of Western Europe from the late 1940s until the Soviet Union finally collapsed. But the notion that nuclear weapons were the best, or perhaps the only, thing standing between a stable Europe and World War III is also popular but equally unprovable. Advocates of this line of reasoning tend to ignore other factors that contributed to the peaceful outcome of the Cold War, including the NATO alliance and the military forces deployed by the European allies; the massive U.S. investment in conventional military forces; actual Soviet intentions toward Europe (as distinct from the Soviet Union's seemingly formidable military machine); and in the mid- to late 1980s, the impact of Mikhail Gorbachev.

Kyl claimed that "many new [nuclear weapon] designs were required during the Cold War to sustain deterrence," ignoring the fact that the genesis for the majority of the 65 types of warheads the United States manufactured was not a specific military requirement but the result of interservice rivalries and competition between Los Alamos and Lawrence Livermore. Each of the services wanted a variety of their own weapons to guarantee control over new missions and mission funding.

When Al Gore and William Cohen made statements supporting the test ban, opponents produced their speeches from many years before, arguing just the opposite. And not a single treaty proponent pointed out that the world was a very different place back then. In a series of "Decision Briefs" prepared by Gaffney's Center for Security Policy, pro-treaty statements by retired military officials, including former chairman of the Joint Chiefs of Staff Colin Powell,

were juxtaposed with their earlier anti-test ban remarks—some from as long as 21 years ago.

Treaty opponents insisted that the United States, hobbled by a test ban, would be powerless to prevent aggression against itself or its allies. But none of the proponents of the treaty pointed out that a considerably larger and more diverse arsenal had failed to prevent Iraq from invading Kuwait in 1990. And what about the bombing of the marine barracks in Beirut in 1983? Or Afghanistan in 1979? Or Czechoslovakia in 1968? Or Vietnam?

Kyl, in a discussion of whether a test could evade detection under the treaty, opined that "decoupling"— excavating a large, spherical underground cavern to muffle the noise of a nuclear blast—"is technologically simple to achieve." In fact, decoupling is an expensive, uncertain, and time-consuming undertaking that offers no guarantee of success, particularly for a state with little or no underground testing experience (which includes everyone except the United States, Russia, Great Britain, France, and possibly China).

Senator Inhofe argued that North Korea has a missile "called the Taepo Dong I that will reach Washington, D.C., from anyplace in the world." This missile, which North Korea test-launched for the first and only time in August 1998, broke up before the end of its flight. It is hardly operational, and even if it were, at its estimated maximum range it could reach only Hawaii or Alaska from its launch site in North Korea.

Inhofe also got carried away at one point, insisting that "virtually every country has weapons of mass destruction," a remark that Dorgan did not let pass unchallenged. But when another Republican charged that the Clinton administration has presided over the worst period of nuclear proliferation in history, specifically citing India and Pakistan, no Democrat rose to point out that the Reagan and Bush administrations had turned a blind eye to Pakistan's nuclear program for at least five years, the better to funnel aid through that country to the mujahideen fighting Soviet forces in neighboring Afghanistan.

Lott declared, "It is through [explosive] testing of the U.S. nuclear stockpile that the United States has maintained its confidence in the safety and reliability of our nuclear weapons," citing a controversial 1987 report from Livermore to buttress his case. That report, however, was challenged not only in a series of three reports written in 1987 and 1991 by Ray Kidder, a physicist and weapons designer at Livermore, but also in a 1995 joint report by Livermore, Los Alamos, and Sandia national laboratories.

What those reports reveal is that the United States has *never* relied primarily on nuclear testing either to identify or fix problems with nuclear weapons. Of approximately 830 "findings" of defects in stockpiled weapons between 1958 and 1993, fewer than one percent were discovered via nuclear tests and only one test out of the 387 conducted since 1970 was for the purpose of "detecting" an age-related problem in a weapon. (That problem was resolved without modifying the weapons' nuclear components.) No more than three percent (11) of the 387 tests since 1970 were conducted for the purpose of ensuring warhead reliability. The primary purpose of nuclear testing was, and remains, the development of new types of nuclear weapons.

Brave new world

Whether intended or not, the arguments the Republicans deployed against the CTBT illuminate the desire to establish what might be termed Pax Americana II. This was most clearly demonstrated in comments by Senators Inhofe and Sessions. Inhofe, quoting colleague Phil Gramm of Texas, said, "We have to remain strong. We all wish for the day and hope for the day when the lion and the lamb can lie down together. But when that day comes, I want to make sure we are the lion." As Jonathan Alter wrote in *Newsweek* the week of the vote, "Nice line, but it doesn't mean much if the lamb is packing nuclear heat."

Sessions warned his colleagues about international treaties in provocative terms. "We have to watch them, I think. It is Gulliver in the land of Lilliputians, stretched out, unable to move, because he has been tied down by a whole host of threads."

President Clinton excoriated the senators who led the charge against the CTBT as the "new isolationists." But isolationism is hardly what senators like Helms and Kyl and Lott are seeking. What these senators and their counterparts in the House of Representatives seem to want is to dominate the world militarily, economically, and maybe even culturally. They want to return to Cold War-era levels of military spending, resume the production and, yes, testing of nuclear weapons, and deploy a nationwide defense against ballistic missile attack so that the United States can do whatever it wants, whenever it wants, wherever it wants, without having to seek the approval or cooperation of anyone else. Or, as an anonymous Senate aide told the *Washington Times* after the vote, "The CTBT is just the warm-up exercise for the Anti-Ballistic Missile Treaty."

Whether the American people, not to mention the rest of the world, will embrace or reject this world view remains to be seen. In the meantime, a majority of U.S. senators, including many who do not subscribe to this military-based unilateralism, have cynically ensured that there will be more, and more sophisticated, nuclear threats to challenge as yet unbuilt and unproven ballistic missile defenses, thereby ensuring that a renewed and difficult-to-constrain cycle of strategic weapons procurement is the most likely outcome of their shortsighted political maneuvering.

Stephen I. Schwartz is the publisher of the Bulletin *and executive director of the Educational Foundation for Nuclear Science. He is the editor and coauthor of* Atomic Audit: The Costs and Consequences of U.S. Nuclear Weapons Since 1940 (*1998*).

A Four-Star Foreign Policy?

U.S. Commanders Wield Rising Clout, Autonomy

By DANA PRIEST
Washington Post Staff Writer

When the Pakistani army staged a coup last October, the Clinton administration sent a stern protest to the new, self-appointed ruler, Army Gen. Pervez Musharraf. A nuclear-capable, unstable nation had plunged into fresh turmoil, and Washington waited anxiously: How would Musharraf respond?

When the general finally placed his call, it was not to President Clinton, Secretary of State Madeleine K. Albright, Defense Secretary William S. Cohen or the U.S. ambassador in Islamabad. Instead, Musharraf telephoned Marine Corps Gen. Anthony C. Zinni, who happened to be sitting with Cohen at an airfield in Egypt.

"Tony," Musharraf began, "I want to tell you what I'm doing…"

Zinni may not be a household name, but as the recent head of the U.S. Central Command, which oversees U.S. military operations in the Middle East, the four-star general was among a quartet of American military leaders who have exerted more political influence abroad over the past three years than most civilian diplomats.

Zinni, along with Adm. Dennis C. Blair, Gen. Wesley K. Clark and Gen. Charles E. Wilhelm, served as regional commanders-in-chief, or CINCs. The CINC offices were expanded 14 years ago to promote efficiency by giving them command of operations involving the Army, Air Force, Navy and Marines in assigned regions of the world. Since then, the CINCs (pronounced "sinks") have evolved into the modern-day equivalent of the Roman Empire's proconsuls—well-funded, semi-autonomous, unconventional centers of U.S. foreign policy.

In a decade when Congress significantly reduced the State Department and civilian foreign aid budgets, the CINCs have enjoyed a budgetary boom unscrutinized by Congress. There is no reliable accounting of the hundreds of millions of dollars the CINCs spend each year, and congressional oversight committees have not asked for one. The Pentagon intentionally keeps its classified, piecemeal version of their budgets out of Congress's hands.

The CINCs control headquarters budgets outside of Washington that total $380 million a year, more than twice what they had when the Cold War ended. They travel nonstop, oversee multimillion-dollar foreign study institutes and round-the-clock intelligence centers, host international conferences and direct disaster relief.

American generals and admirals, emissaries for 50 years of the world's strongest military, have long exercised independent influence abroad, and in doing so, they jockeyed with diplomats and intelligence agencies to shape U.S. foreign policy. But the swelling institution of the CINC has shifted this balance during the 1990s. Sheer budgetary prowess is one reason. Another is that the nature of post-Cold War U.S. military engagements, emphasizing peacekeeping and nation-building, has steadily pushed the uniformed CINCs into expanded diplomatic and political roles.

The pronounced role of the U.S. military is criticized in parts of the world—especially the Americas, Europe, the Philippines and Japan—where resentment runs deep over the conduct of U.S. forces on foreign soil. Human rights groups and some members of Congress believe the military already exercises too much foreign influence and that increased reliance on the Pentagon to solve complex problems is causing civilian agencies to atrophy. Conservatives charge that the diplomatic and nation-building missions drain resources and dull the armed services' ability to fight and win wars.

At a time when the U.S. presidential candidates are debating whether the military has been drawn too far away from its core

Four Corners of American Power

U.S. European Command

Most of the headquarters staff of 1,200 is at Patch Barracks in Stuttgart-Vaihingen, Germany. An additional 3.000 people are on service headquarters staffs, mostly in Germany, England, Italy and Spain. The Command covers 89 countries in Europe, Africa and the Middle East, with 109.000 troops assigned throughout Europe. Army Gen. Wesley K. Clark, 55, was commander until he retired in June. Air Force Gen. Joseph W. Ralston, 56, former vice chairman of the Joint Chiefs of Staff, replaced him. The European commander also is always NATO's top military commander, and works from the NATO military headquarters in Mons, Belgium.

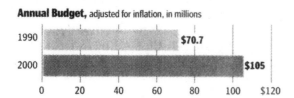

Annual Budget, adjusted for inflation, in millions

| 1990 | $70.7 |
| 2000 | $105 |

0   20   40   60   80   100 $120

U.S. Pacific Command

Most of the headquarters staff of 3,600 are at Camp H.M. Smith and other posts in Hawaii. An additional 2,521 work in other service headquarters staffs in Hawaii. The command area includes 43 countries and 30 territories in the Pacific and Southeast Asia, including four of the world's largest armies and 60 percent of the world's population. About 300,000 troops are permanently assigned to the command and are based mainly in Hawaii, Alaska, Korea and Japan. The commander is Adm. Dennis C. Blair, 53.

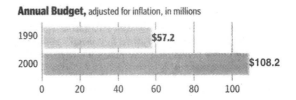

Annual Budget, adjusted for inflation, in millions

| 1990 | $57.2 |
| 2000 | $108.2 |

0   20   40   60   80   100

U.S. Joint Forces Command

Formerly the U.S. Atlantic Command, it is located in Norfolk, Va., and has responsibility for Greenland and much of the Atlantic and Artic oceans. Unlike the other regional commands, its main missions are to train, develop and experiment with "joint" war-fighting techniques and doctrine using more than one service; and to provide troops to other regional commanders. It is excluded from the series for that reason.

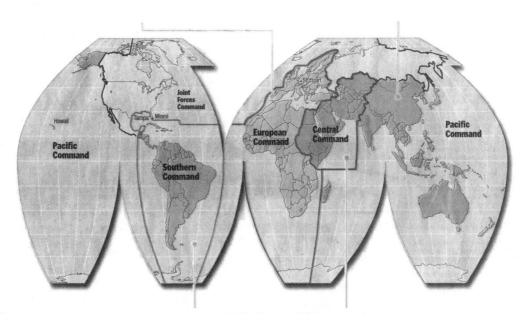

U.S. Southern Command

There is a headquarters staff of 1,200 in Miami, with an additional 1,900 in component commands in Puerto Rico, Arizona and Honduras. The command has no permanently assigned troops. Its theater is the 19 countries of Central and Latin America, and 13 Caribbean nations. The commander was Marine Gen. Charles E. Wilhelm, 59, until Sept. 8. He was replaced by Marine Gen. Peter Pace, 54.

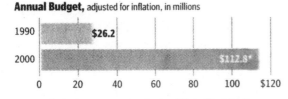

Annual Budget, adjusted for inflation, in millions

| 1990 | $26.2 |
| 2000 | $112.8* |

0   20   40   60   80   100 $120

*Includes $27 million in counter-drug funds and $8.4 million in intelligence funds. Much of the increase came from money shifted from other Army units.

U.S. Central Command

The headquarters staff of 1,050 is at MacDill Air Force Base in Tampa, with an additional 450 people at component headquarters staffs in the United States and Bahrain. The theater is 25 countries from the Horn of Africa, the Middle East and Central Asia. No combat forces are permanently assigned. The commander was Marine Gen. Anthony C. Zinni, 54, until he retired in July. Army Gen. Tommy R. Franks, 55, succeeded him.

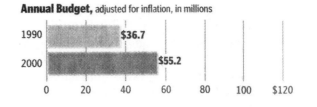

Annual Budget, adjusted for inflation, in millions

| 1990 | $36.7 |
| 2000 | $55.2 |

0   20   40   60   80   100 $120

SOURCE: Department of Defense, Unified Commands

mission of fighting wars, the rising authority and independence of the CINCs offer a little-examined twist on the issue.

Republican nominee George W. Bush has criticized the Clinton administration for diverting military resources to peacekeeping missions in Kosovo, Bosnia, Haiti and elsewhere. He argues that years of Pentagon budget cuts, combined with a heavy peacekeeping load, have hurt military readiness.

In fact, during the 1990s, the Clinton administration found it easier to win funding from a Republican-controlled Congress for foreign policy initiatives handled through the Pentagon rather than the State Department—an approach that Vice President Gore helped to shape.

The Clinton team was abetted by the CINCs themselves. Flanked on their travels by caravans of staff, welcomed by kings and prime ministers, these four CINCs came to believe by the new millennium that their own uniformed services were too parochial, that U.S. relations abroad suffer because the Pentagon's leadership foolishly shuns deep contact with the State Department. The National Security Council, they complain, is too small and ineffective to bring together competing bureaucracies, and too focused on crises to implement long-term strategies.

If today's Pentagon is too engaged in non-military missions, it is partly because the CINCs feel they need to fill a void.

"The system is badly broken," sighed Zinni one midnight in May, his eyes red from fatigue nine hours into a flight to Bahrain. "We use chewing gum and bailing wire to keep it together."

"I look longingly at the foreign affairs intelligentsia, but no one is addressing the cosmic issue; everyone's going tactical," said Blair, heading home one day from Indonesia. "What's the United States going to do with its superpowerhood? It drives me crazy. We're looking at our wake instead of looking ahead."

To assess the world of the CINCs, The Washington Post spent several months this year observing the work of Zinni, Clark, Wilhelm and Blair. All but Blair were in the final months of their tenure and have since retired, yet in their last days in the job they traveled frenetically—to Pacific and Central Asia, Europe, the Persian Gulf and Central America. During their trips, the four gave relatively unfettered access to meetings with staff and foreign dignitaries and granted hours of interviews in which they shared their views, vented disappointments and described their challenges.

Clark, until recently the commander of NATO and the U.S. European Command, hopscotched across Europe each week to help westernize former Soviet bloc countries.

Blair, the Mainer who heads the U.S. Pacific Command, made day-long flights across the international date line twice a month to promote multinational security pacts among Asian countries, an idea once opposed by the Pentagon and the State Department.

Wilhelm, head of the U.S. Southern Command, led a $30 million U.S. relief effort in Central America after Hurricane Mitch in 1998, then lobbied Congress to lift its informal prohibition on contact with the once Marxist Nicaraguan military. He became the first CINC on Nicaraguan soil in 20 years.

In Pakistan, Zinni, commander of the U.S. Central Command, pushed the Clinton administration to open the diplomatic door with Musharraf when many demanded it be slammed shut. Convinced that Pakistan could be a regional stabilizing force, he helped persuade Clinton to visit Musharraf in March. With

Zinni's intervention, Musharraf turned over several suspected terrorists in secret sweeps around New Year's Day.

From vantage points thousands of miles from Washington, the CINCs see problems with some U.S. policies abroad and with their own Pentagon leadership.

"Washington reacts to Beltway issues," said Zinni, so influential in the Persian Gulf that one U.S. ambassador there half-jokingly compared him to God. "It doesn't mean anything out here."

The Unified Commands

The CINC position was created in 1947 as part of the newly formed Department of Defense, but the job did not become influential until after 1980, when five servicemen died in an aborted attempt to rescue American hostages in Tehran.

Gen. David Jones, then chairman of the Joint Chiefs of Staff, complained that the disaster might have been averted if he had had the authority to order more qualified Air Force special warfare pilots to fly the mission from Navy ships.

Congress responded by passing the Goldwater-Nichols Department of Defense Reorganization Act of 1986—over the opposition of the chiefs of the Army, Navy, Air Force and Marines. Designed to override debilitating service rivalries, the law elevated the chairman of the Joint Chiefs of Staff to principal military adviser to the president. It gave the power to direct and unify weapons use, training and tactics from each service to the "unified combatant commands," a term for the commands run by the CINCs.

Their main job is to manage U.S. military operations in separate parts of the world. Clark directed the air war against Yugoslavia; Zinni led missile strikes against Iraq, Afghanistan and Sudan; Blair would lead the response in the event of conflict between Taiwan and China, or between North and South Korea; Wilhelm, the only CINC without war plans on the shelf, would manage operations should Cuba implode.

Unlike the heads of the Army, Navy, Air Force and Marines, who must answer to presidentially appointed civilian secretaries, the CINCs report directly to the secretary of defense and the president. Former defense secretary William Perry had a close relationship with most of the CINCs, but the more insular Cohen has delegated almost all contact with them to the chairman of the Joint Chiefs of Staff, Gen. Henry H. Shelton.

The CINCs' jobs always have been loaded with perks. They live in well-appointed homes, draw $135,000 salaries for terms that usually run three years and have lavish entertainment and travel budgets. But as the demands have broadened, the jobs have attracted a different breed—military leaders not known as company men.

Clark and Blair were Rhodes scholars and White House fellows. Clark was not the Army's candidate for a CINC job, and Blair left the Navy's inner circle for a year to work for the CIA. Zinni, one of the Marine Corps' most unconventional thinkers, got his job over the wishes of the chairman of the Joint Chiefs of Staff, Army Gen. John M. Shalikashvili.

The 1986 legislation also cemented a tug-of-war for resources between the CINCs and the service chiefs. The CINCs in the European and Pacific commands have hundreds of thousands of troops at their disposal for armed conflicts. But in "peacetime engagements," they and the other CINCs must appeal to the service chiefs or to the chairman of the Joint Chiefs for troops and equipment. The CINCs complain bitterly about what they are allotted, but at the Pentagon's Army War Plans Division, staffers besieged with requests from the field voted tongue-in-cheek to rename themselves "The CINC Requirements Task Force," a sign that the CINCs' tug is felt within the very heart of the services.

Three CINCs have staffs as large as the executive office of the president. More people—about 1,100—work at the smallest CINC headquarters, the U.S. Southern Command, than the total assigned to the Americas at the State, Commerce, Treasury and Agriculture departments, the Pentagon's Joint Staff and the office of the secretary of defense.

The CINCs control their own aircraft, can call up a fleet of helicopters, and often travel with an entourage approaching 35. The commanders routinely are received by heads of state who offer gifts, share secrets and seek advice.

The CINCs spend $50 million a year on four foreign study institutes for U.S. and foreign officials. Another $20 million a year goes for conferences that include non-military topics such as environmental degradation, medical care, mine clearance, piracy, drug trafficking and policing. Each operates a huge intelligence center staffed 24 hours a day.

Bountiful resources and an open-ended mandate allow the CINCs to engage with tiny countries and on obscure foreign policy issues if they feel inspired.

Because Zinni loved the Seychelles, his staff spent untold hours finding old U.S. patrol boats the islands could use to equip a coast guard to ward off illegal fishermen. Clark wrangled $3.5 million from the Pentagon for a computer simulation to show leaders in the former East bloc the economic impact of their decisions.

Because Blair admires the Gurkhas of Nepal, he ordered his staff to help improve the elite troops' medical program. Since his groundbreaking first visit to Nicaragua, Wilhelm has returned four times and hundreds of U.S. troops followed for exercises.

"We got into Nicaragua on a tailwind supplied by a hurricane," Wilhelm laughed as he flew home recently from Central America.

Guiding Strategic Shifts

Since the end of the Cold War, the CINCs have helped shift America's strategic thinking. Privately, they hold strong opinions that sometimes differ sharply with the policies they are asked to carry out.

Wilhelm disagrees with the administration's hard-line stance on Cuba, now under a U.S. trade and diplomatic embargo. Several years ago, he publicly declared Cuba no longer a military threat, enraging anti-Castro groups in the United States.

Blair views China as less of a threat than Capitol Hill lawmakers think it is. His determination to open military dialogue with China has helped the administration weather congressional opposition.

Clark wanted the Balkans declared a "major theater war" zone so the services would get a funding commitment for Kosovo and Bosnia deployments. Some military leaders considered even entering the conflict a drain on U.S. troops.

The turf-conscious Pentagon discourages the CINCs from direct contact with other agencies. In July 1998, Shelton was furious with Clark for discussing a limited air strike against Yugoslavia with deputy national security adviser James Steinberg. Both Clark and Steinberg insisted that no specifics were revealed. To keep better control of the CINCs, Shelton began requiring them to file an hour-by-hour appointment schedule when visiting Washington. The rule stands today.

Zinni caught heat when he told a Senate panel that he opposed the Clinton administration's idea of funding an Iraqi opposition group to overthrow Saddam Hussein. Cohen prohibited him from holding on-the-record media interviews. Zinni remembers national security adviser Samuel R. "Sandy" Berger demanding, "What gives you the right to say that?"

"'Well,'" Zinni recalls saying, "'the First Amendment.'"

There are recurrent tussles among the CINCs too, especially when they sit down to adjust their empires, carving up continents like 19th-century European colonialists.

After a battle last year between the colonels of the Central and European commands, Zinni won five Central Asian nations because Clark's unruly territory had grown to 91 countries. When Zinni mounted a campaign to enlarge his Horn of Africa reach, Clark agreed to give him Kenya but hung on to Uganda.

Relationships between a CINC and the countries in his "CINCdom" are heavily colored by history. The contrasts are most striking between Europe, where the United States has long been dominant in security matters, and Latin America, where governments have restricted contacts with the U.S. military because of past U.S. support of abusive regimes.

Traveling with Clark and Wilhelm illustrated these differences. At every stop, Clark sat with prime ministers and foreign ministers and spent as much time with civilian officials and diplomats as with military officers. Wilhelm's most substantive meetings were with his military counterparts; few political leaders sought him out.

Architect of Reform

In Bosnia and Kosovo, Clark used the autonomy and resources that have devolved to CINCs to push NATO troops toward a nation-building role unseen since the military's occupation of Europe and Japan after World War II.

Clark and his subordinates acknowledge that in Bosnia, much of what they did was off the books, the broadest interpretation of the military annexes to the 1995 Dayton Peace

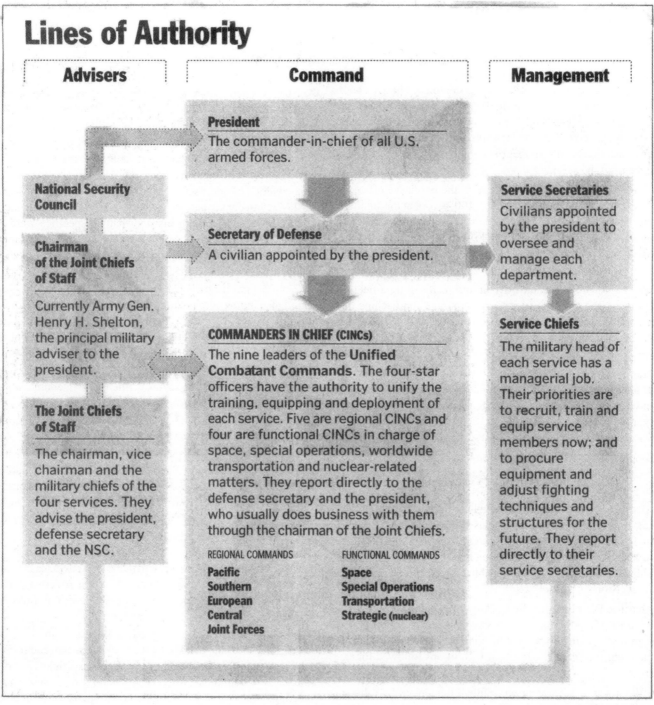

Lines of Authority

Advisers | **Command** | **Management**

President
The commander-in-chief of all U.S. armed forces.

National Security Council

Chairman of the Joint Chiefs of Staff
Currently Army Gen. Henry H. Shelton, the principal military adviser to the president.

Secretary of Defense
A civilian appointed by the president.

Service Secretaries
Civilians appointed by the president to oversee and manage each department.

The Joint Chiefs of Staff
The chairman, vice chairman and the military chiefs of the four services. They advise the president, defense secretary and the NSC.

COMMANDERS IN CHIEF (CINCs)
The nine leaders of the **Unified Combatant Commands**. The four-star officers have the authority to unify the training, equipping and deployment of each service. Five are regional CINCs and four are functional CINCs in charge of space, special operations, worldwide transportation and nuclear-related matters. They report directly to the defense secretary and the president, who usually does business with them through the chairman of the Joint Chiefs.

Service Chiefs
The military head of each service has a managerial job. Their priorities are to recruit, train and equip service members now; and to procure equipment and adjust fighting techniques and structures for the future. They report directly to their service secretaries.

REGIONAL COMMANDS
Pacific
Southern
European
Central
Joint Forces

FUNCTIONAL COMMANDS
Space
Special Operations
Transportation
Strategic (nuclear)

THE WASHINGTON POST

Accords, the agreement that ended the three-year war and sought to create a multi-ethnic, self-governing country.

With an aggressive commander of SFOR, Gen. Montgomery C. Meigs, Clark rewrote the military's Bosnia operational plan in 1998 to go beyond peacekeeping. His allies at the Pentagon and the State Department quietly sold it to the White House.

The new plan tried to make soldiers instruments in political reform. Commanders were encouraged to banish troublemakers and to direct international aid to reform-minded local leaders.

Clark wanted to form an anti-corruption team that would dismantle the Mafia-like organization that supports hard-line leaders. The mission required old-fashioned detective work. The Joint Chiefs of Staff opposed the idea, and the FBI initially declined to help. Clark persisted. He persuaded the State Department to pay for a gumshoe—a U.S. customs agent who had once worked for him in South America.

The anti-corruption team now includes Pentagon officers, Justice Department crime analysts and two battalions of Italian Carabinieri police.

Still, there is Pentagon ambivalence about the operation. Last year, on the eve of a raid aimed at disrupting illegal funding for radical Croat politicians, Cohen overrode Meigs's plan to dispatch a clandestine Navy SEAL team, judging it too risky. French troops went ahead anyway, netting computer tapes that helped demonstrate the Croatian government was funding hardliners. The U.S. pullback highlighted tension between the activist CINC and his more cautious headquarters.

Clark's forceful approach was evident in April, when he traveled with his entourage and a Post reporter to a NATO base in Banja Luka in northeastern Bosnia to deliver a message to a dozen generals and colonels.

Clandestine Delta Force commandos, their index fingers near the triggers of assault rifles, bumped through the rough gray weather with him in a Black Hawk helicopter. A three-layered security perimeter surrounded him when he stepped out and dashed beneath the whirling rotary blades.

Inside, his darting charcoal eyes swept the room as he issued instructions. Use your martial law-like authority; "you can impose any law," he told the officers. Have your soldiers detain and chase out nationalist hard-liners. Find a pretext to search the offices of suspected criminals. Don't be afraid of disorder and isolated incidents of violence against NATO troops.

And most important, he said, don't ask or wait for leadership or direction from superiors in Washington, Paris, London, Rome or Ottawa.

"If you put this strategy down and circulate it," he said. "it's dead."

That attitude mirrored Clark's approach to the Kosovo war, where he pushed for more aggressive airstrikes and lobbied for a ground invasion the Army didn't support. "Never ask 'Mother, may I'" Clark said, "unless you know the answer."

At his retirement ceremony, Clark—ungracefully forced out on June 23 to accommodate his successor—jabbed the Army for what he views as its no-can-do attitude. "Time is passing the Army by," he said, as the Army chief of staff sat beside him. The Army leadership needs "a new mentality.... 'Give us a mission and send us in.'"

Cracking Open Doors

Clark ran operations in a region where the presence of U.S. troops is crucial to stability. In Central and South America, where many newly democratic nations have renounced ties to the U.S. military, Gen. Charles Wilhelm was just trying to gain his footing.

Hostility toward the U.S. military runs deep in the hemisphere, fostered over a century in which the U.S. government supported the oppressive armies of dictators and right-wing governments. For decades, the CINC was based in Panama, but the U.S. military presence was forced out in an expression of sovereignty when control of the Panama Canal was turned over to Panama. Nowadays, at the Pentagon, the Florida-based CINCSOUTH is known as the "stepsister CINC."

But the general with four combat medals from Vietnam said he intends to turn that around.

"The U.S. doesn't have a strategic vision for South America," he said. "I don't take it personally."

To fit his boot in the door, Wilhelm seized upon the U.S.-funded counternarcotics program in Latin America, which the Pentagon all but runs. In June, after rejections from Costa Rica and Peru, he went to El Salvador to seek support for a drug monitoring base. Leftist lawmakers in El Salvador do not want to renew ties with U.S. forces and argue that the country's armed forces need to concentrate on a serious crime explosion.

Wilhelm's allies, however, are the Salvadoran armed forces, who have remained close to the U.S. military in the decade since their civil war ended.

Surrounded by maps marked "Secreto" in the Joint Staff headquarters of El Salvador, Wilhelm laid out his strategy: "Opening the [logistics center] will make El Salvador the focal point of the counterdrug activities in Central America," he told three Salvadoran generals. "We realize, in a diplomatic sense, this plan is for counterdrug only. As a practical matter, all of us know this agreement will give us a superb opportunity to increase the contact with all our armed forces in a variety of ways."

"I hope," Wilhelm continued, "to further exploit this opportunity to provide modest support to you and your modernization efforts."

El Salvador needs help with strategic intelligence, equipment and training, Wilhelm was told. He took notes and instantly offered to host a meeting for police chiefs and military heads of Colombia, Peru and Bolivia so they could discuss joint police-soldier operations.

No country in Wilhelm's theater is threatened by a foreign enemy, and most border disputes and insurgencies are settled. But ask Wilhelm why the region merits a CINC and he whips out his historical chart showing the ebbs and flows of regional democracies. In Peru, Venezuela and elsewhere, there's enough backsliding to warrant U.S. military attention, he argued.

"Every military in the region is rethinking its role," he said. "I'd like to play a larger part in the actual restructuring of the militaries."

Through his own efforts and relations, he already is involved in Panama, El Salvador and Colombia.

In Panama, which abolished its armed forces in 1994, the Southern Command helped experts draft a national security strategy to protect commercial shipping and U.S. nuclear submarines that pass through the canal.

In a more urgent way, Wilhelm also took the lead on the military aspects of Plan Colombia, the U.S.-funded program to create brigades to retake territory controlled simultaneously by leftist rebels and drug traffickers. Neither Wilhelm nor the U.S. Army can be involved with the brigades as closely as they were with El Salvador's counterinsurgency war because Congress has forbidden direct U.S. military involvement. Instead, he must fight through Colombia's army, with its long record of ineptitude, corruption and human rights violations. Just last month the army shot and killed six young children who were on a school nature walk.

Wilhelm scotched a State Department plan to create as many as 15 counterdrug Colombian battalions and argued for three larger, more efficient units. At his insistence, the battalions will fit an American model, with scouts, mortars and forward support, psychological staff and intelligence operations.

He designed a Colombia Joint Intelligence Center, a multi-million-dollar project housed in a watertight tent with sandbag walls. Staffed jointly by U.S. and Colombian analysts, it looks at information collected by both countries.

Congress and the administration have funded a two-year anti-drug program. Wilhelm talks about a six-year strategy— one that will eventually demand more Colombian battalions and an even deeper commitment of U.S. funds and military expertise.

"It ain't no Vietnam," he said, with a slight North Carolina twang. "I wish it were, it would be easier."

Researcher Alice Crites contributed to this report.

UNIT 6

U.S. International Economic Strategy

Unit Selections

27. **Q: Should the United States Renew the Iran Libya Sanctions Act?** Kenneth R. Timmerman and Archie Dunham
28. **The U.S. Trade Deficit: A Dangerous Obsession**, Joseph Quinlan and Marc Chandler
29. **The Death of the Washington Consensus?** Robin Broad and John Cavanagh
30. **Globalization After Seattle**, Jacob Park

Key Points to Consider

- Which type of international system, global free trade or regional trading blocs, is in America's national interest? Explain.

- Which country is the more important trading partner for the United States—Japan, Europe, or Mexico? Defend your answer.

- Select a country in need of foreign aid. What type of foreign aid strategy should the United States pursue toward it? How does this compare with current U.S. foreign aid programs?

- What types of foreign policy goals can be advanced using economic sanctions?

- Should Congress give the president fast-track trade authority? Why or why not?

- Put together an eight-person delegation to the next round of WTO trade talks. Defend your selections. What negotiating instructions would you give them?

 **Links: www.dushkin.com/online/**
These sites are annotated in the World Wide Web pages.

International Monetary Fund (IMF)
http://www.imf.org

United States Agency for International Development
http://www.info.usaid.gov

United States Trade Representative
http://www.ustr.gov

World Bank
http://www.worldbank.org

As in so many areas of American foreign policy, the selection of U.S. international economic strategies during the cold war seems to have been a rather straightforward process and the accompanying policy debates fairly minor compared to the situation that exists today. At the most fundamental level, it was taken for granted that the American economy would best be served by the existence of a global free trade system. The lengthy Great Depression of the 1930s and the accompanying rise to power of extremist governments in Germany, Italy, and elsewhere had discredited the competing policy of protectionism. A consensus existed that, for such a system to work, America's active involvement and leadership were essential. To that end, international organizations were set up whose collective task it was to oversee the operation

of the postwar international economic order. Foremost among them were the General Agreement on Tariffs and Trade (GATT), the International Monetary Fund (IMF), and the International Bank for Reconstruction and Development (the World Bank).

It was also widely accepted that many states would not be able to resist pressure from the Soviet Union or from domestic communist parties, due to the weak state of their economies and military establishments. Thus, containing communism would require foreign aid programs designed to transfer American economic and military expertise, goods and services, and financial resources to key states. Finally, containing communism was seen as requiring economic strategies of denial. Lists were drawn up of goods that U.S. firms were prohibited from selling to communist states because they could contribute to the strength of their military establishments.

Over time, problems arose in all of these areas. Events of the 1960s and 1970s shook the international economic system at its political and economic foundations. There followed a period of more than 20 years in which the international economic system was managed through a series of ad hoc responses to crises and the continued inability of foreign aid programs to produce real growth in the less developed world. U.S. international economic policy during this period was often characterized as one of "benign neglect." Promoting free trade and market-oriented development initiatives became the standard Washington response to international economic issues. The adequacy of this response is questioned today. Rather than operating in a largely favorable international economic environment, policymakers and citizens today see the international economic order as highly volatile and perhaps even threatening. The focal point of their concern is with the process of globalization.

The IMF defines globalization as the growing economic interdependence of countries through the increasing volume and variety of border transactions in goods, services, and capital flows. This is essentially an economic definition but many assert that

globalization also has important social, political, and even military dimensions. Most fundamentally, globalization is change-inducing because of its ability to link activities around the world. From a policy perspective, the most significant aspect of globalization is that international economic activity has become so large, rapid, and dense that it has outstripped the ability of governments and international organizations to manage it. Susan Strange described the situation as one of "casino capitalism" because, just as in a casino, a large element of luck determines the success or failure of international economic policies.

It is against this very changed backdrop of globalization that American international economic policy is now made and carried out. As the debates over the North American Free Trade Agreement (NAFTA), foreign aid to the Soviet Union, establishing the World Trade Organization, and "bailing out" countries whose currencies suffer a sudden and dramatic drop in value make clear, a consensus has not yet taken hold within the American political system on what type of international economic strategy to pursue. The readings in this section highlight several important dimensions to U.S. international economic policy.

The first reading presents a debate over whether or not to lift economic sanctions against Libya and Iran. The second reading, "The U.S. Trade Deficit: A Dangerous Obsession," by Joseph Quinlan and Marc Chandler, asserts that the existence of a trade deficit is no longer a valid measure of the health and global competitiveness of the U.S. economy. In "Death of the Washington Consensus?" Robin Broad and John Cavanagh examine the rise and decline of the consensus that has guided American and World Bank thinking on how best to achieve economic development. They call for starting a new development debate. This theme is taken up in the final reading, "Globalization After Seattle." In it, Jacob Park discusses what lies ahead for the World Trade Organization and examines the role that "soft" power will play in organizing international economic relations.

Q: Should the United States renew the Iran Libya Sanctions Act?

Yes: The Iranian terrorist regime poses a danger to the United States and its allies.

BY KENNETH R. TIMMERMAN

On June 2, a massive blast triggered by a Palestinian suicide bomber ripped through a nightclub in Tel Aviv killing 20 people and injuring more than 80. The terrorist groups Hamas and Islamic Jihad claimed responsibility. Both groups, which are affiliated with the Palestinian Authority of Yasser Arafat, are financed by the government of the Islamic Republic of Iran through official subsidies approved each year by Iran's state parliament, or Majlis.

Terrorists from Hamas and Islamic Jihad regularly travel to Iran, where they are trained by Iran's Revolutionary Guards and by the Ministry of Information and Security (MOIS) in bomb-making techniques. They are taught how to use false documents, pass border inspections and transfer money worldwide. They are instructed how to maintain clandestine contact with their Iranian government handlers. Without state support from the Islamic Republic of Iran, terrorist attacks such as this latest suicide bombing would be far more difficult.

On April 12, 1996, the Israelis arrested Hussein Mohammed Mikdad, a Lebanese Shiite who subsequently admitted that his Iranian handlers had instructed him to hand-carry a bomb onto an El Al flight originating in Tel Aviv. The only reason the Israelis caught Mikdad was his own incompetence. While preparing the bomb in his East Jerusalem hotel room, he suffered the misfortune of setting it off in his own lap. Mikdad entered Israel on a forged British passport provided him by Iranian intelligence.

The Israelis had less luck with the Iranian-trained bomber who drove an explosive-rigged van into an Israeli bus in Gaza on April 9, 1995, killing seven Israelis and one U.S. citizen, a 20-year-old student from New Jersey named Alisa Flatow. Lawsuits filed by her parents led a U.S. court to condemn the government of Iran to pay her family $247.5 million in damages.

Advocates of lifting U.S. sanctions on Iran argue that the re-election of a so-called "moderate" cleric, Mohammed Khatami, as Iran's president on June 8 will end the terror spree and that sanctions only reinforce his hard-line opponents. But since Khatami's first election as president in 1997, he has met repeatedly in Tehran with the leaders of Hamas, Islamic Jihad and Lebanon's Hezbollah. Iran's subsidies to these groups have continued unabated at the rate of around $100 million per year. In fact, as Ministry of Islamic Guidance in 1983, Khatami was one of the original founders of the worldwide Hezbollah movement.

Last October, after one such meeting with Hamas terrorists in Tehran, Khatami proclaimed that only the annihilation of the state of Israel would bring peace to the Middle East. "They are basically an occupying entity," he said of the Israeli government. "Naturally, any government that is based on oppression and injustice may stay in power for a while, but ultimately it is doomed to failure.... Real peace can only be achieved through an end to occupation."

Inside Iran, the reign of terror has accelerated under Khatami's presidency. Despite his claims to promote "liberalization," Khatami's security forces have closed reform-minded newspapers, assassinated dissidents and, in May, shut down Iranian access to the Internet.

On the evening of Nov. 22, 1998, mysterious intruders burst into the Tehran home of secular opposition leaders Darioush and Parvaneh Forouhar, hacking the elderly couple to death and sexually mutilating their corpses. It turned out the murderers were members of Iran's security services, acting on orders from a top deputy of one of Khatami's key government ministers.

Since the gruesome murder of the Forouhars, agents of Iran's security services have executed another half-dozen secular writers. Despite his protests of innocence, Khatami has done nothing to stop such killings or to restrain the intelligence services from their reign of terror.

On the contrary. In July 1999, students at Tehran University revolted against domestic repression and called for greater freedom. In response, the Tehran police stormed student dormitories, killing five students, including at least one person thrown to his death from a three-story window. Instead of backing the students and their calls for reform, the "moderate" Khatami called on students to end their demonstrations.

Many of those who support lifting U.S. sanctions on Iran argue that free trade would subvert the radical Islamic regime by exposing ordinary Iranians to Western culture. But Iranians are very sophisticated, thank you. Many of the current regime's leaders were in fact educated in the West. Tens of thousands of Iranians travel every year from Iran to the United States, while several times that number travel regularly to Europe and even to Israel. U.S. sanctions did not exclude the sale of consumer goods to Iran until 1995. The reason Western notions of freedom and free trade do not flourish in today's Iran is not because they are foreign concepts, but because the regime has demonstrated again and again that it brutally will quash any challenge to its monopoly on power.

Opponents of U.S. sanctions on Iran include some of America's largest and most successful multinational corporations. They stand to gain billions of dollars in potential trade should they succeed in getting sanctions lifted. Put politely, their arguments emit a faint odor of self-interest.

USA*Engage, originally established in 1996 as a mouthpiece for Conoco and Unocal, claims the United States is "shooting itself in the foot" by maintaining trade sanctions on Iran since foreign companies are more than willing to fill the breach left by the U.S. boycott.

There is some merit to this argument. Russia and China are conducting cash-and-carry sales of modern weaponry and the strategic equipment Iran needs to build ballistic missiles and nuclear-power plants. Some U.S. companies might be tempted to follow in their path. U.S. sanctions block these companies from pursuing sales that clearly violate our national interests. If that is shooting ourselves in the foot, then we should keep shooting.

Other countries such as France, Italy, Germany and Japan clearly want to help Iran develop its oil and gas fields. But the lack of laws to protect foreign investment in Iran has helped deter many companies from committing major capital to such projects. Do U.S. oil companies want to invest in Iran without protection? Are they prepared to send American citizens to work in Iranian gas fields while pro-regime thugs continue to trample the U.S. flag on the streets of Tehran?

Liberalizing trade amounts to a cash advance drawn against the hope of future good behavior by Tehran's ruling class.

Added to this high-risk environment are U.S. secondary sanctions, known as the Iran Libya Sanctions Act (ILSA), which is up for renewal this summer. ILSA was passed in 1996 because the U.S. Congress and the Clinton administration agreed it was not in our national interest to help prop up the current regime in Iran by investing in its oil and gas industry.

The ILSA sanctions have helped to deny Iran the technology and capital it needs to rebuild its oil and gas industries, which still account for some 90 percent of Iranian gross national product. New figures released in May by the International Monetary Fund show Iran's economy has shrunk by 12 percent from its size a decade ago, despite surging oil prices. The figures also show Iran to be one of only 11 countries outside Africa and the former Soviet bloc where per capita income actually fell throughout the 1990s while the rest of the world experienced an economic boom.

U.S. sanctions were not the root cause of Iran's economic woes: Chronic corruption and mismanagement by Iranian government planners did the trick. But U.S. sanctions have made a significant contribution—so much so that the Iranian government lodged an official complaint with the International Court of Justice in 1996, accusing the United States of economic "sabotage."

Lifting U.S. sanctions against Iran before significant changes are made in the repressive and terrorist behavior of the Iranian regime only would encourage hard-liners to continue their assault on fundamental freedoms and human decency. Liberalizing trade amounts to a cash advance drawn against the hope of future good behavior by Tehran's ruling clerics.

The previous administration tried throwing sops to Tehran on several occasions without any improvement in Iranian government behavior. The ban on American imports of Iranian carpets, dried fruits, nuts and caviar was lifted last year. Visa requirements were loosened and academic exchanges encouraged. Before that, the administration quietly allowed the sale of U.S. aircraft spare parts to Iran. So far, the Iranian government has yet to make a single gesture in response.

Iran continues to build long-range ballistic missiles while pursuing a clandestine nuclear-weapons program. A major influx of U.S. capital and advanced technology would give these efforts a shot in the arm.

Instead of finding new ways of appeasing a bloodthirsty regime that wishes America no good, the United States should encourage democrats inside Iran to pursue their quest to end the dictatorship of a radical, anti-Western clergy. Lifting sanctions might fatten the bottom line of a few selected U.S. companies, but it would do severe damage to our national security.

Timmerman, a senior writer at Insight, *is a former writer for* Time *and other journals. He repeatedly has testified before Congress on issues concerning Iran.*

No: Sanctions only punish American workers and weaken our national security.

BY ARCHIE DUNHAM

The Iran Libya Sanctions Act (ILSA) should not be renewed. I said publicly five years ago that it should not be enacted; we now have five years of failed policy and ineffective secondary boycotts against non-U.S. companies that prove the folly of this approach.

You may think it odd that I—representing an American oil company—should oppose a law that purports to level the playing field for us against our international competitors. The fact is, ILSA doesn't help my company, and it certainly doesn't help my country. It is not the highest moral choice, it threatens our national security and it doesn't work because it is the wrong tool for the problem it is supposed to solve. It's time for Washington to correct its mistake and get to work on real solutions.

Supporters of ILSA's renewal claim this is the right moral choice, but I believe differently. As I write this, I am in the Middle East. A suicide bomber in Tel Aviv has taken the lives of 20 innocent people. My heart goes out to the families of these victims. It also goes out to the families, known only to God, of those who may pay with their lives if there is retaliation. When the vast majority of peace-loving people in the world witness the atrocious acts of a violent few but seem powerless to exert their will over a small minority to stem the hatred and hostility, what can we do? When each new death, on any side, only deepens the animosities and invites further violence, how do we reverse the momentum and create sustainable conditions of peace, harmony and prosperity?

I am excited that the United States stands at a crossroads in history where unrivaled opportunity intersects self-inflicted consequence. But how will we choose? On the low road lies the invitation to be just another combatant, abandon whatever facade of evenhandedness remains and support the continuing hostilities with attitudes, words, threats, laws, penalties and even arms. We ride down this road on a high horse, pointing an accusing finger and expecting others to be drawn to our "principled" policy.

On this path, American morality looks false and empty, as it refuses to understand all sides and to acknowledge the motivation of all interested parties. We expect to exert leadership from a distant fortress, and we disengage from the hard work of real diplomacy and real defense. We try to punish both friend and foe into toeing our line. This course is futile. Who honestly sees any relationship between such behaviors and our nation's founding values and principles?

On the high road lies the opportunity to lead with a human touch, to engage all sides in discussion, to align exclusively with none and to support all who work peacefully for the good of all. We offer our respect and legitimacy, our active engagement—including investments, diplomacy, aid and international institutional memberships.

Americans like to think of themselves as a Godly nation. We therefore should preach a morality that stems from our common ancestor, Abraham, and that embodies God's commandment to love our neighbor—even the unlovable one. This is characterized by a humility of which President George W. Bush often has spoken. If we lift up our nation's unifying values, we will draw all people to us, just as our economic system and democratic form of government now serve as a beacon for all yearning peoples.

But if we try to punish, bully and coerce others into adopting our choices of behavior, we will drive them away. Indeed, we are driving them away. If we try to push with hatred rather than pull with love, our hope for peace and moderation will backfire. In my travels, I find to my dismay that much of the world resents the power of the United States and is not convinced that we use it responsibly and caringly.

Renewing a sanctions law that has not worked and makes friend and foe both feel victimized only will convince a few million more people that we are uninformed of Middle East culture and values and are not committed to peace in the region. ILSA may be aimed at foreign corporations, but it sends a clear and powerful signal about the prevailing American mind-set toward the world in general, not just toward two critical countries in a region of vital national interest.

ILSA threatens our long-term energy security. It offers a cheap domestic political vote, but it then damages a range of U.S. national-security interests worldwide—interests that all Americans share.

Consider energy. Commercial activity that discovers and distributes energy is a key U.S. national-security interest—a fact that never is appreciated until supplies run short and a crisis descends. California, the world's sixth-largest economy, is instructive. Beyond the blackouts yet to come (on the East Coast as well), Californians face challenges to the public safety, business closures and departures from the state, and potential new investors locating elsewhere to avoid the risks caused by inadequate energy supply and source diversity.

California, long a trendsetting state, is suffering an energy shortfall that highlights the risks faced by the entire nation. Unless America moves quickly to solve its energy-diversity problem, California's predicament could surface in all 50 states. If ILSA is allowed to expire on Aug. 5—as is legislated—and the corresponding presidential Executive Orders that prevent American companies from investing in Iran and Libya finally are rescinded, significant amounts of new energy will be available faster and more plentifully than through any other means. The international-energy industry considers Iran and Libya the two most attractive countries in which to develop new oil resources in the world.

ILSA will not stop those developments from occurring, no matter what Congress passes, but it will cause a trade war with Europe and seriously complicate diplomacy for the president far beyond the Middle East. And, given the message this law conveys toward the Arab world, how will this action square with the hope for Arab producers to favor the United States with increased production? It is a direct conflict. As always with unilateral sanctions, the only losers will be American consumers, workers, farmers and voters.

Vice President Richard Cheney correctly has emphasized that conservation will help, as will increasing domestic-energy supplies. But such actions cannot balance energy supply when demand is increasing globally.

ILSA doesn't work. It has not stopped terrorism or the proliferation of weapons of mass destruction. Nor has it achieved justice and compensation for the Pan Am Flight 103 victims' families—the justifications proffered for ILSA. In fact, many experts believe ILSA and, more generally, unilateral sanctions actually worsen these problems. They encourage the offending actors to establish relationships with other groups and states that profess hostile anti-American ideologies or that are eager to sell weapons and technologies.

We should be using instruments that attack terrorism. If we wish to promote political change, economic engagement is a proven, powerful tool.

The notion that sanctions deprive these states of energy income that they might use for nefarious purposes is conventional wisdom that cannot stand scrutiny. Prices set by global oil markets nullify any impact of sanctions on government revenues in Iran and Libya. While Iran's production was constant throughout the 1990s, its income doubled from 1998 to 2000 in direct relationship to the world price of oil. Paradoxically, to whatever extent sanctions diminish global energy supply, they push up prices, thus increasing the income of sanctioned states. Lawmakers who wish to renew ILSA prefer to ignore these realities.

Supporters of ILSA need to look carefully at the larger world. Shocks to the global-energy system seem increasingly probable. Because energy supplies are tight, a single shock at any point in the system will have significant negative consequences on all parts and major effects on the most vulnerable (high-consuming) parts unless additional supply is created.

What if the sanctions-supporters' fantasies came true and Iran's government fell? When that happened in 1979, 2 million

barrels per day were wiped off the global market, sending oil prices to $45 per barrel and causing a 2 percent drop in U.S. gross domestic product. Does any member of the U.S. Congress imagine that such a catastrophe could not happen again? Iran, with its population of 70 million people, 70 percent of whom are under the age of 30, should be our friend, not our enemy. We certainly don't have an abundance of friends in the Middle East!

ILSA is the wrong tool. The Middle East has many problems requiring real solutions, not phony policies offering punishment rather than processes that stimulate change. If we are serious about combating terrorism, let's use instruments that attack terrorism. If we wish to promote political change, economic engagement is a proven, powerful tool, as Secretary of State Colin Powell repeatedly has said. It offers a number of high-road opportunities to re-establish broken relations with countries whose interests ultimately are compatible with our own.

To anyone prepared honestly to understand Iran and Libya today, it's obvious that both countries wish to enhance their relations with the United States—not necessarily with our government, but certainly with the American people, whom they like. To any serious watcher of the Middle East, it is obvious that our Arab friends and allies increasingly are becoming distant. They are becoming more aligned with those we choose to demonize and victimize, and they reject our disengagement.

Members of Congress cosponsoring the ILSA renewal bill should brace for some tough questions from their constituents, who may find themselves in gas lines, in the dark or in suffocating heat or freezing cold. Let those lawmakers explain why they lost the Middle East for "the right symbolic vote" or "the need to show resolve." See if the American public buys it.

The media often caricature energy companies as being greedy, with no concern for the national interest. We are, of course, public corporations owned by millions of American shareholders. But first and most importantly, we love America. We profoundly believe the American spirit of free enterprise has a major contribution to make toward promoting peace and prosperity around the world, and engagement always has been the best approach to diplomacy.

Even if relations with Iran and Libya remain rocky, working with them, not against them, is essential to U.S. national security. It also is a moral and historic imperative. ILSA is the low road. Let's take the high road.

Dunham is president and chief executive officer of Conoco Inc., an international energy company in Houston, and is a longtime critic of unilateral sanctions.

The U.S. Trade Deficit:
A Dangerous Obsession

Joseph Quinlan and Marc Chandler

THE WRONG SCORECARD

EVERY U.S. president over the past quarter-century has confronted an annual trade deficit. But the cavernous trade gap inherited by President George W. Bush dwarfs those faced by his predecessors. America's current-account deficit (which measures the cross-border exchange of goods, services, and investment income) averaged more than $1 billion a day last year, reaching a record 4.4 percent of GDP. Many economists worry that the huge trade deficit, which must be financed by foreign investors, could lead to a full-blown financial crisis if and when those investors become unwilling to fund the imbalance. Something as benign as stronger economic growth in another country, for instance, could attract a larger share of the world's savings, leading to higher U.S. interest rates, a weaker dollar, and a grimmer economic outlook for the United States and the world.

Economists offer various explanations for the persistent U.S. trade deficit. Some argue that America buys more from the world than it sells because its companies are growing less competitive. Others blame the "unfair" trade restrictions and labor policies of other countries. Still others point to the underlying strength of the dollar, which makes American goods and services more expensive for foreign buyers.

Whatever the proper explanation, a simple and important fact is absent from the debate: the trade balance is no longer a valid scorecard for America's global sales and competitiveness. Given a choice, U.S. firms prefer to sell goods and services abroad through their foreign affiliates instead of exporting them from the United States. In 1998, U.S. foreign-affiliate sales topped a staggering $2.4 trillion, while U.S. exports—the common but spurious yardstick of U.S. global sales—totaled just $933 billion, or less than 40 percent of affiliate sales. How U.S. firms compete in world markets, in other words, goes well beyond trade.

Still, trade erroneously remains the standard benchmark of global competitiveness. More worrisome, it is the most important factor shaping U.S. international economic policy. Overblown concern about the swollen trade deficit, combined with a slowing economy and the expectation of rising unemployment, could ignite a new round of trade protectionism in Washington, which could spark similar responses around the globe. The greatest danger on America's trade front, therefore, is not the size of the deficit but the nation's obsession with it.

INSIDER TRADING

THE RULE "make where you sell" increasingly governs the way American companies do business. It explains, for example, why Ford Motor Company and General Motors have long owned affiliates in Europe and have recently entered promising emerging markets such as Brazil and China. The principle also underlies Dell Computer's direct-investment positions in Europe and Latin America, as well as those of Cisco Systems and Microsoft in China. And because of the increased globalization of services, U.S. service giants such as American International Group, Citigroup, FedEx, and Yahoo have also set up foreign affiliates, leading the boom in U.S. foreign direct investment (FDI) over the last decade.

American companies simply cannot afford the luxury of staying at home. Multiple market opportunities, incessant technological advances, blurred industrial boundaries, and unrelenting global competition all demand that U.S. firms compete not just through trade but also through FDI. Being an "insider" is increasingly critical in markets around the world.

Numerous factors explain this trend. Contrary to popular perception, foreign consumers' demands vary according to location, requiring firms such as Procter & Gamble, Gillette, and Coca-Cola to be close to their customers. For example, China's vastly diverse cultures, dialects, and above all else, living standards demand that U.S. companies adapt their products to local tastes—that they follow Coca-Cola's mantra, "think local, act local." Chinese consumers, whether buying soft drinks, computers, or automobiles, are very brand-sensitive—which means that a local presence is crucial for success in the Chinese market.

Moreover, fierce competition for global market share compels U.S. firms to be close to their foreign competitors. How else can Eastman Kodak successfully compete in China against Japanese rival Fuji Photo Film? Wal-Mart cannot let its global competitor Carrefour of France enter key markets such as Brazil and Japan uncontested; neither can Citigroup, which battled Germany's Commerzbank for market supremacy in Poland last year. At stake for all these companies are new customers, new resources, new opportunities—and by extension, long-term success.

GLOBAL HEAVYWEIGHTS

CORPORATE AMERICA now has some 23,000 majority- and minority-owned affiliates strategically positioned around the globe. Together they rank among the world's largest economic producers, boasting a combined gross output of $510 billion in 1998—greater than the GDPS of most nations, including Mexico, Sweden, Taiwan, and South Korea. U.S. affiliates also contribute significantly to the GDPS of their various host nations. In 1998, they accounted for more than 16 percent of the GDP in Ireland, more than 9 percent in Singapore and Canada, and more than 6 percent in the United Kingdom.

The strategic objective of most U.S. foreign affiliates is to produce and deliver goods and services to the host market. In 1998, roughly two-thirds of total affiliate sales were made to customers in the host nation—virtually unchanged from the level in the early 1980s. Yet as U.S. multinational corporations increasingly disperse different stages of production among different countries, their affiliates have also become world-class exporters of intermediate goods and components. In 1998, the exports of U.S. affiliates totaled $623 billion. That figure not only matched the total value of U.S. goods exports but also easily surpassed the export levels of Germany, Japan, and China.

Critics often claim that U.S. multinationals export cheaper products from their overseas affiliates back to the United States, thereby contributing to the U.S. import bill and undermining American jobs and income. But in fact, most U.S. affiliate exports do not go to the United States. In 1998, only 30 percent of them went to the United States; the bulk of the rest went to regional markets close to the host nations. Moreover, the majority of affiliate exports do not emanate from low-wage nations such as Brazil, China, or India. Rather, nearly three-fourths of total affiliate exports in 1998 came from high-wage industrialized nations such as Canada, the United Kingdom, and Germany.

U.S. affiliates also stand among the world's top employers, collectively employing more than 8 million people in 1998—a workforce greater than that of most countries. Most Americans assume that the bulk of this workforce toils in developing nations under extreme and unfair conditions. But in fact, corporate America's global workforce is concentrated in the high-wage developed nations. In Europe alone, U.S. affiliates employed some 3.5 million workers in 1998—more than the combined U.S. workforce in Latin America and developing Asia. In Canada, some 935,000 workers were on U.S. payrolls in 1998—more than four times the number employed by U.S. affiliates in China.

LOCATION, LOCATION, LOCATION

NOT ONLY are U.S. affiliate sales significantly larger than U.S. exports, but they are also dispersed differently across the globe. Since the end of World War II, America's FDI levels have soared, and Europe, notably the United Kingdom, has emerged as the favorite destination for U.S. multinationals. As Europe recovered from the ravages of war and moved toward creating a common market, U.S. firms seized the new commercial opportunities presented by its peace and economic stability. By the 1960s, Europe accounted for almost 40 percent of total U.S. foreign direct investment. The following decade, the tilt toward Europe became even more pronounced: the region accounted for nearly half the value of American FDI, largely at the expense of Latin America and Canada. In the 1970s, meanwhile, Asia remained among the least favored destinations for U.S. multinationals.

U.S. Exports vs. U.S. Foreign-Affiliate Sales, 1998
(IN BILLIONS OF U.S. DOLLARS)

Country	Exports to	Affiliate Sales from
U.K.	$39.1	$224.0
Germany	$26.7	$163.1
Canada	$156.6	$209.5
Japan	$57.8	$77.2
Brazil	$15.1	$52.9

Source: U.S. Department of Commerce
Note: Figures are for goods only.

The first half of the 1980s proved an unpropitious time for U.S. multinationals. Courtesy of the 1979 oil shock, the global economy stumbled into recession. After reaching a postwar peak of $13 billion in 1980, U.S. direct investment in Europe plunged to just $3.5 billion in 1982. Investment flows to Canada turned negative in 1981–82 due to that country's adoption of restrictive policies such as the Natural Energy Program, which prompted U.S. companies to sell their existing assets in the politically charged petroleum and mining sectors. Meanwhile, Latin America's debt crisis and subsequent economic recession sharply curtailed U.S. multinational participation in that region.

Across the Pacific, talk of an "Asian miracle," set against debt-ridden Latin America, protectionist Canada, and slumping Europe, inspired a friendlier view of Asia among U.S. firms. As a consequence, cumulative U.S. direct investment in Asia rose 71.5 percent from the previous decade, well ahead of the pace in Europe (64 percent), Latin America (37 percent), and Canada (-13.2 percent). More impressive still was the surge in U.S. investment to the developing nations of Asia, which rose to $14 billion in 1980–89 from $6.1 billion in the 1970s. Still, the region attracted only 8.1 percent of total U.S. outflows in the 1980s—less than half the amount invested in trouble-prone Latin America.

Although the 1980s started with a gloomy investment climate for U.S. multinationals, the decade ended on a decidedly different note. In fact, the global investment backdrop at the end of the 1980s and into the 1990s was nearly perfect. Multiple forces—both cyclical and structural—converged to produce one of the most powerful booms in global FDI, with American firms leading the way. Falling telecommunication and transportation costs allowed U.S. firms to broaden the geographic dispersion of their operations. The end of the Cold War opened new markets to U.S. firms, as did the proliferation of regional trading blocs such as the North American Free Trade Agreement, Mercosur (which comprises Argentina, Brazil, Paraguay, and Uruguay), and the common market of the European Union (EU). Moreover, low interest rates and surging equity prices around the world provided copious amounts of cash for global mergers and acquisitions.

All of these developments converged in the 1990s to trigger the most robust wave of U.S. foreign direct investment in history. During that decade alone, U.S. firms invested more capital overseas—$802 billion—than they had in the prior four decades combined. But the geographic preference of U.S. firms did not change, despite all the hype about new markets in central Europe, economic reform in India, privatization in Brazil, and liberalization in mainland China. The developed nations—by a wide margin—remained the biggest recipients of U.S. direct investment.

A number of motives drive the global strategies of U.S. multinationals, but reducing the wage bill tends to be near the bottom of the list. More important are wealthy markets, along with access to skilled labor and technology. These advantages reside in the developed nations, which accounted for two-thirds of total U.S. foreign direct investment during the 1990s. Europe remained the preferred destination, accounting for nearly 55 percent of the total. Canada represented another 8 percent, attracting $2 of U.S. investment for every $1 invested in Mexico during 1994–99. Meanwhile, Asia's total share of U.S. investment

during the 1990s (roughly $122 billion) lagged behind other major parts of the world. And even in the Asia-Pacific, the most favored location of U.S. multinationals was neither China nor Japan, the two largest markets in the region, but Australia, whose labor force and consumer markets are smaller than those of most U.S. states.

During the 1990s, Australia accounted for more than 20 percent of total U.S. direct investment in the Asia-Pacific region, placing the nation among the top 10 foreign destinations for U.S. companies. Australia's attractiveness may owe to its technological capabilities and its well-educated, English-speaking labor force. On a per capita basis, Australia is one of the world's heaviest users of computers and the Internet and is therefore a prime location for U.S. technology firms. Industry deregulation in the late 1980s and early 1990s was another draw for U.S. investment.

At the other end of the spectrum lies India. Although it is often viewed as one of the most promising emerging markets in Asia, with a massive and cheap labor force, India attracted a mere $1.1 billion of U.S. investment in the 1990s—roughly half the level of U.S. investment in Colombia during the same period. Meanwhile, the so-called crisis economies of South Korea, Thailand, the Philippines, Malaysia, and Indonesia together drew only 3.2 percent of U.S. foreign direct investment. Even in Taiwan, one of the region's hottest economies, U.S. direct investment amounted to less than that in South Africa during the 1990s. By the same token, U.S. multinationals invested more capital in tiny Chile than in massive China over the same time frame.

TUNNEL VISION

WHILE U.S. multinationals were enjoying their best decade ever, developing countries around the world were suffering successive economic crises. In 1995, Mexico fell victim to a currency meltdown. In mid-1997, it was Asia's turn. Russia rolled over the next year, followed by Brazil shortly thereafter. Each traumatic event set off a mad scramble on Wall Street to determine the collateral damage to the United States, using trade linkages as the standard benchmark.

As the Asian crisis unfolded, the flurry of attention surrounding U.S.-Asian trade linkages was understandable. Of the top 15 U.S. export markets in the world, 7 were in Asia. Collectively the region accounted for nearly one-third of U.S. exports in the year prior to the crisis, notably higher than the export shares of Europe (22.4 percent) and Latin America (17.8 percent). Using trade as the key variable, then, Asia factored heavily into the U.S. equation. But trade linkages were only half the story—if even that. Viewed from the lens of affiliate sales, the Asian meltdown was significant but hardly fatal to the U.S. economy, given that developing Asia accounted for only about 10 percent of total U.S. affiliate sales.

A trade spat with the EU over bananas and beef risks America's large investment stake in Europe.

In contrast, Europe took credit for more than 50 percent of such sales. The United Kingdom, for example, accounted for $224 billion in U.S. affiliate sales in 1998, versus just $39 billion in goods exports—a ratio of almost 6 to 1. Similarly, in nearly all developed nations, U.S. affiliate sales surpassed exports by a wide margin. Italy, Spain, and Switzerland, for example, do not even appear on the export radar screen, giving the false impression that U.S. commercial links with these countries are insignificant. But in fact, they are substantial when measured by foreign affiliate sales. Thus, when the euro plunged against the dollar in 2000, so did the overseas profits of U.S. multinationals such as Gillette, IBM, Ford, Heinz, and DuPont. And since a shift in exchange rates has a more immediate impact on affiliate sales and income than on trade, these pains were quickly felt by corporate America.

Just as a myopic focus on U.S. exports can distort the true picture of U.S. global competitiveness, so can a singular focus on imports. Many foreign companies compete in the United States the same way U.S. companies compete abroad—through affiliate sales rather than exports. Although American firms adopted FDI-led strategies earlier and more aggressively than did their foreign counterparts, many Japanese and European companies have also begun to prefer affiliate sales over exports as their main approach to foreign markets. According to a 1998 report by the Japanese Ministry for International Trade and Industry, Japan's affiliate sales surpassed its exports for the first time in 1996. The same thing happened in Europe in the late 1980s. By the mid-1990s, affiliate sales of European companies totaled almost $3 trillion, or 1.2 times the value of EU exports.

For many foreign multinationals such as Reuters, Daimler-Benz, Royal Ahold, and British Petroleum, the answer to globalization was to plow billions of dollars into the United States, the growth champion and technological leader of the world. As Krish Prabhu, chief operating officer of Alcatel, remarked to the *Financial Times* in September 1999, "So much company strategy is driven out of the United States today. No serious player can afford not to have a presence there." Indeed, foreign multinationals pumped nearly $900 billion into the U.S. economy in the 1990s, more than the amount invested over the preceding four decades combined.

In 1998, U.S. imports of goods and services totaled $1.1 trillion. But as impressive as that number is, it falls short of the $1.9 trillion in sales by foreign-owned affiliates in the United States that same year. A fixation on imports ignores the extensive presence of foreign-owned affiliates in the United States, which numbered more than 9,700 at last count. It also overlooks the fact that such affiliates contributed nearly $420 billion in output and employed more than 5.6 million Americans in 1998.

Germany, for example, may not be a significant exporter to the United States, but German affiliates here employed nearly 800,000 Americans and racked up sales of roughly $240 billion in 1998—nearly five times the value of German exports to the United States in the same year. Similarly, import figures suggest that China has greater stakes in the United States than the United Kingdom does. But that is hardly the case, given the latter's deep and long-standing direct-investment ties with the United States. U.S. imports from the United Kingdom totaled only $36 billion in 1998, roughly half the value of that year's imports from China. But affiliate sales of British firms operating in the United States—$192 billion in 1998—greatly exceed those of Chinese firms.

GOODBYE, ADAM SMITH

FOREIGN DIRECT INVESTMENT has changed the face of the international economy. Since the early 1970s, it has grown faster than either world output or global trade and is the single most important source of capital for developing economies.

But America's foreign economic policy still centers on trade at the expense of FDI. A trade spat with the EU over beef and bananas, for example, risks America's large investment stake in Europe. And the suggestion of some in Congress to devalue the dollar to promote U.S. exports would only make it more expensive for U.S. affiliates to do business abroad while making it cheaper for foreign companies to buy American assets. An attempt to improve the trade balance, therefore, would actually end up hurting the FDI balance.

Corporate America risks losing out on the best opportunities of the global marketplace if Washington continues to make trade its top priority in the world economy. With China's entry into the World Trade Organization, for example, many observers will carp on the U.S.-China trade imbalance (which recently surpassed the U.S. trade deficit with Japan), even though the real, more substantial penetration of the Chinese market will likely come through direct investment and affiliate sales. In 1998, U.S. affiliate sales in China totaled $14 billion—roughly equal to U.S. exports there. This comparison will only grow in favor of FDI. A continued fixation on trade, however, will divert attention from the more promising opportunities of direct investment in China.

Similarly, America's most significant economic imbalance with Japan is not the headline-grabbing U.S. trade deficit but the stark imbalance of FDI. In 1997, Japan's accumulation of direct investment in the United States was worth $64 billion more than the value of U.S. assets in Japan—a deficit 12 percent greater than the trade gap that year. Thus, in dealing with Japan, the Bush administration should not get bogged down in the all-too-familiar battle over automobile trade. Instead, it should concentrate on opening the Japanese market in service sectors such as health care, insurance, and financial services, where the potential payoffs are greater. In other words, Detroit should not set the tone for U.S.-Japan commercial relations; rather, Washington should work on expanding investment opportunities in Japan for companies such as Yahoo, General Electric Capital, and Charles Schwab. Moreover, the Bush administration should actively promote another round of global trade negotiations, putting the liberalization of services at the top of the agenda.

Looking south of the border, America's widening trade deficit with Mexico appears increasingly formidable. But both policymakers and the media should realize that in 1999, nearly two-thirds of U.S. imports from Mexico counted as "related-party trade"—that is, trade between multinational firms and related affiliates. What drives U.S. trade with countries such as Mexico, Canada, and Singapore is the exchange of goods and services within U.S. firms such as IBM, Ford, DuPont, and Motorola. Slamming the door on Mexican imports, then, means slamming the door on corporate America.

U.S. commercial relations with many developing nations are growing more complex as American firms shift from trade-led initiatives to investment-driven strategies. This development should influence how the Bush administration takes up negotiations for the proposed Free Trade Area of the Americas. The initial signs, however, are discouraging. Just when U.S. firms are striving to integrate more developing nations into their global production networks, the Bush administration is proposing broad cuts in the Overseas Private Investment Corporation, which provides insurance and loans to companies investing in developing nations. That proposal must be music to the ears of policymakers in Europe, who are actively promoting their own commercial interests in strategic markets such as China, India, Mexico, and the Mercosur trade group.

In the end, U.S. exports and imports neither represent America's global linkages nor indicate how or where U.S. firms compete. Yet many still view global competition though the 200-year-old eyes of Adam Smith and David Ricardo, who saw trade as the chief form of economic exchange. Others harbor equally archaic mercantilist prejudices, assuming that exports are good while imports are bad. These observers regard a trade deficit as a sign of national weakness, a warning signal that something is amiss. But U.S. global engagement involves far more than just trade. If policymakers continue to interpret a large trade deficit as a loss of global competitiveness or a result of unfair trade practices, protectionist backlash could result, which could trigger retaliations around the globe. Under this scenario, there would be no winners—only losers.

The United States' obsession with its trade deficit belies the fact that corporate America has never been better positioned to compete in the global marketplace. It is time to say goodbye to Adam Smith's outdated framework of global competition and to embrace instead a more complex understanding of America's economic engagement with the world.

JOSEPH QUINLAN is Senior Global Economist at Morgan Stanley Dean Witter and author of *Global Engagement: How American Companies Really Compete in the Global Economy*. MARC CHANDLER is Chief Currency Strategist at Mellon Financial Corporation.

Reprinted by permission of *Foreign Affairs*, May/June 2001, Vol. 80, No. 3, pp. 87-97. © 2001 by the Council on Foreign Relations, Inc.

Society

The Death of the Washington Consensus?

Robin Broad and John Cavanagh

Between the early 1980s and the late 1990s, an elite consensus swept the globe that unfettered free markets provided the formula to make rich countries out of poor. In policy circles, this formula came to be known as the "Washington Consensus."

As we approach a new century, however, deep cracks have appeared within this consensus. Its legitimacy has come into question in the face of an increasingly effective citizens' backlash in North and South, and there is growing dissension within the ranks of its backers, as the effects of the financial crisis of the late 1990s are felt around the globe. While not yet dead, the consensus has been wounded—and potentially fatally so.

Our essay analyzes the reign of the Washington Consensus and what we see as its loss of legitimacy in the global economic upheavals of recent years. It is written neither to help rebuild the consensus nor to mourn its possible fall. Let us be clear from the start: we were never part of the consensus. In numerous articles written over the last decade and a half, we have chronicled the human and environmental wreckage of consensus policies. Our goal here is to dissect the reign and ana-

lyze the cracks in the consensus, and to reflect upon the lessons learned in terms of a new development agenda.

What is needed, we argue, is not a new Washington-driven and Washington-dominated consensus, but a vibrant new debate, a debate that must involve the supposed beneficiaries of development—workers, farmers, the urban poor, indigenous communities—in determining the goals and policies of new paths to development.

The Reign of the Washington Consensus

In the first three decades following the Second World War, there was a lively debate over the respective roles of government and the market in the development process. Prior to the 1980s, most developing countries favored a strong governmental role in development planning and policies, fearing that unfettered markets in a world of unequal nations would put them at a disadvantage. As a result, most of these governments maintained trade restrictions of some sort, gave preferences to national over foreign investment, and regulated capital flows in and out of the country.

In the United Nations, these countries backed a "new international economic order" agenda to close the North-South gap through collective government action to raise commodity prices and stimulate technology transfers and development assistance. Particularly during the 1970s, the U.S. government rallied rich country governments to oppose most of these proposals.

This development debate was extinguished with the emergence of the governments of Margaret Thatcher, Ronald Reagan, and Helmut Kohl in the early 1980s. With strong corporate support, these governments championed free trade, free investment, deregulation, and privatization as the best route to growth. Exxon, Ford, and the rest of the Fortune 500 flourished as they spread their assembly lines, shopping malls, and American culture around the world. In 1990, the economist John Williamson (then of the Institute for International Economics and now of the World Bank) summed up this growing policy consensus in ten areas of economic reform that reflected free-market strategies to achieve export-led growth—with specific policies ranging from trade liberalization to privatization of state-owned firms.[1]

The Washington Consensus, he argued, was shared by "both the political Washington of Congress and senior members of the administration and the technocratic Washington of the international financial institutions, the economic agencies of the U.S. government, the Federal Reserve Board, and the think tanks."[2]

The power of the Washington Consensus over development theory and practice in the 1980s and 1990s is hard to overstate. That once vibrant debate about development all but disappeared as the consensus took on almost religious qualities. The high priests of the consensus—the U.S. Department of Treasury, the International Monetary Fund (IMF), and the World Bank—were in Washington. Converts to the cult of the consensus spread far beyond the Beltway—as with other religions, through a combination of the appeal of its simplicity, proselytizing by its believers, and outright coercion.

Indeed, beginning in 1982, the majority of developing countries lost substantial leverage over their economic destiny as foreign debts incurred during the preceding two decades fell due at a moment of historically high interest rates. The U.S. government, working with the governments of other rich nations, pressed developing countries into the free-market paradigm as a condition for new loans. The IMF was assigned the role of enforcing the policies; the World Bank urged similar reforms through its new "structural adjustment" loans.

As a result, by the 1990s most developing country governments—with the exception of such East Asian "tigers" as South Korea and Taiwan—had become converts to free-market policies. Over the course of the 1980s and 1990s, the governments of developing countries substantially reduced trade barriers, and many removed longstanding restrictions on capital inflow and outflows.

The high priests of the Washington Consensus were arrogant and

acted as if there was no further need for debate and discussion about what development entailed or how to make it happen. They saw little need for country-specific experts, and detailed field studies were deemed a waste of time. One of us worked as an international economist in the Treasury Department from 1983 to 1985, where it was an article of faith that the IMF and World Bank formula was the only route for countries to follow. Those of us daring to criticize the consensus were treated like heretics.

By the early 1990s, the consensus steamroller was changing the contours of development policy and practice across the globe. Its backers pressed successfully for an acceleration of corporate-friendly globalization rules, leading to the passage of the North American Free Trade Agreement (NAFTA) in 1993 and the creation of the World Trade Organization (WTO) in 1994. Each victory whetted the appetite of consensus backers for more. The IMF and World Bank, in tandem with the U.S. Treasury Department, pressed for investment liberalization in South Korea, Thailand, the Philippines, and elsewhere. The European Union, the United States, and other governments launched a flurry of negotiations in pursuit of a multi-lateral agreement on investment (to outlaw governmental "affirmative action" in favor of domestic industries over foreign) and for regional agreements along the NAFTA model.

Attacking the Consensus

Yet, even as the steamroller plowed on, the consensus never gained widespread legitimacy in the developing world outside of a technocratic elite. As the 1980s unfolded, citizen groups in the South, often campaigning in collaboration with Northern environmental, labor, and antipoverty groups, exposed the adverse development impact of the policies of the World Bank and the IMF, the two institutions that have most zealously enforced the Wash-

ington Consensus. In Africa, Asia, Latin America, and the Caribbean, anticonsensus groups, such as the Freedom from Debt Coalition in the Philippines and the Malaysian-based Third World Network, became forceful actors on the global stage. They mounted opposition to the goals and decried the effect of consensus policies.

The consensus was focused solely on promoting economic growth. As John Williamson later admitted, "I deliberately excluded from [my] list [of the ten areas] anything which was primarily redistributive… because I felt the Washington of the 1980s to be a city that was essentially contemptuous of equity concerns."[3] Likewise, noted Williamson, the consensus "had little to say about social issues… and almost nothing to say about the environment."[4] But in those countries where consensus policies were actually applied, it turned out that the social impact of these policies could not be separated from the economic. From the Philippines to Mexico to Ghana came evidence that the free-market policies of the consensus were having negative effects on workers, the environment, and equity.

Inequality. As shown by numerous studies carried out by the United Nations and other organizations, growing inequality has accompanied economic liberalization in the majority of countries. To dramatize the stark reality of this, critics charted the growing divide between the world's richest and the world's poorest. By 1999, the combined wealth of the world's 475 billionaires exceeded the income of the poorest half of the world's people.[5]

The Environment. Twenty years ago, many developing countries, from Chile and Brazil to the Philippines and Indonesia, were still endowed with abundant natural resources—lush tropical forests, rich fishing banks and mineral deposits, and fertile land. In these and other countries, the increased emphasis on export-led growth has led to long-term environmental costs that were not factored into the Washington Consensus's measurements of economic success. In country after country, export-led growth depended on the plunder of these resources. Forests were cleared, for example, as Costa Rica, encouraged by the World Bank, expanded cattle production for meat exports, and as Indonesia expanded palm oil production. And, with the widespread destruction of natural-resource systems, the very survival of the poorest populations of these countries, those who live off the natural resources, was threatened.

Workers. Countries were encouraged to offer tax and other incentives to woo foreign investment. As a result, factories exporting apparel, electronics, toys, and other consumer goods sprang up in southern China, Vietnam, Guatemala, Malaysia, and dozens of other countries. Indeed, on average, close to one factory a day has opened along the 2,000-mile U.S.-Mexico border since the advent of NAFTA in 1994. Yet, even as countries compete with each other for foreign investment, in what critics have dubbed a "race to the bottom," workers in most of the Third World's new global factories are underpaid, overworked, and denied fundamental rights, including the right to organize and strike, and the right to a safe working environment.

Citizen outcry against the free-trade policies of the Washington Consensus was not limited to the South. Environmentalists in the North began launching campaigns against the damaging environmental impact of the World Bank policies in the early 1980s. Labor unions in developed countries jumped on the anti-free trade bandwagon as companies used the threat of moving production to China or Mexico to bargain down wages and benefits.

As free-trade policies implemented in the South rebounded with adverse effects on factory workers, small farmers, and small businesses in the North, public opinion polls in the United States began to show that a majority of Americans were skeptical of the merits of free trade. By the end of 1998, the U.S. public was not simply opposed to expansion of the free trade agenda: according to a December 1998 *Wall Street Journal/NBC* News survey, 58 percent of Americans polled said that "foreign trade has been bad for the U.S. economy."[6]

This widespread popular opposition was fed by unions, small farmers, environmentalists, and citizen leaders such as Jesse Jackson and Ralph Nader, who echoed their Southern counterparts' critique that free trade undermined workers, the environment, farmers, communities, sovereignty, and equity.

The broad public opposition in the North gained backing in diverse elite circles during the battles over free trade in the 1990s. In the United States, many Democratic members of Congress began to call for "fair trade"—a critique that in many ways mirrored the cry in nongovernmental organizations (NGOs) in the South. On the other side of the aisle, roughly 60 to 70 Republican members of Congress have consistently opposed free-trade agreements. While the Republican and the "fair trade" camps opposed to free trade diverge dramatically on an alternative vision, the two camps have, on key occasions, joined forces to slow the advance of the Washington Consensus.

Indeed, by the late 1990s, anti–free trade forces were strong enough to stall new free trade and investment initiatives from the U.S. government (legislation granting "fast track" trade authority to the president went down in defeat) and on a global level (negotiations over a multilateral agreement on investment were derailed in 1998). But the combined strength of these outside critics only slowed the momentum of the Washington Consensus; it was the 1997 Asian financial crisis that shook its very foundations.

In order to understand the actual cracks that have appeared within the consensus, it is necessary to understand the roots of the financial crisis.

Hot Money

Over this past decade, the World Bank, the IMF and the U.S. Treasury expanded their initial focus from the free trade and long-term investment stand of the consensus to the financial planks, pressing governments around the globe to open their stock markets and financial markets to short-term investments from the West. The resulting quick injections of capital from mutual funds, pension funds, and other sources propelled short-term growth in the 1990s, but also encouraged bad lending and bad investing.

Between 1990 and 1996, the amount of private financial flows entering poorer nations skyrocketed from $44 billion to $244 billion. Roughly half of this was long-term direct investment, but most of the rest—as recipient countries were soon to discover— was footloose, moving from country to country at the tap of a computer keyboard.

In mid-1997, as the reality of this short-sighted lending and investing began to surface, first in Thailand, then in South Korea, and then in several other countries, Western investors and speculators panicked. Their "hot money" fled much faster than it had arrived—leaving local economies without the capital they had come to depend on. Currency speculators like George Soros exacerbated the crisis by betting against the local currencies of the crisis nations, sending local currency values to new lows.

IMF advice seemed only to quicken the exodus of capital. Currencies and stock markets from South Korea to Brazil nosedived; and as these nations slashed purchases of everything from oil to wheat, prices of these products likewise plummeted. The financial crisis stalled production and trade in such large economies as Indonesia, Russia, South Korea, and Brazil, leaving in its wake widespread pain, dislocation, and environmental ruin. Exact figures are hard to come by, but the main international trade union federation estimates that, by the end of 1999 some 27 million workers in the five worst hit Asian countries—Indonesia, South Korea, Thailand, Malaysia, and the Philippines—will have lost their jobs.[7]

As economies collapsed, elite support for the Washington Consensus began to crumble. In the pages of the *Wall Street Journal*, former secretary of defense Robert McNamara likened the crisis to the Vietnam War, implying that then treasury secretary Robert Rubin, his deputy (and successor) Lawrence Summers, IMF managing director Michel Camdessus, and the other top managers had lost control.

Elite Dissent

Two sets of elite actors began launching critiques at Rubin, Summers, and Camdessus—not quietly, but in a very public and vocal fashion, using the op-ed pages of the *New York Times*, the *Wall Street Journal*, and the *Washington Post* to make their cases. One group, led by such highly regarded free-trade economists as Jagdish Bhagwati of Columbia University, Paul Krugman of MIT, and World Bank chief economist Joseph Stiglitz, supports free markets for trade but not for short-term capital. (The group also includes such well-known Washington figures as Henry Kissinger.) Bhagwati argued that capital markets are by their nature unstable and require controls. Krugman outlined the case for exchange controls as a response to crisis.

However, as dramatically interventionist as some of their proposals are and as heated as the debate may sound, these critics largely seek to repair the cracks in the consensus—by allowing national exchange and/or capital controls under certain circumstances—not to tear down the entire edifice.

Some within this first set of consensus reformers have focused more on the folly of IMF policies during the crisis. Some prominent economists, such as Harvard's Jeffrey Sachs, himself once a proponent of "shock therapy" in Russia, faulted the IMF for prescribing recessionary policies that transformed a liquidity crisis into a full-fledged financial panic and subsequently into a collapse of the real economy in an expanding list of countries. "Instead of dousing the fire," Sachs wrote last year, "the IMF in effect screamed fire in the theater."[8] While still subscribing to the goal of free trade, Sachs and others argue that the IMF needs to revise its standard formula for economic reform, make its decisionmaking more transparent, and become more publicly accountable for the impact of its policies.

A second set of consensus dissidents goes further in criticizing the IMF, arguing for its abolition. The critique of this group is rooted in an extreme defense of free markets, and its members fault the IMF for interfering in the markets. They charge that IMF monies disbursed to debtor governments end up being used to bail out investors, thus eliminating the discipline of risk (or "moral hazard") in private markets. This group is led by such long-time free trade supporters as the Heritage Foundation and the Cato Institute (whose opposition to publicly funded aid institutions is nothing new), but its ranks have recently swelled with such well-known, vocal converts as former Citicorp CEO Walter Wriston, former secretary of state George Shultz, and former secretary of the treasury William E. Simon.

These two camps of elite dissent within the consensus in the United States have their counterparts in other rich nations and among some developing country governments. West European economies, while not in the dire straits of Japan and much of the rest of the world, continue to be plagued by high unemployment, and their new joint currency, the euro, has gotten off to a shaky start. The European Union has also been involved in widely publicized trade disputes with the United States, several involving the European public's growing skepticism over genetically engineered foods.

As a result, a number of politicians in new center-left governments in Europe have raised their voices to question parts of the consensus. Even Clinton's closest ally, British prime minister Tony Blair, has a reform plan that includes a new intergovernmental global financial authority to help prevent future financial crises. Most West European governments support at least limited capital controls. And some members of the Canadian parliament are supporting an international tax on foreign currency transactions to discourage speculative transactions.

Japan is also looking for openings to rewrite parts of the consensus. The Japanese government has been both weakened and disillusioned by a decade of recession. Over the past two years, it has waged high-profile fights with the United States over Japan's proposal to create an Asian economic fund to help countries in crisis (Japan lost), and over whether a Thai candidate backed by Japan and much of Asia, or a New Zealander backed by most of the West, should lead the World Trade Organization (a compromise was worked out).

In the developing world, there have also been a number of recent instances where elite actors have departed from specific aspects of consensus policies. In Hong Kong, long heralded by consensus adherents as a supreme example of free-market trade and finance policies, the government reacted to the crisis spreading through Asia by intervening in the stock market and acting to prevent currency speculation. Malaysia grabbed the world's attention in 1998 by imposing a series of capital and exchange controls that were successful in stemming short-term speculative flows. Several developing country governments have moved beyond their discontent over certain IMF prescriptions to openly question whether the World Trade Organization should heed American and European calls for new trade talks to further liberalize foreign investment rules and agricultural protections among member states.

The combination of these criticisms and actions has begun to influence even the IMF and the World Bank. In Indonesia, where the crisis has been particularly brutal, the IMF implicitly acknowledged that there were occasions when the costs of consensus policies were likely to be unacceptably high. Initially the IMF hung tough—until riots greeted the removal of price subsidies on fuel and precipitated a chain of events that actually led to the fall of the long-reigning Indonesian dictator Suharto.[9] In its dealings with the post-Suharto government, the fund responded to the pleas of the Jakarta government for increased social spending and the maintenance of subsidized prices for fuel, food, and other necessities.

The World Bank's president, James Wolfensohn, has taken small steps to distance himself and his institution from the more orthodox policies of the IMF. In 1997, he agreed to carry out a multicountry review of the bank's structural adjustment policies with several hundred NGOs led by the Development Group for Alternative Policies. And more recently, Wolfensohn's speeches and the bank's publications have included what amounts to blistering attacks on the social and environmental costs of consensus policies.

In the final analysis, however, these elite dissenters share a strategic goal: to salvage the overall message of the Washington Consensus while modifying the pillar of free capital flows. Indeed, the heat of the debate between these elite critics and consensus adherents Michel Camdessus of the IMF and Secretary of the Treasury Summers over capital mobility has made it easy for observers to overlook a key reality: the consensus still largely holds with respect to trade policy.

Cracks in the Consensus

Even though it is not the goal of the elite dissenters to kill the consensus, the appearance of any dissent at all is significant. Dissent from within ranks had been unheard of in the last two decades. Now, in their tinkering with the ten commandments of the consensus, and in their desire to capture the limelight, elite critics are not only undermining the legitimacy and credibility of the consensus but are also unwittingly opening the door to broader mass-based anti-free trade criticism. These elite critiques have opened cracks in the consensus in three keys areas, cracks that could become deadly fissures at the hands of outside critics.

First, there is the question of in whose interests consensus policies are sculpted. The language some use in their elite critiques raises questions about the narrow interests that the consensus serves. Free-trade champion Jagdish Bhagwati, writing in *Foreign Affairs*, has decried free capital mobility across borders as the work of the "Wall Street-Treasury complex" (a term that builds on President Eisenhower's warnings of a "military-industrial complex").[10] Bhagwati points fingers at individuals who have moved between Wall Street financial firms and the highest echelons of the U.S. government and who, in Bhagwati's words, are "unable to look much beyond the interest of Wall Street, which it equates with the good of the world."[11] This should create ammunition for the outsider critique: if the U.S. Treasury (and international financial institutions) are not able to look beyond such narrow "special interests" in terms of capital, why should they be trusted to do so with broader economic policies?

Second, what goals should economic policies serve and who should determine these goals? One of the elite critics, the World Bank's Joseph Stiglitz, has recently begun to call for a "post-Washington Consensus" that moves beyond the narrow goal of economic growth to the more expansive goal of sustainable, equitable, and democratic development.[12] In speeches that have surprised many observers, Stiglitz argues that the debate over national economic policies and the debate over the new global economy must be democratized. For example, workers must be invited to sit at the table when their country's economic policies are being discussed in order to be able to argue against policies that hurt them. Outside critics need to push for Stiglitz's words to be turned into action. Why not invite workers—and environmentalists and farmers and others—who represent the broader national interests to participate?

Third, the elite dissenters are reigniting the Keynesian belief that the state has a legitimate role in development. Indeed, whatever comes of the global financial crisis, the widespread fear of an unregulated global casino that can devastate individual economies overnight is negating the consensus rejection of an activist state role. While most elite critics allow for a government role only in the realm of short-term financial flows, outside critics should exploit this crack to open up a larger debate about government intervention. With the acknowledgment that government is needed to check the markets on one front, there can be more intelligent debate over the role of government in other areas. The development debate, so lively in the 1960s and 1970s and so stifled in the 1980s and 1990s, can be revived.

High Priests Respond

In the face of the spreading dissent and criticism, the U.S. Treasury Department is attempting to hold the line. Triumphant, with its booming stock market, its low unemployment and inflation, and its victory in Kosovo, the U.S. government is trying to reassert a Wall Street-centered approach that differs from the old one only in minor details. Mild U.S. Treasury proposals to increase statistical disclosure by financial institutions and improve surveillance of national economic policies by the IMF won the day at the June 1999 meeting of the Group of Eight in Cologne, Germany. Secretary of the Treasury Lawrence Summers and his minions will attempt to consolidate their agenda and glue the cracks together at the late September IMF and World Bank meetings in Washington.

Whether Summers wins the day with this status quo approach depends at least partially on a number of factors that are quite beyond his and both his inside and outside critics' control. First, will the U.S. economy continue to hum along in aggregate terms and will the U.S. stock market continue to soar? Any significant downturn in either will strengthen both the dissenters and the outside critics of the consensus. Second, can the beleaguered economies of Russia, Indonesia, Brazil, and other countries get back on their feet under the current set of rules? Summers and the IMF point to rebounding stock markets and currencies in several of these crisis countries, yet in country after country the employment and ecological crises remain acute. The future of a global economy in which inequality is growing, and only the United States and the world's wealthy are beneficiaries, is inherently unstable, both economically and politically.

Among most leading consensus pundits outside of the ranks of the IMF and the U.S. Treasury Department there is a new—admittedly begrudging—acknowledgement that the consensus has lost much of its legitimacy in the view of the public and that there is a need to factor more social and environmental concerns into economic policies. In this climate of elite discord, there is greater space for the citizen groups on the outside to press for more far-reaching and desperately needed reforms in global economic institutions.

At key moments in the recent past, unions, environmentalists, and other citizen groups have grown strong enough to stall the implementation of consensus policies, as we have seen in the fights over fast track authority and the multilateral agreement on investment. The challenge now for these outsiders is to exploit the internal discord among consensus supporters, to establish links with dissident voices within governments, and to fire up the debate over development goals and the role of government. The Philippine social scientist Walden Bello sums up the clamor of citizens for change around the world with this sentence: "It's the development model, stupid."

A New Development Debate

New development proposals from citizen groups are based on both expansive goals and trade and finance policies that would shift the beneficiaries of these policies from a narrow group of corporations and wealthy individuals to a much broader swath of the public.

On the trade front, the upcoming ministerial meeting of the WTO, to be hosted by President Clinton in Seattle this December, will provide a dramatic backdrop to a major confrontation over the future of trade rules. Joining several developing country governments in opposing an expansion of trade and investment liberalization will be tens of thousands of organized steelworkers and apparel workers, family farmers, members of Ralph Nader's Public Citizen, and environmentalists who are planning a week of educational activities and protests.

Labor unions are calling for a halt in new talks on all issues except strengthening workers' protections under WTO rules. Most other citizen groups will argue for a pruning back of the WTO's powers in favor of once again permitting individual governments to set investment and government procurement rules and for keeping food safety and environmental rules off limits to challenges by other nations.

On the finance front, the IMF and World Bank annual meetings in late September should provide a venue for bringing into focus the different agendas for a "new financial architecture" as well as the issue of debt relief for poor nations. Many of the same outside groups that led the trade fight have shifted their attention to addressing the financial crisis. Over the past year, Friends of the Earth, the International Forum on Globalization, the AFL-CIO, the Malaysia-based Third World Network, and Thailand-based Focus on the Global South have convened hundreds of experts—activists and researchers—from both North and South to sketch out an institutional framework that would reorient financial flows from speculation to long-term investment at the local and national levels.[13]

Collectively these proposals suggest that local and national governments should be given greater authority to set exchange rate policies, regulate capital flows, and eliminate speculative activity. A priority at the international level is the creation of an international bankruptcy mechanism outside the IMF. When a country cannot repay its debts, the mechanism would oversee a debt restructuring in which there would be a public and private sharing of costs. When the next Indonesia, Russia, or Brazil teeters on the brink of a deep financial crisis, it would turn to this mechanism, not to the IMF, for help. With such a facility in place, the IMF could return to its more modest original mandate of overseeing capital controls as well as providing a venue for the open exchange of financial and economic information.

Anti-consensus groups, led by religious coalitions in many countries and rallying under the banner of Jubilee 2000, also argue that current debt reduction initiatives should be expanded substantially to cover a more significant amount of bilateral and multilateral debt, and that debt reduction should not be conditioned on a country's adherence to IMF and World Bank austerity policies.

Finally, many critics are picking up on an old proposal by Nobel Prize winner James Tobin of Yale University, who suggested a tiny global tax on foreign currency transactions. In today's flourishing global financial casino, Tobin's tax would both discourage harmful speculation and generate revenues that could help the nations in crisis.

The growing strength of citizen opposition, however, has not yet been translated into a new overall consensus based on such proposals. Much as we would like to be town criers heralding the death of the Washington Consensus, such news is premature. Too many members of the policymaking elite, particularly in the United States, still cling to the precepts of the old consensus. While another global economic downturn would no doubt lend weight to the outsider critique, the future of these opposition proposals depends in the final analysis on the political sophistication of their proponents. Can citizen movements translate growing discontent into effective political pressure both at a national level and jointly in the WTO, the IMF, and the World Bank? Can they shift the debate beyond the confines of the free market dogma of the Washington Consensus?

In the closing months of the Second World War, a small group made up primarily of men from the richer countries sketched the architecture of the postwar global economy. The institutions they created are no longer serving the needs of the majority of people on earth. In the closing months of the twentieth century, there is at last the opportunity for a larger, more representative group to create new global rules and institutions for the twenty-first century. Indeed, since the Washington Consensus swept the globe two decades ago, the possibility of reading its obituary has never been greater.

Notes

1. The ten areas of consensus in terms of neoliberal, free-market policies, as noted by Williamson, are: "fiscal discipline" (i.e., policies to combat fiscal deficits); "public expenditure priorities" (to cut expenditures through the removal of subsidies, etc.); "tax reform"; "financial liberalization" (toward market-determined interest rates); competitive "exchange rates"; "trade liberalization" (to replace licenses with tariffs and to reduce tariffs); "foreign direct investment" (i.e., removing barriers); "privatization"; "deregulation" (of impediments to competition); and "property rights." See John Williamson, *The Progress of Policy Reform in Latin America*, Policy Analyses in International Economics, no. 28 (Washington, D.C.: Institute for International Economics, January 1990).

2. Williamson, *Progress of Policy Reform in Latin America*, p. 9.

3. John Williamson, "Democracy and the 'Washington Consensus,'" *World Development*, vol. 21, no. 8 (1993), p. 1329.

4. Williamson, *Progress of Policy Reform*, p. 83.

5. Calculated by the Institute for Policy Studies from data published in *Forbes* magazine, July 5, 1999, and in United Nations Development Programme, *Human Development Report 1999*.

6. Jackie Calmes, "Despite Buoyant Economic Times, Americans Don't Buy Free Trade," *Wall Street Journal*, December 10, 1998. Pro-free trade think tanks dismiss such poll results as coming from an ill-informed public plagued with "globaphobia." See Gary Burtless, Robert Z. Lawrence, Robert E. Litan, and Robert J. Shapiro, *Globaphobia: Confronting Fears about Open Trade* (Washington, D.C.: Brookings Institution, Progressive Policy Institute, and Twentieth Century Fund, 1998).

7. International Confederation of Free Trade Unions, *ICFTU Online*, January 21, 1999.

8. Jeffrey Sachs, "The IMF and the Asian Flu," *American Project*, March–April 1998, p. 17.

9. See Michael Shari, "Up In Smoke," *Business Week*, June 1, 1998, p. 66.

10. Jagdish Bhagwati, "The Capital Myth: The Difference Between Trade in Widgets and Dollars," *Foreign Affairs*, vol. 77 (May/June 1998), p. 7.

11. Bhagwati, "Capital Myth," p. 12.

12. Joseph Stiglitz, "More Instruments and Broader Goals: Moving toward the Post-Washington Consensus," 1998 World Institute for Development Economics Research annual lecture, Helsinki, Finland, January 7, 1998.

13. See Friends of the Earth, International Forum on Globalization, and Third World Network, "Call to Action: A Citizens Agenda for Reform of the Global Economic System," Washington, D.C., December 10, 1998; and Robert Blecker, *Taming Global Finance: A Better Architecture for Growth and Equity* (Washington, D.C.: Economic Policy Institute, 1999). For papers from the March 1999 Focus on the Global South conference in Bangkok, see Walden Bello, Nicola Bullard, and Kamal Malhotra, eds., *Cooling Down Hot Money: How to Regulate Financial Markets* (London: Zed Press, forthcoming).

Robin Broad is a professor of international development at the School of International Service, American University. John Cavanagh is director of the Institute for Policy Studies. They are the coauthors of Plundering Paradise.

Globalization After Seattle

Jacob Park

The recent World Trade Organization (WTO) meeting in Seattle can be called many things, but no one would call it business as usual. The opening ceremony was delayed as protesters trapped Madeleine Albright, the U.S. secretary of state, and Kofi Annan, the United Nations secretary general, in their hotels. Environmentalists and labor union members marched to protest the poor environmental and labor record of the WTO. In a scene reminiscent of Ridley Scott's futuristic movie, *Blade Runner*, the Lesbian Avengers and conservative presidential-hopeful Pat Buchanan became marching partners—however briefly —against the policies of the WTO. Instead of launching a new round of talks to liberalize international trade, the WTO meeting in Seattle produced an unprecedented degree of doubts, disagreements, and dismay regarding what is commonly referred to as globalization. For one week in 1999, Jose Bove, the French farmer who gained fame for vandalizing McDonald's in France, overshadowed Bill Gates, chief executive officer of Microsoft, as the human face of globalization.

The failure of the WTO negotiations cannot be blamed on one single factor. Some of the blame must be laid on the complexity and diversity of the trade issues. The lack of transparency and the secretive manner in which international trade rules are negotiated might have been acceptable in the past, but nonstate actors such as environmental groups and labor unions decided they were no longer satisfied with waiting on the policy sidelines. With 2000 presidential elections less than a year away, U.S. domestic politics no doubt played a key role in energizing the WTO protests. The usual lack of concern for the developing world's trade interests, coupled with new issues such as genetically modified foods and the environmental impact of liberalizing the international

commerce of forest and paper products, provided the ideal platform for anti-WTO rhetoric from all sides of the political spectrum and from all corners of the globe.

Whether or not the WTO meeting in Seattle is the harbinger of what global governance may look like in the twenty-first century may depend on how successfully U.S. policymakers cultivate what Joseph Nye, the dean of Harvard University's Kennedy School of Government, calls America's "soft power." Unlike "hard power" that is exercised through economic sanctions or military force, soft power is the ability of a country to get what it wants through cooperation rather than coercion. The United States has become so successful at using hard power in places such as the Balkans and the Persian Gulf that the public sometimes forgets that hard power is not really an option when trying to forge global consensus on international business, labor, and environmental matters. The United States remains the world's only economic and military superpower, so the tendency just to bully other countries to accept its policy agenda has unfortunately become a normal part of our diplomatic reflex. This is why many people around the world resist the inevitability of globalization since the concept is so often tied to U.S. hegemony.

Soft power is often the only diplomatic tool at the disposal of small, less powerful states that do not have the luxury of having a permanent seat on the UN Security Council nor of ranking as the most influential shareholder of the International Monetary Fund. A good example is the way small island nations have organized themselves into the Alliance of Small Island States, an effective lobbying group to promote the UN Framework Convention on Climate Change and the 1997 Kyoto Protocol, which sets legally binding emissions targets for industrialized countries. Barba-

dos, Marshall Islands, and other island states know that their policy objectives are attainable only by working together in a carefully planned alliance, an idea the United States often preaches but rarely commits to. Both dimensions of power are important expressions of U.S. foreign policy. But the ability to cultivate soft power, particularly within the framework of regional organizations such as the Asia-Pacific Economic Cooperation forum and global policy forums such as the International Standards Organization, is likely to determine the strength of U.S. leadership in world affairs.

The failure of the WTO negotiations cannot be blamed on one single factor.

One way to cultivate soft power is for the U.S. government to develop a strategy to include nonstate actors such as environmental groups and labor unions in future international policy negotiations. In a press conference held a month before the WTO meeting, President Bill Clinton told reporters that he supports bringing labor and environmental interests into the trade deliberations. Yet, it took a lawsuit by a cadre of environmental groups to force the U.S. Trade Representative's office to appoint environmentalists to its advisory panels on forest and wood products. President Clinton practically issued an invitation to the labor unions and environmental groups to participate in the trade negotiations, but they found riot police and tear gas when they arrived in Seattle. If the Clinton administration was serious about broadening the framework of the trade negotiations, the White House should have been more explicit in how this increased participation was to be achieved.

There was an opportunity in the spring of 1999 to do just that, but it never materialized. More than six months before the WTO meeting, the Sierra Club, National Wildlife Federation, and other environmental groups distributed a proposal that would give the White House the negotiating authority on trade while ensuring that environmental and health laws were not undermined by its goals. The proposal to establish a special standing committee on international trade, consisting of leaders, committee chairmen, and senior minority members from both parties, did not receive political support from the White House and Congress. The failure to establish such a committee is unfortunate because it might have partly addressed the concerns of labor and environmental groups before the WTO meeting in Seattle.

Another way to ensure America's soft power is for labor unions and environmental groups to understand that demonizing the WTO as a group of faceless international bureaucrats is not only wrong, but also counterproductive. Such criticism only reinforces the power of those who prefer that the United States reduce its role in international affairs and ignore the special global responsibility that comes with its status as the dominant economic and military superpower. With a budget of only $80 million and 500 staff members, the WTO does not wield nearly as much power as some environmental and labor groups would like to believe. The so-called power of these international bureaucrats is illusory, as the policy agenda is initiated and set by the 135 member states that make up the WTO. The WTO is not a world court with unlimited power to trample on U.S. sovereignty (as some of its critics would like to describe it), but a multilateral arbitration forum to settle a wide array of trade disputes.

The WTO is not a world court with unlimited power to trample on U.S. sovereignty.

The problem is not that the WTO is too strong, but that comparable environmental and labor-related international institutions are too weak. Instead of criticizing the WTO, labor unions and environmental groups should work together in cooperation with the developing countries to ensure that policy priorities of the International Labor Organization and the UN Environment Program are on par with the WTO. Vilifying the WTO will only make it difficult for environmental groups to gain public acceptance for the Kyoto Protocol and for labor unions to garner support for fair trade legislation. After all, are the international bureaucrats that staff the UN climate change secretariat and labor organization different from those that work for the WTO?

Whether the United States should serve—and under what circumstances—as the world's police officer is a question that often gets debated whenever international conflicts hit the news screen. If one did use the police officer metaphor to explain U.S. foreign policy behavior, it is important to recognize that police officers do more than use their weapons (hard power) to arrest criminals. More often than not, police officers have to use their negotiating skills (soft power) to settle disputes and work with individual citizens and community groups to prevent criminal activities. Though often criticized as an outdated policy framework, modern police work provides a good model for what constitutes effective U.S. foreign policy in the new millennium: less guns and car chases and more community policing.

Jacob Park is a fellow in the Department of Government and Politics, University of Maryland, and a fellow in the Environmental Leadership Program.

From *The Washington Quarterly*, Spring 2000, pp. 13–16. © 2000 by the Center for Strategic and International Studies. Reprinted by permission.

UNIT 7

U.S. Post–Cold War Military Strategy

Unit Selections

31. **Responding to Terrorism**, David Tucker
32. **War on America: The New Enemy**, The Economist
33. **Musclebound: The Limits of U.S. Power**, Stephen M. Walt
34. **Ending the Nuclear Nightmare: A Strategy for the Bush Administration**, Jim Wurst and John Burroughs
35. **Mission Impossible**, Henry D. Sokolski

Key Points to Consider

- Is military power an effective instrument of foreign policy today? What problems is it best able to and least capable of solving?

- Does arms control have a future? Can it make the United States more secure, or does it weaken U.S. security?

- How should we think about nuclear weapons in the post–cold war world? What is their purpose? Who should they be targeted against? What dangers must we guard against?

- How has your response to terrorism changed since the events of September 11, 2001?

- How great did you think the terrorist threat to the United States before the terror attacks was? What suggestions do you have for dealing with the present situation?

- Under what conditions should the United States engage in peacekeeping activities?

- Should the United States build a national missile defense system? Why or why not?

- Is disarmament an alternative to a national missile defense system?

 **Links: www.dushkin.com/online/**
These sites are annotated in the World Wide Web pages.

Arms Control and Disarmament Agency (ACDA)
http://dosfan.lib.uic.edu/acda/

The Commission on Global Governance
http://www.cgg.ch

Counterterrorism Page
http://counterterrorism.com

DefenseLINK
http://www.defenselink.mil/news/

Federation of American Scientists (FAS)
http://www.fas.org

Human Rights Web
http://www.hrweb.org

During the height of the cold war, American defense planners often thought in terms of needing a two-and-a-half war capacity: the simultaneous ability to fight major wars in Europe and Asia plus a smaller conflict elsewhere. The principal protagonists in this drama were well known: the Soviet Union, China, and their developing world allies. The stakes were also clear. Communism represented a global threat to American political democracy and economic prosperity. It was a conflict in which both sides publicly proclaimed that there could be but one winner. The means for deterring and fighting such challenges included strategic, tactical, and battlefield nuclear weapons; large numbers of conventional forces; alliance systems; arms transfers; and the development of a guerrilla war capability.

Until September 11, 2001, the political-military landscape of the post–cold war era lacked any comparable enemy or military threat. Instead, the principal challenges to American foreign policy makers were ones of deciding what humanitarian interventions to undertake and how deeply to become involved. Kosovo, East Timor, Somalia, Bosnia, Rwanda, and Haiti each produced its own answer, which presented American policymakers with a new type of military challenge in the form of humanitarian interventions. The challenge of formulating an effective military policy to deal with situations where domestic order has unraveled due to ethnic conflict and bottled up political pressures for reform remains. However, they are no longer viewed as first-order security problems in the post–cold war era.

With the terrorist attacks on the World Trade Center and the Pentagon, a more clearly defined enemy has emerged. Formulating a military strategy to defeat this enemy promises to be no easy task. One must first identify the threat. In December 2000 and January 2001, two government commissions published reports warning of the danger of international terrorism. Neither the "Report of the National Commission on Terrorism: Countering the Changing Threat of International Terrorism," nor "Toward a National Strategy for Combating Terrorism," identified terrorism comparable to what occurred on September 11, 2001. Identification is necessary to be able to target an enemy. While the threat of terrorism is personified by Osama bin Laden, virtually all agree that the specter of global terrorism transcends him. Finally, in order to succeed, a military strategy needs a workable definition of victory.

This is not the enemy or the military agenda that the Bush administration had expected to face. In the months preceding the terrorist attack, Secretary of Defense Donald Rumsfeld had directed his energies to reforming the American military by cutting the production of weapons systems such as the B-1 bomber, closing military bases, and reducing the size of the military. Rumsfeld met significant resistance from the military services and their congressional allies and all but gave up on his reform efforts. In this new environment his challenge is to take a military establishment geared for war with a twentieth-century enemy and mold it into a policy instrument capable of fighting the first war of the twenty-first century.

The first set of essays in this unit examines the range of conflict situations that will confront American forces abroad and some of the key issues that need to be addressed in formulating a new military strategy for the United States. Two articles, "Responding to Terrorism" and "War on America: The New Enemy," investigate the current strategies in place to combat terrorism.

Stephen Walt, in "Musclebound: The Limits of U.S. Power," discusses the reasons why the United States can be simultaneously the unrivaled superpower in the world and yet find itself unable to achieve its policy goals when it uses force.

With changes in the nature of the military threats confronting the United States has come a change in the arms control agenda. The old arms control agenda was dominated by a concern for reducing the size of U.S. and Soviet nuclear inventories. A much broader agenda exists today and it is one with many more players.

Two readings contribute to our understanding of the arms-control issues now confronting the international community. No longer does the transfer of large-scale and sophisticated weapons represent the sole conventional weapons arms-control problem. The growth of ethnic conflict has created situations where the transfer of small and light weapons now has the potential for altering regional balances of power. These essays offer opposing views on one of the most politically charged issues on the policy agenda: the construction of a national missile defense system. Jim Wurst and John Burroughs, in "Ending the Nuclear Nightmare," argue for disarmament as the proper course of action. The final essay "Mission Impossible," by Henry Sokolski, looks at the politics of counterproliferation. His essay is a cautionary tale of efforts to implement grand new national security initiatives.

Responding to Terrorism

David Tucker

Terrorism is back. Over the years, it has waxed and waned. Having reached high points in the early and late 1970s and again in the mid-1980s, and a low point in the late 1980s and early 1990s, it is now again on an upswing. Domestic terrorism—the bombings of the World Trade Center in New York and the Federal Building in Oklahoma City—caused a significant loss of life. Fear of international terrorism has shadowed our involvement in Bosnia, restricting our scope of activities. A poison gas attack in the Tokyo subway in 1995 highlighted what many fear is the growing willingness of terrorists to use weapons of mass destruction, while reminding us of our own vulnerability to such attacks. Two bombings at U.S. military facilities in Saudi Arabia in 1995 and 1996 took the lives of 24 Americans, strained our relations with the Saudis, called into question our ability to maintain our presence in this vital area, and, as we implemented additional security measures, added significantly to the cost of this presence. Terrorism has undermined, if not destroyed, a major U.S. foreign policy initiative, the Middle East peace process. Globally, U.S. casualties from terrorism have increased in the mid-1990s. The resurgence of terrorism and fears for the future recently led Secretary of Defense William Cohen to list terrorism as one of his principal concerns.[1]

As attacks on Americans and the attention paid them have increased, officials have reportedly conducted the same debates about how to respond to terrorism that their predecessors had 10 years ago, when terrorism was last at a high point. Once again, they have debated the relative merits of preemptive attacks, covert action, economic sanctions, military retaliation, and diplomacy, and whether to target the states that sponsor terrorist attacks or the organizations and individuals that carry them out—all of this, apparently, with little or no reference to our nearly 25-year experience combating terrorism.[2] But this experience should not be ignored. If we are to handle terrorism effectively in the future, at whatever level it threatens us, we should learn from what we have done before. Not only will doing this improve our ability to deal with terrorism, it will also tell us something about how we must operate in the post-Cold War world.

How the United States Has Responded to Terrorism

Over the years, the United States has combated terrorism in nine ways. It has negotiated international legal conventions, implemented defensive measures, addressed the causes of terrorism, followed a policy of making no concessions to terrorists' demands, imposed economic sanctions, retaliated militarily, prosecuted suspected terrorists (in some cases, following extradition or rendition from another country or seizure overseas), preempted terrorist attacks, and disrupted terrorist organizations. Today, "no concessions," prosecution, and economic sanctions remain the principal weapons we employ against terrorism, but all three present problems.[3] We will begin to develop wisdom in combating terrorism only when we can recognize these problems.

OPTION 1: THE POLICY OF NO CONCESSIONS

Policymakers use as their principal argument to support the policy of no concessions the belief that paying ransom or making other concessions only encourages more terrorism. Moreover, for fear of granting terrorists standing in the international community or among their peers, some analysts argue that a policy of no concessions should exclude even talking with terrorists. Former president Ronald Reagan, for example, announced that although his administration would honor the terms of the agreement Jimmy Carter's administration reached with Iran during the 1979 hostage crisis, it would not have negotiated with the Iranians in the first place. However strictly they interpret it, those who support a policy of no concessions do so for the same reason: If we make concessions, they say, the terrorists win and will only demand more, while other groups will follow their example and pick on the nationals of any government that gives in.

But terrorists do not necessarily make demands because they want them met, and terrorist groups do not necessarily have the same fundamental motivations and modus operandi; hence they may not respond to external stimuli in the same ways. Some terrorists benefit from violent acts even if their targets do not yield to their demands. Rather than immediate concessions, terrorists may seek publicity or the destruction of a society's sense of security and order. The Tupac Amaru seizure of the Japanese ambassador's residence in Lima appears to have been a case where the terrorists acted not only to force the government to meet demands but also to gain recognition and public standing following a period when they had lost both. That terrorists do not need to have demands met explains in part why we see terrorist acts like the World Trade Center bombing, in which demands do not play a central role.

Terrorists do not necessarily make demands because they want them met.

In fact, conceding to terrorists may have no direct correlation with the level of violence. British firmness during the seizure of the Iranian embassy in London in 1980 and U.S. firmness following the kidnaping of Brig. Gen. James Dozier in Italy 1981 did not prevent the subsequent kidnaping of Britons and Americans in Lebanon. Nor did publicity concerning Washington's effort to trade arms for hostages with Iran in the mid-1980's lead to an increase in terrorist attacks or hostage-taking. Again, when the Colombian government—which earlier had taken a hard line with terrorists and responded forcibly to terrorist attacks—made concessions to terrorists in the early 1980s, terrorism began to decrease. Indeed, studies have concluded that refusing to make concessions may not limit terrorism, despite what proponents of "no concessions" claim.[4]

The United States should not adopt a rigid policy of no concessions.

Less effective in combating terrorism than its proponents claim, "no concessions" is also less relevant than it was when first articulated as a policy in the 1970s. Then, terrorism constituted part of struggles for so-called national liberation; Palestinian terrorism was the archetype. Negotiating with terrorists in these cases undermined the legitimacy of governments the United States wanted to protect. Therefore, we rightly resisted negotiating. Now, however, states sponsor terrorism directly. The United States works with or makes deals with these state spon-

sors, because we could not secure our regional or more general interests otherwise. Our relations with Iraq when we hoped to make it a counter to Iran or with Syria during the ongoing Middle East negotiations exemplify the degree to which we will deal with a state sponsor of terrorism if doing so serves our interests.

For several reasons, then, the United States should not adopt a rigid policy of no concessions. It may not work in every case and is less relevant in fighting modern-day terrorism. Besides, making concessions may even help us catch a terrorist: The *Washington Post* and *New York Times* conceded to the Unabomber's demand to publish his 35,000-word manifesto, because federal officials thought that doing so might lead to a suspect; according to media reports, it did. As a practical matter, therefore, policymakers will make exceptions—and concessions—when they have good reasons to do so. We should not worry that this will make us look weak. A flexible policy to which we can adhere consistently will work better and make us look stronger than a rigid policy we consistently violate.

OPTION 2: PROSECUTION

Washington has always used prosecution as the principal response to terrorist acts committed in the United States. For several reasons, it has come increasingly to rely on the same response in dealing with terrorist acts committed against Americans or their property outside the United States. Those who have worked to combat terrorism generally agree that apprehending terrorists outside the United States deters terrorism or makes it more difficult for terrorists to carry out their plans, primarily because it complicates their travel. They must be careful where they set foot and what kind of documentation they use—and as international terrorists require mobility to work, this significantly disrupts their activities.

Further, prosecuting specific acts, such as killing, hijacking, or hostage taking, rather than focusing on the contentious political issues that surround these acts, removes an impediment to interstate cooperation. In addition,Washington's counterterrorism actions have greater credibility when the government bases its claims about a terrorist act on the exacting standards of U.S. criminal procedure and on evidence that can be used in a public judicial process rather than on intelligence that we cannot make public without compromising sources and methods. Finally, we may have no other available response than to arrest individual terrorists and bring them to trial if the connection between the terrorists and their sponsors does not suffice to allow us to retaliate against the latter.

As an example of successful prosecution, one may note the case of Pan Am Flight 103, destroyed in a mid-air explosion over Lockerbie, Scotland, in 1988. After a three-year investigation, the U.S. and British governments indicted two Libyans for the bombing. The two governments, with the help of France—whose airliner, UTA 772, Libyans bombed over Niger in 1989—then persuaded the United Nations (UN) Security Council to endorse a series of demands on Libya based on the indictments. When Libya failed to meet these UN demands, the United States and Great Britain persuaded the Security Council to impose sanctions on Libya. Although this legal process has unfolded slowly, it has kept pressure on Libya since 1991. During this time, as far as we can tell and apparently in response to legal pressure and sanctions, Libya has ceased to sponsor international terrorist attacks. It continues to support terrorist groups, attacks Libyan dissidents, and retains its capacity to commit other terrorist acts, but the legal process so far has effectively countered Libyan terrorism directed at the United States and its allies.

The judicial approach has led to arrests and prosecutions in other cases as well. In 1996, after Pakistan turned over Ramzi Yousef to the United States, a federal court in New York City convicted him, as the man behind the 1993 bombing of the World Trade Center in New York, of a conspiracy to bomb U.S. passenger planes in East Asia. After the FBI seized Omar Mohammed Rezaq in Nigeria, a U.S. district court convicted him of air piracy in connection with the hijacking of an Egyptian airlines flight in 1985 that resulted in the death of a U.S. citizen and the injury of two others. An Asian country turned over Tsutomu Shirosaki to the United States for trial in connection with a mortar attack on a U.S. embassy in 1986. In 1997, the FBI arrested Mir Aimal Kansi in Pakistan on charges that he murdered two Central Intelligence Agency (CIA) employees outside the agency's headquarters in 1993.

Despite the general enthusiasm for prosecuting terrorists, supporters of the judicial response admit its limitations. The United States can conduct foreign criminal investigations only with the cooperation of the governments involved. Exercising extraterritorial legal authority without permission would likely damage our relations with other countries, and it could also weaken the international cooperation necessary to combat terrorism. Finally, in some cases our powerful forensic abilities may be useless. Had the bomb aboard Pan Am Flight 103 exploded while the plane was over deep ocean, authorities might have faced insuperable challenges to investigating the crime scene. The difficulties investigating the explosion aboard TWA flight 800 when its pieces fell into waters off Long Island, New York, highlight this problem.

Although proponents of the judicial approach present these political and practical restrictions as only minor limitations, this approach is less effective than its supporters tend to acknowledge. To avoid political disputes over what may or may not be legitimate uses of force for political reasons, prosecution focuses our attention on individual terrorists and thus does not affect the traditional core of the terrorist threat: state sponsorship. Moreover, the effectiveness of the sanctions against Libya in the Pan Am 103 case resulted not from a judicial process, but from

a political process at the United Nations and in foreign capitals that got UN members to agree to act against Libya—a political process that has not always worked to U.S. advantage in other cases. Washington found it difficult to get international agreement to impose sanctions against Syria in 1986–1987, for example, and the administration faced constant pressure, even inside the government, to lift them. For similar reasons, the UN has hesitated to impose meaningful sanctions on Sudan for its support of terrorism.[5] The judicial process, then, provides limited leverage against terrorism and depends largely on an international political process that it does little to shape.

Furthermore, the judicial approach can prove misleading. First, by emphasizing the criminality of terrorism, it may make us less able to respond flexibly—some might say cynically—to the irreducible political core of terrorism. Second, in adopting the judicial approach, we set the burden of proof for overseas action as high as that for domestic action, an impractical standard that will hinder our counterterrorism activities abroad. Proponents of the judicial response claim that we can, in effect, pick and choose when and where to use the standard, but given our attachment to the rule of law, the domestic judicial standard may become the only standard. Where it cannot be applied—in cases where, for example, the forensic evidence is inconclusive—we may come to believe that we have no justification for action.

This problem has a long history. Even before the legal response became so important in our counterterrorism efforts, we faced political pressure to find a "smoking gun" before responding forcibly to a terrorist attack. The Reagan administration, for example, sought such evidence before U.S. forces launched the raid on Libya. With increasing reliance on the judicial approach, this attitude may become even more pronounced. For example, while the Clinton administration deliberated its response to the Iraqi assassination attempt on former President Bush, the *Washington Post* reported that

> intelligence analysis… [based on circumstantial evidence] had been considered adequate proof of complicity in previous U.S. policy deliberations, but officials said senior Clinton administration policymakers—a group dominated by lawyers—indicated from the outset they wanted to act only on the basis of evidence that would be sufficient to produce a courtroom conviction.[6]

According to another press account, President Clinton asked the Federal Bureau of Investigation (FBI) and the attorney general to take the lead in investigating the alleged assassination attempt, involving the State Department and the National Security Council (NSC) only in the very final stages of the decision-making process.[7] A similar attitude seems to prevail in the case of possible Iranian involvement in the bombings of U.S. military bases in

Saudi Arabia. This makes the emphasis on prosecution a dangerous double-edged sword. If detailed forensic investigation gives credibility to U.S. government responses to terrorist acts, [t]hen the absence of such an investigation or its inconclusive results will detract from this credibility and may make officials hesitant to act, thus restricting our scope of international action.

The judicial approach is a double-edged sword for another reason: It establishes a precedent we may not want other nations to follow. The Iranian death sentence against novelist Salman Rushdie, for example, is an application of Iranian law outside its borders, similar to the application of our counterterrorism laws outside ours. Some will object that there is no moral equivalence between the United States applying the law to terrorists and Iran condemning Rushdie for exercising his right to free speech. Indeed, any right-thinking democrat rejects such an equivalence. But this only highlights the problem with applying a country's laws overseas: If we assert our right to do this, we can deny the right of other nations to do so only by arguing that their laws are inferior to ours—or even illegitimate. Inevitably, by making this case we will have to insist on moral and political distinctions between nations that, for the sake of diminishing the causes of war, have been excluded for the most part from legitimate international discourse for more than 300 years. This can hardly enhance our security.

OPTION 3: ECONOMIC SANCTIONS

"No concessions" and prosecution therefore prove problematic and less effective methods of responding to terrorism than the U.S. government claims. But economic sanctions—a government's decision deliberately to curtail or cease customary economic or financial relations so as to coerce another government—is *less* problematic and *more* effective as a response to terrorism than generally assumed.

In 1973, the United States used economic sanctions for the first time, to punish Libya for sponsoring international terrorism. Since then, in combination with Libya's own economic mismanagement and corruption, the array of U.S.- and UN-imposed sanctions has seriously weakened Muammar Qadaffi's regime, even though the sanctions have not touched the core of Libya's economy: its ability to export oil. The sanctions have produced this effect, moreover, at relatively little cost to the United States. Likewise, economic sanctions helped to change Syria's behavior. The United States last imposed economic sanctions on Syria in 1986 following a particularly vicious terrorist attempt. Since then, according to the State Department, Syria has not sponsored any terrorist attacks, although it continues to provide safe-haven and training facilities for terrorists.

Of course, economic sanctions alone cannot explain this change in Syria's behavior. The collapse of the Soviet Union and changes in Middle East politics have also played important roles. But for a country like Syria, with a weak economy and little in the way of valuable resources, sanctions—especially multilateral ones such as those imposed in 1986—can inflict serious economic damage. In the view of diplomats who have dealt with the Syrians on terrorism, sanctions had a significant influence in stopping Syrian-sponsored attacks. And even in Iran, sanctions have had an effect, impairing Tehran's ability to get the long-term financing its oil and natural gas industry needs.[8]

Economic sanctions are more effective as a response to terrorism than is generally assumed.

Imposing economic sanctions places fewer moral, political, and, often, economic costs on the United States than using military force would, while producing better results than diplomatic démarches alone. But sanctions are far from an ideal policy tool. They are more effective if imposed multilaterally, but the time it takes to organize such a sanctions regime can allow the targeted country to adjust to the impending sanctions, weakening their effect. Unilateral U.S. sanctions will likely become increasingly less effective as global economic integration increases and the U.S. economy becomes a smaller part of the world economy. Finally, sanctions are a blunt instrument; as we have seen in the cases of Iraq and Haiti, they may hurt only the little people and not their leaders, who are their real targets. This increases the difficulty of sustaining them over a long period of time.

Reconsidering Other Methods

The limited effectiveness of the three methods the U.S. government currently considers most useful in fighting terrorism suggests that we look at the six others we have used to see what help they might offer. I will discuss the most oft-considered tactic, military force, at length, and then consider more briefly each of the other five: treaties and conventions, addressing the causes of terrorism, defensive measures, preempting terrorist attacks, and disrupting terrorist groups.

OPTION 4: MILITARY FORCE

On April 15, 1986, U.S. Air Force and Navy jets attacked targets in Libya as retribution for both the bombing of a Berlin discotheque on April 5 that killed 2 and injured 64 Americans, and other, earlier Libyan actions. This was the first use of military force by the United States to combat terrorism. Its primary purpose was to deter future acts of Libyan-sponsored terrorism against the United States. It was also intended to indicate to the world the intensity of U.S. resolve to deal with this kind of violence.

Generally speaking, the raid achieved its secondary more than its primary purpose. As far as we know, after an initial outburst of revenge attacks, Qadaffi did not sponsor an attack on Americans for roughly 12 months after the raid. Following this hiatus, and excluding a spate of anniversary attacks in 1988, five of which took place in April and one of which allegedly was the bombing of Pan Am Flight 103 in December, Libyan terrorist attacks against Americans returned to their typical level of one or two a year. Sanctions and political pressure following the investigation into the bombing of the Pan Am flight probably explain, at least in part, the absence of Libyan-sponsored attacks on Americans since 1990. The most telling statistic concerning the raid, however, is that Libyan-sponsored terrorist attacks killed and injured more Americans after the raid than before—*not* counting those killed in the Pan Am bombing.[9] If the Reagan administration launched the raid primarily to deter Qadaffi from killing Americans, it failed in that purpose.

The raid met more success in achieving its secondary purpose: proving U.S. resolve. According to diplomats in charge of our counterterrorism policy at the time, this proof of our seriousness got the attention of the Europeans and made them more willing to cooperate in efforts to combat terrorism by imposing sanctions on state sponsors (such as those imposed on Syria) and by expelling from European countries the "diplomats" from countries that supported terrorist activities, undoubtedly curtailing terrorist operations. According to records made public since the collapse of the Warsaw Pact, the raid also impressed the East Germans, who cited it in discussions with Palestinian terrorists when trying to persuade them to curtail their terrorist activities.[10] In these ways, the raid probably saved American lives and thus contributed indirectly to its primary purpose. Even so, the number of lives saved by the indirect effects of the raid do not likely outnumber those lost in the Pan Am bombing and other Libyan-sponsored terrorist operations launched after the raid.

On balance, then, our experience with Libya calls into question the utility of using military force to combat terrorism. Indeed, the economic and political pressure that Great Britain, the United States, and France could organize through the UN in response to the bombings of Pan Am Flight 103 and UTA Flight 772—rather than the U.S. military reprisal for the Berlin bombing—seems finally to have stopped Qadaffi's attacks on Americans.

Generally stated, using military force to combat terrorism will always involve an asymmetry of both force and opportunity between the United States and countries that sponsor terrorism. The activities of the United States and its citizens around the world present many more lucrative targets to terrorists than they or their sponsors present to us. More important, terrorists and their sponsors accept the killing of innocents, making them much less restrained than we are in the use of violence. Our military activity may kill innocents, as it did in the raid on Libya, but we do not deliberately target them.

Moreover, we place other constraints on our use of force. A raid on Libya's oil production capabilities would have been a devastating blow to Qadaffi, but the Reagan administration ruled out such an option in favor of attacks on targets associated with terrorism, since this would fit within the international legal understanding of self-defense. Finally, coercing good behavior—our objective when we combat terrorism—may require applying the coercion again and again, which the United States has difficulty doing, given our official and public attitudes toward the use of force. When Qadaffi launched his attacks on the second anniversary of the raid, for example, we did not respond with military force. In any violent confrontation outside of a conventional military engagement, then, we are likely to be at a disadvantage.

OPTION 5: NEGOTIATING TREATIES AND CONVENTIONS

Establishing international norms for dealing with terrorism helps to focus attention on terrorism and encourages like-minded countries to work together. It does not necessarily overcome political differences or the self-interest that guides national decision-making, however, which limits the utility of the resulting treaties and conventions. For example, in January 1994, the French prime minister cited his country's national interests while ignoring the Swiss government's request to extradite two suspected terrorists. Whenever the United States criticizes continued German contacts with Iran, which have included discussions between intelligence officials, the Germans defend these contacts by referring to Germany's economic interests.[11]

OPTION 6: ADDRESSING TERRORISM'S CAUSES

The U.S. government has sought to combat terrorism by addressing its socioeconomic and political roots. But no one has clearly proven what specifically causes terrorism. Both poverty and the unequal distribution of wealth, for example, often thought to cause terrorism, exist in areas free from political violence. Where poverty and terrorism coexist, economic growth might remove this cause of violence, but economic growth can also threaten traditional ways of life and thus *generate* terrorism; much of the fundamentalist religious rebellion around the world exemplifies this dynamic. Moreover, encouraging the establishment of democracy so that grievances may find peaceful expression does not necessarily decrease terrorism. The Soviet Union did not have a problem with terrorism, but Russia does, and Spain's terrorist problem also worsened as it democratized. Encouraging economic growth and democracy may help resolve some conflicts only to generate new ones or create new opportunities for the violent expression of old ones.

OPTION 7: DEFENDING AGAINST TERRORISM

For more than 25 years, the U.S. government has taken steps to make its personnel and facilities overseas harder targets for terrorists to hit. These defensive measures have had notable effects. By following proper procedures with appropriate seriousness, U.S. personnel overseas have made themselves and the facilities in which they work demonstrably more secure than they were before these programs began. In 1980, terrorists launched 177 attacks on U.S. diplomats, military personnel, and other U.S. government officials; in 1995, 10. Terrorists have not stopped targeting Americans, of course, and greater security measures for U.S. officials overseas has probably only deflected some attacks to easier targets, such as American businesspeople or other civilians, or compelled terrorists to devise more sophisticated or lethal means of attack. Still, it is a positive development that America now conducts its official business overseas with more security from terrorist attack than it once did. This success has come at a price, of course, in dollars and personnel resources, costs that will increase in response to the Saudi bombings, and the imposition of these costs constitutes some degree of success for terrorists and their sponsors.

OPTION 8: PREEMPTING TERRORISM

Whereas addressing the causes of terrorism works, if at all, only in the long term, a country can take short-term steps to stop, or preempt, a specific terrorist act. Americans often think of preemption in terms of lethal force or believe it to be a euphemism for assassination. But preempting a terrorist attack might require nothing more than warning another country that a terrorist group is planning to use its territory, or organizing a police raid that arrests suspects before they can carry out a terrorist attack.

More than any other method of combating terrorism, preemption requires specific, accurate, and timely intelligence. A warning to the wrong country or the arrest of the wrong suspects will not stop a terrorist attack. Accurate intelligence is even more important if a situation requires lethal force. We can apologize to another country for a false warning and free mistakenly arrested suspects, but we cannot raise the dead.

OPTION 9: DISRUPTING TERRORISTS

Whereas addressing terrorism's causes has only limited effectiveness and preemption has only limited application, disruption offers a middle ground. Disrupting ter-

rorist activity means targeting a terrorist organization and taking measures not to stop a particular operation but to render all its activities more difficult and, eventually, to make the organization ineffective. Unlike addressing causes, disruption allows us to focus our resources on targeting a specific group. Unlike preemption, disruption does not require that we act before a specific attack takes place, and it thus allows for the gradual buildup of intelligence that permits accurate targeting. In the mid-1980s, the United States conducted a successful campaign to disrupt the Abu Nidal Organization (ANO), one of the most deadly terrorist groups. As reported in a series of newspaper articles, this campaign combined public diplomacy with diplomatic and intelligence initiatives to shut down ANO operations.

As with all the methods we have examined, disruption has its weaknesses. Like preemption, disruption depends critically on intelligence. And it tends to work best against well-developed organizations, like the ANO, that have a significant infrastructure. Groups that do not present such a target prove more immune to disruption.

How the United States Should Respond

As this survey suggests, we should not single out any one—or even three—of the methods we have used to combat terrorism as the most important. To some degree, all suffer from limited effectiveness and applicability, or both. For this reason, success has come when we have combined them and taken advantage of circumstances. Libya's current restraint, for example, is the result of relentless diplomatic pressure, sanctions, public diplomacy, disrupting its terrorist operations, and direct and indirect military action (such as the raid in 1986 and support to Qadaffi's opponents in Chad). This campaign took advantage of such circumstances as falling oil prices (Qadaffi kept supporting terrorism as oil revenues declined but his support became more circumscribed and deprived him of money for other purposes), the disappearance of a powerful ally (the pre-Gorbachev Soviet Union), and the inefficiencies of Libya's domestic arrangements, which have prevented it from adapting well to external pressures.

Our success combining counterterrorism methods suggests in turn that we find additional ways to combine these methods. Carefully targeted sanctions combined with the discreet use of military force may prove more effective than our current tactic of using sanctions and force successively. If the trend toward more independent groups backed by wealthy individuals or religious sects continues, finding and prosecuting individuals will remain an important way to combat terrorism. But, under certain circumstances, we might usefully supplement this approach with disruptive techniques including sabotage, legal proceedings, and information welfare, to attack the assets of the individuals and sects that support terrorism.

If the likelihood of terrorist use of weapons of mass destruction increases, we may become willing to accept measures currently deemed too risky.

Combining methods will not by itself increase our effectiveness against terrorism. We must employ these methods in a strategy that counters terrorism slowly but relentlessly. The horror and shock at a terrorist attack may encourage calls for immediate violent revenge, but this will seldom be an effective response: The asymmetry between the terrorists and their victims will always place us at a disadvantage in the use of violence. As a result, the United States should use conventional military force sparingly in combating terrorism, emphasizing instead public diplomacy, diplomatic and economic pressure, the discreet use of force, and, when possible, prosecution. Such an approach will prevent us getting involved in a tit-for-tat exchange that we will likely lose.

More generally still, our efforts against terrorism will be no more successful than our overall foreign policy and national security strategy. Those devoted to fighting terrorism sometimes forget that the purpose of combating terrorism is to enhance our security and that combating terrorism is only part of this broader effort, because terrorism is not the greatest threat we face. We should remember, especially as calls for stronger action against terrorism mount, that imposing sanctions, using military force, or snatching a terrorist from the streets of a foreign capital—any effort we make to combat terrorism—should be undertaken only if in striking a blow against terrorism it does not undermine our overall well-being.[12] In particular we must recall, as we contemplate how to respond to terrorism, that without the cooperation of our allies and other nations, we would have a much more difficult time combating terrorism, and preserving our security. Integrating counterterrorist efforts into our overall foreign policy and security strategy should also allow us to moderate our attachment both to the policy of no concessions and to an overly legalistic approach to combating terrorism.

Finally, this survey should encourage us. The different methods we use to combat terrorism did not develop all at once or arbitrarily. We have developed and adapted our methods as terrorism has changed. We should be able to do so as terrorism changes in the future.

This record should encourage us not only about our ability to combat terrorism in the post-Cold War world but also about our more general prospects in this world. We must now accommodate ourselves to a geopolitical situation that does not play to our strengths. For the time being, we have no grand reasons to go to war, and we confront few if any threats that the arsenal of democracy can overwhelm with decisive force—the two traditional U.S. ways of responding to threats. Nor as time passes will we have the economic or military weight to tip the balance of power in our favor singlehandedly. The threats and problems we confront with military resources diminishing and our weight in the world declining will likely be smaller and more difficult to assess and counter.

To prevent the slow but sure erosion of our security in this world, we will need patience, a willingness to accept partial and inconclusive results, an ability to absorb setbacks, and the determination to employ policies that take time. Maintaining favorable balances of power will require allies and thus an ability to accept compromise and ambiguity and a willingness to act for something less than the establishment of worldwide democracy. Because these new attitudes so starkly contrast with our past behavior, several authoritative commentators have suggested that the United States will have difficulty adapting and may not be able to do so.[13] Our campaign against international terrorism is at least somewhat reassuring in this regard, however, because for the past 25 years, under administrations of both parties, with only occasional lapses, we have fought terrorists and their sponsors using the modern equivalent of Roman methods of siege warfare, which one of these commentators argues we should emulate.[14] We have been patient, accepted inconclusive results, suffered setbacks, but struggled on. We have worked with allies, applied sanctions, practiced other economic forms of statecraft, undertaken slow but steady criminal investigations, engaged in diplomatic cajolery, gathered intelligence, and operated clandestinely. We have, in the case of terrorism, pursued our goals with the persistent application of diplomacy and force that the United States was supposed to be incapable of achieving. To the extent that the problems we now confront resemble terrorism—in its indirect, slow, but persistent method of attack—we can learn and draw some consolation from our history of combating it.

The views expressed here are the author's and not those of the Department of Defense or the U.S. government.

Notes

1. Patrick Pexton, "Cohen Focuses Sights on Terrorism," *Navy Times*, September 22, 1997, p. 4.
2. David B. Ottaway, "U.S. Considers Slugging It Out With International Terrorism," *Washington Post*, October 17, 1996, p. A25.
3. *Patterns of Global Terrorism: 1996* (Washington, D.C.: Department of State, 1997), p. iv.
4. Richard Clutterbuck, "Negotiating with Terrorists," *Terrorism and Political Violence* 4 (Winter 1990), p. 285; *The Impact of Government Behavior on Frequency, Type, and Targets of Terrorist Group Activity*, (McLean, Va.: Defense Systems, Inc., December 15, 1982), pp. 6–55, 56; Martha Crenshaw, "How Terrorism Declines," *Terrorism and Political Violence* 3 (Spring 1991), pp. 74, 79.
5. John M. Goshko, "UN Remains Reluctant to Impose Tough Sanctions on Sudan for Terrorist Links," *Washington Post*, November 24, 1996, p. A32.
6. R. Jeffrey Smith, "Iraqi Officer Recruited Suspects in Plot Against Bush, U.S. Says," *Washington Post*, July 1, 1993, p. A18.
7. "Commander for a Day," *Economist*, July 3, 1993, p. 25.

8. Thomas W. Lippman, "U.S. Economic Offensive Against Iran's Energy Industry Is Bearing Fruit," *Washington Post*, March 3, 1997, p. A8.

9. David Tucker, *Skirmishes at the Edge of Empire: The United States and International Terrorism* (Westport, Conn.: Praeger, 1997), p. 97.

10. "Stasi Assistance for PLO 'Terrorists' Alleged," *Die Welt*, April 16, 1991, p. 3; in *Foreign Broadcast Information Service, West Europe*, June 27, 1991, p. 29.

11. Sharon Waxman, "France's Release of Iranians Triggers Swiss Complaint," *Washington Post*, January 1, 1994, p. A15; Steve Vogel, "Allies Oppose Bonn's Iran Links," *Washington Post*, November 6, 1993, p. A18; "EU Nations' Envoys Going Back to Iran," *Washington Post*, April 30, 1997, p. 15.

12. As an example of increasing calls for a stronger response to terrorism, see David Morgan, "Gingrich Backs Preemptive Acts on Terror," *Philadelphia Inquirer*, August 21, 1966, p. 11.

13. Henry Kissinger, "We Live in an Age of Transition," *Daedalus* 124 (Summer 1995), p. 103; Samuel P. Huntington, "America's Changing Strategic Interests," *Survival* 33 (January–February 1991), p. 16; Edward Luttwak, "Toward Post-Heroic Warfare," *Foreign Affairs* 74 (May/June 1995), pp. 109–122.

14. Edward Luttwak, "Toward Post-Heroic Warfare," pp. 116–118.

David Tucker is a Member of the Board of Advisors at the Ashbrook Center for Public Affairs at Ashland University and an Associate Professor of Defense Analysis at the Naval Postgraduate School. He is the author of the book, Skirmishes at the Edge of Empire: The United States and International Terrorism. *The views expressed here are his own and do not reflect the position of the Naval Postgraduate School, Navy Department or Department of Defense.*

From *The Washington Quarterly*, Winter 1998, pp. 103-116. © 1998 by MIT Press Journals, Cambridge, MA 02142-1407, for the Center for Strategic and International Studies. Reprinted by permission.

War on America:
The new enemy

The assault on the United States will forever change the way America looks at itself and at the world.

SEPTEMBER 11th 2001 will be a date that America never forgets. Early on Tuesday morning terrorists simultaneously commandeered four passenger aircraft flying from Newark, Boston and Washington, DC. On the evidence of cellphone calls from inside the hijacked airliners, groups of between three and six terrorists herded passengers and crew into the back of each craft, threatening them with knives and cardboard-cutters.

Two of the planes flew straight into the twin towers of the World Trade Centre, felling both structures an hour later while thousands of people were presumably still trapped inside. A third ploughed into the Pentagon. The fourth crashed into a field in Pennsylvania, apparently after the passengers decided to overpower the hijackers when they heard, again over cellphones, of what had happened in New York. The aircraft had been aimed, it seems, at the heart of Washington.

For Americans, these terrible events are epoch-making, changing the landscape of geopolitics as indelibly as they have defaced the skyline of Manhattan. Current debates about budget deficits and the Internet boom now seem frivolous. The country's sense of invulnerability, built on its superpower status, has been violated. America has learned that it is not merely vulnerable to terrorism, but more vulnerable than others. It is the most open and technologically dependent country in the world, and its power attracts the hatred of the enemies of freedom everywhere. The attacks have shattered the illusions of post-cold war peace and replaced them with an uncertain world of "asymmetric threats".

The parallels with Japan's attack on Pearl Harbour in 1941, which brought

The administration
Delayed reaction

WASHINGTON, DC
Who was running the country?

THE terrorists may not have succeeded in paralysing the American government, as they clearly intended. But they certainly sent it into a defensive crouch. Until dusk on Tuesday the need to protect the lives of leading politicians, particularly the president, seemed to override all other considerations, such as rallying public opinion.

George Bush was told that a second aircraft had hit the World Trade Centre while he was visiting a school in Sarasota, Florida. He wanted to return to Washington. But the gigantic security apparatus that surrounds the president had different ideas. Convinced that the president was a target, they kept him airborne on Airforce One for much of the day. At one point, officials contemplated keeping him overnight in an underground bunker at the Strategic Command near Omaha, at the controls of the country's nuclear arsenal.

The obsession with security was pervasive. Dennis Hastert, second in the line of presidential succession, was whisked away on helicopters to an undisclosed "secure location". So were other congressional leaders. The vice-president, Dick Cheney, and Condoleezza Rice, the national security adviser, remained in an underground bunker in an otherwise evacuated White House.

With key officials either in the air or underground, the job of reassuring the country fell, for the most part, to local politicians and retired dignitaries. Rudy Giuliani was a pillar of strength. Old hands such as Lawrence Eagleburger put the horror in context. In mid-afternoon, Mr Bush's counsellor, Karen Hughes, appeared at FBI headquarters to insist that "your federal government continues to function effectively."

The vacuum was filled at about 7pm when Marine One, the presidential helicopter, ferried Mr Bush to the South Lawn of the White House. Mr Bush had finally decided that this hopscotching could not continue. In an important symbolic moment, he snapped a salute to his Marine guards and strode across the lawn to the Oval Office.

In the evening, a succession of cabinet ministers addressed the country; Donald Rumsfeld spoke from the shattered Pentagon. About 150 members of both houses of Congress massed on the steps of the Capitol to listen to Mr Hastert and Tom Daschle pledging that America would stand united against terrorism. They then burst into a spontaneous rendition of "God Bless America".

Just after 8.30pm, Mr Bush spoke to the country from the Oval Office. He was forceful and to the point; but the important thing was the sight of the president back in place, in charge at last.

The perpetrators
Who did it?

The prime suspect is Osama bin Laden. Proving his guilt will be another matter

EARLY on in the assault, George Bush talked about an "apparent" terrorist attack. Although suspicion immediately fell on the FBI's most wanted man, Osama bin Laden, Mr Bush's caution is reasonable. The last time America witnessed an outrage on a remotely similar scale, in Oklahoma City in 1995, officials were quick to blame Muslim fanatics, only to discover that an American had done it.

That seems unlikely this time around. Americans are not prone to suicide attacks. The right-wing militia movement that spawned Timothy McVeigh, the Oklahoma bomber, is a shadow of its former self. The group to which McVeigh himself once belonged no longer has enough members with military experience to conduct proper training exercises. The likelihood of one of its counterparts marshalling the expertise to hijack and fly four commercial airliners is small. And the militia movement is now closely watched.

On the other hand, American intelligence about the Middle East has suffered lately, thanks to Arab anger at the plight of Iraqis under sanctions and Palestinians under Israeli occupation. Since the Palestinian intifada began last year, the State Department has worried that an outraged Arab might imitate the suicide bombings now common in Israel. It has issued several warnings about the threat of terrorist reprisals, including one on September 7th suggesting that militants might target Americans in Japan or South Korea. That implies that America had indeed expected an attack, but had disastrously bad intelligence about its nature.

Investigators have already turned up evidence pointing to Arab involvement. The *Boston Herald* has claimed that several men from the United Arab Emirates, including a trained pilot, had boarded one of the hijacked flights. Flight-training manuals in Arabic were reportedly found in a car parked outside Boston airport, where two of the planes were hijacked. Two suspects flew down to Boston from Portland, Maine—close to the Canadian border. There were also reports of triumphant telephone calls after the attack from Mr bin Laden's followers. On Wednesday, arrests apparently connected to the investigation were made in Boston and Florida.

But even if, as seems likely, the authorities soon establish that the perpetrators were Muslim militants, they will find it harder to work out who sent them. Latter-day Islamic terrorists operate more through a loose fraternity than through rigidly hierarchical organisations. Past arrests of suspected militants in Canada, Germany, Britain, France and Jordan, as well as the United States, leave a picture of like-minded individuals providing one another with frequent support, occasionally coalescing into groups for specific attacks.

Many of these comrades, including Mr bin Laden, made one another's acquaintance while fighting in Afghanistan. It may be possible to show that Mr bin Laden knew the perpetrators, but the paper trail is unlikely to reveal more than that. According to a Pakistani newspaper, he has already denied direct involvement.

Nonetheless, there are several reasons to suspect Mr bin Laden. First, he is one of the few terrorists capable of orchestrating such a daring and complicated series of attacks. He was blamed for the audacious assault on the *USS Cole* in Yemen last year, when suicidal militants steered a dinghy full of explosives into the American warship in Aden harbour. Mr bin Laden specialises in multiple attacks. Members of his organisation, al-Qaeda, carried out simultaneous attacks on the American embassies in Kenya and Tanzania in 1998, according to testimony given in a trial this year by some of those convicted for the bombings. Again, however, prosecutors could not prove that Mr bin Laden ordered the attacks. America also fingered him for another (foiled) plot, to bomb a string of airports and aircraft on the eve of the millennium.

Next, Mr bin Laden recently released a long video, during which he repeated his usual fulminations against America. An Arab journalist in London says he had heard talk of an "unprecedented" action against the United States. That fits Mr bin Laden's habit of circulating virtual advertisements of forthcoming attacks.

Above all, the World Trade Centre has particular resonance for Mr bin Laden. It was there that the first big terrorist attack on American soil was mounted, in 1993, when a group of Egyptian, Pakistani and Palestinian terrorists planted a car bomb in the basement car park of one of the now-toppled twin towers. American investigators have long suspected that Mr bin Laden was involved.

A doubt is raised, however, by recent testimony in the trial of the East African bombers. Mr bin Laden's former associates suggested that he was running short of funds. They also described endless bickering and confusion among his men. His former accountant, America's star witness, stormed out of al-Qaeda after being refused a loan. If he was behind yesterday's horrors, Mr bin Laden had clearly found some more dedicated employees.

The killing fields

Major single acts of international terrorism(number killed)

United States as main political target		Other political targets	
Apr 1983	US Embassy, Beirut, suicide bomb (63)	Jun 1985	Air India flight over Irish Sea (329)
Oct 1983	US Marine barracks, Beirut (299)	Apr 1987	Bus in Colombo, Sri Lanka (150)
Dec 1988	Pan Am flight over Lockerbie (270)	Sep 1989	UTA flight over Chad (170)
Feb 1993	World Trade Centre, New York city (6)*	Jul 1994	Jewish centre in Buenos Aires (96)
Apr 1995	Federal building, Oklahoma City (168)	Oct 1994	Suicide bus bomb in Tel Aviv (23)
Jun 1996	US military complex, Saudi Arabia (19)*	Nov 1997	Tourists gunned down in Luxor (62)
Aug 1998	US embassies, Kenya & Tanzania (224)*	Aug 1998	Omagh town centre bomb (29)
Oct 2000	USS Cole, Aden, Yemen (17)*	Sep 1999	Apartments bombed in Moscow (118)

Source: The Economist
*Osama bin Laden suspected of involvement

Afghanistan
A bitter harvest

The sufferings of Afghanistan come to New York

IN ITS understandable rage for justice, America may be tempted to overlook one uncomfortable fact. Its own policies in Afghanistan a decade and more ago helped to create both Osama bin Laden and the fundamentalist Taliban regime that shelters him.

The notion of *jihad*, or holy war, had almost ceased to exist in the Muslim world after the tenth century until it was revived, with American encouragement, to fire an international pan-Islamic movement after the Soviet invasion of Afghanistan in 1979. For the next ten years, the CIA and Saudi intelligence together pumped in billions of dollars' worth of arms and ammunition through Pakistan's Inter-Services Intelligence agency (ISI) to the many mujahideen groups fighting in Afghanistan.

The policy worked: the Soviet Union suffered such terrible loses in Afghanistan that it withdrew its forces in 1989, and the humiliation of that defeat, following on from the crippling cost of the campaign, helped to undermine the Soviet system itself. But there was a terrible legacy: Afghanistan was left awash with weapons, warlords and extreme religious zealotry.

For the past ten years that deadly brew has spread its ill-effects widely. Pakistan has suffered terrible destabilisation. But the *afghanis*, the name given to the young Muslim men who fought the infidel in Afghanistan, have carried their *jihad* far beyond: to the corrupt kingdoms of the Gulf, to the repressive states of the southern Mediterranean, and now, perhaps, to New York and Washington, DC.

Chief among the *afghanis* was Mr bin Laden, a scion of one of Saudi Arabia's richest business families. Recruited by the Saudi intelligence chief, Prince Turki al Faisal, to help raise funds for the jihad, he became central to the recruitment and training of mujahideen from across the Muslim world. Mr bin Laden fought against the Russians on the side of the ISI's favourite Afghan, Gulbuddin Hikmatyar, whose Hezb-e-Islami party became the largest recipient of CIA money.

After the Russians withdrew from Afghanistan in 1989, the Americans quickly lost interest in the country and a struggle for power erupted among the mujahideen. But since no group was strong enough to capture and hold Kabul, the capital, Afghanistan slumped into anarchy. In 1995–96, a movement of Pathan students—Taliban—from religious schools in the border regions of Afghanistan and Pakistan swept the country, promising a restoration of order. They enjoyed Pakistani backing, and almost certainly the approval of the Americans.

Meanwhile, Mr bin Laden had become a self-avowed enemy of America, appalled at the presence of American troops on holy Saudi soil during the Gulf war. Exiled to Sudan, he was soon forced to leave. He secretly returned to Afghanistan, becoming a guest of the Taliban, whose interpretation of Islam and hostility to the West he shares. After attacks on two American embassies in 1998, America tried to persuade the Taliban to surrender him. When the regime refused, the Americans retaliated by raining cruise missiles on guerrilla camps in Afghanistan. The Taliban have steadfastly refused to hand Mr bin Laden over. As their guest he remains.

America into the second world war, have been widely drawn and are in large part justified. There was the same shock of surprise. Colin Powell, the secretary of state, said there had been no credible warning. The enemy struck at the symbols of American might—its economic, military and (in intention at least) political power. The principal difference was that the targets were on the mainland, not thousands of miles offshore.

Even though the dead will not be counted for days, the casualties were almost certainly greater than the 2,403 who died at Pearl Harbour. This was the deadliest day's military action against Americans since the civil war. It represents a profound change both in the scale and the complexity of operations mounted by any terrorist group.

At Pearl Harbour, America could immediately identify its aggressor. The experience of the Oklahoma City bombing—blamed at first on Middle Eastern action,

but later discovered to be perpetrated by an American—enjoins caution this time. But a growing amount of evidence points towards Islamic extremists, including, some say, the date itself. September 11th 1922 was the day when a British mandate came into force in Palestine, over the heads of unyielding Arab opposition.

In particular, America's leaders seem increasingly convinced that Osama bin Laden was responsible. He is one of the very few terrorists with the organisational power to carry out such an operation. Mr bin Laden's people recently talked of planning "very, very big attacks" on America. As Peter Bergen, the author of a forthcoming book on Mr bin Laden points out, all his operations have been preceded by boasts of this sort. They were not, alas, credible enough for the CIA.

Assuming that the enemy is Mr bin Laden, then the biggest difference from Pearl Harbour may eventually be that America has no clear idea about what it

means to go to war with him. In the immediate aftermath, America briefly behaved as if war had been joined in the old way. Financial markets were closed. Traffic into the capital was turned away. The ordinary business of life—airline flights, sporting events, shopping malls, Disneyworld—was shut. For a few hours, the government itself seemed headless, as the secret services spirited away the president and leaders of Congress to secure, secret spots.

Yet the assault of September 11th presents America not with a military challenge of the old definable sort but with a dilemma of a new type. The attacks were essentially on America's way of life. The temptation is to defy those attacks by going about the nation's business as usual. But that, of course, is not possible or desirable. At a minimum, stricter airport security will be imposed. The bigger question is how America, without compromising its own open society, can defend itself against a suicidal enemy who uses the very infrastructure of an open economy in order to wage war.

The answer will not be clear for years, and will depend crucially on the outcome of America's likely reprisals, unlaunched as *The Economist* went to press. But a few conjectures can be attempted.

Mr Bush called these "not acts of terrorism but acts of war". In other words, he will treat the assault not as a matter for an international criminal tribunal (as happened after the destruction of Pan Am 103 in 1988) or a cause for pinpoint cruise missiles (as after the bombing of America's embassies in Kenya and Tanzania in 1998) but as a *casus belli*. Who then would be the targets of that war? Mr Bush answered: "We will make no distinction between the terrorists who committed these acts and those who harbour them." This must mean America is considering attacks on the military bases and government buildings of the countries that give Mr bin Laden and his like safe harbour: Afghanistan, of course, but possibly also Iraq (implicated in an earlier attempt on the World Trade Centre) and Iran, with the fainter likelihood of Pakistan, Sudan and Syria.

Such a policy would obviously challenge America's allies, some of whom, notably France, have condemned mild attacks on Middle East terrorists. But the scale of the killings may change allied minds. The day after them, NATO invoked Article 5 of its treaty for the first time: this says that an attack on one member is an attack on all. Mr bin Laden has previously shown an interest in acquiring chemical and nuclear weapons. The mass murders in New York and Washington show the seriousness of that possibility. NATO may well take the view that the next time he strikes, there will be a mushroom cloud.

Counter-terrorism will also take centre-stage in America's reordering of its defence priorities. In March, a commission on national security chaired by former Senators Gary Hart and Warren Rudman argued presciently that a "catastrophic attack against American citizens on American soil is likely over the next quarter-century. The risk is not only death and destruction but also a demoralisation that could undermine US global leadership. In the face of this threat, our nation has no coherent or integrated government structures."

The report argued that the Pentagon should be reorganised to reflect these threats; that the special operations division dealing with "low intensity" conflicts should be given more clout (critics claim it has been downgraded by the priority given to missile defence); and that a counter-terrorism tsar should be created, with cabinet rank, to co-ordinate the many different agencies that get in each other's way when responding to terrorism. On May 8th, the vice-president said he would take over this task.

Lastly, the attacks may seem to vindicate critics of Mr Bush's proposed missile defence, who say the biggest threat to America comes not from missile programmes of rogue states, but from terrorists' "suitcase bombs". Logically, that point may be justified. But in their new vulnerability Americans may want defence of all sorts—and be willing to pay for it. You don't tear up your fire insurance because your house has been flooded.

Such arguments will form the debates of a new era of shadow war. No one can know in advance where they will lead. But wherever it is, the starting point is the awful wreckage in lower Manhattan under which so many Americans lie buried.

Musclebound:
The limits of U.S. power

By Stephen M. Walt

AP/WIDE WORLD

Operation Desert Fox: A U.S. destroyer launches a cruise missile from the Persian Gulf

THE END OF THE COLD WAR LEFT the United States in a position of preponderance unsurpassed since the Roman Empire. It has the world's largest and most advanced economy, and its military forces now dwarf those of any other country. Although the collapse of the Soviet Union left it without a major rival, the United States continues to spend more on defense than the next five largest military powers *combined*. English is the language of choice in science and in world business, American media and popular culture are increasingly pervasive, and the ideals of free market democracy have found new converts around the world. The international position of the United States may not be perfect, but Americans could hardly ask for much more.

Yet this extraordinary position of power does not guarantee that the United States can achieve its foreign policy objectives. Wherever one looks, in fact, there is abundant evidence of the limits of U.S. influence. In the Middle East, for example, the Israeli–Palestinian peace process has stagnated despite repeated U.S. proddings and President Bill Clinton's personal intervention at Wye Plantation. In Iraq, neither eight years of crippling economic sanctions nor a punishing series of U.S. air strikes have been able to remove Saddam Hussein from power, and the inspections regime established at the end of the 1991 Gulf War is now in tatters.

In the Balkans, the peace agreement negotiated at Dayton has failed to quell ethnic suspicions and only the continued presence of NATO troops prevents a new round of ethnic bloodshed. The situation looks even worse in Kosovo, where the cease-fire arranged by U.S. envoy Richard Holbrooke in October 1998 is unraveling rapidly, and the killing continues.

In Asia, explicit U.S. warnings and the threat of economic sanctions failed to halt India's and Pakistan's decision to test nuclear weapons; meanwhile, China continues to ignore U.S. concerns about its human rights practices and its sales of sensitive military technology.

Relations between the United States and Russia remain edgy at best, and Moscow has re-emerged as a persistent critic of U.S. policies in Eastern Europe, the Middle East, and the Balkans. All things considered, being the world's sole superpower may not be so wonderful after all.

If the United States is so powerful, then why doesn't it get its way more often? Is it due to a failure of will, as some of President Clinton's critics contend, or is it the result of pursuing the wrong goals at the wrong

time with the wrong strategy? If the United States is really the "one indispensable power," to use Madeleine Albright's self-flattering phrase, then why does its recent track record seem so discouraging?

Even the most powerful state in the world will not get its way on every issue and it may sometimes find itself thwarted at every turn.

The belief that the United States is both all powerful and impotent rests on a fundamental misunderstanding of the nature of power in international politics. For starters, the United States does get its way a good deal of the time, but Americans rarely notice when other states do what the United States wants without making a fuss about it. Focusing on the most difficult or persistent problems inevitably understates U.S. influence, because it ignores all the problems that were avoided because other states followed the U.S. lead, and it omits all the disputes that have already been resolved.

More important, the inability of the United States to get its way on every issue should not be surprising, because that is not how power works in the international system. Being bigger and stronger gives a state more influence, to be sure, in the sense that strong states can do more to weaker states than weaker states can do to them. Thus, the United States has a larger overall impact on world affairs than, say, Bolivia, Pakistan, or Denmark. Moreover, a powerful country like the United States can pursue a more ambitious range of goals than can a weaker state, and it will be better equipped to deal with unforeseen events. For these reasons, states prefer to be strong rather than weak.

Yet even the most powerful state in the world will not get its way on every issue and it may sometimes

find itself thwarted at every turn. The reasons are many.

Who cares more?

One obvious reason why the United States does not always get its way is that other states care more about certain issues than the United States does. The United State lost the Vietnam War in large part because the North Vietnamese cared more about unifying their country than Americans cared about preventing unification. Similarly, the United States worries about the possibility that Iraq might acquire weapons of mass destruction, but it is a safe bet that Saddam Hussein cares more about Iraq's strategic situation than the United States does. He is willing to endure far more punishment than Americans are, just as Americans would be willing to run greater risks and bear greater costs if their security were more directly at stake.

In the same way, U.S. influence over Israel and the PLO is limited by the fact that they care more about the final peace terms than most Americans do. Both sides are willing to stand up to U.S. pressure when disputes arise, even if opposing the United States is costly.

Americans would like to coerce others to do what they want, but they aren't willing to risk much blood or treasure to make sure they do.

The tendency for other states to care more than the United States does is a direct result of the favorable position the United States enjoys. In addition to being wealthier and stronger than any other state, the United States is insulated from the other major powers by two enormous oceans and protected by a large and robust nuclear deterrent. Although no state is perfectly safe from harm, the United States is easily the most secure great power in

There are limits to U.S. influence: Despite President Clinton's personal intervention at Wye River Plantation, the Israeli-Palestinian peace process appears stalled.

AP/WIDE WORLD

history. Other states have to worry a lot about how certain issues are resolved; the United States can often take a more sanguine view.

That condition leads to something of a paradox: Although solving many global problems requires active U.S. involvement, Americans do not see them as vital to their own interests and they are unwilling to expend much effort addressing them. U.S. officials were visibly reluctant to send U.S. troops to the Balkans, and they were clearly aware that public support would evaporate if there were even a modest number of U.S. casualties. Similar concerns explain why economic sanctions and air strikes by *unmanned* cruise missiles have become the preferred tool of U.S. diplomacy. Americans would like to coerce others to do what they want, but they aren't willing to risk much blood or treasure to make sure they do.

This tendency is not caused by a lack of vision, leadership, or courage within the U.S. government. Rather, it is a direct result of the favorable international position that the United States now occupies. The reluctance to "bear any burden" also reveals the tacit recognition that the problems

the United States is trying to solve may not be worth an extraordinary level of effort. The bottom line is clear: When other states care more about an issue than does the United States, Washington won't use all the power at its disposal—and it will be less likely to get what it wants.

It's lonely at the top

A second reason why U.S. influence is less than one might expect follows from the familiar principle of the balance of power. In a world in which each state must ultimately provide for its own security, the most powerful state in the system will always appear at least somewhat threatening to others. This tendency will be muted if the strongest state appears to be fairly benevolent (and especially if its interests are generally compatible with those of the other major powers), but it never vanishes entirely. Even when a strong state seems relatively benevolent, other states may try to keep it from becoming even stronger and may band together to contain its influence.

The well-known tendency for states to "balance" against the strongest power helps explain why France and Russia have joined forces

to undercut U.S. efforts to pressure Iraq, and why Russia and China have been working to improve relations as well. The desire to free Europe from its subordination to the United States is one reason why many Europeans favor continued progress towards European economic and political union.

Efforts to balance against the United States have been restrained thus far. This is partly due to the legacy of good relations established during the Cold War, but an even more important factor is America's geographic separation from the other major powers. Just as the Atlantic and Pacific oceans have long protected the United States from potential rivals, they also protect the Eurasian powers from the possibility of U.S. domination. Although European and Asian elites may resent U.S. high-handedness and worry about American cultural hegemony, they don't have to worry about the United States conquering them militarily. Further, the United States has been a relatively well-behaved great power, which makes it less likely to provoke others into joining forces to keep it in check.

Nonetheless, there are growing differences between the United States and a number of its traditional allies, and these differences are partly the result of the preponderant U.S. position. For example, the United States has dragged its heels on many environmental issues, in part because it fears being forced to pay a disproportionate share of the costs. It also stood apart from its allies over the proposal to create an International Criminal Court to try human rights violators and over the treaty to ban landmines, largely because U.S. officials feared that these initiatives might impair their ability to meet important military commitments both now and in the future.

A similar desire to preserve its own superiority and freedom of action explains why the United States seeks to keep countries like India and Pakistan from acquiring their own nuclear arsenals, while steadfastly preserving its own nuclear deterrent and opposing proposals for NATO to adopt a no-first-use doctrine.

Other states are more willing to oppose U.S. policy because they have less need for U.S. protection. During the Cold War, for example, differences between the United States and its allies were muted by the larger objective of preserving Western unity in the face of the Soviet threat. Now that the Soviet Union is gone, traditional allies are more willing to line up against the United States when they do not agree with its position. Despite—or more precisely, *because*—the United States is so obviously the biggest kid on the block, even its traditional allies may be looking for ways to keep U.S. power in check.

Dreaming impossible dreams

The apparent gap between U.S. power and U.S. influence also reflects the nature of the goals that American leaders have chosen to pursue. The euphoria that accompanied the end of the Cold War encouraged them to adopt an ambitious set of international objectives, and if anything that policy has intensified during the Clinton administration. Americans have always been inclined to remake the world in their own image, and that temptation is especially hard to resist when the United States seems to possess so many advantages.

Since the end of the Cold War, the United States has tried to broker a peace settlement between Israel and the PLO, sought to prevent the spread of nuclear weapons to other states (including several with active nuclear programs), and worked (successfully) to reduce the Russian nuclear arsenal and to disarm the former Soviet republics of Kazakhstan, Ukraine, and Belarus.

It has also committed itself to expanding NATO eastward and enlarging the sphere of democratic rule around the world, and it has provided the military and diplomatic muscle behind the prolonged campaign to eliminate Iraq's residual weapons capability. Finally, the United States also took on the mission of trying to reconstitute a stable, multi-ethnic society in war-torn Bosnia, while simultaneously trying to foster a solution to the simmering conflict between Serbs and ethnic Albanians over Kosovo.

This is a breathtaking array of foreign policy goals, and some of them were clearly quixotic from the beginning. Take Bosnia, for instance. As John Mearsheimer, my colleague at the University of Chicago, has pointed out, history offers not a single case where contending ethnic groups have agreed to share power in the aftermath of a civil war. Yet the 1995 Dayton agreement committed the United States to achieving this historically unprecedented outcome.

In much the same way, the effort to deny nuclear weapons to states like Iraq, North Korea, India, and Pakistan flies in the face of the powerful norm of national sovereignty and it ignores the powerful incentives that each of these states has for acquiring such a capability. It is also transparently hypocritical, given U.S. reluctance to give up its own far larger nuclear arsenal. Slowing the spread of nuclear weapons is a good idea, and U.S. policy has clearly helped achieve this goal, but it is not surprising that it did not achieve 100 percent success.

Knitting with one hand, unraveling with the other

The U.S. position as the sole superpower creates a final constraint on the effective exercise of U.S. influence. The United States is actively engaged in an enormous array of issues and in virtually every area of the globe. As just noted, many U.S. objectives are quite ambitious, and one would probably expect a low success rate under the best of circumstances. Unfortunately, given the number of goals the United States is trying to pursue, it is virtually inevitable that its efforts in one area will undermine its efforts somewhere else.

For example, the U.S.-led campaign to expand NATO is intended to help to defuse potential tensions within Europe and to nurture the new democracies in Poland, the Czech Republic, and Hungary. This is a laudable goal, but it directly undermines the equally laudable goal of improving relations with Russia and the related objective of obtaining Russian adherence to the START II arms control agreement. A similar example is the contradiction between U.S. efforts to promote trade with China, its desire to improve human rights conditions there, and its equally strong desire to build a more cordial political relationship with the Chinese government.

In the same way, U.S. leaders are strongly committed to supporting Israel, yet they also want to hasten a peace settlement, which requires putting pressure on Israel. They also want to avoid becoming the target of terrorist attacks, which are partly a reaction to close U.S. ties with Israel. No matter what the United States does, it will be difficult to achieve all these objectives simultaneously.

AP/WIDE WORLD

But sometimes U.S. influence works: Former U.S. Sen. George Mitchell, shown here with Irish Prime Minister Bertie Ahern and British Prime Minister Tony Blair, helped broker a peace agreement for Northern Ireland.

All states face tradeoffs between different goals, but they are likely to be more numerous and more complicated for a state that has its fingers in lots of different global problems. Paradoxically, America's extraordinary capacity for action is sometimes self-defeating. The more successful it is in one area, the more elusive success becomes somewhere else.

How much is enough?

In the immediate aftermath of the Cold War, many Americans rejoiced at the prospect of a "new world order" in which international conflict would be consigned to the dustbin of history. Instead of debating which weapons to buy, national security experts began to discuss how the country could convert defense industries and spend the anticipated "peace dividend."

Some eight years later, the much-ballyhooed "end of history" has yet to materialize. Although defense spending and weapons levels have fallen steadily since 1989, international conflict did not cease and U.S. military forces have been extremely busy. Indeed, President Clinton recently proposed the first real increase in U.S. defense spending since the Reagan era, to ensure that the United States could still meet its current level of commitments. Americans are discovering what other imperial powers learned long ago: the world is a complicated and messy place and trying to run it is a costly and difficult business.

This situation raises awkward questions for those who simultaneously believe that the United States is still spending too much on its military and that U.S. foreign policy should seek more than the pursuit of selfish national interests. International influence cannot be had on the cheap, and those who want to use U.S. power to deter aggression, halt genocide, or discourage proliferation will have to provide U.S. leaders with the means to ensure that their voice is heard and their actions are felt. In doing so, however, they must remember that even enormous advantages in relative power will not get the United States everything it wants.

Similarly, those who favor continued reductions in U.S. military power must confront the fact that U.S. influence would be even smaller if this policy were followed. Reasonable people can disagree about which course the United States should take; but we should begin by recognizing that there is a very clear choice to be made.

Stephen M. Walt is a professor of political science at the University of Chicago and a member of the Bulletin's *Board of Directors.*

Reprinted by permission from *The Bulletin of the Atomic Scientists*, March/April 1999, pp. 44–48. © 1999 by the Educational Foundation for Nuclear Science, 6042 South Kimbark, Chicago, IL 60637. A one-year subscription is $28.

Ending the Nuclear Nightmare: A Strategy for the Bush Administration

Jim Wurst and John Burroughs

In a presidential campaign scarcely distinguished by visionary language, candidate George W. Bush did utter some lofty and generally forgotten words about national security. Russia "is no longer our enemy," he declared last May, and our "mutual security need no longer depend on a nuclear balance of terror." But almost in the same breath, he restated familiar Reagan-era Republican doctrine: "It is possible to build a missile defense and defuse confrontation with Russia. America should do both." Since his Inaugural, President Bush and his national security team have continued the balancing act, mixing talk of unilaterally reducing the U.S. nuclear arsenal and of taking weapons off hair-trigger alert with pursuit of a missile defense shield that would require modifying or withdrawing from the Anti-Ballistic Missile Treaty, which Secretary of Defense Donald Rumsfeld dismisses as "ancient history."

Yet few elsewhere agree. Russia and China oppose U.S. missile defense plans, and NATO allies are skeptical. For the past two years, Russia and China have sponsored a United Nations resolution calling for strict adherence to the ABM Treaty. The General Assembly adopted the resolution last year by a vote of 88 to 5, with 66 abstentions. Washington's allies might have sided with the United States, saying they had faith in U.S. plans to reduce the risks of nuclear attack through credible defenses. Instead, they abstained. Only Israel, Micronesia, Albania, and Honduras joined the United States in opposing the resolution. To most of the world, the ABM Treaty is not ancient history, but an integral link in the chain of agreements that have produced a sharp downturn in the stockpiles of nuclear weapons. And most nations are well aware that the ABM Treaty also stands in the way of the next likely military push by the United States—deploying systems in space usable against satellites, missiles, and even ground targets.

Secretary Rumsfeld's last act before returning to government was to chair the Commission to Assess U.S. National Security Space Management and Organization. While noting "the sensitivity that surrounds the notion of weapons in space," the commissioners warned against a "Space Pearl Harbor" and argued that the United States should pursue policies "to ensure that the President will have the option to deploy weapons in space to deter threats to and, if necessary, to defend against attacks on United States interests."[1] Placing weapons in space was on the agenda even before this report was issued. The defense appropriations bill for 2001 allocates nearly $150 million for development of space-based laser systems banned by the ABM Treaty.

Should the United States proceed with the deployment of weapons in space, a qualitatively new arms race would result. Even if Russia were to agree to change the ABM Treaty to permit limited deployment of land- or sea-based missile interceptors, it is inconceivable that Moscow and Beijing would permit Washington to dominate space militarily. American claims that such a system is "defensive" would not persuade other countries looking up at lasers, micro-satellites, and targeting devices; they would seek their own space-based weaponry.

Yet none of this is written in stone, especially given emerging constraints on U.S. military spending. Popular movements committed to nuclear abolition and U.S. allies who believe in arms control need to mobilize to take advantage of the divisions in the Bush administration between the hawks, led by Rumsfeld, and the more moderate players, led by Secretary of State Colin Powell. The purpose of this essay is to suggest how President Bush can avoid a headlong rush to a new arms race and proceed down a safer and less costly path, bringing the world closer to the abolition of weapons no nation sanely wishes ever to use.

Deterrence vs. Abolition

The commitment to a missile shield, now central to Republican ideology, represents a rejection of deterrence, or more precisely that part of deterrence doctrine asserting that *mutual* vulnerability to nuclear attack creates stability. Although the rationale of a life-or-death struggle with communism can no longer be invoked, nuclear deterrence remains the cornerstone of the U.S. military posture. The United States has a declared policy of certain and overwhelming response to nuclear attack (with an unstated option of a preemptive strike against enemy nuclear forces on "strategic warning"); it also reserves the option of first use against an overwhelming conventional attack, or against the threat or use of biological or chemical weapons. The Pentagon views the reductions in U.S. forces contemplated in the Strategic Arms Reduction Treaty (START) process as consistent with the fulfillment of all those missions.[2]

At the same time, nuclear deterrence has been seriously challenged from a disarmament perspective. Disarmament proponents contend that the risks of an ongoing reliance on nuclear arms are too high, and that living with the threat of mass destruction as a central tenet of security policy is erosive of the nation's moral fiber. They have come to recognize that initiating and sustaining a process of abolishing nuclear weapons will require rejection of deterrence.[3]

In the early days of the nuclear age, elaboration of a balance of terror calculus as the basis for national and global security accompanied development of the atomic and hydrogen bombs, missile technology, and the computer. The advent of game theory, which analyzes human behavior in terms of instrumental calculations of self-interest, powerfully reinforced the elaboration of deterrence doctrines. One could even say that all those elements were embodied in one person, mathematician John von Neumann, a Manhattan Project consultant who in the late 1940s directed the building at Princeton of a prototype computer used in nuclear weapons design and who was a principal founder of game theory. A half-century later, there is an emerging understanding of the need to replace deterrence with a normative framework of moral and legal rules and political commitments and institutions.

In a 1996 advisory opinion, the International Court of Justice affirmed that under humanitarian law states must "never use weapons that are incapable of distinguishing between civilian and military targets" and held the use or threatened use of nuclear weapons to be "generally" contrary to international law. While a divided court failed to reach a definitive conclusion regarding the threat or use of nuclear weapons in an extreme circumstance of self-defense involving a state's survival, the overall thrust of the opinion was toward categorical illegality.[4]

This evolving debate has fundamental implications for the Bush administration. If the president is seriously going to press ahead with ballistic missile defense (BMD), he has to deal seriously with the reality that he will also have to pursue disarmament or face a global arms race. He has already made political statements to this effect, but he has not articulated a serious program.

A ready-made blueprint for such a program exists, and it has the benefit of being endorsed by 187 nations, including the United States. In May 2000, all the parties to the Nuclear Nonproliferation Treaty (NPT) agreed on a document containing "practical steps for the systematic and progressive efforts to implement Article VI." The article contains the promise to engage in negotiations leading to nuclear disarmament.

The 1970 Nonproliferation Treaty is the most adhered-to arms control agreement in existence (with only India, Pakistan, Israel, and Cuba outside the regime). It is also the only such treaty that permits two classes of members: those recognized as nuclear states (the United States, Russia, Britain, China, and France) and those who have renounced these weapons. The United States has consistently placed a high value on the NPT. Without it, Washington might have to keep an eye on a dozen potential proliferators. The fact that the treaty also commits the nuclear powers to eliminate their weapons has been steadfastly overlooked. Selective reading permits the focus to remain on proliferation rather than disarmament.

That is, until its last review conference. Every five years the parties assess compliance and lay out goals for the next five years. Nearly all review conferences have failed to reach a consensus, usually faltering on the nuclear powers' insistence that they are fulfilling their disarmament commitments, and with most of the non-nuclear parties refusing to go along with the charade. The conference last April and May succeeded in finding common ground. Central to the agreement was "an unequivocal undertaking by the nuclear-weapon states to accomplish the total elimination of their nuclear arsenals leading to nuclear disarmament, to which all states parties are committed under Article VI." In a subsequent resolution last fall, the U.N. General Assembly, with the support of the United States, Britain, and China, strongly reaffirmed the NPT disarmament agenda, with only India, Israel, and Pakistan in opposition, since they reject joining the NPT as non-nuclear-weapon states.

The impetus for the NPT outcome and the resolution came from a "New Agenda" group of nations—Brazil,

Egypt, Ireland, Mexico, New Zealand, Sweden, and South Africa—which negotiated the disarmament provisions with the nuclear-weapon states. The group has weight since it includes states with real expertise (several of which had nuclear weapons programs before joining the NPT) and a long history of commitment to disarmament. Their resolve was fortified by the May 1998 tests conducted by India and Pakistan, a challenge to the nonproliferation regime and a warning of the potential consequences of its breakdown. Ironically, the fear that India would "go nuclear" following China's 1964 test was a major reason the United States promoted the NPT.

The Blueprint

The current NPT agenda is not a perfect blueprint. Its lack of time frames, its sometimes imprecise language, and its generous use of such phrases as "as soon as appropriate" provide a great deal of wriggle room. The "unequivocal undertaking" to eliminate nuclear arsenals undoubtedly will stand as the authoritative statement of the purpose of Article VI, reinforcing the unanimous holding of the International Court of Justice that this article requires the *conclusion* of negotiations on nuclear disarmament in all its aspects. Generally, the new agenda represents consensus-based political, not legal, commitments regarding the steps needed to implement Article VI. But the agenda is comprehensive, sophisticated, and specific, and demonstrates an acceptance that nuclear weapons not only should be but can be abolished. What follows is a brief look at some of the most important commitments under the new agenda.[5]

• *A diminishing role for nuclear weapons in security policies*. This is a polite way of saying that it is time to abandon deterrence. In the United States, and abroad as well, there has long been too little attention paid to the strategies behind the question of numbers. The subject of quantitative reductions in nuclear arsenals mesmerized and distracted us, first as unrealized aspiration during the Cold War, then as reality in the last decade as reductions were implemented. This commitment illustrates that the lesson has been learned that abolition will require focusing on and challenging policy rationales. It will serve, as the NPT agenda states, to "minimize the risk that these weapons will ever be used and to facilitate the process of their total elimination."

The weapons laboratories have drawn the opposite conclusion: sustaining their enterprise will require new rationales. In effect, the nuclear establishment has tried to turn the widening credibility gap with respect to deterrence based on mass destruction to its advantage. For example, Stephen Younger, associate director for nuclear weapons at Los Alamos National Laboratory, has called for consideration of lower yield warheads to be combined with precision delivery systems or "tailored output" weapons that "produce enhanced radiation for the destruction of chemical or biological weapons with

minimum collateral damage." Absent such options, he observes, against some adversaries "reliance on high-yield strategic weapons could lead to 'self-deterrence.'"[6]

The congressionally mandated review of U.S. nuclear posture to be accomplished by the end of 2001 provides a ready-made process under which the Bush administration could revise America's nuclear doctrines. A revision in line with the NPT commitment to a "diminishing role for nuclear weapons" would reject the doctrine of certain massive retaliation and its historically associated posture of "launch on warning." During the campaign, candidate Bush described "preparation for quick launch within minutes after warning of an attack" as an "unnecessary vestige of Cold War confrontation."

Another such revision would eliminate qualifications to the assurances of non-use given to non-nuclear states in the context of the NPT and regional nuclear weapon-free zones. This would help to end the ideological and technical preparations for use, including preemptive use, of nuclear weapons in response to chemical and biological threats or attacks. It would recognize that continuing the practice of non-use that has been maintained for more than five decades since the U.S. attacks on Hiroshima and Nagasaki, and thus reinforcing the nonproliferation norm, is far more important than retaining a nuclear option for implausible scenarios of chemical or biological attacks to which the United States could not adequately respond with conventional means.

A more far-reaching revision in line with the NPT commitment would also encompass "no first use" in any circumstance, including against conventional attack by a nuclear power. In addition to raising further the nuclear threshold, this approach could help wean Russia from its increasing reliance on the nuclear threat to offset declining conventional strength.

• *Concrete agreed measures to further reduce the operational status of nuclear weapons systems*. This provision is diplomatese for dealerting, and refers to a wide range of measures to decrease, from hours to days to weeks to months, readiness to use nuclear weapons. Centrally, it involves separating the warhead from the missile, or the bomb from the aircraft. Dealerting is *not* the same thing as detargeting, which is essentially meaningless, since retargeting can be accomplished in seconds.

President Bush himself has made the argument for dealerting. In a world where there is no danger of a massive surprise nuclear attack, there is no rationale for the United States and Russia to keep more than 2,000 nuclear weapons each on hair-trigger alert. In fact, with the deterioration of Russia's command-and-control and early-warning systems, dealerted nuclear weapons offer greater security than those ready to launch at the push of a button. Because of the Clinton administration's lack of imagination and/or nerve regarding dealerting, this is now the most promising opening for the new president to prove he is more serious than his predecessor about reducing nuclear risks. During the presidential campaign, candidate Bush said that the "United States should remove as many nuclear weapons as possible from high-alert, hair-trigger status. "The "as possible" is the hedge phrase. But if President Bush listens to the likes of Bruce Blair, a former missile control officer and now head of the Center for Defense Information, the goal should be "global zero alert."[7] Britain, France, and China are already at much lower levels of alert than the United States and Russia.

• *Conclusion of START III as soon as possible; further efforts to reduce nuclear arsenals unilaterally; further reduction of non-strategic nuclear weapons.* Under START I, Russia and the United States are to have no more than 6,000 deployed strategic warheads each by the end of 2001. The United States currently has over 7,000 warheads, and Russia about 6,000. START II, not yet entered into force, sets limits of 3,000 to 3,500 warheads. START III negotiations have not yet begun, but in March 1997, Russia and the United States agreed to aim to reduce their arsenals to between 2,000 and 2,500 warheads. Russia, due to its growing inability to maintain its arsenal, has proposed going to 1,500 or lower, but the Pentagon has so far rejected the proposal, arguing that its targets in Russia require no fewer than 2,000 warheads.

The U.S. Senate and Russia's Duma have been uncooperative. The Duma approved START II in 2000, conditioned on adherence to the ABM Treaty. Meanwhile, Republicans in Congress balk at ratification because this would involve approval of agreements concerning permissible testing of anti-missile systems under the ABM Treaty. The knot can be cut with the sword of unilateralism, called for by the NPT agenda. If President Bush is looking for a role model, he need look no further than his father. The simple fact is that the elder Bush did more for nuclear disarmament in one year (1991) than Bill Clinton did in eight. And he did it unilaterally. George W. Bush made this point during the campaign when he said changes in nuclear forces "should not require years and years of detailed arms control negotiations." Pointing to 1991, when the United States and Soviet Union made reciprocal unilateral cuts in thousands of tactical (short-range) weapons and the United States dealerted bombers and hundreds of land-based missiles, candidate Bush said, "Huge reductions were achieved in a matter of months, making the world much safer more quickly." While Congress, in a constitutionally dubious action, barred reductions below START I levels prior to completion of the nuclear posture review, Bush unlike Clinton should be able to bring Congress along.

It is little understood by the public that reducing and eliminating deployed strategic weapons is only part of the disarmament equation. Both the United States and Russia have thousands of reserve warheads, referred to as a "hedge" by the Pentagon. A related problem is that of tactical weapons. This is one area where Moscow would have to pull more of the weight. Russia has perhaps 4,000 tactical weapons, while the United States

has about 1,000. These weapons are the ones experts worry about when they talk about Russian "loose nukes." The 150 or so bombs deployed by the United States in Europe under NATO auspices are a provocation to Russia, and the United States is deeply concerned about the exact number, whereabouts, and status of Russian tactical weapons.

• *Engagement as soon as appropriate of all the nuclear-weapon states.* In the NPT context, this means bringing in Britain, France, and China. While the United States and Russia have weapons in the many thousands, the other three have them in the hundreds. The conventional view is that once U.S. and Russian numbers of deployable strategic warheads are in the 1,000 range, nuclear disarmament will become what most of the world has always insisted that it should be—a multilateral concern, rather than a game of two countries with the rest of the world as passive spectators. But much could be done now to draw all nuclear states, including India, Pakistan, and Israel, into a disarmament process, beginning with transparency, accounting, and dealerting.

• *Ratification of the Comprehensive Test Ban Treaty.* So far as the world is concerned, this is the sine qua non for demonstrating a commitment to nuclear nonproliferation and disarmament. The treaty foundered in the Senate in 1999, partly due to animosity toward and mistrust of President Clinton, and partly because some Republicans doubted that a test ban would permit the United States, as the Clinton administration claimed, to maintain its nuclear superiority indefinitely. The Bush administration may reconsider its stated opposition to ratification as part of an effort to win support from allies for BMD. Disarmament campaigns must first block any move to resume testing (there has been no U.S. testing since 1992), and then seek to resuscitate the test ban treaty on different grounds, based on its historical purpose as a disarmament as well as nonproliferation measure. They should also oppose the ongoing huge expansion of laboratory computing and experimental capabilities to "replace" testing as contrary to the principle of irreversible disarmament endorsed in the NPT agenda.

• *Establishment of a committee to deal with nuclear disarmament in the Conference on Disarmament; negotiation of a fissile materials treaty.* The Conference on Disarmament in Geneva is the only permanent multilateral disarmament negotiating forum, with the Chemical Weapons Convention and the Comprehensive Test Ban Treaty to its credit. The Clinton team resisted the creation of a conference committee to *negotiate* nuclear disarmament, proposing instead that such a committee be limited to *discussions.* The U.S. view has been that the priority is to negotiate a treaty banning the production of fissile materials (plutonium and highly enriched uranium) for weapons. While rhetorically resistant to a multilateral approach, the Bush team has yet to formulate a position. In principle, there is no reason why negotiations cannot begin on both fronts. The real problem is that BMD is casting a shadow over Geneva. China is pulling back from its endorsement of a fissile materials ban, apparently concerned that it may need to produce more materials for an arsenal buildup aimed at maintaining the capacity to overcome a U.S. anti-missile system. China has also insisted on the establishment of a committee to negotiate prevention of an arms race in outer space.

•*Further development of verification capabilities.* Effective, good-faith verification has a multiplier effect. We know the missiles removed from Europe in the late 1980s were destroyed because we saw it happen. We know the Russian tanks removed from the European theater under the Agreement on Conventional Forces in Europe have not been redeployed because we can see them rusting away out in the open on the far side of the Urals. American and Russian/Soviet officials have gone to the bases of their counterparts and seen chemical weapons destroyed. Once the Comprehensive Test Ban Treaty monitoring organization is fully functioning, its global array of sensors will be able—despite claims to the contrary—to detect significant cheating on the treaty. Creating new arrangements to verify steps such as dealerting missiles, ending fissile-materials production, and a test ban adds to the growing body of expertise on verification which, in turn, will aid the next arms control regime.

Indeed, development of verification capabilities makes possible the creation of a nuclear weapons-free world. The New Agenda Resolution in the General Assembly, adopted with U.S. support, states that such a world "will ultimately require the underpinnings of a universal and multilaterally negotiated legally binding instrument or a framework encompassing a mutually reinforcing set of instruments." Since 1997, a broad international coalition of grass-roots and research groups has lobbied for a nuclear weapons convention that would ban nuclear weapons in the same way chemical weapons are outlawed.[8] The United States has not endorsed this approach, even as the endpoint of a process of disarmament to which it is committed in principle. But it is a key demand for disarmament campaigners, because it dramatizes and makes concrete the imperative to create a comprehensive regime eliminating nuclear weapons within the foreseeable future.

The NPT as a Victim of Star Wars

The Nonproliferation Treaty itself could be part of the collateral damage caused by "Star Wars." Absent any new treaty constraints on strategic nuclear weapons, ballistic missile defense will provoke Russia and China to maintain or acquire large numbers of nuclear weapons in order to overcome any defensive advantage of the United States. The only way in which BMD would not be such a destabilizing force would be for it to function as an element of "strategic stability" (a phrase currently favored by Russia) in a trilateral arrangement under

which Russia and China would maintain a nuclear capability sufficient to deter a nuclear-armed and BMD-equipped United States. Therefore, deployment of BMD would require three of the five nuclear parties to the NPT to violate their commitment to negotiate nuclear disarmament. A newly minted "gentlemen's agreement" to keep nuclear weapons in place would be the definitive breaking of faith with the rest of the world, and could irrevocably erode the nonproliferation regime.

The destruction of the ABM Treaty is BMD's first target. Many of Star Wars' most vocal proponents have a fundamental contempt for all arms control. (We are talking about people who opposed the 1988 treaty that eliminated all medium-range U.S and Soviet nuclear missiles from Europe, the downside of which is hard to find.) For START to wither on the vine would not cause them much lost sleep. But the NPT enjoys greater support among hawks because it helps keep proliferation in check. The irony is that BMD, by eroding the nonproliferation regime, would help create the very threat it is supposed to protect against.

A Political Path

Why would a president who turned to such steel-tipped hawks as Richard Cheney and Donald Rumsfeld pursue a disarmament agenda? One possibility—which has already been alluded to as the Bush administration takes shape—is that the United States has to give up something to get BMD. For all its talk of forging ahead alone, it is hard to picture the administration abandoning the ABM Treaty, START, and the Comprehensive Test Ban Treaty without damaging the NATO alliance. The Bush administration will also face severe budgetary problems as it seeks to reshape the U.S. military while cutting taxes. Disarmament advocates can exploit the contradiction between Bush's arms control rhetoric and the push for BMD. While not conceding BMD deployment as inevitable (not the least because BMD does not work), they can campaign hard for unilateral cuts and dealerting. In so doing, they must remain grounded in an abolition perspective. In his confirmation testimony, Gen. Colin Powell said that he shares the "goal" that "at some point in the future, we would see a world where there were no nuclear weapons [and] no need for missile defense." That future needs to be created sooner rather than later, before global competition in high-tech militarism featuring rationalized nuclear capabilities, anti-missile systems, and space-based weapons accelerates and becomes entrenched.

Notes

1. *Report of the Commission to Assess United States National Security Space Management and Organization*, Executive Summary, January 11, 2001, pp. 12–13 (www.space.gov/commission/report.htm).
2. For U.S. deterrence doctrines, see, for example, William S. Cohen, Secretary of Defense, *Annual Report to the President and Congress 2001*, chaps. 1–2 (www.dtic.mil/execsec/adr2001).

212

3. Networks and campaigns committed to abolition, or at least to progressive arms control leading eventually to abolition, include the Abolition 2000 Global Network to Eliminate Nuclear Weapons (http://www.abolition2000.org/), the Middle Powers Initiative (http://www.middlepowers.org/), Project Abolition (http://www.project-abolition.org/), the US Campaign to Abolish Nuclear Weapons (www.wslfweb.org/abolition/scamp.htm), and the Coalition to Reduce Nuclear Dangers (http://www.crnd.org/).

4. See Committee on International Security and Arms Control, *The Future of U.S. Nuclear Weapons Policy* (Washington, D.C.: National Academy Press, 1997), p. 87 (www.nap.edu/catalog/5796.html).

5. *2000 Review Conference of the Parties to the Treaty on the Non-Proliferation of Nuclear Weapons, Final Document*, vol. 1, NPT/CONF.2000/28 (parts I and II), pp. 13–15 (www.un.org/Depts/dda/WMD/2000FD.pdf).

6. Stephen M. Younger, "Nuclear Weapons in the Twenty-First Century," Los Alamos National Laboratory, June 27, 2000, LAUR–00–2850, pp. 13–15 (lib-www.lanl.gov/la-pubs/00393603.pdf). See also National Institute for Public Policy, *Rationale and Requirements for U.S. Nuclear Forces and Arms Control*, vol. 1 (January 2001), pp. 4, 7, 14 (http://www.nipp.org/). Several of the participants in this study are now serving in the Bush administration.

7. Bruce G. Blair, "De-Alerting Strategic Nuclear Forces," in *The Nuclear Turning Point: A Blueprint for Deep Cuts and De-alerting of Nuclear Weapons*, ed. Harold A. Feiveson (Washington, D.C.: Brookings, 1999), pp. 101–28.

8. See Merav Datan and Alyn Ware, *Security and Survival: The Case for a Nuclear Weapons Convention* (Cambridge, Mass.: International Physicians for the Prevention of Nuclear War [http://www.ippnw.org/], 1999).

Jim Wurst is the program director of the Lawyers' Committee on Nuclear Policy. John Burroughs is the organization's executive director and the author of The Legality of Threat or Use of Nuclear Weapons: A Guide to the Historic Opinion of the International Court of Justice *(1997).*

From *World Policy Journal*, Spring 2001, Vol. XVIII, No. 1, pp. 31-37. © 2001 by World Policy Institute at New School University. Reprinted by permission of Perseus Books, LLC.

Mission impossible

The United States wanted to achieve the ability to neutralize any proliferation threat, anywhere, any time.

Described as "preventive defense" or "extended deterrence" by its supporters—but decried as "a new form of gunboat diplomacy" by its detractors—a new program called the "Counterproliferation Initiative" was unveiled in December 1993 by then–Defense Secretary Les Aspin.

There was considerable controversy over what "counterproliferation" meant. But it was widely interpreted as indicating that the United States—having recently demonstrated overwhelming military superiority in the Gulf War—would now flex its muscles even further, looking into the ways and means of preemptively striking regional troublemakers or would-be attackers.

Although there was talk of building conventional weapons capable of destroying deeply buried targets like command centers (Aspin said both new strategies and new military capabilities were needed), the initiative envisioned the use of U.S. nuclear weapons to defeat chemical or biological weapons. The idea, simply, was to "locate, neutralize, or destroy" others' weapons of mass destruction before they could be used. For the first time, the United States openly added targets in the Third World to its nuclear-weapons targeting plan.

Now, after eight years of reality, the initiative has morphed into something much less than promised. Author Henry Sokolski describes the process.

by Henry D. Sokolski

THE FATE OF PRESIDENT BILL Clinton's "Counterproliferation Initiative" was tethered to its strategic assumptions. An initial interest in devising plans for preemptive strikes against foreign proliferation activities simply ignored the American culture's bias against launching Pearl Harbor-like attacks. More important, the initiative at first presumed that some military-technical means could neutralize proliferation problems. And that, in fact, turned out to be inherently difficult, if not impossible.

Strategic weapons (long-range missiles and nuclear weapons) are of proliferation concern, after all, precisely because no ef-

fective military countermeasures against them are yet available, and because only a few strategic weapons can produce war-winning or victory-denying results. To presume that there could be some finite military solution to proliferation is to seriously underestimate what the threat is about.

The sources of these initial misunderstandings can best be understood by tracking the origins of the initiative, which were rooted in the fallout from the war against Iraq.

First, despite clear U.S. military superiority over Baghdad, Iraq's missiles and chemical and biological weapons stock-

piles—and its fledgling nuclear program—heightened concern that the United States would eventually face enemies armed with strategic weapons.

Second, critics of the first Bush administration complained that U.S. export controls had failed to prevent Iraq from acquiring the advanced technologies needed to develop these capabilities. Together, these two events (and the presidential election in 1992), put tremendous pressure on the Bush administration to come up with some sort of response.

Late in the summer of 1992, the Office of the Principal Deputy Under Secretary of Defense for Strategy and Resources suggested a reorganization aimed at strengthening Defense Department efforts against strategic weapons proliferation. The proposal called for a new deputy under secretary of defense to be created to oversee the activities of the Defense Trade Security Administration, the Office of the Deputy for Nonproliferation Policy, and the Deputy Assistant Secretary for Conventional Forces and Arms Control Policy.

Counterproliferation, May 1996

"If you don't think the United States government is doing anything to combat NBC [nuclear, biological, and chemical weapons] proliferation and terrorism, then you don't know what's going on. But if you think it's enough, you don't know the gravity of the threat."

Ashton Carter
Assistant Secretary of Defense

Ironically, the suggested title for this deputy—"Deputy Under Secretary for Counterproliferation"—had been considered for the director of proliferation countermeasures three years before, but rejected as too vague.

Intriguing questions

Did creating a deputy for counterproliferation mean that the Defense Department intended to neutralize weapons of mass destruction with advanced technology? Or was "countering" to be accomplished with more traditional military counteroffensives or with counterintelligence? Did counterproliferation—whatever it was—include traditional nonproliferation efforts, or were these activities at odds with one another?

By 1992, these questions seemed intriguing. Literally hundreds of draft view charts were composed explaining what counterproliferation might mean and what a deputy under secretary implementing it might do. But none of these briefings was ever used.

In September 1992, Deputy Defense Secretary Donald Atwood thought the better of reorganizing the department during the closing months of a presidential campaign and put a freeze on the creation of new offices. Then, two months later, President George Bush lost the election.

True believers

President Bill Clinton and the new officials he brought on were eager to reorganize the government, including the offices focused on proliferation issues. Several senior Clinton defense advisers had already considered what was needed while serving as members of the Defense Policy and Defense Science Boards of the Bush administration.

The Defense Science Board, in particular, had spent more than a year analyzing what new defensive and counteroffensive technologies might be developed to respond if other nations threatened to use chemical, biological, or nuclear armed ballistic missiles. The board concluded that, with enough advanced sensors, counteroffensive missile technologies, and intelligence, the U.S. military might be able to destroy the bulk of an enemy's offensive missiles before they ever left their launchers.

Two key Democratic board members—John Deutch, who later served as under secretary for acquisition and then deputy secretary of defense in the Clinton administration, and Ashton Carter, who became assistant secretary of defense for nuclear security and counterproliferation—warmly embraced the board's findings.

In an essay on intelligence requirements written for the Council on Foreign Relations prior to his appointment, Carter argued that combating the spread of weapons of mass destruction with precision weapons required precise and timely intelligence. What was most critical, he argued, was to know when a nation was about to acquire one or two weapons and where these weapons might be. It was one thing, he noted, to collect intelligence on nations acquiring fissile material to make their first bomb, but:

"Planning an air strike on the nuclear facilities of a nation approaching construction of a first bomb, by contrast, requires entirely different types of collection and analysis. Military planners need to study the building the raid is supposed to destroy. The aircraft delivering the bombs will require information about the location, radar frequencies, and signal structures, and command and control of air defenses surrounding the target. If cruise missiles and other 'smart weapons' are to be used, terrain contour maps, terminal area images, global positioning coordinates, and other precision guidance information will have to be assembled."[1]

Although this kind of planning would naturally be useful to limit damage once a new nuclear nation went to war against the United States, in another section of his essay, titled "Attacking a Fledgling Program or Arsenal," Carter also emphasized that it would be particularly useful if the United States were planning an offensive attack.

The counterproliferation initiative

Planning to fight proliferation and even to launch preemptive strikes was something new. More importantly, the idea resonated with Les Aspin, the new defense secretary, who as chairman of the House Armed Services Committee had argued that the spread of weapons of mass destruction was now the country's number one security concern. On December 7, 1993, after months of briefings on what a counterproliferation initiative might be, Aspin announced the program before an audience at the National Academy of Sciences.

Much of his speech was straightforward. In addition to working with the State Department to try to prevent the proliferation of weapons of mass destruction, Aspin called on the Defense Department to work harder to protect against these weapons' possible use. But what caught most people's attention was the secretary's assertion that providing such protection constituted a new, unique military mission, and that he had formally directed the military services to "develop new military capabilities to execute it."[2]

Although Aspin left the Pentagon soon after announcing the initiative, he tried his best to institutionalize it. First, he established a new post for Carter—assistant secretary for nuclear security and counterproliferation. Second, he instructed the military services to identify research and acquisition programs that needed to be funded to accomplish the new counterproliferation mission. He also had his deputy, John Deutch, make counterproliferation a Defense Department acquisition priority. Finally, he saw to it that language was introduced in the National Defense Authorization Act for fiscal year 1994 requiring his successor to identify precisely what additional counterproliferation spending was needed.

Not surprisingly, the first half of 1994 was a busy one for the initiative's supporters. In addition to Carter and his deputy assistant secretary for counterproliferation, another deputy assistant secretary for counterproliferation was created within the Office of the Under Secretary of Defense for Acquisition.

This new deputy was immediately put to work to answer congressional reporting requirements concerning what new spending would be required. In May, Deputy Secretary Deutch asked the military services to find $400 million a year to fund 14 "underfunded" counterproliferation programs that his acquisition staff had identified. (These programs included development of radars that might find underground command centers, systems that could acquire mobile Scud missile launchers before they fired their missiles, and non-nuclear munitions that might interfere with an adversary's electronic command, control, and communications systems.)[3]

The military services were hardly enthusiastic. After months of review, they had earmarked no more than $80 million for possible use to fund programs supporting the counterproliferation mission. The Office of the Secretary of Defense dropped any further talk of securing hundreds of millions of dollars for counterproliferation, and instead, Clinton's defense appointees began to claim that the entire defense budget was in one way or another dedicated to counterproliferation. The Office of the Joint Chiefs of Staff, meanwhile, contended that the counterproliferation "mission" was not a separate undertaking but was incorporated into all existing military missions.

Why was the military's initial support of the counterproliferation initiative so weak? Several Pentagon observers believe that the Clinton Pentagon simply asked the military to make too great a financial sacrifice. While Deputy Secretary Deutch was asking the military to find $400 million in existing budget authority for counterproliferation, the White House was demanding significant cuts in overall Defense spending. This undermined the secretary's credibility.

The services also resented having counterproliferation forced on them as a separate mission requirement with little or no prior consultation. Certainly, the services could see the need to do more to prepare to fight in nuclear, chemical, and biological warfare environments. But that preparation was something they believed had to be done as part of existing military requirements to assure command of sea, air, and land.

Finally, some in the military were uneasy about the idea of preemptive war, although their concerns were generally not shared by Special Operations staffs: But what were the legal, moral, and operational ramifications of using U.S. military force before open hostilities began?

The military's concerns were amplified by the U.S. arms control community. They too suspected that the preemptive war aspect of the initiative was far more significant than publicly stated. They also were concerned that the Defense Department was abandoning its hardline opposition to lax export controls, especially over dual-use items (computers, diagnostic equipment, and other items useful for making strategic weapons). Counterproliferation was what the Defense Department would do *after* export controls had failed to prevent proliferation: The department's traditional use of military threat assessments to fortify other agencies' export control efforts no longer seemed to be a priority.

Finally, arms control supporters worried that nonproliferation itself was being challenged. On the one hand, counterproliferation's backers were arguing that with enough military effort (and spending), the United States could so mitigate the threats posed by weapons of mass destruction that it and its allies could prevail on the battlefield even if those weapons were used.[4] Yet, if this were so, existing nonproliferation taboos against their use, which the United States had always been eager to strengthen, would be undermined.

Then there was the problem of deterrence. Lacking chemical or biological weapons, the U.S. military reserved the option of deterring their use (and the use of nuclear weapons as well) by threatening U.S. nuclear counterstrikes. Yet the more the Pentagon developed this option, the more arms control advocates worried that it would make other nations' acquisition of nuclear weapons seem justified. All of this and the initiative's feared flirtations with preventive war encouraged extensive debate.

Death by definition?

Counterproliferation also prompted substantive and bureaucratic worries at the State Department, which had traditionally maintained control over proliferation issues. But the Defense Department's initiative now threatened this. In the weeks following Aspin's announcement of the Counterproliferation Initiative, debates broke out between State and Defense officials and even within the Defense Department itself over what the initiative covered. Some officials wanted all proliferation concerns, including advanced conventional weapons, to be included; others did not.

> ## Counterproliferation, July 1999
>
> "According to Sen. Arlen Specter... 96 agencies are pursuing counterproliferation efforts. Creating a national director to oversee them 'is like putting a Band-Aid on a bullet wound to the head.'"
>
> *Ivan Eland*
> Cato Institute

There also were disagreements over who was in control of counterproliferation policy. The State Department insisted that it should be in command of the initiative since State chaired the interagency working group on proliferation. Defense, meanwhile, was just as insistent that it have a free hand because the counterproliferation initiative was its idea, and it was footing most of the bill. The Arms Control & Disarmament Agency (ACDA) and the Energy Department also had a stake in the matter, as did the intelligence agencies that were trying to budget and reorganize themselves to respond to new requirements.

In January 1994, the National Security Council (NSC) staff was asked to resolve the issue. By mid-February, the council settled the key dispute between State and Defense by brokering a set of definitions that both departments could accept but that favored State. Proliferation was defined descriptively: "The spread of nuclear, biological, and chemical capabilities and the missiles to deliver them." Meanwhile, nonproliferation was defined as Washington's comprehensive policy against proliferation, which employed the "full range of political, economic and military tools to prevent proliferation, reverse it diplomatically, or protect our interests against an opponent armed with weapons of mass destruction or missiles, should that prove necessary. Nonproliferation tools include: intelligence, global nonproliferation norms and agreements, diplomacy, export controls, security assurances, defenses, and the application of military force."[5]

This definition of nonproliferation reduced counterproliferation to Defense Department activities "with particular responsibility for assuring that U.S. forces and interests can be protected should they confront an adversary armed with weapons of mass destruction or missiles."[6]

Although somewhat confusing, this definition had three clear advantages.

First, by keeping nonproliferation as the comprehensive term to describe U.S. efforts against the spread of weapons capable of mass destruction, the policy focus was kept on the most horrible and indiscriminate weapons and on existing international and U.S. diplomatic nonproliferation efforts in general. It gave the State Department ultimate control over any counterproliferation effort; by definition, counterproliferation was subsumed under nonproliferation.

Second, it avoided the vagueness inherent to any set of prescriptive definitions. A prescriptive definition might help clarify why weapons of mass destruction were of proliferation concern and what else might qualify and why. But those definitions were certain to generate the kind of debates over what should be included that the NSC definition memo was crafted to avoid.

Finally, by limiting proliferation to weapons of mass destruction and the missiles to deliver them, the NSC definition kept conventional military systems and dual-use items that the United States wanted to export to its friends out of the web of nonproliferation export controls.

The bureaucratic advantages that these definitions offered, however, came at price. As long as proliferation concerns were limited to weapons of mass destruction and ballistic missiles, any hope of developing truly effective military countermeasures (distinct from defenses and damage-limiting measures) would necessarily remain distant. More important, the NSC definitions and their preoccupation with weapons capable of mass destruction kept counterproliferation from addressing the technical revolution in military affairs that even smaller nations were engaged in.

Thus, some of the most interesting of emerging strategic threats were placed beyond the initiative's reach. This was regrettable because some new threats (particularly those posed by conventional cruise missiles, crude information warfare, and submersibles) were precisely the ones that were most amenable to the development of effective military countermeasures and targeted export controls.

The concept in operation

The military services' staffs began to take more serious steps to evaluate the damage-limitation requirements that nuclear, chemical, and biological weapons might impose against U.S. forces, and in 1993 they created a Joint Program Office to address the shortcomings in U.S. preparations to fight adversaries who might use such weapons.

More important, the military finally began to conduct annual war games that focused on the effects that nuclear, chemical, and biological weapons might have on U.S. forces. A little more than a year after Aspin's announcement of the counterproliferation initiative, the navy incorporated nuclear, biological, and chemical weapons threats into its annual Navy War College war game, "Nimble Dancer." Serious problems were encountered in playing out these games, but the navy decided at the highest levels to continue to highlight chemical, biological, and nuclear weapons threats in follow-on war games.

Financially, however, the initiative enjoyed only mixed success. As noted before, Deputy Secretary Deutch attempted in 1994 to increase government-wide funding for counterproliferation-relevant research and hardware acquisition by some $400 million annually. Yet even the White House requested only $164 million. Moreover, the Joint Chiefs earmarked only a third of the $230 million in Defense Department counterproliferation shortfalls Deutch had identified (the other shortfalls were associated with the intelligence community and the Energy Department).

Two years later, things had not improved. In fact, an internal Pentagon review in 1996 concluded that the department was still failing to fund some of the highest priority counterproliferation programs (biological agent detectors, for instance). Finally, in 1999, the department announced it would spend approximately $1 billion over the next five years to address these deficiencies. In one controversial program, many in the military forces were vaccinated against anthrax, but the safety of the vaccine was questioned.

As for the operational implementation of counterproliferation, the Defense Department initially did some planning and actually considered two offensive campaigns.

In 1993 the United States acted on intelligence that the Chinese were shipping chemical weapons–related materials to Iran. The White House considered interdicting the shipment, but the suspect ship, the Yin He, turned out not to be carrying the illicit materials.

Second, during the 1994 nuclear crisis with North Korea, the U.S. Air Force briefed Defense Secretary William Perry on how it might bomb the North Korean nuclear reactor at Yongbyon, although the White House chose a diplomatic approach instead. In exchange for several billion dollars in oil and nuclear energy assistance, North Korea pledged not to operate its known nuclear facilities, eventually to allow inspections, and ultimately to dismantle the facilities.

The two largest counterproliferation operations that the services actually executed came four years later. In 1998, U.S. cruise missiles were fired against a suspected Sudanese chemical weapons plant and against Iraqi chemical, biological, and missile production plants.

Neither campaign was a clear success. Following the attack against Sudan, evidence emerged that the plant U.S. missiles destroyed was a pharmaceutical facility, not a weapons factory. As for Operation Desert Fox against Iraq, its effects were only temporary. As Gen. Anthony Zinni, the commander in chief of U.S. Central Command, publicly noted, bombing Saddam's biological and chemical plants could hardly stop those programs because making chemical and biological weapons is relatively easy.

None of these events helped the initiative bureaucratically. Unable to secure large sums for a new, separate, counterproliferation mission, Defense Department officials began arguing that nearly the entire defense budget was targeted against the threat of proliferation.

In 1996 Defense Secretary Perry eliminated the posts of assistant secretary for counterproliferation and deputy assistant secretary of defense for counterproliferation. By 2000 all that remained within Defense was a counterproliferation directorate. Its most public function was to coordinate proliferation-related meetings with NATO and other nations. The bulk of the initiative's acquisition activities, which focused on passive biological and chemical weapons defenses, continued.

The initiative's emphasis clearly had shifted. Originally the initiative was animated by the prospect that offensive military operations might neutralize or rollback the threat of strategic weapons proliferation. Seven years later, however, the initiative had been reduced to a less heroic but still critical concern of limiting whatever damage U.S. expeditionary forces might suffer if, as seemed likely, chemical, nuclear, or biological weapons were used against them. In short, the word counter-proliferation had survived, but the hope that the initiative might neutralize the proliferation threats the United States and its allies faced, had not.

Notes

1. Robert D. Blackwill and Ashton B. Carter, "The Role of Intelligence," in *New Nuclear Nations: Consequences for U.S. Policy*, Robert D. Blackwill and Albert Carnesale, eds. (New York, N.Y.: Council on Foreign Relations Press, 1993), p. 234.

2. "Remarks by Honorable Les Aspin, Secretary of Defense, National Academy of Sciences, Committee on International Security and Arms Control, December 7, 1993," reprinted in *The Counter-Proliferation Debate* (Washington, D.C.: Carnegie endowment for International Peace, November 17, 1993).

3. Office of the Deputy Secretary of Defense, "Report on Nonproliferation and Counterproliferation Activities and Programs," May 1, 1994, p. ES-2.

4. See, for example, Office of the Secretary of Defense, *Proliferation: Threat and Response* (Washington, D.C.: U.S. Government Printing Office, 1997), p. iii; and Ashton Carter and Celeste Johnson, "Beyond the Counterproliferation Initiative to a Revolution in Counterproliferation Affairs," *National Security Studies Quarterly*, Summer 1999, pp. 83–90.

5. Daniel Poneman, Special assistant to the President and Senior Director for Nonproliferation and Export Controls, Memorandum for Robert Gallucci (Assistant Secretary for Political Military Affairs, Department of State) and Ashton Carter (Assistant Secretary for Nuclear Security and Counterproliferation, Department of Defense), "Agreed Definitions," February 18, 1994.

6. Ibid

This article is adapted from Best of Intentions: America's Campaign Against Strategic Weapons Proliferation (2001), *by Henry D. Sokolski. Sokolski, executive director of the Nonproliferation Policy Education Center in Washington, D.C., served in the Defense Department as Secretary Dick Cheney's deputy for nonproliferation policy from 1989–93.*

Index

A

Abu Nidal, 12
Adams, John Quincy, 90–94
"affirmative action," 181
Afghanistan, 10, 12, 13, 99, 100, 101, 102, 201
Africa, challenges of, 82–87
Agreement on Conventional Forces, 212
AIDS pandemic, 82, 84, 85, 86
Airborne Warning and Control System (AWACS), 124, 125
Albania, 58, 60, 64
Albright, Madeleine, 34, 133, 135, 150, 187
Al-Jihad, 12
al-Qaeda, 10, 11, 20
al-Quds, 80
America, terrorist war on, 199–202
Anti-Ballistic Missile (ABM) Treaty, 28, 43, 120, 155, 161, 208, 212
apartheid, in South Africa, 109
Arafat, Yasser, 78–79, 171
Arkin, William, 160
Asia, balance of power in, 67–72
"Asian Miracle," 70
Asia-Pacific Economic Cooperation forum, 187
Asia-Pacific regional security, 74
Asmus, Ron, 56
Aspin, Les, 128, 148, 149, 150, 215
Association of Southeast Asian Nations (ASEAN), 70, 71
Atlantic Alliance, 56
Atwood, Donald, 215
Atwood, J. Brian, 125–126
Australia, 177

B

Baker, James A., III, 56, 149
"balance of power" concept, 42
Balfour Declaration, 79
Balkans, 58–66
ballistic missile defense (BMD), 23, 28, 43–44, 69, 120, 211–212, 214
ballistic nuclear submarines, 54
Bandow, Douglas, 115
Barak, Ehud, 79, 80
Bartholomew Memorandum, 54
Bateman, Herbert H., 114–115, 116
Begin, Manachem, 80
Bello, Walden, 185
Berlin, Isaiah, 27, 78, 79
Biden, Joseph, 156, 157
bin Laden, Osama, 10, 13–14, 99, 100, 101, 200, 201
biological weapons, 12, 214, 217
bipolar systems, 33
Blair, Bruce, 211
Blair, Dennis, 76, 162, 164, 165
Blair, Tony, 10, 51, 53, 54, 101, 183

Bosnia, 8, 58–66, 128–129, 165, 166, 206
Brazil, 176
Bretton Woods system, 5
Bryd, Robert C., 155
Brzezinski, Zbigniew, 46, 150, 153
Buchanan, Pat, 114
Buckley, James, 125
Bunker, Ellsworth, 123, 124
Burma, 71, 109, 110, 111
Burns, Nicholas, 149, 151
Bush, George, 54, 96, 160, 211
Bush, George W., 10, 18–24, 55, 58, 65, 58, 82–87, 99, 122, 163, 175, 179, 199, 202, 208, 211, 212, 214

C

Cambodia, 60, 67, 69, 70, 71
Canada, 176
Capitol Hill press conference, 113–118
carbon dioxide emissions, 83
Carter, Ashton, 215
Carter, Jimmy, 123–124, 125, 126
Celestial Throne, 70
Central America, civil wars in, 61
Central Command, 162–168
chemical weapons, 12, 211, 214, 217
Chemical Weapons Convention, 155, 211
Chen Shui-bian, 68
Cheney, Dick, 83, 174, 199
Chile, 106–107
China, 4, 6, 7, 8, 9, 19, 20, 25–32, 35, 62, 67, 68–72, 73–77, 172, 177, 211, 212
Chirac, Jacques, 54, 101
Christopher, Warren, 129, 148, 149, 150, 151, 152
civil liberties, 12, 15, 16
civil-military gap, 141
Clark, Wesley, 162, 164, 167
Clinton, Bill, 18–24, 54–55, 58, 59, 82, 85, 96, 97, 98, 127–130, 133, 134, 136, 142, 147, 149, 151, 155, 156, 163, 185, 187, 193, 204, 205, 206, 211, 214
Clinton-Gore Pre-Transition Planning Foundation, 127
Cohen, William, 53, 160, 191
Cold War, 3, 6, 140, 203, 206
Colombia Joint Intelligence Center, 168
commanders-in-chief (CINCs), 162
Committee of Santa Fe, 126
Common Foreign and Security Policy, 51, 52
communist ideology, 40
Comprehensive Test Ban Treaty (CTBT), 95, 155, 156, 158, 159, 161, 211, 212
concessions, on terrorism, 191–192
Conference on Disarmament, 211
Constitution, U.S., powers of federal government in, 109
Cooper, Roger, 53
Cordesman, Anthony, 15
corporations, multinational, 176, 177
CO_2 emissions, 83, 84

counterproliferation: deputy for, 215; initiative, 214–218; programs for 216
"Counterproliferation Initiative," 214–218
Coverdell, Paul, 157, 159
Croats, 58
Cuba, 126
Cuban Missile Crisis, 6
Cyprus, UN role in, 61

D

Daaldeer, Ivo, 60
Davis, Lynn, 148, 149
Dawes Plan, 3–4, 5
Dayton Accords, 60, 62
debts, bilateral, with Africa, 85–86
Declaration of Independence, 137
Defense Science Board, 215
democratic societies, 139
Dempsey, James, 16
Deng Xiaoping, 68
Department of the Treasury, 181, 182, 185
Deutch, John, 215, 216, 217
disrupting, terrorist activity, 196
Dole, Robert, 115
domestic terrorism, 191–198
Danilon, Thomas, 148, 149, 150
Donnelly, Thomas, 115

E

East Asia, security and complexity of, 67–71, 74
Economic and Monetary Union (EMU), 52
economic liberalization, and inequality, 181
Eisenhower, Dwight D., 24
El Salvador, 126, 127, 130, 167
Eland, Ivan, 14, 15
election, presidential, 122
elite dissent, 183–184
energy: domestic supplies of, 174; commercial activity and 173; foreign sanctions, effect on, 173–174
environment, Washington consensus and, 181–182
environmental issues, African, 82–84
Europe, as superpower, 51–57
European Central Bank, 51
European Command, 163
European Security and Defense Identity (ESDI), 53
European Union (EU), 36, 51, 52, 53, 64, 148, 177, 183
exports: multinational, 176, 178; U.S., 179
extradition, 106–107

F

family planning, in Africa, 84
Fiscal Year 2000 Defense Authorization, 117
fissile materials, 211
Flanagan, Stephen, 148

Index

foreign direct investment, 176, 178
foreign operations budget, 135
foreign policy, and states' rights, 109–112
foreign-affiliate sales, 175
Four-Power Treaty, 4
France, 4, 54, 211
free trade, 182
Free Trade Area of the Americas, 179
Freedom from Debt Coalition, 181
Freeman, Charles, 74
Fried, Daniel, 151
FY 2001 State Department budget, 135–136, 138

G

"gap researchers," 139
Gati, Charles, 150
gays, in military, 127, 128, 130
Gaza, 79, 80
General Agreement on Tarriffs and Trade (GATT), 5
genocide, in Africa, 82
Germany, 2, 3, 4, 25, 52, 54, 176, 178
Gingrich, Newt, 115
Giuliani, Rudy, 199
"global gag rule," 84
global policy forums, 187
"global unilateralism," 35
global warming, 82
"global zero alert," 211
globalization, 20, 21, 110, 187–188
Goldwater-Nichols Department of Defense Reorganization Act, 164
González, Elián, 95–96
Gore, Al, 152, 155, 160, 164
Goure, Dan, 14, 15
Great Britain, 2, 3, 4, 8, 10, 52, 211
Great Depression, 5
Greece, 90

H

Haiti, 91, 93
Hamas, 12, 171
Hamilton, Alexander, 111
Haram al-Sharif, 80
Harding, Warren, 4
Harries, Owen, 49
Hastert, Dennis, 199
Havel, Vaclav, 148, 153
Heavily Indebted Poor Countries (HIPC), 86
hegemony: global, 4, 23; regional, 71, 76–77
Helms, Jesse, 119–121, 123, 155, 159
Heritage Foundation, 124
Hezbollah, 12
HIV/AIDS, 82, 84, 85
Holbrooke, Richard, 53, 147, 151, 152, 204
homosexuals, in military, 127, 128, 130
hubris, problem of, 122
human rights, 28, 204; in China, 73
Hundred Years Peace, 2, 4
Hungary, 148, 153
Huntington, Samuel, 9
Hussein, Saddam, 19, 43, 101, 160, 217
Hutchison Doctrine, 116–117
Hutchison, Kay Bailey, 117

I

Ignarieff, Michael, 27
India, 35, 51, 61
Indonesia, 67, 71, 184
Inhofe, James, 159, 160–161
insensitive high explosives (IHEs), 159
International Court of Justice, 209
International Criminal Court (ICC), 105, 107–108
International Criminal Tribunal for the Former Yugoslavia (ICTY), 107–108
India, 177, 210, 211
interagency working group (IWG), 148
International Monetary Fund (IMF), 5, 181, 182, 183, 184, 185, 186
International Standards Organization, 187
International Trade Organization (ITO), 5
internationalism, apathetic, 95–98
Iran, 35, 171–174
Iran Liba Sanctions Act, 171–174
Iraq, 18, 19, 91, 93, 200, 214
Islamic Jihad, 99, 171
Israel, 56, 78–81, 100, 126, 171, 200, 211
Islam, 78, 99, 100
Islamic Movement for Uzbekistan, 49
Italy, 52

J

Jackson, Jesse, 182
Japan, 4, 28, 67, 69, 70, 71–72, 76, 176, 177, 178, 179, 183
Japan's Peace Constitution, 76
Jiang Zemin, 68
Joint Chiefs of Staff (JCS), 127, 152, 165, 166
Joint Forces Command, 163
Jordon, Hamilton, 123
Jubilee 2000, 185

K

Kagan, Donald, 25, 114
Karimov, Islam, 49
Kashmir, 61
Khatami, Mohammed, 171, 172
Kidder, Ray, 161
Kim Jong Il, 71
King, Rachael, 15, 16
Kissinger, Henry, 46, 68
Klare, Michael, 125
Kohl, Helmet, 180
Korea, 68, 71, 75
Kosovo, 8, 29, 52, 58–66, 95, 165, 167
Kozyrev, Andrei, 42
Kyl, Jon, 157, 159, 160
Kyoto Protocol, 83

L

labor, skilled, 177
labor unions, 185
Lake, Anthony, 147, 148, 151
Laos, 67
League of Nations, 4, 5
Lebanon, stability of, 61
Li Peng, 30

Libya, 171–174, 193, 194, 195, 196
Lindsay, James, 12
Linowitz, Sol, 123, 124
long-range missiles, 214
Lott, Trent, 156, 157, 158, 159, 160, 161
Lugar, Richard, 116

M

Maastricht Treaty, 52, 54
MacArthur, Douglas, 140
Macedonia, 63
Madison, James, 111
Mao Zedong, 68
Marshall Plan, 5
Massachusetts Burma Law, 110, 111
McCain, John, 114
Mead, Walter Russell, 119, 120
Mercosur, 177
Messervy-Whiting, Graham, 53
Mexico, 179
Mexico City Policy, 84
Middle East, 67, 78–81
military: gays in, 127, 128, 130; readiness, 163; role of, 162; supremacy of, 22, terrorism and, 194–195, 217; expenditures in Japan, 70
Millennium Plan (Africa), 87
Mischief Reef, 69
missiles: ballistic, 23, 69, 217; long-range, 214
Moscow, 42
Moynihan, Daniel Patrick, 158
Mt. Kilimanjaro, 82, 83
multinational corporations, 176, 177
multipolar systems, 33
Musharraf, Pervez, 100
Muslim world, 100

N

Nader, Ralph, 182
National Foreign Trade Council v. Natsios, 109, 110, 111
national missile defense (NMD), 23, 28, 120
National Security Council (NSC), 147, 148, 166, 216
Natural Energy Program, 176–177
Navy War College, 217
Neustadt, Richard, 122
New Agenda Resolution (UN), 212
New Independent States (NIS), 149
Nicaragua, 126
"Nimble Dancer," 217
Nine-Power Treaty, 4
Nixon, Richard, 68
nongovernmental organizations (NGOs), 110
non-Social Security surplus, 134
North American Free Trade Agreement (NADTA), 177, 181, 182
North Atlantic Cooperation Council (NACC), 148, 149
North Atlantic Council (NAC), 148
North Atlantic Treaty Organization (NATO), 22, 28, 29, 40, 52, 53, 54, 59, 62, 64, 99, 147–154, 155, 208
North Korea, 19, 68, 69

Northern Ireland, separation of, 62
nuclear arsenal, 208, 209
nuclear disarmament, 211
Nuclear Non-Proliferation Treaty (NFT), 159, 209, 210, 211, 212
nuclear weaponry, 12, 208–213, 215
nuclear weapons, 69, 208–213
"nuclear-free zones," 109

O

Office of Homeland Security, 12, 16
Ogawa, Shin'ichi, 65
Oklahoma City, federal building, 191, 201
Old City, 80
Omar, Mullah Muhammad, 99
"one percent solution" game, 133–138
150 Account, 133, 134
openness, promotion of, 21–22
Operation Safe Sword, 52
Orwell, George, 6
Overseas Presence Advisory Panel (OPAP), 135
Overseas Private Investment Corporation, 179
Owen, David, 129

P

Pacific Command, 163
Pakistan, 61, 100, 162, 164, 210, 211
Palestine, 62, 78–81, 200
Pan Am Flight 103, 192, 193, 195
Panama, 130, 167
Panama Canal Treaty, 123, 124, 125, 130
partition, of states, 64
Partnership for Peace (PFP), 147, 148, 149, 150, 151
Pastor, Robert, 123, 126
peacekeeping, U.N., 136
Peña, Charles, 15
Pentagon, bombing of, 10, 13, 199
petroleum, 55–56, 177
Philippines, 69, 71
Pinochet, Augusto, 106–107
Pipes, Richard, 46
Plan Colombia, 167
Poland, 148, 149, 153
Policy Planning Staff, 148, 149
Pollard, Neal, 12, 16, 17
Popular Front for the Liberation of Palestine General Command, 12
Posen, Barry, 60
postmodern military, U.S., 139–144
Powell, Colin, 18, 20, 82, 83, 86, 100, 160, 201, 209, 212
Powell Doctrine, 18
presidency, transition of, 122–132
Presidential Transition Act, 124
Primakov, Yevgeny, 41, 42
Prodi, Romano, 51
Putin, Vladimir, 29, 41, 102

Q

Qadaffi, Muammar, 194, 195, 196

R

ratification, of test ban treaty, 155–161
Reagan, Ronald, 124–126, 130, 180, 191
"realistic empathy," 26–27
religious coalitions, 185
Republican party, 113–118
Rice, Condoleezza, 20, 23, 199
Ridge, Tom, 12, 16
Roman Empire, 203
Roosevelt, Theodore, 113, 114
Rough Riders, 113
Rumsfeld, Donald, 208, 209
Russia, 5, 6, 7, 8, 25–32, 40–44, 62, 69, 101, 172, 210

S

Saudi Arabia, 100, 125, 126, 130
Schuwirth, Rainer, 53
sea-lanes, commercial, in South China Sea, 69, 70
Serbia, 63; encroachment by, 62; partition of, 64
Sergeev, Igor, 29
Sino-U.S. relations, 73–77
Skaggs, David, 96
Smith, Robert, 159
Smithson, Amy, 12
Social Security surplus, 134
"soft power," 187, 188
Somalia, 91
South Africa, democratization of, 61
South China Sea, 69, 71
South Korea, 67, 68
Southern Command, 163
Soviet Union, 3, 6, 201, 203, 204
space, weapons in, 208
Spain, 52, 195–196
Spencer, Jack, 10
Spratly Islands, 69
START I, 209, 211
Start II Treaty, 43, 211
START III, 43
State Department budget, 135
Summers, Lawrence H., 34
Syria, 61, 194

T

Taiwan, 7, 28–31, 62, 68, 71, 73, 74–75
Talbott, Strobe, 34, 54, 149, 150, 151
Talent Inventory Program, 123
Taliban, 10, 99, 100, 101
technology, 177
Temple Mount, 80
terrorism, 10–16, 99–104, 191–198, 199–202, 215
test ban debacle, 155–161
Thatcher, Margaret, 180
theater missile defense (TMD), 75, 76
Tibet, 62
Tobin, James, 185
Toepfer, Klaus, 83
trade deficit, 175–179
transition syndrome, presidential elections and, 122–132
Treaty of Versailles, 3

Triangle Institute of Security Studies (TISS), 141
Trident II/D-5 missiles, 159
Turkey, 55, 56, 61, 90

U

"unilateral globalism," 35
uni-multipolar systems, 33–37
United Kingdom, 176, 178
United Nations (UN), 5, 53, 60; nuclear weapons and, 212
United Nations Transitional Administration for Cambodia (UNTAC), 60–61
United States of Africa, 87
universal jurisdiction, pitfalls of doctrine of, 105–108
USA*Engage, 98, 172
USS Cole, 11, 200
Uzbekistan, 49

V

Vance, Cyrus, 129
Vandenberg, Arthur, 120
Vienna Convention on Consular Relations, 110
Vietnam, 67, 69, 70

W

Walesa, Lech, 148, 153
War on America, 199–202
Warner, John, 158
Warsaw Pact, former, states, 148
Washington Consensus, 180–186
Washington Naval Treaty, 4
West Bank, 79, 80
White Paper, 126
White, Ralph K., 26
Wilhelm, Charles, 162, 164, 165, 167
Williamson, John, 180, 181
Wilson, Woodrow, 3, 25
Wolfowitz, Paul, 23, 100
workers, global factory, 182
World Bank, 136, 137, 182, 183, 184, 185
World in Depression, 1929–1939, The, (Kindleberger) 4
World Trade Center, 10, 13, 191, 193, 199–202
World Trade Organization (WTO), 111, 181, 183, 187, 188
World War I, 2, 3, 6, 25
World War II, 4, 5, 6
Wye River Plantation, 205

Y

Yeltsin, Boris, 42, 43, 152
Yugoslavia, 60

Z

Zimbabwe, expropriations in, 61
Zinni, Anthony, 162, 164, 217
Zionism, 78

Test Your Knowledge Form

We encourage you to photocopy and use this page as a tool to assess how the articles in *Annual Editions* expand on the information in your textbook. By reflecting on the articles you will gain enhanced text information. You can also access this useful form on a product's book support Web site at *http://www.dushkin.com/online/*.

NAME: _____ DATE: _____

TITLE AND NUMBER OF ARTICLE: _____

BRIEFLY STATE THE MAIN IDEA OF THIS ARTICLE: _____

_____

LIST THREE IMPORTANT FACTS THAT THE AUTHOR USES TO SUPPORT THE MAIN IDEA:

_____

WHAT INFORMATION OR IDEAS DISCUSSED IN THIS ARTICLE ARE ALSO DISCUSSED IN YOUR TEXTBOOK OR OTHER READINGS THAT YOU HAVE DONE? LIST THE TEXTBOOK CHAPTERS AND PAGE NUMBERS:

_____

LIST ANY EXAMPLES OF BIAS OR FAULTY REASONING THAT YOU FOUND IN THE ARTICLE:

_____

LIST ANY NEW TERMS/CONCEPTS THAT WERE DISCUSSED IN THE ARTICLE, AND WRITE A SHORT DEFINITION:

We Want Your Advice

ANNUAL EDITIONS revisions depend on two major opinion sources: one is our Advisory Board, listed in the front of this volume, which works with us in scanning the thousands of articles published in the public press each year; the other is you—the person actually using the book. Please help us and the users of the next edition by completing the prepaid article rating form on this page and returning it to us. Thank you for your help!

ANNUAL EDITIONS: American Foreign Policy 02/03

ARTICLE RATING FORM

Here is an opportunity for you to have direct input into the next revision of this volume.
We would like you to rate each of the articles listed below, using the following scale:

1. **Excellent: should definitely be retained**
2. **Above average: should probably be retained**
3. **Below average: should probably be deleted**
4. **Poor: should definitely be deleted**

Your ratings will play a vital part in the next revision.
Please mail this prepaid form to us as soon as possible.
Thanks for your help!

RATING	ARTICLE
	1. The American Way of Victory: A Twentieth-Century Trilogy
	2. War on Terrorism
	3. Different Drummers, Same Drum
	4. In From the Cold: A New Approach to Relations With Russia and China
	5. The Lonely Superpower
	6. Russian Foreign Policy: Promise or Peril?
	7. Against Russophobia
	8. Europe: Superstate or Superpower?
	9. The Lesser Evil: The Best Way Out of the Balkans
	10. East Asia: Security and Complexity
	11. To Be an Enlightened Superpower
	12. A Small Peace for the Middle East
	13. Bush's Global Agenda: Bad News for Africa
	14. On American Principles
	15. The New Apathy
	16. Allies in Search of a Strategy
	17. The Pitfalls of Universal Jurisdiction
	18. States' Rights and Foreign Policy: Some Things Should Be Left to Washington
	19. The Folk Who Live on the Hill
	20. Farewell to the Helmsman
	21. Perils of Presidential Transition
	22. The One Percent Solution: Shirking the Cost of World Leadership
	23. America's Postmodern Military
	24. NATO Expansion: The Anatomy of a Decision
	25. Outmaneuvered, Outgunned, and Out of View: Test Ban Debacle
	26. A Four-Star Foreign Policy?
	27. Q: Should the United States Renew the Iran Libya Sanctions Act?
	28. The U.S. Trade Deficit: A Dangerous Obsession
	29. The Death of the Washington Consensus?
	30. Globalization After Seattle
	31. Responding to Terrorism
	32. War on America: The New Enemy
	33. Musclebound: The Limits of U.S. Power

RATING	ARTICLE
	34. Ending the Nuclear Nightmare: A Strategy for the Bush Administration
	35. Mission Impossible

(Continued on next page)

BUSINESS REPLY MAIL
FIRST-CLASS MAIL PERMIT NO. 84 GUILFORD CT

POSTAGE WILL BE PAID BY ADDRESSEE

**McGraw-Hill/Dushkin
530 Old Whitfield Street
Guilford, Ct 06437-9989**

ABOUT YOU

Name   Date

_____   _____

Are you a teacher? ❏   A student? ❏
Your school's name

_____

Department

_____

Address   City   State   Zip

_____

School telephone #

_____

YOUR COMMENTS ARE IMPORTANT TO US!

Please fill in the following information:
For which course did you use this book?

_____

Did you use a text with this ANNUAL EDITION?   ❏ yes ❏ no
What was the title of the text?

_____

What are your general reactions to the *Annual Editions* concept?

_____

Have you read any pertinent articles recently that you think should be included in the next edition? Explain.

_____

Are there any articles that you feel should be replaced in the next edition? Why?

_____

Are there any World Wide Web sites that you feel should be included in the next edition? Please annotate.

_____

May we contact you for editorial input?   ❏ yes ❏ no
May we quote your comments? ❏ yes ❏ no